Gare du Nord
RUE DE MAUBEUGE
RUE LA FAYETTE
BOUL. DE SEBASTOPOL
Gare de L'Est
CANAL ST. MARTIN
Porte St. Denis
DE MAGENTA
BOULEVARDS
Porte St. Martin
RUE DE RICHELIEU
Bourse
RUE MONTMARTRE
Palais Royal
RUE DE TURBIGO
Place de la République
BOUL.
BOUL. BEAUMARCHAIS
RUE DU TEMPLE
Les Halles
RUE DE RIVOLI
Palais du Louvre
VOLTAIRE
BOUL. LENOIR
Hôtel de Ville
Palais de Justice
Notre Dame
Place de la Bastille
SAINT GERMAIN
SAINT MICHEL
Sorbonne
St. Étienne du Mont
Panthéon
Jardin des Plantes
Gare de Lyon
Gare d'Austerlitz
DU PORT-ROYAL

LIBRARY
EMORY & HENRY
COLLEGE
EMORIUM et HENRICENSE COLLEGIUM
MACTE VIRTUTE
MDCCCXXXVI
WITHDRAWN
EMORY, VIRGINIA

ACTION FRANÇAISE

⚜

Action Française

ROYALISM AND REACTION IN
TWENTIETH-CENTURY FRANCE

EUGEN WEBER

STANFORD UNIVERSITY PRESS
STANFORD, CALIFORNIA
1962

Stanford University Press
Stanford, California

Library of Congress Catalog Card Number: 62-15267

Printed in the United States of America

Published with the assistance of the
FORD FOUNDATION

To Edward Welbourne

Master of Emmanuel

PREFACE

Modern History touches us so nearly, it is so deep a question of life and death, that we are bound to find our own way through it, and to owe our insight to ourselves.

LORD ACTON

THIS IS THE STORY OF THE MAJOR royalist and nationalist movement of twentieth-century France; a movement which between 1899 and 1944 provided the fundamental doctrines of practically the whole Extreme Right in France and of important nationalist and traditionalist groups in Belgium, Italy, Portugal, Spain, Romania, and Switzerland, as well as the theoretical background of the National Revolution of Vichy.

The literary and political influence of the *Action Française* was immense: its columns were responsible for launching Proust, Bernanos, and Céline to public favor, for driving at least one Minister to suicide and hounding others out of office—even into jail—for shaking the foundations of several cabinets and, at one time, of the Republic itself. It was among the first to warn of Nazi dangers and it fired the first shots against aid for Spain. It had one of the finest literary pages, and the most pungent, venomous, and Rabelaisian among polemicists.

Its history is full of paradoxes: responsible in great part for the moral rearmament of France before 1914, its campaigns seem to bear an equal responsibility for France's being caught morally disarmed by the Second World War. It was a determined foe of idealism and of "romantic incoherence," but its followers nonetheless reflected the idealistic mood they scorned, and finally fell away, abandoning its principles for the sake of action. The fiercest champion of the Catholic party, it was condemned by the Pope; responsible for making royalism a fashionable cause, it was disowned by the princes it professed to serve; above all patriotic and anti-German, it came into its own when France reached her lowest point since Joan of Arc rode into Bourges, and gave unreserved support to a Head of State whose policy included collaboration with the German enemies of France.

And yet not only did the Action Française persist and grow stronger, but it kept its integrity to an extent unknown among political groups—a fact which might explain its own ineffectiveness as a *political* group. It held its own against the Catholic Church and braved its princes with very little loss. It challenged the Republic and impaired its credit until it sagged and creaked for all to see. It stood in the still center of the storm it had predicted, a new Cassandra, and refused to bow. It left its mark on friends and enemies, and upon France itself, where few men now maintain liberal democracy as a political ideal.

I thought that it would be well to learn how a small group of intellectuals, with but a handful of influential friends to start with and very thin resources, whose paper at its height did not print much more than 150,000 copies, whose movement could not marshal a third that many votes, managed to do so much—and what it was they did.

Such an ambition might well seem excessive when the subject of my story lies in the recent past. Like all investigations conducted into contemporary history, mine would have benefited from the broader perspective which only time allows, and from the information which will be made available through the years. A hundred years from now the historian who cares to investigate the subject will possibly have access to official documents and private papers which I sorely lacked. A hundred years from now, however, the men who lived through the events in question will be long dead, and many of their papers will have been destroyed. There will be none left who will remember how situations *felt,* or who can be asked to clarify moot points. Time, which makes available some sources of evidence, will have destroyed others, perhaps quite as rich. (I have, for instance, obtained access to copies of Foreign Ministry papers, the originals of which were destroyed in 1940. Where will these copies be a hundred years from now?)

It seems to me that arguments for action and delay are six of one and half a dozen of the other. Evidence from "official" sources is often estimated far above its worth, and it tends, moreover, to discourage searchers from striking out farther afield where evidence is more elusive but sometimes more reliable. Had I not gone to a great deal of trouble to elicit membership or circulation figures from provincial leaders of the Action Française, in good part because the simple way of looking up official figures was closed, I could not have checked the ones against the others when, by a stroke of fortune, official estimates came into my hand.

Besides, scholarly patience has its limits. The Action Française is not something that can be packed away in an historical freezer until the Archives open. It is a part of our time, and it was an important factor in forging a mentality we want to understand. An account of its history, even imperfect, is overdue; and I have tried to make it as complete and as objective as the available information will allow.

The available information, when one looks for it, is quite impressive, particularly that which an attentive reading of the *Action française* will reveal. I have been fortunate in obtaining interviews with over seventy persons, and sometimes lengthy letters and statements from eighteen more, all of whom as leaders, friends, or enemies of the Action Française were able to give me much useful information. I should particularly like to express my thanks to M. and Mme Jacques Maurras and Mlle Hélène Maurras, who generously opened great portions of their uncle's still unsorted papers to my hungry curiosity. I have also profited greatly from the rich private records and information which MM. Pierre Boutang, Paul Courcoural, François Daudet, Paul Dresse de Lébioles, Francisque Gay, Count Louis de Gonzague de Reynold, Roger Joseph, Count Olivier de Roux, and René Rancoeur have permitted me to use. I am most grateful for their patience and their help.

I owe thanks, too, to Professor Pierre Renouvin and M. André Chamson, Director of the Archives Nationales, for helping to make available files relevant to my inquiries which the fifty-year rule would otherwise have closed. Nor must I forget the debt I owe to my friend Professor Donald Harvey, to my research assistant, Mlle Yvonne Dusser, and to Mrs. Shirley Taylor of the Stanford University Press, whose scrupulous editorial work went a long way to improve my manuscript.

But it would be difficult to discriminate, other than on a quantitative basis, and my thanks go out as unreservedly to all those who in varying degrees allowed me to enjoy their confidence, their patience, and, sometimes, their friendship: M. le Comte de Paris, Mmes L. Blanchet-Courcoural, L. M. Pujo and P. Varillon; MM. Salvador Abascal, Simon Arbellot de Vacqueur, Emmanuel Beau de Loménie, Georges Bidault, Henri Boegner, Maurice Bardèche, André Blumel, Claude-Philippe Bodinier, Raymond Batardy, Professor Henri Bernard, Professor Rafael Calvo Serer, Professor Marcel De Corte, Coutant, Pierre Cot, Georges Calzant, Michel Déon, Baron Drion du Chapois, Adrien Dansette, Aquiles Elorduy, Bernard Faÿ, Alfred Fabre-Luce, Jean Fayard, Eugène Frot, Bertil Galland, Raoul Girardet, Pierre Gaxotte, Georges Gaudy, Darsie Gillie, Kléber Haedens, Robert Havard de la Montagne, Vintila Horia, Louis Jasseron, Marcel Jouhandeau, Elie Jacquet, Henry Jamet, Louis Kraft, José Le Boucher, Joseph Lémery, Jean Longnon, Pierre Lecoeur, Roland Laudenbach, Pierre Longone, Bernard Lecache, François Mauriac, Dr. Pierre Mauriac, Louis Michaut, Michel Missoffe, Henri Massis, Armin Mohler, André Nicholas, Roger Nimier, Baron Pierre Nothomb, Count Yves O'Mahony, René Pléven, Jacques Ploncard d'Assac, Max Richard, Lucien Rebatet, Henri Rambaud, Marcel Regamey, Théo Ripoull, Canon A. Simon, André Thérive, Henri Torrès, Pierre Taittinger, Bernard de Vaulx, André Voisin, Xavier Vallat, and Georges Wurmser; as well as those of my informants who have preferred to remain anonymous and who may occasionally recognize themselves or their remarks below.

While I am engaged in thanking, I ought to add some very special thanks: to the Social Science Research Council, whose Faculty Research Fellowship enabled me to spend two years completing my research in France; to the American Philosophical Society, whose support helped me in starting out; and, very particularly, to the University of California, Los Angeles, for their great generosity with leave and, in the case of its Research Grants Committee, with grants. I hope they will find their money and their kindness have not been too ill-spent.

Since this is not an obstacle course for apprentice scholars, I have not bothered to append a lengthy bibliography, usually consulted only in order to discover gaps in the author's information. There will be no need to turn to the back of the book to do that. In any case, books that relate directly to the subject are few, and those that have been found useful or relevant are cited in due course. There is no commendable history of the movement as a whole, and no really thorough history of its time, though partial and partisan instances of both exist and are referred to when needed. Professor Edward Tannenbaum's *Action Française* (New York, 1962) appeared too late for me to take its argument into account. The reader who cares to compare the two books will see that, although many of our impressions are similar, our points of view differ markedly. Mr. Tannenbaum's "café intellectuals" appear in my pages as influential publicists and public figures.

My own sources of information are indicated, whenever they can be, as I go along. The information itself is in my pages, references and occasional comments in the notes. If the latter are numerous, that is because so many things are too little known or too outrageous not to call for some remark or confirmation. The pages may be a bit numerous also, but this is an unexplored subject, and, as it is, I feel that my presentation is woefully sketchy, no more than the preliminary spadework in a field in which books need to be written where there are chapters now.

Most of my European informants are or have been devotees of the Action Française and admirers of its leaders. They knew that my interest in the Action Française did not mean agreement; they helped me in the belief that objective treatment would be better than either prejudice or panegyrics. I hope the results will bear them out. I doubt whether they will agree with my conclusions; for that matter, I doubt whether their enemies will. But I hope they will be able to recognize a determined attempt to be fair.

By being fair I mean specifically that I have tried to see the Action Française in terms of its own purposes and intentions, and also in terms of those to whom it appealed, before hazarding a personal judgment on its achievements or on its work. I have avoided making the movement a simple plaything in the hands of social, economic, or psychological forces. When one has explained something away by manipulating these, the people still remain, their attitudes and their thoughts, quite unaware of deep historic factors, but often knowing well some more immediate and specific motive, whether they own to it or not.

There are, I think, general explanations that must serve as background; and there are underlying factors that play the part of Caliban or id: I hope the reader will occasionally recognize them, in the background, where they belong. But the lives of men and movements are more than seismic incidents, explicable in deceptively mathematical terms: they are a series of acts and decisions, of impulses, rationalizations, and reasonings, particular and responsible and unique.

This is the story of one of these complex wholes—like every life, the focus of many others; like every story, partial and incomplete. The Action Française was born in crisis and ended in disaster. The Chinese wish that their enemies may live in interesting times. *It* did. It was exciting while it lasted. And now it is history.

E. W.

CONTENTS

MAPS

PART I: THE RISE, 1899-1918

Tout comprendre, c'est tout pardonner.

MADAME DE STAËL

Prenons garde de ne pas trop expliquer, pour ne pas fournir des arguments à ceux qui veulent tout excuser.

ALBERT, DUC DE BROGLIE

I

PREPARATION, 1899–1908

About noon on a spring day in 1908, Maurice Barrès, deputy of Paris, and Henri Massis, walking past the Paris Halles, saw the walls covered with fresh posters. "*L'Action française*," they read, "a daily organ of integral nationalism." Barrès shrugged—"An absurd undertaking . . . won't last six months!"

The undertaking was absurd enough, but it lasted. The daily paper born on that day lived for thirty-six years, until the summer of 1944, when it came to an abrupt end, along with the regime it had done its share to inspire, leaving behind an intricate web of political and ideological influences that still exists after nearly twenty years. It will be the purpose of this book to show how the Action Française movement, and later the newspaper of the same name, came into being, how they lasted through the years, and how they affected the society in which they prospered for so long.

If, as Bergson once suggested, the life of nations, like that of men, can be greatly affected by small, very small, accidental circumstances, it follows then that men of action can greatly affect events and that the evolution of society is certainly, though often unwittingly, influenced by the efforts of tenacious wills. Wills, however, are at their most effective in the service of a purpose, and before the Action Française could assign itself a task, it had first to define its nature and its aims. Its leaders and creators knew this, and we shall see that, of the political movements of our time, none was more self-conscious or more aware of its ideology, and of the importance of ideology, than this. The search for a doctrine occupies the first decade of its existence and defines it from the very beginning as an intellectual movement and a highly didactic one. Its nature, however, must appear more clearly when viewed against the background of contemporary events, particularly the Dreyfus affair.

The Dreyfus case began in 1894 when a Jewish officer on the General Staff was accused of espionage on the flimsiest of grounds, court-martialed, and sentenced under illegal conditions, the Court's decision having been largely determined by documents to which it alone had access. Jailed, dishonorably discharged in a public ceremony, and shipped to Devil's Island under a life sentence, the traitor was soon forgotten. But at the Ministry of War, where the disappearance of secret documents had started the espionage alert, leakage of information continued. Lieutenant Colonel Marie-Georges Picquart, who had in 1895 taken over the Second (Intelligence) Bureau, began to suspect another officer, Major Ferdinand Walsin-Esterhazy, debt-ridden and a known bounder, but with good connections. Picquart's suspicions were based on the discovery of an express-letter form, the famous *petit bleu,* addressed to Esterhazy, which a cleaning woman had fished out of a wastebasket in the German Embassy in Paris. On examination, Esterhazy's handwriting was found to be the same as that on the *bordereau* which had been the chief evidence against Dreyfus. But if Esterhazy were to be proved guilty, Captain Dreyfus would be cleared, and, even worse, the prejudiced and superficial inquiries that had led to his accusation would be made public. To prevent such awkwardness, another officer of the Second Bureau, Major (later Colonel) Hubert Henry, got hold of the *petit bleu* and rubbed out and then rewrote Esterhazy's name, to make the letter seem a forgery. Then, as a precaution, he bolstered the evidence with a pure forgery—a purported note from the Italian military attaché in Paris, Colonel Panizzardi, to his German colleague, in which "the scoundrel Dreyfus" was specifically mentioned.

Alarmed at Picquart's interference in what was considered a closed case, the Army ordered Picquart to Africa. Before he left, however, he confided his suspicions, and the nature of the evidence, to a lawyer friend, who soon afterward communicated them to an eminent politician, the vice-president of the Senate, August Scheurer-Kestner. In the meantime, the Dreyfus family, still trying to prove the Captain's innocence, had also concluded that Esterhazy was the real traitor, and in November 1897 Mathieu Dreyfus publicly accused Esterhazy of the treachery for which his brother Alfred had been condemned, and asked that the sentence of 1894 be reconsidered on the grounds of new evidence. The court-martial which examined Mathieu Dreyfus's charges, however, found nothing to justify a revision. Esterhazy was not guilty, and the General Staff, momentarily shaken, was back in the clear. Then, on January 13, 1898, two days after Esterhazy's public vindication, Clemenceau's *Aurore* published Emile Zola's long open letter "J'Accuse" in which Zola charged the generals and the Staff with having knowingly convicted an innocent man. Zola in his turn was brought to trial and sentenced to a year's imprisonment, but despite the judge's deliberate stifling of relevant evidence and the ruling that no reference could be made to the Dreyfus case, Zola's lawyers were successful in revealing the illegal maneuverings that lay behind the condemnation of 1894.

The "case" had become an "affair," but it had still not attained national proportions. The arguments of Dreyfus's defenders, the revisionists, did not convince even all of the relatively few people who would lend them an ear. Anti-revisionist assertions, backed by all the authority of Army leaders, were enough for the respectable and patriotic majority. Revisionists and counter-revisionists succeeded only in making the confusion worse.

The first to take sides on issues where principles, documents, and evidence played such a large part were scholars and intellectuals. Not only were they inclined by training and orientation to consider such things important, but they were also less likely to accept the unsupported pronouncements of established authorities. It was thus that many of the earliest champions in the Dreyfus debate came from the University or, like Zola, from its intellectual and artistic borderlands. The intellectuals who defended Dreyfus against his Army accusers may have had their impartiality jogged by the military service to which they had been subjected since 1889, and which had impressed a good many among them with the fallibility and narrow stupidity of an officer corps whose prejudices failed to match their own. They certainly responded, too, to a call to defend the critical and moral principles of the University and of the Republic against the challenge of alien authorities and values embodied in social groups—Army, Church, "society"—that they both envied and suspected. When, in February 1898, the Ligue des Droits de l'Homme was founded in response to Zola's appeal, they flocked to its ranks.

Intellectual debate around issues that remained obscure was not, however, sufficient to fascinate the general public. The elections of May 1898 seemed but little influenced by the Parisian debates, and most Dreyfusards who campaigned on the issue got nowhere. Criticism of the Army leaders had led, on the contrary, to a revival of the earlier Boulangist agitation, chauvinistic, popular, and authoritarian in tone, which affected the mood of the Right as a whole and even contributed to the election of a baker's dozen of nationalistic and anti-Semitic deputies.

In July 1898, a few weeks after the elections, the Minister of War, Eugène Cavaignac, arose in the Chamber to expose the proofs of Dreyfus's guilt. Among other documents he produced at the time, he made the mistake of insisting upon Henry's forged letter from Panizzardi to his German colleague. But another Intelligence officer had been taking a hard look at the evidence, and the forgery was exposed. Henry, now a colonel, admitted its authorship and was imprisoned. On August 31 he was found dead in his cell, perhaps a suicide, perhaps murder.

After Esterhazy, who in the meantime had proved his foresight by leaving for England, Henry: the revelation of the forgery, and perhaps even more the dramatic circumstances surrounding the revelation, strengthened the case for revision. Its opponents were disoriented. One of the liveliest among them, a thirty-year-old Provençal royalist who had just taken a week off to admire the Elgin marbles in the British Museum, was hurriedly recalled from London by his editor. A week after Henry's violent death, under the signature of Charles Maurras, the royalist *Gazette de France* declared that Henry's forgery was the result of patriotic devotion, and his death "the first blood" shed in the Dreyfus affair.[1]

[1] Numbered notes will be found at the back of the book, pp. 537–76.

Henry's great, and only, mistake, the article said, had been to let himself be caught. Rhetorically addressing the dead man himself, Maurras laid down more than a justification, indeed, a declaration of faith:

> Force, decision, shrewdness, none of these you lacked, only a little luck . . . In all circumstances, you have displayed superior gifts of initiative and resolution. You have used them frantically, to the point of misleading your superiors, your friends, your colleagues, and your fellow-citizens, but, it is true, for the good and the honor of all. Your slogan, "Allons-y," which had become proverbial, is now invested [by your sacrifice] with a profound and mysterious significance; it remains the motto of a moralist or a statesman. We shall see to it that it remains immortal.[2]

The young reporter who thus entered the lists brandishing a cutlass of *raison d'état* had been writing philosophy and poetry for the last twelve years. His first article, in February 1886, had been a scholarly review in the *Annales de la philosophie chrétienne*; his first distinction, in 1888, a prize for a Provençal poem. At twenty-three, he was referred to as "the learned critic Charles Maurras" in the manifesto for the new "Ecole Romane,"[3] issued by the poet Jean Moréas, and he and his friend Frédéric Amouretti were the leading lights of the Félibrigian movement of Provençal revival.

Charles Marie Photius Maurras was born at Martigues, a small fishing village near Marseille, on April 20, 1868. His father, the local tax collector, came from Roquevaire, an inland village not far distant, and cherished the classical culture associated with high-minded secularism. The names of Maurras's father—Aristide—and of his seven uncles and aunts had been drawn from Plutarch and Titus Livius, their standards from the same source. Aristide served the state in a number of undistinguished but respectable posts with the same conscientiousness with which he read his Byron; but he was no traditionalist. Disillusioned by the failure of the Second Empire and of Thiers, he died, still young, in 1874.

Where Maurras's father had been liberal and romantic, his mother was devout and royalistic. In 1848, Charles Marie's grandmother, a devoted legitimist, could be told of the new republic with only the greatest circumspection, and, in spite of all precautions, could not forbear to faint. His grandfather had served in the navy under Louis-Philippe's son, the Prince de Joinville, and it was only on this account that the old lady had accepted the family of Orléans. Naval service was a favorite in this respectable provincial family of officers, magistrates, doctors, and builders, still close to the soil and to its peasant origins in the *midi blanc*; and a commission in the navy had been the boy's ambition until, at fourteen, he was struck by the first symptoms of the deafness that would torment his life.[4] He never got over the bitter disappointment, but the ideas of his youth and of his mother's family remained, the tradition of soil and service, the passion for Provence harsh as the landscapes of his native countryside and sharp as its spices, the royalist devotion of the southern "whites," and, overlaid by a touch of bohemianism and a thick rationalistic veneer, the lofty bourgeois idealism of provincial society.

When Maurras was imprisoned in 1944, at the age of seventy-six, he set out to compose in his inimitable scrawl a "moral, magical, and detective story," cast, in spite of his denials, in a strongly autobiographical vein. As in all his writings, the fictional structure of *Le Mont de Saturne* (Paris, 1950) is only a thin pretext for the elaboration of poetic recollections, philosophical discourses, and numerous anecdotes. Under a halfhearted camouflage, certain revealing personal traits appear. In their light, Charles Maurras's ideas on love and marriage, for instance, appear to be of the most conventional kind. The double standard, wholeheartedly accepted, permits sexual and sentimental adventures for the male but requires absolute purity in his life companion: "In their own house, my father and my mother had never imagined their daughter-in-law other than an untouched maiden. The name which did not belong to me alone could not serve the trivial purpose of regularizing a passing Paris affair." Along with this flat pompousness there is a highly idealized picture of "true love" between two poets working together on a vast anthology, citing obscure versifiers to each other in the most sterile and high-minded of literary courtships, and sacrificing their love, almost unspoken except in quotations, for the sake of principle. What to the uninitiated reads like a rather heavy-handed parody of fin-de-siècle *feuilletons* is to Maurras the picture of high and perfect love, the communion of two fellow souls, essential and self-justifying.

That life and love should be envisaged within the limits and through the lenses of petty bourgeois respectability is nothing to condemn. It is worth noting, however, that like Comte, whom he admired, this advocate of empirical reasoning, logical even to recklessness, was a conformist in his social morality; and that like the *philosophes,* whom he detested, he was a profound, though unconfessed, romantic. Had he been nothing more than that, life might have treated him more kindly and history allowed him to die ignored. That he was more he may have owed to the crisis of his youth, to a spark of his mother's indomitable spirit, or to some other inherited source of strength and courage, a hunger for *his* truth along with which went the determination to affirm it, whatever the odds. "Mau-ras," the Provençal poet Frédéric Mistral had jestingly called him—ill-fed, or, better still, insatiable; he might have added indomitable as well.

"For man," says the hero of *Mont de Saturne,* "to live is to enter into conflict with nature, to resist . . . all the forces that tend toward his death. One would have to be stronger than they are. But how can one be stronger than one's own nature?" And, further: "I struggle against Nature, a diabolic, devilish Nature. I have no other foe than this figure of evil [whose dark designs] are printed in my palm. Against its folly, my reason."[5] The hero struggles against a fate which a seer once read in the lines of his hand—Maurras struggles against the fate that overtook him in his youth. The arbitrary design that maddens the one is like the arbitrary affliction of deafness that mined the other's young hopes; both grimly faced and angrily opposed, and with a certain success.

It is difficult not to see in the evils Maurras spent his life denouncing the reflection of the immediate evil that afflicted him and, behind it, of the Great Evil that he hated in the world. It seems clear, in any case, that his personal pain left him little patience for the optimistic nonsense of democratic equalitarianism, his resentment against blind injustice no time for humanitarian elegies—hence, probably, his hatred of "Hebraic thought and all the dreams of justice, of happiness, and of equality it drags in its wake." To one who had known grievous injustice in his bones, justice was a delusion; goodness, either of God or of men, a dream. Good was not merely unattainable, it was indefinable: right, being positive, empirical, and human, was not. Only the stoic acceptance of such facts could permit man, caught in the chaos of an anarchic world, to establish and maintain the precarious, limited, and fundamentally disillusioned order which is peculiarly his, the disciplined order of a society capable of culture, of art, of a life the more human as it became less "natural," more reasonable, more coherent, more refined.

It was this thought that made him appreciate the grand achievement of a Catholic Church which, withstanding the pressures of "Judeo-Christian barbarism," had rebuilt and defended its lands against the forces of disorder. "An intelligent destiny," he wrote in May 1894, "has seen to it that the civilized peoples of southern Europe should only know the turbulent Oriental writings [of the Bible] when they had been mutilated, recast, transposed by the Church." Catholic order had organized the Middle Ages for the reign of beauty and the salvation of the world. Both had been in great danger since the Reformation, and now a bizarre romantic Jesus was being called up to the aid of disorder. But "I know no other Jesus than that of our Catholic tradition," declared the Catholic agnostic, citing Dante's "Sovereign Jove who was on earth crucified for us." "I shall not leave the learned retinue of Fathers, of Councils, and of Popes, and all the great men of the modern elite, to put my trust in the scriptures of four obscure Jews."[6]

The gospel of Maurras was not a gospel of love; his idea of justice was legal, not divine. Evil, once discovered and described, must be attacked and punished. Not for him discretion and detachment. "After the evidence of sage and scholar, the silence of the judge would be a form of injustice." But the evidence may be one-sided, the court prejudiced: "Maurras est sourd à force de ne pas écouter," Julien Benda told Maurice Martin du Gard. And another enemy recognized that what he hated most about Maurras and his disciples was "this determination to slander, to discredit the opponent, who is never given the credit of acting in good faith."[7]

It is hard to say to what extent a court judging on fixed principles can vary in their application. In such circumstances it is irrelevant to give anyone the benefit of the doubt. When principles are firm—as Metternich told Guizot when they met in London exile after the upheaval of 1848—error never enters the mind. Nor can there be tolerance for evil, once it has been recognized as such. All means are good to extirpate it. To fail to use them is to fail in one's duty. It may be that Maurras was deaf only to arguments that he discounted from the first.

Such firmness, however, involves considerable temptations, and it is difficult to tell at what point rocklike reason becomes deaf, deliberate rationalization. Maurras had a great capacity for believing only what he wanted to believe, and for turning supposition into fact. There is no lack of evidence, even from friendly sources, for his facile mythomania and for the stubbornness with which he clung to favorite ideas. "Nothing can alter judgments that Maurras has decided to make on people," his admiring prison companion Xavier Vallat noted ruefully; "I shall not be able to persuade him to give up a misunderstanding he likes."[8]

An expert witness, a judge, and an executioner: Maurras would try to be all these at once. Even before he succeeded, his personality merged in his task like that of Minos in the Minotaur's mask. "My life?" he said. "My life is my ideas and my books." That is where we shall find him.

The philosophy of Maurras, a system he himself considered positive and one that might be called Machiavellian in the best sense of the term, was grounded in the overwhelming mood of decadence and disgust that followed the French defeat of 1870. It was a time when many thought that greatness, glory, and adventure had deserted France, and that, as Colonel Jean-Baptiste Marchand wrote to a friend, "La génération qui vient sera bien obligée pour faire quelque chose de prendre le contre pied de ce que lui a enseigné celle qui passe en ce moment."[9]

The origins of Maurrassian ideas, like the origins of nationalism in certain critical campaigns of Maurice Barrès, were literary and artistic rather than political. It was disgust with prevailing barbarism, Maurras later declared, that sent him looking for the principles of order "first in art, then in the rest of society." This was not accidental. "We had seen the ruins in the realm of thought and taste before noticing the social, military, economic, and diplomatic damage that generally results from democracy." And so it was "by analyzing the literary errors of romanticism that we were led, indeed dragged, to study the moral and political error of a State involved in revolution." There could be no beauty without order, no order without a hierarchy of values, no hierarchy without authority both to define and to endorse it.[10]

The outline of Maurras's literary ideas appears most accessibly in an essay, less well known than some of his other works, that he wrote in 1896 on the urging of a friend.[11] For the twenty-eight-year-old Maurras, man's distinguishing characteristic was reason, but reason is merely the instrument man uses to balance the many elements in his make-up, all of which must have an opportunity to express themselves in the well-rounded human being. Balance, indeed, is a term more misleading than just: man must not *balance* the elements of his nature, but *order* them. Man fulfills himself when he uses first his reason to determine what we may call his own internal order, and then his will to express and enforce these decisions.

As long as man acted on these lines, Maurras argued, he could be trusted to show a sound judgment and a healthy standard in literature as in other fields. Thus the artist of, say, the seventeenth century could rely on the instinctive taste of his public, which, taken as a whole, was likely to be sound because it stemmed from the conscious and unconscious application of known values. Since then, however, and especially during the nineteenth century, public taste had been corrupted: private principles, education, fashion, all had contributed to the decline, and now the duty of the critic, who once merely expressed and applied prevailing standards, was to breast the tide, reformulate the canon of a healthy "taste," and educate the public.

How was this to be done?

The first step in the reform of art and taste must come by re-establishing the function of an aspect of writing which had suffered from misunderstanding and neglect: style. The form in which thoughts and values are expressed is not a secondary consideration, but the very essence of the thought one wants to formulate. Style is all-important, and style is simply the order and the movement one gives to one's own thoughts. *Le style*—and here Maurras quotes Buffon—*c'est l'homme.* In other words, form (or style) is the pattern man imposes on his own natural diversity and on the disparate, confused, and confusing impressions he receives from the outside world; it is his way of assimilating and synthesizing the *other,* and of expressing his inner self. Thus, says Maurras, style and thought are one, because when one is thinking, everything that is not style—everything, that is, that is not order and movement—is not thought, but merely the dross or residue of the act of thinking.

It would follow from this that when one attempts to express something, what matters is less what one wants to say than the way one says it, and that content acquires meaning in terms of style. Every man has his own style, and every nation, too; and their style is their true expression. And here Maurras points out that the French, after being wakened by Romanticism to a concern with French themes, made the mistake of writing in an un-French way, only to find that their "French" subjects were far more foreign than *Le Cid* or *Esther* because, though insisting on national themes, the new writing had accepted an alien, "gothic," cosmopolitan mentality more insidiously corrupting than mere subject matter could ever be.

From this disease, French literature had to be cured by being shown the merits of style—good style. The first rule of good style is simplicity, which shuns lushness, vagueness, impressionism, and other sources and reflections of confusion. To achieve simplicity one must perceive what is essential, and subordinate everything else to the central point or theme. It is also wise not to mix one's methods, and to choose a method in harmony with the tradition in which one works, in this case the language and the literature of France. "All else being equal, something written in conformity with the tradition of a language or a literature succeeds better than something cast in terms that go against old, established habits: this is obvious."

If the artist looks to tradition, he is bound to find counsel and aid; nor is anything worth while done without such help. Literary history, wrote Maurras, does not show us a single outstanding poet as indifferent to his great predecessors as the poets of the present affect to be. Of course, these arrogant contemporaries also feel the burden of the tradition they deny, but it is only an unexamined residue which they breathe in with the fashions and the climate of their time: unconscious, unfiltered, and useless. "A true tradition is examined before being accepted. False freedom ignores even the yoke its weakness makes it wear."

So, the writer must fall back upon tradition. But all traditions are not of equal worth. Differences exist between different men and between different nations, which may well be attributable to nature, but which create or reflect the superiority of one man or one nation over others. The same differences exist between traditions. Fortunately, however, there is one among all others "whose most striking characteristic is its almost complete conformity with the principles of taste which are the expression of the highest and best in man." Born in Greece out of Homer's ashes, this paragon of traditions had found a new fatherland in Rome, had survived in France and the Italian cities during the Middle Ages, and had then revived to conquer all of Europe. Its focal point was Paris, as once it had been Athens, and its high-water mark was reached in the France of the late sixteenth and seventeenth centuries.

Here was a tradition both essential and natural to France. History shows clearly, wrote Maurras, ever on the lookout for laws commanding the evolution and the well-being of his land, that if the French structure remains firm it is because it has been put together by classical architects: the language, the Catholic Church, the Roman administration and its law, with all the influence these exercised on the policies of the kings of France. And this classical tradition, which is France's own, is also better than all others: stronger and more forceful, more brilliant, more delicate, and more enduring than anything that one can find elsewhere.

Indeed, Maurras goes on, one is justified in calling barbarous all that is alien to classical letters, not only because it is cut off from the treasury of Greco-Latin creations, but because it is contrary to the noblest in man. Barbarism, in effect, begins when man prefers his impulses to his reason, and insists on having his own way regardless of his own wisdom or of the accumulated wisdom of his people. There is barbarism when man's disorderly impressions and impulses pretend to express themselves, unordered and unrefined, in a work of art. There is barbarism when out of the mists of undisciplined minds men produce an incoherent patchwork of ideas. And there is barbarism, too, in the eclectic toying with different ideas, techniques, or styles, the turning of words and rhymes into the gewgaws and baubles that prevailed around the end of the century, a pastime degrading to the material as well as to the artist.

In Maurras's eyes this was exactly what the Romantics and their heirs had been guilty of, in abandoning the creative discipline of their own tradition to choose at random among alien experiments and trinkets, or simply to indulge their own anarchy of thought. Aside from Anatole France, no one in the older literary generation had bothered to maintain the classical values, and few gave classical letters a thought before Maurras, Jean Moréas, and a handful of others founded the Ecole Romane, to restore a flaccid literature to the clear virility of yore. Maurras was in a good position to know that the literary reformers of the Ecole Romane were not meeting much success. And yet the prevailing degeneration which set their teeth on edge was bound to have more serious effects in France than elsewhere, because the classical spirit was not only the highest tradition mankind had produced, but the essence of the nation itself. Frenchmen ignored it at their peril. They must rediscover it and return, like Atlas, to their natural source of vigor; only then would they be able to contribute to the common fund of human creativity from which of late they had done no more than draw.

It was natural and easy to translate this point of view into political terms. It is possible to discover the laws of a saner, more virile literature; but, as Comte once wrote, "Pour compléter les lois il faut des volontés." Will always loomed large in Maurras's scheme of things, and it would become ever more important with time. We can find the clearest statement of his view in *Les Vergers sur la mer,* published in 1937:

> There is nothing more certain than the fact that no man is his own master, that no man rules or possesses that obscure physical realm where the tides and tumult of our blood are stirring. But one must *will* to rule it, one must *tend* to it; however insolent the claim, it is man's only guarantee against the world of darkness he carries in him. To react against one's internal sphere is a condition of an energetic and prosperous life.[12]

A reasoned, cultivated (hence, inevitably, tradition-inspired) discipline and self-discipline is the condition of success in every sphere of life: for politics as for literature, for society as for the individual. But, in order to be sound, the political structure, like the literary one, must obey certain rules: "There are certain truths in politics which everything affirms and nothing denies, and against which the orator's verbiage or the intriguer's maneuver is powerless.

These truths shall triumph . . . gradually, as the world shall feel the need to verify them."[13]

The need to discover such truths as these was making itself felt even as the young Maurras scribbled his meditations on literature in his small room above the rue du Dragon. For what was true in art was true in society, too. One did not have to look far to see that a decadent art was no more than a reflection of the decadent society in which it thrived. This decadence, one of the major tenets of Maurrassian doctrine, was proved by the defeat of France in the War of 1870, by the subsequent loss of Alsace-Lorraine, and by the decreasing birth rate. All these were both causes and effects of the country's general decay, and the moral and social upheaval that was only too obvious, as it nearly always is, was cited as additional evidence.

From Athens, where he had gone in 1896 to report on the first of the newly revived Olympic games, Maurras looked back at his homeland and was dismayed to see how insignificant it appeared, how strong the German influence loomed over the Greek court, how solidly the British had established their power in the Mediterranean. The factions he saw tearing Greece apart were the same as those at work in France, both stemming from the liberal and democratic misconceptions which the French Revolution had broadcast through the world. Humiliated and alarmed, Maurras calculated the debit balance of the Revolution, which was responsible in his eyes for the decay and corruption of the moral and political fiber of every people it had touched.

Back in France, his impressions were confirmed. Only a corrupt society could split so brutally over issues like those of the Dreyfus affair. And this was stressed by the growing number of foreigners to be found in public life and public affairs, metics (as he had called them in an article of 1894), who could not react to French problems in a French way because they had no roots in French tradition and carried with them none of that intuitive understanding that would belong to men who shared a common heritage. As long as these aliens were left free to colonize France and increase their influence in every walk of life, the country would be not only divided "but betrayed, occupied, exploited by an internal enemy." Thus, before any attempt at synthesis or union, these foreign or ill-assimilated bodies—Freemasons, Protestants, foreigners, and Jews—must be either regulated or expelled.[14]

The problem presented by the metics, however, was only the expression of a deeper disease, a more general disorder. Deprived of any definite or discernible purpose, French patriotism was disoriented, French policy lacked coherence. There was only one solution: "French patriotism needs a permanent expression, which can be nothing but a king or, more correctly, a succession of kings."[15] The common purpose that France ignored, the principle of unity it so obviously lacked, the embodiment of the common weal that alone had made the power and the greatness of the country in the past, could be found in the monarchy. Around its kings, the French people had awakened to their peculiar unity. Slowly, perseveringly, the nation had been forged, its territory assembled, its self-consciousness hammered out by a long line of men who identified themselves with the nation that they ruled and led, who devoted themselves to the nation so completely that even natural human selfishness operated in favor of national interests. As Maurras saw it, this monarchy would be limited, but its legitimacy, ensuring public peace, would protect the people from those movements caused by the ambition of achieving supreme power. It would be "a kind of government in which the throne, with a precise, appointed, legal place, would find itself a necessary part of the whole but far from being the whole."[16]

At their best, the forty kings who in a thousand years had forged France had made the country greater, more powerful, more prosperous. At worst, the hereditary principle had ensured at least some continuity of purpose, and prevented the squandering of national energy in disputes over the succession to power. The monarchy had also ensured that no divergency and no dispute shattered national unity. In the last resort, all parties were one in their loyalty to France, a France embodied in the person of the king, and no one party could ever "own" France to the exclusion of all others. A party out of power could, and would, still consider itself "His Majesty's Opposition."

As long as this state of affairs had lasted, Maurras believed, the land had prospered. It may not have been perfect; but it worked, and for a long time, to the greater glory and the greater good of France. But then, theorists, men who thought they could perfect what needed no perfecting, interfered. At the most, what the country required in 1789 had been certain reforms. As ignorant of historical realities as they were of human nature, the revolutionaries sought to tear down the existing structure and rebuild it on the basis of ideas that were false because they ignored the real nature of man, which was selfish and imperfect, and of society, which could only subsist when the naturally lawless instincts were tamed, taught, and harnessed, not left free to wreak havoc at the general expense. The chaos of 1789, the instability that followed, were the results of this wrongheaded meddling. The murder of Louis XVI broke the great contract between France and her kings and left her at the mercy of adventurers and factions, all of whom tried to capture power in order to further their own ideas or interests. Except for the brief interlude of Restoration, the story of France since 1793 could be told in terms of a struggle for power between diverse groups, all eager to run the country in their own interests. But these interests coincided only by chance with the interests of France, for no man, no faction, no party could identify itself with the whole nation as the king had done.

It followed that present disruption could be traced back to the unfortunate moment when, having made the helmsman walk the plank, the French allowed the ship of state to sail about uncontrolled, at the mercy of winds, tides, and drunken members of the crew. But if the cause of their present ills was clear, so was the solution: monarchy must be restored, rival factions must learn to submit to its nonparty rule, rival interests must be ordered by the one figure whose interest is in the good of the nation as a whole. With the return of the king, the nation could begin purging itself of the harmful humors and evil habits it had picked up during the previous century. To advance the restoration, to persuade Frenchmen of its need, all means were good—even legal ones. And the end would justify the means.

Persuasion, however, was not enough—first, because no guarantee existed that a sufficient number of people could be persuaded to see where their true interests lay; second, because in any case democratic principles were corrupting and false. A moment always comes, however, when success depends on readiness to seize the initiative. The main thing is to be prepared. To talk of armed uprisings would be to ignore reality, but a *coup d'état* was within the realm of possibility.

In *Si le coup de force est possible* (1910) Maurras made these ideas explicit. The future belonged to men of action, and only by action would political truth be re-established in the land. The coup which would achieve this could be carried out by a general, a prefect, or a minister who controlled some part of public force, or by a resolute group following an energetic leader. The occasion might be furnished by a military mutiny, a conspiracy, a popular rising, or simply a major riot, or by someone who, like General Monck in 1660 or Talleyrand in 1814, would throw his weight into the scales of restoration. But an essential prerequisite was "a royalist frame of mind," which, since it did not exist, must be created. French opinion must be introduced to the idea that such a coup is not only possible but necessary, and familiarized with the solution to national problems it had so far ignored. "Il faut créer une mentalité conspiratrice": one must persuade the public that royalists really meant what they said.[17]

In the parable of *Mademoiselle Monk* Maurras at a much later period personified his dream in the fashionable, fanciful Aymée de Coigny, born before the Revolution but still charming in Napoleon's day, whose royalist lover, the Marquis de Boisgelin, converted her to the idea of restoring the exiled Louis XVIII to his legitimate throne. Convinced by Boisgelin, Aymée in turn catechized Talleyrand, who, without her intervention, might not have taken the Bourbon side in the crucial days of 1814.

The accuracy of the story is, in this case, irrelevant; to Maurras it seemed the perfect illustration of his theme. Professional politicians have to be inspired; men with power or with the opportunity to use it must be prompted by those who know what would be best for them to do. The work of new-model royalists, like the work of the Comtesse de Coigny, should be educational, suggestive, one might almost say Fabian. In the meantime, the possibility of an intermediary dictatorship could not be spurned. As Maurras had written in 1888, "We are all a little Bonapartist." And so, though a dictator would be far from perfect, and would lack, in particular, the stability that the country needed, he might at least be left to pulverize the prevailing elements of disorder and clear the way for the necessary restoration. "S'il fait la besogne, s'il nous rend ce service, on lui pardonnera facilement d'y avoir mis quelque vivacité. Grâce à lui, l'institution d'un ordre sera redevenue possible dans notre pays."[18]

Such arguments appeared impressive. Even more provocative were the circumstances of their formulation. Arguments drawn from history can be twisted all ways to prove a desired point, but arguments based on present circumstances, even misinterpreted, have a certain convincing force. Even before the Dreyfus affair had gained momentum, colonial difficulties, financial scandals, and the revelation of corruption at the highest levels of politics and government argued impressively in favor of Maurras. Many people, tired of religious strife and parliamentary finagling, were looking for a force that could heal social and intellectual rifts and in some way discipline the national energies.

The contemporary revival of interest in the Catholic Church appears as a result of the same reaction. It was part of a trend in favor of authority, hierarchy, and discipline, rather than a search for ultimate truth, which did not seem nearly so interesting. Shortly before the First World War, when Renan's grandson, Ernest Psichari, was converted to Catholicism, he delighted to find in it "clear duties, well-defined dogmas, an internal and external rule." Psichari, as we shall see, was an admirer of Maurras and of the Action Française. Another young man, soon to be active in its ranks, would mark the point in describing his feelings for the new royalist doctrine: "Comme c'est clair! Comme c'est à l'emporte-pièce!"[19]

But all this lay far ahead, and, though the general lines of the doctrine we have glimpsed had already shaped themselves in Maurras's mind, their elaboration remained to be worked out. On his return from Greece, Maurras, convinced now that royalism was the only salvation and that the country's interests must be placed above all else, found in the vagaries of the Dreyfus case his first opportunity to apply his ideas to events. That an innocent man should suffer, he argued, is a terrible thing. But to endanger or harm the French Army would be much worse. If alleged injustice can be put right only at the cost of French security, the cost would be too great: the Army would be disorganized, the country's defenses would be imperiled, and thousands of innocent people would risk suffering and death for the saving of one.[20] By 1898, however, he no longer accepted even the presumption of the Jewish Captain's innocence: Dreyfus's supporters were too suspect for his guilt not to be reaffirmed by association. Hence, when Maurras wrote his apologia for Henry, he could do so in the serene conviction that no one would be hurt by his words except those who richly deserved to be.

"The apologia for Colonel Henry," an early adherent would write a long time later, "was the starting point of the Action Française, its foundation, the password by which its supporters recognized each other. Maurras had handled the matter with a decisiveness that surprised and scandalized the opposition. For all those, however, whom idle moral fancies did not deprive of common sense, what could be clearer than the innocence of the forgery, provided one knew Dreyfus guilty?"[21]

It was becoming more difficult, however, to be certain that Dreyfus was guilty, and a series of ministerial resignations and collapsing cabinets did not help matters. In the autumn of 1898, the Criminal Chamber of the High Court of Appeals was asked to consider Mme Alfred Dreyfus's new petition that a revision be granted. Five months later, the case was transferred to the High Court of Appeals sitting as a body, where it was probable that revision would be viewed less sympathetically. Within a few days of the transfer, on February 16, 1899, the sudden death of anti-revisionist President Félix Faure brought on a political crisis that would last the rest of the year.

It was in the midst of these confused events that the Ligue de la Patrie Française was founded, to oppose the efforts of Dreyfus's defenders, notably the Ligue des Droits de l'Homme. Where the older organization recruited its members from the intellectual Left, the new one sought them on the intellectual Right. Against the University it raised the Institut and the Académie Française; against the dull, scrupulous scholars the fashionable critics and men of letters. Only three days were needed, the first days of January 1899, to collect twenty-five Academicians; a little longer to flaunt the support of fourscore members of other academies, besides other, lesser lights in the hundreds and thousands. Catholics, conservatives, nationalists, university teachers like Louis Dimier, Gabriel Syveton, and Henri Vaugeois, writers like Georges Fonsegrive and Maurras, gravitated toward the Ligue. It was in the Ligue's ranks that they met, that they talked, and, as we shall see, that before too long they went on to further action.

For events, which until 1898 had moved so slowly, were being precipitated by the death of President Faure and the election in his stead of a moderate—but a moderate revisionist—Emile Loubet.

It is difficult to know exactly what took place behind the scenes in the course of 1898; but nationalists and royalists, in separate conspiracies, seem to have plotted the overthrow of the regime, possibly with the help of Army officers offended by the disrespect and criticism to which they had been subjected. These plans must have been confused and hastened by the President's unexpected death. A rash attempt to carry them through on the day of his funeral failed. A little later, in June, a nationalist attack on the new President, coming in the wake of the unremitting violence of the preceding twelve months, stimulated a lively Republican reaction. The nationalist Paul Déroulède and the royalists André Buffet and Eugène de Lur-Saluces were implicated in the conspiracies and subsequently brought before a High Court of Parliament in December 1899, where they were sentenced to varying terms of exile.

In the meantime, the High Court of Appeal had quashed the first judgment against Dreyfus and ordered the reopening of his case. A warship sped off to bring him back from Devil's Island, and hopes of a pardon ran high as Dreyfusards and anti-Dreyfusards dueled and fought. But on September 9, 1899, a second court-martial, held in the dreary town of Rennes, again found Dreyfus guilty, although two officers of the five-man court voted for acquittal. The inconsistent verdict found the accused guilty of treason, but added "mitigating circumstances," unspecified, and reduced the original sentence to ten years' detention—too little for a traitor, too much for an innocent man, unlikely to satisfy anyone. Dreyfus was soon released with an official pardon, but his supporters continued to struggle for complete rehabilitation, and were finally successful, though in circumstances which, as we shall see, continued to the end the equivocal nature of the case.

While the legal side of the affair was drawing to an animated close and the conspirators against the Republic were being brought to book, the anti-revisionists found themselves blocked and frustrated at every turn. The great affair had finally been resolved, and they had lost. The ruling government of Waldeck-Rousseau showed itself determined to affirm the Republic and cow its enemies in the Church, in the Army, in the leagues, and in the streets. The sometime-swaggering Ligue de la Patrie Française began to disintegrate. Funds, once plentiful, were drying up. Only the faithful and enthusiastic few would ride out the doldrums—those who really knew what they were about, and thought it worth a long, hard struggle. Among these Gideon's men, some of the firmest and the most clearheaded were to be found in the circle formed by those whose rallying cry had been furnished by Maurras's 1898 apologia for the forgery of Colonel Henry.

Born of the confusion of the Dreyfus affair, the Action Française was from the first an attempt to work out the broad lines of French recovery. Early in the 1890's some of those who had been interested in such matters before the name of Dreyfus had ever been heard had joined Paul Desjardins's liberal Union pour l'Action Morale, founded to unite men of all political opinions and religious confessions in an effort to establish the reign of virtue and morality in the world.

It was in the spring of 1898 that two such men of good will, Maurice Pujo and Henri Vaugeois, sickened by their country's plight yet unwilling to follow the Union into the Dreyfusard camp, founded a Comité d'Action Française to influence the elections of that year. The Comité's appeal to the electorate presented the Dreyfusard campaign as a revival of *panamisme,* a diversion to serve the interests of corrupt politicians and financiers. The two founders were quite unknown: Vaugeois, at thirty-four the more impressive and the older of the two, a teacher of philosophy by profession and somewhat left of center by inclination, had all the patriotic Jacobinism one might expect from one who counted among his forebears a regicide member of the Revolutionary Convention. Pujo, eight years his junior, had studied at the Orléans *lycée* at the same time as Charles Péguy, had won a prize at eighteen with an essay on Spinoza's moral philosophy, and thence had wandered into vague intellectual pursuits overlaid by Wagnerism and an interest in German poetry. Since the age of twenty, in 1892, he had directed a self-founded review, *L'Art et la vie,* one of many publications then drifting down the narcissistic waterways of the fin-de-siècle Left Bank. They enlisted Vaugeois's cousin, Captain Jules Caplain-Cortambert, and fire-eating Colonel Comte Georges-Henri de Villebois-Mareuil, soon to die fighting for the Boers in South Africa. But their appeal seems to have gone unheeded. Unable to influence the election results, the Comité languished during the summer, but its moving spirits had only begun their work. On December 19, 1898, Ernest Judet's nationalist *L'Eclair* published a letter signed by Pujo explaining how intellectuals interested in contributing to "French action" should go about getting started. For Pujo, at this time, the purpose of such action should be "to remake France, republican and free, into a State as organized at home, as powerful abroad, as it was under the Old Regime." And this "without recurring to the forms of the past," for, Pujo was careful to explain, "nothing can be done with the dead"—*on ne fait rien avec les morts.*

Meanwhile, a group of men who believed strongly in the uses of the dead as providing the traditions and firm bases of all human societies, had founded a movement that would at first overshadow these timid fumblings. Organized, as we have seen, to defend the country against subversive Dreyfusards, the Ligue de la Patrie Française started off, on December 31, with a tremendous surge of activity. For the next few months, the men of the little Comité d'Action Française, who had played a crucial part in its founding, were engaged in helping to marshal those intellectuals who would defend order against the theoretical preachers of morality and justice.

Pujo's article in *L'Eclair* had not been to the taste of the Patrie Française's respectable hierarchy, which was anxious to remain politically neutral, and above all to avoid the harsh words and hard knocks that can endanger well-run political and literary careers. In the circumstances Vaugeois and his followers did not take long to conclude that the Patrie Française was too weak, too soft, altogether too pusillanimous a vehicle for the salvation of France. In January 1899, Vaugeois for the first time met Maurras, who was then thirty, and the two agreed that the Patrie Française was not moving fast enough, or, indeed, toward any definite goal. They began to canvass possibilities of separate action, tried unsuccessfully to raise the funds needed to start a five-cent evening paper, and finally, in despair, set out to organize their independent existence.[a]

On June 20, 1899, in a public lecture presented under the aegis of the Patrie Française and presided over by one of its luminaries, François de Mahy, Vaugeois introduced the Action Française to the nationalist public. A prospectus published at the same time claimed a strength, probably exaggerated, of six hundred and the aim of "creating a closer relationship between the people and the men of high culture whose initiative has brought about as a first result the magnificent expansion of the Patrie Française." When this relationship had been achieved, they could work together to stimulate "the revival of more honest politics."

At last, on July 10, 1899, there appeared under a gray duodecimo cover the first number of the new movement's *Bulletin,* or as it shortly became, *Revue de l'Action Française*. The "little gray review" would be issued in this format every two weeks until it increased its size and changed its color to blue in 1904. Blue or gray, the fortnightly remained the center of Action Française activities until 1908, and its pages reflect the shifts, discussions, and heart-searchings that turned what started as a patriotic republican movement into a royalist one—the most *sui generis* and the most successful neo-royalist movement of the twentieth century.

The paradox of this change appears when we remember that of the men who first launched the Action Française on June 20, 1899, only one was a professed royalist. Vaugeois, a professor of philosophy at the College of Coulommiers and a sometime radical; Pujo, who not long before had dabbled in anarchism; the first and short-lived president of the society, François de Mahy, a former Minister of the Navy, were all republicans. There were Bonapartists, Catholics, freethinkers, positivists, and democrats. As for Maurras, apparently the only royalist among them, he was still overshadowed by better known or more active figures, and he reserved much of his energy for the royalist publications in which he regularly wrote. The evolution that the Action Française underwent during the first two years of its existence was due to the rigor with which some of its original postulates were followed to what seemed increasingly logical conclusions. And the most striking aspect of the process was the original detachment of men who, once they had thought out their position and all that it implied, would become tenaciously committed to their beliefs.

[a] On February 10, 1899, Maurras wrote to Maurice Barrès: "Voici une lettre officielle. Le groupe qui se réunit au Café Voltaire (Vaugeois, Pujo, etc.) et dont je suis toutes les délibérations me charge de vous demander si l'on peut citer votre nom dans la liste des collaborateurs possibles du journal? . . . La nuance est nationaliste, avec quelques propensions au socialisme." Though pessimistic about their chances, Barrès agreed (in a letter of March 8, 1899, Maurras papers). See Archives Nationales, Action Française, F^7 12862 (subsequently only file number given), 1/3 of May 24, 1899, for reports of Vaugeois's and Caplain's efforts to found a newspaper, and the displeasure of Patrie Française directors, who call them "l'élément tapeur de la Patrie Française."

In the public lecture of June 20, which was reprinted in the first issue of the *Revue,* Vaugeois described the Action Française as a guerrilla band, turned toward the future in its inspiration and its aims. More important, perhaps, he voiced the empirical religious views that would remain one of the movement's distinguishing characteristics: "French morality," he declared, "does not depend on theories . . . It can be atheistic." (This statement was greeted with loud approval.) The wonderful thing about the Catholic faith, "this attenuated form of Christianity, filtered by the happy genius of France," was its practical sense. The whole address was in this tone: Vaugeois was a Catholic, he said, because Catholicism was French, and a republican for the same reason. The Republic was not capable of any sustained resistance to the general sense of the national instinct. It could not be long, therefore, before it reflected the authoritarian trend, whose rise he was glad to welcome. Some people in the audience stirred uneasily at this; others applauded. François de Mahy protested: the tone of the speech, the mood of the audience, were both too revolutionary, too authoritarian, for his taste. But Vaugeois was quick to reassure him: nothing was further from his mind than Caesarism or revolution. No one knew better than he the terrible dangers inherent in illegal action, brute force, or *pronunciamentos,* all of which the Action Française would shun. The only kind of reform worth having, the only kind that the Action Française would seek, was one obtained by legal means. As for dictatorship, "I have been, I am, and I shall remain a republican, that is to say a friend of freedom."[22]

This diffidence was of short duration, however. By August 1, Vaugeois, who three weeks earlier had asserted that the Action Française turned not to the past but to the future, had changed his mind: "Réaction, d'abord." Above everything, he now asserted, the Action Française was a turning back, a reaction. "This is what, in fact, we think, and we shall not hesitate to admit it, for there is nothing frightening about such a turning toward the past." A week later François de Mahy resigned the presidency because of Vaugeois's too explicit anti-republicanism, and Vaugeois had to explain himself again:

> There are a lot of us young republicans torn asunder by the conflict of two needs. On the one hand, there is the need of order, authority, governmental force, the basis of the reactionary spirit and of monarchy. But, unfortunately [here an echo of his friend Pujo], monarchy in France is dead and there is nothing to be done with the dead! On the other hand, there is the need of freedom, of progress, of an opening toward the future, all the things that go to make up the republican spirit. But the present republic satisfies neither of these aspirations. It is feeble and anarchic, without being really liberal—or free.[23]

French character and national needs are defined more explicitly in another exploratory article of 1899: France is Catholic, and so must be rid of Protestants, Freemasons, and Jews; France is agricultural, and so needs a protectionist policy and a back-to-the-land movement; France is military, hence her glory and the glory of her arms are a condition of her happiness; France is republican, but not democratic. But the empiricism was still eclectic: a month after this statement of France's republican character, Maurras in the same pages proclaimed that he, for his part, was no republican. The republican doctrine was absurd and puerile, the Republic the last degree of French decadence. The serious reader, consistent in his patriotism, persistent in his will to do the best for France, must make up his mind once and for all that France would not be saved until the people decided to abandon legalism in order to reaffirm justice.[24] Not surprisingly, many readers were shocked by such assertions, and the next issue of the *Revue* had to reaffirm the principle that debate among patriots was free, and to make it clear that the Action Française as such was not royalist and intended to remain aloof from any sovereign family.

To begin with, then, the Action Française circle was looking for a political doctrine and trying to formulate one by talking. It began by eliminating what it did not like, democracy and parliamentarianism, but it refused to accept royalist or, for that matter, Bonapartist ideas, with their exclusive implications. Although they were sympathetic to the Orléans family, most of the group clearly felt that the Republic was in France to stay and that restoration was an impossibility.[25]

But Maurras was at work. In the royalist *Gazette de France* of May 6, 1899, he had defined his view of what restored monarchy should be: "To the hereditary institution of the *family,* add the permanent ruling entities of the *commune* and the *province,* and the professional stabilizing institution of political *authority*: there you have the formula of monarchy." A few weeks later, as the government started proceedings against royalist leaders, he decided to answer the government's challenge with a challenge of his own. He drew up a brief, specific royalist manifesto, "Dictateur et Roi," outlining the double role of dictator and king that he envisaged for the restored prince, "first meting out justice to those who have committed crimes against the State; then proceeding to reconstruct and run the country."[26]

In manuscript form, the essay contributed to the conversion of several who read it, including Pujo. Maurras then solicited the ideas of the two banished royalist leaders, Buffet and Lur-Saluces, who were living in Brussels. "Dictateur et Roi," expanded with their help and annotated with great talent and dialectic skill, became the neo-royalist bible, *L'Enquête sur la monarchie* (1900). After reading it, Vaugeois told Maurras, "You are the only royalist in France." To which Maurras replied, "Join me and there will be two of us!" It took a little more than that to convince Vaugeois, but by 1901 he too had succumbed. Two articles of that summer expressed his new-found royalism. To seek a better republic, he wrote, was to follow a false hope. The only tenable principle was that of monarchy, because it provided the only logical conclusion to any serious search for order and stability.[b]

In November 1899, Maurras had sought to still Barrès's fears of his subversive influence. His friends on the *Revue de l'Action Française,* he reported, never failed to find objections to his monarchist ideas: "I have no hold on Caplain, or on [Paul] Copin-Albancelli, or on [Maurice] Spronck, or on [Paul] Delbet, or on Colonel de Villebois-Mareuil. . . . I am a tiny minority, ever opposed by Moreau and Vaugeois, themselves solidly backed by fourteen or fifteen champions who are ready to take their place. It seems to me that the Republic is well defended." But these defenses soon crumbled before the trumpets of Maurras. In December 1900, the original association was dissolved and replaced by a new one. Caplain, with Vaugeois, had been a joint director of the *Revue,* but he, Copin-Albancelli, and their friends drew away from an enterprise "which was now going to be run on principles quite different from the *republican and national* program on which the first Action Française appeal had been based." Within a few months, Vaugeois, now sole political director, Montesquiou, and Moreau all publicly acknowledged their conversion.[27]

During all this time, the Action Française had remained for the most part out of the public eye, just another little clique of the sort that flower briefly and fade away when funds and juvenile enthusiasm run out. Its shift to the royalist point of view attracted little attention. Sometime republican friends veered away, and royalists remained wary—partly because the new recruits seemed too poor and insignificant to matter, partly because bred-in-the-bone royalists had little in common with such highly rationalistic converts. Indeed, the Action Française was more readily accepted by the real Chouans, who appreciated its enthusiasm and hard-boiled enterprise, than by the domesticated royalists of urban journalism and politics. Most of the latter, having abandoned every principle but live and let live, disliked the new men's brash talk and reckless action.

By the turn of the century, the great business and financial families had shifted their interest, if not their allegiance, to the Republic, and sources of income for royalist activity had begun to dry up. Former contributors abandoned a cause already lost when royalist leaders appeared before the High Court of 1899, and moved toward a republican opportunism that promised better pickings and better hopes of order. The Church itself, the most important of royalty's props, had shifted its support to the established order and thus removed the last excuse of many who had hesitated in their allegiance. After 1892, royalism, which had missed every opportunity since Sedan, be-

[b] *RAF,* July 15, Aug. 1, 1901; but it is only on November 1, 1901, in an article of hyperbolic rapture, that Vaugeois accounts for the assurance of his new-found revelation by a visit to the Duc d'Orléans at Karlsruhe.

came a really lost cause; and the first to realize this and to act upon it were those whose business it was to invest in winning causes only.

But it was not simply the royalist press that suffered from lack of funds; the popular nationalist press, notably Edouard Drumont's *Libre Parole* and Henri Rochefort's *L'Intransigeant,* which appealed to the chauvinistic radicalism that Boulangism had revealed, was also short of readers, and therefore of funds. The newspaper-buying public preferred the mush of the great dailies like *Le Matin* to the definite and sometimes disturbing opinions of the *feuilles d'opinion.* Serious people read *Le Temps,* of course; unserious people, the penny press. As for "society," it sought either the solid social pages of a few fashionable dailies (*Gaulois, L'Echo de Paris*), or else the novelty that persistent old fighters had lost long ago.

Most people paid their pennies to papers that ground their axes more discreetly, and turned to opinion sheets only in times of crisis, when the banalities of the great dailies no longer sufficed. From this point of view, crisis and scandal were the lifeblood of the political papers. It is no accident that the great scandals that shook the Third Republic were all revealed, set up, or triggered by publications like the *Libre Parole* or the *Action française.* The former had got its start by revealing the graft and parliamentary corruption of the Panama affair. The Dreyfus affair—also, to begin with, sparked by Drumont—served in its turn to launch a thousand sheets.[c] When, with the botched compromise of Rennes, public interest in the Dreyfus affair began to wane, and when the new government of Pierre Waldeck-Rousseau affirmed its grip and smashed all hopes of effective agitation, the briefly prosperous political journals had to battle among themselves for the attentions of a rapidly dwindling public.

This was the background of the Action Française's entrance upon the scene: too insignificant to exploit the possibilities of 1898 and 1899, it made its way in a period of public indifference. Along with a score of other nationalist and royalist organizations, it had to struggle for limited funds and a limited public. Part of its achievement lies in the fact that it created for itself what might pass for a new public: it combined and almost reconciled the popular radicalism of nationalism with the reactionary elitism of the royalists. For the first time in almost a century students could be both royalist and radical.

The achievement was original. But it meant that the movement and its publications would grow mostly at the expense of two other hard-pressed movements, would prosper only as their competitors withered. It is not insignificant that when, in 1907 and 1908, the Action Française seriously began

[c] As Gaston Méry wrote Léon Daudet on December 18, 1898 (F. D. papers): "Et puis, croyez-vous que cette bonne foule qui se bouscule dans nos escaliers pour apporter son obole à la souscription se trompe! Cet élan, voyez-vous, ce ne sont pas des sentiments faux qui le provoquent!"

to think of a daily paper, it first considered buying the old royalist *Soleil,* then the once great, now shaky *Libre Parole.* It could think in these terms because it had developed a doctrine that would appeal to the readers of both papers. And this, in turn, was a result of the Dreyfus affair.

It is always said, and rightly, that the Action Française was born of the Dreyfus affair. What is less clear is that the Action Française, as we know it, could not have existed had not the Affair shuffled established political positions so as to permit the kind of alliance the new movement would represent.

On December 10, 1898, the *Gazette de France* had published a declaration of the Jeunesses Royalistes de France affirming that the nation had broken in two: "On one side true France and the Army, on the other the Republic and the Jews." The situation was a little more complex than that: for beside the Army, the Church, and the familiar Conservatives now stood the republican troops of nationalist radicalism, men of Jacobin temper who had followed Déroulède and Rochefort instead of the Dreyfusard champion Georges Clemenceau. And once they had been defeated, memories of common struggle, hatreds surviving against the same enemies, created a new bond between them. Equally important, however, the success of the Dreyfusard forces had entrenched the Left in the seats of power and turned them into beneficiaries and defenders of established order. In the wilderness, the nationalists remembered their radical origins; if one did not look too closely, their social chauvinism could be connected with the social Catholicism of patriotic conservatives. Since the latter held the purse strings, arguments for a closer look seemed unconvincing. It was a junction that could be effected only in the opposition, where opportunities of application were lacking and reconciliation could be maintained in theory even though agreement might be difficult in practice. But someone had to see the possibility, and formulate the doctrine that would achieve it. This was the intuition of Maurras, and the achievement of the Action Française.

One of the things that qualified the Action Française for its new role was the fact that its members were untainted by any association with the classical royalist movements. Practically none of its early leaders could boast any royalist antecedents. Vaugeois had been a Radical-Socialist; Léon Daudet, the scion of a great republican family, had been radical and anti-Boulangist; Léon de Montesquiou, grandson of the governess of the King of Rome, had rallied to the Republic; René Quinton, the first famous scientist to join, was a great-nephew of Danton; young Eugène Cavaignac, the first winner of the Action Française's history prize, was the grandson of a Jacobin. Lucien Moreau, a member of the solid Larousse family, never baptized, had been converted by Maurras from moral and philosophical anarchy; Jacques Bainville's clan had been radical republicans, his father a supporter and friend of the hirsute Camille Pelletan; as for Jacques Maritain, he was the grandson of one of the founders of the Republic, the austere Jules Favre. Others, like Colonel Georges Larpent or Frédéric Delebecque, had come from the Bonapartist camp. Maurice Pujo had royalist forebears, but he had ignored them to become an idealistic anarchist. And if Frédéric Amouretti was a staunch royalist, Maxime Réal del Sarte could pride himself on descent from a member of the first Paris Commune.

What brought these men together was an overriding love of France, a great respect for order, and faith in the orderly processes of reason. Convinced by the failure of nationalist agitation and by the results of the 1902 elections that the time for a coup had passed, they set out to prepare the way for its return by educating people to see things their way.

As early as August 1899, when Waldeck-Rousseau ordered the arrest of the chief royalist leaders, Maurras and Vaugeois had called for active reprisals, including attacks against certain witnesses at the Rennes trial and other enemies of the nation. They found themselves in a minority before the rest of the Action Française editorial board, who believed in more restrained tactics. The two men drew their own conclusions: "They don't want to do anything," said Vaugeois. "They may be right in thinking that the time for action is past. It may be an indication that we have to get down at once to education, to teaching." "And," said Maurras, "to establishing the subject matter to be taught!" *Si non e vero, e ben trovato*: first the *Revue,* then the student groups founded shortly after, then the Institute, planned in 1905, opened in 1906, and finally the newspaper, in 1908, were all pedagogic enterprises designed first to define a doctrine, then to explain and inculcate it as effectively as possible.

In January 1899, a police report on the Jeunesses Royalistes, which had been working since 1895 to reorganize royalist groups disbanded after the *ralliement* and the 1893 elections, described it as the only royalist group with a serious organization and representing any real interest. Nearly five years later, another police report on royalist activities and royalist leagues still contained no word of the Action Française. When, in March 1905, the Action Française at last appeared in a police report, it was mentioned only briefly.[28] Eight months later, however, the tone had changed: the Action Française was active in student circles, its propaganda had achieved an important number of conversions; the violence it advocated, the activities it inspired, must be watched. But the new movement, whose "philosophical and scientific tone attracts a good many people," was still far from alone and unchallenged: The Ligue des Etudiants Patriotes and a monarchist movement called Le Rayon were quite as lively. By May 1906, however, police informants had concluded that other reactionary groups would henceforth follow in the wake of the Action Française.[29]

What had happened between 1899 and 1906? How had the small group that met at the Café de Flore come to be recognized as the leaders of French reaction? Persistence was part of their success, capacity also, and luck, and the talent and readiness to seize the right moment.

The men who gathered at the Flore in 1899 were young: Vaugeois, at thirty-five, was the oldest. Maurras was thirty-one, Moreau twenty-four, Pujo twenty-seven; Bainville, only twenty, looked as if he were still in school. Beside the celebrities of the Ligue de la Patrie Française, neither their names nor their activities could count for much. What they did not like about the vast new Ligue was that by aiming for numbers it had become a mob; that to attract as many followers as possible it had adopted slogans that would please everyone. In speeches pitched, in the best demagogic tradition, to attract as many and disturb as few as possible, the orators of the Ligue—Jules Lemaître, François Coppée, Gabriel Syveton, Louis Dausset—had avoided formulating a concrete program to which anyone could take exception, had indeed avoided any clear doctrine at all. Hence, complained Vaugeois and his friends, the Ligue's public action was, as it was bound to be, divided and ineffective.

Worst of all, the Ligue, although founded in response to ideological attacks upon the instruments of order, hierarchy, and social discipline, did not realize that these could not be defended or affirmed without first discarding the liberal ideology that had allowed things to come to such a pass. Dreyfus had been judged and found guilty. The heads of the Army and of the State affirmed him guilty. To question the authority of the court that had condemned him, of the men who stood by it, was to question the principle of authority itself, and with it the existence of society, which could not endure without it.

Compared with the welfare of the State, the guilt or innocence of the condemned officer was a minor issue, and those who thought otherwise could only do so on the basis of values which, if applied, were bound to reduce State and society to a shambles. Thoughtless or deliberate, the Dreyfusards were the enemies of France because they proclaimed principles that must bring France to perdition. Their opponents insisted that the general good must come before the individual. *Salus populi suprema lex esto.* When the structure, order, and survival of the nation are at stake, a man's fate must be treated as immaterial, an injustice as irrelevant. As Paul Bourget said to Maurice Paléologue shortly before the High Court of Appeal pronounced on the Dreyfus case in 1899, "La Justice? Eh bien, je m'en moque de la justice!"

Not, they would add, that in the case of Dreyfus an injustice had been committed. Colonel Henry's forgery had played no part in the judgment of 1894, for it had not been manufactured until two years later. It thus proved nothing at all—or only that the ignorant manifestations of public opinion out of its depth could drive honorable and patriotic men to forgery, in order to defend the secrets in their keep. If Dreyfus was guilty—and to question the court that had convicted him would be to question the State itself—then Henry's forgery was innocent: a fabrication, yes, but in a good cause and perhaps no more than a paraphrase of facts *raison d'état* made it impossible to reveal. Henry had been rash to present as a document what was a mere précis of the information in his possession. But "the apocryph was telling the truth; the forgery was true."

Raison d'état is another supreme law. In so far as it laid down this essential principle, Maurras's apologia for Colonel Henry's act was the starting point of the Action Française. And we can see now why he and his friends would find the evasions of the Patrie Française's respectable leaders exasperating. For these eminent liberal conservatives persisted in ignoring the impossibility of reconciling a liberal policy and a strong, effective executive, the one based on the right to doubt and question, the other on superior knowledge above and confidence below.

And so it was that, from the very beginning and against the law-abiding conservatism of temporizers like M. de Mahy, this group of ruthless reasoners insisted on drawing the conclusions of their logic and, what is more, on stating them. They had begun by shocking those who, when they proclaimed their readiness to do anything at all, meant that they were ready to do anything within the law. They were now going to shock the tenants of an even stronger myth, by questioning the uses of liberty.

During the autumn of 1899, in a series of meetings and newspaper articles, Barrès had argued that the gains of the Dreyfus affair, the new patriotism, the concern for public order and national advantage, would gradually be lost if an enduring doctrine based on this surge of feeling were not created to inspire future action.[30] Within a few weeks, the Action Française had drawn up for him a declaration of what the principles of French nationalism should be.

The Declaration of November 15, 1899, was in effect an extended critique of liberty as the basis of social order. The Rights of Man had dominated political thought for over a century; the Dreyfusards brandished them to justify their opposition to the State. Against the Dreyfusards and the tradition for which they stood, the Action Française set out to refute individualism, democracy, and the whole Protestant conception of free will. Ignoring ultimates, it based its arguments on one principle only: the existence of the nation represented by the State. As Maurras would soon write, in *L'Enquête sur la monarchie,* "La volonté de conserver notre patrie française une fois posée comme postulat, tout s'enchaîne, tout se déduit d'un mouvement inéluctable. La fantaisie, le choix lui-même, n'y ont aucune part."[31] Starting from this point, and through a thousand arguments, Maurras convinced his fellows that only one conclusion remained open: "Si vous avez résolu d'être patriote, vous serez obligatoirement royaliste . . . La raison le veut."

A society could hope to survive only if it was capable of unity and discipline; without them it was bound to be torn apart by the clash of many differing elements. Men and factions of diverse interests could be reconciled, and their energies harnessed to the common good, only by a superior arbiter, uncommitted to any particular interest yet completely devoted to the general, and invested with the power and prestige to make his will and his decisions effective. Democratic rulers, their position based on public approval, lacked the authority which alone could make government effective, and dictators, relying on force or on transitory public emotions, lacked the acceptance that tradition and habit commanded, the acceptance without which no margin for error existed. Besides, both of these forms of power suffered from one grave drawback; they were, by their nature, temporary, and they exposed society to recurring crises of succession to power.

Only one form of rule was subject to none of these vices—hereditary monarchy. Kings could never be identified with any interest but the general one of their subjects and their realm; they ruled for life and could therefore undertake long-range policies impossible to republican governments; and, being in a position of unchallenged authority, they could afford to relax and would therefore trespass far less on the freedom of particular men and bodies.

This last was an essential point, for, in their argument against individualistic democracy, the reasoners of the Action Française had set out to prove that the liberal society was in effect less free than the monarchic order which they extolled. By their lights, the atomized society in which individuals appeared as free and separate entities before the law actually wrenched the individual away from such natural societies as his family, his trade, and his region, only to incorporate him into a much vaster and less natural one. The individual who moved with complete freedom and counted for something in family, corporation, guild, or village, had been "liberated" only to become an item in the books of a vast, distant bureaucracy, indifferent to his real being and needs.

The individual had thus gained a theoretical freedom which he could only use, so far as he was capable, anarchically—that is, by asserting himself without regard to all the other equally free, equally isolated individuals around him, and with regard only, in the end, to his own judgment and his own free will. He lacked the intermediate bodies which, at the local and professional levels, had once offered him guidance and which could cope, as he could not, with the now overwhelming central power.

In destroying these intermediate bodies and giving men an anarchic or illusory freedom, the Revolution of 1789 had torn France away from her true and natural line of development. It had induced the French to act on principles that could only bring them harm. And it had begun a process of moral and physical disintegration whose results were evident all around and must be convincing when compared with the prosperous stability of an earlier day. The inescapable conclusion of all this was, Maurras argued, that if you began as a patriot you must end as a royalist. And furthermore, since the nation's survival hinged on an early restoration of the monarchy, all means were justified in seeking this essential end.

The last postulate both shocked and attracted: it was a novel point of view to voice on a Right dominated for nearly a century by its concern for security and order. That violence might be necessary to attain security and order, illegal violence especially, most conservatives had never seriously contemplated—not even those who cheered Thiers in his bloody repression of the Paris Commune. To the angry young rationalists of the Action Française, however, violence and force and guile seemed more likely to succeed than the sloth and inefficiency of legal expedients, from which the opposition had so far reaped only impotence and defeat. They sneered at gentlemen who had been conditioned by years of sterile electoral activity to do nothing more than fight the game by the enemy's rules. Elections were useful only as furnishing better opportunities for propaganda; a seat in Parliament was desirable only as offering a better platform. The ultimate resource of national restoration must rest in a *coup d'état,* which alone could hope to triumph over the powerful interests vested in the present shambles.

In other words, as it progressed, the doctrine of Vaugeois and Maurras developed into a theory of civil war. They were determined to subvert the regime by every means in their power "including legal ones," and openly declared this to be their intention. If it was a novelty to see such subversive ideas appear on the Right, it was even more novel to have them aired in public with every intention of being taken seriously. Maurras declared that to gain his end he would not hesitate to murder or to use the explosives and the tactics of the anarchists he abhorred, and royalist admirers shuddered deliciously at the new sense of dynamic conspiracy his bloodthirsty articles produced. As Louis Dimier would comment in retrospect,[32] neither Maurras nor his friends took such blood-thirsty approval altogether at face value, but they derived from it the reassuring "impression of an absolute will to win." A good many other parties that opposed the regime also preached civil war, but the Action Française really meant what it said, and prepared for action.

The fact that it took itself and its intentions seriously was only the first step and not the most remarkable in its climb. While their doctrine was still being worked out and given its first expression in a series of articles, events were developing to the point where the small intellectual clique could begin to apply theory in action.

The chance was to come unexpectedly, but not from a wholly unexpected quarter. Since the elections of 1902, the Ligue de la Patrie Française had merely been marking time, but within it a few energetic men continued to fight for the aims of 1899. The center of this unrelenting activity was the Ligue's able secretary, Gabriel Syveton. A brutal, greedy, and sensuous man,

Syveton had been dismissed from the University post in which he taught history for expressing his anti-Dreyfusard views too forcibly. He became a deputy of Paris in 1902, and thereupon assumed main control of the Ligue, whose most active members had left it by that time for more profitable or livelier organizations. With the aid of a rich supporter, Count Boniface de Castellane, and the platform of a great daily, *L'Echo de Paris,* Syveton became in a few short years "the very incarnation of reaction"[33] and the recognized leader of the extreme Right. The Action Française had nothing to do with the movement he was trying to arouse, although it was on friendly terms with him. Some Action Française members, among them Maurras's great friend Frédéric Amouretti, were suspicious of the plebiscitarian overtones in Syveton's demagogic nationalism, but most of them followed his activities with sympathy, and Maurras himself may well have hoped to persuade the brilliant demagogue to move his troops over to the royalist camp.

Events, however, worked another way. In order to attract attention and support, Syveton needed a concrete issue on which to build his case against the regime and to incite antiparliamentary agitation. He found it in the policy adopted by the man who had been War Minister since 1901, General Louis André. André decided to purge the Army of officers disloyal to the Republic, and one of the officers on his staff, a Captain Mollin, enlisted the aid of the Masonic Grand Orient in gathering information on officers' religious beliefs and the assiduity with which they and their families attended church and church schools. The information was filed on forms or cards (*fiches*) in the offices of the Grand Orient, whence it was communicated to Mollin at the Ministry of War.

News of this policy was not long in leaking out, and when, in 1904, an employee of the Grand Orient sold Syveton a large collection of the *fiches,* the nationalists had the ammunition they needed for a first-rate public scandal. The government, attacked first in the press and then in the Chamber, could muster only a weak and uncertain defense. At this point, Syveton, apparently fearing a whitewash, astounded France by publicly slapping General André. The deed was not particularly valorous, since André was sixty-six years old, but it prevented the issue from being quietly smothered by a vote. Moreover, Syveton would presumably be brought to trial, where he could no doubt manage to present all the distasteful evidence republicans had worked so hard to keep hidden. The country, embarrassed by the violence but disgusted by the revelations of government spying, awaited less the outcome than the disclosures of the trial. The civil war Maurras recommended had been started by Syveton, as he said in explaining his act. The next step, before a jury of his countrymen and before the country itself, would be to convert the humiliation of André into an indictment of the system and the regime that André represented.

The regime, however, was ready to defend itself, especially against opponents who, like Syveton, had failed to keep their private affairs above reproach. Faced with charges of embezzling the funds of the Ligue de la Patrie Française and accused of sexual relations with a stepdaughter who conveniently remembered to regret her lapse, Syveton committed suicide on the eve of the trial. With him died the last hopes of republican nationalism and of the Ligue. Henceforth, as Dimier felt, the country's only hope would rest in the Action Française.[34] The country was a little slow to recognize its salvation. A police report on "the dislocation of Syveton's troops" estimated that not more than one per cent of them would take their money and their support "to the unregenerate monarchists of the Action Française."[35] At that time, the judgment was probably correct.

But the death of Syveton helped to force a realignment. With him, the last intelligent and active right-wing leader was gone, and his movement, discredited, was left to disintegrate. Those who remained were old and tired. The other of the two great mass organizations of the Extreme Right, Déroulède's Ligue des Patriotes, had also been foundering for some time, and shortly after Syveton's death it sank.[36] Slowly, almost reluctantly, the nationalist public began to turn to the only remaining organization with any unity and voice. By the beginning of 1906, royalist electoral candidates supported by the Action Française were replacing regular nationalist candidates.[d] And one police informer, at least, had come to take them seriously: "At the present moment," he wrote, "the royalists alone in the opposition seem capable of doing something. They organize for action and await their opportunity."[37]

The Syveton affair had been a lucky accident for the Action Française. The second of their early opportunitites for action was self-created. The Catholic Church, both clerical and lay, had played a conspicuous role in the verbal battles of the Dreyfus affair. Despite papal attempts to keep the Church outside the dispute, despite the efforts of a few progressives like the founders of the Comité Catholique pour la Défense du Droit to remind the faithful that charity and even justice are, in Christian eyes, virtues higher than patriotism, the Church had ranged itself against the party of revision, as it had done in 1830, in 1851, in 1871, and again in 1889 during the Boulangist agitation. "All the friends of the Church are on the anti-Dreyfus side, and all its enemies, Jews, Protestants, freethinkers, are on the other."[38]

There was nothing particularly astonishing about the stand the clergy took; what was unfortunate was the virulence with which some of its members expressed their opinion. When, in December 1898, Drumont's anti-Semitic *Libre Parole* announced a subscription to aid Colonel Henry's widow, Catho-

[d] F[7] 12564 of March 3, 1906, reports that in the 20th Arrondissement of Paris a good many Socialist electors will vote for the royalist Castillon de Saint-Victor, not because their political opinions have changed, but because they are tired of the Socialist candidate, Dejeante.

lic priests accompanied their gifts with remarks hardly reflecting the principles of their faith. One *abbé* wished for a "Kikeskin bedrug he could trample morning and night"; another said he would like to crush Jew Reinach's nose under his heel.[39] One of the loudest of the anti-Dreyfusard papers was the Assumptionist order's *La Croix*. At the start of the Zola trial in February 1899, Father Bailly took an uncompromising editorial stand: "Free thought, advocate of the Jews, the Protestants, and all the enemies of the Church, stands in the dock with Zola, and the Army is forced, in spite of itself, to open fire against it." And later: "On every side, people demand a strong man, a man ready to risk his life to wrest France from the traitors, the factious, and the imbeciles who are handing it over to the foreigner . . . Ah! who will deliver us from this gang of hoodlums?"[40]

It was scarcely Christian but not altogether surprising that the hoodlums thus admonished should seek revenge. But *La Croix*'s bitter campaigns had also served as a reminder that the Republic must heed this great unharnessed power of the regular congregations, active, wealthy, influential, and persistently opposed to many of the policies of the existing regime. Within a few months of his coming to power, in the autumn of 1899, Waldeck-Rousseau opened his campaign against the religious orders, which since the Concordat of 1801 had proliferated in vast numbers, unregulated and legally unrecognized, yet educating the children of the elite, confessing and advising their parents, interfering in politics, and refusing to pay taxes (their real estate alone in 1900 was worth something like a billion francs). Under the new regime, businessman monks and politician monks would have to go; the rest could stay, but they could no longer be a state within the State. Their establishments and their activities must henceforth be registered and regulated like those of their secular brethren.

Before the issue had been settled, however, the elections of 1902, disastrous to the extreme monarchist and nationalist Right, furnished indications of the mood in which the Church-State controversy might be debated. They also furnished a new government, headed by Emile Combes, that was much further to the anti-clerical Left than its predecessor of 1898. At Lourdes in 1901, a Jesuit had proclaimed that the only candidates in the 1902 elections would be Barabbas and Jesus Christ. The choice for Catholics was clear. The Archbishop of Paris himself had charged the faithful with their electoral duty: "The question is whether society will continue to be ruled by the teachings of Scripture, or whether it shall follow the advances of anti-Christian sects that proclaim the absolute independence of human reason."

Now Barabbas sat in the seats of the mighty, determined to use his reason, and whatever else came to hand, not only against the regular clergy but against their secular brethren as well—indeed against Catholicism itself, which seemed to him, and not without reason, a symbol and citadel of the anti-republican tradition. To the moderate Alexandre Ribot, who complained that one cannot limit the governmental policies of a great country to the struggle against religious orders, the onetime seminarist Combes replied, "I have come to power only for that reason."[41] Under the rule of this anti-religious monomaniac, what had begun as a regulatory campaign became a massacre: religious orders were suppressed, church schools closed in mid-term. Backed by a fanatic anti-clerical majority and egged on by extremist demagogues like Charbonnel, the unfrocked priest-editor of *L'Action,* who called the priest "the mad dog every passer-by has the right to destroy for fear he may bite the people and infect the flock," Combes forced the passage of measure after measure designed to destroy the influence and then the existence of religious orders in France.

In the spring of 1903, most of them were dissolved and ordered to close their schools, disperse, and leave France. Some tried to resist, and troops were ordered to dislodge them, often against the opposition of local citizens. Army officers, unable to reconcile duty and faith, resigned. Riots broke out at the Grande Chartreuse, at Tréguier, and at Lorient, where the workers of the naval arsenal attacked a Catholic procession. The crucifix was removed from tribunal walls, membership in officers' religious clubs was prohibited, the highest teaching credential, the *agrégation,* was forbidden to clergymen, the monopoly of burials was transferred from clerical to municipal hands. The property of the persecuted orders was confiscated for sale by the State, and crooks and swindlers swarmed to enjoy the spoils of principle.

During the suppressions, in the summer of 1903, Leo XIII died. His successor, Pius X, was unaccommodating, and Combes, who had looked for trouble, was not long in finding it, first at the Vatican, then in France itself. Within two years of Pius X's election, diplomatic relations with the Vatican had been severed. Within three years, Church and State, united by the Concordat of 1801, had been separated, the former freed of a constricting though convenient tutelage, the latter of its responsibility and costs. There remained to be decided the fate of Church property, buildings, and goods belonging to or used by ministers and establishments of public worship but administered by State or local authorities. The conditions under which Catholics might henceforth avail themselves of these, first accepted by a majority of the French hierarchy, were finally rejected by papal decision. In the meantime, the inventory of Church property ordered by the government seemed but a preliminary to confiscation. When revenue agents attempted to list Church assets, they were met with boos and sometimes with blows. In Paris, they were able to enter several churches only on the heels of the military. In Brittany, in the central provinces, in the pious Basque country, peasants and gentlemen leagued together to prevent the intruders from carrying out their sacrilegious mission. On both sides, men were beaten up, injured, even killed. Once more, indignant Army officers resigned their commissions rather than disperse the rioters or march against their Church. The *ralliement* had died a second time: all hopes of reconciling Republic and Church were, for the time being, dead.

The disturbances surrounding the *inventaires* afforded the Action Française its first great opportunity, and this it seized with alacrity. The group that moved to protect the Church was not a Catholic group: many of its leaders, as we have seen, held views much opposed to orthodox ones. Maurras himself seems to have respected Catholicism primarily for having saved mankind from an inherently corrupting and anarchic Oriental Christianity, but he was tactful enough not to say this outright, lest he shock his Christian friends.[e] Whatever his views on Catholicism, he knew the value of the Catholic alliance; while this alliance lasted, analysis could wait. In the Action Française, he insisted, religious questions were not their concern. "Nous ne voulons traiter que de politique—we see religious matters in political terms. And, politically, a patriotic Frenchman knows no other religious interest than that of Catholicism." As a member-priest remarked, "If one is not politically a Catholic, one does not join the Action Française; metaphysically, you can be whatever you like."[42]

Among its old-fashioned royalist supporters the Action Française counted a good many Catholics; in politics it fought the regime the Catholics were also fighting; inevitably, a good many of those who rallied to the aid of the Church in 1906 were of the Action Française. And the struggle itself recruited more. The nature of the royalist league had ensured that its Catholic members would take a leading part in the riots. This naturally attracted other Catholics who had taken a similar stand, some of them young officers like Bernard de Vésins and Robert de Boisfleury, who resigned their commissions to join the Action Française.

Henceforth for some twenty years, members of the Action Française—and especially the Camelots du Roi when these appeared in 1908—were to be among the most zealous of the papacy's supporters. Simultaneously, Fontaine tells us, the French episcopate slowly came to be filled with their friends. A rumor circulated about 1910 that Maurras himself nominated the bishops.[43] It was unfounded, but true to the extent that for a long time bishops were nominated by Cardinal de Lai, who was secretary of the Consistorial and apparently an outspoken defender of the Action Française at the Holy See. In France, of the group particularly favored by Pius X and his intimates, all, according to Fontaine, felt more or less directly the influence of Maurras. Among them, by all accounts, could be numbered three cardinals—de Cabrières, bishop of Montpellier; Sévin, archbishop of Lyon; and Andrieu, archbishop of Bordeaux—and a growing number of other dignitaries: Mon-

[e] He came very near saying it, however, in *Trois Idées politiques* (1912), p. 10: "Old France professed the sort of traditional Catholicism which, while submitting Jewish visions and Christian sentiment to discipline inherited from the Hellenic and Roman worlds, carried within itself the natural order of mankind."

seigneur Penon, bishop of Moulins, Bishop Guillibert of Fréjus, Cardinal-Archbishop Luçon of Reims, Monseigneur Laperrine d'Hautpoul, the rather mysterious and very powerful Monseigneur Benigni, Father Billot (later cardinal), and many influential scholars and teachers of the religious orders. Their activities, exasperating to more moderate prelates, continued well past the death of Pius X, until in the middle 'twenties Pius XI decided to transfer episcopal nominations from the Consistorial congregation, which they dominated, to the congregation of extraordinary ecclesiastical affairs. Not until then, says Fontaine, did the influence of the Action Française on Church politics begin to decline.[44]

During the early years of the new century, Maurras and his friends were equally busy in a field more properly their own, that of education in the service of their cause. The origins of these educational ventures lay in the fortnightly dinners of their sympathizers at a restaurant in the Palais-Royal called the Boeuf à la Mode. Paul Bourget was one of the circle. Others were Furcy-Raynaud, director of the Arsenal library; the royalist leader Lur-Saluces, back from his Brussels exile after the amnesty of 1900; a Breton deputy, Jules Delahaye; the historian Gustave Fagniez, cofounder, with Gabriel Monod, of the *Revue historique*; Camille Bellaigue, musicologist and papal chamberlain; and, to maintain a certain balance, Antoine Baumann, a positivist and one of the executors of Auguste Comte's will. There were also several officers, a few priests, and, of course, the staff of the *Revue de l'Action Française*. These dinners were followed by discussions, and occasionally lectures, on the literary, historical, and political implications of Action Française doctrine. Emboldened by the success of these informal beginnings, Vaugeois, who presided, and his friends soon organized public lectures and meetings. The medievalist Auguste Longnon, sympathetic to their ideas, helped to launch the first of these, appropriately devoted to Joan of Arc. Léon de Montesquiou followed him, then the group's academic members, Vaugeois, and the Catholic art historian Louis Dimier. Their lectures deliberately avoided demagogy and attempted instead to disprove, factually and logically, the detested myths which they believed were weakening France. At first there was little attempt at vulgarization, or, rather, at making the vulgarizations popular. The initial aim was to equip a limited group with facts and arguments designed to counter the prevailing republican nonsense. Once this group was ready, however, it became necessary to have publicity, to concentrate on some striking act that would draw attention to the new ideas and give their proponents a wider audience.

Dimier thought an opportunity offered with the approaching seventy-fifth anniversary, in 1905, of the birth of the noted medievalist Fustel de Coulanges. Although Fustel, who had died in 1889, had been neither a royalist nor a practicing Catholic, he satisfied the new royalists because of his "historical patriotism and his refusal to accept theories relating French institutions to Germanic origins."[45] He had another great advantage: he was little read and little appreciated by the prevailing masters of the University. His memory, therefore, was not tinged with republican associations, and his immediate cult was nobody's preserve. True, the celebration of a seventy-fifth anniversary, when no earlier one had been noticed, might seem odd. True also, the Action Française had no apparent qualification for undertaking the celebration of a fame heretofore ignored even by Fustel's students. On the other hand, no one better qualified to celebrate the anniversary had shown any interest in it.

After securing the permission of the historian's widow, Dimier gathered a committee for the memorial celebration and, carefully excluding anyone tainted by Dreyfusard associations, went ahead with his arrangements. The committee included Barrès and Bourget, Jules Lemaître and Auguste Longnon, Fagniez, Louis Léger of the Collège de France, Gustave Schlumberger of the Académie des Inscriptions, the cartoonist Jean Louis Forain (who was one of the most biting of the critics of Dreyfusism), Alfred Rambaud, former Minister of Education (who had split with Ernest Lavisse over the Dreyfus affair), and a number of other dignitaries; but it was chiefly notable for its omissions. As an unsympathetic conservative, E. Melchior de Vogüé, pointed out to Dimier, Lavisse would have seemed a better choice than Forain—but Lavisse had the wrong ideas, so Forain it had to be.

Inevitably, news of the preparations leaked out. Fustel's former students were furious, and their protests were echoed in the scholarly press: the alumni of the rue d'Ulm, where Fustel had taught, got into the fray: Jean Jaurès, Albert Petit, and Paul Guiraud denounced the royalist plot to kidnap a corpse and deprive republican historiography of one of its hitherto unsuspected glories. The *Journal des débats,* conservative and highly influential, pressed the case, and committee members began to fall away. Mme Fustel withdrew her permission, and Emile Gebhart of the Académie Française, who had agreed to preside at the ceremonies, begged off. But the faithful Longnon promptly replaced Gebhart, the Collège de France the Académie; the speakers hesitated but did not change their minds, and the meeting of March 18, 1905, was a great success.[f] The outcry that preceded it, the press polemic, the scandal of impertinent royalist annexationism, had all served Dimier's purpose of providing free publicity for the Action Française. The hall of the Sociétés Savantes, just off the Boulevard Saint-Germain, was packed, and the new pedagogic campaign had been well launched.

The year 1905 proved to be a seminal year. In January, as an outgrowth

[f] Maurras, *La Contre-révolution spontanée* (Lyon, 1943), p. 73. One historian attracted by the Fustel episode was Franz Funck-Brentano; another, not long after, was young Eugène Cavaignac, first winner of the Fustel Prize, who died in the First World War. The furor may have played its part in the publication, beginning in 1905, of a revised edition of Fustel's works.

of the public lectures, a Ligue d'Action Française had been founded, largely for financial reasons, to solicit funds and contributors for the *Revue*. In December, Lucien Moreau gave student sympathizers a rudimentary organization in the first Action Française student group, which began by meeting twice a month in term-time for lectures and discussions.[g] But the Institute, which opened its doors in February 1906, was the liveliest of these creations.

Like the new Ligue, the Institute grew out of the Fustel campaign. The lectures had been a success, but it was important not to lose the momentum of such a fortunate start. A brief, concentrated campaign had brought Fustel de Coulanges to public notice, and the Action Française as well. If a public that had heretofore ignored Fustel's ideas could be persuaded so quickly to take an interest in him, even to read his works, the same could probably be done for other thinkers in other fields dear to the heart of the Action Française. Teachers were needed, a hall where they could speak, and a prescribed set of courses. First of all, however, the money was wanted to make all this possible. This was found with the help of Colonel Fernand de Parseval, a regular guest at the dinner discussions of the Boeuf à la Mode and one of the directors of a royalist lecture group called Tradition et Progrès. The money found, plans were worked out in the home of another Boeuf à la Mode regular, the Comte de Courville, a director of the great Schneider steelworks at Le Creusot—or, more precisely, in the *salon* of his wife.

Mme de Courville, a great friend of Maurras and Barrès, and especially of Mme Barrès, would prove herself over the years to be one of the Action Française's most loyal and helpful friends. All her charm, energy, and social finesse were enlisted in its service, and she also made use of her connections in the Catholic world. Her son, Xavier, and her two sons-in-law, Jean Rivain and Pierre Gilbert, were among the Action Française's earliest bright young militants. She herself presided over the discussions in which the Action Française Institute was born.

The Institute was designed to provide instruction in all essential aspects of neo-royalist doctrine. It offered courses in politics, social science, foreign relations, nationalism, and regionalism—that is, national and provincial history. Following the pedagogical precepts of Auguste Comte, much admired by Maurras for his royalist ancestors, his Catholic proclivities, and his systematic authoritarianism,[h] each course and hence each professorial chair was given a symbolic name: nationalism was represented by Maurice Barrès, provincial history by Louis XI, politics by Sainte-Beuve. This last chair was held by Maurras, who taught a course concerning organizational empiricism—the

[g] The student groups were never very numerous before the war, as can be seen from F[7] 12862 of December 9, 1911, which counts only 72 members in Paris; but they spread through the Faculties and *lycées* in the years that followed the Agadir incident.

[h] Comte, a native of "white" Montpellier, had made a point of mentioning his royalist and Catholic ancestry in his will.

famous formula of *l'empirisme organisateur*—which he defined as the middle ground where reason and experience meet in practical politics, unencumbered by empty systems or rash, shortsighted practice. A special course in positivism, taught by Léon de Montesquiou, carried the name of Comte himself, in whose philosophy the individual is subordinated first to the family, then to society, then to the state, which tends toward an almost Hegelian absolutism. Another special course, in Catholic politics, was named after Pius IX's *Syllabus of Errors,* the chair to be held only by a priest—to begin with, the Abbé Appert, vicar of Attigny, near Chalons-sur-Marne. Lucien Moreau, one of the first to congratulate Maurras on his apologia for Colonel Henry, was the first holder of the Barrès chair of nationalism. Another member of the Boeuf à la Mode circle, a portly Jesuit named Georges de Pascal, philosopher, historian, economist, sociologist, collaborator and friend of the influential Marquis René de la Tour du Pin, taught the social science courses before taking over those of the *Syllabus.*

Dimier accepted the responsibilities of direction. With Vaugeois, he was able to attract some acquaintances from the University, including Pierre Lasserre, a critic of French romanticism, and the historian Franz Funck-Brentano. The lectures became chapters, the courses became books, the books needed a publisher: to fill the need, Rivain, who had a sizable income from a great religious-objects firm in the shadow of Saint-Sulpice, set up the Librairie Jean Rivain to publish and sell the writings of Action Française members and their friends. The Institute, the *Revue,* the Librairie—the apparatus for intellectual action had been set up. Those responsible now delighted in comparing their enterprise with that of the Encyclopedists, against whose influence they had begun by rising, against whose legacy they would not cease to fight.

But fighting implied something more than writing and talking. The doctrinal foundations of action were being laid: it was time to move on to action itself.

The circumstances of the Dreyfus affair had furnished the inspiration for the creation of the Action Française; now, its closing incidents were to afford the opportunity of effective action. In May 1900 an immense majority of the Chamber had voted a motion "inviting [Waldeck-Rousseau's] government to energetically oppose the revival of the Dreyfus affair,[46] but in 1903 Jaurès rose to demand this very revival, and in 1904 the High Court of Appeal ordered a new inquiry, which lasted until the end of 1905 and resulted in the annulment of the sentence against Dreyfus.

The several preceding inquiries had seemed to show conclusively that Dreyfus had been condemned on evidence either defective or forged, and that the essential evidence leading to his conviction fell into the latter category. The Court's final decision, however, rested on a reading of Article 445 of the Code of Criminal Instruction that was, to say the least, debatable. This article, soon to become notorious, authorized the Court to decide a case without referring it back to a lower court for retrial "when the annulment pronounced concerning a living person leaves no charge standing that can be qualified as a crime or misdemeanor."

Such a stipulation, however, refers to quite exceptional conditions which do not seem to have been fulfilled in this particular case. The High Court of Appeal in France is called the Cour de Cassation. As its name implies, its function is not to judge the essence and detail of cases brought before it, but to annul the judgments of lower courts if there is reason to do so. Having been condemned in 1899 by the Rennes court-martial, Dreyfus could not be properly discharged of its sentence without retrial before a court of the same order. So, at least, said eighteen judges, but thirty-one others considered that the case had been exhausted. The presiding judge of the Cour de Cassation, Alexis Ballot-Beaupré, the man who had ordered the retrial of 1899, stood with the minority in 1905. On July 12, 1906, the Court, having quashed the verdict of 1899, declared Dreyfus innocent. On the following day, in the Chamber, the government completed his rehabilitation by proposing to reinstate him and his champion, Picquart, in the Army from which they had been drummed out—the one as Major, the other as Brigadier General.

In the debate that followed, a Socialist, Francis de Pressensé, called for reprisals against the generals he held responsible for the injustice now being repaired, beginning with General Auguste Mercier, "the greatest criminal of them all," who had been Minister of War at the time of the first court-martial and had testified against revision on every subsequent occasion. In the same debate another speaker, the Radical Adolphe Messimy, attacked "the madmen, the wretches, and the imbeciles" who had led the Army astray in those days of strife. Now, to cap everything, the vote of a Socialist proposal to transfer the ashes of Emile Zola to the Panthéon marked the full victory of the Dreyfus party.

Extreme words and actions have a way of evoking echoes similarly extreme. The conservative leader Denys Cochin had protested against the insults flung at officers perfectly entitled to their own opinions, but he had accepted the Court of Appeal's verdict that showed these opinions to have been wrong.[i] Such faintheartedness, however well wrapped in righteous protests, could not satisfy the more extreme anti-Dreyfusards. The case which had

[i] A letter written that week by François Coppée to Léon Daudet (F. D. papers, July 17, 1906) reflects the mood prevalent among anti-Dreyfusards: "Les derniers événements me désespèrent," writes the *poète des humbles*: "L'apothéose du Juif était prévue, sans doute. Elle fait horreur, quand même, dans cette France où périt tout ce que nous aimons, tout ce que nous respectons, la foi, le patriotisme, l'honneur, absolument tout. Il semble que la vraie France soit morte. Elle est, dans tous les cas, chloroformée. Peut-être les jeunes, comme vous et votre vaillante femme, verront-ils le réveil. Mais moi qui ne suis plus jeune et qui me sens tout à fait vaincu et désarmé, je n'ai plus d'espoir et j'en souffre cruellement."

begun with an injustice was ending with what seemed to be another; if a case for believing Dreyfus guilty had apparently been rigged up, this was no reason to rig up a case for his innocence. If the conservatives accepted the new arguments of the High Court, the Action Française did not. On the contrary, it found in its verdict fuel for a fresh campaign that would last until the outbreak of the First World War.

Their protest began with a *triduum,* meetings on three consecutive days devoted to the presentation of proof of Dreyfus's guilt and the guilt of his defenders. Critics had warned them that the public had had enough of the story, that renewed agitation could never be sustained in the face of general indifference, but surprisingly enough the meetings attracted a numerous audience, which responded warmly to the denunciations that established conservative leaders had failed to make.

The Action Française was providing the lead for other nationalists to follow, as it would for the next thirty years. In January 1907, on the twelfth anniversary of Dreyfus's public degradation, a special Action Française meeting drew such a large crowd that overflow meetings had to be held in neighboring cafés. At about the same time, in the fall of 1906, replying to the attacks to which General Mercier had been subjected, the Action Française decided to strike a commemorative medal honoring Mercier as the judge and justiciary of Dreyfus. The nationalist *Eclair* lent its pages to the subscription campaign, and its lists reflected the smoldering resentments of the anti-revisionist public. The medal was presented at a crowded meeting in the Salle Wagram, at which the cream of nationalist leadership, assembled on royalist initiative, reasserted their belief in Dreyfus's guilt and the justice of their own cause. There was a striking parallel between this public and the one that had cheered Boulanger's lieutenants some seventeen years before. But Dimier, among others, sought to show that if the emotion was the same and the motives similar, supporting a legitimate king was a far cry from supporting a mere adventurer. The misinterpretation and misrepresentation of Article 445 became a nationalist slogan to be exploited against the believers in truth and justice, who were invited to reflect on the arbitrariness of their own side. On the Left Bank, young enthusiasts like Georges Bernanos, Jean Longnon (son of Auguste and later Librarian of the Institut), Eugène Marsan, and an old student of Dimier at Valenciennes, Abel Manouvriez, flaunted the Court's tainted decision in the faces of the self-satisfied Left; and the enemy began to show signs of dismay at the revival of nationalist agitation.[47]

There was nothing but talk until the reinterment of Zola's body in the Panthéon, which had been postponed by the government because of nationalist opposition and the popular outcry that it stirred up. After repeated delays, the ceremonial transfer was fixed for June 4, 1908. President Fallières's carriage rode up to the Panthéon between two lines of soldiers presenting arms, amid scattered hoots of demonstrating Action Française members. As the ceremony itself was being conducted, the journalist Grégori, a well-known military analyst, suddenly fired two shots at Dreyfus, wounding him in the arm. Another enthusiast, André Gaucher, a writer for the royalist *Soleil,* had volunteered for the same task, but Maurras had forbidden him to attempt it. On September 10, when Grégori was brought to court and promptly acquitted by twelve good men and true, the impetuous Gaucher interrupted the judge with a challenge of the trumped-up verdict of 1906.

Gaucher was routinely jailed for contempt, but his act began to assume heroic proportions among his friends. And in fact, by brandishing the "talisman" of Article 445 in a crowded courtroom, under the very beards of judges used to more respect, he did more to bring the Action Française's campaign to public attention than all the pamphlets turned out by Jean Rivain for the edification of the faithful. A public scandal was just what the authorities, deliberately ignoring the Action Française's earlier campaigns, had been trying to avoid. Public scandals they were henceforth to get. Within a few weeks Gaucher's scandalous outburst was imitated by another partisan, the twenty-year-old art student Maxime Réal del Sarte. On October 16 the High Court of Appeal opened its new judicial year. The usual opening speeches were suddenly interrupted by a loud voice: "Et l'article 445? Magistrats faussaires! qu'avez-vous fait de l'article 445?" Réal del Sarte was arrested and jailed, and it was expected that he would be severely punished. Instead, however, he was soon released on orders of a government that prized discretion above honor. Such events made Article 445 a byword. In Le Havre, a pastry cook exhibited a monumental cake crowned by the fateful number. At Quiberon, someone inscribed it on the pedestal of General Hoche's statue. In more commonplace locations, a rash of graffiti served the same purpose in a humbler fashion.

The triumphant revisionists had also marked their success by promptly erecting statues in honor of the deceased leaders of their cause: Scheurer-Kestner, one of Dreyfus's earliest champions; Gabriel Trarieux, originator of the Ligue des Droits de l'Homme; and Bernard Lazare, enemy of anti-Semitism and defender of Dreyfus. Young royalists thereupon attacked the statues with stones, crowbars, and hammers—Scheurer-Kestner's statue in the Luxembourg gardens, Trarieux's at Denfert-Rochereau near by, Lazare's at Nîmes, all were mutilated and chipped. Of course the vandals got publicity, and soon no one could ignore the existence of these prankish, violent, overweening young men, who claimed that nothing they were doing was so harmful as what was being done to France by the regime they hated.

The mood of the public made even such extreme actions surprisingly acceptable. The heroic days of the Republic, when to a vast majority the regime seemed the reflection of France, worthy of struggle and faith, were over. The years of the Dreyfus affair had affirmed the Republic's capacity to survive, but success and its aftermath, and especially the separation of Church and State, had brought about a division between republicans whom crisis had united. Some were beginning to forget their high moral principles in the glories of power; others, having achieved their moderate ends, were beginning to have doubts about the real intentions of their erstwhile Socialist and syndicalist comrades; all continued to mouth the slogans of republican unity while maneuvering for position against one another.

In the years after 1906, the most active section of the Republic's troops, that represented by the Socialists and the syndicates, was affected by extreme dissatisfaction with the fruits of the common fight and by a growing disenchantment with the regime. A vocal opposition on the Extreme Right had been, of course, a constant feature of Third Republic politics. But now an Extreme Left opposition was taking form. If the Right did not accept the political order, the Left did not accept the social order, and this opened up possibilities to the men of the Action Française at the same time that it weakened the positions of successive republican governments.

The extent of serious concern with the political issues involved in the struggle between Right and Left should not, however, be exaggerated. It is interesting to see, as we shall in the pages to come, that the agitation and violence of the Camelots in the years before 1914 caused much more alarm among conservatives, and even among conservative royalists, who were shocked and disturbed by illegal action and the vulgar display of force, than among workers, who for the most part were but indifferent or amused spectators of these bourgeois dissensions. And when, a little later, an imprisoned Camelot would be liberated from the prison of Clairvaux on the telephoned orders of another who pretended to be the President of the Republic himself, even the hosts of Midian could not forbear to grin, though perhaps a little wryly.

By then, such exploits could be given first-rate publicity in the Action Française's own daily newspaper, long planned, long awaited, and at last, in 1908, a reality.

2

RECOGNITION

THE MAN WHO MADE IT POSSIBLE for the Action Française to realize its dream and achieve the daily platform it had coveted for so long was a recent recruit and one whose appearance in royalist ranks could not fail to create a stir.

Léon Daudet was the son of one of the glories of republican letters. His father, Alphonse, the creator of Tartarin and Nouma Roumestan, was a man of Nîmes, his roots deep in the part of Languedoc that borders on Provence, and a great friend of the poet Mistral. Although the novelist was himself an unbeliever and a good republican, his parents had been pious and conservative. Léon's grandfather, Vincent Daudet, had been a royalist; his grandmother spent a large part of her life in church and was in the habit of repeating, "God blesses large families!"—which did not prevent her from losing fourteen of her own seventeen children, including the oldest, Henri, a priest. The paternal "white" tradition was balanced by the maternal side. Léon's maternal grandfather, Jules Allard, had been a *bleu de Bretagne* in the Jacobin tradition, a friend of the revolutionaries Barbès and Blanqui, and Alphonse had proved in this respect to be more of an Allard than a Daudet.

Léon grew up in the best republican society, along with Hugos and Berthelots; he was a friend of Zola and was acquainted with every writer of any importance. After an early try at medicine, which he abandoned because of an injustice suffered, or assumed, in a competitive examination, he turned to writing, and got his revenge on the medical profession by ridiculing its pompous mandarins in *Les Morticoles* (1894). Twenty-two at the time of the Boulangist agitation, he took the Republic's side with the same zeal with which he would later oppose it. The students of 1889 were not nationalistic and hardly admired Boulanger. But Daudet already had a way of passionately expressing his feelings that could get him into trouble. Years later he claimed to have been briefly arrested for crying "Down with Boulanger!" long before he had suffered for crying "Long live the king!" More accurately, perhaps, J.-H. Rosny remembered having met him and Georges Hugo on the boulevards the night of Boulanger's election, January 27, 1889. The young men were indignant at the braying crowd, and, unable to contain their feelings, they began to shout back. "Ce fut un moment incommode. Des centaines de poings nous menaçaient, des voix furibondes: 'A bas les Juifs!'

(Nous étions tous trois bruns, avec des nez recourbés.) Avenue de l'Opéra, il y eut une ruée, et je comprends mal encore comment nous ne fûmes point passés à tabac."[1]

All this was only to be expected from an energetic young man whose closest friendships lay in the Hugo family circle. In 1891, Léon married Jeanne Hugo, sister of his best friend Georges and granddaughter of the poet. The marriage, a civil one only, was not a success; they had a son and were divorced in 1895. From this unfortunate experience, Daudet seems to have carried away an enduring resentment of his former friends. His memoirs, always biting but generally good-humored, cloud over when the Hugos appear, and it is not impossible that these private resentments had a good deal to do with his later public attitudes.

In 1903, at the age of thirty-six, Daudet married again, this time closer to home. His second wife, Marthe Allard, was doubly his first cousin, being an offspring of the marriage of his father's sister to his mother's brother. It was Marthe who brought him back to Catholicism; it was she, too, who influenced a second conversion quite as important as the first, by turning him toward the royalist cause to which he would henceforth devote his life. Like others, he made his way from anti-Semitism to anti-Dreyfusism, and thence to the Action Française.

Daudet's anti-Semitism was a complex sentiment, partly inherited, partly rationalized, partly opportunistic, as were many of his momentary fancies. Unlike most fancies, however, it was a constant—fluctuating in intensity, occasionally discriminating as anti-Semites generally do in favor of "good" Jews, but never disappearing for long. His father, too, despite his republican sympathies, had been an anti-Semite, a close friend and collaborator of the cranky agitator Drumont. Léon grew up in a house at which Drumont was a frequent and intimate guest. Before he was twenty, he joined Drumont's new Ligue Antisémite, and during the Dreyfus controversy he wrote occasional biting articles for the *Libre Parole*.

His anti-Semitism fed upon the degradation of Dreyfus and grew fiercer as the Dreyfus affair released upon the country its burden of disunity and rage. From a mere set of inherited prejudices, it became a rationalized part of his nationalist position. A Jew had betrayed France; other Jews and their friends continued to hurt her. These seemed sufficient reasons to want to eliminate the Jews from a body politic which it was their tendency to corrupt and harm. But, now that the original anti-Semitism had been overlaid by nationalism, it had become more searching, more discriminating. The early prejudices had been tempered by bonhomie; the later would be tempered by concern for national welfare, which allowed him to support "good" Jews like Georges Mandel.

The second Mme Daudet, known to her friends as Pampille from the pen name she adopted for her occasional sartorial and gastronomic excursions, was more extreme than her husband. In January 1899 she had been one of the first and most enthusiastic members of the Ligue de la Patrie Française, and when the Ligue went into a decline, it was she who drew Daudet to the Action Française, which she liked for its uncompromising royalism. Syveton's death raised doubt in the minds of Jules Lemaître and others, who could not accept the murder theory that Syveton's friends had evolved, but Daudet saw only that the dead man's task must not be abandoned. His first public appearances for the Action Française date from 1904. But we cannot tell how long he took to fully accept the "integral nationalism" of his royalist friends. An undated letter from Maurras, after Daudet's second speech in public had shown him to be the rousing sort of orator the Action Française was looking for, suggests that he had not quite made up his mind. He cannot, however, have taken very long about it after the end of 1904. His character inclined him to "heroic medications," such as the Action Française promised to provide. His father's incurable locomotor ataxia had driven him not only into his medical studies, but into a search for miraculous and lightning cures for the incurable, reflected in his political enthusiasms as well as in his scientific ones. There could be no halfway remedy for Alphonse Daudet's mortal illness; thereafter, the son looked upon all halfway cures as no cure at all.[a]

The first benefit of his joining was that the Action Française gained a lively and amusing public speaker. It could do with one, for its leaders, intelligent and capable though they were, were not at their best on a platform. Vaugeois was charming but nervous, and despite flashing eyes and a ringing voice was not effective in a large hall; Pujo not only stammered but always held his manuscript up before his face; Montesquiou spoke clearly but coldly and could not excite an audience; Maurras's voice, hollow and low, did not carry beyond the first few rows. Even so, like Major Cuignet, whose anti-Dreyfusard clichés never missed the mark, and Bernard de Vésins, he never failed to draw enthusiastic applause. But it was Daudet who became the public's favorite. Rabelaisian in person as well as in print, he was Maurras's complement: where Maurras explained dispassionately and logically, the sanguine Daudet seduced by his fire and verve, providing a body for what had so far been only a doctrine.

His presence thus brought the Action Française a living symbol of its own character. Edmond de Goncourt had long before been struck by the mixture of hoax and violence, brag and brains, of the brash young man. He had noted in his *Journal*: "Il m'étonne, ce sacré grand gamin, par ce mélange chez lui

[a] See his statement, quoted in Dresse, *Léon Daudet vivant,* p. 68: "Je rêvais de médications héroïques qui eussent résolu les scléroses de la moelle et du cerveau, de fonte miraculeuse des pachyméningites et des tumeurs, de guérisons par la volonté, par un sérum, par une inoculation de vénin, par l'aimant, même par les forces inconnues que nous groupons sous le nom de pesanteur. L'inertie de la thérapeutique, en face de lésions qui devraient être curables ou au moins modifiables, me surprenait et m'indignait. Alors, à quoi bon l'étude, à quoi bon les concours, à quoi bon le sacrifice des plus belles années de l'existence, si l'on devait aboutir à ce *nihil,* à cette abstention, à des palliatifs pires que tout, comme la morphine?"

de fumisteries inférieures, de batailles avec des cochers de fiacre, et en même temps par sa fréquentation intellectuelle des plus hauts penseurs et ses originales rédactions sur la vie médicale."[2]

By 1904, the *sacré grand gamin* had proved himself as ready with a rapier as with a pen, with his tongue as with his cane, a tough, relentless polemicist with a gift for sharp ridicule. He was also, less happily from his new friends' point of view, the author of some very risqué novels, whose lack of literary merit did not detract from their sales. *L'Astre noir* (1894) and *Suzanne* (1896) did not reach the semipornographic lengths of Daudet's postwar novels or the public success of his *L'Entremetteuse* (1921), but they did not improve his fame in the Catholic circles to which his new wife and new enthusiasms had led him. When asked how she reconciled the new recruit's political ideas with the dubious morality of his novels, the Marquise de MacMahon did her best: "Nous faisons crédit au polémiste. Quant au romancier, nous l'ignorons. C'est un autre homme."[3]

The selective blindness that enabled some Catholics to ignore in Daudet the unacceptable author of *L'Astre noir* just as they ignored in Maurras the agnostic and fundamentally anti-Christian doctrinaire of the *Chemin de paradis,* did not last forever. For the moment, however, it sufficed. And it permitted, in a rather roundabout way, the financing of the *Action française.*

There is some disagreement about how much money it took to start the new venture, and about just where this money came from. One authority speaks of 287,000 francs, more than a third of it furnished by the Daudets; Daudet himself refers a little vaguely to an original capital of something less than 500,000, with the greatest single contribution (80,000 francs) coming from his wife. Arthur Meyer, the director of the socially dominant *Gaulois,* who was at first a friend, then a patron of Daudet before becoming the target of his insults, seems to think that Mme Daudet's contribution was closer to 200,000. Maurras, telling the story to Xavier Vallat, talks of 100,000. With one exception, the figures quoted seem to indicate an *ordre de grandeur* rather than a precise amount. Daudet would be the witness most likely to know, and his statement, although mentioning his wife's support specifically, does not exclude the possibility of other capital of his own. Since the original capital was not raised at once, and since it was increased, as we shall see, shortly after the paper's founding, it seems likely that these various figures are more reconcilable than they would at first appear to be.[4]

There is no doubt, at any rate, that Daudet money was the core of the original capital. The origin of this hard core is thus of some importance, and not the least of the paradoxes in the history of a movement that seems at times to be paradox incarnate. The story goes back to the days of the Second Empire and to the adventures of a lady best known as the Comtesse de Loynes.

In the days of *La Belle Hélène* the future countess came to Paris to make her way as best she might, and she was soon one of the city's most fashionable courtesans, known by the flowers that she constantly wore as the "Dame aux violettes." She had certain literary predilections, and managed to become the friend of Alexandre Dumas *fils* and of the journalist Emile de Girardin, then of Prince Napoléon, whose *salon* she conducted for some years, and finally of Ernest Baroche, the rich son of an Imperial minister. Baroche died during the siege of Paris in 1871, leaving her his considerable fortune, and after his death she was married *pro forma* to the Comte de Loynes, who managed one of the Baroche sugar refineries. In this position she attained success as one of the great hostesses of the Third Republic. She had been, we are told, the confidante of Sainte-Beuve, then of Mistral. Under the new regime she took up Jules Lemaître, who was beginning his career as a literary critic, paved his way to the Académie Française, and established herself as the protector of right-wing journalists and writers.

She knew Alphonse Daudet first, then Léon, and was delighted by the young man's ideas and vitality; she approved of the enthusiasms of his wife, and of Lemaître's increasing interest in the Action Française and the royalist cause. When she died at a great age in 1908, she left 200,000 francs to Marthe Daudet. The Daudets used it to set up the *Action française,* and thus it was Bonapartist money that went to create the most virulent Orléanist paper France has ever known.[5]

Founded on a shoestring, though a most expensive one, the newspaper was never free of financial difficulties. Within seven weeks of its first appearance more capital had to be called for; within seven months its funds had dried up again. In January 1909 a third lot of shares was issued, and in 1912 a fourth lot. André Gaucher, who was on the staff of the newspaper for five years before the war, says that between May 1908 and March 1913 the *Action française* augmented its capital by 512,000 francs—an average of more than 100,000 francs a year. Since the figures he quotes are almost twice what subscribers actually paid, most of the difference must have been made up by a few rich friends who were persuaded to come to the rescue as the original operating capital drained away. Gaucher affirms that losses such as the *Action française* continued to face could be made good only by blackmail campaigns. But, although such campaigns were apparently undertaken, they seem to have been designed more to attract attention by spectacular allegations than to make money from actual pay-offs. As for the running losses, they could have been covered easily enough by the income from the almost continuous subscription campaigns. In the seven years from 1908 to 1915, drives to raise funds "against Jewish gold" brought in some 283,000 francs, mostly from small subscribers, many of them members of the provincial gentry who loyally dipped into their slender funds to keep the royalist flag flying.[6]

One quarter from which money could have been expected yielded very little—the rich Pretender himself, Philippe, Duc d'Orléans. The Duc, more interested in travel and mistresses than in his claims to a rather distant throne, did his best to play the part that fortune had assigned him. Apart from the fact, however, that by 1907 he felt nothing but distaste for the anti-Dreyfus policy of the Action Française, his royal funds had to suffice for a score of political enterprises, among which the Action Française, though not the least demanding, was the youngest. Other old and well-established papers—the *Soleil,* the *Gaulois,* the *Gazette de France*—carried the royal banner and sought the royal franc. Even when the daily *Action française* had been no more than a plan, the royalist political bureau, hard pressed for funds, had considered ending the subsidy it paid to Gustave Janicot's *Gazette de France* and giving the money to the more up-and-coming *Action française*.[7] In the end, Janicot continued to get his subsidy and something was found for the new sheet, too. But the dole was pitifully small. A newspaper whose straight losses (not counting interest on debts) would rise by 1912 to over 11,000 francs a month was being paid only 1,000 francs a month by its reluctant patron.[8]

The financial problem was made worse by the movement's active propaganda. A stagnant organization has steady costs; its subscribers may be few but they are dependable; its printings remain the same and its losses are stabilized at a predictable figure. But an ambitious movement, and its budget, are liable to violent oscillations. The *Action française* deliberately printed more copies than it could sell, sent out hundreds of free subscriptions, then thousands, published special editions, spattered the hoardings with stickers and posters, the pavements with handbills—all devices that its resigned competitors had long ago given up. It became involved in costly court actions and had lawyers to pay, and costs, and fines; it increased its staff, recruiting propagandists and simple hangers-on, and generally played havoc with its budget. A shortage of funds was bound to be the chronic condition of its existence. The only time the paper's budget seems to have been balanced was shortly before it ceased publication, during the Lyon period, when its sales were sure and its other activities were halted.

There appeared to be only two ways of balancing the budget without subsidies: by eliminating the paper's competitors, or by increasing its reading public. The two solutions were practically the same, since the disappearance of competitors would bring new readers, and the capture of the royalist public would deal a fatal blow to the already moribund royalist dailies. Early in their planning, the directors of the *Action française* had approached the aging but still nimble-penned Rochefort and asked him to join it. He rebuffed them: "You are mad," he said. "You won't last three months, and what will I do then?" As it turned out, the *Action française* drew readers not only from the *Soleil* and the *Gaulois,* but from other nationalist papers as well. Royalists who had subscribed to the republican *Libre Parole* because it was anti-Semitic, or to the Bonapartist *L'Autorité* because of its determined tone and steadfast anti-Dreyfusism, turned to a paper that was all these and monarchist too. Republicans, on the other hand, delighted perhaps by its firm authoritarian doctrine, took it up despite its royalist ideas. Donations for the new adventure trickled in from Paris and the provinces; and the money thus acquired, however insufficient, was that much less for the competition. Thus the first concrete result of the *Action française*'s appearance on the newsstands of Paris was trouble for the publications and the movements closest to it. The tottering *Libre Parole* slipped out of Drumont's hands; equally threatened, royalists of the *Soleil* and Bonapartists of *L'Autorité* considered a merger that would save them both; and at the *Gazette de France,* Gustave Janicot openly expressed disgust at the ruthless tactics of the *Action française.* The new paper, in the meantime, hungrily watched its stodgy rivals, impatient at their persistence in staying alive when it could have put the money they got from the Duc's funds to such good use.[9]

It had been clear from the beginning that, as Pujo was to explain, "The only really effective means of making ourselves heard will be by attacking the façade of public order that hides scandals and by creating the timely news item that will bring such scandals into the open."[10] Obviously, when scandals were lacking, they would have to be created: agitation in the streets would provide fuel for the paper's campaigns while the paper feverishly stoked the fires of the disturbances on which it fed.

The first number of the *Action française* appeared on March 21, 1908. The lead article, signed by the principal contributors, called on all good Frenchmen to turn against the Republic. Not for the last time, the paper asserted that the few who still had any faith in the regime were rare and becoming rarer. A few minutes' thought was bound to convince everyone that a king was necessary if France was to be turned from the downward path it had followed since the Revolution. Beside this article, signed by Henri Vaugeois and Léon Daudet, who were the joint directors, and by Maurras, Léon de Montesquiou, Lucien Moreau, Jacques Bainville, Louis Dimier, Bernard de Vésins, Robert de Boisfleury, Paul Robain, Frédéric Delebecque, and Maurice Pujo, two columns carried a triumphant interview with Jules Lemaître, who had "found his haven" at last in the royalist faith. Lemaître expressed satisfaction that Action Française doctrine was gaining in intellectual circles and among "studious youth, the young men of the Faculties who have had enough of vague democratic anarchy." The old Academician was somewhat premature, but the new daily did benefit from a revival of nationalistic passions.

Fortunately for the *Action française,* its beginnings almost coincided with the government's budgetary request for funds to reinter Zola in the Panthéon. The uproar this occasioned astonished the ruling Radicals, many of whom thought that passions of this sort had vanished in the last two years. The credits were voted, but, disturbed by the violence of the outcry, the government decided to postpone the ceremony until early summer. The *Action française* was jubilant: "At the very moment our paper enters the scene, nationalist agitation flares up and Paris stirs."[11] In fact, Paris stirred only slightly. By the newspaper's own testimony, it took the nationalist and anti-Semitic crowds and converted them to royalism.[12] Probably even this was an exaggeration. It merely helped to mobilize, and in the process attract to itself, a heterogeneous public of royalists and anti-Semites, reactionaries and earnest patriots. Its success, and its eventual importance, stemmed from the fact that, in a world of loose associations based on loose arguments, the Action Française insisted on discipline and organization, and presented a coherent doctrine as the respectable basis of its activities. These activities attracted the traditional nationalist forces, the same that had been attracted by Boulangist and anti-Dreyfusard appeals. In spite of their insistence on the importance of the crown, the influence of the Action Française increased rather despite than because of their royalism. As Joseph Denais, a nationalist deputy of Paris, would later remark, "Royalism—no one took it seriously."[b] The Action Française provided a rallying point; it kept the flag of nationalism flying and inspired many a student disgusted by the vagueness of democratic theory and practice, but its serious converts to royalism were few.

Lemaître had been right when he claimed that the influence of the Action Française was growing in the University and in intellectual circles. Jules Renard, a soured man but still anti-nationalist and anti-clerical only a few years before, by 1908 found the Action Française pretty much to his taste. And the future editor of the *Nouvelle Revue française,* then an adolescent in Bordeaux casting longing looks at the capital, wrote his friend Henri Alain Fournier in Paris:

> I take sides for reasons unconnected with clear, reasonable thought; I take sides by my childhood, by all my Catholic, reactionary upbringing. I still prefer the Action Française, none of whose stupidities escape me, to the Radical-Socialist league, for which I feel a truly physical repugnance. In spite of everything, when I hear talk about Radicals and Socialists I feel the same slightly superstitious horror that I had as a child for the Dreyfusards. I always imagined these latter as more or less deformed, with something of the devil about them. This sentiment has persisted, even after my mind sloughed off its misconceptions. Naturally, I do nothing to rid myself of it . . .[13]

Jacques Rivière's lines shed a light not only on the scars left by the Dreyfus affair, but also on the kind of prejudices and sympathies on which the nationalist revival of those years, and the Action Française as the most active of its

[b] Joseph Denais, personal communication. In the autumn of 1908, the Action Française, more interested in the articulateness of its recruits than in their royalist convictions, attempted to enlist a man named Massiani, a former secretary of Denais and vice-president of the Jeunesse Plébiscitaire Bonapartiste, who, a police informer reported, "finds himself without a position at the moment" (F^7 12862, 2/85 of Oct. 15, 1908). Massiani eventually became a contributor to Doriot's *Liberté.*

battalions, could count.[14] But such sympathies had to be nourished. From the very beginning, each issue of the paper carried its list of traitors; each week brought another shocking scandal, some familiar, some fresh. The republican press began to notice the unusual vivacity of "nationalist and reactionary polemics." Nationalism had been smoldering; under the Action Française bellows it flared up, and even in the provinces radical papers began to pay attention.

The unsuspecting Sorbonne was first to furnish the nationalists with a really good pretext for righteous indignation. An eminent professor of German at the Sorbonne, Charles Andler, had taken a student group on a visit to Germany during the Easter holidays. The trip had been arranged to foster better understanding between the two countries and was, in fact, given something of an official turn by the German hosts of the visiting party. The idea of such officially, or semi-officially, sanctioned visits, led by a University professor who also happened to be a leading disciple of Jean Jaurès and a close friend of the Socialists' gray eminence Lucien Herr, exasperated the nationalists, who were opposed to any sort of temperate move that might weaken their countrymen's desire to avenge the defeat of 1870–71. When the summer term began, organized riots protesting Andler's tour broke out in and around the Sorbonne. The German visit had been criticized by the *Action française* on April 24. On May 4 it had called a meeting, "Contre l'oubli de '71," as a prelude to the demonstrations at the Sorbonne and in the Latin Quarter which were designed to force suspension of Andler's lectures. In a letter to *Le Temps* of May 10 Andler explained that the trip had been organized chiefly to allow the students to travel at half-cost as members of a group led by a professor, as regulations required. The demonstrations only grew worse. Sordid material reasons were no excuse for the corruption of French youth, who had better and less dangerous things to do than learning German at the source. On May 16, Vaugeois rejoiced over the nationalist awakening his campaign had achieved: "Nationalism, our sentiment of 1898, our initial movement. That is what we rediscover, identical, intact, in these young men."

The comparison with 1898 was not unjustified. Serious clashes took place in the streets, in the courts of the Sorbonne, even in lecture halls. Andler's lectures were not suspended, but on the days when they were scheduled the police station in the Place du Panthéon was packed to overflowing. The *Dépêche de Toulouse* was dismayed: "One could have thought nationalism dead and buried. But here it is again . . . and on the Boulevard Saint-Michel cudgels are selling like hot cakes once more." The agitation rose to its highest point on June 4, when Action Française students seem to have sparked the hostile demonstrations that greeted President Fallières and the other luminaries of the Republic on their way to and from the Zola ceremonies at the Panthéon. There were no riots that day, and the shots of Grégori did not carry very far, but it all helped to convince the Action Française—and even its opponents—that nationalists now dominated the Latin Quarter.

Grégori's acquittal in September came as a surprise. It confirmed the feeling that had been growing since spring that the wind had turned once more toward the Right, that the public was beginning to favor anti-republican ideas, and that the time might be coming for new outbreaks of violence. In this favorable situation, the leadership of the Action Française was by no means universally recognized by the Right. A police agent's report of the time says that other nationalists did not want to play the Action Française's game or cooperate in the "talisman" campaign. When the government failed to dignify Gaucher's outburst at Grégori's trial by treating it as a political crime, the right-wing press was slow to support the Action Française in its efforts to promote Gaucher from misdemeanor to martyrdom. By the end of September Action Française leaders were discussing ways of forcing the government to notice them and bring them to court, especially into the Assizes, where a public trial by jury would offer them an excellent opportunity for propaganda.[15] In October Maxime Réal del Sarte made his violent, and no doubt carefully planned, challenge of the Cour de Cassation, and more demonstrations soon followed at the Palais de Justice and the Théâtre de l'Odéon, the latter occasioned by a reading from the detested Zola. Then, on November 16, 1908, young royalists for the first time joined some of Lucien Moreau's student group in selling copies of the *Action française* on the streets of Paris. The Camelots du Roi had been born, equipped with hawkers' licenses from the Prefecture of Police, recruited partly from a royalist group from the wealthy 17th Arrondissement which had been raised by Henry des Lyons to sell royalist papers at church doors on Sundays, and partly from Firmin Baconnier's royalist workmen and clerks of the Accord Social. Thus they included upper-class students like the three Réal del Sarte brothers, Théodore de Fallois, and Armand du Tertre, as well as recruits of humbler station like Marius Plateau, who ran errands at the Bourse, Lucien Lacour, a carpenter, and Louis Fageau, a butcher boy. Some Camelots made their living by selling the paper; others sold it for a lark. Probably most of them, like Georges Bernanos, were not much concerned with the theoretical or "Maurrassian" ideas they were supposed to defend. But, in spite of moral difficulties which resulted in repeated purges, the Camelots were to serve the Action Française well.[16] Their first president was Maxime Réal del Sarte; des Lyons became secretary; but the real decisions rested with Maurice Pujo, who was responsible for relations with the central organization and for ultimate discipline. Their numbers increased rapidly. Nonexistent in October 1908, a handful in November, they were several dozen when December offered a fresh occasion for displaying their force.

Four years earlier, Professor François Thalamas, while teaching history at the Lycée Condorcet, had expressed opinions on Joan of Arc that caused a minor scandal and resulted in his being transferred to another school. Since the new school was also in Paris and had perhaps even better standing, Thalamas did not suffer, but he remained from that day one of the nationalists' pet aversions. The announcement that he had been permitted to give a series of public lectures in the Sorbonne moved them to transports of rage.[17] The subject of the lectures, pedagogical method, was irrelevant to the symbolic importance attached to his presence in the halls of the Sorbonne. The nationalists were, indeed, not altogether wrong in taking Thalamas's appointment as a personal affront. In the summer of 1908, when the Faculty Council of the Sorbonne had received Thalamas's application for permission to lecture, it had decided that a refusal would seem to be a concession forced by nationalist attacks against him, and its decision was thus a reaction against, almost a defiance of, nationalist threats.[18]

The Camelots du Roi played an active part in disrupting first the courses of the winter term, then those of the spring term in 1909, in riots that involved large forces of police and led to pitched battles, both inside and outside the Sorbonne, between Thalamistes and Anti-Thalamistes. On one occasion, the lecturer himself was hunted out and soundly thrashed by Camelots who had managed to enter the heavily guarded amphitheater by a forgotten side entrance. There were other incidents: Jewish lecturers, as well as the dean of the faculty, the eminent Hellenist Croizet, fell victim to Camelot-staged campaigns. Once, Pujo took over a hall and, fending off the professor who was attempting to lecture, proceeded to deliver a lecture of his own on the Action Française, its grievances and aims. Hilarity was mingled with exasperation in the public's reaction to all these doings. The great majority of those arrested were less than twenty years old; few were over thirty. Not all were students—some were students only by virtue of being habitués of Left Bank cafés. But the Action Française had made its point: its power in this milieu would be an important asset and one that it jealously protected.

Even there, however, the beginning was slow. Grit and imagination got the Camelots through the Thalamas affair, but they faced some awkward moments when republican students, far more numerous, decided to put up an opposition. Several times early in 1909 they were routed, and they avoided humiliation only when the Bonapartist supporters of Cassagnac and his paper *L'Autorité,* with whom relations had previously been strained, decided to come to their aid.[19] The risk had deliberately been taken, in the hope that the "tumult policy" would bring attention and recruits. There were riots at the Père Lachaise cemetery, incidents in the national theaters, demonstrations in the Latin Quarter, all this with the slenderest of means. If we are to believe a police informer, the Action Française could count for its riots on less than 180 persons. The informer gives details and numbers: sixty students and Camelots; fifty men of Baconnier's Accord Social; some forty socialites, who could only rarely be brought out by one of their social equals—Daudet, Montesquiou, or Boisfleury—for some fashionable romp like jeering in the lobby of the Comédie Française; ten newspapermen, including Gaucher and Pujo; and twenty hired rowdies. To the question why the Action Française should undertake its rough campaigns with such feeble forces, the informer replies that it does this in order to recruit others and to keep the royalist cause before the public.[20]

The policy worked. Within a year there were sixty-five Camelot sections throughout France, and some six hundred members in Paris alone.[c] But Camelots' duties were hard—they had to sell the paper on Sunday mornings and be on call at all times for parades and demonstrations—and only about a quarter of the Paris membership seems to have been really active. In theory, such dereliction of duty would result in expulsion, or at least suspension. In practice, and since the Action Française cared about the figures of its membership, a compromise was reached in 1910 by creating an elite of the elite, the Commissaires, for use in all possible circumstances. Armed with loaded canes and clubs, the Commissaires maintained order at meetings, marched on either side of Action Française parades, guarded the leaders and the offices, and provided a task force for adventures of every kind.

Camelot demonstrations at republican ceremonies and Camelot irreverence and larks would set police and press by the ears. By 1909, the police considered the Camelots the most troublesome of all the right-wing organizations. Their talk of a *coup d'état* in friendly houses like that of the Duchesse de Rohan raised apprehensions in official quarters. When President Fallières went south to Nice on an official visit, one of the authorities' prime concerns was to protect him from some violent Action Française outburst. The movements of local and Parisian Camelots were watched, and the police were clearly more worried about their intentions than about any left-wing threat. Nor did the summer holidays bring a lull: "Of all the leagues and of all the opposition," reported one of the Sûreté's untiring spies in August 1909, "the Action Française is the least on holiday. In contrast to what usually happens in the other movements, its headquarters are almost as lively and active as usual."[21]

The kind of activity the integral nationalists best liked to indulge in was not designed to endear them to certain people on their own, royalist, side. More revolutionary than conservative, the Action Française pursued its anti-democratic and anti-republican campaigns without looking too closely at the kind of support it could get. And the sympathies it showed for the economic claims of postmen, naval conscripts, and railroad workers, whose demands and strikes filled the whole of 1909, enraged more conservative royalists, whose original

[c] F^7 12864 of Nov. 28, 1909. Provincial recruitment was helped by similar tactics. The Action Française seized the opportunity offered by the provincial tour of *Le Foyer,* in 1909, to organize demonstrations and attract attention in towns where the road company performed. In the wake of this campaign, sections sprang up at Angers, Cahors, Montauban, and Toulouse; see Gaucher, *L'Honorable Léon Daudet,* pp. 28–32.

suspicion of their recent allies was heightened by the feeling that the new organization no more supported the established order than the embattled workers did. In effect, as a left-wing paper remarked, the Action Française stood at the extreme Left of royalism; and old-fashioned royalists had never suspected that royalism could have a Left. In April 1909, the Pretender's political bureau ordered all open participation in working-class activities to cease, and for a brief time the Action Française submitted.[22]

There was a certain opportunism in the Action Française's courting of labor; there was also, as we shall see, a sincere effort to win workers over to a program of social reconciliation. Neither was likely to appeal to the older Orléanists, who were as suspicious of social concern as they were of force. Such men would agree with the observer who, in the summer of 1909, felt sure that in their search for revolutionary opportunities the Action Française would not hesitate to associate with their enemies of yesterday, "be they anarchists, collectivists, etc., provided they were revolutionaries."[d] These revolutionary proclivities were further proved by their irreverent statue-smashing, cane-wielding activities, by their disruption of public ceremonies and attacks on public persons, and by their generally hooligan-like behavior.

If the men of the Action Française were more revolutionary than royalist, the old fashioned followers of the Duc d'Orléans seem to have been less royalist than conservative. Their attitudes had been formed in the days when the parliamentary majority had been monarchist, when a royal restoration by legal means had not been a vain hope. Their resentment of the competition of these johnny-come-latelies was partly jealous complacency and reluctance to change, partly a genuine fear that such violent techniques would wreck the cause. Even though past results had not been brilliant, things should be done the way they had always been done. More important, things should not be done that might rock the boat, even though the boat, becalmed, had for some time been drifting over an ocean of indifference toward the shoals of final failure.

Vaugeois, Daudet, and Maurras, on the other hand, could not hide their impatience at the old fogies who had charge of the Pretender's affairs in a country that he was not, by law, allowed to enter. The fact that the Action Française was officially independent and not in any way considered to be the responsibility of the Pretender's political bureau only made things worse. For the gentlemen of the bureau felt entitled to a say in activities that took place under the royal aegis, and the Action Française objected to any advice or criticism.

The friction between the two parties came to a head early in 1910 at the official unveiling of a statue of Jules Ferry, when a Camelot, Lucien Lacour, stepped out of the crowd and smartly slapped Premier Aristide Briand. Ferry

[d] F7 12862, 4/78 of June 21, 1909; *ibid.* 2/52 of July 1, 1908, for a report that François de Ramel, royalist deputy of Alais (Gard), who does not like the Action Française, is doing his best to deprive it of the sympathies, support, and subsidies of the royalist aristocracy of Paris.

was the father of secular education, against which the French Catholic hierarchy was just then once more protesting; Briand was the best-known politician associated with the separation of Church and State. Lacour's slaps therefore were intended as more than mere assault; but it was the assault, and against the Premier, that shocked respectable persons on all sides. Breaking statues was bad enough, roughing up professors in the halls of the Sorbonne was worse, but men who manhandled premiers, even republican ones, could not be trusted to refrain from manhandling *bien pensants* themselves.

The *bien pensant* offensive began on March 20, 1910, when Arthur Meyer's *Gaulois,* which was the favorite reading of fashionable circles, published an interview with the Duc d'Orléans at Seville in which the Duc expressed disapproval of Camelot violence and hinted that if it went on he might be forced to disown both the Camelots and the Action Française. The move was motivated less by Lacour's act than by the dispute that had broken out in its wake between the more conservative royalists and the supporters of Camelot guerrillas. The dispute was embittered by another issue: the *Action française* had reported complaints that Maxime Réal del Sarte, then serving his term of military service, was being unfairly treated by his superiors. The *Action française* was here attacking the representatives of established order; it did not hesitate to criticize the Army, most of whose officers were conservatives and Catholics themselves.

In his interview, the Duc d'Orléans reprimanded such insubordination and imprudence, which might lead (as indeed, it already had) "to the unforgivable mistake of attacking the nation's Army." He would not hesitate, he declared, to disown his overeager partisans "if they failed much longer to discriminate between enemies and friends, and if a persistent error of maneuver caused them to direct their fire against the main body of royalist troops."

In whole or in part the interview was reproduced by most of the Paris and provincial press, and it struck Action Française leaders with dismay. That obviously had been the effect intended. The Pretender's personal friend, the Duc de Luynes, wired to Seville: "Article en général très bien reproduit dans toute la presse." If the stroke had been deliberate, and there is no reason to doubt that it was, the reaction was electric. Telegrams flew back and forth between Paris and Seville—congratulations from old royalists like François de Ramel and Gustave de Lamarzelle, expostulations from friends of the Action Française.

On the surface, the Action Française put up the best front it could, protesting that the Duc's words had been misleadingly reported and that the whole interview was a deliberate attempt to divide the royalist camp. Behind the scenes it worked feverishly to reach the Duc and regain his favor. On March 21, without having received permission for an interview, Maurras, Montesquiou, Pujo, and Major Cuignet boarded the Sud-Express for Spain. In a cable the next day to their friend Roger Lambelin, a nationalist councilman from Paris, the Duc repeated his refusal to meet the delegation; but at the same time he was preparing his retreat. Under heavy pressure in Paris, the journalist G. de Maizière, to whom the interview had been granted, cabled Seville for a word confirming his account, which the Duc's Paris office, claiming utter ignorance of the matter, refused to endorse. In the version the *Gaulois* had published, the Duc's expressions had been, if anything, toned down. But if Maizière believed the Duc would stand by his word, he was due for a disappointment. The Paris press of March 28 heralded the return of the Action Française pilgrims from Seville, their faces somewhat red but their spirits far from low. The note the delegation published, with the Duc's approval, showed that they had at least talked him to a draw.

The Duc declared that his words concerning them had been misunderstood. He had in no way blamed the Action Française, with whom he found himself in full ideological agreement. On March 28 the *Gaulois* admitted defeat: "Our duty is to comply." *Gil Blas* quipped wryly: "He denied without denying, while denying all the same." The general knowledge that not Maizière but the Duc had gone too far only made Vaugeois's success seem the more striking. And very few people saw the piteous private cable from the Duc to Maizière, letting down the man he had so clumsily used without being able to mention a single error or exaggeration in the interview's printed text. Few could remonstrate with a prince, even with one in exile. Only Luynes had the temerity to express his disapproval, by cable, of the Duc's retraction, which, instead of soothing royalist dissensions, distinctly encouraged the violence of the Action Française.[23]

For the moment, the Action Française was glad just to get its breath. A police informer reported the immense relief in Action Française circles at having got away with it, for, knowing the Duc's disapproval of their policy and tactics, they had expected the worst. When the delegates returned from Seville, reprieved if not approved, one of the founders commented, "Enfin nous voici sortis du cauchemar." They had promised to give up the use of force; there would be no more violence in the streets: "La politique des barricades est abandonnée."[24] Outwardly successful, the Action Française had in truth had a tight squeak. The humiliation of the *Gaulois,* against which it had concentrated its fire, was incidental to the real issue. Meyer and his paper had simply tried to capitalize on the conflict between the old royalists and the new, and Daudet and Maurras erred in thinking that the conflict itself was due to Meyer's intrigues. The *Gaulois* was apparently defeated, but the real conflict was in no way lessened.

The old bears were still in control of official royalist activity. On the steering committee of the political bureau, Mayol de Luppé, Castillon de Saint-Victor, the Duc de Luynes, and President Legrand of the Jeunesses Royalistes (who had fought a duel with Daudet) held the majority. They considered Lur-Saluces a hothead and no more trustworthy than his rowdy Camelot friends, and looked askance at the conspiratorial posturings of all these extremists. The only supporter of the Action Française on the steering committee, Roger Lambelin, resigned in disgust only to be replaced by the Comte Henry de Larègle, who was a friend of Meyer and had long disliked the Action Française. (In 1907, when Maurras had attacked a friend of his in the *Gazette de France,* he had furiously canceled his subscription.) The Action Française pretended to consider his appointment of no significance and declared itself determined to remain royalist, even, if necessary, against the Pretender, but it sensed breakers ahead. Though Vaugeois publicly attributed Larègle's appointment to the charms of the Comtesse de Larègle, he and others knew better. The respite obtained at Seville might be short-lived.[25]

The Action Française leaders were in a quandary: much as they might want to appease the Duc and his advisers, they had their own party to consider. They maintained their troops, stimulated interest, and attracted readers by the very activities of which the conservatives disapproved; if they gave them up, they would be abandoning their most characteristic attraction and would be reduced to the level of the conformist opposition they despised. If they persisted, however, conflict with the political bureau was inevitable, and behind the bureau stood the Duc, who had warned them that he would not tolerate any more "untimely demonstrations." When, during the summer, cries of "Vive le Roi" and "Vive Orléans" and insults to Fallières had risen from the crowd as he rode by with the visiting king of Bulgaria, a telegram from Marienbad had expressed anger at the incidents and forbidden their repetition. The *Action française* had cautioned its readers to restrain themselves in the future and attributed the demonstrations against Fallières to *agents provocateurs.* But it knew that by trying to restrain its supporters too much it ran the risk of losing them. Restless colts can be driven only with a very loose rein; but on a loose rein they can bolt to trouble.

Larègle's opportunity came in October when dissatisfied railroadmen tried to back up claims that had been too long ignored with a strike that briefly immobilized rail transport throughout France. Premier Briand countered by calling up the strikers for military service, and this broke the syndicalist resistance. The Action Française, which disliked Briand and the railroad owners far more than it did a strike, showed sympathy for the syndicalist side. Indignant, the royalist political bureau advised the Duc d'Orléans that such a stand would badly hurt his cause in staunchly conservative provincial areas. The leaders of the Action Française, thus threatened again from the Right, were obliged to explain themselves in a series of articles, pointing out that when they declared themselves on the same side of the barricades as the revolutionary strikers this applied only in certain contingencies—against, for instance, "the Jewish sword" of the generals charged with putting down the strike.[26]

But this time they could not get away with it. The crime of leftism had compounded "the unforgivable mistake of attacking the nation's Army." On

November 30, the *Correspondance nationale,* the official organ of the royalist political bureau, printed an article which, for all those in the know, was a direct condemnation of the Action Française. To prevent all possible misunderstandings this was followed by a statement from the Duc himself, in the form of a letter to Larègle, in which he disowned the Action Française and criticized their attacks against Larègle as "unworthy of devoted royalists," "an act of revolt and indiscipline that I cannot tolerate." The Action Française had always been completely free to act as it wished, since its members "never speak in his name or commit him in any fashion." He could not, however, admit that they should use this freedom, against his express injunctions, for violent and unjustified attacks on other royalists: "When I command I expect to be obeyed, and I am the only judge of the direction and political orientation of my party." The Duc, the press reported, no longer knew those who had revolted against him. The leaders of the Action Française could return to the royalist party only "after their complete submission and after having furnished proofs and categorical guarantees that their submission is sincere."

As Dimier would later explain, in an otherwise confused account of these events, two reactions are possible when one is faced with this kind of outright and unequivocal excommunication: either say that one serves the cause regardless of its leader, or allege that the leader has been deceived. "Neither is any good. We could not, however, be silent, for we did not want to disband. We chose the second excuse as being the less implausible, as in a way reserving our obedience, finally as leaving room for some arrangement."[27]

And so the paper was filled with passionate denunciations of Larègle and his gang, evil counselors of their prince, sowers of discord and dissension. The old royalists replied in kind. After two years of sparring, the issue was out in the open: it was who should control the royalist organization and its funds, who should have the Duc's ear. The *Action française* began a subscription for a fighting fund and published endless subscription lists from its backers. Some of the lists were rigged, showing gifts that dated back six months or more, before the conflict started, and thus hardly to be counted as an endorsement of the paper's present policies. To pad out the lists even further, certain large donations were divided into several small anonymous ones. Mme André Buffet, listed for 500 francs at the beginning of the campaign, was embarrassed enough to write the Duc explaining that she had donated the money before any trouble had occurred.[28]

The struggle between old royalists and their rivals went on through the winter of 1910 and the spring of 1911. The *Gaulois* and the *Correspondance nationale* were losing "disgusted subscribers"; the *Action française* seemed to be gaining. Both sides recruited butchers and other toughs to defend them, and each sometimes called upon friends in anarchist or social revolutionary circles to disrupt the other's meetings. The conflict had a certain paradoxical aspect, because the Action Française had gained the support of legitimist families for whom the Orléans pretenders were upstarts. Reluctant to accept the Orléans succession on the death of the Comte de Chambord, some of them had not returned to the royalist fold until Maurras stirred their faith and sense of purpose with the arguments of his *Enquête sur la monarchie.* To these old *chouans,* heirs of legitimist *ultras,* the Action Française was the only movement to show some sense and spirit. Its break with the descendant of Philippe Egalité delighted them. They would not let it down; and their qualifications and their devotion to the royal cause could not be gainsaid. To Dimier, as to everybody else, names like that of the Comte de Damas evoked the very essence of royalism.

The support of such men gave the rebels hope, but far more hope came from the surprising number of latent royalists who had apparently been awaiting a break before choosing the activism of Maurras over the inactivity of its bureau. "You just cannot imagine," wrote Maurras's secretary, Henry Cellerier, to a young Swiss friend, "what the state of mind is in France concerning the Action Française. Many people were prevented from rallying to the cause of monarchy only by the entourage of the Prince; and don't think they didn't give us a lot of trouble! From now on we are free, and *already* people are joining up at a tremendous rate. We are going to make an enormous impact on the masses. Our movement will increase tenfold. *I assure you.*"[29] Cellerier apparently thought there was good reason to expect success. And the fighting fund grew daily.

The success of the rebels did not go unnoticed by the Duc, and meanwhile Lur-Saluces and the Marquise de MacMahon were working hard to re-establish the Action Française in royal favor. A reconciliation was ultimately arranged, and one that satisfied both parties. On April 28, 1911, the Action Française board wrote the Duc assuring him of their devotion, expressing their regrets at having had to defend the royal interests at the risk of incurring his disfavor, and pledging themselves his humble subjects and servants. This was answered in a conciliatory and friendly vein, sufficient to show that the Action Française was back in royal favor and that Larègle had lost his battle to keep them out. The old gang could not fight as savagely as the new; their invective was poorer, their will to win less intense. It was not for them to defend the colors of the king.

The exchange of letters was made public on May 19. A police note of the same day declared the issue settled in favor of the Action Française and the use of force. By elimination of its opponents, in part deliberate, in part accidental, the Action Française had now been "left alone at the head of the royalist movement." On June 15, this was confirmed by royal writ: the *Correspondance nationale* was excommunicated and Larègle's resignation from the political bureau was accepted. Henceforth, for more than a quarter of a century, the bureau would be dominated by the Action Française, speaking as the official mouthpiece of the king.[30]

By the end of 1911, the reconciliation between the Duc d'Orléans and his strong-minded supporters seems to have been complete, despite some problems concerning the liquidation and replacement of the defeated royalist organization. Many of the important Orléanist leaders refused to have anything to do with the political bureau because they were unwilling to risk the fate of their predecessors; others declared themselves unable to afford the expense such responsibilities would entail. In the end, unable to rally volunteers, the Duc seems to have relegated the central organization in Paris to a secondary role, and supplanted it by a system of strong regional delegates. Eugène de Lur-Saluces in the southwest, Picot de Pledran in the east, Flachaire de Roustan at Lyon, and the Marquis de Suffren at Toulouse were the first royal delegates thus appointed, and "naturally these gentlemen would act especially and altogether at one with the Action Française."[31]

Ultimately, it was the old crowd's refusal to play the game under Action Française leadership that left the field free to the integral nationalists. Not all the regional positions were accepted eagerly. For example, when the Duc de Bourbon-Busset refused to take charge of the central region, saying he would not work to find money for the Action Française to waste, the Comte de Montlaur had to be persuaded to fill the gap. But one way or another, all the royal delegates chosen in November 1911 either belonged to the Action Française or were close to it.[32]

The time has now come to take a closer look at the organization which, for the next three decades, would play such an important part in the destinies of royalist and nationalist movements.

In December 1910, while the conflict between old royalists and new was at its height, the Third Congress of the Action Française met in the Salle Wagram. We are fortunate to have the detailed account of a police agent who conscientiously attended every session and described what would still be the pattern of such functions even fifty years later.

The Congress, the agent reports, was a success. It reflected Action Française gains throughout the country, and the League's readiness to absorb the rest of the royalist movement and establish itself as the official party organization. This was no congress, the agent observed, where delegates discussed and voted on various questions. It was "a school where provincial members come to receive instructions decided on in advance, orders in which they have had no voice and which they listen to and accept without discussion." The important reports were read to the meeting by the Paris leaders, the others by the most loyal of the provincial lieutenants; but all had been submitted to Maurras in advance. Everything was done to dazzle the provincial delegates, to convince them of the movement's vitality and influence, to attach them securely to the Action Française leadership, and to imbue them with confidence, indeed with fanaticism. Such efforts did not go unrewarded: the enthusiasm, greater than at previous congresses, rose to heights of religious fervor. But—and the but is important—the focus of the new enthusiasm was more and more the personality of Charles Maurras and his lieutenants, less and less the royalist idea itself.

Some three hundred persons attended the meeting, three times the number who attended the First Congress in 1907. The majority of them were, of course, Parisians. Only sixty-five were from the provinces, the police agent reported, half of them very young men "incapable of any serious influence or of important local results." Since all the provincial delegates were supposed to be heads of sections, it followed that half of the Action Française groups in the provinces existed only on paper. Some members of the remaining half were between thirty and forty-five and could be "serious"; among these, ten were retired officers of noble descent. The remaining ten or so were "old and without importance, too wildly fanatical to have any influence."[33] Allowing for the agent's prejudices, the result is not unimpressive. Any congress where even a quarter of the provincial delegates might possibly be "serious" deserves some respect. Apart from the Paris region, the two-hundred-odd sections represented by these delegates were concentrated mainly in the west, southwest, and south, in Normandy, in those parts of the Nord and Pas-de-Calais where Catholic and patronal influence was strong, and in the Rhône Valley from Lyon and Saint-Etienne due south.

More than half of these sections were headed by titled persons, an unusually high figure in comparison with other political movements. In so far as it can be identified, between 15 and 20 per cent of Action Française support at this time seems to have been drawn from people with titles, real or assumed.[34] Clerical supporters must have been almost as numerous. Even so, the bulk of support came from the Third Estate, especially from the Army and the intellectual professions. There were many lawyers, some of them section heads. The Société des Jurisconsultes Catholiques, soon to become an Action Française stronghold, numbered a good many sympathizers: among them the sons of its founder (the royalist Senator Emmanuel Lucien-Brun of Lyon) and its secretary, Antoine Lestra. Faculties of medicine, especially those of Paris and Bordeaux, had not yet turned into the Action Française bastions they would become after the war; but, perhaps by a process of natural selection among traditionalists, the Ecole des Chartes, had already contributed its share of enthusiasts, who could in after years be found throughout the Archival administration, in Paris and the provinces. Perhaps the most numerous were the recruits from the lower middle class—shop and clerical workers, teachers and librarians, noncommissioned officers, insurance agents, and commercial travelers. The propaganda value of these last was so great that the League had a special section for them, open to "all members whose profession consists of persuading clients."

The petty bourgeoisie was traditionally patriotic, even chauvinist. This was the class which, Jacobin or other, had furnished the core of nationalist troops in the days of Boulanger and Dreyfus. Its members liked the Action Française for being as extreme in its opposition to the government as they themselves would have liked to be. To Maurras, their sympathies seemed to be based on devotion to the past: "No break in continuity," he wrote with the provinces in mind, "no schism, between national elements in whom consciousness of the past endures: peasants, workers, bourgeois, small and middling nobles in the country or in the services, all have remained united and bound together." Maurras, who had rightly noted how the society of Paris, royalist and reactionary only shortly before but knowing on which side its bread was buttered, had been drifting into the republican camp, here exaggerated the unity and breadth of royalist support. Some peasants certainly backed him, but—outside of certain White departments like the Gard, the Hérault, and the Vendée—only patchily, out of deference to gentry or priests or for some special reason of their own. There were few workers in the ranks, and the number would grow less—railwaymen, especially on the Paris-Lyon-Méditérranée lines, some miners and textile workers in the north, and the traditionally White working-class families in Lyon. As for the lower middle classes, their sympathy stemmed less from the survival of traditional loyalties than from resentment against a regime which they blamed for their economic difficulties, and against democratic doctrines which seemed to them responsible for the many puzzling social and economic pressures they had to bear. Any party that energetically opposed government and democracy, capitalism and collectivism, could expect their support. Indifferent to the monarchy, a growing section of the petty bourgeoisie was beginning to turn against the regime and to support those who opposed it, be it in the name of the king.[35] The bourgeoisie also contributed the largest contingent of Camelots. Before 1914, the Camelots seem to have consisted largely of shop clerks and office workers with a sprinkling of young bloods. Some Camelots were recruited from Catholic institutions, both educational and charitable; some were students of one sort or another. Since *lycéens* and undergraduates often joined the Etudiants d'Action Française, it seems likely that most of the student Camelots came from technical schools and other establishments less exalted than the Sorbonne.[36]

In the frenzied days of March 1815, when Napoleon was marching up on Paris from Golfe Juan, students of medicine and law had furnished the main body of royal volunteers, had been among the first, and last, to cry "Vive le Roi!" before Louis le Désiré had left them stranded. Almost one hundred years were to pass before progressive-minded students could again cry "Vive le Roi!" and feel themselves in the vanguard of events. But fashionable as integral nationalism had become on the Left Bank by 1911, and much as it would impress Jean Barois about 1912, students remained in a minority among the gangs of roughneck hawkers led by Pujo and Réal del Sarte. Among the fifty Camelots arrested during the July 14 demonstrations in 1911, there were twenty-four clerks and five artisans; only six were students (and one was a professor).[37]

If the areas of Action Française recruitment were socially heterogeneous, they were almost uniformly Catholic. Since 1905 and 1906, increasing numbers of priests and monks had shown their sympathy to the new league and to the newspaper, which many of them received free. Their comments, quoted in the pages of the paper, indicate that it was less the Republic itself that they hated than "the monstrous Judeo-Masonic regime," of which they thought themselves the victims. But this was sufficient reason to persuade a good many that when the Action Française labored to restore the monarchy it also "prepared for the Church the holy freedom needed to lead men's souls to their supernatural end." Forgetting the monarchy's steadfast struggle to control the Church, clerics like Dom Besse could assert that "The remedy for France's ills lies in the intelligent return to the political constitution and to the social institutions the revolutionaries destroyed. On the day these are restored, France will find herself once more the *eldest daughter of the Church,* the most Christian kingdom."[38]

Right or wrong, such arguments were persuasive, and while many of the episcopacy surviving from Concordat days continued to follow policies that were far too restrained for the new Pope's taste, "all that was combative among French Catholics passed to the Action Française."[39] The Assumptionist fathers of *La Croix,* reprimanded a decade before but still active, were very sympathetic, and so was the whole "integrist" clan—enemies of modernism like Jacques Rocafort, a professor at the Lycée Saint-Louis and "the principal agent of the Pope's policy in France";[40] Monseigneur Jouin, the publisher of the anti-Masonic *Revue internationale des sociétés secrètes*; and the *Revue*'s editor, Abbé Boulin, who was also the editor of the extreme integrist publication *La Vigie.* Catholic seminaries became hothouses of integral nationalism; the Catholic military organization Notre Dame des Armées was reported as helping to spread the new doctrine; and soon the great Catholic organ *L'Univers* (Louis Veuillot's old *Univers*), which was already infiltrated by sympathetic integrists, would be bought by a monarchist group, "friends or members of the Action Française."[41]

Heavily dependent on the Catholics for money, sympathy, and support, the Action Française could no more dispense with them than it could have dispensed with royalist endorsement. Yet it was threatened on its Catholic flank from two directions at once. The more obvious line of attack was the one voiced by an old teacher of Maurras, Bishop Guillibert of Fréjus, when he wrote to a correspondent hostile to his former student:

> It appears to take some courage to attack the stronghold of the Chaussée d'Antin [where the Action Française offices were in 1910]. You see how our great Catholic dailies dare not speak up, and how, when at last they

> do, it is only to give the straight news. All tremble before those daring men who with incomparable virtuosity have found the means to set forth the detestable doctrines of the most brutal paganism, or the most subtle modernism, under the immaculate attire of a highly proclaimed confidence in the Catholic Church, as a principle of social order and a necessary ingredient of French unity.... [They do this at the price of] misrepresenting the Semitic scriptures, forgetting or civilizing the Hebrew Christ, and concealing other insanities and blasphemies in their splendid pages, pages by which the naïve let themselves be taken in, at which the royalists applaud, and at whose success those who play this grand new game must swell with real pride.[42]

But views such as these would have to wait many years before they came into their own.

More immediate was the threat of Christian Democracy, of the social Christianity first promoted by priests like the Abbés Naudet and Garnier, and later by a man of charm, drive, and rhetorical talent, Marc Sangnier. Sangnier, the scion of a wealthy Catholic family and the grandson of the famous Bonapartist barrister Georges-Alexandre Lachaud, had launched in 1898 a social pietist movement with populist and Tolstoian overtones known as the Sillon. With its mixture of high-flown oratory and informal camaraderie, of pious mysticism and enthusiastic populism, the Sillon was not attractive to integral Catholics, who were anti-modernist in religion and anti-democratic in politics. Father Le Floch, the rector of the French Seminary in Rome, who was a Breton from Finistère and a friend of the Action Française, spoke for a good many other priests when he declared, "They had to be condemned. They would have made Breton priests accept the Republic."[43] As Le Floch perceived, the Sillon was a powerful force on the Left, as capable of eliciting devotion and loyalty as the Action Française itself. When in May 1908 Sangnier appealed for contributions to start a daily paper, a poor student at Nantes, Raoul Villain, nearly starved himself to death for a whole year in order to save the wherewithal of an anonymous thousand-franc donation. Within a year, over 260,000 francs were collected; within another, the first number of the Sillon's *Démocratie* appeared.[44] It came only a few days ahead of a papal letter which, on August 25, 1910, condemned Sillonists and other Christian Democrats for wanting "to make religion accessory to a political party." "In order to justify their social dreams," explained the Pope in words that could have been applied to the Action Française simply by replacing *social* with *political,* "they appeal to the scriptures interpreted after their fashion and, what is graver still, to a disfigured and degraded Christ."

The papal letter was interpreted on all sides as a success for the Action Française and the integralist point of view. Sillonists and integral nationalists had for some time struggled for dominance in Catholic circles. Active in the provinces, the Sillon attracted country priests, members of Catholic youth organizations, and also members of the more conservative Action Libérale. It had organized workingmen's circles, which the Action Française eyed greedily, and now it had entered another competitor in the already overcrowded field of political journalism.[45] The heaviest guns of integral nationalism had been trained on these dangerous opponents, and their condemnation by the Pope was a reason for rejoicing at the Chaussée d'Antin. The Christian Democrats were, for the moment, defeated, but the Action Française had made powerful and persistent enemies, and only the most persuasive interventions were to keep them from being likewise condemned during the prewar years. But revenge is a dish that even Christians can eat cold; and the friends of the Sillon would not rest until the shame of 1910 had been avenged.

3

ALARUMS AND EXCURSIONS

TRIUMPHANT OVER THE ROYALISTS, well established in the Catholic world, the Action Française would be less successful in another of its enterprises: the wooing of labor.

An essential part of Maurrassian doctrine concerned the egalitarian individualism which had helped to disintegrate a society hitherto united. The democratic revolution had destroyed the old structure of natural corporate bodies and had left men isolated before the encroaching powers of mammoth capital and the leviathan State. One result had been a moral anarchy in which men felt responsible only to their own interests or desires. Another, of which the current social agitation was symptomatic, had been the creation of artificial and selfish class divisions and interest groups. The nation was a whole. To levy war against any of its parts was to diminish it and at the same time oneself. It was not class war that was needed, but class cooperation; and the first step in this direction could be taken by reconciling employers and employed, by integrating workers morally and socially in the national whole and showing them that their natural interests, like everybody else's, lay in the prosperity of their trade, in which the welfare of employer and employed was one.

Heretofore, these doctrines of social conciliation had been preached mostly by Catholics. In 1871 two dedicated Army officers, the Comte Albert de Mun and the Marquis de la Tour du Pin, resigned their commissions in order to found the Oeuvre des Cercles Catholiques d'Ouvriers to promote the union of capital and labor in Christian guilds under the patronage of the Church and the upper classes. Given the traditionalist backgrounds of the two men, it was not remarkable that from the first, despite the best intentions, the Oeuvre was tainted with reaction. After a brief Boulangist excursion, de Mun followed the *ralliement* into the conservative republican camp; but La Tour du Pin continued a royalist and in 1905 joined the Action Française. His support was flattering but somewhat constraining owing to his undiminished faith in his corporatist ideas, which were heavily tinged with paternalism and, as Dimier would put it, quite out of touch with current questions.[1]

In the wake of the Oeuvre, sometimes inspired by a genuine concern for the welfare of workers, sometimes by awareness of a handy counter to Socialist and syndicalist pressures, there grew up a series of "independent" or "yellow" unions, anti-syndicalist, anti-Socialist, anti-Marxist, opposing decentralization to Red centralism, patriotic fervor to Red internationalism, and friendly relations with employers to Red theories of class war. Whatever the program, the Jaunes (their name was derived from the strips of yellow paper with which their local at Montceau-les-Mines repaired the windows broken by striking miners) were mostly strikebreakers. Their first national congress, in 1902, claimed strength comparable to that of the class-conscious Confédération Générale du Travail (CGT), then, as now, the largest labor union in France. Soon, under the influence of their leader, the shrewd Socialist renegade Pierre Bietry, the movement adopted a title appropriate to its claims, and called itself the Socialist National Party.[2]

The new name was no more than an opportunistic label. It fitted, however, in a tradition parallel to that of the Catholic social conciliators and one closely connected with nationalist reaction throughout the Third Republic. Where the Catholic corporatists were paternalist and *bien pensant,* the National-Socialists were rebellious, opposed to the established order and the bourgeois capitalism that thrived upon it. Enemies of plutocracy and of smug self-satisfaction, they scorned the degenerate barbarians of a society they would gladly tear down. Elitist in temperament and taste, they preferred the workers they did not know to the middle classes they knew and despised. They sought social justice as a prelude to national revival, or at least they used this as an excuse to pursue their own ambitions.

Bietry was but a feeble flash in the National-Socialist school, however. Its best-known and most intelligent representative had been Maurice Barrès, a man who never feared to insist on the intimate union of nationalist and socialist ideas. At Nancy, where he was elected as a Boulangist in 1890 and where he unsuccessfully sought re-election throughout the 'nineties, he campaigned on a platform of "Nationalism, Protectionism, and Socialism," and his supporters were the Republican Socialist Nationalist Committee. It was he who first gave nationalism and socialism the chance to meet in print, in the *Cocarde,* which he published from September 1894 to March 1895. In its pages could be found such unlikely companions as René Boylesve, Charles Maurras, Frédéric Amouretti, Camille Mauclair, and extreme syndicalists like Augustin Hamon and Fernand Pelloutier. As resolutely socialist-minded as they were nationalist, the editors greeted President Casimir-Périer's resignation in 1895 as "one of the milestones of the Social Revolution that is slowly taking place . . . and whose fulfillment no power can henceforth prevent." Writing the paper's story in 1910, Henri Clouard, by then a convinced Maurrassian, found it "exactly socialist in that it led a relentless struggle against economic liberalism and called for the organization of labor and the suppression of the proletariat, that is to say, its integration in society."[3]

Clearly, the national-socialists and the integral nationalists had certain mutual dislikes, but they came from different poles. The Action Française proposed to replace economic liberalism with a corporate order that the embattled workers would not accept, wanted to organize labor but in guilds that would be out of the workers' hands, wanted to suppress the proletariat by developing a system of corporatism and small ownership on almost Jeffersonian lines. They rejected bourgeois order and bourgeois democracy, but only in favor of a new hierarchy with elitist implications for which the working class had no use.

None of this was very clear, however, when the Action Française first set out to capture the labor element. The leaders knew that without a substantial working-class following the movement was doomed to insignificance. They wanted to impress *bien pensant* supporters and avoid being labeled as wholly reactionary, but, even more, they wanted to propagate their ideas in a section of society that had so far proved impervious to them. As a first attempt, they tried a *rapprochement* with Bietry, who seemed to have all the right qualifications, including a readiness to accept royalist subsidies for the good work his movement claimed to do among the working class. But the flirtation with Bietry did not last long. By 1908, the Action Française seems to have decided that the man was something of a fraud and that they could use their money more profitably alone. They cut Bietry's subsidies and made an effort to draw the Jaunes away from his influence; the result was that he became their enemy.[4]

The next move in the courtship of the workers was more direct. With Bietry cut adrift, the Action Française began to think of setting up its own workers' groups. After devoting several weeks in the summer of 1908 to an ineffectual wooing of working-class readers, it sought the advice of Firmin Baconnier, a self-educated printer and royalist convert who had set out to bring the gospel of monarchy to "workers and men of humble condition such as he had been himself."[a]

A drive for an *amicale royaliste,* led by a sometime revolutionary syndicalist named Mahon and operating from Action Française headquarters, tried to advance the royalist cause in syndicalist circles. The royalists took the side of the Draveil strikers against Clemenceau's police; Emile Janvion, one of the founders of the CGT and now a royalist, was one of four syndicalists prosecuted for hanging the bust of Marianne from the front of the Paris Bourse de Travail; young noblemen begged provincial *bien pensants* to offer

[a] Baconnier's Avant-Garde Royaliste, which had been very active in 1904–6, had gained the sympathy of old-line royalists like Larègle and even of the Pretender, who wanted to win workers over to corporatism and hoped Baconnier would undertake the task. After dissolving the Avant-Garde, Baconnier founded L'Accord Social, set up a weekly review, and established a national network of local committees. His relations with the Action Française were excellent, especially on the personal plane, until they became strained by the sympathies of the younger generation for revolutionary syndicalism, which Baconnier did not like at all. Suspicious of the Action Française's new drift and resentful of its attempts to indoctrinate some of his own working-class followers, Baconnier cooled toward the Maurrassians after 1908 and broke off relations altogether in 1910–11 at the time of the Larègle fight; some years later, however, he returned to become the *Action française*'s specialist in corporative affairs. See F^7 12862, 4/158–65 of Dec. 23, 1909, which explains that the Action Française proposes to reconcile royalism and revolutionary syndicalism, hence opposes Baconnier's corporatist and unrevolutionary efforts.

the workers a fraternal hand, and older ones told their listeners that a Socialist fatherland would be the fatherland still. "Même sous le drapeau rouge nous servirions la France!" affirmed Etienne de Resnes to a working-class audience at Béthune, to the wild approval of Socialists and Nationalists alike. Vast meetings were organized, at which Daudet declared his sympathy for the CGT and Pujo praised the syndicalists who had been imprisoned—just like the Camelots—for their political beliefs. The workers showed curiosity; they were not displeased by the violent opposition of the Action Française to the government, and one syndicalist spokesman even praised Lacour's attack on Briand. But they had no intention of restoring the monarchy.[5]

Daudet thought he knew the answer to working-class indifference: anti-Semitism. "You give us the king, and we'll give you the Jews!" But his attempts to catch proletarians with Jewish bait failed like previous ones baited with Catholic paternalism or benevolent monarchy. Daudet was remembering the lessons of Drumont, whose anti-Semitism had been in part inspired by a hatred of what the Duc d'Orléans called "anonymous and vagabond wealth" and its corrupting effects upon society and State. During the 'eighties this point of view was not far different from that of many Socialists, who also equated moral and political action and to whom anti-Semitism seemed natural at a time when Jew was still synonymous with usurer or banker, and Rothschilds and Péreires were the symbols of high finance.

Drumont's *Libre Parole,* "ce curieux journal qui est lu par des curés et des communards," was founded in 1892 partly on the proceeds, both moral and material, of his most socially conscious book, *Le Secret de Fourmies.* Fourmies was a small northern town in whose streets, on May 1, 1891, government-ordered troops shot down striking miners as well as women and children, until, wrote horrified observers, the gutters ran red with blood. Drumont's description of one of the dead, a young working girl named Marie Blondeau, offers a perfect example of his approach and his appeal:

> The child of the people had begun her day by working from the very first rays of light, and the light was not yet gone before she fell before the bullets of other children of the people like herself. . . . She was literally scalped; the whole top of her head was torn off. The *curé* gathered the bits of her brain scattered on the pavement, but no one ever found the magnificent fair hair of which she had been so proud.
>
> Legend has it that this hair was stolen and sold. It probably went to deck the bald head of some old Jewish baroness; and some bankrupt gentleman, playing the comedy of love before the crone in the hope of a loan from her husband, may, in a boudoir of the fashionable quarter, have covered with his kisses the fair remains of the murdered working lass.

Drumont, here, gives us everything: the pure and suffering poor, the Jewish profiteers, the corrupt aristocracy, the indirect lie based on both fact (the girl's death) and speculation (the disappearance of her hair), and, finally, the conversion of speculation into fact, with the implication that such crimes cannot be allowed to go unpunished by men with any sense of chivalry or justice. Thus social indignation, like anti-Semitism, becomes a question of *noblesse oblige,* and hence acceptable to men who might otherwise reject it.

With more vivacity and verve, with fewer organ stops, Daudet carried on the social romanticism of Drumont. As a patriot, he denounced the ill-hidden hand of Judeo-Masonic conspiracies in the service of corrupt and corrupting capitalism; as a lover of humanity, he heaped abuse on the plutocratic enemy, busily planning the downfall of the proletariat and the ruin of France. It did not occur to him that by trying to convert popular anti-capitalism into anti-Semitism he might render it less effective. Bankers, creditors, union organizers and powerful businessmen, Socialist agitators and wage-squeezing employers, collectivists and individualists, all these Daudet identified with the Jews, and inevitably the anger of his audience turned away from its original objectives toward a few choice scapegoats. Gabriel Péri would say of French National-Socialists: "They rail against plutocracy the better to guard its privileges." This was not always true. Drumont really cared about social injustice; Daudet cared more for effect than for the privileges of plutocracy. Objectively, however—as Péri would have said—the result was the same.

Objectively, Daudet's campaigns deserved a better fate. In Drumont's time, as we have seen, a good many Socialists might have agreed that nineteenth-century economic history could be summarized as "the bourgeoisie exploiting the people and being despoiled in turn by the Jews."[6] But the Dreyfus affair had forced the Socialists to discard their demagogic anti-Semitism and admit that racial, if not religious, identification of their class enemies was impossible. So Daudet's anti-Semitism did not get very far. French workmen had no more reason to hate their Jewish employers than to hate their gentile ones, and they knew it; the recently unified Socialist party, SFIO, and the syndicates had their men in hand where doctrine, at least, was concerned. Anti-Semitism was the socialism of idiots: syndicalists knew better.[7]

The Action Française, though not the first movement in France to combine a reactionary appeal with an anti-Semitic one, was the most persistent in directing its propaganda toward the working class. By sheer dint of repetition, it helped to prepare the way for later movements with a similar appeal, which were to find French workers familiar with and hence more receptive to arguments they had previously shunned.[b]

[b] Its activity did not pass unnoticed by the young German Socialist, Robert Michels, then preparing his famous study of *Political Parties*. In the introduction to that work, published in 1911, Michels speaks of the enemies of democracy turning democratic in order to gain their ends: "they endeavor, as did very recently the royalists in the French Republic, to ally themselves with the revolutionary proletariat, promising to defend this against the exploitation of democratic capitalism and to support and even to extend labor organizations—all this in the hope of destroying the Republic and restoring the Monarchy. . . . *Le Roy et les camelots du Roy* . . . are to destroy the oligarchy of the bloated plutocrats." See the 1962 ed. (New York), p. 45.

As a matter of fact, the theoretical arguments of Maurras and Vaugeois proved more attractive to such workingmen as cared to listen than the demagogic anti-Semitism of Daudet. And it was in the theoretical field that the movement's social concerns produced the most interesting results. "We are nationalistic and consequently social-minded," Maurras declared in the third number of the daily *Action française,* on March 23, 1908. "Do you know that the Action Française has a social program far more 'advanced' than the Radicals?" Robert de Traz asked the readers of *Le Génèvois* on January 5, 1911. This continued to be so in theory even when concern for social conservation got the better of concern for social progress, and it was to this that Thierry Maulnier referred when, on the eve of the Popular Front of 1936, he told the conservative readers of the *Revue universelle* that "at the beginning of the century the battalions of the Action Française were the harbingers of this new Right, which, not satisfied with being the party of resistance, meant to be—it, too; it *above all*—the party of movement."[8]

It was perfectly true, as Maulnier would say, that Maurras's critique of individualism and liberalism led him to positions very similar to those of the Socialists, who were as concerned as he was with a public good superior to the private and as aware of the dangers of anarchy and tyranny in a completely free society. Where Maurras differed from the Socialists was not in matters of social concern, but in matters of social order. He denounced their equalitarian myths and their belief that authority stems from the masses; for him, authority was clearly established only by the natural hierarchy of talent or birth. In opposing Socialist democracy, Maurras also opposed, of course, Socialist internationalism. In his *Dictionnaire politique et critique,* under "Socialism," he says: "There is opposition, contradiction, between equalitarian and international Marxism and the protection of nation and of fatherland. But a socialism that has been freed of democratic and cosmopolitan elements can fit nationalism as a well-made glove fits a beautiful hand."[9]

Such a hand-in-glove relationship would be tried and found wanting before the First World War in the stormy courtship of Charles Maurras and Georges Sorel. The man who served as go-between was a strange and forceful admirer of both, Alfred Georges Gressent, better known as Georges Valois.

Born in 1878 and therefore ten years younger than Maurras, Valois in his youth worked his way around the world and for a time lived in India and in Russia, where he served as tutor to the children of a noble family. Back in Paris in 1904, he found work in the publishing business. He was an omnivorous autodidact, and in 1907 he published a book expounding his "philosophy of authority," a heady blend of revolutionary syndicalism and authoritarianism entitled *L'Homme qui vient.* Maurras liked the book and its author, and found him a place in Jean Rivain's publishing house, now called the Nouvelle Librairie Nationale. But though Maurras was pleased to have gained a proletarian recruit to the monarchist cause, he did not care for Valois's basic philosophy, which was derived largely from Proudhon, Sorel, and Nietzsche. Nietzsche, much as some of Maurras's friends appreciated him, was to Maurras anathema.[10] Proudhon could qualify as a patriotic anti-plutocrat with the right ideas about corporate interest and family. Sorel was acceptable only in small, diluted doses. But Sorel, the only one of the three who was alive, was favorably disposed toward Maurras, and soon, with some prodding from Valois, became even more so. It was through him that the attempt would be made to combine nationalist and syndicalist efforts.

We know that about 1907 Sorel began to edge away from the syndicalist movement from which he had expected so much. As the syndicates showed a growing inclination to cooperate with political parties, Sorel found them just as "greedy," just as "hungry," as the reviled bourgeoisie. Within a few years the old theoretician had come to agree with Croce that "socialism is dead," and to appreciate the potential public that Action Française circles offered him. In an essay called "The Rout of the Boors," published during the summer of 1909, Sorel attacked the corrupt politicians and the Socialist rhetoricians who, like Jaurès, played the losing parliamentary game. He praised the Action Française royalists as being alone able to stimulate any protest against the prevailing decadence. No other social group had the necessary intelligence, faith, and courage to launch an all-out attack on the boors who had corrupted France. "Their merit will stand high in history, for we can hope that, thanks to them, the reign of stupidity and loutishness will come to any early end."[11] On April 14, 1910, the *Action française* published an article by "the most powerful and penetrating of French sociologists" on "The Awakening of the French Heart." This was followed on September 29 by an interview with Sorel in which he declared his support for "reaction."

It was in this mood that projects were mooted for a review, to be called (shades of Fustel!) *La Cité française* and to be issued jointly by syndicalists and nationalists. Sorel even went so far as to draft a manifesto: "The review addresses itself to reasonable men who have been sickened by the stupid pride of democracy, by humanitarian drivel, by the fashions come to us from abroad." The proposed *Cité* was eventually abandoned, to be replaced in the spring of 1911 by the most intriguing of national-socialist reviews, *L'Indépendance.* Its editorial board included Sorel, the novelists Emile Baumann and René Benjamin, the composer, Vincent d'Indy, Paul Jamot, the two brothers Tharaud, and Jean Variot. Elémir Bourges was added in 1912, and Barrès, Bourget, the playwright Maurice Donnay, the literary historian Henri Clouard, the painter Maurice Denis, and the poet Francis Jammes the following year—representatives of philosophies running from the most esoteric sort of mystical Catholicism to the most brutal revolutionary syndicalism. The steadiest contributor was Sorel, a patriotic, nationalistic, anti-Semitic Sorel, who compared France's struggle against the Jews to America's struggle against the Yellow Peril[12] and who worked side by side, as it were, with the Camelots.

But the more intellectual members of the Action Française wanted to go beyond Sorel's somewhat anarchic social criticism. They wanted to clear up the persistent confusion between liberty and disorder, and they wanted an opportunity for national-socialist studies of economic problems. In answer to their demands, in December 1911 the Cercle Proudhon held its first meeting, with Charles Maurras in the chair. A month later there appeared the first *Cahier du Cercle Proudhon*. Its contributors, who were also the founders of the Cercle—Georges Valois, Henri Lagrange, Gilbert Maire, René de Marans, and Edouard Berth—all agreed that "democracy is the greatest error of the past century," the enemy of both culture and productivity. Democracy was responsible for destructive capitalism, and for the exploitation of labor. Soon thereafter, while a special number of the *Cahiers* sang the praises of Georges Sorel, Sorel's disciple Berth published *Les Méfaits des intellectuels,* which rerevealed nationalists and syndicalists at one on the necessity of destroying the capitalist regime, of restoring monarchy, and, in the process, of reconciling Sorel and Maurras in "a new and fertile synthesis."[c]

Soon after the First World War, which destroyed these hopes by reinforcing the established order and decimating the *Cahiers'* leading spirits, Pierre Drieu La Rochelle, who had been attracted by the activity of those early days, wrote of the Fascist climate that reigned in those circles about 1913, of young men in Lyon who called themselves royalist-socialists, of other young men drunk with heroism and violence who dreamed of destroying both capitalism and parliamentary socialism. After Lagrange had died of wounds received in battle, his great friend, the *chansonnier* Maxime Brienne, reaffirmed what they had had in mind and what he still hoped for:

> Le vieux conflit, soigneusement prolongé et limité par les partis, d'un patriotisme trop sentimental, inopérant, naïf, où le conservatisme cachait son ignorance—et l'incurable égoïsme de la Sociale grasse, décorant un matérialisme utilitaire et grossier; tout cela, vieilleries bourgeoises ou rengaines avancées, à faire taire, à disperser; le rapprochement du syndicalisme laborieux et pratique, et du nationalisme vivant, réaliste, qui fonderait une France solide, sainement détachée et délivrée de cette mystification ploutocratique: le suffrage universel.

As late as 1936, other survivors of these golden days would find the essence of Fascism in "prewar national-socialism and syndicalism" and lament the ruined hopes of "1913 Fascism."[13]

As a matter of fact, the hopes of the moment and the wistful backward glances exaggerated the chances that the slender national-socialist movement might survive. There was no ground for a real understanding between Sorel and Maurras. Both were prima donnas; both knew what they wanted; and

[c] See *L'Indépendance,* June 1, 1912, p. 336, where at the end of a long, three-installment article on "Quelques prétensions juives," Sorel declares that "the defense of French culture is today directed by Charles Maurras."

their minds, however superficially similar they may have been when it came to means, were miles apart on ends. Sorel appreciated the contribution of monarchy and Church to an authoritarian regime, but he believed these institutions dead and impossible to revive. Unlike Vaugeois, he did not change his mind. Maurras, for his part, suspected Sorel's syndicalism and resented the influence he might have over his disciples.

Besides, all this talk of syndicalism, socialism, and revolution dismayed the more orthodox friends of the Action Française. Conservative Catholics began to draw away. The Marquis de la Tour du Pin withdrew his support. Maurras decided that social concerns were too costly for the results they brought. He himself had no interest in economics; his ideas of social justice were either ad hoc or romantic, and in any case, politics came first. There was clearly little political gain in disturbing one's *bien pensant* friends for the sake of unappreciative proletarians.

Maurras' waning enthusiasm for ventures which might give the old respectables cause for alarm was also reflected in his relations with another Action Française enterprise, the *Revue critique des idées et des livres*. It was the fate of Maurras, like that of all teachers, to be overtaken and left behind by his disciples. Attracted by the excitement of ideas in action, many bright young men worked briefly with the Action Française only to break away, or drift away, when they felt they had exhausted the possibilities that had initially fascinated them.[d] For in its time, especially during the years just before the First World War and those immediately after, the esthetic and literary doctrines of the Action Française offered an original tool for minds keen to explore the intellectual world. Against a romanticism dulled by age, degraded, irrational, confused, and imprecise, its neoclassicism stood out clearly as what the times demanded: a bold effort to reaffirm man as a reasoning being within a reconstructed hierarchy of spiritual and intellectual values.

But the empirical rational approach that Maurras recommended bears within itself an independent life of its own which cannot be constrained within narrow limits. A valid critical technique is applicable to everything, even to the ideas that originated it. Men who find truth and beauty in literature or art cannot withhold their appreciation for political reasons. Thus, a good many

[d] One such young man was Henri Lagrange, a Camelot at the age of fifteen, to whom Barrès devoted several pages as a representative traditionalist in *Les Familles spirituelles de la France* (1917). The preface that Maurras contributed to a posthumous collection of Lagrange's essays, *Vingt Ans en 1914* (1920), conceals the serious friction between the impetuous secretary of the Etudiants d'Action Française and the old leaders, jealous of their authority. Lagrange began to write for the *Revue critique* in 1910, and Romain Rolland expressed surprise that a youth of sixteen should be such an acute critic. But within a few years Lagrange was expelled. Drafted at the outset of the war, he visited the Action Française offices, then in the rue Caumartin, to make up and say good-bye, was not received, and left in a fury, shouting "Salauds!" This was forgotten after his death in 1915 from wounds received in action, and the heretic redeemed by death was conveniently made one of the movement's dead heroes.

young men of intelligence and sensitivity were drawn to the Action Française by the esthetic appeal of its doctrines and left it when they found they liked some things outside the canon, because they could not help it, and disliked some things within.

Furthermore, although Maurras was remarkably tolerant with sympathetic outsiders, he was capable of great rigidity when dealing with his own adherents. He lacked the flexibility of appreciation, the breadth of taste that would have helped him to understand the plight of others who transgressed the limits of his esthetic doctrines. This intolerance, to some extent implicit in the principles themselves, must have been in some way associated with the fact that in many ways the neoclassical theories appeared as a form of morality. "The firmness and inflexibility of a train of thought, the unity of a plan, the order of its execution, are literary qualities, but alike to moral virtues in that they are the outcome of a will and demand a character."[14] Lagrange was here referring to Proudhon, but the description is equally applicable to Maurras.

We know that Maurras himself had come to politics by way of esthetics, and that his theories of society and politics had grown out of his criticism of literature. He had been brought to make a distinction between romantic idealism, the mother of anarchy and evil, and a classicism, equally ideal, that stood for the principles of order: form, hierarchy, and discipline. The distinction, easy enough to make, was difficult to apply. Maurras's older friend, the poet Jean Moréas, died telling Barrès: "There are no classics and romantics . . . That's nonsense." This was a judgment Maurras himself would echo at the end of his life.[15] But in his prime he insisted that there was a difference: on the one side, invigorating and clean-limbed, Dante, Racine, Poussin; on the other, the corrupters—Musset, Baudelaire, Rimbaud, and the worst of them all, Jean-Jacques Rousseau.

Barrès, who was in a position to know, declared that in the literary field it was Maurras who opened the campaign against the glittering, un-French evil of romanticism. Addressing a nationalist audience, Barrès observed that Maurras's classical criticism could serve as a firm base for more than literary studies. "Nationalism is more than merely politics: it is a discipline, a reasoned method to bind us to all that is truly eternal, all that must develop in continued fashion in our country. Nationalism is a form of classicism; it is in every field the incarnation of French continuity."[16]

More than Barrès, who was too romantic, Maurras could symbolize classic, reasoned, nationalist sentiment. When during 1912 and early 1913 Henri Massis and Alfred de Tarde interviewed scores of students and fledgling writers to determine the climate of opinion among French youth, they asked for comments on passages from Renan, Anatole France, and Barrès. Renan and France were not liked at all. About Barrès, most young men seemed uneasy; they admired the artist, but they looked on his ideas as "transitional stuff, a plank to cross the ford." The writers these young men cared for were

Maurras, Péguy, and Claudel, who were better suited to their need for affirmation and for faith—especially Maurras, even when they did not accept his royalism. Royalist or not, there was a trace of Maurras in everyone: "Criticism of the parliamentary regime, reaction against those who disturbed the social order, against Germanism, against romantic excesses . . . Their very vocabulary seemed to have been affected by it, and the word *French* on their lips sounded more rigorous, more offensive, almost warlike, a sound whose Maurrassian accent was easy to recognize."[17]

This influence is very clear when Clouard, writing the story of Barrès's *Cocarde,* devoted a whole chapter, one-seventh of the book, to Maurras, "the restorer of the intellectual powers," although Maurras's contribution to Barrès's short-lived paper was negligible.[18]

But the best-known representative of neoclassical ideas was Pierre Lasserre, a descendant of a representative of the Third Estate to the Estates General of 1789, and, like Dimier and Vaugeois, an *agrégé de philosophie.* He was a revisionist on legal grounds in 1898, but his Nietzschean, nationalistic proclivities brought him over to the anti-Dreyfus side the following year, and eventually to the Action Française. The young *agrégé* was not a disciple but an ally, and in his articles for the *Revue de l'Action Française* he worked out his own ideas, later published as *Le Romantisme français* (1907). Rousseau, who embodies romanticism, who is indeed "le romantisme intégral," is there considered among the most important agents of the Revolution. As for himself, Lasserre could not but regret, though he did not always say so, the traditional monarchy that the romantic ferment had helped to overthrow—natural, historical, misunderstood, and corrupted by revolution and revolutionary principles.[19] Views such as these, reflected more or less in his doctoral thesis, could not fail to bring Lasserre into conflict with Alphonse Aulard, one of the great pontiffs of the Sorbonne. As his relations with the University grew worse, his ties with the Action Française grew stronger, and when the first issue of the *Action française* appeared he was its literary critic. At the same time, he continued as editor of the *Revue.*

"Have you read Lasserre's book on French Romanticism?" wrote one of his admirers, Pierre Jourdan, to a friend not long before he was killed in the war. "It was my bedside book, and I can tell you, as a matter of fact, that it was he who led me to the ideas of the Action Française." But the doctrine was a bit restrictive. "You see," Jourdan went on, "the question of Classics and Romantics works out this way: Racine, Molière, La Fontaine, are our masters and our dearest friends. But that cannot prevent us from having a passion, perhaps a shameful one, for Lamartine, Musset, Verlaine, Baudelaire, and still others."[20]

Lasserre himself eventually grew impatient with the excessive vulgarization of his thesis, with the oversimplified "primarisme de droite" of some of his followers, and with Maurras's rigid exclusion of all romantics from the literary pantheon of the Action Française. After some years, friction between the two men finally came to a head when Maurras tried to edit Lasserre's articles, and in 1914 Lasserre left the *Action française* altogether. A few years later he had settled down in a chair at the Ecole des Hautes Etudes.[e]

After 1908, moreover, the *Revue de l'Action Française* was subordinate to the *Revue critique*. When plans for the daily newspaper were being worked out, it was thought that the old blue review might be ended, since most of its contributors would be busy with the new daily; and a number of young men whom Jean Rivain had brought together for discussion in a Cercle Joseph de Maistre suggested that they might continue its publication themselves. This plan did not work out, but their interest had been aroused; too many ideas had been mulled over, too many sparkling articles planned, for them to abandon the project. With the support of Rivain, Eugène Marsan, and Rivain's brother-in-law Gilbert, a new monthly was founded: the *Revue critique*. The first issue appeared on April 25, 1908, in a format markedly similar to that of the *Revue de l'Action Française*.

The editor of the new publication was Pierre Gilbert, a poet who had been lost behind a desk in the War Office; the editorial secretary was Clouard, followed in 1912 by Jean Longnon, a future librarian of the Institut; the publisher was Jean Rivain. Along with Marsan, who was still a fervent Maurrassian and classicist, some of the regular contributors were Bordelais Nel Ariès, Lagrange, André Thérive, and Antoine Baumann. Edouard Berth wrote for it; Ernest Denis, Emile Bernard, and P.-J. Toulet contributed regular notes on art; Jean-Marc Bernard sent poems; and Emile Henriot, Henry Bordeaux, and Henri Martineau wrote critical articles. There was regular syndicalist news from a royalist syndicalist, Emile Para (who ended up on the *Bonnet rouge*); and the very first number carried an "Inquiry on the Monarchy and the Working Class" by Georges Valois.

The new publication rapidly gained ground at the expense of the old, now somewhat neglected, review. At the end of 1911, there was some talk of consolidating the two, but plans fell through when it became evident that Lasserre thought the younger review should be absorbed by the older. Then, in January 1912, the *Revue critique* appeared in a larger, brighter format. Financially it was now more independent of the Action Française than before, owing to Rivain's personal support, but it was no less devoted to the movement and to the league. This devotion later proved embarrassing when the *Revue cri-*

[e] See André Thérive, *Moralistes de ce temps* (1948), pp. 209ff; Dimier, *Vingt Ans d'Action Française*, p. 317. Lasserre, says Thérive, disapproved of theories like that of the Maurrassian Louis Reynaud, who in, e.g., *Français et Allemands, histoire de leurs relations intellectuelles et sentimentales* (1929) and *Crise de notre littérature* (1931), argued that German romanticism was corrupting French cultural values. Pierre's brother Henry (Pierre Tuc) stuck with the *Action française*; he compiled the paper's press review until his death in 1938 and also contributed to the extreme-right-wing weekly *Choc*, as "Observateur."

tique took up political or literary positions that clashed with the interests or doctrine of the Action Française.

The list of contributors has indicated how deeply writers of the *Revue critique* were involved in the flirtation with Sorel, in the abortive planning of the *Cité Française,* and, finally, in *L'Indépendance.* Gilbert, Clouard, Maire, and their friends had little patience with Maurras's conservative allies, and did not hide their interest in a possible alliance with the Left, seeking out opportunities for friendly discussion in the Cercle Proudhon and elsewhere.[21] They not only criticized Maurras's tactics, but annoyed him with their extravagant admiration for figures he did not care for, notably Stendhal.

The enthusiasm of the *Revue critique* for Stendhal was to have considerable effect on French literary life and that author's reputation in the years to come. With the advantage of hindsight, we may term the sympathy predictable. Stendhal combined in his writing and in his person the mixture of passion and would-be self-control, idealism and calculated appraisal, romantic fervor and cold analysis, that typified the new literary generation. His lucid criticism, his biting tongue, his sensitive detachment, all these gifts appealed to young men who had to work as hard as he had worked to master them. "To act, but without being deceived, and yet to act," one of Stendhal's many mottoes, could easily have become the motto of his admirers—proud, as one of them would boast, of "the unidealistic frame of mind that the books of Maurras and of Barrès maintain among young people."[22]

Shortly after the July Revolution of 1830, Stendhal wrote: "I think the current Chamber is leading us to the sorry condition of a republic, a condition that is horrible everywhere but in America. This is the true plague. Our society tends to annihilate all that rises above mediocrity." Here were sentiments to suit men of elitist, anti-republican, and anti-parliamentary temper; and, indeed, their first encomiums of Stendhal referred to the aristocratic elitism they discerned in his work, his clear-sighted egotism, his realism, and the anti-democratic nature of his views.[23]

It was no accident that Stendhal's greatest modern champion, Henri Martineau, began his literary career in such a circle. He was involved in nationalist affairs during his days as a medical student at Poitiers, where he was a friend of the young royalist Marie de Roux. In 1901 he edited the royalist students' publication, *Poitiers universitaire,* which was backed by the Action Française. A few years later, he applied his medical knowledge to a critique of Zola's scientific conceptions. As a result of his collaboration with Longnon, Clouard, and Maire, he became convinced of Stendhal's importance and resolved to devote his life to him, thus reconciling his political and literary interests. His Maurrassian views occasionally affected his later, better known, work; for example, he explains Stendhal's evolution from republican sentiments to monarchism and even Catholicism as a reaction against a doltish society that he feared would stifle art, liberty, and the life of taste. Happily, "as the best minds always knew—*cette mauvaise tête était patriote*."[f]

Thus it was that in his presidential address at the *Revue critique*'s fifth-anniversary banquet, Paul Bourget could rejoice at the completion of a new edition of Stendhal's works and add: "We are among nationalists, and there is already a slight *Beylist* tradition. Let us maintain it, as we do all others."[24] The *Revue critique,* which had been of great influence in the revival, worked steadily to maintain it. The March 1913 issue was a special number dedicated to Stendhal, and a Stendhal Prize was established "for reasons that, beyond his work, affect French intelligence and art." All this did not fail to excite comment, for by now the *Revue critique* was becoming on the Right what the *Nouvelle Revue française* was on the Left. In *Le Figaro,* Alfred Capus marveled how in the midst of political and diplomatic activity, between discussions of electoral reform and arguments over the three-year military-service law, with the country on the alert for foreign danger, attention could be focused even for a moment on Stendhal. Such a literary phenomenon, of more than literary significance, would not have been possible twenty years earlier, said Capus, for twenty years earlier Ibsen and Nietzsche had reigned in cultivated circles, and their admirers would not have appreciated Stendhal's models of "regulated energy and intelligent exaltation of life." And why was Stendhal so important to the nationalists? Because, Capus said, Stendhal stood up against Rousseau and Tolstoi, against the demands of sensibility that derived from them. All that was really strong in Nietzsche and in Ibsen, all that the French could assimilate with profit, could already be found in Stendhal's works. But whereas Nietzsche's principles would tend toward anarchy, Ibsen's toward extreme individualism, Stendhal's would lead to the highest civilization.[25]

None of this was designed to please Maurras. Although he had some reservations about the honesty of Stendhal's anti-romantic views, he did not personally mind Stendhal; what he disliked were the attacks to which the *Revue critique*'s praises of Stendhal exposed him from priestly pamphleteers and others on the lookout for Action Française godlessness. Threatened with public condemnation and under heavy fire from his enemies, the worried leader was ready to do anything to avoid displeasing Rome.[26] In defense, he sought to disavow the *Revue critique*; and a special chapter of *L'Action Française et la religion catholique,* published in 1913, made it clear that the *Revue critique* and the Action Française were completely separate. The disavowal

[f] Martineau, *Coeur de Stendhal,* pp. 182–84, 224. Martineau diagnosed his own congenital jaundice as bound to kill him by the age of forty. He gave up practice three years before the fatal date, invested his fortune in publishing, the one thing he had always loved, met with success and lived to be over seventy. See Anne André-Glandy, *Le Marquis de Roux* (Poitiers, 1957), pp. 19, 23, 100.

was made with the knowledge and agreement of the staff of the *Revue critique,* and had it been true there would have been no need to insist on it. But discord between the parties would soon be turning a statement of expediency into a matter of fact.

Maurras thought that he discerned too much sympathy for Germany in certain articles of the *Revue critique.* He was also incensed by the appreciation shown for Henri Bergson by Clouard, Maire, and their followers, who were determined to assert their independence. In a bitter evocation of the brilliant circle that dissension and then death were soon to ravage, Clouard has explained how to him and his friends Maurras seemed a prisoner of his Catholic readers—people who were badly out of touch with the modern world. Heedless of the Church and of the *Syllabus,* Clouard and company sneered at Catholic criticism of Bergson and Claudel. Recriminations flew back and forth, the young men would not back down, and finally, in February 1914, relations were severed.[27]

The breach thus opened was not mended until France entered the war, and not properly even then. Gilbert, soon to die in action, never forgave Maurras; Clouard and Maire never quite overcame their feelings of injustice and incomprehension. The impression remained, as Longnon would put it, that to keep on good terms with the Action Française it was best to stay away from it. But however unjust or opinionated Maurras might be, even those who never looked back except in anger continued to live in an atmosphere impregnated with his thought. When the *Revue critique*'s guiding spirits had departed, their passions and ideas preserved on dusty bookshelves still remained to draw recruits to the cause that most of them had given up. Thus it was, for example, that Gilbert Charles, a young Bordeaux student indifferent to politics, discovered "the efforts of young writers whose thought Maurras had so powerfully helped to shape," and followed the pure stream backward to the source.[28]

By the eve of the war the Action Française was becoming accepted as the chief exponent of nationalism, the nationalist party *par excellence.* In late 1910, the old but vociferous *Libre Parole* had changed hands: Drumont stayed on to write for it at a magnificent salary, but editorial policy was in the hands of liberal Catholics, conservative supporters of the established order who were loathsome to the integral nationalists. There were other nationalist publications, Judet's Bonapartist *Eclair,* Cassagnac's even more Bonapartist *Autorité,* even the *Echo de Paris,* for which Barrès and Bourget wrote regularly; and the tone of the press as a whole, in the years before 1914, grew increasingly bellicose and chauvinistic. But only the Action Française and its paper combined the printed and the spoken word, the slogan and the blow. In 1911 at Nancy, to the patriotic citizens of Lorraine, Jules Lemaître boasted: "The Action Française is a complete entity. It has the means to act upon all Frenchmen and upon all categories of Frenchmen. It has its newspaper . . . For students, it has its Institute . . . it has the *Revue de l'Action Française* and the *Revue critique des idées*." It also had the Camelots, who could reap some of the less intellectual advantages of opinion leadership.

The Camelots' feats of arms had been restricted largely to the undergraduate atmosphere of the Left Bank, where they could be written off as mere student pranks; but the beginning of 1911 brought them an opportunity to mobilize nationalist opinion in the very center of Paris. The occasion was a decision by the Comédie Française to produce Henri Bernstein's *Après moi*. Bernstein had been something of a playboy in his youth. Disgusted with the rigors of military service, he had deserted after seven months and fled to Brussels, from where he wrote to a Paris newspaper the kind of letter that foolish young men regret when they are no longer so foolish or so young. By 1911, he was a successful playwright; his youthful peccadillo had been officially forgiven, and, it was assumed, forgotten. But the announcement of the production of *Après moi* brought a prompt reaction from the *Action française*, which was determined to prevent this desecration of France's national theater.

The play went on as announced, but to the accompaniment of such demonstrations both in the theater and outside that the author withdrew it a fortnight later, after discreet official requests. The keynote of the campaign had been anti-Semitism. On the opening night, all the *affiches* in Paris and on the theater itself were pasted over with Action Française stickers denouncing *Le Juif Déserteur*. During every performance the voices of the actors were drowned out by disturbances in the hall. Cartoons in the *Action française* showed the interior of the theater with every other seat occupied by a policeman. Those who had paid no attention to the student riots around the Sorbonne could not ignore disturbances that now had moved into the very heart of Paris.[29]

Even the *Paris Daily Mail* was sufficiently aroused by what it called the "recent Bernstein incident" to print a study of anti-Semitism in France, in which it declared:

> All the latest disturbances prove that anti-Semitism is a political weapon wielded by two minorities . . . the Action Française . . . and a few revolutionaries like Urbain Gohier . . . The only lesson taught by the events is the eternal fact that patriotism and militarism are still predominant characteristics of the people of France.[g]

[g] March 12, 1911. The odd figure of Gohier appears here as another instance of the revolutionary side-tracked into anti-Semitism. He left the conservative press to join in the defense of Dreyfus, but, dissatisfied with his treatment, he soon turned upon his new allies, accused Jaurès of opportunism, and developed a vicious anti-Semitic vein which appealed to the petty bourgeoisie of Paris. Employing his vitriolic talents in the service of the highest bidder, he henceforth combined racist arguments with revolutionary ones and found many points of agreement with the Action Française until the latter's break with his employer, François Coty.

The nationalists exulted. "Yesterday the Latin Quarter carried Paris with it," wrote Xavier de Magallon in the *Libre Parole*.[h] "Youth is with us. The future is ours." No one had expected to find nationalist anti-Semitism so lively, and kicking so hard, after all these years.

The Republicans were uneasy. *L'Aurore* warned against possible nationalist plots and urged that a stern eye be kept on the Army, whose loyalty it considered doubtful. To another Radical, writing in the *Dépêche de Toulouse*, the anti-Semitic victory seemed ominous: "Around it the neoroyalists, frantic with joy, are sounding their call. And there are revolutionary syndicalists who echo their words." The *Petite République* noted the apparent alliance of the *Action française* with Gustave Hervé's left-wing Socialist *Guerre sociale*, an alliance which police reports described as based on "a common anti-Semitism directed against great bosses or bankers, and members of big companies' boards." A veteran Socialist, Eugène Fournière, also expressed concern that the working class might have been influenced by the anti-Semitic campaign.[30] Only shortly before, Maurras had suggested that it would be in terms of their anti-Semitic program that nationalism and monarchism could be carried from conception into execution. But this was the first time Socialists themselves had been worried that "this doctrine of hatred and reaction" was making progress among workers.[31]

The flirtation of the Action Française with the extreme Left, which had already proved disturbing to its own more moderate supporters, was proving equally disturbing to the men of the moderate Left. In jails and in police stations, arrested Camelots had become friendly with syndicalists and anarchists who had also been arrested for their beliefs. The camaraderie of the prison cell, where all parties met around a game of cards and learned to sing one another's battle songs, persisted after release. Their enforced *rapprochement* not only had made them appreciate one another's toughness but also had revealed an unsuspected, if superficial, similarity of views. Anarchists, syndicalists, and integral nationalists saw themselves, at least for the moment, as enemies of the State working more or less together in their fight against democracy. Proudhon had opposed the absolute of property to the absolute of State power and declared that these two absolutes were fated to live together, face to face, political movement and social life arising from their constant interaction. Thus it was possible for men like Edouard Berth to argue that a new and better social balance could arise from the free opposition of nationalist and syndicalist movements, the one destined to affirm the State, the other to give social and economic groups an equally absolute autonomy.[32]

A common enmity makes for passing friendships, but passing friendships are the best one can expect in politics. The brightest lights of the extreme

[h] March 14, 1911. See *AF*, Oct. 3, 1922, in which Maurras announced a 300-franc contribution to a benefit performance of Bernstein's *Judith*, the proceeds of which were to be used for equipment for French laboratories.

Left—Gustave Téry, Eugène Merle (later of the *Merle blanc* and *Paris-Soir*), and Miguel Vigo-Almereyda—hobnobbed with the royalists. When Téry produced a play in May 1910, he invited a score of royalists to the dress rehearsal. Almereyda, Merle, and the future Communist Victor Méric (the founder, with Hervé, of the *Guerre sociale*) spent all the intermissions chatting agreeably with Maurice Pujo and half a dozen Camelots. Daudet was also there, and many revolutionaries sat with Camelots in seats arranged two by two.[33] It was not surprising that at the Action Française Congress in December of the same year the two Camelots hawking the paper at the door were also selling copies of Téry's "anarchistic" *Oeuvre.*

These glances to the Left, however, came to nothing. Even though the Action Française had several lines dangling, it soon gave up this sport, and, indeed, soon forgot it. It was difficult, in any case, to reconcile leadership in the nationalistic revival and the championing of Army claims for credits and for men, with friendships on a Left that despised all patriotic trappings and thought in terms of strikes and barricades.

Already, in 1911, there was some talk of war. On July 1, 1911, the German gunboat *Panther* dropped anchor in the Bay of Agadir, ostensibly to protect German interests, but actually as a gesture of defiance by the Kaiser. Lloyd George had warned the Germans that they would not find France alone, and suddenly the possibility of war seemed real; reservists were called up, and the grand maneuvers were canceled so that troops could be held in readiness. The crisis passed and war was for the time being avoided, but the result of the summer's excitement in French politics did not disappear at once. A colonial settlement brought about, it seemed, by German pressure revolted moderates who usually ignored international affairs, cast down the politicians who favored policies of conciliation, and added grist to nationalist mills. From 1912 on, the government of France was in the hands of hard-headed republicans like Raymond Poincaré, Alexandre Millerand, and Louis Barthou, who were now convinced that France must be morally and materially prepared for war. The tone of the press, even that of hitherto mild-spoken elements, became increasingly patriotic and bellicose. Tattoos and torchlight parades, revived by the sometime-Socialist Millerand, turned into anti-German demonstrations; anti-militarists were manhandled in working-class districts; military reviews became enthusiastic patriotic displays, the like of which had not been seen since the days of Boulanger. "It is a long time," wrote *Le Figaro,* "since there has been such tension in the talk of the street, of drawing-rooms, and of clubs."[34]

To the chronicler Alfred Capus, the tone of the year 1912 was reactionary. Jacques Bainville agreed. So did the Socialist leader Marcel Sembat, who at the year's beginning had published *Faites un Roi, sinon faites la paix,* in which the Action Française was suggested as the beneficiary of conflict if a conflict could not be avoided. The neoroyalists had come a long way. Another observer, the republican André Chéradame, admitted that whereas a few years earlier no one would have thought seriously of restoring the monarchy, now the idea deserved consideration because of the vigor and talent with which it was supported by Charles Maurras and his "young, ardent, disinterested" friends. The young bourgeois who fifteen years before had called themselves Socialists and joined collectivist student groups were now joining the Action Française, or cheering it from the sidelines.[35]

When the royalists came out to oppose the celebration of Rousseau's Bicentenary in June 1912, "Not a voice," wrote the *Guerre sociale*[36] "was raised to answer the Camelots du Roi, no countermanifestation organized to shut them up." What little opposition there was came from their embittered competitors on the Right, the followers of Déroulède and of the old Sillon, who were jealous of the neoroyalists' growing public and angry at their intriguing at the Vatican and at home; or who were simply afraid of being compromised by associating with a movement that had become the very symbol of reaction. Thus, in 1913, on Joan of Arc's Day, which Poincaré had proclaimed a national holiday, instead of one parade there were four: those of the Action Française, the Action Libérale and the Sillon marching together, the Ligue des Patriotes, and the Jeunesse Catholique. The last two, of course, were negligible in numbers; the others infinitesimal or overwhelming, according to the prejudices of the counters. But, even though estimates differed widely, the 25,000-odd Action Française marchers were probably double the numbers of their rivals.[37]

Quietly, the nationalist organization grew. Its friends turned up in unexpected quarters, as Maurras learned when the president of the Republican Progressive Students' group called on him one day in 1911 to assure him of his royalist sentiments and his devotion, or as Professor of Mathematics Gaston Marcellin could testify about the circles he frequented. An intelligence service in the hands of Marius Plateau kept track of royalist fortunes in every corner it could reach. Armed support was canvassed, and plans for a possible coup were prepared. Much of this activity was no doubt superficial, but by 1913 the Action Française thought that it could rely on armed bands in Roussillon, in the Jura, and in the following towns: Alais, Armentières, Aurillac, Bourges, Lorient, Montpellier, Moulins, Nancy, Nantes, Nîmes, Orléans, Le Puy, Roubaix, Rouen, and Toulouse. The numbers were usually inconsequential: Le Puy reported "fifteen men with guns, probably more"; Armentières, "eight men with guns and cudgels." These small bands were meant to converge on Paris on receipt of a prearranged message, there to join the main body of royalist troops.

Plateau may have relied greatly on help from the armed services. Officers were, of course, forbidden to join political organizations; but their sympathies were well known. "At Bourges," said one of Plateau's reports, "many of the officers read the *Action française*. Daudet's *L'Avant-guerre* stands in the library of the Cercle Militaire."[38] Friendships born in Dreyfus days had been maintained. Colonel du Paty de Clam, a leading figure in the Dreyfus case now in retirement at Versailles, had Pujo, Daudet, and Bernard de Vésins as frequent guests at his table, with officers of the local garrison and high-ranking clergy.[39] There was sympathy for integral nationalism in lower ranks as well. Ernest Renan's two grandsons, Michel and Ernest Psichari, one the son-in-law of Anatole France, the other already a colonial hero of the young flag-waving Right, both admired Maurras.[40] And in the spring of 1914, Navy Lieutenant Dominique-Pierre Dupouey, on board *La République,* drew up a letter to Maurras which André Gide forwarded after its writer's death at Nieuport the following year: "Around me I see more and more young people filled with real disgust for this regime of elementary formulas, of spiritual downfall. In you they have found the vein of decency and of national honor."[41]

Sympathies like those of the Psicharis and of Dupouey, of Péguy's friend Joseph Lotte and of Alphonse Séché, were symptomatic. As D. W. Brogan has commented, "The clever young man who did not turn socialist joined the Action Française." After the Congress of December 1913, a Socialist observer noted the importance the Action Française had attained and its growing influence in academic and professional circles, which had formerly been the core of republican strength. "One cannot afford to ignore the royalists any longer: the time has come for serious concern with their doings."[42]

"I do not approve the conclusions of Maurras and of the Action Française," wrote Romain Rolland to Séché. "But their party is logical and well organized." The Action Française had become accepted, as it had wanted to be, as the great analyst of political possibilities and the only serious proponent of alternatives to the established order. It was possible for Daudet to boast that the only significant patriotic movements taking place in Paris were those directed, supported, and led by Camelots du Roi and members of the Action Française league and student organizations.[43]

Daudet exaggerated, but not by much. Paul Déroulède, a mediocre poet and quixotic politician who had risen from repeated failure to become the embodiment of *revanchard* patriotism, died on January 30, 1914, at Nice. One hundred thousand people turned out on February 3 to honor his remains as they were carried from the Gare de Lyon to the Church of Saint-Augustin, and when the cortege halted before the black-shrouded statue of Strasbourg in the Place de la Concorde, the statue that had been the symbol of the dead man's hope, no Camelot was needed to direct the spontaneous "Vive la France" that rolled over the square and up the great avenues. Dead, the veteran who in 1882 had founded the Ligue des Patriotes now seemed to inspire the crowd that had so long ignored him and call it to the trials ahead:

> En avant! tant pis pour qui tombe!
> La mort n'est rien. Vive la tombe!
> Quand le pays en sort vivant.
> En avant!

The Action Française, whose column at Déroulède's funeral was said to have numbered some 3,000 persons, was determined to keep the mood alive. On March 1, while Action Française student leaders organized similar demonstrations at Nancy and Grenoble, they turned out over 7,000 Paris students for an "apolitical demonstration" before the statue of Strasbourg. Less than three weeks later, Gaston Calmette, editor of *Le Figaro,* was shot by Mme Caillaux, the wife of the Minister of Finance, for something approaching blackmail. At his funeral, which threatened to turn into a riot, between 4,000 and 6,000 *ligueurs* paraded. On March 29, the forty-four sections which made up the Action Française Federation of Paris and the suburbs ended their congress with a meeting attended by 10,000 royalists. Then, on May 24, well over 30,000 marched in the Joan of Arc's Day parade. By June, the Action Française was strong enough to hold its own in fights with the Socialists on their home ground, in the Marais and in the working-class streets near the Place de la République.[44]

To the Socialist *Vorwaerts* of Berlin, the Action Française appeared as "beyond dispute the best-led fighting organization in France, not excepting the working class itself." Its members did not seem particularly intelligent, but they were "energetic, brutal, and fanatical." "Among French non-Socialist papers, the *Action française* is incontestably the most interesting. It offers the most bizarre mixture of intelligence and vulgarity, science and stupidity."[45]

4

WAR, 1914-1918

THE ACTION FRANÇAISE had been founded out of concern for national security; its campaigns had always been intended to prepare Frenchmen for the war to come, to forge national unity, and to make sure that a strong army would be ready—ready not only to meet an attack, but to recover the lost provinces of 1871 and re-establish French supremacy in Europe. In the years after 1911, as the international situation grew more tense, as the rearmament race progressed, as major crises like the Balkan wars and minor ones in Alsace and elsewhere kept fear and hatred at a high pitch, the *Action française,* like the rest of the French nationalist press, campaigned loudly for military preparedness and issued warnings against German spies and stooges in politics, business, and the labor unions. It backed the efforts of Millerand and Poincaré to raise the period of military service from two years to three; and its staff fought in print and in the streets against those who, like Caillaux and Jaurès, thought that a more conciliatory German policy could preserve the peace.

Late in 1911, inspired by the Agadir crisis, Daudet set out to investigate the activities of German and German-Jewish "spies" who, behind the respectable façade of doing business, were preparing the way for the enemy's invasion. Throughout 1912, Daudet revealed to his appalled readers the incredible extent to which these German agents now controlled essential industries. The tale of his campaign to unmask Berlin's infiltration, published in March 1913 under the ominous title *L'Avant-guerre,* provided the author's first great publishing success. Eleven thousand copies had been sold by the beginning of the war, 25,000 by January 1915; by 1918 it had passed through fifty printings, and the men it pilloried had suffered the torments of hell.

The foundation of all Daudet's argument was the belief that firms with German connections or men of German extraction could not be trusted. Starting from this assumption, it was easy to convert potential into actual and deliberate treachery, the opportunity to serve the enemy being considered sufficient proof of the fact. How this worked in practice may be seen from the case of one of Daudet's chief targets, Maggi-Kub, an international dairy-products firm which had its headquarters in Switzerland but held extensive interests in both Germany and France, and had a board of directors drawn from all three countries. Throughout 1913, flourishing documents that seemed to prove his case, Daudet attacked the Maggi dairies. In July, the corporation sued him for libel. The documents were proved to be forgeries and the corporation won its suit, but the allegations that had been brought against them stuck. Subsequent inquiries proved inconclusive. Though Daudet's arguments had been ill-founded, it would appear that his charges were not altogether without foundation; and they were remembered in August 1914. The pro-German directors of Maggi-Kub were safe enough beyond French borders, but some who did suffer were the French *concessionnaires* of Maggi shops, against whom there was the additional complaint that, with the higher standards and resources of a great international concern behind them, they had threatened to undercut and outsell their unorganized competitors in the dairy trade.

The tale was typical of many an *Action française* campaign. Lashing out wildly in most directions, the chauvinistic champions of the French injured mostly their own compatriots. They had an inkling of possibilities that did not occur to others, they had the nerve to speak out, but they did not pause to check their facts or to consider the seriousness of the charges they so lightly made, let alone their effects. For them, France was in a state of siege, and the forces they denounced had to be exposed lest they betray the already imperiled country.

It cannot be said that the Action Française wanted war. In the midst of the last prewar crisis, although already preoccupied with the trial of Mme Caillaux, the paper devoted a full column to Jacques Bainville's comments on the Austrian ultimatum to Serbia. The Quai d'Orsay, Bainville thought, should press the Serbs to accept humiliation and so avoid disaster; this would save France from the perilous choice between going to war for a Pan-Slavism it did not want or destroying the Russian alliance.[1] But if a war should come, the Action Française wanted the French to be united—and this would be impossible as long as socialist agitators like Jaurès continued to stir up class dissension and to preach an internationalistic pacifism that could only leave France disarmed before a more determined foe. There is no reason today to doubt the patriotism of Socialist leaders like Jaurès, but it does seem that they feared war itself almost as much as any defeat that could result from one; for, if a defeat could be the end of France, a victory, so Jaurès thought, would be the end of the Republic.[2]

When Jaurès was assassinated by Raoul Villain on the evening of July 31, 1914, French nationalists who would not themselves have raised a finger against him could not but rejoice. A few days after the crime, Villain wrote proudly to his brother: "So I have felled the flag-bearer, the great traitor of the Three-Year Law, the furnace-mouth that swallowed all appeals from Alsace-Lorraine. I punished him, and my act was the symbol of a new day."[3] In the *Journal d'un cochon de pessimiste,* the Comtesse de Martel de Jonville, better known to her readers as Gyp, notes the receipt of a letter from Jules

Soury, a friend of the *Action française,* who wrote "to express his joy at the death of Jaurès, whom he abhorred." She herself thought those mistaken who, having first attributed the responsibility for Jaurès's death to the Sillon, to which Villain had once belonged, later attributed it to the Action Française. Any unbalanced person, any simple-minded patriot, she argued, could easily have got the idea, when war was imminent, of destroying the man who had prevented France from arming. "But if the *Action française* and its editor have really done the country [this] signal service," they have done "a jolly good job."[4]

It would be hard to say just what part the *Action française* and its editor played in Jaurès's assassination. It is certain that they had no direct part. Joseph Paul-Boncour, pleading for the injured party, stated this categorically at Villain's trial in 1919, and nothing leads us to think otherwise. But, throughout July 1914, Maurras's attacks were steady and virulent, denouncing Jaurès as a traitor and a German agent, and rising to what could easily be taken as incitements to murder.[5]

There is no doubt that around 1908 or 1909 Raoul Villain had been devoted to the Sillon, but his subsequent activities are not at all clear. Accounts of his trial in 1919, after five years of war had dulled memories, dispersed witnesses, and buried much evidence, give the impression that, behind the most proper of fronts, there was some odd juggling of what evidence and witnesses were still left. Some of the witnesses declared that Villain talked a great deal about politics, always carried a copy of the *Action française,* and regularly attended Action Française meetings. Neither the Court nor the prosecution, however, made any attempt to follow up such statements.

It would appear that Villain, the erratic and maladjusted son of a respectable middle-class family, with aspirations well beyond his talents and a small allowance that allowed him to do nothing in particular, did frequent political circles and did read political papers. He belonged to several organizations, including the Ligue des Jeunes Amis de l'Alsace-Lorraine, a highly nationalist and *revanchard* group whose personal links with the Action Française were close and whose meetings were generally attended by Camelots. The friends of Villain who testified in his behalf at his trial were all nationalists; at least one of them was a royalist. But it is difficult to be more precise. In particular, there is no reason to believe that Villain, who was highly impressionable, was any more influenced by the *Action française* campaign against Jaurès than by the similar sentiments of the other reactionary sheets that he habitually read.[6]

If the murder of Jaurès has stuck to the Action Française for nearly half a century, it is largely because by July 1914 the newspaper was the best known of the whole nationalist and reactionary press, its comments widely noticed, unlike those of similar but more obscure publications. But the Action Française itself does not seem to have felt entirely in the clear. The day after the assassination it published and circulated a statement denying that Villain was a Camelot and claiming that he had nothing at all to do with the movement. The crime, it asserted, was contrary both to the letter and to the spirit of all recent instructions to its members, who had even been warned against attacking Caillaux to avoid aggravating an already tense situation.

On the same first day of August, Daudet, leaving Paris for Touraine to avoid possible retaliation, was involved in an automobile collision, in which he suffered a head injury that would keep him away from the capital for some time. Gyp noted unsympathetically: "M. Daudet quit Paris just as things were becoming really interesting, on the morrow of Jaurès's murder and the plundering of Maggi shops, on the eve of the exciting times that we anticipate." As Gyp remarked, in the heady excitement of a new war, some persons who could not start for Berlin at once had sought compensation in attacking those of Berlin's agents whom the *Action française* had helped point out. During the first few days of war, while the Army was seeing to the removal of Maggi-Kub hoardings for fear they might guide an advancing enemy, there was organized pillage of Maggi shops by small gangs of young hoodlums, watched by silent or approving crowds. "C'est un énorme succès pour M. Léon Daudet et une grande joie pour les laitiers du quartier."[a]

Riots and violence were no longer, however, what the Action Française wanted. With the enemy at the gate, Maurras called for civil union, praised the rabid anti-militarist Gustave Hervé and the Socialist deputy Barthe when they volunteered for military service, and, for his part, announced suspension of the "talisman," the number 445 which had been printed for eight years as a daily reminder of the "Dreyfusard crime" of 1906: "Yesterday it was necessary to call attention to the things that threatened to weaken us before the foe. Today the enemy is here. Let us think only of victory." In theory—and for a good while in practice—this expressed the movement's position throughout the war. A few months later, Maurras repeated the idea: regardless of the nature or composition of succeeding governments, the Action Française would support every one of them: "Only one thing matters—victory. We shall not win by internal divisions, by abetting the disorder, the incoherence, the scandalous governmental instability that has been the essence of the present regime; this can and must be overcome owing to the enemy's presence."[7]

Throughout the early part of 1915 the *Action française* gave strong support to René Viviani's government, and particularly to Millerand, the Min-

[a] See *AF*, Aug. 1, 3, Sept. 8, 1914; Gyp, *Journal d'un cochon de pessimiste*, pp. 55–61, 77. Daudet always referred to the Army High Command's orders enjoining local authorities to destroy Kub advertisements in their area as proof that his charges had been valid. On the contrary, they were proof of the standing he and his paper enjoyed in military circles. Thus Daudet was able to justify his unproved assertions by referring to an official action taken because of the assertions themselves.

ister of War, who was then under severe criticism for what was said to be his misuse of manpower. *La Croix,* on July 9, 1915, commented sarcastically: "It is strange that the duty of defending the thesis of the Radical government's necessary authority against the Radical conspirators should fall to M. Maurras." Strange, yes, but not inconsistent with Maurras's doctrines of authority, for which he had at last found takers outside his own ranks.

A few months later, when the Ligue des Droits de l'Homme opened a campaign against press censorship, the royalists refused their aid. Whatever its faults, censorship was necessary in wartime both to check the leakage of military secrets and to ensure internal order and high morale. Any campaign against it was against the national interests and thus objectionable to the *Action française.* It is true that at the time the royalists themselves had little cause for complaint, and the indulgence which the authorities showed them surprised not only observers but Maurras himself.[8] The honeymoon was sweet while it lasted. Police reports praised the irreproachably patriotic attitude of royalist militants, and wondered that "utter calm [should] reign in Action Française circles where everyone declares himself a patriot above all else." Though propaganda continued—especially in the provinces and at the Front—*Action française* readers found reason to complain that the contents were becoming too moderate, almost "governmental."[9]

As President Poincaré noted in 1917, "Since the beginning of the war, Léon Daudet and Charles Maurras have forgotten their hatred for the Republic and republicans, and think only of France." In effect, it was true that they supported men of all parties, including even the hated Aristide Briand, who would live to hear himself accused in the Chamber of adopting the line Maurras was advocating in the *Action française* and to be praised, however halfheartedly, by the paper, which was obviously determined to do its duty to the end.[10] But, most of all, they supported Georges Clemenceau, once their bitterest enemy, when he eventually came to power. In the summer of 1918, in the dark days just before the turning of the tide, when the German offensives were threatening the Allied front, the paper insisted that France's military and political leaders deserved complete confidence: civilians should not bother military experts, nor the ignorant those in a position to know. No more partisan political debate should distract the energies of the country's leaders.[11] This point of view was a mere application of basic principles: unity, discipline and confidence in the leader.

By 1918, the *Action française* believed that the right leader had at last been found. Heretofore it had been less sure. At another critical moment, in the winter of 1916, when Bucharest had fallen to the Germans, the Russians were in retreat, and the war was going badly, the paper had campaigned for confidence and efficiency. The British were just setting up a small war cabinet numbering only five men; for France, Maurras suggested, a single dictator would do, a *podestat,* or lieutenant general (he did not add "of the kingdom"), preferably chosen from the Army.[b] The good thing about the war was that it had forced the country out of its democratic pretense. It was no longer opinion, wild and unstable, that governed the land but the experts, the soldiers, the administrators—at least in theory. At last one could say that the few were governing the many. One could hope, furthermore, that sooner or later the trend would come to its logical conclusion and a single dictator would take office. As Vaugeois had pointed out at length, national welfare demanded that the most serious matters of national concern should remain outside the control of a capricious public opinion. "Il ne faut plus que chacun puisse dire son mot sur tout et en toute circonstance." There were times, and it was the movement's mission to make this clear, when national unity had to be formulated and imperiously imposed from above.[12] The war was one such time, and the Action Française made the most of it.

And yet, governmental as it was, the paper had lost none of its bite. Throughout 1914 and 1915 it led the offensive against the internal enemy, keeping an eye out for latent defeatism, Socialist slips, false moves by Caillaux, and the treacherous proclivities of foreigners in general.[13] It attacked recently naturalized Germans and Austrians, asserting that their secret sympathies were with the enemy; it attacked German-owned commercial and industrial enterprises and other firms that seemed of doubtful loyalty because of German shareholders or connections, notably Bouillon Kub and Osram;[c] it campaigned against the left-wing Russian exiles in Paris, "Juifs Russes insoumis," who endangered national security; it encouraged Jules Delahaye to introduce a bill that would suspend all naturalizations for the duration of the war; it hounded the authorities to intern more aliens and catch more spies.

In the climate of war, Daudet's anti-foreign campaigns were extremely influential, the more so for his apparent prescience prior to the outbreak of the war. Other papers took them up—such as, in January 1915, *Le Figaro*—but, more important, they could affect the reputation and even the safety of persons cited. As Daudet's frequent retractions indicate, people were often accused by mistake. One has the impression that every story furnished by what must have been a host of voluntary informants was indiscriminately printed, on the principle that some might well prove true and God would recognize his own. Anyone with German, Swiss, or Dutch blood, or with relatives of those nationalities, might easily be a spy or a potential spy. "The pursuit of German firms" never slackened. Daudet called for the confiscation of all property owned by or connected with Germans, and for the punish-

[b] *AF*, Dec. 10, 1916. He had begun by inviting Poincaré to take over, and the President had himself envisaged some such possibility, abandoning it for fear of precipitating a crisis. Poincaré to Maurras, Dec. 30, 1919.

[c] Even their friend Ambroise Rendu, a Paris municipal councilor and president of the charitable Oeuvre du Bon Lait, found some of their assertions excessive and unjust; see *AF*, Feb. 1, 1915.

ment not only of their protectors, who were traitors to France, but of persons who had traded with Germany before the war, and of *les embochés*—all those who questioned his methods.[d]

In April 1915, the *Frankfurter Zeitung* devoted an editorial to the Action Française: its gains since the beginning of the war, its hold on public opinion, and (not without a certain *schadenfreude*) the threat that all this constituted to the *union sacrée.* But the French champions of the *union sacrée* do not seem to have been alarmed. Barrès praised the courage and clairvoyance of Daudet's prewar anti-spy campaigns. In the Senate, the Bonapartist Sylvain Gaudin de Villaine paid tribute to the man "whose political preferences one may not share, but whose patriotic clearsightedness before the war one must salute." From Reims, the Archbishop, Cardinal Luçon, sent fifty francs for the *Action française,* with his respectful congratulations to Daudet, the brave and farsighted denouncer of German invasion. The eighty-year-old Juliette Adam, who had long ago founded the *Nouvelle Revue* to aid Gambetta and the republicans, now read only the *Action française,* feeling unable to do without Daudet's daily blows against the hydra of treason. André Gide wrote Maurras an admiring letter and enclosed a contribution to the paper, to which he also subscribed.[14]

Meanwhile, the League continued in existence, its position strengthened by the disappearance of royalist competitors like the *Soleil* group, by the adherence of a good many old royalists reassured by the paper's new tone, and by the decision of the Duc d'Orléans to grant Maurras and Daudet a confidence and exclusiveness of representation he had previously begrudged them. The war provided an unexpected opportunity to solidify the position painfully built up over the preceding few years. Competitors eliminated or reconciled, the Action Française henceforth *was* the royalist movement.[e]

Anti-republican propaganda also continued, despite the newspaper's expressions of loyalty. In June 1915, the Arras section printed and circulated a

[d] See, e.g., *AF,* Feb. 2, 3, July 2, 1915. Some of Daudet's favorite targets were naturalized German Jews in high business or banking positions, such as Caillaux's friend Emile Ullman, the director and vice-president of the great Comptoir National d'Escompte, and Lucien Baumann, the director of the Grands Moulins de Corbeil, which was vital to the capital's bread supply. Both these men were driven to resign by his sustained campaigns. See the Paris press of Oct. 30, 31, 1915; Gaudin de Villaine in *JOS,* Dec. 23, 1915; *La France de demain* quoted in *AF,* Dec. 9, 1915; *AF,* Nov. 5, 1915, April 29, May 26, 1916. But on July 4, 1916, Daudet is careful to distinguish between honest businessmen and bloodsucking war profiteers. He insists that it was never his intention to incriminate the powerful industrial forces whose praiseworthy efforts have permitted the saviors of France to be supplied with ammunition. It was not big industry he meant to attack but the men, "generally of foreign and vagabond race," who were profiting without decency or scruple from France's need. A convenient distinction, this combined the advantage of seeming precision with that of complete pointlessness.

[e] F[7] 12863, No. 4, of Jan. 28, 1915: "On peut donc considérer que l'Action Française tient dans ses mains, désormais, toutes les forces royalistes de France. De ces forces elle fera, quand elle jugera le moment venu, ce qu'elle voudra. Elle ne rencontrera plus chez les royalistes que de l'enthousiasme. Et nul doute que le royalisme ne sorte fortifié de l'épreuve que nous passons."

tract denouncing republican inefficiency and disorder, calling on all good Frenchmen to choose between republicanism and France and to cry with the Action Française, "Let the Republic die so that France shall live!" League meetings in Paris and the provinces dispersed to shouts of "Long live the King! Death to the Republic!" In June 1916, some three hundred persons attending a section meeting in the 10th Arrondissement of Paris rose to their feet with cries of "Long live the King! Long live France! Down with the Republic!" Throughout 1917, military units friendly to the movement were carefully watched, particularly cavalry regiments close to Paris, in which a good many officers were known to be anti-republican. Marius Plateau, invalided home from the trenches and discharged, had not given up the preparations for the hoped-for coup.[15]

Clearly, there was more than one point of view in the movement's counsels; from different extremes both Louis Dimier and Edouard Berth would later complain that had Maurras been more of a man of action, the Republic might have been overthrown at some time between the murder of Gaston Calmette and the end of 1917. Not everyone in the movement endorsed its wartime policy of supporting the government. Toward the end of 1915, Maurras refused the collaboration of a friendly republican on the ground that such a step would disorient his readers and lead them to fear a possible *ralliement*.[16] There were probably other reasons for Maurras's refusal, including lack of space in a paper that was now limited to a mere two or four pages. But it is suggestive of the uneasy speculations that the new policy must have aroused. Private reassurances were also in order.[f] One wonders to what extent Daudet really believed what he told his listeners at a closed meeting in 1917: "We must continue our propaganda, so that our friends at the Front may find on their return a united force ready to overthrow the Republic and restore our king."[17]

Except at rare moments, however, it was nationalist activity rather than royalist conspiracy that occupied the attention of the League. With young people in the services, preoccupied by the war, or fascinated by more heroic possibilities than those open to Camelots, recruitment dropped off and almost ceased until the great treason campaigns of 1917, against Caillaux and Malvy, caught public interest. A few young men, among them Alfred Droin and Henri Ghéon, were converted to monarchism during the first year of the war. Droin has told (in the *Revue universelle* of January 1, 1937) how, after he had been gravely wounded in the Château-Salins offensive, he remembered the paper's prewar warnings and realized how much Charles Maurras had tried to do to prepare the country for the war. As for Gide's friend Ghéon, a convert to Catholicism, he was drawn to the movement by reading the

[f] F^7 12863, 4/116, of Sept. 20, 1915: "Certains, parmi la clientèle de l'Action Française, se plaignent de constater que le journal devient de plus en plus modéré, voire gouvernemental! [*sic*] et menacent de raréfier leurs versements réguliers."

letters of Dupouey, killed in the Battle of the Yser, who had written an explicit profession of his integral nationalist faith: "Il fallut bien me rendre à l'évidence. Cela n'étonnera que ceux qui n'auront pas connu le temps où l'on allait au Christ-roi par le roi, ou bien au roi par le Christ-roi, avec une parfaite aisance."

There was good reason for Catholics to feel a particularly close relationship with the Action Française. True to its tradition, it had championed the cause of enlisted priests and seminarists, and of the Church itself, from the very beginning of the war when the Catholic publications had, for a while, been restrained in their support. In the twenty-seven months between September 1914 and December 1916, Maurras wrote 139 major articles defending the Pope, the Church, and the clergy, attacking their critics, justifying every Catholic position, and calling for re-establishment of the Embassy to the Vatican, which had been suppressed in 1905. Collected in a volume and published in 1917 as *Le Pape, la guerre, et la paix,* these articles established him as the most valiant, articulate, and uncompromising defender of the Catholic cause.

The cause had needed a defender. Many Frenchmen objected to the Pope's efforts to remain neutral, to his refusal to condemn German aggression, to his silence before German destruction and atrocities in Belgium and northern France. Certain clerics, and even certain laymen like Mistral with his *Psaumes de la pénitence,* had chosen to treat the sufferings of war as a punishment for French irreligion and anti-clericalism. When protests against such statements threatened to develop into a new anti-clerical campaign, Maurras branded them "the infamous clamor," a breach in what should remain a united national front, and his paper became the clergy's strongest defender. The *Univers* waxed dithyrambic: "We are hundreds of priests who love him, forty bishops support him." Priests like Pierre Rousselot welcomed their new champion, and when, in the spring of 1915, the future Cardinal Verdier, then director of the *Revue apologétique,* published an article defending the Pope, his arguments were essentially those of Maurras.[18]

Consistent in its Catholic policy, the paper was equally consistent in its foreign views. Along with the normal patriotic nonsense about Germany's being on the brink of starvation and collapse, almost every issue contained some statements of the soundest common sense, such as Bainville's lucid explanation, in December 1914, of "Why the War Is Long," and why it was likely to be a good deal longer.[19] At the outset, Bainville had assumed Cato's task, and also adapted his famous slogan to the present crisis: *Delenda est Borussia.* On September 23, 1914, he had for the first time stated the essence of his thought and what he considered the French war aim should be: German unity must be broken, and Prussia, for two centuries past the scourge of nations, the spirit of evil poisoning the European world, must be destroyed.

From the beginning of the war the *Action française* had opposed the argument that war was caused by rulers alone, that all would be well once the German people had rid itself of its Hohenzollern overlords. On the contrary, it declared, the Germans would remain a threat to France as long as a united Germany existed; and the first fruits of victory must be the destruction of this menacing monster. Hopes of a democratic revolution in Germany were misguided: a German revolution, Maurras suggested in 1914, could only be national and devoted to furthering national unity. It was not Germany's regime that counted, but its unity and its size. As long as the unifying German monarchy had not been destroyed, as long as an amorphous federation had not taken the place of the existing Reich, the royalists would continue to warn of the peril to France, and to point out the remoteness of disarmament. Monarchy was good for France because it would be a unifying force, but it was undesirable for Germany, from the French point of view, for the very same reason. The same was true of nationalism, and Bainville could only hope that the principle of nationality would be abandoned as an Allied war aim, since its logical application could only increase German power.[g]

There is something paradoxical at first sight about anti-monarchist monarchists, about anti-nationalist nationalists; but the Action Française was empirical, not logical—inspired not by general principles but by its particular view of what was good for France. Whatever one's opinion of integral nationalism may be, it lent itself to the most pragmatic of applications. Bainville's insistence that nationalism running wild could not be tamed by good intentions alone went against the prevailing propaganda of his time, and distinctly against the desires of a public that wanted to look upon militarism and ruthlessness as the preserve of a few highborn criminals, whose elimination would henceforth allow peaceable lions to lie down with self-determined lambs. When Bainville said that France's problems would not be settled until Germany returned to a state structure similar to that of 1648, he was being hopelessly anachronistic, though not so much concerning German particularist fancies as concerning the intentions of France's powerful allies. But he was far from wrong when he assumed that under any regime a monolithic Germany in the center of Europe would be a constant threat to her neighbors' security. It took more generations and several million lives before his views could find a wider acceptance.

The kind of common sense that some, though not all, of Bainville's articles reflected could also be found in some of Maurras's campaigns. Nothing had been done in France by way of economic and financial preparations for a war that had been envisaged largely as a series of brave charges with colors flying and white cassowary feathers fluttering in the breeze. Yet the war was to last

[g] See Bainville in *AF,* Sept. 23, 1914, and Aug. 4, 1916; Dimier in *AF,* Oct. 28, 1914; Maurras in *AF,* Nov. 27, 1914. Dimier's *Les Tronçons du serpent* and Bainville's *Histoire de deux peuples,* both published in 1915, preached the necessity of dividing Germany. Dimier's book, which was the result of his lectures at the Institut d'Action Française, made quite a stir in its time; but it was Bainville's work that really attracted the reading public. By 1960, it had sold nearly 90,000 copies.

over fifty months and to cost more than 150 billion gold francs. The mobilization of the nation's human and economic resources had to be improvised, the latter largely by means of indirect taxes and loans. And, at the very time when the national potential was most strained, it became apparent that some of the richest lands in France, instead of contributing their share to the general war effort, would on the contrary have to be succored by the rest of the country. German occupation and German devastation would have to be made good somehow, the ruined inhabitants set on their feet again, and destroyed property and installations rebuilt.

It was with all this in mind that the Belgian Minister of Justice, Henry Carton de Wiart, in a speech before the University of Lyon in 1915, first called for reparations. His Chef de Cabinet, the future Baron Pierre Nothomb, who drew up the speech, was a prewar friend of integral nationalism, and the *Action française* gave Carton de Wiart strong support, even against King Albert himself. "If the enemy does not pay, who will?" Maurras asked.[20]

The point was not ill-taken, but it had the disadvantage of encouraging the enemies of direct taxation to go on drawing checks on future bankruptcy. It is impossible to pay the huge cost of modern war simply from income taxes; but the French bourgeoisie had no intention of trying to pay even part of it. They did not wish to modify their primitive tax structure, in which loans had come to be increasingly important. Yet, if the war was lost, such loans could be redeemed only by bankruptcy; if it was won, a similar bankruptcy of the enemy, which might prevent him from footing the bill, was never envisaged. A revolutionary crisis called for revolutionary measures to cope with it; but few Frenchmen, and no one with political influence, could see the situation as much different from that of 1871, and the *Action française,* heedless as always of economic matters, was no help at all.

A more constructive, though historically less significant, development of Maurras's insistence that the enemy should pay occurred when he demanded that fighting men be rewarded for their sacrifice and courage by more than mere praise. In the good old days, there had been spoils for victorious armies. Men moldering in trenches or risking a dank death at sea deserved as much. From this was born the idea of a bonus, a *part du combattant,* for fighting soldiers. The first suggestion of it was made in October 1916, when an editorial by Maurras deplored the elimination of naval prize money, which had been abolished by an ordinance a few months before. Patriotism and praise were all very well, but men were only human. They should, they could, be offered more. Idealists were foolish in hesitating to assure the soldiers that war would pay, not only collectively but individually as well, and that Germany had quite sufficient means to pay. The soldier must be shown that he was fighting for himself, for his own *material* advantage. This was not his only motive for fighting, but it was only reasonable to take it into account and plan to satisfy it.

With the French counteroffensive in the Battle of Verdun at its height and as the French people rejoiced over the taking of Fort Douaumont and Fort de Vaux, Maurras continued the argument. He repeated that heroes should get rewards more concrete than the mere burning of incense. France must not fear "to realize the just profits of victory." "We are governed by the vain and stupid spirit of stoicism and hypocrisy." Why not approach the matter honestly and admit that a bonus would be the best incentive for battle-weary soldiers?[21]

It would take the fatal spring of 1917, the bloody failure of the Allied offensives on the Somme and in Champagne, the industrial strikes of May, the military mutinies of June, to stir some interest in an idea to which Maurras returned whenever the news seemed worst. As the much heralded Nivelle offensive was bogging down in the middle of April 1917, Maurras took several columns to develop at length the plan for a *part du combattant.* The argument was simple: the fighter produces victory, the fighter has a right to a share of his product, and it should be more than pensions—cash, with special bonuses for elite troops. France must not fear, like the senators of Rome, to sell the lands on which Hannibal was camping. A Military Gratuities Bank should be set up out of a public loan to be looked upon as an advance on the sums to be recovered from Germany after victory had been attained. This would have the double advantage of renewing the bonds between the military and civilians, which had been loosened somewhat in recent months, and interesting the French public directly in a profitable peace, one that would not permit Germany to escape paying France the reparations that were her due.[22]

Ignored a few months before, the idea now received widespread support. *L'Intransigeant, L'Echo de Paris, Le Journal, L'Heure,* even *La Petite République* agreed with the advanced republicans of the *Revue libre* that "the idea is just . . . No need to be royalist; one need only be fair-minded to demand a *part du combattant.*" And in the *Journal,* under the heading "Patriotic Realism: The Right to Loot," Maurice Talmeyr demanded: "Existe-t-il encore des esprits assez hypocrites pour prétendre que le gain noblement mérité avilit ceux qui le reçoivent?"[23]

To show that its proposals were really serious, the *Action française* opened a subscription to begin the *part du combattant.* The first list, published on April 15, 1917, totaled over 43,000 francs, including 20,000 from the Duc de Vendôme. Several other newspapers soon started lists of their own, and the Left began to be alarmed at the prospect of subversion. The Right, it asserted, was illegally conspiring to buy the Army for its nefarious ends. On January 18, 1918, a Socialist deputy, Paul Poncet, rose in the Chamber to ask the government whether such subscription lists were legal. The government, unwilling to take a direct stand on an issue it would have preferred to postpone, declared that it had been giving the matter thought and that every fighting soldier would get a combat bonus of three francs a day. By this time, however, the idea had become identified with the men who launched it, and politicians tended to take sides according to their view of the royalists. The debate, in which the Action Française and its ideas served as a key point of reference for both sides, degenerated into a brawl, and it was clear that the *part du combattant* would be forgotten in arguments about royalist loyalty and in charges and countercharges occasioned by the coming of the Clemenceau administration.

It may well be that a bonus scheme predicated on income from the bear in the bush, from almost unobtainable reparations, had little chance from the start. Probably, also, the government's other concerns were more important than a bonus plan based on what for a long time seemed a doubtful victory. Yet Maurras's scheme, presupposing income from the Saarland mines, was not unsound if the principle of reparations be accepted at all. The Second World War has shown the value of postwar planning undertaken before the end of hostilities. And, of course, Maurras never considered the possibility that France might not in the end be victorious.

Not for the last time, one of Maurras's proposals had become entangled in irrelevant political concerns and rejected not so much because of its faults as because of the suspicion and opposition excited by the Action Française. Meanwhile, a Military Gratuities Bank established by the government received the proceeds of the royalist subscription, and in June 1918, some 160,000 francs were given as recompense to the men of three regiments that had distinguished themselves in the recent combats. Each corporal got ten francs, each other noncommissioned officer fifteen; the remainder, divided into lots, was raffled off.[h]

The debate of January 1918, the angry questions of Paul Poncet, and the blows exchanged by nationalist and Socialist deputies had really been concerned not with bonuses but with another campaign of the *Action française,* one which for the first time threatened the very safety of republican leaders.

In March 1916, as the Battle of Verdun developed, Daudet had presented the idea that France was waging a total war, involving every aspect of national life. It followed, therefore, that all complaisance toward Germany or Germans, in whatever domain, must henceforth be considered treason.[i] Pub-

[h] *AF,* June 19, 1918. This was not the end; echoes of the scheme continued to be heard for several years thereafter. Thus during the discussion of bonuses and demobilization in 1919, when the Right proposed a bonus for front-line soldiers, to be paid for by the Germans, the Left recognized this as Maurras's *part du combattant* (*JOC,* Feb. 26, 1919). In the Radical Party Congress of 1921, a motion for a *rente du combattant* was killed ignominiously by the assaults of numerous critics, who found it too similar to the royalist idea (*Petit Parisien,* Oct. 30, 1921). On February 15, 1930, Poincaré could still write in *L'Est républicain,* "Voici la retraîte du combattant qui rappelle sous une forme du reste très différente et peut-être moins heureuse, cette part du combattant que Charles Maurras réclamait dès 1917, en faveur des ouvriers de la victoire."

[i] *AF,* March 11, 1916, "Une Guerre totale: eux ou nous." The idea was inspired by Séché's remarkably prescient *Les Guerres d'enfer* (1915), one of many successful books that Daudet was responsible for launching.

lic opinion seems to have been on Daudet's side when he affirmed that "every naturalized German must be considered a suspect" and that "every German living in France is necessarily a spy." In January 1917, a court at Melun acquitted him of slander and defamation, on the ground that he had acted in the national interest. Although Daudet's charges were unjustified, the court declared, it was the duty of the press to point out all individuals who might seriously be suspected of being friendly to the enemy.[24]

In pursuit of this duty, the *Action française* had been squabbling ever since the war with several left-wing publications which it considered too defeatist, and most particularly with one called the *Bonnet rouge,* which was directed by an old acquaintance, Miguel Vigo-Almereyda.[j] Toward the end of the summer of 1916, while a slander action brought against them by Vigo was pending, the royalist leaders were approached by a friend in official quarters who offered them secret information that would convict their enemy of treason. The *Bonnet rouge,* which the *Action française* never mentioned except as *Le Torchon* (The Rag), was being supported, their informant said, by German funds brought in from Switzerland by its financial administrator, one Raoul Duval. Vigo himself had been in touch with enemy agents; he and his henchmen had traveled to Spain on passports delivered by the Paris Prefecture of Police. Better still, his newspaper, which had lately taken on a particularly critical and defeatist tone not calculated to improve morale, had at one time received private subsidies from Caillaux and public ones from another Radical-Socialist, Louis-Jean Malvy, Minister of the Interior since June 1914.

The information was as explosive as it was doubtful. If true, or even partly true, it could not only destroy a nest of spies but seriously compromise important politicians and high officials connected with Malvy and Caillaux, perhaps even with the Premiers, whose responsibility would also be involved. The identity of "the very highly placed official figure" who contacted the *Action française* remains hidden to this day, but he seems to have reckoned carefully in picking the paper as a cat's-paw for what looks to have been essentially a machination against the Caillaux-Malvy wing of the Radical group. Other newspapers had cast a suspicious eye on the activities of writers and financiers moving in the twilight zone of near-illegal action, but only the *Action française* would so readily believe the implications of outright treason in high places which the secret information carried; only the *Action française* would

[j] The *Bonnet rouge* had attracted the particular hatred of the *Action française* by attacking its directors throughout the summer of 1915 with slanderous charges, for some of which it was actually condemned later that year. Maurras was especially irate at being ascribed "the mug of a masturbator," and he was incensed that friends like the Comtesse de Courville nevertheless plunged into the "vile rag" every evening to see what fresh insults it would come up with. Some of the rag's information was remarkably accurate, being provided by disaffected royalists. See *AF, Le Bonnet rouge,* June–November 1915; F[7] 12863 (1915), 4/71 of June 15, 4/73 of June 22, 4/75 of June 26, and *passim.*

be brave enough, or reckless enough, to publish such charges and stand by them.

On September 9, 1916, Maurras began his campaign against Vigo and the personnel of the *Bonnet rouge,* branding them as German agents. He had no real proof of his allegations, which were in any case proved to be incorrect in detail and within a few months brought him a heavy fine for defamation.[25] This, however, did not stop the paper's almost daily attacks against alleged German spies. Marius Plateau was being supplied with information from friendly sources in the Prefecture of Police and the Sûreté Nationale. The head of the Second (Intelligence) Bureau in the office of the Paris Military Government (which was in charge of the capital's security throughout the war, by reason of the state of siege), a Major Baudier, had been in 1912 an unsuccessful Action Française candidate for municipal councilor at Levallois-Perret. He and some of his subordinates were for some time a precious source of private information. Other information was furnished by friends in the censorship and postal services, among them the Abbé Cochin, who was employed as a censor in the post office at Bellegarde, on the Swiss border. Cochin examined the correspondence of prominent political figures and sent copies of their most interesting letters to Daudet, Dom Besse, and another nationalist leader, Charles Maignen. As Daudet himself declared in testimony before Malvy's judges:

> During 1915, 1916, and 1917 I received documents from the Prefecture and the Sûreté. They were, I think, what are commonly called "leaks." By these documents, I was able to note that if one part of the executive personnel of the Prefecture and Sûreté was not doing all its duty, another part of this same personnel did its duty in very thorough fashion and procured information for me as best it could.[26]

An anti-subversive Ligue de Guerre d'Appui, with offices in the new Action Française headquarters in the rue de Rome, was established in June 1917. Its honorary president was the aged but symbolic General Mercier; its manager was Etienne de Resnes, who also presided over the Action Française board of directors. Its avowed purpose was to furnish useful information for Daudet's campaigns and to collect contributions in support of his patriotic endeavor. An "apolitical" Ligue de Défense Anti-Allemande followed a few months later, with a short-lived bulletin called *On les aura.* Bolstered by this and other support, Daudet kept up his fire, and it began to tell. In the early summer of 1917 an *Action française* reporter who met one member of the *Bonnet rouge* staff on the street found him looking haggard and worn. "Daudet's campaign against me is making me ill," Paul Marion complained; "it's driving me mad. All the journals where I used to get work are closing to me."[27]

Soon, a great many things would be closing in on Marion and his friends. Their arrest came at the beginning of August, and within a week Vigo was found dead in his cell, strangled with a narrow cord or shoelace, possibly murdered to keep him from telling whatever he knew. The *Action française* had triumphed. As the republican *Dépêche de Lyon* (August 10, 1917) pointed out, for more than a year the *Action française* had been exposing Vigo's criminal record. Now Vigo's friends had better look out. On July 22, Clemenceau had risen in the Senate to call for the repression of treason and of defeatist propaganda. His speech had been an open attack against Malvy, and a covert one against Caillaux, who was suspected of still favoring some kind of understanding with Germany. Finally, on August 31, Malvy, discredited, resigned, stating clearly in his letter of resignation that he was doing so because of attacks on him by the press.

J. Coudurier de Chassaigne, the London correspondent of *Le Figaro* and president of the Foreign Press Association in the British capital, took this opportunity to explain to the English public the rash of espionage cases in France and their role in the political crisis. Malvy's resignation, Chassaigne wrote on September 6 in an article for *Land and Water,* had been the result of Clemenceau's speech in the Senate, the ground for which had been prepared by Léon Daudet's long campaign. Without Daudet, it was doubtful whether Clemenceau could have brought off his attack.

Chassaigne described Daudet to English readers as a farsighted patriot and prophet, a man only at that time coming into his own. He himself had never attached much importance to the propaganda of Daudet and Maurras and their Camelots until shortly after the outbreak of the war, when a friend gave him a copy of *L'Avant-guerre,* which he devoured in one night. The very next day he bought a copy of the *Action française,* and he had read it regularly for the past three years. Although he did not always agree with its editors, "he was forced to admit that *alone* in the Paris press they had sufficient intelligence and courage to pursue day by day the patriotic campaign against hidden foes."[k]

The end of September brought more arrests, and further requests from Daudet that he be allowed to testify against Malvy. He stated the burden of his charges in a letter to President Poincaré, who, by all accounts, thought rather highly of his enlightened patriotism, and in reply was informed that he and Maurras would be received on October 1 by Premier Paul Painlevé, the new Minister of the Interior Théodore Steeg, and Raoul Péret, the Minister of Justice, who promised a thorough inquiry. Then, unexpectedly, following Malvy's own request that the charges be made public, Painlevé read to an agitated Chamber the letter in which Daudet accused the former minister of treason:

[k] Quoted in full by *AF,* Sept. 14, 1917. But one should remember that *L'Oeuvre* had been foremost in criticizing slipshod security and speaking of other cases that ended before the courts and in the death ditch of Vincennes: convicted spies like Bolo Pasha, Lenoir, and Turmel had first been mentioned by Gustave Téry, but without the *panache* and without all the political overtones that the *Action française* carried.

> M. Malvy [Daudet had written] is a traitor. For the last three years, with the complicity of M. Leymarie [his Chef de Cabinet] and several others, he has betrayed the national defense. The proofs of this treason are overwhelming. It would take too long to state them. . . . M. Malvy has caused Germany to be exactly informed of all our military and diplomatic projects, particularly by the spy gang of the *Bonnet rouge* and his friend Vigo . . . and by a certain Soutters, director of Maggi-Kub. This is how, to cite only one example, the German high command learned point by point the plan of attack on the Chemin des Dames . . . as soon as M. Malvy was admitted to the [cabinet's] War Committee. . . . Documents of undisputable authenticity also show the hand of Malvy and that of the Sûreté in the military mutinies and the tragic events of June 1917 . . . The only way to destroy the German plan is . . . to refer to a military tribunal the miserable creature by whom France has been handed over, bit by bit, to the enemy.[28]

These assertions were as false as they were extreme. With the agreement of his successive Premiers, Malvy had paid Vigo out of secret funds, as he had paid scores of others, to keep him from making trouble; but he had discontinued the subsidies when the *Bonnet rouge* turned pacifist in 1915. He had sought to appease left-wing agitation, not to arouse it by censorship and suppression, and his policy on the whole had proved a success. The workers had stayed at work, the machines had kept turning, and industrial disputes and friction had been held to a minimum. All this had caused suspicion and resentment, however, in quarters ready to interpret any concession to the Left as potentially treasonable. What was worse, Malvy had laid himself open to reproach by his easygoing manner, a kind of amoral *bonhomie* which, although common in political circles, seemed reprehensible in a time of crisis. The outstretched hand, the easy *tutoiement,* and the apparently friendly relations he entertained with petty crooks may have been harmless enough, but as represented by Daudet they proved disturbing to the general public and even to a few of Malvy's colleagues in the Chamber—while more thought well to pretend that they were troubled.

Daudet's charges were declared to be without foundation even before Malvy was tried, and were subsequently given the lie by every investigation, but they opened the door to other, lesser, charges of negligence and dereliction of duty which might otherwise never have been made.[l] Where Daudet was concerned, however, Malvy was not merely a normally fallible being, or a fool who had given Germany's friends and agents too much rope: he was the

[l] See *Revue des causes célèbres,* 1918, pp. 25ff, 63, 250, for the opening reports of Malvy's trial on July 16–17, 1918, and for the opinion of Public Prosecutor Mérillon on July 18 and August 2, 1918. In his testimony (p. 124), André Maginot, whom Daudet had visited at the Ministry of Colonies in July to denounce Malvy's treason, expressed as tactfully as he could the feeling that Daudet had never proved or substantiated any of his charges. The final verdict of the High Court was blunter: it found that Daudet's charges had been entirely refuted.

deliberate agent of Germany herself. What Daudet said carried the ring of conviction to deputies like Henri de Monplanet, who declared: "I do not know the men of the Action Française, but I cannot help noting that well before the war Daudet had pointed to the organization of German espionage in France . . . for three years he had to repeat his warnings every day before measures were taken." The Right was aroused against Malvy and no explanation would satisfy them. The debate went on and on, growing increasingly bitter. "For the last six hours," a Socialist complained, "in this overexcited hall, we have argued on a question brought up by Léon Daudet. On one side a calumniator, a professional defamer, on the other the Chamber and the whole country. What is this person who can thus occupy the country's representatives for six hours? What is his importance? What is his power? I cannot find an explanation consistent with the dignity of this Assembly!"

The answer was supplied by another Socialist, Marius Moutet: "Men like Léon Daudet have only the importance given them by the government's weakness."[29] It is true that Daudet was at his best in moments of governmental incoherence. But he also excelled in helping to create such moments. At any rate, the last half of the Third Republic, which was remarkable for its executive weakness, would offer him every opportunity to exercise his talents. For the moment, his accusation of Malvy had made him famous. The title he had assumed of King's Prosecutor—Procureur du Roi—was now being attributed to him, more or less angrily, more or less wryly, by enemies and friends. *Vive Léon Daudet* began to appear scribbled upon Paris walls.[30]

First seized and then suspended for a week, the newspaper had itself become a *cause célèbre*. In the fight over Daudet's letter and Malvy's guilt, the fragile union of Left and Right which had endured since the beginning of the war disintegrated. Painlevé was attacked by the Right for reading Daudet's private letter, by the Left for not prosecuting Daudet, and under the double pressure not only his government but its majority disintegrated. Daudet had helped touch off a parliamentary division that would end only with the coming to power of Clemenceau and the departure of the Socialists from the coalition.[31]

On Saturday night, October 27, 1917, police raided and searched Action Française offices in Paris, Bordeaux, Lyon, Nîmes, and Montpellier. The homes of Maurras, Daudet, Plateau, Dimier, Emmanuel Buffet, Maxime Réal del Sarte, who had been invalided home, and other leading figures were also searched either that night or on the following day. The searches were not without reward: fifty guns, 250 loaded canes, and a quantity of brass knuckles and blackjacks were seized, and also the files in which Plateau kept the movement's plans for insurrection.

From the first, however, the *Action française* minimized and ridiculed the raids and the booty they yielded, and the public generally believed the newspaper's assertions that only a ridiculous token supply of arms had been found, along with out-of-date documents referring to plans the royalists had never sought to hide. The story circulated that what arms had been found had been bought out of secret funds by an *agent provocateur.* Criticized by other newspapers on every side, the government retreated, and on November 4 the case was dismissed.[32]

There was a good deal more to the so-called *affaire des panoplies,* however, than a frame-up that had failed to stick. It was true, as the prosecutor said in dismissing the case, that most of the files found in Plateau's home dated back to 1913, and that they revealed only conspiracies admitted by all and abandoned at the outbreak of the war. But there had been other files as well, which pertained to the sentiments of officers in military units stationed near Paris in 1917. And there had been much more than a token store of weapons. As one Socialist pointed out several months later—of course, Socialists were prejudiced—had but a quarter of the things seized in the homes of certain Action Française members been found in the home of a union secretary, he would long since have been arrested, and he would not be about to leave jail, either.[33]

On the other hand, Dimier remarked wistfully, the ridicule with which the news of an Action Française plot was greeted, not least by the royalist leaders themselves, reflected how little they had come to believe in their own ostensible aims. In saying that the Republic had conjured up an imaginary royalist threat, they passed sentence on their own failure to make the threat come true. "There was no conspiracy, that was only too true," wrote Dimier. "There had never been one." There may have been one once, and there may still have been fleeting thoughts of plotting and revolt among the younger men, but it is hard to believe that the surviving leaders—Vaugeois and Montesquiou were dead—had not by now abandoned all serious thought of any *coup de force.*[34]

The Painlevé government fell on November 13, 1917, on a vote concerning the date when its internal policy should be debated by the Chamber. The debate, turning on the recent searches and "persecution" of the Action Française, and on the charges that Daudet was pressing in its pages, had been fixed sometime earlier for the 13th. In the meantime the Italian front had collapsed at Caporetto, the Bolsheviks had risen in Petrograd, and an Allied conference had been called to discuss the serious military situation. Preoccupied by all these matters, Painlevé requested that the day's discussion be adjourned to the 30th of the month. All sides opposed him, and he was voted down, 277 to 186.

It was the only government during the whole course of the war to be overthrown by a vote of the Chamber. Socialists and Right voted almost solidly against Painlevé, each side because it felt he had given in to the other. When the result of the voting was announced, there were cries from the Socialist benches: "Down with Clemenceau! Long live the Republic!" They both reflected and predicted a conjunction which, though perhaps fortuitous, seemed clear to many. Without Daudet, as Coudurier de Chassaigne had said, the ground for Clemenceau's July speech would not have been prepared. But by this speech, and subsequently by his articles in *L'Homme enchaîné,* Clemenceau seemed to confirm Daudet's accusations and enabled the *Action française* to carry on as if it had his backing.[35]

When, on November 20, Clemenceau's new government faced the Chamber, his brief, determined declaration of policy was generally well received, especially on the Right. The Socialists, however, went into opposition. The former Minister of Armaments Albert Thomas explained why they would refuse to Clemenceau in 1917 a support they had not begrudged Briand in 1914: "The situation in 1914 was quite different from that created by the battles waged in the country during the last few months. Today, party activity has revived, whether you like it or not."[m]

The Socialists had unpleasant memories of Clemenceau, as they had had of Briand. Could they have buried them, as they had managed to do before, in order to preserve the *union sacrée*? Perhaps, if the union had not collapsed during the mud-slinging and political accusations of the previous months. Bitter campaigns, in which *L'Homme enchaîné* and the *Action française* had played the leading parts, had torn down the fragile structure of party cooperation, and not all the king's horses could put it together again. The king's men certainly did not want to do so.

A perhaps apocryphal story claims that on the night when the Tiger set up his cabinet, which must have been the night of November 15, he sent the royalist deputy Jules Delahaye to Action Française headquarters in the rue de Rome to learn what the integral nationalists wanted. In answer to their three requests, he refused to re-establish an embassy at the Vatican, declared that he would consider the *part du combattant,* and agreed to pursue spies and traitors vigorously. The last was obviously the most convenient as well as the most popular coin by which Action Française support could be paid for. Whether such overtures were ever made—and Georges Wurmser, who was then a member of the Premier's staff, formally denies that they were—the movement could congratulate itself. For, from the moment he took power, Clemenceau proceeded to apply their program.[n]

The conjunction might seem strange at first: few republican politicians had been so abhorrent to the royalists, or so roughly handled, as this Anglo-

[m] *JOC,* Nov. 20, 1917. Before the month was out, representatives of the Left and Right would express the feeling that the *union sacrée* had been broken and that Clemenceau had come to power in circumstances closely connected with Action Française activities: see Pierre Renaudel in *JOC,* Nov. 22, p. 3001; Paul Poncet in *JOC,* Nov. 28, p. 3069; and Jules Delahaye in *JOC,* pp. 3074–75. Like Maurras himself, Albert Thomas might have welcomed an executive led by President Poincaré (Poincaré to Maurras, Dec. 30, 1919).

[n] Maurras, *Pour un jeune français* (1949), p. 135; *La Contre-révolution spontanée,* p. 164; Dimier, *Vingt Ans,* p. 270. Note that on December 1, 2, and 3, 1917, the Action Française

phile Dreyfusard and "most mischievous of Frenchmen." True, at the beginning of the war Maurras had advised that Clemenceau be given the choice between Conseil de Guerre and Conseil des Ministres. But he had not expected "the eternal father of disorder, the Commander in Chief of anarchy," to accept the latter. Indeed, Maurras commented in 1917, no one was more responsible than Clemenceau for the country's present misfortunes.[36] Right-wing approval came only slowly. Daudet, who had once called Clemenceau "a dolt deemed a Caesar," was still calling him a maniac and a perverse macrobite in 1915; in 1916 he was an evil demolisher, a surly old carcass; and in 1917 he was the sinister gaffer of *L'Homme enchaîné*. But by 1918 the sinister old gaffer had become a symbol of moral pluck, standing in the first rank of patriots. Even without a secret understanding, however, there was by then good reason for the change in tone.[o]

On November 28, 1919, Malvy's case was referred to a High Court of the Senate for inqury, then trial. The motion deciding this incorporated parts of Daudet's letter, and the debate did not fail to recognize his role. On December 11, the Chamber removed parliamentary immunity from Caillaux. The Radical leader had imprudently expressed the view that a negotiated peace was preferable to a long-drawn-out war; worse still, he had compromising friends and connections and had not been able to prevent their being used against him. Even more than Malvy's, Caillaux's impeachment was the reflection of political feuds dressed up as *raison d'état*; but since the autumn of 1914 the *Action française* had insisted on the Radical leader's moral collusion with the Germans. Now, it seemed clear that the paper had been right all along. It dominated public opinion, or could be said to represent it. When Clemenceau warned Parliament that public opinion was wrought up and demanded executions, a Socialist retorted, "Who unleashed it? The *Action française* of Daudet and Maurras!"[37] Caillaux's arrest in January 1918 seemed to confirm the justice of such patriotic intuitions. The left-wing press attributed the decision

---

instructed all members and friends to abstain from demonstrations against defeatists being organized at the Concorde and on the Left Bank, advising them that order should come before all other concerns. Against the story is Georges Wurmser's letter of February 21, 1961: "Il n'y a eu aucun lien d'aucune sorte à aucun moment entre Clemenceau et l'Action française." In a more detailed interview, M. Wurmser maintained and emphasized this assertion. All the other actual witnesses are dead.

[o] *La Libre Parole,* Nov. 10, 1907; *AF,* Aug. 19, 1915, Aug. 27, 1916, Sept. 1, 1917, April 5, 11, 1918. Maurras himself never quite changed his mind; as his correspondence with Poincaré shows, he regretted seeing Clemenceau in power and especially representing French interests at the Peace Conference. Some years later, however, after the break between the Action Française and the supporters of Georges Valois, rumors began to circulate about subsidies that Mandel was said to have paid the royalists during Clemenceau's tenure of power. Marcel Bucard of the *Nouveau Siècle* claimed to have had the story from Tardieu; another supporter of the Faisceau asserted he had heard it from Réal del Sarte. See F[7] 13198, Jan. 9, 1926.

to arrest Caillaux to Daudet's campaigns and Clemenceau's desire to please the royalists.[p]

Clemenceau cared very little about the royalists, and it is not likely that he gave their desires much thought. The coincidence, however, was striking, and Clemenceau's Socialist and Radical opponents did all they could to stress it. It suited them to denounce Clemenceau's campaigns as identical to, perhaps inspired by, those of the arch-reactionaries. But it suited the royalists, too, for they could enjoy the feeling of influence that this implied and bask in the popularity of policies far more widely noticed and approved than their own had been.

The opposition's hostility was shown more clearly in a debate that took place four days after Caillaux's arrest. On this occasion a motion singling the royalists out as the chief menace to internal peace was almost approved despite Clemenceau's clearly expressed wish to the contrary. The Premier had to introduce the question of confidence before the Chamber would extend the censure meant for the Action Française to "others" who also tended to divide the country. But if the Action Française had powerful enemies, it had strong supporters as well. A moderate, Charles de Boury, said in the debate: "There were many of us who held the *Action française* in horror; it is not our fault that it has been made attractive to us." To which Poncet replied: "That implies, M. de Boury, that your republican convictions were not very solid, and that those who doubted your *ralliement* were right."[38] But it was not Boury's anti-republicanism that made him sympathetic to the *Action française* during the war; it was his dislike of the men the newspaper attacked and his appreciation of the patriotic work accomplished by these attacks.

When the treason cases eventually came to court, these feelings reached their height. In April 1918 the trial of the *Bonnet rouge* band and of Malvy's right-hand man, the former Prefect Jean Leymarie, appeared as the logical, necessary, and salutary end of the *Action française* campaign against them.[q] Malvy's trial and conviction the following July brought fresh triumphs: "Daudet and Maurras have done as much as Clemenceau to uncover Malvy, and

[p] Cf. *L'Humanité, Journal du peuple, AF,* Jan. 15, 1918. See, however, the "Rubicon" plans, akin in their unreality to the Action Française's own, discovered in Caillaux's safe-deposit box in Florence. They included the arrest of leading personalities, the dissolution of Parliament, the occupation of Paris by loyal troops, and also a plan for "having the men of the Action Française and their accomplices on the large-circulation newspapers arrested and brought to trial." At his trial (see *Revue des causes célèbres,* 1920, pp. 180, 368–71, 418) Caillaux spoke very seriously of the potential danger of the Action Française to the Republic, and expressed the wish that republican bands could be set up to counter the Camelots du Roi.

[q] Maunoury, *Police de guerre,* p. 141, says that the Colonel presiding over the Court was a member of the Action Française. It is interesting that General Dubail's report of December 10, 1917, in which the military governor of Paris requested the Chamber to suspend Caillaux's Parliamentary immunity, mentions the *Bonnet rouge* only as *Le Torchon,* using the sobriquet applied to it by the *Action française.* Is it possible that the officer who drew up the report knew the activities of the *Bonnet rouge* only from accounts in the royalist paper? See the report in *Revue des causes célèbres,* 1920, pp. 158, 160.

they had the merit of being first to start." According to Albert Thomas, one had only to read a copy of the *Action française* to know what would be the tone and spirit of the morrow's press.[r]

Naturally, in such a friendly atmosphere, the business of the League was looking up. Under Dimier's guidance the Institute continued to offer regular courses. In hospitals and barracks, even at the Front, the paper circulated, infuriated, proselytized. In 1916, all officers of the 233d Infantry Regiment had simultaneously received free subscriptions to the *Action française*,[39] and there is no reason to think this an isolated case. The results were not always predictable, but the public grew. In 1917, the *Action française* lost 3,254 subscribers and gained 10,516, a net increase of 7,262. Marcel Proust, André Gide, the poet Joachim Gasquet, the young historian Augustin Cochin, Auguste Rodin—all read and admired the paper. Guillaume Apollinaire, who appreciated Maurras for his literary talent, devoted his last review to praising Maurras's "Ode à la bataille de la Marne," comparing its author to Pindar and Ronsard.[s]

Articles, hostile or admiring, bore witness to the movement's growing importance. Its enemies complained that integral nationalism was being supported by a host of Paris papers (*L'Echo, Le Figaro, L'Excelsior,* where Bourget, Bainville, and Capus had a foot in the door; *La Liberté, L'Intransigeant,* and *La Croix,* "acquises à toute une partie du programme de *l'Action française*"), by provincial satellites (of which the Toulouse *Télégramme,* the *Soleil du Midi* at Marseille, and *L'Eclair* at Montpellier were the most important), and by numerous periodicals. The Jesuit *Etudes religieuses* was sympathetic, the *Mercure de France* was considered so, and so, for a while, was the *NRF* itself.[40] In September 1917, when Barrès presented to the readers of *L'Echo de Paris* a new league founded to ensure a "French peace" of restitution and reparations, its republican complexion guaranteed by sponsors like Léon Bourgeois, Ernest Lavisse, François Aulard, and Charles Seignobos, his article was one long panegyric of Charles Maurras, who had foreseen the dangers of intellectual and moral corruption from across the Rhine.[41]

Even the money was rolling in. A call for a million francs made on De-

[r] *Revue des causes célèbres,* May 16, 1918, p. 72; *ibid.,* July 28, 1918, p. 13; Maurras, *La Contre-révolution spontanée,* p. 165; *Pour un jeune français,* p. 136; Dimier, *Vingt Ans,* p. 279. Xavier Vallat, *Charles Maurras,* p. 41, claims that Albert Thomas's mistress was the sister of a member of the Action Française whom he knew well and who later became one of General de Castelnau's assistants. By way of this convenient connection, Vallat says, Maurras and Thomas, who was first Minister of Armaments and then director of the International Labor Office, exchanged certain messages concerning proposed political moves and press campaigns. This seems to be confirmed by statements in letters exchanged after the war between Maurras and Poincaré.

[s] *AF,* Jan. 1, 1918; Proust, *Contre Sainte-Beuve* (1954), pp. 438–41; *AF,* July 10, 1916; Rodin to Léon Daudet (F. D. papers); *Mercure de France,* Nov. 1, 1918. Toward the end of the war, Apollinaire, still hospitalized with his head wound, wrote Daudet to congratulate him on his new book, *L'Hérédo,* and to offer to help him in his patriotic campaigns: "Il faut bien que ceux qui sont de votre avis vous aident." "Vous pouvez toujours correspondre avec moi," he added in a postscript, "par la voie du journal sous le vocable *trépané*."

cember 16, 1917, had by the 31st brought in a quarter of that sum. The *Canard enchaîné* maliciously began to print lists to parallel those that filled the royalist paper's pages:

L. M. Luçon, archevêque	50.00
"Vive le Roi!" 2 écoliers (prélevé sur leur petit goûter)	0.15
Général Serrefilles	1.00
Bloch, Aaron, curé de St.-Jean	2.00
Vicomte Sosthène de la Clé de la Porte du Parc	10.00
Mlle Tarte (2e versement)	3.50
Pour que la République crève	3.50
Mlle Hivnani Troulalahijan. "La France aux Français."	10.00
Pour le Roy. Vive Philippe IX!	5.00
	85.15

Manque encore 2.999.914 francs et 85 centimes. Courage!
A nous les millions! On les aura![42]

More symbolically perhaps, the new-found prosperity was reflected in new and more prosperous-looking offices. Until 1908 Action Française headquarters had been situated on the Left Bank, in the rue du Bac. They were moved in that year to No. 3 Chaussée d'Antin, and thence in 1910 to equally dingy quarters in the rue Caumartin, also not far from the Opéra. In February 1917 the League moved again, to a more spacious building opposite the Gare Saint-Lazare, Nos. 12 and 14 rue de Rome, where it would remain for the next fourteen years.

Some of the earliest leaders did not live to see the rue de Rome. Jules Lemaître died within a few days of the outbreak of the war. Léon de Montesquiou was killed in action a year later. So was Octave de Barral, president of the Paris Federation of the League. Henri Vaugeois died in April 1916, hardly past fifty, leaving behind him a much younger widow and many regrets. Daudet and Maurras now found themselves alone at the head of the movement, accompanied by several only slightly lesser lights, some of which time would dim, others render brighter—Bainville, Dimier, Pujo, Plateau. The important question was in what direction they would lead a movement that seemed in so short a time to have reached such unexpected heights.

PART II: THE GOLDEN DAYS OF PEACE

On oubliera. L'oubli est en train.

CHARLES MAURRAS, FEBRUARY 2, 1918

5

FOREIGN POLICY, 1918-1925

WHEN BUGLES SOUNDED AND church bells pealed on the 11th of November, 1918, to mark the end of fifty-one months of war, it was the *Canard enchaîné* that expressed the dominant feeling when it headlined simply "OUF!" The *Action française* was one of the few newspapers to realize that the Armistice marked no more than a suspension of hostilities—to what purpose and for how long, the decisions of the next few months would tell. All the energies of the royalists were henceforth turned toward securing a "French peace," one that would in their eyes best serve the country's interests. For a long time their opinion of what these interests were agreed with that of the patriotic Right, and it emerged as the most forceful expression of an uncompromising policy which had a brief fruition in 1923 with the occupation of the Ruhr.

In November 1918, however, the solution of 1923 was still far away, and the royalist view of peace conditions was far more stringent. It called for the division of Germany, the annexation by France of Landau and the Saar, and something like a French protectorate over the other Rhineland regions.[1] National self-determination was not a general principle to be used without discrimination, but one to be considered empirically, in terms of Allied interests. Germany's eastern neighbors had to be helped because this would serve the interests of France, but Germany herself must be weakened. It was naïve to fear a possible Bolshevization of Germany by the Spartacists or others acting in the wake of amputations and humiliations that had debilitated the ruling conservatives; on the contrary, revolution in Berlin would speed the disintegration of the Reich, which was what all Frenchmen should wish for, not reconstitution under any government whatever.

Jacques Bainville, more lucid than most, warned that fear of Bolshevism was no reason to permit German reorganization. Bolshevism was a new force to be reckoned with in international calculations, but it did not change the basic relationship between Germany and the rest of the Western world. Between Germany and France, there still remained the problems of Alsace and "the never ending dispute for the Rhine."[2]

Nor was the League of Nations anything more than a dead formula out of a dead past. To put one's faith in European unity was vain. European unity, in so far as it had existed, had been a remnant of the Christian unity that was shattered by the Reformation. A society of nations could be reconstituted only after a community of thought and spirit had been recreated. Until then, international relations would continue to depend on separate national units, which the growing division of languages, cultures, and points of view showed to be increasing in number rather than diminishing. The *Action française* regarded the League's begetter, President Wilson, with suspicion, and, after a while, found his determination to make peace on terms that would ruin France explicable only by his being a disguised agent of Germany and the Elders of Zion.[a] Beset by general stupidity and international conspiracy, France, the *Action française* insisted, must in no way lower her guard. Only a strong air force and a strong regular army could prevent the Germans from seeking their revenge as the Prussians had done after their defeat at Iena.[3]

There had been a brief hope that Germany would not accept the "mad and deplorable" treaty terms the Allies sought to impose: early in 1919, it looked as if hostilities might again break out.[b] But nothing happened. The Germans knuckled under. The peace treaty was signed, too weak in its severity, too severe in its weakness, as Bainville would say, and it was greeted with mitigated joy.[4]

Having failed to weaken Germany territorially, the French could still hope to weaken it by severe reparations. Reparations were meant to be what the word implied: compensation and, to some extent, atonement for damage. Of what the war had cost France—an estimated 210 billion—only 32 billion had been covered by normal budgetary means. In the German-occupied areas of the north, 893,792 buildings had been damaged or destroyed, 9,332 factories had been destroyed, 200 mines had been put out of production, and two million acres of land had been devastated and must be restored before they could again be productive. To France, which knew that Germany had been the aggressor, the principle of reparations seemed eminently just. But Bainville did not hesitate to proclaim that the reparations must not only repay France but also weaken Germany.[c] Properly used, they might perhaps achieve that end.

[a] There was already a hint of this on March 25, 1917. In February 1920 the attacks on Wilson began to include his second wife, who was described as a German, the sister of Masaryk, and the power behind all the current anti-French and anti-Italian plots. When the New York *Herald* explained that the former Miss Bolling was generally supposed to be a descendant of Pocahontas, the *AF,* February 28, 1920, accepted the correction, persuaded by the thought that her royal blood guaranteed integrity, but it added that President Masaryk had married an American—"Would it be a relative of Mrs. Wilson?" In *AF,* March 14, 1921, Maurice Talmeyr referred to Wilson as having been a well-known agent of Germany and of Jewish interests since before 1914.

[b] *AF,* July 24, 1920. Glandy, *Maxime Réal del Sarte,* p. 82, quotes a letter of the Duc d'Orléans to Réal del Sarte, dated February 18, 1919, asking him to intercede on his behalf with Clemenceau should war break out once more: "Si l'armistice est dénoncé, si la guerre se réveille, je demande instamment à M. Clemenceau de ne pas mettre d'opposition aux nouvelles démarches que je pourrais faire pour aller rejoindre les armées et me battre pour la France . . . j'irai n'importe où."

[c] *AF,* Jan. 2, 1922. The amount of income from reparations was consistently subordinated to the need of curtailing the power of Germany by reducing the amount of its territory; see, e.g.,

To use them properly, however, the stress had to be placed on other ends than Machiavellian ones. Inherent justice and national need were called upon to secure what *sacro egoismo* might not have seemed to warrant. "The most elementary justice requires Germany to make good the damages for which she is responsible," wrote a member of the Lyon branch of the Action Française. "The French have shed enough blood not to be called on to give their gold." "Solvent or not, the Boche shall pay because he must," declared Maurras. If France needed supplies that Germany could not at once provide, not taxes on capital or income but forced loans, backed by expectations of future reparations income from Germany, would be the right solution. A tax would imply that the legislators were not expecting Germany to pay. "All the responsibilities are the enemy's; consequently, so are the costs." Above all, one should be careful not to speak in terms of a definite figure: "However high, it might still be letting the Germans off too lightly."[5]

A more moderate suggestion came from an *Action française* reader who explained in detail how a war debt of 150 billion, payable (with interest) at 12 billion a year, could be settled in no more than half a century.[6] But this was a game that most of the press was playing. *L'Avenir du Loir-et-Cher* said it would settle for 10 billion a year, to be paid within "twenty, forty, or fifty years—however much time is needed"; *Le Matin* calculated that Germany's debt should amount to over 300 billion, which, at 6 per cent interest, could be an income of 19 billion a year for a long, long time.[7]

The question of how the payments should be made was less easily answered. Germany must pay, but France was warned to look out for an influx of German goods. Germany should help rebuild the devastated north, but without deriving employment thereby for its own workers and profits for its industries.[8] The impasse was insoluble: Germany must become prosperous to pay her debts. But once prosperous, she would have not only the means to pay her debts but the power to refuse to pay them. It therefore seemed clear that France would receive her due only if she were strong enough to enforce payment. The vicious circle applied not only to reparations but to the budgetary balance: if reparations were first and foremost a question of force, if payments depended on an Army sufficient to intimidate the debtor, then France would need a vast military budget in order to ensure a balanced general budget.

Since the balancing of both a huge military budget and a general budget by revising the tax structure could have been interpreted, as the *Action française* had warned, as foregoing claims for compensation, the government financed the necessary expenses of the reparations policy with money bor-

---

AF, Jan. 27, 1920. Five years later (Sept. 26, 1925) Bainville could wryly point out how right he had been in refusing to take long-range reparation schemes seriously: far from having lasted sixty-two years, reparations were already dead. Other, equally thoughtful Frenchmen perceived the danger implicit in the reparations-revival equation, but none so clearly or so soon as he. See also Philippe Berthelot's letter to Briand, quoted by Pierre Renouvin, *Histoire des relations internationales*, VII (1957), 236, but dating from January 1923.

rowed on an income that was never received. Inflation inevitably followed, and it not only weakened the economy of France but also limited her ability to enforce the collection of reparations from her defaulting debtors; she was forced to make concessions, and the whole policy of reparations became a costly failure.

The realities of the situation as it developed, however, had to be hidden from a country that was sure both justice and power were on its side. Concession after concession had to be presented to the public as hard-driven bargains. For a long time French and German nationalists would go on talking of all the golden billions, some indignant that they had not yet been paid, others that they should still be mentioned; but by refusing to face the facts France lost both moral and material advantages. Not even Bainville could explain how Germany could be made to pay without being driven to ruin, or, if she were saved from ruin, tell how to make her pay. In the end, foolishly exaggerated nationalist claims and the vacillating pusillanimity of governments influenced by nationalist arguments combined to give France the worst of a bad deal.[9]

All this was soon to be reflected in an economic crisis which, although not actually attributable to it or restricted to France alone, served to heighten the anxieties of those who feared an early German bid for revenge. The end of war, the need for reconstruction and for the rebuilding of stocks of raw material and food, the easy availability of foreign credit, and the maintenance of high wartime wages had resulted in a brief production boom in 1919–20, accompanied by galloping inflation. The Price Index, based on the average of 1901–10, with a mean of 100 for those years, had stood at 118 in 1914. By the end of the war prices had nearly quadrupled; the Index rose to 392 in 1918, to 412 in 1919, and to 589 in 1920.[10]

With the cutting off of American credit, the departure of heavy-spending foreign troops, and the satisfying of the most urgent needs in equipment and consumer goods, the market began to shrink and prices fell, but not sufficiently to stimulate demand. Heavy industry was seriously affected, and retailers who had bought stock when prices were inflated held on grimly waiting for better times, held on and went down to bankruptcy or into liquidation with the wry satisfaction of not having marked down a single item. As 1920 turned into 1921, the bankruptcy rate rose steeply, and unemployment rose along with it. We shall see later that the *Action française* did not fail to draw the political lessons of all this in its own way. It was possible to blame even these economic difficulties on the ill will and the delay with which Germany fulfilled her treaty obligations.

Things might have been different but for the troublesome Allies, particularly the British, who refused to envisage either a Europe dominated by France, or a Germany entirely ruined. British foreign policy, Bainville pointed out, which was determined by British interests, was ready enough to sacrifice the interests of others. France could balance her budgets only by collecting her war debts from Germany, but for Britain this was tantamount to economic paralysis in central Europe: a paralyzed Germany would mean a loss of trade and profits, and, in turn, trouble for the British budget. In such circumstances, Bainville realized, an understanding must be supremely difficult, and all the more so since it would have to be a compromise; a compromise implies sacrifices, and France had made too many sacrifices already to tolerate any more.[11]

What actually was needed, it would seem, regardless of the falling price of coal, was a firmer stand all around. By the beginning of 1920, the British ally, still prized a few months before, had begun to irk, and soon annoyance turned to vexation. "To whom does the *Daily Telegraph* think it is talking? To idiots, to debtors, or to children?" asked Bainville, and he warned against the dangers of the Anglo-Saxon delusion that Germany could be conciliated by being allowed to remain big and strong: "It all leads straight to another war and to a German-Russian alliance." By April, Bainville was urging that France go it alone: "Nous retrouverons toujours l'Angleterre." It was good advice, but, given the economic situation, not easy to follow.[12] In December 1920, Daudet insisted: "Il faut occuper et encercler la Ruhr." His was the most forceful voice in a concert that soon drove the moderate Leygues cabinet out of office as not strict enough in its defense of treaty terms.[13] The influential *Temps* had by now been convinced: "The more we cede," it wrote, "the more the Germans ask . . . We must, if we are not to be ruined, seize the reparations money where it is to be found—in Germany." And Bainville insisted: "We must make up our minds to occupy the Ruhr."[14] In pursuit of this policy during the course of the year 1921, the *Action française* turned with increasing violence against the British and against the principal supporter of British policy in France, "the sometime pimp and revolutionary" Premier Briand.

Every time France sought to apply against Germany the sanctions foreseen in the Treaty of Versailles, said Bainville, subsequent inter-Allied conferences and commissions settled things at her expense. The Belgians came off well (although this was not surprising, since Belgium was a monarchy); the British came off well; and France was left to pay the piper. Inevitably, it would all result in directing German hostility against France alone, without France's receiving any assurances of money or security. All that the "British party," which stood for better Franco-German relations, could show for its policy was a long series of losses and concessions. For the sake of the alliance, the Republic had sacrificed the Rhine frontier, reparations, a fleet, an army, even independence. It had accepted and aggravated the risks of war, bankruptcy, and revolution. The reason for all this was obvious: the republic was the government of the foreigner—British, Jewish, Bolshevik, and German.[15]

Such resentments reached a boiling point in 1921, when the ghost of reparations rose once more to bedevil French affairs. After Germany defaulted on her reparations payments in the spring of 1921 and appeared determined not to fulfill her commitments, it became increasingly clear that Britain might favor a moratorium. Briand himself inclined toward a policy of conciliation, which, by easing German resentments and strengthening the German peace party, would favor the recovery of the defeated and secure the support of the estranged ally. The French public, on the other hand, tended to think that British friendship bought at the cost of lost reparations and a revived Germany would be dearly bought indeed. It was against this background that, on January 10, 1922, Daudet, now a deputy from Paris, proposed in the Chamber that Briand be recalled from Cannes, where he was attending the Allied conference on reparations. What time limits were being set on a moratorium, Daudet asked, what guarantees were being secured in exchange for more concessions? Let Briand leave the golf course and salons of Cannes for a special sitting on the morrow, where he could reassure the Chamber that no compromises would result from his doubtful maneuvers. Two hundred forty-nine deputies voted for Daudet's motion, only 334 against. In a year of decisive majorities, this was the first serious challenge that Briand's German policy had yet encountered.[16] Briand returned to Paris in haste and promptly resigned, to be succeeded by Poincaré, who was firmly opposed to gratuitous concessions.

Briand's fall—or Briand's departure, for he may well have chosen to leave office on an issue raised by the Right which would make him increasingly available to the Left—had repercussions throughout Europe. In Britain the Conservatives attacked Lloyd George for his excessive friendliness to Germany and to the left-wing friends of Germany. In Italy, Romania, Germany, Poland, Austria, and Greece, governments fell or foreign ministers were replaced. A whole political orientation was coming to an end, and the end reflected a noticeable shift in international public opinion. This was soon seen in the firmer stands of Poincaré and the German Chancellor Joseph Wirth, and finally, in April, in the failure of the International Conference at Genoa. On Easter Sunday, April 16, the German and Russian delegations, at a private meeting in nearby Rapallo, signed a separate treaty renouncing all mutual reparations claims and re-establishing normal consular and diplomatic relations. As a result, the general prospects of the conference were damaged, although the meetings actually broke up over the question of foreign-owned property in Russia.

The royalists in France, along with many other observers, saw the Treaty of Rapallo as bearing out their predictions. Two years before, Bainville had warned against the danger of a Russo-German alliance and had called for measures which, in harming Germany, would also strike at Bolshevism.[17] To the *Popolo d'Italia,* the *Action française* was now the voice of French public sentiment: "The man in the street plainly echoes what the paper writes."[18] The *Petit Havre* praised Maurras and his paper for having foreseen the crisis and having pleaded for the policy the government now planned to follow: "Bainville's word carries authority not only in royalist circles but in many republican publications from the *Liberté* to the *Revue des Deux Mondes,* in which Poincaré has often paid tribute to his discernment."[19] Daudet noted with satisfaction the astounding progress of integral nationalism, to an extent unmatched by either Boulangism or the Patrie Française.[20] For Bainville, the implications were clear: "We must make up our mind to it. We are the most reactionary country in the world. Let us, then, boldly become the leaders of reaction. In the Europe of today, this is the reason for our existence." The inevitable outcry this raised in the left-wing press showed that for the moment his statement seemed pretty close to the truth.[21] When, at the end of May 1922, a great debate in the Chamber raked over all the questions of general policy, the question of occupying the Ruhr was in the air, and Edouard Herriot, rising to criticize Poincaré's anti-democratic stand, could find no better symbol for the ideas he wanted to oppose than Maurras's own "politique d'abord."[22]

But, as it turned out, the Action Française had no more helpful agents than the Germans and the British themselves. Although Maurras strenuously advised the use of force, there is no evidence to show that Poincaré contemplated such action except as a last resort. The Germans, with British encouragement, forced him to it by their repeated refusals to make their payments and deliveries on time. Poincaré had declared that France would not proceed with the payment of her inter-Allied debts until Germany paid the amounts owing under the Treaty of Versailles; nor would France agree to suspend payments without some security to guarantee that such payments would eventually be made. British proposals completely ignored French demands; to Poincaré they seemed to lead the way toward a revival of German supremacy in Europe. In late December 1922, the Reparations Commission, under French pressure, announced that a German failure to deliver shipments of wood and coal had been intentional and that the case was clearly one in which the Allied powers might take other measures as needed. Accordingly, Poincaré at last conceded the necessity of what others had long predicted, and on January 11, 1923, French and Belgian troops entered the Ruhr.

Although Sir John Bradbury of the British Treasury declared that wood had never been so misused since the Trojan horse, Poincaré's decision seems fully justified. It can be argued that the arrangements at Versailles should have been revised, and it can be shown that the French themselves had not made the most of the possibilities of reparations. But even though France, partly from bureaucratic inertia, partly to protect home industries, had failed to place orders to the limit of the French quota, this could only mitigate the burden Germany complained of. Further, any proposal to revise the treaty, to which in any case a majority of Frenchmen was opposed, only made sense coming together with some *quid pro quo*. In the final analysis, responsibility for the breakdown of 1923 must be laid in greatest part to German inertia and ill will, to some extent to Britain's policy of readiness to cede other nations' rights, and least of all to Poincaré's stubborn insistence on the letter of the law.[23]

Bainville was exultant: "We have at last recovered our freedom." But freedom proved to be a cold and costly state. England was hostile, Belgium and Italy halfhearted, the French Left menacing, international finance unfriendly, and the Pope disapproving.[24] Germany, resisting in the Ruhr, showed signs of deeper trouble. In October the return of the Crown Prince to his homeland started talk of a possible Hohenzollern restoration. At the beginning of November, the Ludendorff-Hitler putsch in Munich raised up the bogey of a military dictatorship. In such circumstances, the French policy of going it alone began to seem too risky. "A country must have the army of its policies," André Maginot had said at the start of the occupation. But France could not afford the army, and Parliament began to wonder whether it could afford the policy. "Heroic times are over," wrote the influential Léon Bailby in *L'Intransigeant*; "With elections still a year off, most deputies are thinking less of the Ruhr than of their campaigns."[25]

Poincaré was not himself concerned about the elections—although some members of his majority thought he should be—but he knew that France was in a bad position economically and strategically. Just when the Ruhr gamble seemed about to pay off, he gave up. In exchange for much-needed foreign financial support, he accepted a new reparations settlement and a milder German policy. It was the end of the strict application of the Versailles Treaty.

The new trend would be ratified by the Left-dominated elections of 1924, and symbolized by the Locarno Pact of 1925, which, said Bainville, merely revived the difficulties from which war had come eleven years before. Its terms, concealing the true awkwardness of the situation, would serve as chloroform to put to sleep those who had reason to fear for their security. Of course, France retained the right to intervene if, for instance, Poland were to be attacked. But would France ever be apt to make use of such a right? Even should she want to, she would no doubt lack the military means, since one could guess that the treaty would hasten disarmament—at least on the French side.[26]

There is no question that here Bainville was right. Far from showing generous or enlightened statesmanship, the Locarno Pact appears in retrospect as a failure of will, which encouraged fuzzy thinking and a shirking of urgent responsibilities. The *Action française* warned against these very dangers, but its conservative readers were too ready to cry over spilled milk and too helpless or afraid to do anything more. Three years earlier, on the signing of the Rapallo agreement, Maurras had cautioned, "Plus on se laissera faire et plus ce sera dur." But after November 1923 no one wanted to listen to Cassandra. The articles of the Locarno Pact gave reassurance; the British guarantee could be regarded as an excuse to ignore any remaining obligations. And the *Action française* would henceforth concentrate on remaining friendly with the least dependable of the signatories to the treaty, the Italy of Mussolini.

6

THE INTERNAL SCENE, 1918-1922

IN THE FIELD OF INTERNAL POLITICS, the Action Française had since the end of the war been enjoying a period of prosperity and progress. It was to score several marked successes before its credit and that of its policies would begin to wane.

Royalist prestige had never stood higher than at the end of the war. A cartoon of the victory parade showed Clemenceau, Poincaré, and Mandel astride a Pyrrhic elephant, with Daudet and Maurras following close behind, and lesser scribes like Barrès and Gustave Hervé bringing up the rear.[1] The royalists inspired gratitude and sympathy for their patriotic and pro-Catholic campaigns, delighted appreciation for their virulent, old-fashioned nationalism,[a] and a somewhat awed respect for the apparent power of a spy system that could intimidate even government officials. Malvy was in exile, his henchmen either dead, jailed, or awaiting trial. Caillaux, who had planned to arrest Action Française leaders and thus destroy the league, had himself been arrested and could fear for his life.[2]

Furthermore, the royalists now represented the most solid-looking bastion against the threats of revolution and disorder. Revolutions and uprisings, first in Russia, then in Germany and other countries in eastern and central Europe, had encouraged agitation in the west and persuaded the property-owning classes that such agitation should be taken seriously. Fear of social revolution had existed in France before the war; but it never seemed so strong or so justified as in the early 'twenties.

The industrial and money market boomed for a time, but continuing inflation brought serious difficulties at the end of 1918 and in the spring of 1919. The franc, which had been printed in paper notes to meet rising wartime needs, had lost three-quarters of its gold and silver backing. The Index of wholesale prices had risen from 100 in July 1914 to 346, which implied a 71 per cent fall in the internal buying power of the franc. Transport, which had been overstrained for years, was breaking down so completely that it was sometimes impossible to supply the devastated north with needed goods. Coal was in short supply, butter and eggs were both scarce and prohibitively

[a] See the letter in *AF,* July 19, 1919, from a reader who, having decided in 1917 to sample the paper that was the reason for so much fuss, had been delighted to rediscover "encore accentuée, ma *Libre Parole* d'antan."

expensive, sugar was a luxury item, and the price of meat kept rising. The black market flourished and even necessities became so costly that the government had to set up barracks in Paris to sell goods at reasonable prices, in hopes of forcing profiteering merchants into line. Finally, in the summer of 1919, a law was passed to regulate high prices, hoarding, and speculation.[b] But none of this prevented the ferment of hunger and distress from boiling over in a series of strikes and demonstrations.

In January 1919 there were strikes on the railroads and in public transport. In February Emile Cottin, an ex-anarchist carpenter turned Communist, attempted to murder Clemenceau. In March there was trouble among civil service employees. In April Jaurès's murderer, Raoul Villain, was acquitted "in the name of victory," and Cottin, who had only wounded Clemenceau, was condemned to death.[c] Trade-union membership was growing by leaps and bounds, their mood every day more threatening. People began to feel uneasy at the approach of May Day and laid in provisions just in case there might be trouble. Hoping to ward off serious disturbances, the government proposed the passing of the eight-hour law, which had been one of the basic aims of labor for nearly thirty years. Voted under the spur of fear, the law was enacted on April 23, but it was too late. On May 1 came the expected general strike, with bloody clashes between strikers and police, and casualties on both sides.

Of course the Action Française made the most of the disorders. It had always maintained that the Socialists were essentially unpatriotic, and now that the threat of revolution had been realized just across the border, now that general strikes and riots were shaming the country under the eyes of the foreign delegates who were gathered in Paris to prepare the peace, their old warnings took the tone of prophecy. Maurras could now reflect that things had changed. They had indeed! Relations with the authorities were excellent, especially in newly liberated Alsace and Lorraine, where freshly installed administrators, often military, regarded the royalists as valuable auxiliaries. One pamphlet, distributed both by the government in Alsace-Lorraine and by the royalists themselves, contained several passages extolling the Action Française influence and doctrine.[d]

The extent of Action Française power was acknowledged even by the opposition. The left-wing deputy Paul Meunier, who had long been an object

[b] An amendment inspired by electoral prudence provided that the law would not apply to agricultural enterprises.

[c] Cottin was given a reprieve at Clemenceau's request and was released from prison ten years later.

[d] *AF*, June 12, 28, 1919; Edmond de Mesnil, *Le Rappel*, July 22, 1919; *La France d'aujourd'hui* (1919), pp. 24–25, 29. See also Rémy Roure's story, quoted by Georges Arthuys in *Les Combattants* (1925), pp. 191–92, of meeting in 1918 a Catholic patriot who said that on his return home from a prisoner-of-war camp he had been utterly disgusted and disillusioned by the atmosphere he found: "Si je n'avais pas lu Maurras, me dit-il tout-à-coup, je serais bolcheviste."

of nationalist slander, declared, "The government rules by means of the Action Française, and the latter makes the most of its protection."[e] The national congress of the Radical and Radical-Socialist Party in September 1919 approved by acclamation a motion attacking Daudet by name and denouncing the royalist campaigns.[f] Further to the Left, Gustave Téry and Robert de Jouvenel presented Daudet's control of police and intelligence services as a threat to the regime: "Half the police force of the Republic is in the service, if not in the pay, of the King's Prosecutor," Téry wrote. Exaggerating for effect, he drew a chilling picture of the many-tentacled power in which the Ministry of War, the intelligence bureaus, and Daudet—*préfet de police in partibus*—worked closely together to the detriment of the Republic. The same sort of picture was the basis of the attacks of Paul Vaillant-Couturier, who concluded, as Sembat had done seven years before, that at the present moment one could be only royalist or Socialist, a partisan of the old order or of the new.[3]

Obviously, such critics meant to confuse the government and its allies, however diverse, by endowing the conservative and opportunistic Right with the characteristics of its most extreme wing, and by crediting the royalists with considerably more power than they actually had. What is interesting is that the royalists believed it. Indeed, the self-confidence acquired partly from such left-wing attacks played no small part in their decision to risk in the electoral races what they had won on the patriotic merry-go-rounds.

Electoral contests were something that integral nationalists professed to despise. Anti-democratic, anti-parliamentary, the expression of a *vox populi* far removed from that of God carried for them no attraction or prestige. Parliamentary action seemed vulgar and confused, resulting only in administrative chaos. Similarly, electoral propaganda was part of a vast process of democratic stupefaction. In actual practice, although it ran no candidates of its own, the Action Française had always supported its friends, especially in the west and the south, where a royalist tradition still existed. It had also worked for less positive allies, sometimes indeed for men with whom it had nothing at all in common except mutual hostility to another candidate. Before the war, at Chambéry, Dimier and the integral nationalist *Réveil savoyard* had caused the defeat of Radical Théodore Reinach, despite his having been a favorite on the second ballot. Similar pressures had defeated the Catholic liberal Henri Bazire at les Sables-d'Olonne, and Marc Sangnier.

During the 1914 elections, Action Française support, sometimes drummed up (as in Savoy) only before the second ballot, seems to have been decisive in many instances. Thus, at Rouen, Amédée Peyroux, whom the Action Fran-

[e] See Bonnefous, III, 292; *La Vérité,* Sept. 17, 21, 1919. Paul Meunier and his friend Mme Bernain de Ravisi were imprisoned on charges of intelligence with the enemy that were never substantiated; not until 1922 were they released and the charges against them dismissed.

[f] See *La Vérité,* Sept. 24, 29, 1919. One of the sponsors of the motion was Angelo Chiappe, a brother of Jean Chiappe, who later became a prefect and a friend of the Action Française.

çaise supported so that the Radicals would brand him "the royalists' candidate," sneaked by with a majority of 300; Jules Roche at Tournon in the Ardèche and François Arago at Cannes enlisted royalist notables like the Pampelonnes to help them; at Rueil-Malmaison in Seine-et-Oise, André Tardieu finally won after his campaign manager solicited the votes of the Action Française; in the Blaisois, where the Socialist candidate Joseph Paul-Boncour was defeated by only 34 votes, the Alliance Démocratique probably owed its narrow victory to the royalist support rallied for them by the *Avenir du Loir-et-Cher*. The same was true at Montargis (Loiret); in the eastern Pyrenees, where the *Eclair* of Montpellier and the *Rousillon* of Perpignan were influential; at Versailles, where Professor Thalamas had to be opposed at any cost; and at Nancy, where nationalist Catholics like Thierry de Ludre and Louis Marin benefited from royalist votes and Major Emile Driant received not only votes but subsidies as well.[4]

On the whole, however, Action Française intervention in prewar elections was negative, although it was effective in certain special contests where a small number of votes could be decisive. But many royalists did not really care for electoral activity,[g] and few, indeed, aside from those in the traditionally royalist regions, had built up even the most rudimentary electoral machine. This was something that professional politicians would take into account when weighing the importance of Action Française opposition or support, but it was something that Maurras and Daudet knew little about.

The elections of 1919 were dominated by the Bloc National, a conservative coalition directed against the mild leftism of the Radicals and against Socialist "Bolshevism." Old-school nationalists of various persuasions—Marcel Habert, who had been Déroulède's lieutenant, Maurice Barrès, the Bonapartist Paul de Cassagnac—joined the Bloc. Although precise evidence is lacking, it would appear that Maurras had thought to do as much.

In July 1919 certain unequivocal overtures of an alliance were rejected by *Le Temps* as too compromising, but early in August new advances met with a friendlier reception.[5] It may have been at this point, when the election lists for Paris were being drawn up, that Alfred Capus of *Le Figaro* appeared at Action Française offices in the rue de Rome with an offer of one or two places on the Bloc ticket in return for the cooperation of the Action Française, and, so the story goes, was refused by Maurras, who was not opposed to a deal but wanted better terms.[6] It is hard to know how much truth there is in the story, or whether anything would have come of the negotiations had Maurras been more responsive. But enthusiastic friends felt sure that the Action Française could send a hundred deputies to the new Chamber if it so wished, and Daudet seems to have shared their optimism.

[g] It is naïve to complain, as Dimier does (*Vingt Ans*, p. 241), of Paul Proust's ingratitude at Chambéry; the royalists intervened on Proust's behalf because they wanted to defeat his opponent, "the foreign Jew" Reinach.

The royalists made little effort to come to terms with other dissident groups, like the National-Socialists of Gustave Hervé and Alexandre Zévaès, who would have welcomed an alliance. They felt strong enough to stand alone.[7] They received support from the great *Croix* syndicate, which declined to ostracize them on republican grounds, and from patriotic conservatives who respected their consistency and their force. But it is clear that, acting on an incorrect estimate of their power, the Action Française leaders miscalculated: they might have got two or three seats on a deal, with a chance for better terms later. By acting on their own, they ended up with far less than that, and it cost them 800,000 francs.[8]

It has been contended that it was Millerand who kept the royalists off the Bloc ticket; it is likely that Millerand had a say in it and that a certain wing of republican nationalists, led by Marcel Habert, would not have welcomed competition from Maurras.[9] But royalism certainly counted for little, far less than more vulgar electoral considerations. The Duc d'Orléans had approved the idea of conservative collaboration, and to the very end, the program of the Union Nationale, as the Action Française called its ticket, gave not a hint of monarchism.[h] The program contained the following points: no amnesty for crimes against the fatherland; legislation to regulate immigration; a reduction of the three-year military service period and the organization of regular and specialized forces; the enactment of the *part du combattant*; a vigorous program to increase the birth rate; a reduction in the number of deputies and governmental departments; a change in budget procedure, reserving the initiative in allotting expenses to the executive; decentralization and regionalism in economic and administrative policies; the re-establishment of a French embassy to the Vatican; a settlement with the Holy See on outstanding religious problems; and the suppression of all measures that might interfere with the Church, the religious orders, or Church schools.

The program was aimed clearly and unequivocally at the patriotic, chauvinistic, conservative, and Catholic vote, and Action Française tickets were filed only in the three electoral divisions of Paris. A fourth ticket for the Paris suburbs was withdrawn on election eve in exchange for a promise of Bloc support in the forthcoming municipal elections. Similar bargains were struck in many provincial areas—Hérault, Vaucluse, Ardèche, and Vendée—where royalists and conservatives met on Union Nationale tickets. In Ille-et-Vilaine, an old republican colleague of Waldeck-Rousseau's ran on the Union Nationale ticket with royalists like Charles Ruellan and the Marquis de Kernier. In the Cher, Pierre Dubois de la Sablonière of the Bloc was elected with the

[h] See *AF*, July 20, Aug. 7, Oct. 4, 1919, and the *Almanach* of 1921. In *L'Honorable Léon Daudet*, pp. 89–90, André Gaucher, who is hostile but well-informed, affirms that Daudet's election in 1919 was achieved by playing down all aspects of royalism, avoiding the label, the slogans, and the songs of the Action Française *qua* monarchist, and singing only the "Marseillaise" at meetings. In fact, Daudet was probably elected for his personality, not for his ideas, beyond the general one of nationalism.

"devoted" help of the royalists of Berry. In Tarn-et-Garonne, a royalist sympathizer running as a Bloc candidate won with the broadest of right-wing support, only to move to the left when the times had changed.[10]

In at least twelve departments tickets of the National Union (Côtes-du-Nord, Cher, Basses-Pyrénées, Vendée, Ille-et-Vilaine, Loire Inférieure, Vaucluse), Republican and National Union (Haute-Garonne, Indre), Patriotic Union (Moselle), Republican and National Union (Ardèche), and the Action Française and National Union (Gironde) came out ahead of their competitors. Fewer than thirty candidates were elected who could be considered close to the Action Française—less than 5 per cent of a Chamber numbering 616. They were characteristically grouped in areas where royalist and Catholic faith was strongest and to this day most enduring: the white south (Vivarais, Comtat Venaissin, Gard, Hérault), the Pyrenean southwest, the west (Vendée, Poitou, Anjou, and Brittany), and the north (Ardennes, Nord).

It was not a brilliant result, and at first it seemed worse than it actually was. The directors of the Action Française had refused to agree to terms they thought unsatisfactory for political effectiveness. They had insisted that, isolated or with few supporters, the most resolute must fall, his voice be drowned out by Socialistic roars.[11] In the end, only a few provincial candidates won, and Léon Daudet was the only candidate to be elected in Paris, in which they had hoped for so much. Yet there were some compensations. Because the moderate and patriotic vote was split in Paris between the Action Française and the Bloc, some Socialists were unexpectedly elected and certain candidates of the Bloc left at the post.[12] More positively, though alone, Daudet would make himself heard. He became the moving spirit of the right-wing independents, the constant critic of all concessions to the internal or foreign enemies of France, the most forceful spokesman of extreme nationalism at a time when extreme nationalism was much in fashion.[i]

From the outset, the new deputy from Paris took the lead in trying to swing the rather loosely formed Bloc more definitely toward the right. He attracted notice by attacking Steeg, the Minister of the Interior in Millerand's cabinet, as being of German descent and, furthermore, the tutor—he alleged—of the

[i] See *L'Opinion,* September 1922, quoted in *AF,* Sept. 24, 1922. Xavier Vallat, in *Le Nez de Cléopâtre* (1957), p. 69, describes Daudet as the most powerful personality of that legislature, and says that the role he played in the Chamber was out of all proportion to his scanty support and isolated position. A similar judgment, and an attempt to explain the phenomenon, is to be found in Georges Bidault's important essay on the Action Française and foreign policy, in *Un Grand Débat,* pp. 147–74. The integral nationalists were to many, he says, the very symbol of patriotism. Under the pressure of royalist fervor and overbidding, other patriots could not but feel that if they failed to carry out Action Française ideas they were themselves falling short of true patriotism. This state of mind, says Bidault, explains why the Action Française enjoyed an influence that many did not suspect because it affected even those whose republican ideas were supposed to make them immune. As he goes on to remark on p. 149: "Parce que l'audience accordée . . . aux écrivains de l'Action Française, considérés comme les interprètes du patriotisme, ne se traduit pas par des adhésions en règle, on aurait tort de croire qu'une telle influence soit négligeable."

bastard offspring of the exiled Malvy and Malvy's former mistress, now deceased, who, he said, had been a German spy. He warned his right-wing friends to resist the pressure of the Left; he opposed government attempts to increase direct taxation, denouncing the unholy alliance of Socialist and banking interests which was bent on ruining defenseless property owners.[j]

Far from inclining to the Left, the majority in the Chamber was moving more and more to the Right. Daudet helped to polarize it. *Le Figaro* remarked, echoing previous Socialist opinions, that the strongest attractions tempting the Bloc were those of socialism and the Action Française.[13] There was little doubt to which the majority inclined. Serious labor troubles were once more plaguing the country. Railwaymen had struck in February and March 1920, and miners were out from March until the end of May. "Civic unions" were being organized to oppose the so-called Bolshevik threat, and in them the integral nationalists shared the leadership, frequently taking the lead and setting the tone. In April 1920, when the National Congress for the Social and Economic Reconstruction of France met under the presidency of Juliette Adam and Louis Marin, the speakers echoed what was then the line of the Action Française. Yet, although the Marquise de MacMahon was there, and Bernard de Vésins, other participants were republican nationalists like Lucien Millevoye and General Bailloud, who headed the Civic Unions in Lyon and Paris, and General Léon Durand, who was president of the largest veterans' organization, the Union Nationale des Combattants. If not all these Civic Unions were, as *L'Humanité* supposed, front organizations of the Action Française, they were at any rate inspired or led by royalist elements like the Camelots.[k]

As May Day approached and the CGT began agitating for a general strike, the bourgeoisie once more expected heads to roll. "Here comes the dreaded hour," one provincial, Joseph Lahille, wrote his daughter in Paris; "If on the first of May you ride [to the scaffold] in the fateful tumbrel, do it with grace." M. Lahille, with all his irony, was whistling in the dark. The strike did take place, as feared, and the clashes between troops and strikers left several dead and wounded. The government opened proceedings against the unions and arrested union leaders, a severe stand which the Left was sure must have been taken under royalist pressure. Behind Millerand and the government, wrote *L'Humanité,* stood Daudet.[14]

A few months earlier, in February, when the Marquis de Vogüé received

[j] *AF,* Jan. 25, 31, 1920, especially Bainville's warning against income taxes "designed solely to deprive [peasants], by underhand means, of their possessions and to confiscate the fruits of their labor."

[k] *AF,* April 8, 9, 16, 1920; *L'Humanité,* June 4, 1920. See also Manouvriez in *AF,* July 1, 1921, for his reply to *L'Ere nouvelle,* which had called royalist sections the "armature réelle" of the Civic Unions. The fact is that whenever conservatives and moderates needed active and hard-hitting auxiliaries against a real or fancied Red peril, they called upon the Camelots. See *AF,* June 22, 1921, for a Radical's doing this.

Marshal Foch into the Académie Française, a member of the public had commented, "C'est un discours d'Action française que je viens d'entendre." In the Brussels *Flambeau,* the veteran journalist Louis Dumont-Wilden referred to the Action Française movement as being so active that it was causing concern not only to the government but to conservative republican circles. A month later, against the fading echoes of the Kapp putsch stranded on a strike, over 12,000 people applauded Daudet at the opening of the Seventh Action Française Congress in Paris.[15]

Feared by some, alarming to others, the royalists seemed nonetheless handy to have around, a reassuring force against a common left-wing enemy, and Daudet's boasts that the Action Française and the Camelots were the main safeguard against a revolutionary attempt from the Left were echoed even by some elements of the left-wing press.[16] The alternative of socialism or monarchy appeared increasingly obvious. When in September 1920 the government, giving in to right-wing pressure and to the *Action française* campaign against the *Sedantag,* abandoned plans for an official celebration of the fiftieth anniversary of the Republic, Daudet had some reason to exult.[l] He had it again a little later, when the Chamber voted to restore diplomatic relations with the Holy See. The *Action française* had campaigned for this with the slogan that republican anti-clericalism had been a "German" policy—"Anti-clericalism is what the Germans want" read its posters all over Paris and Bordeaux. Now at least, though far from home, France was back on the right road.

Events soon belied such optimism, however. The Leygues cabinet, which was formed after Millerand was promoted to the Presidency, fell in January 1921 and was replaced by a cabinet of the Center Left headed by Aristide Briand, the royalists' *bête noire,* the only one of their chief enemies whom they had been unable to touch in 1917 and since, the focus of their loathing between the wars. Their fire had been aimed at him so steadily that some observers considered his first vote of confidence to be a vote against Daudet.[17] During Briand's year in office the Camelots pestered him with posters and tracts, almost drowning out the rival furor on behalf of Sacco and Vanzetti. And finally it was Daudet's pleasure to be the instrument of his fall. Although Daudet's motion which precipitated Briand's resignation was not, in fact, carried by the Right, it was a success of the most surprising sort, and when Briand arrived at the Gare de Lyon from Cannes he was met with whistles and catcalls by a crowd of jeering Camelots and students especially mobilized by the Action Française for the occasion.

There was no mistaking it this time: Daudet was becoming a cabinet-

[l] *AF,* Sept. 4, 1920. The royalists maintained that, rather than celebrating the end of the Second Empire and the beginning of the Third Republic, the republicans were really celebrating the surrender of Sedan. The Fiftieth Anniversary was officially celebrated on the Second Anniversary of the signing of the Armistice, when the body of an unknown French soldier was placed under the Arc de Triomphe.

killer, like Clemenceau before him. "One can criticize, detest, or admire M. Daudet," wrote *Le Temps* on February 25, "but one cannot deny that he is a power." At a great meeting in the Salle Wagram 8,000 people cheered Daudet's demand that the "agent of Anglo-German Jewry" be called to account before a High Court.[18] The apparent royalist ascendancy was further reflected a few months later in the turnout for the Joan of Arc's Day parade, which was more numerous and enthusiastic than ever before. Only a fraction of the marchers were of the Action Française, but the press attributed the success of the parade largely to them.[19]

In the government as well as in the press, the prestige of integral nationalism had reached a new high. It was said that prefects could be made and unmade at the word of the deputy from Paris. Some civil servants thought it politic to have their sons enlist in the royalist ranks. A left-wing publication complained that potential backers had withdrawn, frightened by Action Française attacks. Caricatures appeared of "His Almightiness Daudet."[m] In July, when all the sailors who were imprisoned after the revolt of the Black Sea fleet in 1919 were given amnesty except the Communist ringleader André Marty, it seemed once more as if the government were acting on the dictates of the rue de Rome. *L'Internationale* thought the cabinet was merely rubber-stamping Action Française formulas; Paul Faure in the *Populaire* wrote that it was the will of the Action Française that triumphed, the thesis of Maurras that the government ratified; the *Journal du peuple* saw Marty's staying in jail as the work of royalists; "The Republic at the orders of the King," said a headline in *L'Humanité*.[20] Other newspapers, like the *Liberté*, had also opposed Marty's release, but the *Action française* had become the symbol of all nefarious reaction; it was held responsible for all the victories of the Right, and this was a responsibility it shouldered gladly.

Among other things, henceforth, there would be attributed to the Action Française a new responsibility and a new idea—Fascism. The confusion of Italian politics since the end of the war had resulted in the rise of a new nationalist movement led by the veteran Socialist Benito Mussolini. Throughout 1921 and 1922, Mussolini's Fascist bands had pursued Socialists and Communists who only shortly before had been the terrors of northern Italy, shooting, beating, doping, and burning them out of every stronghold, and finally using the arms and the immunity afforded them by the Army to stage a bloodless make-believe march on Rome. Their swift rise to power could not fail to excite comment, and some admiration, in a neighbor that was also beset by labor troubles.

[m] *Bonsoir*, *L'Internationale*, July 9, 1922; *L'Ere nouvelle*, Sept. 3, 19, 21, 1922; *Le Populaire de Nantes*, Sept. 7; *AF*, July 9, 10, Sept. 8, 20, 21, 1922. Three years earlier a campaign of the *Action française* had prevented the appointment of a man of whom it disapproved as a French delegate to the Peace Conference. See *AF*, Jan. 16–18, 1919, and echoes in other newspapers such as *La Liberté* and *Le Rappel*.

Italian Fascism, Daudet explained, was no more than a reaction of national sentiments to the bestiality, stupidity, and noxiousness of Communism. Following a devastating war, the political tradition of the Italian people had been attacked head-on by a sort of murky Hebraic-Germano-Russian program of expropriation, spoliation, and internationalism. Now the true Italian spirit was fighting back. The analogy was obvious: similar causes might well produce the same effects. The French, also, were waiting for a leader, even a temporary one, who, coming at long last to chastise the traitors and the thieves, would distribute their ill-acquired wealth among deserving war veterans. Everybody knew, Daudet pursued, that it was not Millerand and Poincaré who were in control of France, but Rothschild, Finaly,[21] and the London Sassoons. Jewish and German financiers were the real revolutionary menace, from whom the nation could be saved by a civilian dictator acting in the name of the king.[22]

Both friendly and hostile observers took note of a similarity between integral nationalists and Fascists. Members of the Action Française hoped that Daudet would assume control in Paris as Mussolini had done in Rome; provincial commentators warned against the danger of a royalist coup. The *Populaire* of Nantes bewailed the strength of Daudet's position with the power of the Action Française behind him. Daudet was someone to be reckoned with, and any day, encouraged by Mussolini's success, he might attempt a coup.[n]

Such an idea seems to have occurred to Daudet himself. He received an enthusiastic response from a student audience when, talking about Mussolini, he asserted that the Action Française, too, would soon seize control by force—and the Fascist purges would be nothing beside what France would witness then.[23] This would not be done under Fascist inspiration, however, but as a result of the long-standing doctrine of the Action Française. "We imitate no one," Daudet explained a little querulously; "we are an outgrowth of no other movement, not even Italian Fascism, contemporary or past."[o]

In this he was probably right. André Lichtenberger, in his review of Pietro Gorgolini's book on Fascism, which, in a translation by Eugène Marsan issued by Georges Valois of the Nouvelle Librairie Nationale, first introduced the movement to France, says that Mussolini and d'Annunzio were really disciples of the French royalist movement. Other observers as well thought that Fascism had in many ways simply taken over the doctrines of integral nationalism.[24] Such assertions are considerably exaggerated, however. The ideas of the Action Française did contribute to the hodgepodge that sought to articulate the

[n] *Le Populaire,* Nov. 2, 1922, quoted in AF, Nov. 3. Ten days later, a subscription list included twenty francs sent by an artilleryman who said that he "would like to help the Action Française reach the same point as the *Fascio.*" See also *La Libre Opinion,* Feb. 18, 1923.

[o] *AF,* Jan. 29, 1923. Only a few weeks before Mussolini's march on Rome, on October 1, 1922, the *RU* (XI, 13) began installments of Daudet's *Sylla et son destin,* which, in its praise of Sylla as a man who did not separate the idea from the act "et, concevant juste, appliquait rude," provides the most faithful reflection of its author's political theories.

violence of eclectic Fascist activism, but many similarities were coincidental. The enemies of both movements were the same. Mussolini did not hesitate to describe himself as "Reactionary because anti-parliamentary, anti-democratic, and anti-socialist"; to define his principles as order, hierarchy, and discipline; and to call upon the State to abandon "attributions for which it is not fitted and which it fulfills badly."[25] But differences between the two movements were fundamental: although both had sprung from the same anti-democratic reaction, the one was as resolutely doctrinal and rationalistic as the other was churlishly anti-intellectual. And while the Action Française insisted on the dangers of centralization and State control, Mussolini aimed to capture the State and exploit its power to the full. There was a profound difference between Maurrassian *anti-étatisme* and the Fascist *statolatry* which Pius XI denounced in his Encyclical of June 29, 1931.[p]

It would be true to say that Italian nationalism in its early years strongly felt the influence of Maurras and Vaugeois; the Action Française had been in existence for some time when Luigi Federzoni, Francesco Coppola, and Enrico Corradini established *Il Regno* in Florence. This was succeeded by the daily *Idea nazionale,* which soon became the leading Italian nationalist publication. Its propaganda sought to make the liberal and republican patriotism of the Risorgimento distinct from a more authoritarian nationalism; it derided racial and ideological sentimentalism, promoted the idea of hierarchically and corporatively organized society, and opposed the concept of a struggle between nations to that of a struggle between classes.

In a recent study Salvatorelli and Mira suggest that the Italian nationalist movement drew its doctrinal and sentimental inspiration "above all from French nationalism à la Maurras." And while the nationalists were getting many of their ideas from the *Action française,* syndicalism was splitting into two movements: of workers, who were moving ever closer to revolutionary socialism, and of the intellectuals, grouped around Paolo Orano's *La Lupa,* who, like Berth and others in France, were moving toward a national-socialism of the Sorel-Maurras kind.[26]

That Fascism had a good deal in common with the ideas of the Action Française, the Fascists themselves recognized;[q] and so, necessarily, did the

[p] Mussolini, *Le Fascisme, doctrine et institutions* (1933), quoted in Guérin, p. 178: "The State is the absolute before which individuals and groups are merely relative . . . For the Fascist, all is in the State and nothing human or spiritual exists or has value outside the State."

[q] See Giacomo Lumbroso, *Gerarchia,* November 1923. In "L'Esprit fasciste en France," *Centre international d'études sur le fascisme, Etudes 1928* (The Hague, 1928), p. 179, Homem Christo says grudgingly: "Le fascisme a sans doute appris beaucoup de l'Action Française, qui en fut, sur le terrain spéculatif des idées, la glorieuse aînée. L'Action Française, par contre, n'apprit absolument rien du fascisme, et c'est grand dommage." The final comment apart, this puts the situation in a nutshell. When, in 1930, a leading local Fascist tried to persuade the Nice section of the Action Française to organize meetings in favor of Fascist policy, its president answered that integral nationalists could not support the Fascist form of government, which they found too centralizing and imperialistic. F^7 13202 (Alpes-Maritimes), June 4, 6, 13, 1930.

foes of Fascism like the Ligue des Droits de l'Homme, which during the spring of 1923 organized a series of meetings to fight the so-called French Fascism of the Action Française. The only ones who saw clearly that the differences between the two were more significant than their similarities were the Communists[27] and the royalist leaders themselves. We shall see how in the 'thirties the Action Française gave a great deal of thought to doctrines and enthusiasms that seemed attractive to their members—generally in order to stress the difference between such alien doctrines and their own. For the moment, the situation was simpler. For one thing, as Valois has pointed out, none of the leaders really believed that Fascism would last. Lacking themselves the decisive temperament of men of action, they rationalized their failure to go beyond words by explaining that since France was without a monarchy, it could not, like Italy, benefit from a Fascist revolution or withstand the perils of a Fascist regime.[28]

A Fascist temper did exist, it is true, among the rank and file. Younger men like Valois and Marsan who had been active in the national-socialism of prewar years, as well as veterans like Raymond Batardy to whom the idea of force had always appealed, would certainly have liked less talk and more action. The year 1923 was to be full of demonstrations inspired by events in Italy, all destined to come to nothing because the leaders were determined to avoid any violence that would offend the conservatives.

It is possible, also, that Poincaré's decision to occupy the Ruhr, coming only a few weeks after the march on Rome, drew their attention to more immediate matters. The Action Française was always much more national than insurrectionist. Poincaré's German policy and the success of the movement itself combined to make it quite "governmental" throughout most of 1923. Whatever the temptations and provocations—and we shall see that they were not lacking—the leaders were not ready for any action that might split the tenuous *union sacrée* of a difficult year.[r]

[r] Note that this policy in no way excluded witch hunts and anti-Marxist campaigns directed against "the internal enemy." See, e.g., *AF,* Aug. 17, 1922.

7

1923

As 1922 drew to a close and the press prepared to honor the new year with the usual predictions and post-mortems, a fashionable Pythoness and seer predicted that in 1923 "the royalist party which for a moment will have thought itself the master of the situation would soon see its hopes deceived." And, indeed, in the first days of 1923 the royalists felt that Poincaré, so long hesitant to adopt a definite political orientation, had at last decided to follow their advice by abandoning hopes of holding the uneasy Bloc majority together, and working openly with the Right. On January 11, the *Action française* thought it had cause to celebrate: "After three years, the Republic has conceded that the *Action Française* was right. It has arrested the Communist leaders. It has occupied the Ruhr."[1]

The policy the paper had tirelessly advocated appeared at last to have come into its own. It was hardly surprising that the Left attributed Poincaré's decisions to the influence of Maurras, but more moderate political observers like Eugène Lautier, who had taken over Clemenceau's *L'Homme libre,* did likewise; and even the sober political analyst Roger Mennevée referred to "the considerable influence Maurras and Daudet exercised on Poincaré."[2]

A superficial investigation of the still unsorted Maurras papers has uncovered traces of a correspondence between Maurras and Poincaré which the two men maintained at least from 1918 to 1925. In the sixteen letters so far found, Poincaré appears in the role of an appreciative reader of the royalist publicist, who seems to have presented him with copies of his works, both literary and political. Such meager evidence does not permit any but the most tentative conclusions about a relationship which rested, it would seem, on the mutual respect of two great patriots. As Poincaré explained in a letter of December 30, 1919, he made a distinction between the criticisms addressed to him: "Les uns ne soulèvent que mon mépris, parce que je sens bien comme vous qu'ils sont l'oeuvre directe ou indirecte de l'Allemagne; les autres me touchent, lorsqu'ils émanent de bons français." In the ensuing correspondence, the man who was then the President of the Republic went out of his way to provide Maurras "as discreetly as possible" with the explanations and the information that would justify his policies in the eyes of the royalist sage.

Poincaré answered Maurras's reproaches of injustice to the monarchy with copious quotations from Michelet, Lavisse, Laboulaye, and Guizot, protesting his impartiality and assuring him that he had never thought the Republic could enhance itself by minimizing France's great past (September 7, 1919). He explained at some length why it would be impossible to keep President Wilson out of the Peace Conference or to go himself instead of Clemenceau (December 29, 30, 1919). He also on occasion considered various more concrete matters brought to his attention by Maurras, and one of the first letters written from the study of his new private residence on February 18, 1920 (Paul Deschanel had taken office on the 17th) was to acquaint the royalist leader of his actions in the case of a prisoner on whose behalf Maurras had intervened.

The relationship developed in the Elysée grew beyond the epistolary stage between 1920 and 1922 as Poincaré, then once again Senator of the Meuse, became increasingly dissatisfied with his country's reparations policy. A number of notes and letters beginning in the spring of 1922 suggest that personal meetings were henceforth not infrequent and that Poincaré, busy though he was as Premier, continued to give Maurras advice and information and to welcome suggestions from Maurras in turn.

"Here are the explanations Official Services have furnished [in the matter you have raised]," he wrote on April 2, 1922, "including a remark of strictly confidential nature. I hope this will suffice for your information." "Il suffit que vous ayez à m'entretenir d' une question franco-belge pour que je me mette le plus tôt possible à votre disposition. Vous me trouverez demain Samedi à 6h ½ du soir." By the time these last lines were written, on June 2, 1922, his closing sentiments for Maurras had grown from "distinguished" to "devoted," a nuance revealing closer acquaintance if not greater intimacy. A few days later, on June 11, another note of a similar tenor accompanied "the last telegrams received from Munich," which he sent Maurras "à titre d'information personnelle." Still another letter, of January 1923, which refers to differences between French and British views of the reparations issue, mentions a M. de P——, who had relayed some "interesting information" from Maurras. This sort of exchange continues at least to the end of the year, with brief notes and more lengthy letters, the last of these dated December 30, 1923.[a]

It is safe to suppose that these fourteen letters are only a sample of a larger correspondence. The Premier's note of January 2, 1923, for instance, begins with an apology referring to a previous letter: "I wrote you in such haste this morning that I did not even thank you for your [New Year's] wishes." Three months later, on March 30, a hasty postscript acknowledges the receipt of a note from Maurras on an indecipherable subject (Poincaré's cramped hand is as hard to read at times as the spiny hieroglyphics of Maurras) : he has been attending to the matter for some weeks and promises to write soon. In the absence of the promised letter and, presumably, of a number of others, one retains the impression that there was between the two men a fairly close rela-

[a] Two letters of January 1925, concerning the death of Philippe Daudet, are not considered here.

tionship which, had it been known, might have proved embarrassing to the republican statesman.

There was, in fact, nothing improper about such a connection. What we know of Poincaré should be sufficient assurance that in his dealings with Maurras he disclosed no secrets of consequence and did not abuse his office in any way. He responded to the overtures of a like-minded person, accepted aid from and sometimes furnished it to a natural ally in the circumstances of the moment. A few years earlier the *Action française* had treated Poincaré with as little respect as it treated other republican politicians: "médiocre entre les médiocres," Daudet called him on March 19, 1909, "pauvre larve de portefeuille . . . qui n'a ni talent d'écrivain, ni caractère." Within a few years Daudet was hankering after a portfolio himself, and by January 10, 1921, Poincaré had become "la dernière carte du régime."

Between 1916 and 1923 Poincaré and the *Action française* found themselves on the same side: both mistrusted Germany, both stood for a strong reparations policy, both kept a weather eye cocked for any possibility of detaching the Rhineland from the Reich. It was natural that they should pull together, but such collaboration was not possible in the open, and the punctilious Poincaré showed his regard not only for Maurras's patriotism but for the influence of Maurras's movement when he maintained in private connections he could not admit in public.

None of this is sufficient justification for thinking that Maurras or Daudet exercised any particular influence on Poincaré. But for the moment, and as this chapter will show, the coincidence of their views was striking, and the Premier's stand on the Ruhr while it lasted could not but fill the royalists with glee.

In the *Action française* Daudet, after self-congratulations, praised his colleagues of the Bloc for having decided to move at last. He went on to suggest, not for the first time, that the Action Française could and should collaborate with a government of true patriots. He knew that the Bloc, careful of its republicanism, was wary of the Action Française because of its royalism. But, said Daudet, we are Frenchmen first. As Frenchmen and as nationalists, the members of the League could wholeheartedly join any combination that put such values first, and he was ready to assure his colleagues of the Bloc that the presence of a rightist from his group, presumably himself, in the key Ministry of the Interior would afford them satisfactions more thorough than even Mandel himself.[3]

But such high hopes, unfounded though they were, were soon dashed. On January 22, 1923, Marius Plateau, general secretary both of the Camelots and of the League, one of the movement's most active and devoted executives, was killed by a twenty-year-old Anarchist named Germaine Berton. The young woman had wanted, so she said, to avenge the deaths of Jaurès and Almereyda, had tried unsuccessfully to reach Daudet or Maurras, and had then fallen back on someone not of the first rank but more accessible. She obtained an interview with Plateau, fired several shots into him, and was quickly arrested, being either unwilling or unable to turn the gun against herself as she had first intended.

Events would show that Germaine Berton had aimed more justly than she knew in killing the man who stood at the center of much Action Française activity. But for the moment the murder of their chief infuriated the Camelots. A man who had been badly maimed in the war had survived only to die stupidly under the gun of a political assassin. They wanted revenge, and they turned upon the antagonists who had long called for an end to royalist violence, who had denounced their tightening grip on the regime, who—like the patriotic press before 1914—had singled out royalist leaders as a public menace. At first the Camelots vented their ire in the streets, but what began as demonstrations on the boulevards ended in the wrecking of the offices and printing shops of *L'Oeuvre* and of *L'Ere nouvelle,* then their most constant foes, and—since the offices were shared—of a third newspaper, *Bonsoir.* The premises were almost empty when they were attacked, so no one was hurt, but furniture, files, and linotypes were thoroughly smashed.

The riots and the smashings, perhaps less than completely spontaneous, were a mistake. Boisterous horseplay was all right; Camelot fury running wild was too ugly. It cost the Action Française whatever public sympathy it might have had. The violence served as a reminder that with Plateau's death it was only reaping, although with interest, some of the seeds it had sowed. Only a few days before Plateau's murder, a chansonnier named Lauff, who, like Plateau, had been wounded in the war and trepanned, had died, as the result, some papers said, of blows received in a brawl started by Camelots.[4] The Camelots were being fought on their own terms, remarked a Dutch observer. "Violence and murder have struck the house where daily violence is called for, political murder glorified," wrote the *Populaire.*[b] Provincial newspapers criticized both the crime and the reprisals. In reply, the *Action française* attacked the failure to distinguish between the crime and its just retribution and threatened action against those so obtuse or wicked as to confuse the two.[5]

Plateau's funeral was the occasion for a great demonstration; mourners in the thousands followed the coffin, filing through the wintry streets hour after hour in grim, impressive calm.[c]

[b] *Vaterland, Le Populaire,* Jan. 23, 1923. Commenting on the latter in *AF,* January 24, Robert Havard answered, "Must we repeat that certain acts of violence are necessary and noble?"

[c] As usual, there was disagreement on numbers. *AF,* February 3, 1923, claimed an attendance of about 200,000; *L'Eclair* of January 28 estimated 30,000; *Le Matin* of the same day spoke of an immense column marching along the streets for hours; the *Dépêche de Brest* of the 30th counted only "un millier de personnes et deux mille collégiens." The following month the Lille Socialist *Bataille* wrote disparagingly of four or five thousand at most, including women and children. In total effect, the numbers must have been impressive; and some people later thought it had been an irreparable mistake not to have attempted a rising at this moment when the movement's numbers were so high. See Paul Dresse, *Léon Daudet,* p. 275.

The *Action française* was quick to see a connection between the murder and contemporary events. Germaine Berton's irresponsible and stupid crime, it charged, was part of a vast international conspiracy. Royalist pressure had been responsible for the arrest of Communist leaders. The Ruhr had been occupied after a long nationalist campaign in which Daudet had played a major part. Ergo, all the foes of France whom Daudet had pursued since 1917 had sought their revenge—anarchists, Marxists, radicals and spies, their agents in police and security posts, their journalistic friends. When the CGT went on strike at the printing shop of the *Action française* in retaliation for the wrecking of the *Oeuvre* plant and the linotypists then thrown out of work, the connection seemed proved. Good Frenchmen must now, clearly, stand shoulder to shoulder against the joint forces of Germany, the Soviets, and international finance.[6]

This was not exactly the conclusion that most people seemed to reach, however. The daily barrage of royalist vituperation could easily inspire thoughts of crime. Daudet must have appeared, at least to those whom he hounded, much as Senator McCarthy would do at a later date, as the persistent evil spirit of an uneasy world, recklessly pursuing, with marked success, smear campaigns and witch hunts that left lives and reputations torn to shreds. Many people must have wondered who and what might rid the world of such a wretched man. That someone should set out to do it, and, unable to reach him, turn against a henchman, did not need to be explained by deep-laid plots. A mind more ready than most to follow its resentments to their logical conclusion was all that was needed to arm a murderer's hand. Jaurès had come to his death in much the same way.

Germaine Berton's defenders did not fail to stress this when her case came to court; and when she was acquitted the royalists had to note, as Jaurès's friends had done earlier, how far the human weakness of an Assize jury stretched. They preferred, however, to attribute the acquittal to the republican treachery and injustice to which they had begun by attributing the crime.

Meanwhile, in quite another circle, in which, as a rule, the movement could rely on a great deal of sympathy, there were signs of growing disaffection. In the summer of 1922, after the death of Paul Deschanel, Maurras had declared himself a candidate for the deceased President's seat in the Académie Française. The writer from Martigues had perfectly good titles for consideration. A fertile though pedestrian journalist, a competent though pedantic poet, he had a high literary reputation, perhaps in part because his political opponents liked to display their fairness by an appreciation of his nonpolitical works. Critical discussions had already been devoted to his literary *corpus,* and partly because of his personal prestige, partly because of the impressive-sounding board of the *Action française,* the publication of a new book by Maurras was always a literary event. In a broader, more significant, sense, however, Maurras also stood for a vast and growing intellectual influence. Wrote Eugène Lautier:

> How many novels, plays, and essays will have been forgotten by the time when no discussion of the intellectual movement of our day will be possible without some mention of the Action Française group! It will have taken its place, its great place—and no one can regret this more than I—in history; and the grandson of this or that detractor of today will be admitted to the doctorate of letters with a thesis on *Maurras, Daudet, and their friends*.[7]

But despite a respectful consideration of Maurras as a literary figure, the predominant assumption was that his candidacy was a political one, inviting political rather than literary judgment. Anatole France, kindly disposed to the man, nonetheless declared: "His candidacy is clearly political. It is a deliberate challenge by a partisan who wants to plant his flag on the *coupole*. I shall not give my vote to reaction."[8] Others who felt the same, who either refused to support reaction or shrank from being labeled reactionary by supporting it, favored the—equally political—rival candidacy of Célestin Jonnart, a veteran republican politician whose ideological emptiness could compromise no one.

Although such details always counted little on the Quai Conti, Jonnart's titles to election were almost nonexistent, and Maurras was without doubt the most distinguished in a narrow field. His friends, especially René Boylesve and Henri Bordeaux, worked hard for him, and might even have succeeded had not the *Action française* interfered unwisely by vehemently attacking poor Jonnart and, worse still, the dolts who were backing him. In April 1923, true to form, the Immortals, after several ballots, at last chose Jonnart, giving him twice as many votes as his opponent. Daudet's campaigns on Maurras's behalf probably hurt Maurras more than all his enemies did; and once the results were out the royalist reaction hurt him even more. Not content with dressing up a donkey in an Academician's garb and parading him all over the Left Bank, the newspaper went so far as to reproduce the ballots of the ten men who had voted for Maurras—and since the election was secret, the ballots must have been stolen. This silly gesture annoyed friends as well as enemies and effectively ended any hopes that, after what could be called an honorable defeat, Maurras might soon have been elected after all. It may even have determined the rejection a month later of another Action Française candidate, the historian Louis Bertrand.[9]

More serious developments were to follow these storms in literary teacups. Camelot violence continued, and their sections turned out in force to celebrate their saint, Joan of Arc, who had been "betrayed by Freemasons and burnt by the Boches" as the *Canard* put it. In Parliament and press, meanwhile, Poincaré, who had probably voted for Maurras's election to the Académie Française, was being bitterly accused of leaning too far to the Right represented by Daudet and by François Arago, the leader of the Entente Démocratique. Daudet's influence was more apparent every day,[10] as when, at the end of May, government anti-Communist measures met with opposition in the Senate and Poincaré briefly considered resigning.[11] Soon, however, Daudet would have to defend his own troops and himself, and, at an awkward moment, he would find the Premier oddly but unequivocally on his side.

Before proceeding to the crucial events of June 1923, it is well to point out as a reminder that if to their enemies the royalists seemed a tough and ruthless lot, in their own eyes they were unjustly persecuted patriots. They drew a sharp distinction between their own acts of violence against enemies of France like Caillaux and Briand, for whom any punishment short of death was too mild, and the attacks upon themselves, which could come only from unworthy motives. Their increasing influence had not gone without attracting increasing hostility, and their old complaints of public indifference to their propaganda had now been replaced by complaints about the attacks to which their new prominence exposed them.

Daudet, who was not unaccustomed to threats (he had once been set upon by a Corsican rowdy), was given stern warning in the lobby of the Chamber of Deputies in the spring of 1923 by friends of Caillaux who were angered by the unprovoked assaults on the statesman by Camelots.[12] On May 25 an unemployed metalworker named Georges-Lucien Taupin entered the offices of the *Action française* in the rue de Rome and fired a shot into the ceiling of the waiting room. "This is a warning from the Anarchists," he shouted. "They are always ready for the Action Française!"[d] Besides these indignities, Plateau's murder remained unavenged, Germaine Berton's crime was still untried before a court, and the enemies of France were at work once again. It was clearly time for justice to be given a speedy hand.

The excuse came on the evening of May 31, when well-known republican politicians were due to speak at a left-wing meeting protesting Poincaré's German policy. On their way to address the meeting, Marc Sangnier, Maurice Violette, and Marius Moutet were attacked by Camelots, beaten, and spattered with coal tar and printer's ink. Sangnier narrowly escaped a castor-oil purge, and Mme Violette, who was with her husband, was roughly handled. A fourth republican politician, Fernand Buisson, although spared violent treatment on account of his age, received a threatening letter accompanied by a packet of dung.

It is possible that Maurras had no more to do with these attacks than with the pranks that resulted in his being kept out of the Académie for nearly fifteen years. The royalist leaders always had the problem of trying to keep their followers in hand.[13] But in this instance the leaders at any rate followed their troops by endorsing their actions. In reporting the attacks, the *Action française* stressed the need for individual initiative "in the face of the inertia of the State," and it quoted, for once with evident approval, an opponent's remark that the Action Française was the French brand of Fascism. As for Daudet, he issued

[d] On June 6, 1923, Taupin was sentenced to fifteen days in jail and fined 25 francs.

a "Warning" that the extraordinary moderation which his men had shown heretofore, always acting only in self-defense against the growing arrogance of their enemies, was coming to an end.[14]

The echoes of Fascist bluster had been resounding across the Alps for some time. Daudet had expressed the opinion that Mussolini's actions were restrained, perhaps too restrained; and more moderate members of Parliament had facetiously threatened Communists with similar treatment. As for the Left, they had long taunted royalists about their failure to carry out their threats of violence.[e] But now that they had done so, brutally, childishly, albeit with some provocation, the storm of republican censure would break over their heads and over those of men like Poincaré who, in the eyes of the public, seemed to condone their violence.

On the day following the Camelot aggressions, June 1, 1923, the debate in Parliament brought out all the resentments not only of the frustrated Communists and Socialists but of the more moderate Left, which had on most occasions since 1919 voted with the Bloc in prolongation of the *union sacrée.* The union had been shaky, and, as we have seen, Daudet had done his best to turn it toward the Right, but without ever being able to persuade even Poincaré himself that a smaller but more stable majority, purged of its more doubtful elements (i.e., of the Radicals), was preferable to continued intermittent Radical support. Now it would be the Radicals who, angered by the events of the previous night, would press the cabinet to choose between the royalists and them.

Their leader, Edouard Herriot, stood up to denounce the Camelot attacks. The Action Française, by its own admission, he said, boasted of being French Fascism and aimed at fomenting civil war in France. And the government, if it did not aid the royalists, at least abetted them. "We have had enough!" Herriot declared to loud applause from the left, the extreme left, and various benches in the center. And a voice from the left concurred: "We have had too much!" Thus, speaking in the name of all republicans, "even moderate republicans," the Radical leader called forth in one moment the reaction that was the first really striking manifestation of the Cartel to come.

"At this moment," he said, addressing Maurice Maunoury, the Minister of the Interior, who was sitting in the Premier's place in Poincaré's absence, "at this moment when we must rise to the level of highest principles and count the members of our great republican family [applause on the left and the extreme left], there is here, on this side of the Assembly [the extreme left], an

[e] *AFD,* Nov. 12, 1922, referred to a "façon bonhomme de châtier." In the Chamber on May 8, 1923 (*JOC,* p. 1782), when the Communist Vaillant-Couturier compared the anti-labor activities of the French and German bourgeoisie, Rillart de Verneuil, a conservative, interrupted him by saying, "Vous méritez, jeune homme, qu'on vous administre un verre d'huile de ricin," evoking laughter in the center and on the right. See also P. Renaudel in *JOC,* Nov. 28, 1917, p. 3086, and P. Poncet in *JOC,* Jan. 18, 1918, p. 112.

empty place. It is a place that we still remember, and we still mourn Jaurès's unpunished murder. [On the extreme left, the left, and in the center, the deputies rose and applauded.] Yes, we have had enough." The government, he warned, must make its choice, either for the Republic or against it.

After Herriot had sat down to loud applause from the extreme left, the left, and the center, another republican, of the moderate majority, Emmanuel Brousse, added his support. Not since the days of Dreyfus had the Right faced such united opposition. Perhaps, commented a Radical, the Action Française ought to be thanked after all for having brought the republicans together. Not all republicans, in fact, were united, but most of them were, and from Marcel Cachin to Marc Sangnier, their speeches supported one another. Sangnier's remarks were typical:

> More and more in the country—I don't say in the Chamber—the idea spreads that the government does not want to displease the Action Française [Here a voice interrupted "That's right!"] and does not want to divorce itself from it too publicly. ["Hear, hear!" sounded on the left and the extreme left.] I do not say that this is the case, but almost everybody in the country has come to believe it. [Applause on the left and the extreme left.] . . . Too many of our colleagues seem to fear the Action Française press campaigns . . . too many fear to say openly what they think of certain acts of the Action Française . . . they fear—oh, how wrong they are! I know not what reprisals. . . . The importance attributed to the Action Française is factitious, and I think I can assert that the daring of [Daudet] comes only from the cowardice of many others.[15]

Before the sustained criticism of the Left, the hard-pressed Maunoury could only answer that the government was on guard and quite resolved to defend the Republic against all those who might attack it. But this was not enough to gratify the republicans, who were determined, above all, to extract an unequivocal statement from Poincaré. Even Léon Bailby, who was usually friendly to Maurras, demanded to know Poincaré's reason for treating the turbulent enemies of the Republic with so much patience. The government replies, said *L'Intransigeant,* that patriotic royalists cannot be treated like international Communists; it was true that the doctrine of the *Action française* brought precious help to the national cause, but that was not enough to justify the government's accepting without a murmur the image of being led by the monarchists.[f]

[f] *L'Intransigeant,* June 5, 1923. An anonymous correspondent, writing on June 2 from the office of the Minister of Justice, ruefully informed Maurras: "La très grande admiration, souvent accompagnée d'une vive sympathie, que les meilleurs éléments du Parlement et du Ministère portent, vous le savez, à l'A.F., est certainment amoindrie depuis hier. . . . (L'A.F.) n'apparaît plus à la plupart que comme un allié agité, maladroit et compromettant" (Maurras papers). Less kindly, *Le Canard enchaîné,* June 6, suggested that only Poincaré's personal intervention had saved the playful Camelots from serious trouble. A cartoon in the same issue showed a Camelot advising a neophyte: "D'abord tu le purges. Et après, s'il n'a pas de papier, il est bien obligé d'acheter *l'Action française.*"

On June 5, the Chamber decided that the texts of the speeches by Herriot and Brousse should be displayed throughout France. To offset this, government supporters pushed through a vote affirming that Maunoury's speech should be displayed as well.[g] But Poincaré, back at his place, sat silent through the day's proceedings. In the lobbies there was talk of deep dissensions within the cabinet (which contained three Radical ministers), and it was said that for the first time in ten years a government might fall on a clear issue of internal policy.

Faced with a government unwilling to commit itself, although under fire from both of its extremes, the Right decided that shock tactics must be used. Jean Ybarnégaray, a deputy from the Basque country who would achieve notoriety in later years, set out to force an explanation by questioning "the position the government proposes to adopt in the already heated struggle between the Left and the Bloc National."

On June 15, in the midst of great public excitement (7,000 applications had been received for seats in the public galleries), Ybarnégaray recapitulated the events of the preceding fortnight. On June 1, Herriot's motion of censure, although defeated, had got 181 votes; five days later, the posting of his speech had been endorsed by 280 against 213—to Ybarnégaray and his colleagues on the Right this was a victory for the left-wing minority. As for Maunoury, "abandoned by Herriot's friends," he had received scarcely more votes than the minority leader—320. "This victory of June 5 which you applaud, and rightly, was a victory of the left-wing bloc," said Ybarnégaray. Then, turning to his right-wing colleagues, he continued, "The truth is, gentlemen, that all this business has been very cleverly organized by the *bloc des gauches*. The Left has used this myth [of a royalist plot] to traipse around the country crying 'We have saved the Republic.' But the country has believed you. That, I think, is all you asked for." And now, Ybarnégaray went on, here was the Right cowering in fear of being compromised—tarred with the brush of unrepublicanism—on election eve: "Ces gens à genoux, qui baissent la nuque, sous la crainte . . . de la défaite de 1924, c'est nous, c'est la majorité!" This brought laughter on the left and the extreme left, and applause on the right and in the center.[16]

It did, indeed, look as if a good many of the Radicals who had been carrying the card of national union since 1919 had, during the last two weeks, shifted toward the traditional republicanism of the Left. For men elected on the Union Nationale ticket, the change was largely an opportunistic one, the result,

[g] After Maunoury's *affichage* had been voted, the Extreme Right tried to obtain the same for the text of the entire June 1 debate, and lost by 30 to 510, figures which, after correction, became 17 to 477. These 17 form the hard core of integral nationalist support in the Chamber: Baudry d'Asson, Bermond d'Auriac, Léon Daudet, Hyacinthe de Gailhard-Bancel, César Ginoux-Defermont, Pierre Joly, Jacques de Juigné, Henri Auguste de La Ferronnays, Jean Le Cour-Grandmaison, Xavier de Magallon, Louis Magne, Ambroise Rendu, Victor Rochereau, Charles Ruellan, Alphonse Sevène, Etienne de Seynes, and Xavier Vallat.

as a Communist told them—to Daudet's approving jeers—of their awareness that electoral and popular opinion had changed.

For the true Right the issue was simple. Nationalists must be staunch friends of the Action Française, Xavier de Magallon[h] explained, to applause on the Right, "because of Bainville's admirable foreign policy, because of its social ideas, which they share, because of the unquestioned services in wartime of that great citizen and writer Léon Daudet." They might agree to disapprove what many others would consider harmless pranks, but they could not censure the Camelots without censuring the Communists, too.

This was where the Right and Poincaré found themselves at one. Rising to speak at last, the Premier said that, although he deplored all extremes, he had to recognize that "there are extremes which still continue to serve the fatherland" and must be singled out as favored exceptions. The government would rely only on those that were dedicated to defending the Republic, disavowing all those that believed in class warfare and also all persons who wanted to come to terms with them. Loud and prolonged applause in the center and on the right followed Poincaré's comments, and voices on the right queried the Radicals: "Well, gentlemen?" Voices on the left replied, "We have understood."

For once expressing the general sentiment, Herriot described the session as one that would mark a turning point in the history of the legislature.[17] The Radicals had been restless for some time. With the legislature coming to an end, their political intuition told them that continued collaboration with the Right might cost them their adherents in the next election. Furthermore, the creation of a French Communist Party at the Congress of Tours in 1920 had forced the Socialists to adopt a more conservative platform, thus making possible once more the traditional electoral cooperation of the republican, and increasingly moderate, Left. The Radicals, who had been part of the majorities of both Briand and Poincaré, had not liked Poincaré's hard policy toward the Germans, or his uncompromisingly firm hand with the British allies. As early as the summer of 1922 they had joined the Socialists in criticizing him, although, as *Le Temps* pointed out, not once before that summer, in twenty-seven months, had the Radicals separated from the Bloc National. On every other occasion they had separated clearly from the Socialists, the revolutionaries, and the Communists. Their change of heart at this point has led a recent writer to argue that it was in the summer of 1922 that the Bloc really came to an end.[18] But a closer look shows that this was not so.

In the vote which in June 1922 followed the first signs of Radical independence, 19 Radicals voted against the government, 26 voted for it, and 29 (including Herriot) abstained. Six months later, on the question of the Ruhr,

[h] Xavier de Magallon, who joined the Action Française openly only after losing his Chamber seat in 1924, is mentioned in a letter from Poincaré to Maurras (April 2, 1922) as being an intermediary between the two men.

out of 83 Radicals, 42 voted for the government and 35 abstained. On June 1, 1923, however, the proportions changed: 48 Radicals voted against the government; two weeks later 58 voted against it, 12 for it, and only 8 abstained.[19] The Radicals were moving toward a break, and Poincaré's policy on the Ruhr may have provided the pressure—or the excuse—to ease them out of the ruling coalition. But the crucial rupture clearly came after the Camelot assaults, which forced the deputies to take a stand not only out of recognition of the necessity for maintaining public order and parliamentary solidarity, but also out of a consideration of what effect castor oil and coal-tar shampoos would have on their own constituencies.

The Action Française was certainly not alone responsible for the disintegration of the Bloc, but, as in 1917, it provided the catalyst, the forceful, obvious excuse for the split. The Radicals themselves had been drifting, and they continued to drift; but whereas before June 1923 they had inclined toward the Right, they inclined toward the Left for a little time thereafter.

The loudly expressed support of Magne, Daudet, and other royalists during the long afternoon of June 15 was both compromising and embarrassing to Poincaré, and it proved the final persuasion for hesitant republicans. What the Action Française was really working for, however, was to force the Center Left out of a majority that they wished to purify in order that they might themselves enter it officially at election time. In such expectations they were to be disappointed. Far from bringing about a purer, surer right-wing majority, they provided the impetus for the Cartel des Gauches—the impetus and the raison d'être, for the threat of a French Fascism was a persuasive campaign issue for the Radicals in the absence of other arguments.[i] For the moment, however, the royalists seemed to have been successful. "M. Daudet was the winner of the day," commented André Tardieu in the *Echo national,* "because, purged according to the plan of the Action Française, Poincaré's majority is now no more than the royalists' docile retinue."[j]

[i] Herriot's article in the *Dépêche de Toulouse* of June 16, 1923, the day after the great debate, was a determined declaration of war against the Action Française and anyone who chose to defend it. The Communists did not find the "Fascist" menace of Maurrassism so serious as did the Radicals and others. There was nothing to worry about as yet, declared Amédée Dunois in the *Bulletin Communiste* of June 14, pp. 295–96; the Camelots were a lot of children, drunk with their own excitement. "It is when Herriot, Painlevé, and Léon Blum are in power that big capital, no longer feeling safe, will favor in France a class fascism, anti-Communistic and, in a word, anti-labor." Events would bear out his analysis and predictions.

[j] Quoted in *AF,* June 18, 1923. On June 27, Maurras received a sentence of four months in prison and a fine of 500 francs for his role in the Camelot affair. Two Camelots got sentences of three months and 500 francs, and a third Camelot, two months and 200 francs. There is no record that Maurras ever served this sentence: amnesties always seemed to save him in time.

8

1923-1926

THE MONTHS THAT FOLLOWED the momentous debates of June 1923 were perhaps the high point of integral nationalist influence in politics, and of their self-confidence as well. The right-wing coalition purged of its compromising members, it remained for the royalists to win acceptance as substitutes for the departing Radicals. In addition, electoral changes likely to demolish the work of the past years by changing the friendly majority in Parliament had to be avoided at all costs. The *Action française* now bent its efforts to suggesting that it could become a loyal and effective member of a new political alliance—not revolutionary, not subversive, but safely, reassuringly conservative. But international difficulties, it argued, as well as internal social pressures, made it inadvisable to allow the political upset that elections would involve; times were too critical for changing asses in midstream; the 1924 elections should be postponed.

Even in June 1923, Maurras had told the Tenth Action Française Congress that the elections of 1924 must be prevented. Electoral scandals should not be permitted to harass a government busy with more pressing concerns. All patriots, all men of order, all honest men, could and should rally behind the simple slogan "No enemies on the Right."[1]

In a series of articles on the same theme, Daudet, too, pressed the importance of an electoral alliance, especially with the Entente Démocratique (of men like Louis Marin, Auguste Isaac, and Lefebvre du Prey). The Left, said Daudet, was drawing its lines for the fray. The vital interest of Millerand and Poincaré coincided with the vital interests of the country, in an evidently reactionary sense. More important still, the Action Française should now be recognized as more than just a ginger group: "It has not been sufficiently remarked how much is new and original in the attitude of the royalist Right. Under previous regimes, the opponents of established institutions were in the opposition and nothing but the opposition. But royalists today are far from limited to such a stand, and, what is more, they know how—when the moment comes—to help and to cooperate."[2]

In the right-wing press, friends echoed their support: "We always prefer a good Frenchman, even a royalist, to a dubious one, even a republican," wrote the *Liberté* of Levallois ("journal républicain, indépendant, et patriote"). "And if next year, for an eventual electoral arrangement, we had to choose between the royalists who serve France and, for example, the Radicals who harm it, we should not hesitate in choosing [the friends of] France." In *L'Eclair,* an industrialist, Jean Rey, approved the argument that times were far too critical for holding early elections. The idea seemed to be gaining ground.[3]

Unsympathetic political commentators warned against the possibility of a *coup d'état,* basing their arguments on Action Française influence on Poincaré and Millerand and on wide circles throughout the Right.[a] Their directives, thought Roger Mennevée, influenced French foreign policy; and meanwhile André Maginot, who made no secret of his sympathies for the Action Française, was maneuvering to get the Ministry of the Interior for himself and that of War for his friend Jean Fabry. Moreover it was the Action Française that had launched the idea of naming General Charles Mangin military governor of Paris. The scheme had met the concerted opposition of the Left and had been abandoned, the governorship falling to General Henri Gouraud instead. But Gouraud's sympathies also, it was rumored, were going to the royalists—hardly reassuring at a time when the German army was bidding for power in the East and the Spanish army in the person of Primo de Rivera had just grasped it in the South. It was time to extirpate democracy, clamored Daudet.[b]

Economic conditions did indeed seem propitious for a coup. In the month of September 1923 alone, the price index rose by eleven points. The cost of bread, milk, sugar, and rents was going up. There were demands for the suppression of customs duties on agricultural products, but it was hard to single out farm prices for control while those of industry rose because the franc was dropping as the price of raw materials soared. During the twelve months of 1923, the franc depreciated 50 per cent on the international exchange. The dollars one used to buy for 100 francs now cost 150. The occupation of the Ruhr had led to speculation based on expectation of a falling franc. Anglo-American credits had been cut, and French industrialists were being forced to find ready exchange in order to pay for their imports in cash. Under pressure from Anglo-American banks that did not want to see France use her reparation rights to get the upper hand on German industry, French prices

[a] See the anonymous letter, "Cabinet du Garde des Sceaux," June 2, 1923, Maurras papers: "C'est en soutenant de toutes ses forces depuis 1914 ce qu'il y avait de national dans le personnel républicain que l'A.F. est arrivée naturellement à cette situation privilégiée et presque paradoxale. Les socialistes et radicaux, jusqu'à ces derniers jours, répétaient avec rage que le gouvernement était à vos ordres: C'était exagéré? Mais vous savez mieux que moi ce 'topo' dont la diffusion dans le pays avait, ces derniers temps, accru le prestige de l'A.F. de telle sorte que, par un processus psychologique bien connu, ce qui n'était pas tout à fait vrai hier allait le devenir demain."

[b] See *L'Oeuvre*'s headlines of July 19, 1923: "Mangin Gouverneur de Paris? Le Coup de Force est donc possible?"; *Les Documents politiques,* IV, No. 11 (November 1923), 399–403; and the *Daily Herald,* Feb. 25, 1924. When Mangin died in the spring of 1926, the *Action française* immediately asserted that he had been poisoned.

mounted steadily, and when worried foreign investors sold their francs, the demand for foreign currency caused the position of the franc to worsen. Fearful of being caught, industrialists and merchants rushed out to build up stocks and made the inflated prices still higher. As prices throughout the country rose apace with rising production costs, consumers became restive. Docks and public utilities were struck in August, small businesses in Paris (haberdashers, for example) in the autumn; in November, miners exacted a wage increase and state employees began clamoring for one; and in December a police strike brought bloody riots up to the very gates of the Palais Bourbon.

To face these problems the government sought special powers, thereby leaving itself open to accusations of dictatorial tendencies. The Left again identified the government's policy with that of Maurras and Daudet,[4] and their exaggerations were borne out by Daudet's articles. When the decrees which the Premier hoped would save the critical financial situation came up for discussion, Daudet declared that he and all other reactionaries would vote for them because "they were basically anti-republican" and represented a first step toward "the reactionary measures that I favor and that I would take myself." "Without the twenty-six votes of the Action Française, whose leader, M. Léon Daudet, declared himself in favor of the government's decrees, M. Poincaré would not have got the vote of confidence he requested," observed Tardieu in disgust.[5]

But, helpful though they might be, the royalists were still not wanted in a union of the Right. It was all very well for men of the same mind to cooperate in practice, but when going to the hustings, tradition counted more. A conservative coalition could not afford to ignore the strength of basic republican appeal, and so, once again, the Action Française was forced to go it alone. As February 1924 drew to a close the paper announced that it would run candidates in the four Paris electoral sectors and welcome "honorable alliances" elsewhere.[6] A high general opinion of their effectiveness bolstered the royalists' own optimism. A Dutch Catholic observer who expected the Right to make important gains felt certain that the influence of the Action Française would be predominant: "It is better organized than the Reds and its electoral propaganda shows incredible force."[7]

And, indeed, the paper's circulation (no precise figures are available for subscriptions), which had risen by an average of four thousand copies during the first quarter of 1924, rose almost twice as much during the second quarter. Toward the end of April, in an interview with a *Revue hebdomadaire* reporter, Daudet, in a highly optimistic mood, talked of the great royalist gains to come and proposed when re-elected to press for the formation of "a government of order and authority, a concentration of all reactionary forces," in which he would be glad to welcome such "very pleasant men" as Paul-Boncour, Ferdinand Buisson, and Herriot. "So, no more *coup de force*?" the interviewer asked. "Apart from absolute necessity, no," Daudet replied. "Why force our valiant lads to break their heads against a wall, when I can act more effectively from the inside?"[8]

Although some thirty seats had become vacant in the meantime, no by-elections had been held since November 1919, and there had been but little check on the country's electoral temperature. The weight of press and parliamentary opinion led everyone to think the Right, though not so decisively as before, would repeat its success of 1919. The Radicals, as usual, were split between a minority of moderates and the Cartel majority that favored collaboration with the Socialists. It was possible to think that these dissensions, and the votes that were counted as lost to the Communists, would be a serious disadvantage for the Cartel. Overconfident, the Right repeated the mistake its opponents had made in 1919 and entered the battle separate and dispersed. As it turned out, the competition of the Communists encouraged an understanding between the Socialists and the Radicals, the latter being inclined now to accept their partners as less than dangerous revolutionaries, since such obviously more dangerous revolutionaries existed on the Extreme Left. And the conservatives, having rejected help (perhaps quite rightly) from the most dynamic right-wing publications because they lacked republican *bona fides,* found themselves opposed by a lively publication of the Left, the *Quotidien,* which had been founded in 1923 for this special purpose.

In the end, although the Right did not actually lose any votes, the Left gained a good many. The turnout, 12 per cent higher than in 1919, higher than ever before during the century, showed that the Cartel had managed to mobilize votes heretofore uncommitted. And the nature of the electoral system, which favored massive parties (or party coalitions), meant that the Action Française did far, far worse than anybody had expected. Although the "white" regions were, as always, dependable, Daudet himself, who had predicted the collapse of the Cartel and an absolute majority for the ticket he headed, was not re-elected.[9]

The Action Française and their friends got only 328,003 votes—something more than a third as many as the Communists (875,812), less than half as many as the Socialists (749,647),[c] but hardly impressive. In the Seine—that is, in the Paris area where it really mattered—the averages of the several Action Française tickets, and the votes for the *têtes des listes,* were as follows:

First sector	7,979	(Bernard de Vésins, 9,653)
Second sector	6,027	(Marie de Roux, 7,317)
Third sector	13,513	(Léon Daudet, 17,424)
Fourth sector	11,013	(Georges Valois, 13,246)

In the first two sectors, the royalist vote was much the same as in 1919; in the third, where the Right lost some 12,000 votes, or about 20 per cent of its usual

[c] It should be remembered that in most constituencies the Socialists joined Cartel coalitions, and that the only votes tabulated as Socialist were those cast for straight Socialist, noncoalition, tickets. Hence these figures are somewhat misleading.

electorate, the Action Française lost roughly 2,000 votes, or about 14 per cent. A broader comparison of the averages shows the real place of the royalists in Paris electoral politics:[10]

	Union Nationale	Cartel	Communists	A.F.
First sector	67,641	42,769	41,120	7,979
Second sector	56,356	49,701	40,781	6,027
Third sector	61,416	56,010	43,506	13,513

Thus, in the most sympathetic constituency in the most "nationalistic" city in France, the third sector of the Seine, the Action Française, running on Daudet's name, managed to keep ahead of its liberal enemy Marc Sangnier, but lagged far behind all the other parties, including the Communists. It was no consolation that Sangnier had done more badly still. The blow was hard—and costly. The tribune of the Chamber as a sounding board had served the paper well. It would miss the special ring that Daudet's words acquired in such a setting, as well as the area of maneuver afforded by the sky-blue majority of 1919.

In the provinces, the very men who had nailed the Action Française colors to the mast and sailed in with the nationalist tide of 1919 were now left high and dry. Ambroise Rendu in the Haute-Garonne and Charles Ruellan in Ille-et-Vilaine succumbed before the coalition of the Left. The Catholic west was turning moderate, and the new Christian Democrat elected in Ille-et-Vilaine, Armand Le Douarec, found himself in hot water when he said that he read the *Action française* every day. The solid royalist bastions in the Nord, Vendée, and Loire-Inférieure remained loyal, the latter re-electing all four of its deputies, all sympathetic to the Action Française but none dependent upon it.

The collapse came in the south, which had returned some of the most devoted royalists in 1919. Gard, where integral nationalists had in 1919 helped elect four stalwarts, now had only one. The three royalist deputies of Hérault, including Xavier de Magallon and Bâtonnier Louis Guibal of Montpellier, went down; and so did Isidore Méritan in Vaucluse. Having enjoyed the nationalist swing five years before, all these men were stranded now that the mood had changed. Royalists were re-elected where they had always thrived, but not where the Action Française and a momentary mood had helped them to a brief success. Only in the Ardèche did the defeat of Action Française friends like Hyacinthe de Gailhard-Bancel and Xavier Vallat mean no more than a fluke. There, the more violent whites had joined with moderate traditionalists to hold their own against the Protestant and Radical Left. The Radicals won by less than 300 votes, but they were swept out again in 1928, when Vallat was returned to the Chamber. But the Ardèche, or at least the relevant part of it, provided yet one more traditional bastion of the Right, and it was the Action Française that prospered on these foundations, not the Right that benefited from its activity.

If such results proved anything so far as a history of the Action Française is concerned, it was the electoral ineffectiveness of the movement. The fleeting gains of 1919 may have deluded the men of the rue de Rome into overconfidence. Lacking electoral organization or experience, lacking enthusiasm for efforts about whose value many members had the strongest doubts, the leaders were at last convinced by the dismal results of their second electoral venture. They would not make the same mistake again.

The 1924 elections were far from a decisive victory for the Left. No clear majority existed, although it was always possible to find one for moderate policies. But straightaway the prevailing impression was different—the more so since the Cartel deputies united from the start to get revenge on Millerand, who, as President of the Republic, had too openly taken the side against them. It may be that, briefly, leaders of the Action Française tried to persuade Millerand to stay, and to suggest a *coup d'état* backed by the Army and the people of Paris. If they did, no one took them seriously, and rumors of their having visited the Elysée quickly faded.[11] The President resigned on June 11, and was shortly replaced by the most moderate of moderate Radicals, Gaston Doumergue.

It seemed that *ultra* dominance was over. The power lay with parties of the moderate Left, which showed great interest in the perquisites of office and little in social and economic reform. The issues of political debate were of the symbolic sort on which Radicals and Socialists could agree to join: the reviewing of wartime sentences for "traitors" and of sentences hastily imposed on labor agitators; the pardoning of Malvy, Caillaux, and other Radicals; amnesty for Communists like Jacques Sadoul; the re-employment of railroad workers who had been suspended in the postwar strikes; the extension of the religious measures of 1905 and 1906—indeed, of 1882—to the churches and church schools in Alsace-Lorraine; chicanery against religious orders that had been revived after the war; a more accommodating foreign policy, in closer collaboration with the United States and especially with England.

The government's most active opponents during the first few months were a group of Catholics who tried to set up a party of their own, and General de Castelnau's Fédération Nationale Catholique, which included many men like Xavier Vallat and Henri Groussau, the deputy of Lille, who were very friendly to the royalists.[d]

[d] See *Pour la restauration française* (Langres, 1924). After the "detestable" elections of May 1924, a number of friends of the Action Française founded a group called "Energie." Some of the members were Gaëtan Bernoville, the publisher of *Les Lettres* and later a contributor to *Je suis partout*; Louis Guibal, an ex-deputy and eminent Montpellier lawyer; Louis Latzarus of *L'Intransigeant*; Professor Louis Le Fur, whom Pétain would name to the governing body of the Institut d'Etudes Corporatives and who would later, during the years of Occupation, contribute to the *Petit Parisien* and *Je suis partout*; the Comte de Leusse, an ex-deputy from Alsace and the mayor of Reichoffen; Professor Achille Mestre, another future councilor of the Institut d'Etudes Corporatives and of the Conseil Corporatif; Robert Schuman, a Christian-Democrat deputy of

The Action Française itself remained relatively quiet, licking its wounds, until November brought new opportunities for action. Autumn had seen conservative anxiety growing over (admittedly unsuccessful) attempts of the Radicals and Socialists to find some common ground in plans for social and economic reform. The Communists were busy, but far more alarming were the decisions of the Radical Party Congress of October, advocating more actual and discriminating taxes, cheap housing, social insurance, and the strict enforcement of the eight-hour work law. Portentous, too, had been the government's decision to recognize Soviet Russia. This was the real Communism against which the moderate leaders decided to move.

One of the foremost journalistic spokesmen of the bourgeoisie, Camille Aymard, attacked the government as unwilling to defend itself against the Communist threat.[12] Under the leadership of Millerand, a National Republican League was founded, with strong backing from industrial and financial interests.[e] This only spurred the government's plans to transfer the ashes of Jean Jaurès from Albi to the Panthéon and to give the ceremony unusual pomp. With Radicals and Socialists uneasily not-quite-united, the government thought that a demonstration was in order to prove that there need be no enemies on the Left (not including the Extreme Left, however).

Before the May elections, Poincaré had felt that anything involving Jaurès would only stir up political passions. It is possible that the new Premier, Herriot, hoped that passions thus stirred would simmer down into a more concentrated Left. In any case, the ceremony, fixed for November 23, was planned with great elaborateness and splendor. Jaurès's remains arrived from Albi on the 22d, lay in state in the Palais Bourbon, and on the following day were moved to an impressive stand outside. Covered with masses of flowers and draped with Tricolors, the great funeral pile rose beneath the Chamber's portals, flanked by two huge flaming torches. An apparently endless line of mourners filed by, to the background of an equally endless concert arranged by the composer Gustave Charpentier and transmitted by loudspeaker from within the Chamber where it was being played.

Then, as the orchestra played the grand march from *Aïda,* the coffin, on a bier eighty-two feet long, moved slowly off, borne by twenty-two miners dressed in their working clothes. The long cortege followed: schoolchildren,

---

Moselle; and the Comte Béranger de Miramon. Their manifesto, which was made as an appeal from the existing Parliament to the elite of France, called for the restoration of French spiritual forces, but it was only mildly anti-parliamentary and in no way monarchistic, since not all the members were royalists and some were still in Parliament.

[e] The manifesto of the Ligue Républicaine Nationale appeared on November 7, 1924, signed by Millerand, Anthony Ratier, Emile Bourgeois, P.-E. Flandin, Frédéric François-Marsal, André François-Poncet, Auguste Isaac, Yves Le Trocquer, André Maginot, Louis Marin, Pascalis, Charles Reibel, and Emmanuel Brousse. Their paper would be *L'Avenir.* When *L'Ere nouvelle* on the same day called their program a breviary of reaction, *AF* (Nov. 8) replied "mais de réaction molle."

delegations, republican and Masonic leagues, cooperatives and federations. Behind, and separate, unwilling to let the moderates claim all the glory of the great tribune, some fifty thousand Communists marched silently, in serried ranks. At the Panthéon, President Doumergue and Premier Herriot, with the Cabinet, awaited the arrival of the procession, while speech after speech lauded the dead man in whose greatness everyone now wanted to bask.

The ceremony did little to solidify the Left, but it horrified the entire Right. In spite of their order, and perhaps because of it, the hundreds of red banners and the long, dark, red-dotted flow of mourners as it passed along the Boulevard Saint-Germain and the Boulevard Saint-Michel and up the rue Soufflot, had given the impression of a vast insurrectionist parade, full of latent power. And many could not stomach the sight of a French premier on a public reviewing stand saluting red flags as they passed. An old Parisian felt that he had witnessed the first day of a revolution. For Gustave Hervé, the red banners followed the funeral procession of the bourgeoisie.[f] As Pujo would write a year later, "the revolutionary menace seemed apparent to everyone, and the alarm it caused provoked the setting up in Paris and the provinces of numerous groups of social and national defense."[13]

This sort of reaction could not but benefit the recruitment program of the Action Française. Once more the circulation of the paper rose, its activity redoubled.[14] The old Ligue des Patriotes, whose president, Maurice Barrès, had died a year before, got back into the news by appointing as its joint presidents Millerand, who was now head of the Republican National League, and Castelnau of the Catholic Federation. And a Bonapartist deputy with strong monarchist connections, Pierre Taittinger, founded a League of Patriotic Youth (Jeunesses Patriotes or JP), copying its organizational structure after that of the Communists in hopes of fighting them more effectively.[g] In the provinces too, all sorts of defense committees were set up, like the League of Order and Social Conservation of Amiens, which had enlisted 1,500 members by the beginning of December.

In Action Française circles, fears of a Communist plot for Christmas led to serious discussions concerning the possibilities of armed resistance; and Georges Valois, with a few friends like Jacques Arthuys, began to organize

[f] *Le Rappel, La Victoire,* Nov. 24, 1924. The Action Française tried to organize a counter-demonstration by calling its followers to march to Plateau's tomb. This was not a great success. See *Paris-centre,* Nov. 25, 26, 1924.

[g] See Taittinger in *JOC,* June 30, 1936, pp. 1639–40. Of a Bonapartist family, like his Laniel cousins, Taittinger married a Mlle de Mailly, of royalist family, one of whose uncles was a leading member of the Action Française at Marseille. Many of her royalist relatives, however, like the d'Andignés, one of whom had commanded the Duchesse de Berri's forces in 1832 and had been condemned to death *in absentia,* were legitimists and did not accept the Orléans pretenders. Such royalists, like d'Andigné or Colonel Charles des Isnards, preferred to join the JP rather than the Action Française. Pierre Taittinger, personal communication.

for action. There was talk of machine guns and armored vehicles, and nostalgic arguments engaged the excited veterans (their war experience only a few years behind them) about the relative merits of rifles or pistols and of this or that strategy for counterrevolutionary defense.[15]

The *Action française,* long crying in the wilderness, now found that its fears were shared by a whole pack of bourgeois newspapers, from *Le Temps* and *Le Matin* even as far as the *Quotidien.* In the face of such general clamor, which, said Herriot, bordered upon panic, the government was obliged to act.[16] Communist offices were searched and Communist leaders arrested; the Party Propaganda School at Bobigny, which Maurras had been the first to denounce, was raided and closed down. Accused by the Left of acting to appease his right-wing critics, Herriot replied that he was well aware that in royalist circles men were being advised to prepare for a fight, to buy guns and blackjacks—but he gave no sign of intending to halt the preparations. To the royalist leaders it seemed as if they were back in the fall of 1917, riding a crest of popular support. In the *Paris-centre* of December 27, Abel Lamy quoted from a letter written by a "republican patriot" reader: "The only great force actually organized and capable of opposing a Communist movement is the Action Française. I am no royalist and do not want to be a part of the Action Française, yet at this moment a man of sense can put his confidence in nothing else." Two days later, when a Radical member demanded in the Chamber the dissolution of the royalists "who every day preach civil war," Ybarnégaray defended them as an important rampart against Communist revolt.[h]

The Herriot cabinet had antagonized moderate forces thrice over: it had taken up as a convenient symbol the anti-clerical policies that were the province of the classic Left; it had not shown sufficient firmness against the Marxist threat; its economic and financial policies were too progressive-sounding for business and far too timid for success. The Cabinet would eventually fall on a combination of these issues, but its position would previously be shaken by a minor issue stirred up by the Action Française.

In February 1925, with relations between the government and Catholics already tense, the Cartel majority voted to abolish the French Embassy to the Vatican. The Catholic Federation's protest campaign, which had not abated since the election, increased in violence. Great crowds came to hear their ora-

[h] *JOC,* Dec. 9, 1924; *AF,* Dec. 15, 1924; *Paris-centre,* Dec. 27, 1924; *JOC,* Dec. 29, 1924. in January 1925, *Les Documents politiques,* VI, No. 1, 1, complained: "Les constitutions de ligues se succèdent sans cesse et les appels au coup d'Etat ne sont pas moins nombreux." But it is to be noted particularly that, among the leagues, the Action Française continued to rank foremost. In *Les Lettres,* February 1924, Gaëtan Bernoville, who differentiates between the Action Française and movements of the Fascist type, considers it "the final culmination of French nationalism." Bonapartist R. Giron, "Il compito delle Jeunesses Patriotes" in *Critica fascista,* quoted in *AF,* October 15, 1926, still considers the Action Française to be larger, more active, and better prepared ideologically than the JP or any other royalist group.

tors preach a Christian reaction against governmental paganism: at Rennes some 30,000 people cheered talk of anti-materialist revenge; at Marseille, a Federation meeting ended in bloody clashes that left three dead and more than threescore wounded.

A few weeks later, the Assembly of French Cardinals and Archbishops issued a declaration attacking the very principle of a secular—hence atheistic—State, opposing all concessions, protesting against the suppression of the Vatican Embassy and the revival of anti-clerical passions. Society owed the true God worship; there was no getting round this by professions of religious neutrality behind which hovered only a hostile paganism. The *Action française,* naturally, claimed the credit. When L.-O. Frossard interpreted the Cardinals' declaration—"the most significant act of the French Church in the past fifty years," according to *La Croix*—as an Action Française victory, the paper commented, "The truth is both simpler and more complicated: the declaration is a victory of common sense; but it was the *Action française* which, for twenty-five years . . . maintained against one and all these common-sense positions." The coincidence was clearer than the distinction. As a progressive Catholic complained, Catholicism and reaction were everywhere considered identical: "You are a Catholic, you are a Camelot; you are a Catholic, you are a reactionary," that was what they said in the shops.[17]

It was at this very time, with Catholics up in arms, that a thoughtless move of the Minister of Education, François Albert, would set a thousand student wasps buzzing angrily round his ears.

A chair in the Paris Faculty of Law having fallen vacant, the Faculty Council had, as usual in such cases, submitted to the Ministry of Education a list of three persons recommended for the appointment. Although three names were always submitted, it was customary for the Minister to appoint the first, who represented the University's choice. In this case, however, not the first man named but the second was appointed: Georges Scelle, Professor of Law at Dijon University and chef de cabinet of the Radical-Socialist Minister of Labor, Justin Godart. It was a clear case of political favoritism, which, under usual circumstances, would at most have provoked furious but ineffective protest from professors accustomed to more respect for the traditional forms.

Instead, the student branches of the Action Française stepped in. They denounced the Scelle appointment as a typical display of democratic and Masonic corruption, and they organized riots to prevent Scelle from lecturing in the Faculty of Law. On March 9 the police were called on to intervene, and every day thereafter on which Scelle was due to lecture, fights and rioting occurred. By the end of the month the disturbances had reached frenzied heights. When, on the 28th, a hundred or so of the demonstrators and eleven policemen were injured, and thirty-six arrests were made, things had gone well beyond the bounds of a student rag. On March 30 the Faculty of Law was closed by order of François-Albert, and its Dean, Joseph Barthélémy, a nationalist himself, was suspended for not having put an end to all the troubles.[i]

What had started as a staged protest became a public issue. The right-wing press used the riots as an excuse to blame the government, and in the Chamber Ybarnégaray sounded the note of injured innocence. The students' protest was, he said, a professional corporative movement. Jules Uhry countered, "It is also the line of the Action Française." And Ybarnégaray retorted, "This means that there are five thousand students in the Action Française!" But Herriot, too, agreed that the trouble had been started and kept alive by the royalists: "If we do not resist a movement of this sort, we shall find ourselves helpless in the future against the insolent pressures of this group."[18]

On the day after the debate, the General Association of Paris students, dominated by its well-organized royalist membership, ordered a student strike as a demonstration of sympathy for the Law students. Medicine and Pharmacy students joined those of the Faculty of Letters on April 2, and trouble broke out in the provinces, at Nancy and Angers. Within a few days, the strike had spread to Lyon, Bordeaux, Marseille, Rennes, Rouen, Poitiers, and Algiers.

It was against this lively background that the financial crisis of the Herriot government was to be played out. On April 2, the day the strike began, the Minister of Finance, Etienne Clémentel, resigned, unable to agree with his colleagues on how the fiscal problem should be solved. To cope with the soaring inflation and with the Treasury's loss of funds, the left wing of the government coalition wanted a capital levy; the right called for economies and for an end to "costly" State monopolies (e.g., matches and tobacco), the farming out of which, they thought, could bring in the sums the Treasury needed. The holes in the government were hastily chinked up, but the structure did not long survive. It fell on April 10, voted down by a Senate hostile to its financial proposals and especially to the prospect of a capital levy. But three days before this happened, the Senate had already shown its hostility by voting a symbolic cut of 100 francs in the Education budget.

Although Herriot fell on the financial question, apart from which his cabinet might well have survived, Catholic hostility played an important part in the April votes. So did the fear and resentment of the property-owning classes, large and small, which were alarmed by manifestations like those of November 23, by threats of capital levy, and by a sense of growing Socialist influence which the propaganda of the *Action française,* among others, had done its best to inflame.[19] But we must also give some credit to the forceful action of the Action Française student groups, whose initiative and persistence

[i] See *AF* throughout March and *Candide,* March 19, 1925. Along with André de Fels, Jean Fabry, Le Provost de Launay, Picot de Pledran, Pierre Taittinger, Ernest Pezet, and others, Barthélémy, destined to become one of Pétain's Ministers of Justice, had in 1919 founded the Parti Républicain de Réorganisation Nationale, better known by its weekly review *La 4e République.*

largely determined the disturbances in the Latin Quarter. When Scelle also resigned, on the day after Herriot's resignation, the royalist headline ran, "STUDENT VICTORY." The victory was to some extent their own.[20]

The cabinets that followed Herriot bore the deceptive pinkish tinge still required by certain traditional attitudes of the Left, but in actual practice, Painlevé, who held office if not power from April to November 1925, set out to drop the Cartel's awkward program, although with Cartel support. To do this he made of his cabinet a screen of names which would ensure its not being identified with the Right. The principal figure of this ploy was Joseph Caillaux, recently amnestied, who now made his political comeback in the Ministry of Finance.

Caillaux's appointment was meant to be reassuring to financial interests, which would not have to fear capital levies or other unorthodox measures, and also to enlist the Left, the Socialists in particular, who could be expected to rally round the man whom the Right had martyred. And thus it happened that a very moderate program, smoothing the hackles of the Catholics and appeasing fears of untoward economic measures, was greeted by hostile demonstrations on the Right and won the votes of Socialists, for whom Caillaux's presence on the government benches appeared the symbol of a righted wrong.

Painlevé, who held the premiership jointly with his chair at the Sorbonne and who often prepared his lectures between a cabinet meeting and a parliamentary debate, combined tremendous working capacity with an absentmindedness that was no less impressive.[j] He was artful enough, however, to know that he could expect a left-wing majority for a rather conservative program only if he gave the program the appearance of being anti-Right. Not only Caillaux but other men in his cabinet were anathema to the *Action française*—Steeg and Briand, seeming Radicals like Georges Bonnet and seeming Socialists like Monzie and Laval, who could usually be relied on to be neither.

The appearance of the cabinet did not long deceive any but those who wanted very much to be deceived. Even Maurras soon noted that it leaned as far to the Right as the make-up of the Chamber would permit.[21] It was at this point that diversionary measures proved briefly useful as a means of showing that, despite its moderateness, the ministry was still soundly republican. Caillaux had been a handy way of getting the support of the Socialists as a reaction to the hostile demonstrations of the Right, but it was soon clear that Caillaux's policies would lose the Socialists. Some new demonstration against the Extreme Right was needed to regain the sympathy of their enemies.

[j] One day Painlevé arrived unexpectedly at a political luncheon which he had said he could not attend, to join Charles Daniélou, Briand, Steeg, Léon Blum, and Anatole de Monzie. Halfway through the meal, he jumped up and dashed off, having just remembered that he was due at another luncheon, where, presumably, they were still waiting for him. But he could come out of a parliamentary sitting at four in the morning, deliver a lecture at eight, and be at his ministerial desk an hour later, ready for the day's work. See Charles Daniélou, *Dans l'intimité de Marianne* (1945), pp. 137, 139.

A welcome opportunity for this was provided by the right-wing leagues, which since the end of 1924 had been busily campaigning against the Communist peril, recruiting men and holding meetings. At the end of April a meeting of Taittinger's Jeunesses Patriotes in the rue Damremont in Montmartre ended in disaster when a Communist ambush resulted in four dead and several dozen injured. This had been followed by a number of other brutal skirmishes between the Communists and the leagues, with outcries in the moderate press that the police were doing nothing about the Communist threat.[22] The police were, indeed, doing something, but they were also hard on the leagues, especially on the occasion of the funeral for members of the Jeunesses Patriotes killed in the rue Damremont riot. May 1 demonstrations were forbidden, but so, a little later, were league demonstrations planned for Joan of Arc's Day. The Action Française and the Jeunesses Patriotes, in violation of police orders, demonstrated anyway, and a running battle followed, in which 118 policemen and 150 members of the Action Française were wounded, some quite seriously, and over 200 persons were arrested.

Despite their self-satisfied exhilaration, the nationalists were highly critical of the Jewish Minister of the Interior, Abraham Schrameck, for not appreciating the difference between patriots and Reds, treating both sides with equal severity. Patriotic indignation reached a peak when, as an aftermath of the Damremont bloodshed and subsequent retaliatory threats from armed nationalists, the police began to enforce long-standing regulations (long ignored) concerning the carrying of firearms. Royalist and Nationalist meetings were raided, and those attending them were searched; firearms carried without permits were confiscated and charges were brought against the offenders. This caused an outcry that police forces were leaving Jeunesses Patriotes and Camelots unarmed at the mercy of the Communists. At the beginning of June, when thirty-six members of the League were arrested at one fell swoop for illegal possession of arms, Maurras addressed an open letter to the Paris Prefect of Police, Morain, and to his superior, M. Schrameck, protesting against such measures and threatening reprisals.

In the present circumstances, which republican negligence and complicity with murderous revolutionaries had created, said Maurras, for patriots to carry arms was not a right but a duty. As for Schrameck, if one more life were lost as a result of his orders, he would pay with his own: "It would be without hatred as without fear," wrote Maurras with characteristic sobriety, "that I would give the order to spill your dog's blood, if you were to abuse the public power to open the floodgates of French blood shed under the bullets and daggers of the Moscow bandits you love."

Maurras's threats caused a great stir.[k] Again, there had been some provo-

[k] *AF,* June 9, 1925. Prosecuted for the threats and insults, Maurras was sentenced on July 17 to two years in prison and a fine of 1,000 francs. He appealed, and on October 29, 1926, the sentence was reduced to only one year in prison; after a second appeal the sentence was confirmed *but suspended* on February 8, 1927. This was the fate of several other apparently severe sentences—suspension or amnesty always intervened.

cation: only two weeks before, on May 26, Ernest Berger, the treasurer and administrative secretary of the League, a dim and bearded figure who had been Plateau's right-hand man but had always kept inconspicuously in the background, had been shot in the back as he came up out of the Métro at the Gare Saint-Lazare by an insane woman who harbored an ill-defined grudge against the Action Française. The senseless killing, coming on the heels of the rue Damremont shootings and the rioting on Joan of Arc's Day, was an additional example for the complaints of the Action Française about judicial persecution. Now, by Schrameck's order, it charged, the police had gone beyond harassing the patriots—and, some hinted, rigging their murders—and were bent on disarming them as well.

The Right took up the cry of injustice. The disarming of patriots who carried arms only for self-protection, wrote François Coty in *Le Figaro,* meant that they were being abandoned to all sorts of aggressions in the streets, where the forces of disorder were left uncontrolled. "When the State no longer defends its citizens," Jean Guiraud in *La Croix* argued with dangerous logic, "the citizens must defend themselves." Many law-abiding persons agreed with Maurras when he asked who would stand up against armed revolution if the so-called Fascist leagues were disarmed. Not the police—that was clear.[l]

But not the conservatives, either! Such outbursts as the letter to Schrameck attracted notice and raised the circulation (nonsubscription circulation, 47,500 in January, was more than 56,000 in June), but they scared off the more timid or the more respectable among the moderates. In May, Daudet, keen to be back in Parliament, had declared himself a candidate for the Maine-et-Loire Senate seat left vacant by the death of his friend Jules Delahaye. He received the support of most of the local conservative press, of great Paris dailies like *L'Echo de Paris, Le Figaro, La Liberté, Le Gaulois,* and *La Croix,* and of the Anjou Catholic Federation, which was the local branch of General de Castelnau's great Fédération Catholique.[23] He had the backing of the Delahaye interest, and the nomination of the Conservative Congress of Maine-et-Loire as "sole candidate of all the Rights against the left-wing Cartel." Yet, though ahead on the first ballot, he lost the election when republican Catholics and Radical-Socialists combined their support for his most moderate opponent, a Catholic ex-deputy named Manceau.

The provincial notables and small-town politicians of Anjou did not want a firebrand to represent them in the Senate. Daudet's Catholic enemies circulated information about his semipornographic novels and the pagan proclivities of the Action Française, but, even apart from that, Daudet was far too

[l] *Le Figaro* and *Le Gaulois,* June 10, 1925; *La Croix* and *AF,* June 11, 1925. Arguments like Guiraud's received reinforcement with the news that Etienne de Raulin, the publisher of the *Gazette de l'Ouest* of Rennes and a member of the Action Française, had been attacked by an unidentified gunman one dark night and had just managed to save himself. When a police investigation revealed that Raulin had staged the whole thing and had himself done all the shooting, the *Action française* (June 18) declared this bore all the marks of a police plot invented to discredit *them.*

flamboyant for the conservatives. While Daudet was being defeated, his enemy Caillaux was being returned to the Senate in the almost equally conservative Sarthe, right next door. But Caillaux was reassuring; Daudet was hardly that. And echoes of the Schrameck scandal would not prove attractive to provincials, who distrusted all talk of guns and wanted solid, sober men to look after their interests in Paris.[m]

Sobriety was not always, it was clear, an outstanding characteristic of the movement Daudet led. The leagues were noisily in evidence throughout the summer, and sometimes made the news, as when student members of the Action Française and Jeunesses Patriotes so booed and insulted Herriot as he addressed the prize-giving ceremony of the Lycée Louis-le-Grand that they drowned out his words and got themselves carried off to the police station. Talk of the agitation spread, and even foreign papers noted the new violence of the *Action française,* pointing out that it fed on the unending economic troubles, on governmental instability, on a patriotic concern for France's overseas interests affected by serious troubles in Syria and North Africa, and on disaffection for Parliament and for parliamentary government.[n]

A sensitive deputy, Jean Chastanet, when registering at a Lyon hotel, found it better to give a false name and profession than to admit he was a politician.[24] Tradesmen had started to refuse their tax schedules, and the spring of 1926 would bring shopkeeper protest strikes that seem an earlier, smaller-scale version of Poujadism.[o] "There is a lot of talk right now of leaders and dictators," Daudet commented, and a month later, Charles Benoist: "On parle beaucoup de la dictature"[25]—not an altogether surprising suggestion in view of the three cabinets and six Ministers of Finance who had held office in twelve months, nor in view of the raging inflation; the pound sterling had risen from 83 to 130 francs, the dollar from 18.40 to 26.75.

Against this background of soaring prices, speculation, and deteriorating currency, of personal feuds and theoretical disagreements among political personalities to whom the country looked for a solution to its problems, royalist agitation grew. The Action Française tried to recruit more and more adherents, whether they were royalist or not: "We do not ask you to cry 'Long live the King,' but only 'Long live France,' " it argued, and it helped to foster the idea that only renewed national union round Clemenceau could rescue the country from its present straits.[26]

The Cartel majority was incapable of handling the crisis. The suggestion

[m] It should be noted that the endorsement of the Conservative Congress had come on June 6, three days before Maurras's letter to Schrameck.

[n] See *Frankfurter Zeitung,* July 19, 1925. But *L'Ere nouvelle,* Sept. 30, 1925, pointed out that royalist ideas had their share in present economic difficulties: "Mais qui a donc accepté le plan Dawes, si ce n'est M. Poincaré? Et qui donc a porté M. Poincaré au pouvoir si ce n'est *l'Action française?*"

[o] The Action Française was no stranger to this movement; one of the protesting leaders at Sully-sur-Loire, the owner of the local hardware store, was treasurer of the royalist group there (see *AF,* Jan. 31, 1926). Of course, Poujade's father, too, was a member of the Action Française.

of a radical solution only antagonized the Radicals, and more orthodox solutions which drew the support of the Right threw off the Socialists. In the summer of 1926, as Herriot was forming his most ill-fated cabinet, the pound sterling stood at 235, nearly 300 per cent higher than eighteen months before; in shops the prices rose from one hour to the next as people bought anything at all in order to unload their cash. When Monzie (who would take the Finance Ministry under Herriot) offered the Treasury to Maurice Colrat, the latter remonstrated: "Come now, Anatole, we're both representatives of the Lot; why do you offer me the Treasury when you know there's nothing in it?"[27]

In the boiling summer heat, the *Action française* campaigned harder than ever against the cracking Cartel. No more inflation, it clamored: "Ni impôts, ni emprunt!" The budget impasse could be solved by cutting government personnel 20 per cent, by cutting direct taxes (which would increase the revenue from them), by taxing resident foreigners and their businesses, by raising customs duties, and—most important—by farming out the State monopolies, thus getting ready cash to stabilize the franc.[28]

The *Action française* and its sidekick *Candide* were echoed at great public meetings—at Nîmes on July 11, in Vendée on the 25th, at Strasbourg on the 27th, where tens of thousands cheered the denunciation of a supine Left and a useless Parliament. Camelot violence likewise rose to a high pitch in a series of riots outside the Palais Bourbon, especially when, refused the Chamber's confidence upon its first appearance, the Herriot cabinet and Herriot himself almost ended up in the Seine.[p]

Two days of rioting on July 20–21 ended the Cartel's uneasy hold, and in a near-insurrectionist atmosphere, ushered in the financial appeasement of a Poincaré combination. These days seem to have marked the high point of the leagues born in 1924, and also the high point of the Action Française in political activities. When on the morrow of Herriot's fall Daudet proclaimed that the choice of France lay between the Action Française and revolution, he was wildly wrong—but his error was comprehensible. Like most political enthusiasts, he lived surrounded by like-minded friends; he marked the hold his movement had on students and on the Latin Quarter; he counted—or rather gave up counting—the thousands who swarmed eagerly to meetings throughout the country; and he concluded that, away from the Left, his movement was alone in youth and enthusiastic numbers.[29] Turning his back on economics, he felt quite sure that even Poincaré could not disentangle the dreadful mess of French economic affairs. Only dictatorial methods could do that, and then the loathed republic—*la gueuse*—would be on its way out: "Just wait a little while, you scoundrels, dolts and dupes," he apostrophized in near-triumphant tones. "Nothing, nothing, nothing is going to stop us!"[30]

[p] Valois, *L'Homme contre l'argent,* pp. 244, 258, suggests that the July riots were instigated and to some extent carried out by agents of the police or the Sûreté.

9

PHILIPPE

SOMETHING WAS TO STOP THE Action Française soon, and it would come from an unexpected quarter. But omens for the future were not lacking. In these years, and at the height of its success, the Action Française was involved in difficulties which squandered much of its energy and its effectiveness, and which we must now pause to attend.

The beginnings, most cruel and most publicized, go back to 1923, when, on November 27, a brief note in the *Action française* announced the death of the eldest son of Daudet's second marriage, fourteen-year-old Philippe. Condolences flowed in on the bereaved parents, letters from unknown friends, from parliamentary colleagues, from political acquaintances, and even from opponents. Then, suddenly, five days later, headlines announced to startled readers that Philippe Daudet had died a violent death, and a mystery was touched on that still remains unsolved. The space devoted to its discussion is pertinent not to its historical significance, if it has any, but to the part it played and still plays in the mythology, psychology, and fortunes of the movement that concerns us here.

On Tuesday, November 20, 1923, Philippe left his home in the rue Saint-Guillaume, next door to the building of the Sciences Politiques, for school. But instead of going to school, he took a train for Le Havre and there attempted to secure passage to some Canadian port. He had a good sum of money with him—700 francs of his own, plus 1,000 more that he had taken from his parents. It was not enough for passage to Canada, however, and he had apparently counted on working his way aboard ship. He was a month short of fifteen but looked three or four years older—nearly six feet tall, broad-shouldered and strong.

Such escapades were nothing new in Philippe's life; several times in the past few years he had run away from home, and his parents, resigned, had even gone so far as to sew money and identifying labels into his clothes. This time, however, Philippe could not resolve to return home as he had done on three or four other occasions. The day before his departure he had written a poem that ended, "None will understand the reason of my going. None will guess what made me do it. Two more days and, like the bird on its first flight, I shall be off to faraway lands, new experiences, and adventure."

Unfortunately, adventure was hard to find. At Le Havre Philippe discovered that there were passports and labor regulations, and that employers wanted to hire men with identification papers and with a trade. His money was insufficient for a passage, and his hopes of working his way across were frustrated. For two days he hung around Le Havre, moping in his hotel room and visiting the port. He tried to buy a gun and failed. He wrote to his parents but tore up what he wrote. On Thursday, November 22, he was off again, leaving his books behind in the hotel—Malherbe, Ronsard, Chenier, a mystery story, a list of sailings for Canada, and a copy of *L'Humanité*.

He arrived back in Paris on Thursday afternoon, at the Gare Saint-Lazare, almost opposite the offices of the *Action française* in the rue de Rome. But instead of going to friends, he turned and made for the offices of the Anarchist review, the *Libertaire*. There he talked to one of the editors, Georges Vidal, declaring his sympathy for Anarchist ideas and his desire to strike a blow for the cause. Could not Vidal suggest someone the Anarchists would like to be rid of? Vidal, embarrassed by so much enthusiasm and probably a little alarmed, said no. The visitor insisted: Poincaré, Millerand, perhaps Léon Daudet? Vidal did his best to make him drop these notions. The Anarchists of 1920 had little in common with their bomb-throwing predecessors of an earlier day. They were individualistic, pacifistic, anti-authoritarian, more than a little broke. Their chief enemies now were not so much among the bourgeoisie as at the extremes of bourgeois society: aggressive nationalists of whom the royalists were the most militant symbol, and Communists who tried to drive the Left under Muscovite dictatorship. They did not really care for murders and did far more talking about them than acting. Besides, Germaine Berton's trial was pending, and the unknown visitor might be either mad or an *agent provocateur*. Philippe gave a donation of 200 francs for the paper, a gift "From X—for violent action." He did not reveal his identity.

His new Anarchist friends asked him to dine with them, and one named Gruffy put him up for the night. To his night's host Philippe confided that his father beat and punished him too harshly, that he hated him and all the bourgeoisie from which he had now escaped, and that he wanted to get revenge on the whole crowd by committing some dazzling crime. But here again he was frustrated. Neither Gruffy nor another Anarchist he tackled on the subject would help him by suggesting a good target.

Friday the 23rd seems to have been the day on which Philippe acquired a gun—but probably no bullets. The Anarchists had given him the address of a bookshop kept by another Anarchist, Pierre Le Flaoutter, on the Boulevard Beaumarchais, near the Bastille, and Flaoutter, among whose other professions was that of police informer, may have got the gun for him. But there is no evidence at all that Philippe did visit Flaoutter on Friday, and Flaoutter later maintained that he saw him for the first time on Saturday. Philippe did, however, visit the explorer Louis Frédéric Roquette, whom he had never met but whose writings on Alaska and the Great North had fired his imagination.

Roquette received him kindly, but gave him no encouragement to believe that a trip to Alaska would be easy or the life there uniformly exciting.

Philippe then returned to the *Libertaire* and gave Vidal a sheaf of poems that he had written and a sealed letter for his mother, which, he said, Vidal would learn to whom to send if anything should happen. The letter read: "My darling mother,—Forgive the suffering I cause you. I have been an Anarchist for a long time but did not dare to say so. Now the cause has called me and I believe it is my duty to do what I do. I love you very much. Kiss the kids for me.—Philippe."

The following morning, Saturday 24, he visited Flaoutter's bookshop, asked for Baudelaire's *Les Fleurs du Mal,* and agreed to return for the edition that he wanted some time during the afternoon. He also asked for ammunition—and probably got it—and revealed his plans for murdering Poincaré, Millerand, or Léon Daudet. The bookseller at once passed on the news to Lannes, a high official of the Sûreté, who in turn warned his superior, Marlier. The news of possible murder attempts apparently reached the rue des Saussaies at the beginning of a dull Saturday afternoon, in the awkward period between the end of one shift and the start of the next. Marlier despatched the men he could lay hands on—eight inspectors and commissaires under the orders of a high administrative official, Controller-General Delange. To be on the safe side, he also warned the Prefecture of Police, which sent four police agents to Flaoutter's shop, three of whom remained before it throughout the afternoon.

The two forces ignored each other, as police and Sûreté usually tend to do, at best, but the eleven, sometimes twelve, men remained on duty throughout the cold, gathering dusk of a November afternoon, surveying a shop front about fifteen feet wide, with a narrow door and an illuminated interior that one could see from the street. They watched for the dangerous man who, they had been told, was armed and who planned to kill an important politician; they watched, and, it would seem, they missed him.

And while they watched, a little before half past four, but a few blocks away, a tall young boy hailed a taxi and asked to be driven to the Cirque Médrano. The driver, one Bajot, took the Boulevard Beaumarchais, passing Flaoutter's shop, and then the Boulevard Magenta. Near the Gare du Nord he heard a sharp report that sounded to him like a blowout. He glanced back and saw that his passenger had slumped down on the seat. He stopped, got out, saw that the lad was shot through the head and bleeding heavily, and with a policeman drove him to the Hospital of Lariboisière. It was there that the boy died, unidentified, without regaining consciousness.

Philippe's parents in the meantime had begun to worry. They had grown used to unexpected flights—only the year before Philippe had left them twice at eight days' interval. But this absence was unduly long. They did not like the disappearance of the 1,000 francs, and they did not like the persistent silence. Anxiously, they scanned the newspapers for some indication they may have hoped they would not find. When on Sunday they saw a brief item about an unknown suicide, they sent a family friend to look at the body.

Philippe was buried quietly by his family.[a] No one doubted that he had committed suicide, and to secure him a Christian burial the family doctor certified that this suicide had occurred while his mind had been unbalanced. The doctor could so certify with a clear conscience, knowing that this was perfectly true, that there was no way of telling the degree, but that young Philippe's vagaries were, more than repetitious adolescent pranks, symptoms of a disease whose grip he could do little or nothing to resist.

The suicide was not publicly admitted, of course. Daudet told everyone that his son had died of lightning spinal meningitis, and even when rumors of suicide began to leak out, the press breathed not a word to trouble him. Then, on Saturday, December 1, the *Libertaire* broke the discreet silence with its disclosure that Philippe Daudet and the unknown visitor who had offered his help to the Anarchist cause were one and the same. The dead boy's memory, claimed the *Libertaire* in thus publicly forwarding his last words to his mother, demanded that he be acknowledged for what he was—a loyal Anarchist disciple ready to die for the cause. Nothing could be sweeter to the Anarchists than this melancholy duty of so proclaiming that the son of their loathed enemy Léon Daudet had turned to the Anarchists, and if they were glad to avenge the deaths of some of their friends in this way by drawing public notice to the strange hostility in Philippe's letter, there seems to be no question of their doubting the sincerity of Philippe's conversion.

The sensational revelations of the *Libertaire,* apart from increasing sales a hundredfold, did rather miss their mark. Instead of breaking, Daudet reacted by utter disbelief. If the Anarchists were in it, so, necessarily, were the Germans, the Jews, and the police. His son's death was the work of political enemies always on the lookout for revenge. On December 2, an article in the *Action française,* under the headline "AN ATROCIOUS REVENGE: PHILIPPE DAUDET HAS BEEN MURDERED," explained to its fascinated readers how the German party always sought to strike at France through the Action Française, at particularly crucial moments: a German agent had murdered Marius Plateau just when French troops were entering the Ruhr. Now Philippe Daudet had been caught in a mysterious snare at a moment when new danger of war with Germany had arisen.[1]

To discover how his son's death had really occurred, Daudet lodged a complaint and waited for justice to take a speedy course. But could one

[a] On January 18, 1925, Poincaré, who had been Premier at the time, recalled his part in the events in a letter to Maurras: "Lorsque le malheureux Philippe a été reconnu à Lariboisière, M. Jacques Bainville et M. le docteur Bernard sont venus, de la part du père, me prier de faire ramener le corps à la maison. J'ai immédiatement remis à ces Messieurs une lettre pour le Préfet de Police. Le docteur Bernard m'avait dit: 'Ce jeune homme était atteint de la maladie de la fugue. Il s'est suicidé. C'est le sort de la plupart de ces malades.' La version du suicide m'a donc, dès la mort, paru vraisemblable." Maurras papers.

trust the kind of court that allowed Germaine Berton to go free? When the decision in the Berton case was reached on Christmas Eve, an *Action française* editorial castigated "The Jury's Crime" and affirmed that the failure of police and justice to carry out their tasks meant that the Action Française had the right to improvise its own magistrature:

> No force in the world can prevent a people from wanting its share of justice. If justice is refused, it takes it, it creates it, since public order and public life cannot endure without it.
>
> But the revolutionaries say the same thing.
>
> They do not say or do the same thing at all, because their violence is not in the service of order but of disorder, not in the service of property but in that of theft, not in the service of authority but in that of anarchy, not in the service of the fatherland but in that of the enemy.[b]

Necessarily, since justice was so backward, the Action Française sponsored its own investigations. Witnesses came forward to testify to odd, unsubstantiated things; theories were proposed, tested, and discarded; surprise witnesses announced with great fanfare vanished without further word after an hour in the judge's chambers. Several *juges d'instruction* considered the case without finding the evidence that Daudet expected. The young man had not been coerced into running away or writing his note, either by physical force or by drugs. He had moved freely, and despite some odd gaps remaining in the reconstruction of his five days of wandering, it did not appear that he had been used for any nefarious plan. The Sûreté had bungled again, certainly; but it was difficult to say more than that. Philippe had hailed a taxi, had sat in it alone, and then some minutes later had been found shot through the head. The driver's evidence seemed incontrovertible. In September 1925 the case was dismissed, investigations having uncovered no fresh evidence that could explain the death as other than suicide.

Yet the case remained obscure. There was the question of the victim's clothes, which, carefully labeled when he left home, bore on his death no mark of identification. Had he removed the tags himself, or had someone else? Who, then, and when? Had the Anarchists, despite their denials, been able to learn his identity by some remaining tag? What had happened to his money, of which he had so much on Thursday and so little on Friday that he had to borrow some for the night's lodging? Did all of it go for the gun? Above all, how had a dozen experienced detectives, with a friendly informer to help them, failed to get their quarry? And why, in the first place, had so many of them been mobilized on the strength of some crackpot's threats?

[b] *AF*, Dec. 2, 5, 25, 1923. With the exception of *L'Oeuvre*, the *Quotidien*, and the Marxist papers, all the Paris press of December 25, 1923, found Germaine Berton's acquittal highly regrettable. But then, as Hervé remarked in the *Victoire*: "Que voulez-vous que le jury réponde, quand on vient déballer devant lui toutes les violences de *l'Action française?*"

As *L'Humanité* commented, "If judicially the Philippe Daudet affair is closed, mysterious aspects are still unexplained. The child's death remains an historical enigma."[2]

It would not remain an enigma long if Philippe's father had his way. He saw the poor boy's death as the result of a police plot to get him, Léon. The Sûreté, through one of its numerous stool pigeons, had discovered Philippe's presence among the Anarchists, had followed him, had let its dubious henchman Flaoutter get a gun for him, and then had got him cornered in the bookshop. The plan had been to frame the boy and use the resulting charges as a lever to keep the father quiet. But the scheme went wrong: probably someone panicked—a policeman or the boy. Philippe was shot, put into a taxi, and then "found" as a suicide. And the plan would have worked, but for the *Libertaire*'s having inadvertently aroused Léon Daudet's suspicions.

This theory, or variations of it, usually less convincing, which were advanced at different times, assumed that a great many persons had been involved in murder, by design or by chance, and that in an unusual display of solidarity they had decided to stand or fall together. Flaoutter and his wife lied; policemen, of two rival forces, lied; above all, Bajot the taxi driver lied, out of fear of the police, and his tale was a fabrication from beginning to end.

It was true that Bajot's story contained some discrepancies, but by good luck the taxi driver was able to track down his fares for Saturday afternoon until quite close to his last fateful charge; and it was incredible to suppose that men of the Sûreté, trying to camouflage a shooting, would hail a cruising taxi at random, load in the dying boy, and coach the driver in his part, all within a few minutes. Yet it was Bajot whom Daudet singled out, persuaded that if he broke him down he would also break the conspiracy of silence that surrounded the alleged crime. When, bitterly attacked and challenged to admit the truth, the taxi driver sued Daudet for slander, Daudet had what he wanted: a court in which to present his case and to denounce the vile conspiracy against him by Anarchists, policemen, and their despicable stooges.

It was evident that Daudet's case did not hold water. No one could deny that Philippe's death was odd, and a good many people thought it was not a suicide. But Bajot's story, however challenged, held; and the jury did not seem to think that an apparently innocent witness need be sacrificed to a father's grief. The jury was noticeably unsympathetic when, in the midst of a poignant appeal for justice, Daudet suddenly changed from a heartbroken father into a professional denouncer of the Germans. When he began his tirade, blaming everything on German intrigue, the jurors overcame their emotion; their faces hardened, and his case was lost. On November 14, 1925, Daudet was sentenced to five months' imprisonment and a 1,500-franc fine. Joseph Delest, the manager of the *Action française,* was sentenced to two months' imprisonment and a 300-franc fine, and both Daudet and Delest were ordered to pay Bajot joint damages of 25,000 francs.[3]

Opinion was divided: Edouard Herriot and André Lefèvre, a former Minister of War, seem to have believed that Philippe had been murdered. So, in a different way, did Anarchists like Georges Vidal.[4] The Daudet family continues still to maintain, though without proof, that Bajot was in the pay of the police.

If we discount the Daudet theory, the most reasonable remaining explanation seems to be that Philippe, high-strung and impulsive, had been affected by the atmosphere in which he moved, at a most impressionable age, an age when young boys yearn for action, for heroics, for adventure. His entire life had been colored by the Action Française, his imagination inspired by its hates and loves, by its pranks and its campaigns. Now he thought of Alaska, now of dreadful enemies that swarmed around; his dreams oscillated between faraway lands and the no less fascinating possibilities of adventure and derring-do that Paris held in store. None of this need have gone far beyond adolescent fancy, had not Philippe been slightly unbalanced, subject to runaway fits and uncontrollable impulses.

When Philippe ran away that Tuesday in November, he may have had a definite idea in mind, but it did not survive the hard facts that he learned at Le Havre. Unable to follow his fancy to Canada, he was then torn between remorse and fear at the way he had left home and the money he had taken and, on the other hand, the wish to enact his daydreams in some way, by some ennobling deed. In Le Havre he wrote to his parents, both of them, a pathetic letter, begging forgiveness and announcing suicide—but he did not send it.[c] The thought of suicide may have occurred as one more dream of an absolving act, something spectacular and striking to satisfy the mind, a ransom or a forfeit that would clear away his guilt. But other possibilities offered: in Paris he could walk into the dragon's mouth, seek out his father's enemies, the men who had planned Léon Daudet's murder and executed that of Plateau—the Anarchists.

Did Philippe seek revenge at the *Libertaire,* or was he actually fascinated by them? Like the Action Française, the Anarchists opposed the established order, criticized corrupt society, attacked plutocracy and the political system. The violence of the language was much the same in both. They differed essentially in that Anarchists considered individuals more important than the nation; but how are we to know Philippe's attitude on this score? His poems, "Les Parfums maudits," reflect some talent, much concern with sex, and the strong influence of Baudelaire. They carry no trace of the orderly rigor of nationalist neo-classicism (but then, neither does his father's writing). How

[c] The letter ran: "Mes parents chéris,—Pardon, oh! pardon, pour la peine immense que je vous ai faite. Je ne suis qu'un misérable et un voleur. Mais j'espère que mon repentir effacera cette tache. Je vous renvoie l'argent que je n'ai pas dépensé et je vous supplie de me pardonner. Quand vous recevrez cette lettre je ne serai plus vivant. Adieu mais je vous adore plus que tout. —Votre enfant désespéré, Philippe. . . . Embrassez de ma part Claire et François, mais ne leur dites jamais que leur frère était un voleur.

much of all this would Philippe understand? How much would he consider?

He may have wished to "infiltrate" and to return with glorious tales of having uncovered Anarchist conspiracies. He may have—who can tell?—gone to the movement that seemed from an Action Française perspective darkest and most dynamic, oddly attracted by the diabolic prestige attributed to it. He may actually have thought of killing someone just to cut a dash; perhaps even—why not?—his own father. The tales he told Gruffy are typical enough of adolescent exaggeration, but how many have not invented their like and even for a moment wished that they were true?

But things apparently went wrong: Canada turned out to be inaccessible, the Anarchists did not come up to expectations, no one appreciated his dreams, the unaccustomed amount of money disappeared, the world grew cold and lonely. Saturday must have been dismal, as all accounts agree—even the street lights had to be turned on at an unusually early hour—and through it the boy wandered with his collection of rebuffs. Did he see the policemen at Flaoutter's door, and turn and run? When he asked Bajot to drive him to the circus, was it an excuse and did the grim determination flood him on the way? With the intuition that knows intention to be the better part of crime, he may have thought his guilt so overwhelming that no escape remained. Tragedies are terrible at fifteen, far, far worse than at fifty, and the despair that whispered suicide before would now seem more decisive, and so he raised the gun.

Shortly after the Daudet-Bajot trial, Mme Marthe Daudet wrote a book about her son and his death. After reading it, a friend sent her a letter of sympathy:

> How can it be that so many men should hide the truth or fail to discern it! Such complicity in some, such blindness in others! It is a baffling mystery to me how the party spirit can to such a degree stupefy so many minds otherwise enlightened, degrade so many consciences to which, after all, the idea of good is not completely foreign.

A year later, when the High Court of Appeal affirmed the verdict of Assizes, another friend, Léon Mirman, wrote to Mme Daudet: "I am quite certain that a day will come—it cannot fail to come—when in the abominable network of complicities a thread will snap to let the whole truth out. What a collapse there will be that day, what a stampede, what rushing *sauve-qui-peut*!"[5]

But the thread has not yet snapped. The revelation that one could reasonably expect had Daudet's theory been right has not been made in nearly forty years. Under such circumstances, it would seem safe—though not absolutely certain—to assume that no further revelations will be made to change the historian's verdict of "Not proven."

10

THE LEAGUE: DUTIES, DUES, AND DOCTRINE

In the reorganization of royalist activity that followed its prewar triumph over the "old gang," the Action Française had divided France into ten zones, each covered by a delegate of the Duc d'Orléans and a regional secretary of the Action Française. The zones were made up as follows:

Zone 1, Northern Region: Pas-de-Calais, Aisne, Nord, Somme, Oise.

Zone 2, Northwest Region: Mayenne, Calvados, Seine-Inférieure, Manche, Sarthe, Eure, Seine-et-Oise, Orne.

Zone 3, Western Region: Loire-Inférieure, Côtes-du-Nord, Finistère, Ille-et-Vilaine, Morbihan, Maine-et-Loire.

Zone 4, Eastern Region: Vosges, Ardennes, Meurthe-et-Moselle, Aube, Haute-Marne, Meuse, Marne, Seine-et-Marne, Belfort.

Zone 5, Loire Region: Cher, Loiret, Loir-et-Cher, Indre, Indre-et-Loire, Eure-et-Loir, Yonne, Nièvre.

Zone 6, Southwest Region: This had two regional secretaries—one at Bordeaux: Gironde, Dordogne, Lot-et-Garonne, Landes, Hautes-Pyrénées, Basses-Pyrénées; the other at Poitiers: Deux-Sèvres, Vendée, Vienne, Charente, Charente-Inférieure.

Zone 7, Massif Central: Allier, Corrèze, Creuse, Cantal, Haute-Vienne, Puy-de-Dôme.

Zone 8, Lyon: Rhône, Ain, Ardèche, Isère, Savoie, Haute-Savoie, Drôme, Saône-et-Loire, Haute-Loire, Loire. (The departments of Côte-d'Or, Haute-Saône, Doubs, and Jura came under the Delegate's authority but not under the authority of the Action Française regional secretary.)

Zone 9, Toulouse: Haute-Garonne, Aveyron, Ariège, Gers, Aude, Tarn-et-Garonne, Pyrénées-Orientales, Lot, Tarn.

Zone 10, Midi: Hérault, Alpes-Maritimes, Hautes-Alpes, Basses-Alpes, Bouches-du-Rhône, Gard, Vaucluse, Var, Lozère, Corsica.

At the beginning of 1923 a new regional secretariat was set up for Algeria, including the departments of Alger, Oran, and Constantine, with its headquarters at Oran.[1]

Except for the Algerian zone, these administrative divisions corresponded neither with the ancient provinces of France nor, exactly, with the new departments. A good example of this was Zone 2, the Northwest, which included the departments of what was the province of Normandy, but also Mayenne and Sarthe. The most active royalist centers in that zone were not Rouen or Le Havre but secondary cities like Caen, Evreux, and Alençon, where conservative traditions would be more helpful than in, for example, booming Cherbourg. In effect, the zones overlapped traditional administrative and physical limits, and the newspaper itself did not appear any too certain of their boundaries, listing certain towns now in one zone, now in another. The centers chosen for regional and district activities did not always coincide with important economic centers or geographical areas. The most discernible basis for their choice seems to have been as follows:

1. Chance: a compromise between some pre-existing order and the initiative or the convenience of a local leader, patron, or enthusiast.
2. The desire to reinforce already existing royalist organizations.
3. The presence of a university. New groups were set up in university towns where contacts could easily be made with young people, mostly of the middle class.
4. The presence of small and medium industry, which provided good opportunities for propaganda.
5. The existence of a strong local clergy. An attempt was made to exploit the possibilities of regions where the clergy was strongly critical of the State and State schools.

The Action Française *Almanach* of 1911 listed 182 sections and groups; by 1912, over two hundred were claimed; by 1914, a hundred more.[2] During the war, for obvious reasons, the organizations these numbers represented largely disintegrated, with the young men in military service, the old ones busy with other tasks, and with organizers and lecturers from Paris no longer available to keep the royalist network together. By the end of the war, only a skeleton of the prewar structure remained. Sections shown on the books as having three hundred members numbered less than ten; and of the few remaining members a good many had neither signed the conditions of membership nor kept up the payment of their dues. Nor were most of them particularly restoration-minded. "Our friends," wrote Louis Dimier, "had ceased to believe in the old aim of the Action Française, in the restoration, and even less in the idea of a *coup de force* supposed to be its means." As for the Paris office, nobody cared what went on in the provinces, except when it came to raising funds.[3]

The end of war did not bring any sudden change; soldiers could not shed their horizon-blue at once, and then there was the problem of a job and the resumption of civilian life after years of war. There were also, of course, many gaps that could never be filled. Some 2,500 Camelots were dead or missing in action. The Limoges section, for one, was decimated; the Rouen section lost twenty-three dead, that of Nîmes, forty-three. In all, several

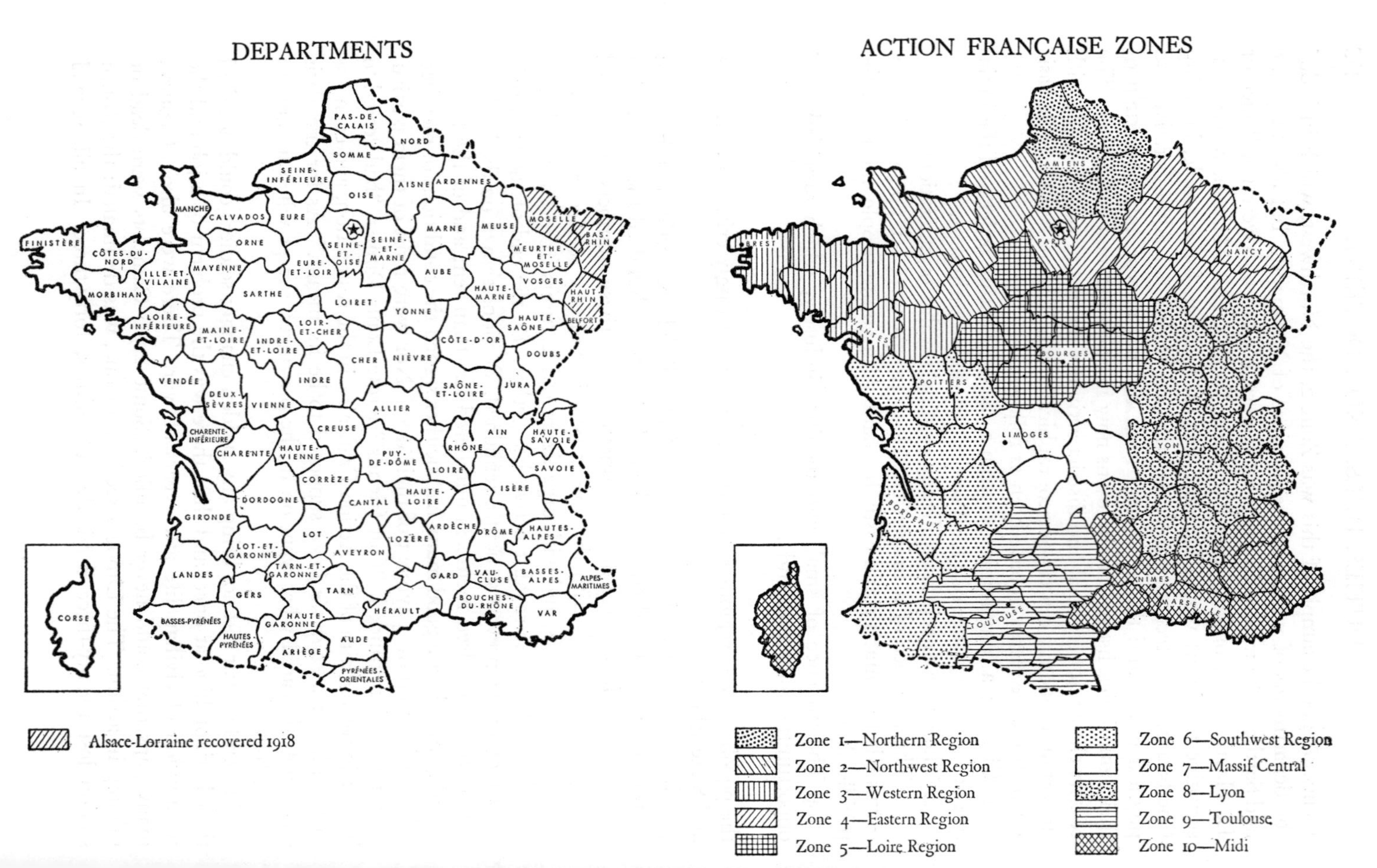
DEPARTMENTS
PAS-DE-CALAIS
NORD
SOMME
SEINE-INFÉRIEURE
OISE
AISNE
ARDENNES
MANCHE
CALVADOS
EURE
MOSELLE
BAS-RHIN
FINISTÈRE
CÔTES-DU-NORD
ORNE
SEINE-ET-OISE
SEINE-ET-MARNE
MARNE
MEUSE
MEURTHE-ET-MOSELLE
ILLE-ET-VILAINE
MAYENNE
EURE-ET-LOIR
AUBE
VOSGES
MORBIHAN
SARTHE
LOIRET
HAUTE-MARNE
HAUT-RHIN
LOIRE-INFÉRIEURE
MAINE-ET-LOIRE
LOIR-ET-CHER
YONNE
HAUTE-SAÔNE
BELFORT
INDRE-ET-LOIRE
CHER
NIÈVRE
CÔTE-D'OR
DOUBS
VENDÉE
INDRE
SAÔNE-ET-LOIRE
JURA
DEUX-SÈVRES
VIENNE
ALLIER
CHARENTE-INFÉRIEURE
CREUSE
AIN
HAUTE-SAVOIE
CHARENTE
HAUTE-VIENNE
PUY-DE-DÔME
RHÔNE
LOIRE
SAVOIE
CORRÈZE
DORDOGNE
CANTAL
HAUTE-LOIRE
ISÈRE
GIRONDE
LOT
ARDÈCHE
DRÔME
HAUTES-ALPES
LOZÈRE
LOT-ET-GARONNE
AVEYRON
LANDES
TARN-ET-GARONNE
GARD
VAUCLUSE
BASSES-ALPES
ALPES-MARITIMES
GERS
TARN
BOUCHES-DU-RHÔNE
HÉRAULT
VAR
CORSE
BASSES-PYRÉNÉES
HAUTE-GARONNE
HAUTES-PYRÉNÉES
AUDE
ARIÈGE
PYRÉNÉES-ORIENTALES
Alsace-Lorraine recovered 1918
ACTION FRANÇAISE ZONES
AMIENS
BREST
PARIS
NANCY
NANTES
BOURGES
POITIERS
LIMOGES
LYON
BORDEAUX
NIMES
MARSEILLE
TOULOUSE
Zone 1—Northern Region
Zone 2—Northwest Region
Zone 3—Western Region
Zone 4—Eastern Region
Zone 5—Loire Region
Zone 6—Southwest Region
Zone 7—Massif Central
Zone 8—Lyon
Zone 9—Toulouse
Zone 10—Midi

FRENCH POLITICAL ORIENTATION*

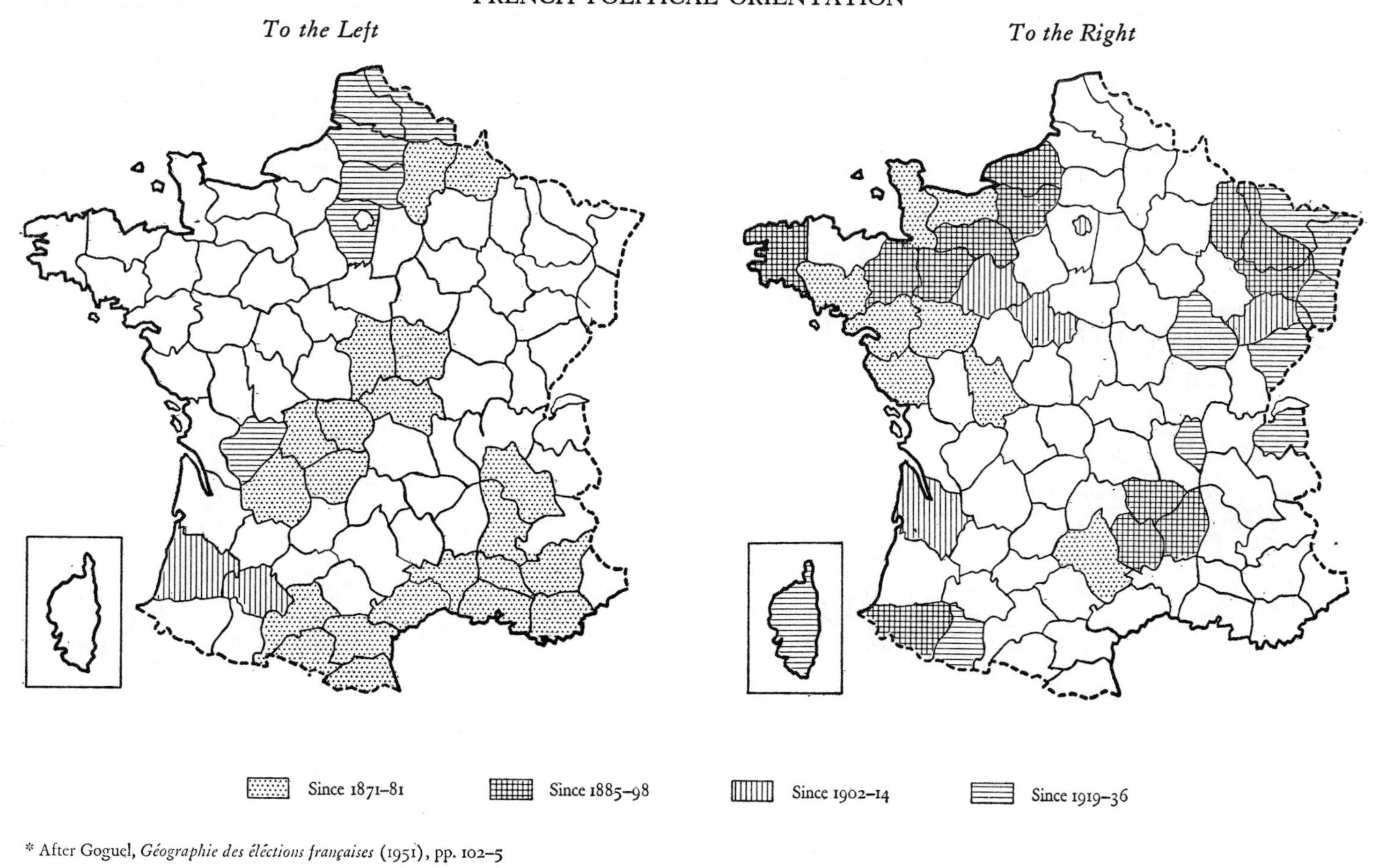

* After Goguel, *Géographie des éléctions françaises* (1951), pp. 102–5

THE ACTION FRANÇAISE IN 1910

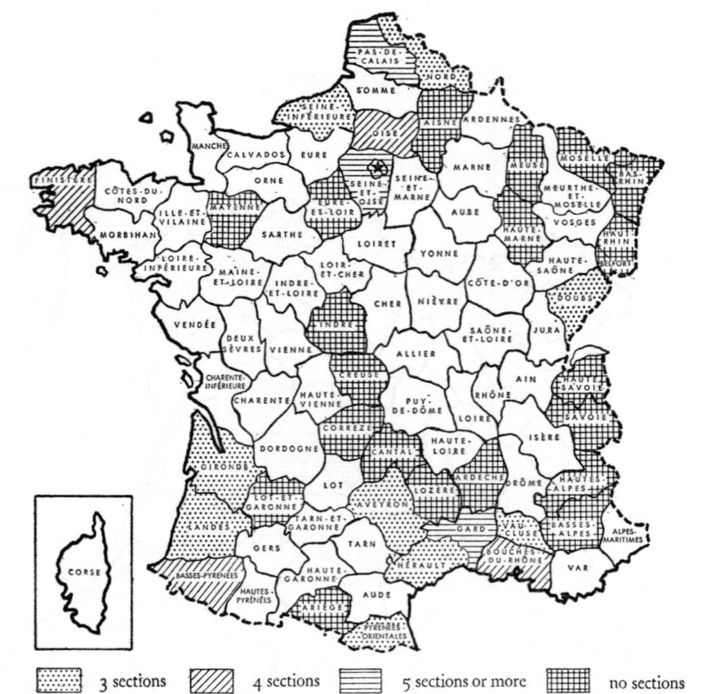

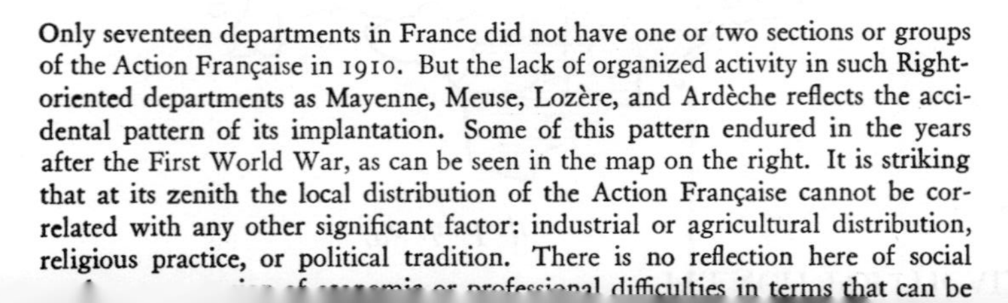

THE ACTION FRANÇAISE IN 1928

Only seventeen departments in France did not have one or two sections or groups of the Action Française in 1910. But the lack of organized activity in such Right-oriented departments as Mayenne, Meuse, Lozère, and Ardèche reflects the accidental pattern of its implantation. Some of this pattern endured in the years after the First World War, as can be seen in the map on the right. It is striking that at its zenith the local distribution of the Action Française cannot be correlated with any other significant factor: industrial or agricultural distribution, religious practice, or political tradition. There is no reflection here of social [illegible] of economic or professional difficulties in terms that can be followed through. In Tarn-et-Garonne, where artisan industries were facing ruin, the Action Française flourished; but in the neighboring Tarn the local textile industry prospered and the Action Française did too. Aveyron, fervently Catholic, showed less Action Française activity than the religiously indifferent Pyrénées-Orientales or Seine-et-Marne. Both Nord and Meuse were highly industrialized: one had fifteen sections, the other none. Nothing can show better the ideological and somewhat artificial character of the Action Française. It transcended concrete differences because it appealed to ideas which had little connection with existing political and social realities.

THE ACTION FRANÇAISE AND CONSERVATIVE OPINION

Four representatives or more (Paris and Seine, 13)

Three representatives Two representatives

On November 11, 1936, one hundred Deputies and Senators signed a protest "contre la rigueur inaccoutumée des mesures prises à l'égard de l'un des plus éminents représentants des lettres françaises." The distribution of the signers gives a classic map of the French Right, reflecting the prestige of the Action Française in conservative circles, even those Republican in name.

THE ACTION FRANÇAISE IN 1959

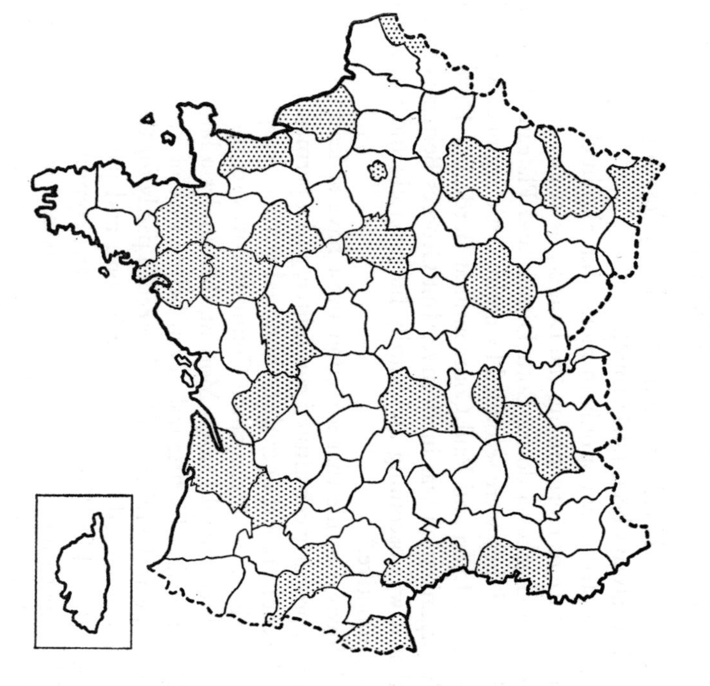

The Redressement Français, direct heir of the Action Française, in 1959 had twenty-three sections besides its organizations in Paris and Algiers. Once again, there is no obvious coincidence between this distribution and any current political, social, or economic realities, even that of Poujadism, which made a good showing not only in Isère and Maine-et-Loire, where the Redressement Français was active, but also in Charente-Maritime, Vaucluse, and Aveyron, where it did not even exist.

thousand members were killed or maimed—a heavy loss for a movement whose numbers had always been fairly small.

The leaders, interested now not only in money but also in electoral action, realized the importance of reorganizing the League, or at any rate of giving those who wanted a chance to do it. Both Dimier and Plateau made some attempt at revival, and they were seconded by enthusiastic regional secretaries like Louis Jasseron at Lyon and Paul Courcoural at Bordeaux. Dimier complained that the organization was ineffective. But Georges Bernanos felt, on the contrary, that it was becoming awkwardly bureaucratic and was stifling the old Camelot initiative.[4]

Plateau laid down the rule that a section must have at least forty dues-paying members, a properly constituted committee, and a permanent meeting place. By 1922 he could report over three hundred sections, propaganda centers, and representatives.[5] A Propaganda Committee was set up in 1920, first under Maurras's trusted friend Lucien Moreau, then under a lawyer devoted to the cause, Paul Robain. Its first task, even before that of arranging provincial lecture tours, was the raising of funds, needed partly for the newspaper budget, partly for free or reduced-rate subscriptions, and partly for posters, public meetings, and the like. The propaganda service commissioned and circulated pamphlets, generally in first printings of 100,000, which sometimes went into several editions. One pamphlet by Jean Gazave, on the Action Française, its leaders and its doctrines, was printed, the Eleventh Congress was told, in a run of a million copies. Some of the propaganda for Alsace-Lorraine was printed in German, like the special editions of the Action Française *Almanach, Kalendar der Action Française für Elsass und Lothringen.* Occasional newspaper reports describe meetings in the Colmar region held in German or in the local Alsatian dialect.

The 136 lectures that the central lecture service organized in 1923–24 had grown to 828 in 1926. During the last years of the 'twenties, Paris and its suburbs were treated to an average of 550 propaganda lectures a year, about twice as many as in the provinces.[6] The columns of the newspaper were filled with accounts of meetings designed to spread the word. Dozens of propaganda rallies were held every Sunday in hotels, ballrooms, barrooms, and cinemas, and in the open air, many of them drawing hundreds of idle, curious Sunday-afternoon listeners.[a]

[a] See, e.g., *AF,* Feb. 15, June 5, Sept. 3 and 30, Oct. 25, Dec. 18, 1921. At Angers in February, 800 attended a meeting; at Tourcoing in June, 1,800; in October 500 turned out at Argenton-Chateau (Deux-Sèvres) and 400 at Ancenis, and a banquet at Pignan (Hérault) drew some 300 members and sympathizers from all over the department; in December lectures at Amboise and Tarbes were attended, respectively, by 600 and 200 persons. Figures like these cannot be taken at face value. On the other hand, many more meetings were held than are mentioned here. In the Pas-de-Calais, for example, one of the least active of Action Française Departments, fifteen meetings of different sorts were announced in the first half of 1925.

Numbers at these meetings varied from satisfyingly large to embarrassingly scanty. After a propaganda center was set up near Belfort, only thirteen people came to a meeting in Vesoul, a town of over ten thousand, from the whole of Haute-Saône. In February 1924, three members of the League from Toul (Meurthe-et-Moselle), out to spread the word in the little village of Ochey, talked for ninety minutes before some thirty persons, of whom a good many were staring children with their fingers up their noses. On the other hand, at Metz and Brive thousands of persons turned out to hear the royalist orators. Clearly, a small but active group could move a large mass of the uninitiated but curious. Thus, in April 1923, at Dôle in the Jura, a morning meeting held for the regional membership gathered some threescore *ligueurs,* and the grand evening rally in the Catholic Club Hall drew over seven hundred.[7]

In the southwest, where the Action Française had early gained the support of the local royalists, things did not get started again after the Armistice until January 1921, when the first regional congress was held at Bordeaux. By 1924–25, the Bordeaux region was the scene of great activity, thanks to its regional organizer Paul Courcoural and to the sympathy of strong local Catholic organizations. After a meeting held in Libourne (on February 8, 1925) by Georges Valois and the former Communist mayor of Périgueux, Marcel Delagrange, now converted to royalism, the independent *Chronique du Libournais* expressed surprise at the progress the Action Française had made "among a population more reluctant than most to oppose the established order."

Between December 1924 and March 1925, the Libourne section held seven meetings. The stir was increased in April 1925 by the appearance of a new royalist journal, the *Nouvelle Guyenne,* which would only wither away under the rigors of German occupation. Support also came from *Le Paysan du sud-ouest,* printed at Tonneins and read mostly in Lot-et-Garonne where the peasantry furnished 80 per cent of Action Française membership. But the most vigorous activity was to be found in the Gironde, chiefly in and around Bordeaux. There, the Action Française had not only proper quarters but also its own lending library, run by the Dames Royalistes and boasting 1,697 volumes in June 1926. Furthermore, membership was swelled by over a hundred *étudiants* as well as some younger *collégiens.* Great public meetings at the Alhambra theater drew crowds of 3,000 in 1925, 4,000 in 1926. In August of that year the *Nouvelle Guyenne* listed eight sections and seven propaganda centers in the departments, with a record during the previous months of twenty-six propaganda meetings in Bordeaux itself, seven in the city's suburbs, and thirty-three more in the surrounding area.[8]

As we can see, the real numbers were to be found in the cities where, as in Lyon, the royalists were numerous and well organized; and most especially in Paris. Reorganized in 1920, the Paris Federation reported fourteen sections that year, eighteen in 1921. Its strongest positions were, of course, on the Left Bank, which was, by all accounts, completely dominated by students, Camelots and *commissaires* of the Action Française.[9] In 1920, the secretary of the Etudiants d'Action Française, Emmanuel Beau de Loménie, reported his body to be the leading student group in Paris, much stronger and more active than any other. Royalist students had held the presidency of the General Students Association and now held posts in its administration and committee. They would not cease until the late 'thirties to hold the upper hand around the Sorbonne, and, for the present, their only serious rivals were the Socialist student groups. As Alfred de Tarde told *L'Ere nouvelle,* which watched its enemies with a baleful, vigilant eye, prewar republicans had vanished, leaving only Socialists behind. "Young people," the president of the Jeunesses Républicaines declared, "are either royalists or Socialists."[10]

Beginning in 1920, the students began issuing their own monthly review *L'Etudiant français,* which became the nursery of several generations of French right-wing intellectuals. Its columns would see the signatures of Claude and Gabriel Jeantet, Jean de Fabrègues, Jean Humbert, Claude Roy, Philippe Ariès, Pierre Boutang, Jacques Laurent, Raoul Girardet, Philippe Brissaud, Robert Brasillach, Firmin Roz, Jean Dufour, and the historians Pierre Gaxotte and Jean Héritier—a group of whom many had scarcely been born when it first appeared.

But publications came second to the traditions of an earlier day—the prank, the swift blow, the riot remained a favorite means of student action.

Throughout the spring of 1921 an anti-Sorbonne campaign, led by René Benjamin in *L'Echo de Paris* and taken up by the *Action française,* inspired numerous *chahuts* which disrupted lectures in the University so severely that some of them could not go on. Police were called to intervene and clear the lecture hall when riots were organized against Victor Basch, because, as one of the leaders of the Ligue des Droits de l'Homme, he had spoken up in favor of imprisoned Communists.[11] At the Ecole Normale, once a stronghold of the Left, sympathies abounded; even more so at the Ecole des Chartes and in the Faculty of Law. In the rue d'Ulm, room 16 on the first floor sported a mural showing a Camelot group demonstrating at the near-by Sorbonne, and an inscription in both Greek and Latin commemorating the artistry of Franciscus Poncet, *pictor* before he became *Ambassador.*[12]

The Institute, which had offered seven courses in 1920–21, had eleven in 1921–22, all heavily attended; by 1926, the *Revue des cours et conférences,* first issued in 1923, had 2,000 subscribers. The *Etudiant français* was even more successful, and in 1924 it began to appear twice a month. A rival republican review called *Jeune Europe* had to suspend publication after three issues.[13] By 1925, the Etudiants d'Action Française claimed twenty-six student groups, twenty-eight groups in lycées, with 2,200 members in Paris alone.[14] A good many of the members were Camelots, although the term had now come to mean almost any active member of the Action Française.[b]

"The Camelots are not the only ones who represent the monarchy," remarks a character in a novel about the time. "Yes, I know," comes the reply: "For old ladies and for the naïve there are Maurras and Daudet . . . but for the masses, only the Camelots exist."[15]

They rained handbills denouncing Briand all over theaters and cinemas and even from the Eiffel tower. They attacked and sought to beat up Caillaux and Malvy.[16] They daubed paint on statues and broke up lectures. They interrupted the showing of films they thought misrepresented Frenchmen and French history[c] and intervened against the performances of immoral and unpatriotic plays, successfully forcing the withdrawal of Denys Amiel and André Obey's *La Carcasse* from the Comédie Française, despite a Parliamentary vote against such a step.[17] They sold the newspaper, of course, and fought the Reds as the occasion demanded. But they also helped to make friends. On Easter Sunday 1925 they ushered and guarded a Catholic meeting at Bergerac in the southwest; in March 1926 they defended a meeting of the Catholic Federation at Marseille; in June, near Lille, two hundred *commissaires* intervened to open the way for a Catholic procession.[d] When René Benjamin on a lecture tour was bitterly opposed by the teachers' syndicates which he had ridiculed and which had threatened to silence him in return, the Action Française came to his defense, at Loches, Bordeaux, Lyon, and Saint-Etienne, against syndicalists and, when necessary, against police as well.[18]

Their activity, and their good organization, made them appear more nu-

[b] Before 1914 there had been squads of Camelots and *commissaires,* backed by other squads of students and *ligueurs* regarded as reserves. After 1918, eight squads of *commissaires* were set up in Paris, each 100-strong and divided into three or four sections. By 1926, the number of these squads was given as twenty-six, by 1927 as thirty: see *AF,* Nov. 26, 1926; Nov. 26, 1927. But some of the recruits counted in these figures were merely honorary members, which anyone could become on payment of 500 francs (equivalent to about $20 then or $30 now)—a fund-raising invention related by Charlotte Montard, *Quatre Ans à l'Action Française* (1931), pp. 105–6.

[c] The Action Française early became aware of the possibilities and dangers of the cinema (*AF,* Sept. 9, 1916: Léon Daudet, "Le Cinédrame et son avenir"). In September 1922, over forty Camelots and students were arrested for trying to prevent the showings of foreign films that did not present French history in what they considered the proper light (*AF,* Sept. 9, 16, 17, 18, 1922); in March 1926, another film misrepresenting Louis XVI and his court was withdrawn from the screens of Bordeaux and Saint-Etienne (*NG,* March 1, 1926) as a result of their "vigorous protests." Even *Ben Hur* was attacked, for being too pro-Jewish and anti-Roman. (*NG,* Feb. 1, 15, 1929; *L'Action catholique,* Feb. 5, 1929).

[d] One result of this activity was the progressive identification of royalist and Catholic organizations, reflected in a police report from Tarbes: "L'activité de l'Action Française et de ses filiales, ligue d'Action Française, Unions paroissiales, etc. . . . devient chaque jour plus manifeste . . . des zélateurs et des zélatrices recrutés parmi des personnes bien pensantes, très honorablement connues, font de la propagande sous prétexte de défense religieuse. . . . Dans bien des cas [le succès] est réel." F^7 13120 (Hautes-Pyrénées), May 28, 1926.

merous than they were.[e] For a special task or a meeting, they would assemble from all over a region, coming to Lille from all over the north, to Bergerac from Libourne, fanning out over lower Brittany from Nantes;[19] and though their roughness drew criticisms from many a quarter, as it had done before the war, it also elicited the enemy's respect. Thus, Jean Prévost, who at the Lycée Henry IV had joined the Revolutionary Socialist group but had soon become fed up with their endless wrangling, reached the conclusion that if one had to have an ideal, one might as well stick with the fatherland and join the Action Française: "The straightforwardness and the courage of the Camelots that my fellows hotly denied seemed to me, on the contrary, quite evident. —J'imaginais leur doctrine comme un égoïsme et une volupté."[20]

All this activity sprang from the urban centers: speakers, Camelots, *ligueurs* went out on week ends to address meetings and sell the newspaper in rural areas where the movement was weak or nonexistent.[21] The paper sold fairly well when hawked in these outlying districts, but those who bought it rarely joined the movement or contributed to it, and since no effective distribution plan existed, there was seldom a follow-up.

Spasmodic propaganda stirred up curiosity, but little else. Few people cared to sign the League's terms of membership, including the declaration that they would fight the Republic by every means in their power. Conservatives and liberals opposed royalist influence and did their best to keep it from taking root in centers where it might compete with them for local authority or simply prove troublesome to the peace. The feeling spread that Action Française sections were something young men joined, but that serious persons seldom belonged to.[22]

This means that an equation between the movement's activity and its membership would be hard to draw. Plateau's rules about minimal section membership were still enforced, but the result was chiefly that sympathizers from a wider area, sometimes from a department (as in Vendée in 1921), would join one central section. When this happened, as it did at Fontenay-le-Comte, or at Toulouse, the active membership of sections was very small and leaders hesitated to exclude those who fell behind with payments or to strike names off the books, in order to keep the section going and its prestige still high.[23]

The movement seldom published any definite figures of its membership. At the beginning of 1924 Maurras mentioned 30,000 dues-paying members of the League, adding that few of these were also subscribers to the paper. But speakers generally seemed to think that royalist support could be identified with the circulation of the paper and its subsidiaries, and in boasting of the

[e] More subtle methods were also employed. Thus, on November 28, 1926, when the League organized a pilgrimage to honor its dead in the cemetery of Vaugirard, police reported the turnout of 900–1,000 ligueurs. However, "pour donner l'impression d'une assistance plus nombreuse, 700 ligueurs qui avaient déjà défilé devant les tombes se sont replacés à la queue du cortège pour saluer à nouveau leurs morts." F^7 13198, Nov. 28, 1926.

numbers that banquets and rallies could attract, they tended to speak in terms of subscription figures.[24] Circulation figures for this period during which the newspaper was in the ascendant and its directors not so reluctant as usual to disclose their situation can be traced with fair accuracy, the statements made by leaders tallying as a rule both with each other and with independent sources. Here, very roughly, are the figures available for the years 1913 to 1926:[25]

	Action française		*Action française du dimanche* *Action française agricole*	
Year	Subscriptions (to nearest 1,000)	Average Nonsub. Circulation	Subscriptions (to nearest 1,000)	Average Nonsub. Circulation
1913	7,600	20,000		
1914	11,000	20,000		
1915		36,000		
1916				
1917		156,000		
1918				
1919			2,500	
1920	24,000		8,000	55,000
1921	20,000	21,000*	13,000	
1922			15,000	
1923	24,000	41,000		
1924	29,000	45,000	19,000	24,000
1925 (April)	35,000	55,000	20,000	
1925 (August)	48,000	53,000	17,000†	
1926 (August)	45,000	45,000	25,000‡	

* Indicates provincial circulation only; no figures are available for Paris.
† *Action française agricole* only.
‡ Probably remaining stationary thereafter; the *Action française agricole* ceased publication suddenly on July 5, 1931.

Clearly, such figures can be accepted only with the greatest caution: they have been taken from statements that are sometimes contradictory and always, naturally enough, try to put the best possible face on things. They do not seem far from the truth, but the truth itself calls for certain explanations. First, of course, circulation for a newspaper does not mean sales: it simply means the number of printed copies of the paper that have been distributed for sale. Perhaps 20 per cent of these are never sold; in the case of the *Action française* this proportion was always higher, reaching sometimes as much as fifty per cent. But even subscription figures can be misleading. A good proportion of the *Action française* subscriptions were free, sent for promotion purposes for three, six, or twelve months, and sometimes longer, to people who might or might not read the paper, much less resubscribe themselves when the gift subscription expired.[26] With these qualifications in mind, we can review the figures and note that even at its peak, in the late summer of 1926, the *Action française* was being printed in editions of well below 100,000, with something like 15,000 more for its Sunday subsidiary.

We shall see that Action Française ideas actually reached more people than those who bought the paper or its Sunday publications. But before that, a word is in order concerning the *Action française du dimanche.*

Like many other Parisian newspapers, the *Action française* was published seven days a week. The *Action française du dimanche,* which first appeared on October 19, 1919, was therefore not simply a Sunday edition but a separate four-page newspaper, designed to reach a special public, mainly farmers. Dedicated, as the motto on the masthead declared, "to National and Social Defense," the *Action française du dimanche,* although carrying on its front page features signed by Daudet and Maurras, emphasized agricultural and regional news. An entire page was taken up with stockyard prices, the *cours des engrais,* columns of advice like "Les conseils du Père Sylvain sur les engrais," and a regular feature "Pour une politique du cheval." On the other pages, political articles warned against the coalition of capital and socialism, and courted the small landowner. The Left threatened property; but the Enemy was more complex than just the Left: a compound of Bolsheviks, Germans, Jews, and financiers, conspiring with one another to tax, to rob, and to confiscate hard earned savings and the fruit of honest labor.[27]

Early in 1920, in an effort to combat the success of the *Action française du dimanche,* the Socialists brought out a publication of their own directed at the peasants, the *Voix paysanne.* By the end of 1920 the *Action française du dimanche* claimed over 11,000 subscribers (mainly in Touraine, Berry, Limousin, and the Paris area), but the *Voix* had barely reached a third of that figure.[f] And in the summer of 1921, when the royalist paper announced the publication of three regional editions, it could triumphantly quote the words of an opponent, rural Socialist Deputy Charles Baron, that the best agricultural weekly he knew was the *Action française du dimanche.*[28]

By 1924, with nearly 19,000 subscribers and additional sales of 4,000–5,000, the paper was issuing regional editions for Savoy and for the Limousin; and by special arrangement articles by Daudet and Bainville appeared in the Sunday edition of the *Gazette de l'Ouest* at Rennes. Moreover, the first two pages of the *Action française du dimanche,* which contained the important political features, were reprinted in half a dozen other provincial publications: the *Nouveau Berry,* the *Nouvelles Bazadaises,* the *Clarion de l'Ardèche,* the *Echo du Maine,* and the Basque *Argia.*[29]

Late in 1925, the *Action française du dimanche* became *Action française*

[f] *AFD,* Nov. 7, 1920; *L'Humanité,* Dec. 23, 1920. In January 1921, after the Congress of Tours, the *Voix paysanne* was taken over by the Communists, along with *L'Humanité*; when on March 1, 1922, Renaud Jean jubilantly announced in *L'Humanité* that the *Voix* counted 8,000 subscribers, *AF,* March 2, rejoined that the *Action française du dimanche* had 15,000.

agricole, thus confirming an obvious trend. The last number of the *Action française du dimanche* appeared on November 29, 1925, the first number of the *Action française agricole* on the following Sunday, December 6. The new publication, under the management of Ambroise Rendu, a former deputy and farmer, and of Henri de Castillon de St. Victor, an agronomist, was clearly aimed at the agricultural reader. Only the front page was devoted to politics, and even there the slant was agricultural. The newspaper represented the Action Française Corporation Française de l'Agriculture[g] and sponsored also a Ligue de Défense Rurale, whose purpose, as the name implied, was to defend the landed interest. Defense was needed against Socialist and Communist schemes for confiscation, against lying press campaigns misrepresenting the true state of French agriculture, against taxation—for there was talk of increasing property taxes to catch up with reality—against every action of a State caught in the mire of creeping socialism.

The new agricultural venture did very well at first. By 1926 it was publishing regional editions for Savoy, Limousin, the North, and Franche-Comté; but the regional situation varied, and at different times special agreements were concluded with friendly local papers like the *Gazette de l'Ouest,* the *Nouveau Berry,* the *Courrier des Alpes,* and the *Petit Provençal,* to supplement or replace a regional edition of the *Action française agricole* itself.[30] The paper continued to be prosperous in 1926 and 1927, but thereafter it was affected by the general decline in Action Française fortunes as well as by internal dissensions. At the end of 1927 Rendu, and a few months later Castillon de St. Victor, left it, just when sales stopped rising and perhaps even fell off. Subsidies kept it going, with about one-fifth of the subscriptions free, until it ended suddenly and without warning in July 1931, another casualty of the depression.[31]

Such publications, run directly from Paris, did not exhaust the web of Action Française influence throughout the provinces. In the early years, as integral nationalism got the upper hand on older royalist organizations, it had also taken over or inherited a slew of royalist publications. In many cases, relations between these and the Action Française were far from cordial, old-fashioned royalists resenting the newcomers and fearing their competition, the Paris leaders desiring to suppress all notions of independence from possible critics and competitors for funds. The Action Française therefore sponsored or encouraged the efforts of devoted friends who ran local sheets on which they could rely: the *Aunis-Saintonge* of Rochefort, which moved its gaze inland to become *Aunis-Saintonge-Angoûmois*; the *Brigade de fer* in Franche-Comté; the *Petit Patriote* in Normandy and Maine; the *Bulletin* at Rennes; the

[g] The Corporation Française de l'Agriculture set up eleven departmental committees, in the Aisne, Charente, Côte-d'Or, Dordogne, Isère, Maine-et-Loire, Marne, Seine-et-Marne, Seine-et-Oise, Rhône, and Yonne.

Avant-garde de Normandie, which Bernanos would briefly edit at Rouen; Robert Havard's *Nord Patriote* at Lille; the *Bulletin savoyard* and *L'Action pyrénéenne.*[32] Some of these were short-lived: Paul Courcoural's *Aunis-Saintonge,* a monthly, ran just two years, from March 1909 to April 1911, and had a press run of about 1,400. But they were supplemented by a number of well-established papers that had rallied to the new monarchism and usually echoed its directives, among them the *Nouvelliste de Bordeaux* (which ended in 1920), *L'Eclair de Montpellier,* the *Messager de Valence, L'Avenir du Loir-et-Cher,* the *Réveil de la Haute-Saône,* the *Courrier de la Vienne,* the *Journal du Loiret, L'Indépendance Bretonne,* the *Télégramme des provinces de l'Ouest,* the *Gazette du Centre,* and the *Mémorial des Pyrénées.*[33]

After the war, although the Action Française position had been considerably reinforced, and assured of a wider hearing, by the new prominence of its leaders, many of its prewar provincial publications had disappeared. Some had been one-man undertakings whose editor, like Henri de Bruchard, had died, or, like Georges Bernanos, had drifted off to other things. It was this situation that the *Action française du dimanche* was designed in part to remedy.

But while Action Française interest and funds favored direct enterprises and national publications, like the *Revue universelle, Candide,* later *Je suis partout,* the provincial press was certainly not ignored, and friendly—sometimes feudal—relations were maintained with a variety of publications. It is difficult to say just how many papers owed direct allegiance to the rue de Rome apart from the *Soleil de Nice,* the *République lyonnaise,* the *Salut du Centre* (Clermont), the *Salut national* (Limoges), the *Nouvelle Guyenne* (Bordeaux), the *Courrier lorrain,* and the *National d'Alsace-Lorraine,* a German-French weekly published by the Action Française in Strasbourg.[h] The *Clairon de l'Ardèche,* which had suspended publication during the war, reappeared in 1923, one of a host of similar sheets all drawing their inspiration from the Action Française: the *Echo de la Sologne,* the *Courrier du Midi,* the *National d'Artois* (Saint-Omer), the *Fanion picard* (Amiens), the *Gazette de l'Hérault* (Béziers), the *Pays d'Orléans,* the *Restauration nationale* (La Rochelle), the *Action Algérienne* (Blida), and the monthly bulletins published for certain areas and zones, like the *Echo* in the North, the *Chroniques* in the department of the Rhône, and the *Ordre provençal* at Marseille.

Older publications—the *Nouvelliste de Bretagne,* the *Nouvelliste de Lyon,* the *Express du Midi,* the *Roussillon,* the *Soleil du Midi,* the *Tablettes des Deux-Charentes,* the *Nouvelle Bourgogne*—continued to be friendly, and

[h] Pujo argued that, with the vast majority of Alsatians knowing only German, untoward pressure would antagonize them. They should be taught not French grammar, but French history and culture, even if it had to be done in German. Make France attractive, and the French language *because* of it. *AF,* July 12, 1921.

new ones like the *Réveil national* at Versailles and the *Réveil de Saint-Brieuc* appeared to join the ranks.[i]

It is harder to tell where less definite relations ended: nonroyalist papers like the *Indépendant du Berry* (owned by a conservative republican deputy), the Catholic *Indépendant de la Nièvre,* the *Tablettes de l'Aisne,* and the *Télégramme de Toulouse* repeatedly took the royalist side. Coty's friend Martin-Mamy, in his *Progrès du Nord,* seldom failed to lend support. A similarly friendly echo could be expected from some of the rabid anti-Masonic publications like the *Conquête* of Versailles, the *Echo du Cher,* and the *Petit Oranais.*

The significance of this array of titles should not be overestimated. The provincial press of France was a multitude in which these few dozen held only a modest place. In any case, political issues were allowed only a small space in the pages of the provincial papers. Whereas in the nineteenth century, politics, both national and local, had been of prime concern to the provinces, the years around the First World War had seen such matters taken over by the Paris press or by the great regional dailies like the *Dépêche* at Toulouse or the *Progrès* of Lyon, which reached rural areas heretofore untouched by any but the most parochial influences. Between the wars, the small provincial papers gradually dwindled into simple local news sheets, awakening to politics only at election time and then with far less gusto than before. In 1885 a ministerial crisis might take up nearly half the columns of a paper; by the 1930's it rated less than a tenth. The electoral campaign of 1885 got an average of one page a day; that of 1936 seldom reached even two columns.[34] This being so, the exact political coloration of many newspapers was hardly noticeable, their royalism—when royalism it was—impinging but little on their general conservative and Catholic tone.

The disappearance of more frankly political publications that did not hew to the Action Française line may well have reflected a deliberate policy that discouraged provincial friends of the Action Française from supporting editors and publications that the rue de Rome did not entirely trust. But it was a symptom, too, of a more widespread malaise affecting all the *presse d'opinion.* Publications that had kept going before the war with only a few faithful readers and perhaps some additional funds from the publisher were gradually dying, not because they had lost readers or subsidies but because rising paper and production costs meant that the old readers were no longer enough.

If this was true in Paris, it was even more true in the provinces, where the

[i] Some of these papers were extremely important locally. *L'Express,* at Toulouse, had 800 regional correspondents and 3,500 sales depots serving eighteen departments; Eugène Delahaye's *Nouvelliste de Bretagne,* at Rennes, published ten departmental editions; Régis Rambaud's *Nouvelliste de Lyon,* nine editions covering twenty-five departments, with a total guaranteed circulation of 230,000 in 1928. In the middle 1930's one could still count some thirty monarchist publications.

Paris press was capturing an ever-growing section of the newspaper-reading public and where those who wanted a *journal d'opinion* could get more lively, better-written ones than the mediocre local journals.

It is all the more impressive, bearing this in mind, that so many small local publications, like the *Nouvelle Guyenne,* did keep the flag of political discussion aloft between the wars, using their pages not to compete with the *Action française* but to support it, often by opening subscription drives for it in their own columns.[j] The real enthusiasts would take both the local paper and the *Action française* and try to circulate them, sometimes by gifts of free subscriptions, throughout the region or the town. As an unfriendly witness would admit, the *Action française* could be discovered in the most out-of-the-way places.[k]

This was what mattered in the last resort, for ultimately the Action Française stood or fell by the paper. "The Action Française is no more than a newspaper," André Gaucher wrote after he had left it, bitter and disillusioned. But if that is all it was—and we have seen it was much more than that—the paper must have served as a titanic lever. Admirers and critics agreed about its influence, agreed that its ideas penetrated even minds one would have thought best able to withstand them, agreed that the rest of the press was intimidated, and, whether critical or respectful, unwilling to risk its ire, agreed that its opponents were the first to read it: "One hears them protesting against the contents; but they cannot avoid the charm of the container."[35]

There is little doubt that the container did have charm: from its earliest days to its last, people read the *Action française* because it was well written, threw it aside because it was exasperating, and found it hard to dispense with even so: "Charles Maurras is so seductive and sometimes so irritating," a critical Catholic wrote before the First World War, "that I find all papers insipid since I have taken up the *Action française*."[l] Anatole France seems to have shared this view;[36] and, shortly before his death, Marcel Proust had this to say:

[j] During its existence from 1926 to 1944, Louis Jasseron's *République Lyonnaise* printed a weekly edition of 6,000 copies. If one accuses the Action Française of driving other royalist publications out of existence, as Professor Osgood does in *French Royalism,* p. 153, one ought to remember the economic conditions of survival in a postwar world where journalistic ventures could not be undertaken or kept up as simply and cheaply as before 1914. An even sterner economic law presides over the French scene today, when no more *journaux d'opinion* exist at all, except as periodicals or "private bulletins."

[k] In *Le Coup du lapin,* p. 280, Gyp refers to a remote village of the Poitou: "Ils connaissent l'AF dans ce pays reculé . . .?"—"S'ils la connaissent! D'abord, ma mère y a abonné les notables, et elle a fait distribuer des numéros. Les paysans aiment autant lire ça qu'autre chose. Ça leur est bien égal!"

[l] G. Marcellin, *Lettres d'un disparu,* II, 76. But six months later (p. 91) he wrote in a different tone: "Je ne comprends pas que Maurras gaspille un talent d'écrivain si magnifique et si rare en controverses polémiques 'd'où le raisonnement a banni la raison.' L'impression d'agacement que je ressens est renforcée par la lecture de l'Action française quotidienne, à laquelle il faudra que je renonce uniquement parce que Maurras et ses disciples sont exaspérants."

No longer able to read more than one newspaper, I now read, instead of those of other days, the *Action française.* I daresay that in this I am not without merit. The thought of what a man could suffer having once made me a Dreyfusard, one can imagine that the pronouncements of a sheet infinitely more cruel than the *Figaro* or the *Débats,* which formerly satisfied me, often give me the sensations of an oncoming heart attack. But in what other newspaper is the front page decorated with a fresco by Saint-Simon himself—that is to say by Léon Daudet? Farther on, upright, unique in its crystalline irrefutability, Bainville's luminous column guides me unerringly across the desert of foreign policy. Then Maurras, who seems today to hold the record for altitude, makes a general comment on Lamartine, and it is better for us than an airplane flight, a cure by elevation of the mind.[m]

Eugène Lautier attributed this influence and success to the importance given by neo-royalists to ideas and the discussion of ideas. Many papers sold more copies, but none, he thought, was more worth reading or was more carefully and thoroughly read.

On this, opinions differed. The Paris correspondent of the *Gazette de Lausanne* evidently appreciated "ce journal remarquablement rédigé et où l'on trouve souvent d'utiles vérités qu'on ne trouve pas ailleurs." Gyp, on the other hand, suggested that a good many subscribers never bothered even to remove the brown-paper wrapper in which their cherished newspaper arrived. Maurras's long and bleak disquisitions held little attraction for royalist young ladies, tennis-playing students, and dowagers. But Maurras in his late years recalled a little Paris electrician who loved the more difficult articles in the *Action française* because in the Métro on his way to work he could use them to quiz and confound his friends who read *L'Humanité.*[37]

"It is fortunate," wrote *L'Homme enchaîné* in admiration, "that, lacking governments that fulfill their obligations and great newspapers as well informed as they were in the past, there should exist the *Action française,* which in our country takes the place of all authority, all research, all effort."[n]

Such praise was flattering, but the research and effort cost a great deal of

[m] Marcel Proust, "Léon Daudet," *Contre Sainte-Beuve,* pp. 438–41. This unpublished article was probably written in 1920. Both the *Revue universelle,* founded that year, and the *Action française* refused to print it, protesting embarrassment over its excessive praise. They may have disagreed also with criticisms implied rather than expressed. Proust found other occasions to state his admiration for Maurras as a literary figure in letters to Maurras, and in a long dedication on a presentation copy of the first edition of *A L'ombre des jeunes filles en fleurs,* which won the Prix Goncourt in 1919 due in good part to the efforts of his self-styled "grand électeur," Daudet. Proust did not forget that twenty-three years earlier Maurras had given high praise to the author of *Les Plaisirs et les jours,* than whom, he wrote, he could name no one "d'une pénétration ainsi délicate, ainsi sûre, et d'une si simple élégance." See Maurras, "La Vie littéraire," *Revue Encyclopédique Larousse,* Aug. 22, 1896, p. 584, and *L'Amitié de Platon* (1936), pp. 70–71; *Cahiers Charles Maurras,* No. 5, April 1962, pp. 29–34.

[n] Jan. 6, 1922. The Clemenceau group was at the time on excellent terms with the Action Française.

money. From the very first, the Action Française had had to face unusually large expenses, because of its extensive propaganda, its disputes with printers, which sometimes, as in 1923, made it miss entire issues, its careless editorial practices, which Maurras stubbornly refused to alter, and the costs of court actions, generally for libel or slander, sometimes for incitement to murder, from which it was never free after 1913. These suits not only were costly in actual money[38] but frequently meant also that entire pages of the newspaper had to be given over to apologies and retractions ordered by the courts. Several times during 1920 three-quarters of the front page was consumed in this way by judgments in favor of the Maggi-Kub, and after a while the paper took to inserting such matter upside down. Alongside such expenses, the normal income was small indeed; advertising was never an important source of revenue, and since the selling price of the paper was kept purposely low, income from sales was less than the budget demanded.

Most French newspapers have known similar problems, and their quandary was clearly expressed by Jean Luchaire at his trial for collaboration in 1946:

> I want to make quite clear, and newspapermen in this court are well aware of it, that political papers and publications before the war could not subsist without private support. We had the choice: we could choose between foreign funds and between the funds of capitalist societies commonly called trusts. The least bad source to draw on was the State itself.[39]

To this rule that none denied and few evaded, the *Action française* tried throughout its life to be an exception. From the beginning, it managed to make up its losses by small gifts from readers and sympathizers—first as an expedient, then, in 1917, as a calculated practice. When circulation tripled at the time of the *complot des panoplies,* new financial problems arose, simply because the increase in paper costs was not matched by the increased sales revenue, or by much rise in advertising revenue. It was then that, desperate for funds, Maurras launched his first great appeal for contributions. On December 16, 1917, he asked for one million francs by the paper's tenth anniversary in March. He got over a quarter of a million more than he asked for, and, his appetite whetted, he seldom stopped asking from then on.[40]

The money was sorely needed: in the seven years 1920–26, the losses of the paper totaled nearly five million francs.[41] Some of these losses were made good by exceedingly large gifts, like that left by the will of a young millionaire who was killed in the war,[o] others by subsidies from the perfume-rich François Coty, who seems to have paid Maurras some two million francs between 1924

[o] Maurras, *La Contre-révolution spontanée,* pp. 117–18, mentions rich, enthusiastic young Pierre Villars, who drew up a will leaving his fortune equally to Maurras, Maritain, and Sorel. Just before entering the Army in 1914, however, Villars cut out Sorel, "qui avait passé du mauvais côté de la barricade"; thus when he died at Verdun in 1916, Maurras and Maritain shared his fortune between them.

and 1928;[42] but most of the money came from people of limited means, in gifts ranging from a few centimes to 10,000 francs. Of the 14,014 contributors who responded to Maurras's first appeal, 800 gave sums of 100 to 10,000 francs, 784 gave between 50 and 100 francs, and the remaining 12,430 gave less than 50 francs apiece. Although the possibility that these figures were doctored cannot be excluded, they are eloquent, and they continued to be representative of the mass of the newspaper's support. The newspaper encouraged supporters to undertake firm commitments for so much a year. At the Ninth Congress in 1922 such contributions were reported as having risen to 416,000 francs in the previous year, with another 150,000 in occasional gifts. The voluntary contributors were not, as a rule, the same as those who sent money for the open subscription lists, and the sums they contributed (when they did not forget) were generally larger:[43]

	1924–25	1925–26
Below 50 francs	2,149	2,180
50–99 francs	1,320	1,344
100–199 francs	1,039	1,059
200–499 francs	311	313
500–999 francs	135	142
1,000 francs and over	130	119
	5,084	5,157

As Gyp, a faithful though impatient guide in the vagaries of the petty nobility, tells us, when Maurras appealed, "la Normandie, le Poitou, la Vendée, marchent comme un seul homme," poor provincial royalists, very often silly women who did not even read Maurras and would not have understood him had they tried, responded to appeals from women's committees in Paris and deprived themselves and their families in order to contribute.[44]

That the fund-raising activities of the Dames and Jeunes Filles Royalistes, the feminine auxiliaries, should have acquired something of the snob value of certain community drives is not particularly surprising. But there were loyalties, too, and enthusiasms of the sort that Jean de La Varende has depicted in his novels, for which Maurras's sober appeals and Daudet's boisterous assurance could promise justification and perhaps an early vindication. The people who gave could feel that they were being useful, and that their contributions were keeping the *Action française* locomotive stoked to pull the train of royalism to an eventual goal or, at the very least, to spit its fiery steam at everything they loathed—Reds, Masons, Germans, British, Jews, bankers, politicians, the Y.M.C.A., or merely the Republic. But no dry listing of this sort could equal in flavor the contributors' own expressions in the subscription lists regularly published by the paper, which in themselves constituted a further encouragement for those to whom this was a rare chance to see themselves in print.

The lists also constitute a precious indication of the make-up and mentality of the newspaper's reading public. Here, culled at random over several years, are some of the signatures and remarks that accompanied gifts: A druggist from the Orléanais. An Action Française grocer. Mgr. H. bought the paper in front of Notre-Dame-de-la-Garde Cathedral. He brought me luck; sold twenty-five numbers in twenty minutes. A postman. A secular schoolteacher. To fight against cosmopolitan high finance. A disgusted Radical-Socialist electoral agent. M. Durand against Bolshevism. A fervent royalist: that Léon Daudet may kick with vengeful boots the German arse of our Bolshevizing Anarchists. A patriotic driver. A disillusioned proletarian. To buy the dozen bullets that Caillaux deserves. A republican. A student of the Ecole Normale. Against the modernist and gallican spirit. Against the maneuvers of the Y.M.C.A. Against theosophy. Against Zionist propaganda. Against Protestant, liberal, and Masonic infiltrations. Against Lutheran infiltration. Against the Action Libérale. God in his place! To liberate us from Jewish servitude. Divine heart of Jesus, hasten the King's return, Mlle Désirée P. Money I did not expect. To buy a blackjack, Louis Deschanel. In memory of Marius Plateau, Comte de Tocqueville. An *agrégé* professor. A stifled member of the middle class. For the execution of F ∴ Bringer, dishonorer of Lozère in Parliament. For the Action Française against the clan of Masons, liberals, and Jews under the tutelage of pimps and public whores.[45]

Something of the diversity of the integral nationalist following is evident in these remarks, as well as in police reports of the time. Thus, in March 1926, a report from Beauvais lists thirteen Camelots who had applied for a permit to sell the paper: two farmers, two industrial representatives, two students, two with no profession (probably with a private income), one lumber merchant, one carpenter, one mechanic, one railroad worker (who may, however, have been a clerk), and one commercial employee, very likely a shop assistant. Although the leading militants of the Senlis section included a good proportion of prosperous and titled individuals, the royalists of Thionville drew upon a humbler public: as listed by the local police in April 1926, they counted one Air Force officer, one notary's clerk, one shopkeeper, one milliner, one gardener, one railroad worker, one liquor merchant, the local tax collector and his son, and five employees of the Maison de Wendel (the government metallurgical works).[46] In addition, a good many politicians—some said all members of Parliament—read the *Action française* to see what it would spring next.[47] A certain public read it for the literary columns, those of Daudet carrying immense prestige.[p] Some looked particularly to Bainville. Many who had nothing to do with the movement approved of its revolutionary

[p] Pierre Benoît, in *Aspects de la France,* March 23, 1958, has told of his excitement and delight when in July 1923 Daudet devoted a column to his new novel *Mademoiselle de la Ferté*: "On ne peut imaginer l'importance que pouvait avoir, dans la vie littéraire d'alors, un pareil coup de clairon. Un article de Léon Daudet, c'était la lumière faisant fondre subitement les nuées les plus opiniâtres."

policies.[q] Others who, like the father of Simone de Beauvoir, held the idea of a royal restoration to be utopian but were disgusted by the Republic, were friendly to the movement without actually belonging to it, and admired Maurras and Daudet.[r]

Among those who read and appreciated the paper, officers were far from last. In front-line messes the *Action française* had been very widely read. To flaunt the paper had been in certain spheres a manner of conformity, a means of fitting into new circles when promotion or a posting brought a change. The officer corps was widely believed to be full of royalists and sympathizers. In novels, characters conformed to this belief by sporting the opinions *de rigueur*; and in real life adherents kept turning up in the news, to bolster the impression. When the warship *Liberté* blew up, one hero of the disaster, Lieutenant Gabolde, was found to belong to the Action Française; when the airship *Dixmude* crashed in 1923, its commander, Lieutenant du Plessis de Grenadan, belonged to the Action Française; when in the Ruhr the Germans killed a French officer, Lieutenant Colpin, he, too, belonged to the Action Française. One of the great heroes of the war, Joseph Darnand, commanded a squad of Action Française *commissaires* at Nice. No wonder the *Action française* was kindly looked upon in the world of camps and barracks, in which other political publications were seldom found.[48]

During the early 'twenties Catholic seminaries were hotbeds of the Action Française faith, and many priests like the Abbé Laudel of Saint-Germain l'Auxerrois were proud of their membership in the League. Seven bishops and archbishops sent Maurras their condolences in November 1922 when his mother died. Two months later, forty-four priests and canons were mentioned by name among the scores attending the funeral services for Marius Plateau. And many more clearly endorsed Cardinal Billot's opinion that against liberalism and democracy there was nothing better than Maurras.[49]

Academic friends were scarcer. It was not until 1927 that a professor of classics, a convert from Protestantism and nephew of Francis de Pressensé—Henri Boegner—founded the Cercle Fustel de Coulanges to carry the Action Française word into the teaching profession. But the academic world was not without its admirers of Maurras, especially in Catholic Faculties and among medical men. Friends were not lacking in other fields, however. A former Sorbonne professor and student of Propertius, Frédéric Plessis, ran in the 1924 election on Daudet's list. And when Jean Izoulet, after a five-year break, again resumed his lectures at the Collège de France in 1923, the first lecture

[q] Like the Saint-Nazaire lawyer who wrote Daudet (*AF*, Oct. 16, 1921): "Je ne suis pas de l'Action française, bien que je lise volontiers votre journal et suive avec intérêt le courant de réaction que vous avez créé dans ce pays."

[r] Simone de Beauvoir, *Mémoires d'une jeune fille rangée* (1958), p. 38. M. de Beauvoir detested metics, disliked Jews, was persuaded of Dreyfus's guilt, considered *L'Oeuvre* a rag, and thought the Camelots' castor-oil pranks very funny.

of his course in social philosophy was partly devoted to a sympathetic analysis of Maurrassian theories—"true catapult of counterrevolution"—whose influence he compared with that of the *Encyclopédie* in the *ancien régime.*[50]

The liberal professions—doctors, lawyers, notaries, minor local officials[51]—were always well represented, and so were men of letters. Regional leaders in 1924 were almost all newspapermen or lawyers, often stemming from families with a legal or journalistic tradition. Maurice Dupont in the North, André Feildel in Anjou, Jean Jamain in Poitou, Paul Courcoural at Bordeaux, Elie Jacquet at Limoges, Alban Castelbert at Toulouse, were all professional journalists; Brunel in the south and Jasseron at Lyon were law graduates from magistrate families who lived on a private income and ran royalist publications; the Marquis de Roux was chairman of the Poitiers Bar; Georges Calzant, head of the student association, was a lawyer.

Well represented, too, were businessmen and manufacturers, usually of the lesser ranks. Druggists, who, like notaries, made excellent propagandists in country towns, were fairly numerous.[s] When Valois lectured at Lille in 1920, Charles Nicolle, who was president of the Société Industrielle du Nord and a man of some prominence, presided at a meeting attended by "the elite of Lille's industrial society." When in 1923 the *marchands forains* of Paris wanted to erect a statue honoring their comrades who had fallen in the war, it was Maxime Réal del Sarte whom they commissioned. Réal del Sarte, who had indeed almost cornered the memorial market, received numerous commissions from municipalities for statues of Joan of Arc, and he did the statue of General Mangin for a distinguished soldiers' committee.

Particular attention was still paid to commercial travelers, who had been allotted a special section of their own in the League. Reorganized with some fifty members in 1920, the section soon grew, in size and propaganda value, and by 1927 it was regularly distributing enormous quantities of tracts and flysheets.[52] Railwaymen also had sections of their own—the center of the eastern network being at 208 bis, rue Lafayette—and a delegation of workers of the Paris-Lyon-Méditerranée line followed in Plateau's funeral procession. By 1929, as many as 180 railroad workers marched in the Joan of Arc's Day parade, and 124 signed an address to Daudet on the anniversary of his son's death.[t]

When all was said and done, however, as Bernard de Vésins affirmed, "C'est chez l'employé et l'ouvrier que l'Action Française trouve les plus beaux dévouements: avec les étudiants, ils constituent l'élément le plus actif, celui

[s] One of them, Paul Dreyer-Dufer, a Paris chemist, directed a royalist periodical *La Droite* and in 1924 ran on the Action Française ticket in the first sector of Paris. See also *AF*, April 2, 1920, June 22, 1921, Feb. 23, 1923.

[t] See *AF*, May 23, 1929. French railroad workers, especially before the First World War, were by tradition not so much proletarians as middle-class employees, who built their own houses and took pride in working for a great company, so it was not surprising that they should furnish recruits for the Action Française. The P.L.M. railway probably had the most prestige. See Raymond Long, *Les Elections législatives en Côte-d'Or depuis 1870* (1958), p. 254.

qui fournit les meilleures Commissaires et Camelots du Roi."[53] There is no gainsaying the diversity of the area of support; and this diversity went even so far as to include elements of the groups the Action Française professed to abhor—odd foreigners, like the *jeune Arménien d'Action Française* born at Nizhni Novgorod, Berdj Minassian, whom Robert Brasillach encountered in prison, like Sergeant Pierre David, "le héros juif d'Action Française," whom Maurras and others never ceased to praise, like the many Protestants who joined the royalists and collaborated with them.[54]

As Professor Schram has told us in his study of *Protestantism and Politics in France,* after the war some Protestants moved away from their traditional progressive politics toward a sort of neo-Calvinism that attacked democracy, while praising hierarchy, virility, and order. Royalist Etienne de Seynes had been returned to the horizon-blue Chamber of 1919 by the once republican, Protestant middle class of Nîmes. His election was an indication that the Protestants, like the Radicals, were shifting toward a new conservatism, and also toward a nationalism in which the disillusions of the war years may have been of some significance.

Foremost among Protestant nationalists, René Gillouin, a critic of Jean-Jacques Rousseau and an admirer of Fascism, produced some telling criticisms of Action Française thought before he himself turned Maurrassian.[55] Pastor Noël Vesper warned against the false doctrines of collective salvation (akin to collectivism) and emphasized that only faith could save. The divine order was reflected in the social, and, like the divine world, the social also had need of a sovereign. These basic ideas were to be found also in the Association Sully, in which Vesper played an important role.

The Association Sully claimed to be absolutely independent, but its activities were close to those of the Action Française. We might describe it as a fellow-traveling organization within the Protestant world, comparable to the Cercle Fustel in the academic world. Their members, who were sometimes the same, as in the case of A. Lecerf, neo-Calvinist theologian and leading Protestant member of the Cercle Fustel, shared a common feeling that France was going to the dogs, that the social order, Christian civilization, national security, and modern culture were imperiled, their vigor sapped by democratic ills for which a new order was the only cure.[56]

No Jewish counterpart of the Association Sully existed, but there were always some Jews who were fascinated by the Action Française, as the persecuted often are by their persecutor. Not long before the First World War, Henri Lagrange reported the case of Jean Lévi, an Alsatian Jew who was a student at the Ecole Normale. Lévi declared himself as patriotic, as anti-democratic, and as anti-Semitic as the *ligueurs* whose acceptance and approval he sought, but when he realized that however much he struggled he could never be more than a second-class citizen, he ended by drowning himself in the Seine.[57] Other Jews insisted that, as good Frenchmen, they could join the

League; and in 1919 one of them had come to his feet in an electoral meeting demanding to know by what right Jews were kept out of the Action Française if they wished to join.[58]

Actually, some Jews did become members of the League, or, more often, "allies," like Georges and Pierre-Marius Zadoc; Raoul-Charles Lehman, who left Jonnart's Parti Républicain Patriote for an even more loudly patriotic movement; Marc Boasson, killed in 1918 but earlier a secretary of the Ecole d'Hautes Etudes Sociales, whose desire to become truly French led him to become both a Catholic and a royalist; and René Riquier, who from his Provençal teaching post contributed to the *Revue fédéraliste* and remained a lifetime admirer of Maurras.[59] Subscriptions and correspondence often arrived from Jews, curiously eager to approve, or to engage in a dialogue with, their detractors. And Jewish journalists like Louis Latzarus and René Groos never ceased to defend and praise the great work the Action Française and its leaders were doing for France.[60]

In theory, it was quite possible for Jews, or Protestants, to appreciate the Action Française or to belong to it, for the doctrines of Maurras were only incidentally anti-Semitic, as they were against anything or anyone that was harmful to France.

If one began by assuming that national unity was a good threatened by diversity, by a multiplicity of factions, faiths, or alien traditions, it followed that men who did not share the historic national religion (or at least acknowledge its superiority), whose habits and loyalties were determined by other values than those derived naturally from a long background in France, were but dubious Frenchmen, despite what their papers said. Even if they wished, they could not possibly respond to France's problems as, without even thinking, a real Frenchman would, steeped as he was in the rich heritage compiled over many centuries by his ancestors, who had lived on the soil of France, tended it, and shed their blood for it.

Theories in which order is the greatest good and individualism a danger, if not a sin, in which the cry of freedom is taken as the warning voice of anarchy, must necessarily regard Protestantism as an insidious force that trains its adherents to a factious pride, sets private conscience above public good, and persistently ignores the sacrifices that apparent justice must sometimes make to the superior interests of *raison d'Etat*.

It was only when, ceasing to emphasize the duty of personal decision before God, some Protestants began instead to speak of certain needs to conform before Society, to care about stabilities that conscience might injure—it was only then that they found some common ground with the Action Française.

In the case of the Jews, the problem was more awkward, complicated by a historical context which royalist analysis did not begin to consider. For several thousand years Jews had stood apart and emphasized their differentness in the societies in which they moved. Within the Christian world, they were pictured as a manifestation of the principle of evil. Forgetting that Jesus and the apostles were Jews, the Christians remembered only that Jews had killed or spurned them; and this unforgivable crime became to simple minds a justification for any kind of secular revenge. Gradually enlightenment, revolution, economic change, the waning of religious prejudice, freed the Jews throughout Western Europe. As the nineteenth century advanced, they were incorporated as equals—at least in the eyes of law—in nations where increasingly the differentiating factors were economic ones. But in a world that was beginning to define itself in national terms, the Jews appeared—whether they liked it or not—refractory to the new values as to old. They had been alien in a Christian world, and alien they remained in the new world of clear-cut nationalities. Wherever men sought an object for their national hates, the Jew was the resident alien. Nothing could be more natural—men being what they are—than that the Jew should be a symbol of hated foreigners, whoever those might be.

This seemed especially obvious in societies where, as in the Third Republic, many Jews were recent immigrants, often of German origin or at any rate with German-sounding names, and thus readily attacked as being insufficiently loyal to their new culture, national interests, and flag.

Despised for religious reasons, distrusted on nationalistic grounds, the Jews also became a focus for strong economic resentment. Medieval discrimination had done its share in forcing Jews to become merchants and usurers, men without a land, who traded without producing. The strengthening of capitalist sentiments and the rise of anti-capitalistic hatreds found in them a ready object of aversion. They were already alien, already in the popular mind connected with obscure, perhaps nefarious, practices; and it was easy to assume that those who had crucified God on Good Friday would no more hesitate to crucify than to exploit his children. What would Jews care, whose closest ties were not with compatriots but with coreligionists, about furthering the interests of some foreign power if at the same time they could advance their own?

Thus it was, as chauvinism and class resentments grew, that Jews became the chief target of both. In the United States, the popular agitators of the 1890's identified the British and the Jews. In Populist demonology, as Professor Hofstadter has shown, anti-Semitism and Anglophobia went hand in hand.[61] In France, where after 1871, and especially after 1905, the major enemy was Prussia, anti-Semitism went hand in hand with Germanophobia.

But nationalist arguments were reinforced by other, socio-economic, resentments: for as the importance of capital grew, as the existing social order began to shift, the umbrage of those whom economic change endangered focused upon the Jews. The Jews, like the Protestants, had played an important part in the creation and in the politics of the Republic and of the new society, the new world of which the Republic was the political incarnation. Not only in the banks, but also in the University, in letters, the theater, and in the press, throughout the complex society of Paris, their role seemed increasing and increasingly obvious. Not surprisingly, the once-privileged social groups found it easy to blame them for their loss of position, their dwindling incomes from land or careers in the public service, their bad financial investments, their losses in crashes and speculations, in which the dealings of Jews were always prominently featured.

What sometimes manifested itself only in snobbery and social discrimination was given direction by campaigns like those of Edouard Drumont, bolstered by the animosities of the Dreyfus affair, and was sometimes expressed in the violence of anti-Semitic gangs like those led by the Marquis de Morès and, later, by Jules Guérin.[62] The anti-Semitic doctrines of the Action Française were influenced by all these, but their explicit source lay in the statement of Philippe d'Orléans, who, in February 1899, attributed the Jewish problem to the difficulties arising out of the growing importance of movable property:

> Governments that lacked the necessary vigilance did not realize that this economic revolution—for which everyone had reason to rejoice since the growth of movable property knows no limits—created for them the obligation to defend by appropriate laws and without racial exceptions the man who loves his land and puts his heart and soul into the soil of the fatherland, against his being crushed by anonymous and vagabond wealth. [With government so neglectful] who then should profit from this state of things but those who not only care nothing for the land, but bridle at its bonds?[63]

The language might be muddled, the composition weak, but the implications of the statement were clear, and the Action Française clung to them. Movable property might be an excellent thing, but excellent also was real estate, especially land, and one should not be crushed by the other. A State that ignored its responsibility to regulate and to protect left Jews and other protagonists of irresponsible capital power free to exploit their opportunities at the expense of defenseless Frenchmen. This was the cause and the nature of the Jewish problem. Reform the State and regulate the Jews, and the Jewish problem would no longer exist.

As aliens who were free to follow their particular interests without restraint, the Jews were a disruptive element in republican France, but "under a prince who would progressively raise them to our nationality, who would protect them against their too Oriental fellows whose invasion a good many among them already deplore, they would be perfectly capable of becoming useful servants of France." And Fagus, an anti-Semitic poetaster, explained that he could quite well imagine Jewish families "freely prospering in France, loyally serving it by their particular talents, and by their blood . . . under the protection of the law and of the King. Indeed—why not, if they should wish —becoming in time, by alliance or by marriage, very excellent Frenchmen."[64]

This is what certain Jews also wanted. Alarmed at the influx of "Oriental" Jews, refusing to be classed with coreligionists whom they considered far more strange than their fellow-Frenchmen, the offspring of long-established Jewish families did their best to prove how truly and loyally French they were. One way of displaying their Frenchness was to appeal for acceptance and approval to their severest judges, the men of the Action Française. Sergeant Pierre David wrote thus to Maurras shortly before he died:

> Born of a Jewish family, I came to feel completely detached from the Jewish tradition, completely French. It was enough for me to be a good Frenchman and to be logical with myself, to adopt the doctrines of the Action Française in all their consequences. . . . Thanks to the meditations inspired by your ideas, Fatherland and Family have become for me powerful realities within which persons considered individually are no more than abstractions.[65]

There was no real hope for such open attempts at integration; the Action Française could tolerate Jewish heroes only when, like David, they were safely dead. Alive, they could not expect more than negative acceptance, since it was beyond their power ever to acquire what they and their nationalist friends thought essential—tradition and descent.

There was furthermore the fact that, although the anti-Semitic doctrine was moderate, its application was often brutal and indiscriminate. Anti-Semitic theory may at times be expressed in a seemingly reasonable way, but since logic is too apt to destroy it, it can thrive only on appeals to the emotions. When Henri Vaugeois called for anti-Semitism he meant an instinctive, quasi-physical repulsion for the Jew and for his skin.[66] It was on these grounds that the Action Française really made its appeal, whatever the occasional rationalizations either of its doctrinaires or of its Jewish friends.

"One must be anti-Semitic," said Vaugeois. "This is what we must make the nationalists understand: there, in effect, is the psychological root of all the ideas and the feelings that have brought nationalists together." And Maurras, who considered anti-Semitism a natural current for the royalists to exploit, has told how keen he and Daudet always were on the anti-Semitic nuance which "corresponds with our ideas and with the roots, the reasons for being, of our ideas."[67]

There has been some discussion of whether Action Française leaders were personally anti-Semitic. For Daudet, anti-Semitism was most probably a convenient fuel for attacks motivated by quite different animosities, the term "Jew" but one more epithet in a quiverful of insults. But Daudet never held a grudge long, and his malice was of the personal, not the principial, kind. Maurras, over the years, developed an anti-Semitism that was more rabid, more consistent, and probably much more influential. Lucien Rebatet, who became a noted Jew-baiter in his own right, claims that he had no anti-Semitic ideas when he joined the Action Française but soon acquired them under the influence of Maurras, whose private secretary he was for a time.

But whatever their personal sentiments may have been, it was on the shoulders of Maurras and Daudet that Drumont's mantle fell; it was because of the *Action française* and several generations of publicists whom it helped to launch that anti-Semitism spread in France. They provided the theoretical arguments that made base prejudice socially acceptable and even, in a sense, defensible.

Professional anti-Semites flocked to the Action Française—Henry Leroy-Fournier and Commandant Biot from the *Libre Parole,* Jacques Cailly and Edouard Brunet from Left Bank anti-Semitic groups, Lionel des Rieux from Bonapartism, "because the monarchy was anti-Jewish."[68] It was anti-Semitism that brought Roger Lambelin to the movement in its dispute in 1910 with the old royalists, a fundamental issue in the conflict being that the Comte de Larègle and Arthur Meyer had wanted to play down anti-Semitism, whereas the *Action française* insisted on its essential place in royalist doctrine.[u]

Demagogic considerations may also have obtained when, at the close of the war, anti-Semitic sentiment in France was fairly weak. Jews had fought and died along with other Frenchmen. Even Maurice Barrès was moved to accept them as one of the *familles spirituelles de la France,* even the *Libre Parole* in liberal Catholic hands softened its traditional antagonism. The *Action française* alone, despite occasional denials, kept the anti-Semitic fires burning, maintaining the traditions of Drumont and anti-Dreyfusism. For a self-conscious Jewish politician like Léon Blum's cousin André Blumel, the *Action française* was the focus and the spearhead of French anti-Semitism between the wars.[69]

Where once the Jews had been agents of the Germans, now they were agents also of international Communism. In his articles, Lambelin showed the dark and devious ways by which international Judaism plotted the enslavement of the world. His forebodings were bolstered by the publication in France of the *Protocols of the Sages of Zion,* Urbain Gohier's translation of which was greeted by French anti-Semites as vindicating their tireless campaigns. "Don't imagine," rejoiced Daudet, "that these *Protocols* are a fiction, an ingenious invention, a polemical trick. They are a document, nothing more or less. 'Do you have a text?' Fustel de Coulanges used to ask his students. Urbain Gohier brings us a text."

Texts, however, mattered very little. When, not many months later, *The Times* denounced the dangerous and shoddy nonsense of the *Protocols* for the

[u] See *AF,* Dec. 31, 1910. It has been suggested (F7 12862, No. 2/28 of April 22, 1908) that the virulently anti-Semitic tone adopted at that time by the *Action française* was a deliberate move to attract the public of the *Libre Parole* by making the latter seem "lukewarm and tired." If so, it was successful. Similarly in Algeria, where the growth of integral nationalism was at first slow, anti-Semitism was the most favorable means of approach; see the report of the Tenth Congress, *AF,* June 21, 1923.

wretched forgery it was, Bainville quickly admitted that he had always felt "a certain suspicion about the *Protocols,* whose authenticity seemed to call for some criticism." But, he maintained, their authenticity had no particular bearing on the connection between Bolshevism and Jews: "It is possible that the *Protocols* were forged . . . So what? . . . What does this prove about Bolsheviks and Jews? Absolutely nothing."[70]

Not everyone was so logical as Bainville, or even so willing to admit that the *Protocols* might be fakes. But many would agree with him that although all documents were welcome when they reinforced the case for anti-Semitism, the case was really so obvious that it needed no proof at all. Documents, like miracles, were simply manifestations of a previously known truth. If Jews could not be pelted with facts, prejudices could be just as useful. Several books had outlined the "Jewish conspiracy": first serialized in the periodicals of the respectable bourgeoisie (the *Revue hebdomadaire,* the *Mercure de France,* the *Revue des Deux Mondes*), works like Lambelin's *Règne d'Israël chez les Anglo-Saxons,* Georges Batault's *Le Péril juif,* and the Tharaud brothers' *Royaume de Dieu* and *Quand Israël est roi* left their Catholic middle-class readers with ideas of which the *Action française* was for a long time the most persistent and effective exponent, until overtaken at last by louder, more voracious offspring.

We shall later see how alumni of the Action Française became the backbone of the staffs of the most rabidly anti-Semitic publications of the 'thirties and 'forties, and how, fed by their arguments, a pervasive anti-Semitic mood developed during the years preceding the Second World War, reaching its climax in the anti-Semitic legislation of the Vichy regime, which was inspired by and generally sponsored by friends and allies of the Action Française.

PART III: TWO FAILURES

The stone falls on the egg: alas for the egg!
The egg falls on the stone: alas for the egg!

CYPRIOT PEASANT PROVERB

II

THE WOOING OF LABOR

An analysis of the Jewish question has shown the Action Française caught between ideas and reality: a theory that was fairly rational and moderate would be distorted by the unreasoning proclivities of its supporters. In another field, also, and most notably, ideas and realities clashed again: in the relations of the royalists with labor and in the shifts of their economic policies.

We have seen how, in the years preceding the First World War, the Action Française tried to woo syndicalist workers and how a certain nationalist group, led by Georges Valois, tried to define a consistent social policy. The internal dissensions which, quite apart from working-class indifference, prevented the success of the endeavor were to reappear in postwar years and, after promising beginnings, to end future attempts at forging a valid labor policy.

As in prewar days, the man who directed the activities of the Action Française on the economic front was Valois, assisted now by a young Northern industrialist, Jacques Arthuys, by Firmin Baconnier, who had patched up his differences with the rue de Rome, and by a Catholic syndicalist particularly interested in agrarian questions, Georges Coquelle-Viance. Beginning early in 1919, each Monday a page of the *Action française* was devoted to economic and social matters, always discussed from the point of view that class war (nothing but illusion, though a harmful one) could and should be replaced by collaboration intended to integrate workers into the bourgeoisie.[1]

Within a year, in March 1920, Valois had launched the Confederation of French Intelligence and Production (CIPF), which was designed to organize production on a corporatist basis. Considering employers and employees alike as producers in their occupational groups would cut across class differences between master and workman and reach the "reality" of their common occupation.[2]

Vigorously promoted by Valois and his lieutenants in pamphlets and lectures, the CIPF attracted the attention of businessmen worried by the industrial unrest of the early 'twenties. It received favorable comments in the conservative press[3] and gained the support of some powerful provincial interests. At Nantes, its local president was Jean Babin-Chevaye, a respected representative of local industrialists and senator of the Loire-Inférieure; at Saint-Chamond, its meetings were sponsored by the Union des Industriels; at Le

Havre, Valois was received by the influential Comité de l'Industrie, du Commerce, et de l'Armement; and in the North the owner of the textile complex of Roubaix-Tourcoing, Eugène Mathon, supported the endeavor.[a] The Corporation's monthly bulletin *La Production française* insisted on high production and on the community of interests that all producers, both masters and their workers, must necessarily share.

It was in this spirit that the CIPF organized a series of "Weeks"—conferences designed to promote production and sales in different industries: Semaine du Livre, Semaine du Bâtiment, Semaine du Commerce Extérieur. In June 1922, the last of these, the Semaine de la Monnaie, on whose committee sat men like Mathon and Lucien Romier, discussed the stabilization of the franc, which had to come before there could be any real economic recovery. The Semaines attracted much favorable publicity, and the sympathetic attention given to Valois's ideas by a good part of the business world prompted Romier (who was not a royalist) to ask whether industrialists might not be looking to a king for a solution of the country's difficulties.

It seemed to many observers that Valois had some chance of enlisting the working class in a movement whose energies would be directed away from destructive, to profitable ends. With company unions almost dead and CGT membership soaring, his arguments suggested the possibility of recapturing social peace in a restored prosperity.

Late in 1922, Valois began his campaign for an Estates General of French Production, in which the royalist hand would be less immediately obvious than in the Semaines. It had been carefully prepared with the aim of bringing industrial and union leaders together in a movement representing the social and economic realities that the nation had to control before it could work out a political solution. The national committee, headed by Mathon, included, in addition to Valois, Arthuys, Bernard de Vésins, and Paul Robain, Auguste Cazeneuve of the Fédération de la Mécanique, Etienne Bernard-Précy (director of the influential financial and business magazine *Journée industrielle*), Martin Mamy (who would soon become director of a Coty enterprise), and several others, equally friendly but not members of the Action Française.

All producers, whatever their part in the whole process of production, must unite, Valois argued; every category must set up its syndicate, then all must join economic groups (steel, insurance, haberdashery, publishing, etc.) or regional groups, which would in turn send representatives to a national economic council.

Where the Semaines had helped certain professions to organize and regu-

[a] AF, April 22, 23, May 12, 14, 1920; Valois, *L'Homme contre l'argent,* pp. 50–54. Mathon, president of the Comité de la Laine, supported first Valois, then the Action Française against Valois. After 1925, he made financial contributions toward royalist activities in his region "out of hatred of Christian unionism," and had vast numbers of copies of the paper distributed throughout the North, affirms Valois, p. 181.

late themselves,[b] the Etats Généraux de la Production were meant to affect the structure of French economy and, eventually, of the State itself. At a great meeting in the Salle Wagram on December 18, Valois explained that the Estates General should represent the solid realities of French society—"les familles, les provinces, les grandes corporations, les grands corps de l'Etat, l'Eglise." As a mere parliament of trades and professions, the Estates would be incomplete: "We are not only men of a trade, we are heads or members of families, we are the sons of our provinces; we observe a moral doctrine or follow the precepts of a Church." All these realities should be reflected in the new Estates, whose great task would be the coordination of national forces.

But if this was the practical purpose of the new corporatist Estates, their spiritual task was to purify and revivify the climate of national affairs. Like institutions or social bodies, an "order" is not an end but a means, Valois wrote a few years later in the *Revue universelle*. The nation is a hierarchy of leaders, running from the head of a family to the head of State. A system that recognized this would foster the development of an elite that opposed its sense of national greatness to the self-seeking money values that had too long prevailed: "Il nous faut recréer les conditions de la grandeur. La première des conditions, c'est la rentrée dans la vie publique des valeurs héroïques retrouvées dans la guerre." French unity had to be rebuilt on a heroic as well as on a practical plane, under the stimulus of a national leader who would take the initiative against the false values that soldiers had learned to hate during the war and against those financiers and decadent politicians who had turned the national and social revolution fostered in the trenches away from its true course and back into the corrupt channels of the old order.[4]

As the broader implications of the movement and the lines of Valois's thinking became clearer, strong interests reacted in opposition. Valois has argued that enthusiasm was shattered by the murder of Plateau, which convinced everyone that the Action Française would never carry out either promises or threats. Henry Coston has attributed the eventual failure of Valois's scheme to the hostility of the Comité des Forges and other powerful economic groups. Yet in the late spring of 1923, conservative publications like the *Revue hebdomadaire* were still giving sympathetic attention to the Estates General, and Marc Sangnier was complaining that Valois's plans were getting too much approval and even official cooperation.[5]

It may be that the loss of momentum and then the disintegration of the Estates General hinged more on Valois's disagreements with his supporters than on hostile reactions from without. For, just as left-wing flirtations had once cost the integral nationalists the encouragement of conservative royalists, similarly leftish inclinations cost Valois some of his business backers, who

[b] The Semaine du Livre ensured the success of the Maison du Livre Français, which by 1922 included 130 publishers and 700 booksellers, and still exists today.

were apt to be skeptical of any talk of professional organization or regulation. Valois's obvious contempt for economic liberalism not unnaturally aroused accusations of collectivism, especially when he set out to persuade Communist workers that they could reach their economic aims more readily by cooperating with the CIPF. One can imagine what his business backers thought when they heard of his words to the Communists at Périgueux: "We are both against plutocracy. We are the only active troops in the battle against it. Separately, we risk defeat; so, I propose, let us carry out the revolution together."[6]

Valois had to choose—either to organize production with the bosses, or to revolt with the workers. No argument about common interests could resolve the difficulty, and in the end it was Valois's revolutionary temper that made, or helped others to make, the choice.

In 1924, as for one reason or another the grand schemes of professional organization began to fade away and as the CIPF concentrated more on establishing trade and professional unions—insurance, architecture, publishing, commerce—Valois turned toward the activism that fascinated him, whose prototype he found in Mussolini's Fascism, whose troops he sought among his former companions of the trenches, and whose appeal he hoped would prove a unifying force far stronger than the divisive slogans of class war.

To galvanize the nation one should begin, he felt, by organizing the veterans. But such an effort, if it were to succeed, could not parade under the royalist label. Integral nationalism had in any case been for him only a convenient symbol of authority. Although he accepted Maurras's conclusions and even, for a while, remained loyal to the Pretender, he knew by now that undertakings clearly associated with royalism would not get far. The directors of the Action Française did not object when he proposed to set up his own newspaper and his own movement, to propagate ideas similar to their own but not explicitly monarchic.

On February 26, 1925, accordingly, there appeared the first issue of the *Nouveau Siècle*. It carried a manifesto calling for but one party, that of France, and one policy, that of glory. The nation under one leader should abandon its worn divisions to organize in families, provinces, and trades; religious faith should be left its own master; and social justice must come into its own. The signatures below the manifesto were more significant than the generalities they endorsed. The new weekly review had recruited some of the best and liveliest talent both in the Action Française and outside. Signatories included René Benjamin, Gabriel Bonvalot, Hubert Bourgin, Maurice Denis, Henri Ghéon, Louis Marcellin, Eugène Marsan, Martin Mamy, Henri Massis, Ambroise Rendu, Jacques Roujon, André Rousseaux, Edouard Soulier, Georges Suarez, Jérome and Jean Tharaud and, of course, Valois himself.

The rue de Rome supported Valois fully, and its representatives were in attendance at the official ceremony some weeks later, at Easter, founding his veteran-recruited Legions, "formation de combattants pour la politique de la victoire." The names of the founders read like a roll of honor of veteran and Fascist leaders of the time: one was Maurice de Barral, an official of several veterans' organizations and also of the Parti Fasciste Révolutionnaire; there were also Marcel Bucard, the future head of the Francistes, Emile Fels, who founded the Syndicat des Journaux de Combattants, and Jacques Arthuys, an officer in the First World War and co-founder in the Second of one of France's great resistance organizations, the Organization Civile et Militaire. These men and half a dozen others, all held the Croix de Guerre, and, most of them also the Legion of Honor, won on the battlefield.

Relations between the *Nouveau Siècle,* the Legions, and the Action Française were good. The latter saw in the dynamic veterans' movement a means of influencing men who were otherwise beyond its reach. Valois, on the other hand, hoped to use his royalist connections and the dual membership of many royalists, especially among his movement's leadership, to draw the Action Française, willy-nilly, into the revolutionary plans he envisioned.[c] Each side fully intended to exploit the other, but meanwhile they expressed their mutual admiration and support.[7] On Armistice Day 1925, however, the new team founded its own, openly Fascist, party, the Faisceau, and from then on relations with the Action Française quickly grew worse.

The main cause of friction seems to have been financial: the *Nouveau Siècle* was financed by a group of rich supporters like Serge André, an oil man, and Jean Beurrier the banker, but it also solicited and received subsidies from François Coty and probably also from Jean Hennessy, who used his brandy fortune to support keen national-socialist interests. Its fund-raising campaigns began to cut into the income of the *Action française,* some of whose revenue came from identical quarters, and this was something the neo-royalists had no intention of tolerating. When the *Nouveau Siècle* became a daily paper in November 1925, the competition was more than Maurras could abide. Asked by Valois and Arthuys to urge all monarchists to join the Faisceau, he announced that monarchists would have to choose for themselves, but they could not belong to both organizations.[8]

Thereafter, the quarrel deepened. Valois's idea of Fascism was clearly not the sort that the Action Française would entertain. René Johannet had once expressed the latter's view when, welcoming Mussolini's *coup d'état,* he said that he looked forward to the day when France would follow suit. Then, Johannet had said, the big industrialists would know how to go about breaking the humiliating hold of Red unions. "It is an excellent thing that the bourgeoisie should prove that it is even better able than the proletariat to impose a dictatorship."[9] Valois, on the other hand, honored industrialists not as capital-

[c] *L'Homme contre l'argent,* p. 167: "Ma volonté bien arrêtée était d'entraîner toute l'Action française dans un mouvement révolutionnaire. Je la tenais pour gouvernée par des hommes parfaitement résolus à ne jamais agir, mais comme une force indispensable contre la ploutocratie."

ists but as producers, and saw in Mussolini the enemy both of liberalism and of Bolshevism. "You would not find a man at the Action Française disposed to sacrifice a moment or a hair for what is called the bourgeoisie," he declared.[10] This was wishful thinking, of course, but it indicates the basis of misunderstanding between him and his erstwhile friends.

Valois and the Action Française differed also on the question of political action. Both sides agreed that their disagreement was most profound not as it concerned doctrine, but as it concerned method. Valois felt that Maurras had made a fundamental ideological contribution to French revival, but that, having furnished the ideas, the Action Française was now incapable of implementing them. The action would have to come from his veteran-recruited Legions, which would take over where the older organization, the older leaders, hesitated. In the latter's eyes, Valois was a megalomaniac, riding for a fall. The Action Française, said Bernard de Vésins, would bide its time before deciding on the sort of action into which some were attempting to drag it. It wanted a dictator-king, but its desire for a dictator must always be conditioned by its prior desire for a king; and this was not the case where Valois was concerned.[11]

The immediate causes of the open break, which came within a month after the founding of the Faisceau, were probably only the symptoms of these fundamental differences of doctrine and of temperament. Valois had been criticizing his old companions for their inertia and their hypocrisy. Published in the Italian press,[12] his statements did not improve the climate. Then, on December 12, with the support of two members of the board, he obtained control of the Nouvelle Librairie Nationale, of which he had been the director since 1912, and carried it out of the Action Française. To Maurras and his fellow-directors, the loss of the N.L.N., their own party bookshop and publishing firm, was the last and intolerable blow. That very evening, Valois's supporters on the N.L.N. board, Colonel Milleret and the Comte de Lur-Saluces, were expelled from the royalist organization. More forceful reprisals were planned, in the shape of a surprise raid on a Faisceau meeting that had been announced to recruit student members for a group called the Faisceau Universitaire.[13]

The meeting of the Fascist student group was broken up by a force of Etudiants d'Action Française; after that, for nearly a year, a state of war existed between the two groups, a situation which their opponents on the Left greatly enjoyed. In January 1926, the royalist leaders estimated their losses to the Faisceau around nearly two thousand. The provinces, where membership was more conservative, were less affected, although even there some of the most active militants left to join the veterans' organization. Accused by his erstwhile friends of being a thief, a traitor, and an agent of the police, Valois countered with slanderous accusations of his own.[14] The feud, carried on largely in print but also in street skirmishes, came to a head in a raid of

Valois's Blue Shirts upon the offices of the Action Française in the rue de Rome. The raiders, who managed to turn the offices upside down, were at last beaten off by the regular Camelot guard after a gunfight in which one Blue Shirt was left severely wounded. But by then—November 26—the Faisceau was already on the decline.

During its brief prosperity the Faisceau creamed off the "purest" veterans from all over France. It benefited from the financial crisis and from the Red scare of November 1924; it attracted labor leaders like Marcel Delagrange, the Communist mayor of Périgueux, and Henri Lauridan, who organized the textile unions of the north for the CGTU; and a number of bright young men like the future senator Jacques Debu-Bridel and Philippe Lamour, who is now one of France's great industrial experts. Its great meetings at Verdun and at Reims and its strong hold on veterans' organizations were briefly alarming to the banks, the unions, and Parliament all together.

But as Poincaré began to restore the economy and re-establish the franc, the veterans' movement, which had lost impetus and support in its running fight with the Action Française, began to wither. Disgusted with the Right, Valois returned to his early syndical loves; his followers split, the *Nouveau Siècle* disappeared in April 1928, and Valois himself, although active for another fifteen years, slipped back into obscurity, forgotten by all but a few who still thought longingly of the wonderful spirit that was or that might have been.[d]

It is difficult to estimate what the break of 1925 and the loss of Valois and his supporters meant to the Action Française. Valois, by all accounts, never fitted in and was but grudgingly accepted by the royalist hierarchy, with whom he was often in disagreement. Especially after Vaugeois and Montesquiou were gone, Maurras could not allow the rise of men who might stand up to him, or who would simply rock the boat by suggesting policies that might disturb his more cautious friends. Perhaps if Valois had not left in the explosive context of a Fascist venture, he would have been eased out in any case.

Valois was an economist, even though a self-taught one; nothing was more

[d] Valois's other enterprises were no more successful. A weekly founded in 1928, *Les Cahiers bleus,* expired in 1932; the *Nouvel Age,* started as a literary periodical in 1931 but turned into a political journal in 1934, continued to appear through 1938, reflecting Valois's evolution from anti-socialist syndicalism to sympathy with socialist ideas after the disillusions of his Fascist experience. In the *République,* August 24, 1935, he declared that Fascism erred in thinking that economic ills could be remedied by political (and police) methods, and that no authoritarian solution could prove lasting unless the foundations and structure of the existing economic order were themselves attacked. Valois's economic thought is thoroughly discussed by Georges Mazières, *L'Oeuvre économique de Georges Valois* (Castelnaudary, 1937). During the winter of 1940–41, Valois and several "accomplices" were arrested for "Gaullism," imprisoned at Clermont-Ferrand, and eventually deported to Germany. Pierre Mendès-France, *Liberté, liberté chérie* (New York, 1943), pp. 158–59, attributes Valois's arrest to Action Française vengeance. For Valois's brave end at Bergen-Belsen, shortly before the liberation of the camp, see "Les Derniers Jours de Georges Valois," in *Bergen-Belsen, Bagne Sanatorium,* published by the Librairie Valois in 1947.

foreign to the humanistic leaders of the Action Française. Valois was proletarian; they belonged to the bourgeoisie. Valois wanted a revolution; they praised order—more and more the established order. Valois sided with the workers, they with the middle class. Valois's departure was but one aspect of a shift in basic policy of a movement whose direction, although it may long have been implicit, was not actually decided until the 'twenties. Always a middle-class movement, henceforth the Action Française would more and more fall back on the middle-class attitudes it had been reluctant to accept, particularly in the subsequent evolution of its corporative policy.

In 1924, the CIPF had been transformed into the UCF—the Union des Corporations Françaises—with Valois as president and Bernard de Vésins as vice-president. In 1926, with Valois gone, Georges Coquelle also left, soon to join the Fédération Catholique, and Firmin Baconnier took over the social and economic side, and eventually the presidency, of the UCF after Pierre Chaboche, owner of Salamandre stoves, and Jacques Delafour, of the Etablissements Jacob Delafour, had held the office in turn.

Safe from dangerous new ideas, the UCF stood firmly behind René de la Tour du Pin's old doctrine of professional and trade organization, but it was not interested in doing any organizing itself. As Chaboche told the 1927 Congress, since no effective corporations could be set up under the actual political regime, the UCF would limit its efforts to the capture of elites within all trades and classes. What this actually came to was the establishment of propaganda centers, which were at best lecture and discussion groups enrolling anybody at all who cared to come, and the publication of propaganda pamphlets and reviews. Provincial propaganda centers, no more than three in 1925, numbered twenty-six by November 1927, and eighty-nine by 1928. Besides a monthly journal called *Production française,* regular news-sheets were issued for some special groups like builders, doctors, and engineers.

By 1930, the UCF showed very little trace of working-class support.[15] Like the Action Française, it was, for the most part, in favor of abandoning action for talk and for the printed word.[e] Its policy became increasingly conservative, opposing the eight-hour law and social insurance and proposing to resolve the depression by protective measures and private enterprise. Its membership inevitably followed the policy. In 1934, members of the UCF took a leading part in founding the Institut d'Etudes Corporatives et Sociales, directed by Maurice Bouvier-Ajam (then still a royalist and not yet a Communist sympathizer), with Georges Blondel, Firmin Baconnier, Claude-Joseph Gignoux (of the *Journée industrielle*), and Louis Salleron—the group that would under Pétain furnish the nucleus of the Office Central d'Organisation Corporative.

[e] *AF,* Nov. 30, 1932. In his report to the annual congress of the UCF, the business manager of the *Production française* cited 115 publications (not counting *journaux amis*) that had quoted its articles, and claimed a 20 per cent rise in subscriptions. But in 1933 (*AF,* Dec. 13, 1933) the UCF had only 3,000 dues-paying members.

In the 'thirties, however, with the Vichy government still far off, the most definite public expression of these ideas was that which occurred in March 1936, when, shortly before the legislature ended, six right-wing deputies introduced a bill proposing a full pattern of corporatist organization for French economy. The bill was something of a symbolic gesture, but it expressed the views of the Institut, the UCF, and of the Action Française, with which three of its sponsors—René Dommange, Jean Le Cour-Grandmaison, and Xavier Vallat—had rather close associations. As the *Action française* explained,[16] the intention was to replace "the concept of the individual with those of family, trade, and region."

The proposed measure provided for the establishment of unions for all those making a living in the same profession. These unions were to be set up on a regional basis, with each local union to include one section of employers, directors, and managers, and another section of workers and office staff. The local unions would send delegates to the regional corporation, which would in turn be represented both in the central corporation of the trade and in a regional corporative council on which all trades of the region would have representatives. At all levels, masters and workers were to receive equal representation. At all levels, too, agricultural interest would be heavily favored, their votes and representatives being never less than half of any body on which they sat.

This particular concern with agriculture was characteristic of traditionalist views, and also of preoccupations that Maurras had once expressed in the slogan "Agriculture first!" The Jeffersonianism of Maurras and others who liked to imagine a society where every man should sit under his own fig tree (preferably at Martigues), or where, at least, all other interests should be subordinated to agrarian ones,[17] reflected not only conservative tendencies that were coming to the fore but also the relative strength of royalism in agricultural regions and corporations.

Royalists like Hyacinthe de Gailhard-Bancel had long been active and successful in launching agrarian unions, mutual benefit societies, and credit associations. Many regional unions belonging to agricultural syndicates were dominated by royalists, especially in the west, the southwest, and the central regions. On the eve of the Second World War, some 1,800 agricultural unions were "corporative," led by men who would hold positions of responsibility under the Vichy regime.[18] It was only natural that the Action Française should be concerned about a field in which its followers and sympathizers were doing so extraordinarily well.

The emphasis on agriculture could not but pull the Action Française back in time. The future, Georges Coquelle-Viance had argued, lay in agricultural not industrial societies. France should concentrate on becoming the leader and organizer of countries "that produce bread and wine . . . that have their basis in a fertile soil"—in other words, countries that were underdeveloped and proud of it. But the countries that produced the bread and wine, Poland,

Romania, and Serbia, asked nothing better than to forget about bread and wine and to industrialize as fast as they could. And so, furthermore, did France, which, because of relative industrial stagnation, was rapidly becoming a second-class power.

The true implications of the UCF policy were made very clear in the 1927 Congress of the French Corporation of Agriculture: "The first task of the Corporation," the Congress declared, "is to cling to the ways that express the wisdom of the ages."[19] For this determination, the Action Française would henceforward provide every possible support.

It appears from the foregoing that this chapter of relations with labor, however small a part it played in the complex saga of integral nationalism, was an important one. The questions that it posed forced the leaders of the movement, if not the movement itself, to define for themselves, and then to assume, a clear position on issues they really had no desire to face. In 1908, Daudet spoke of the Pretender as "the King of Labor"—meaning, perhaps, that this could and should come true. As late as 1924 he asserted in the Chamber, "M. Compère-Morel est moins révolutionnaire que moi!"[20] But, under pressure, the dream of revolution had been left by the wayside, along with the dream of labor support, and the Action Française's true milieu recognized for what it was—the world of the bourgeoisie, and of the petty bourgeoisie at that.

Again and again, throughout the early 'twenties, we find the *Action française* expressing the grievances, resentments, and envies of a declining order: the old *rentiers,* who find that working people are eating better than they; the owners of real estate, who have lost their investments while factory workers have been making money; the good sturdy local landowners and farmers, threatened by democracy and by international finance; "la classe des moyennes et petites gens de France," hard hit by Poincaré's *double-décime,* a tax peculiarly burdensome to those with a fixed income; small shopkeepers and shop assistants menaced by department stores and foreign labor; white-collar, bank, and office workers who must have higher wages. Again and again, the paper warned, Action Française speakers warned, against the decline and fall of the middle class.[21]

Such a position did not by any means exclude hatred of plutocracy, for little people feared and hated capital as much as they did collectivism, or the State. The power of plutocracy did not, in fact, seem very different from that of collectivism, its menace no less. There was no paradox in Daudet's taking the side of bank employees when they struck for higher wages, or in his demanding sanctions against war profiteers. And it was understandable even twelve years later to find, in a book dedicated to Maurras and published by the Action Française, the assertion that the future of strong nations lies in national-socialism under a modern, social monarchy.[22] Such positions were perfectly logical and wholly consistent with neo-royalist doctrine; but in another sense they had very little meaning, simply because, although the revolution of reaction was a fact, the Action Française was hardly in any position to lead it.

Socially and psychologically, the directors of the *Action française,* despite what they said, found themselves on the side of established order. True, they detested it; but after the war it happened that their friends detested change even more strongly. A movement that clings stubbornly to established ways, a movement that needs money to survive, a movement that abhors the Republic but sees no way of overthrowing it, a movement that discourages precipitate action and includes under that heading almost any action at all—such a movement will very soon be incapable of understanding the difference between being reactionary (which it would of course approve) and being merely conservative.

The Action Française maintained that it stood for change quite as radical and revolutionary as the change demanded by the professed insurrectionists of the Left: and in some ways it did. But the changes it advocated were institutional and political; and if politics came first, then economics was secondary. But since the movement was politically impotent, its political action had to become didactic and ideological, and therefore largely dependent on economic matters.

In the field of economics, the leaders of the Action Française were hampered by an extreme lack of imagination; even when they had economic ideas, they were of the most orthodox kind. Valois at least understood that organization and production mattered more than the stock exchange, and that industry mattered more than agriculture. Daudet, led by strong though erratic Jacobin sentiments, sometimes touched on the essential role of the money powers; but his explosions never had any morrow, and were in any case easily shunted off into some wild Jew chase. Bainville and Baconnier, each in his way, were utterly conformist. As for Maurras, his economic ideas never got beyond the level of the provincial bourgeois he always, in some respects, remained.[f] His ignorance of economics has often been held against him. What seems much worse, he was, it appears, afflicted with an insuperable bourgeois deference to big money, of the sort that has also afflicted some Presidents of the United

[f] See his letter of July 18, 1930, to the president of the Cercle La Tour du Pin (*La Production française,* July 27, 1930), in which he explains that he never had to look for a social doctrine because, from the first, he had adopted that offered by La Tour du Pin, with its two basic principles: freedom for the State to exercise its proper functions, and freedom for all natural organizations when they do not go beyond the limits of their particular area of competence. This, as he goes on to interpret it, must imply professional freedom—for individuals organized in corporations. Property would be respected, the worker's property of his skill no less than that of the owner and employer. But Maurras failed to consider the crucial difficulty of delimiting the spheres of influence of State, professions, and labor, and the possibility that new products or technical developments might devalue the worker's skill as catastrophically as other modern forces had devalued the franc. La Tour du Pin's principles were clear, and they seemed sensible; there was no need to match them with the realities of the world around.

States. "Les plus sérieuses garanties de tous les droits des humbles," he wrote in 1910, "sont liées au salut et au bien des puissants."[23] This was a view he would repeat with variations for more than forty years.

In one particular sense, his point may be well taken. Maurras rightly saw that the problem of social politics and social peace would be near a solution when the transient worker acquired a stable situation and a worth-while stake in society. He wanted the worker to become part of a working-class bourgeoisie, as it might be called, which would be a sort of continuation of the merchant and the industrial bourgeoisie. Against the government's social insurance measures of 1930, the Action Française, like the Duc de Guise, backed Xavier Vallat's project of a fund to finance the acquisition of property by the working classes. Liberalism, with all the unrestricted freedom it vouchsafed to the activities of capital, was rejected as bitterly as Communism. Not free and unrestricted enterprise, but a policy designed to open the realm of property to workers and to increase the say of trade and professional corporations in their own affairs, was the royalists' recipe for social improvement and peace.[24] But this quite tenable idea was spoiled by a strong sense of hierarchy which affirmed social divisions, even while denying their significance. The welfare of the humble as dependent upon the powerful and rich did not imply great possibilities of enterprise and riches working together to open new horizons that would bring riches to all; it harked back, rather, to "the rich man in his castle, the poor man at the gate," and Maurras would undoubtedly have approved the idyllic scene.

In a deferential, hierarchic society, as Maurras saw it, such a situation could not but translate the necessities, and the security, of a natural and beneficent order. The corporative system was the natural one: it translated into institutional terms realities that both liberalism and socialism ignored. Liberalism made for chaos, socialism for division into warring groups; corporatism alone offered the perfect analogy to the family, which was the basic social unit for all men.

And here, it seems, lay the essential error of Maurras's reasoning. The argument based on organic unity, in which the family appears as the microcosm of the State and the State is no more than one big family, in which an enterprise is a sort of tribe and the State just another paternalistic enterprise, in which the same rules of common sense, family duty, and affection apply at every stage, differing only in scale, forgets that at a certain point quantitative differences become qualitative, and that the difference between an outhouse and the Eiffel Tower is more than one of size.

For one thing, as Julien Benda has pointed out, whereas family, region, and profession are concrete realities, the State is a transcendent one—in effect, and in spite of its many tangible manifestations, an abstract. For another thing, the State is not just an expression or extrapolation of families and regions and professions: by its very nature, it tends to master, to order, to control them.

It may in its own interest turn against them, or against any one of them, oppose, constrain, or even abolish them. Just as a crowd is generally different from the sum total of the individuals who compose it, so the State is different from the groups and corporations that compose *it.* Far from having grown out of them, it has usually grown against them and at their expense, expressing an altogether different will and altogether different interests.

What the Catholic syndicalist Paul Vignaux has called the feudalistic traditionalism of the corporatists looks back with longing to a sort of golden age in which human relations are hierarchic, in which interdependence is really dependence, in which inequality is part of a social order with generous employers and loyal and trusting employees.

In 1920, when monarchist Baudry d'Asson pleaded in the Chamber for abolition of the eight-hour work law, he argued that such a law not only hampered production but curtailed individual freedom. To end class war, he said, capital, talent, and labor must be associated in intimate collaboration, as they had been, he said, in his own factories for the past twenty years.[g] A *roman social contemporain* serialized in the *Action française* put it this way: "The manufacturer was liberal and eclectic, but a determined believer in order, without which no prosperity is possible in a civilized state."[25] This expresses the sort of idealized paternalism that might go down in company unions, but it sounds false and is false in an age in which theoretical equality is the rule and economic relations are based less on mutual confidence than on written contract.

Traditionalists who do not like contractual relations because contracts imply parties, hence a difference of interests, insist on the fact that a workshop, a factory, a profession is a unit whose members share a community of interests. Workers and masters joined in common endeavor labor together for the common profit in the necessarily hierarchized order that empirical reality has imposed. They are a corporation held together by interest and, eventually, by sentiment. And what is true at the workshop or professional level can and must be true at the national level also.

And yet to achieve such results—which, in view of current prejudices, must be imposed by force—and to keep the system going, preventing the corporations from eating each other up, the traditionalists do not postulate a strong, totalitarian State. Far from it: they want the State of Locke in the economic jungle of Hobbes—a weak, noninterfering State that would be no more than an occasional arbiter between rival professional or regional interests, conciliating them all for the common good.

However, the corporatist doctrine being anti-historical (at least in the sense that it denies widely accepted ideas like class antagonism and opposes established institutions like trade unions), it can only be enforced by a State

[g] *JOC*, May 19, 1920. When Baudry d'Asson intervened, Daudet had just called for the dissolution of the CGT.

strong enough to break the opposition it is bound to meet, on both the institutional and the ideological plane. Whether in Italy between the wars, or in Vichy France, corporatist ends justified authoritarian means. Instead of strong corporations supporting a weak State, France got weak corporations enforced by a strong State. And the corporatist vocabulary served to mask increased State interference on behalf of the planned economy that the traditionalists professed to dread, of the great financial interests they abhorred, and of anti-unionism.

And so it was that traditionalist reactionaries justified their revolutionary claims, by trying, so far as they were able, to destroy the existing socio-economic order and to replace it with one of their own devising; and acknowledged the lessons of history by achieving results—where any were achieved—quite different from those they had hoped to get.

12

TWO BEACONS

"Roma locuta, causa finita est."
"??? . . ."

If the break with Valois forced the Action Française to abandon its rather weary hopes of successfully wooing the workers, another crisis, at the same time, would prove more important and much more costly. The Faisceau feud ended what was hardly more than a well-intentioned illusion. The feud with Rome, beginning in the autumn of 1926, would mean the loss of a strong position in Catholic circles, which had been an important source of recruits and of funds, the close not only of a chapter in the development of the Action Française but of its period of ascendancy.

We have already seen what influence neo-royalism had acquired upon the Catholic public, what sympathies it had won among the hierarchy and, in turn, of what importance Catholics and Catholicism had been in its own organization and policy.

The campaigns of the Action Française against liberalism and democracy, and against all tendencies to compromise with them, coincided with the anti-modernist campaigns which, beginning with the century, culminated in 1907–10 in the encyclical *Pascendi,* in the prohibition of works by Loisy, Laberthonnière, and Le Roy, in the persecution of ecclesiastical scholars seeking to interpret Christian doctrine in the light of modern social and scientific developments, and, finally, in the condemnation of Marc Sangnier's Sillon. Modernists were removed from Catholic faculties and seminaries, their publications were suppressed or placed on the *Index,* and an anti-modernist loyalty oath was demanded of the clergy and candidates for the clergy.

The anti-modernist reaction was led by a number of "integral Catholics," including friends and admirers of Maurras like Father Le Floch and Cardinal Louis Billot. Its central figure was Monsignore Umberto Benigni, a close aide of Cardinal Merry del Val, who was Secretary of State to Pope Pius X.

Around his periodical, the *Corrispondenza di Roma,* which in 1908 became, significantly enough, the *Correspondance de Rome,* Benigni organized an anti-modernist league to fight modernist ideas, to track down their exponents and denounce them. Behind the anti-modernist league and the *Correspondance,* a more mysterious body operated, one whose activities still appear melodramatically shadowy: the Sodalitium Pianum or Fellowship of the Pine, a secret international federation of integral Catholic groups. Dispersed throughout the Church, its members and agents kept careful watch on all Catholics suspected of "demo-Christianity," and, in France, worked closely with the Action Française, with whom they shared a mutual apprehension of an international Judeo-Masonic conspiracy.

The policies of the Sodalitium Pianum and of the Action Française had a good deal in common. Both were extremely hostile not only to all forms of social Catholicism but also to the liberals, who, at Leo XIII's behest, had rallied the Republic. As Benigni's network strengthened its hold upon the hierarchy, men sympathetic to integral nationalism rose to leading positions in the Church of France.

Clerical and lay, the leaders of the neo-Thomist revival, which was Catholicism's answer to its subversive exegetes, gravitated toward the Action Française. Unworldly men, great scholars like Billot or Father Thomas Pègues, saw only its single-minded opposition to the worldly forces of modernism. Catholic faculties were crowded with admirers of Maurras who, like the Abbé Maisonneuve at Toulouse, tended to consider his anti-liberal political ideas infallible.[a] Of the Dominicans in particular, like Fathers Georges de Pascal, Jacques Vallée, and Garrigou-Lagrange—not forgetting Dom Besse, the master of novices at Notre-Dame-de-Ligugé—may be said what Raïssa Maritain has written about one of them, Father Humbert Clérissac: "Father Clérissac passionately admired Maurras; in his disgust with the modern world, in his pure enthusiasm for the metaphysical notion of order, he trusted the [Action Française]."

The influence of men like these was very great at a time when young people of the educated classes, ill at ease before the critical ideas of a rationalist Sorbonne, turned in droves toward the Church, hoping to find in it the principles of order and social discipline that might help to stave off the destruction of their world. It was Dom Besse who helped guide Bernanos toward the Action Française; it was Father Clérissac who recruited Jacques and Raïssa Maritain, and also, to some extent, Henri Massis.[1] The Assumptionists' *La Croix* served as another grammar for neo-royalist converts.[2]

By 1913, the excesses of extreme integrism had brought on the inevitable reaction. That year, Merry del Val put an end to Benigni's *Correspondance*

[a] See Commandant Dublaix, *Un apologiste du catholicisme—Charles Maurras* (1924), p. 33. The critical acumen of these scholarly admirers was not, however, without lapses. Father Pègues, well known for his commentaries on Saint Thomas, was also one of the men who defended Léo Taxil's hocus-pocus about Diana Vaughan, the extra-human lady who possessed the tail of the lion of Saint Mark, which, when placed on a table, would raise its hairy tuft and change it into a devil's head. The head would then speak, saying, "I am the devil, Bitru." Bitru had carnally known a daughter of man and engendered the woman one of whose descendants would, in 1962, give birth to Antichrist. To believers in the supernatural it was all most edifying. See Léo Taxil, *Le Diable au dix-neuvième siècle* (1894); Louis Nemours-Godré, *Diana Vaughan et ses répondants* (1897); Louis Dimier in *AF*, June 3, 1914; Abbé Jules Pierre, *L'Action Française en 1923* (1923), pp. 32–33.

de Rome, which Benigni replaced with a less obtrusive information service, the International Agency of Rome. The Sodalitium Pianum itself, however, was not dissolved until 1921; Pius X was much too sympathetic, and until the war the secret of its very existence was too well preserved, for the essential body to be endangered. But the resentment that accumulated against integrist polemics, against their spying, their denunciations, and their campaigns of intimidation, spread to the integrists' allies and notably to the Action Française.

In a pastoral letter of April 1913, Monsiegneur Chapon, Bishop of Nice, warned his flock against the perfidy and blindness of those writers who "with the pretext and the pretense of serving the Church, seek to discredit Christ, his morality and his doctrine." A few months later, in talking to the students of the Great Seminary of Chavagnes, Monseigneur Catteau, Bishop of Luçon, cautioned them that reading a paper like the *Action française* could only harm a priest; harmful, too, were "the polemics and discussions to which this paper gives rise in clerical meetings, and which continue even in railroad trains." Just before Christmas, in a Memoir addressed to Rome, one of Maurras's own teachers, Monseigneur Guillibert, Bishop of Fréjus, denounced his former student's sophistical turn of mind and warned against the interest of the Action Française in a Catholicism it only wanted to use for its own ends.[3]

As a certain coolness toward the Action Française began appearing in sections of the secular clergy and in Jesuit and Franciscan circles, a man as responsive to prevailing winds as Cardinal Paulin-Pierre Andrieu of Bordeaux was reported beginning to turn against the movement.[b] The Cardinal may well have known that at Rome an obstinate battle was being waged to place on the *Index* some of Maurras's most irreligious works and that, in spite of powerful interventions, the royalists' enemies were gaining ground.

Strong criticisms had first been leveled about 1910 against the irresponsible activities of the Camelots and the Action Française student organizations, and the effects they could have on the morals and spiritual values of Catholic youths who participated in them. The intervention of men like Louis Dimier, as well as the memory of the part royalists had played in defending the Church against the secular State, had brought these early attacks to nought. The critics had then turned to the writings of neo-royalists who flaunted their agnostic views in publications like the *Revue critique.* Maurras had had to disavow the latter; it would be more difficult to disown his own past articles and books.

A number of his writings had been submitted to the Congregation of the Index, and although their prohibition would not directly have condemned either the author or the movement he led, it would have been widely interpreted in that sense, almost as a counterpart to the recent condemnation of the Sillon. In July 1913, the music critic Camille Bellaigue, an unreconstructed

[b] See police reports F[7] 12862 of March 21 and Oct. 16, 1912, and Feb. 28, 1913. But, as events would show, the friends of the royalists were more in evidence than their enemies; and even Andrieu made his most complimentary references to Maurras after these dates.

monarchist, while performing his duties as an honorary Papal Chamberlain, handed the Pope a brief in Maurras's defense, including warm letters from the royalist Cardinal de Cabrières and from Benigni's French supporter Abbé Emmanuel Barbier.

The Pope was full of sympathy; he knew Maurras to be a champion of the Church and of the Holy See ("un buon defensore delle Santa Sede et della Chiesa"), and asked for nothing better than to avoid a condemnation. But the hope of avoiding it seemed slight.

"Tant va la cruche à l'eau," Merry del Val had said, and Bellaigue had to admit—at least in the pages of his private diary—that there were things in Maurras's writings deserving of condemnation, and that when Rome was faced with them there would be no way of avoiding an answer.[4]

Maurras attempted to justify himself in *L'Action Française et la religion catholique,* published in the late autumn of 1913, and his integrist friends continued their interventions in his behalf, but no one, as 1913 drew to a close, really believed his books could be kept off the *Index.*[5] However, although unable to arrest the implacable wheels of Roman procedure, the Pope had given his promise to do his best if and when a condemnation should occur.

On January 16, 1914, the Congregation of the Index found that seven of Maurras's books and the *Revue de l'Action Française* were "truly very bad and deserving of censure, the more so since it is hard to keep young people away from these books whose author is presented to them as a master in political and literary questions and as the leader of those from whom the salvation of the country should come." On January 29, Pius X accepted their decision, but he reserved the right to decide when the decree should be made public.[6] Maurras and his friends were reassured—at least the blow had been suspended in mid-air. And the Pope, though well aware of Maurras's paganism, seems to have remained sympathetic toward him and the rowdy activists of the Action Française.[c]

Soon after his final intervention, Pope Pius X died. Pope Benedict XV, who succeeded him in August 1914, had more pressing business than the Action Française to attend to throughout most of his reign, but the enemies of integrism nonetheless breathed more lightly once the old regime was gone. In October 1914, undeterred by war, Monseigneur Mignot, Archbishop of Albi, addressed a long memoir to Cardinal Ferrata, the new Papal Secretary of State, to warn against "the danger to morals and faith of an association whose theorists are agnostic and anti-Christian":

[c] The Action Française maintained that Pius X continued to approve of it even after January 29. But its main argument for this rested on Bellaigue's mistake in attributing a phrase of 1913 to 1914. Its second argument was the recollection of an anonymous witness who heard Cardinal Alexis Charost say that Pius X told him late in July 1914, shortly before his death, "As long as I live [the Action Française] will not be condemned." Published in 1951, this third-hand evidence seems most likely to refer to the Pope's decision not to publish the condemnation. See Robert Rouquette, *Les Etudes,* June 1953, pp. 392–400.

> The ravages made on Catholic youth by these false prophets, several of whom enjoy unlimited esteem, are considerable. They have deformed and paganized many a conscience. They pursue a labor of dechristianization, and in a few years we shall see a good portion of Catholics enlisted in the army of this reviving paganism. Bishops are powerless to stop their propaganda because of local difficulties and because of the interests—even material ones—that they control. They have been allowed to claim a monopoly of Catholic defense, for they were working together with all the branches of occult power. Enemies of Jesus Christ have protested their devotion to the Roman Church, and even theologians have been misled by these artifices. The awakening could be terrible.[7]

Perhaps as a result of such reminders, in 1915 Benedict XV made some inquiries about Maurras's books and the *Revue de l'Action Française.* The secretary of the Congregation of the Index reported that Pius X had ratified their condemnation but postponed publication of the decree until a more propitious moment. So informed, the Pope declared that the moment had not yet come. With the war still on, passions would prevent an equitable judgment—nor was it possible for a Pope already under fire from the French for being too pro-German to condemn a French nationalist movement, especially with no apparent forewarning.[8]

In the ten years that followed this decision the Action Française reached its peak of influence and effectiveness, in Catholic circles even more than in the nation as a whole. Subscription lists were full of seminarists, clerics, and teachers in Catholic schools. Reports to the annual congresses referred again and again to the clergy, which showed its sympathy, which joined, which lent support.[9] Many Catholics read both *La Croix* and the *Action française,* and a good many others who could not afford to subscribe to both read only the latter. Their feelings must have been similar to those of the faithful reader who wrote to say that he thanked God every day for having granted France this movement and these men who would bring Catholic and national regeneration.[10]

When in January 1920 the Archbishop of Rennes, Cardinal Dubourg, forbade the liberal Abbé Trochu, a long-time foe of the royalists, from continuing to write in his own paper *L'Ouest-Eclair,* the *Action française* could count it a personal victory.[11] The *Action française* (so it said of itself) was the only really Catholic journal, the only one to defend the interests of the Catholic religion.[12] A Catholic revival was taking place in politics—first in the Right-dominated Chamber of 1919, then as a reaction to the anti-clerical measures of the Cartel of the Left—and all this the paper took as a welcome sign of growing national purpose.[13] *La Croix* and *L'Echo de Paris,* which were accused of following the *Action française* lead, were, if not followers, at any rate highly sympathetic. And in 1923, the *Libre Parole,* which had been in the hands of liberal Catholics for over fifteen years, was passed on to good friends of the

Action Française, who proved their sentiments by supporting the royalist electoral candidates the following year.[14]

With but few exceptions, all reviews that reached Catholic circles felt its domination. Young Catholic novelists, poets, journalists, and critics, like Robert Vallery-Radot, Henri Massis, René Johannet, Montherlant, Henri Ghéon, Maritain, and others of less importance, looked to Maurras as the first thinker of his time.[15]

Yves Simon suggests that at this time Action Française "dictatorship" of Catholic intellectual circles was practically complete:

> An admission of democracy in such a climate exposed one to ironical and disdainful pity; one passed for anachronistic, a survivor from another age. . . . In order to appear fashionable and to make one's way, one had to speak of liberal errors with a superior air, scoff at liberty, equality, or fraternity, joke about progress, assume a vague look when human conscience or dignity were mentioned, affirm loudly that any project of an international order was a bloody fancy, and jeer at the League of Nations.[16]

In November 1922 the funeral of Maurras's mother showed the breadth of Catholic sympathies. Monseigneur Penon, Bishop of Moulins, who had taught Maurras in the Catholic college at Aix, came to walk in the funeral procession bareheaded and on foot, like any member of the family. Archbishop Rivière of Aix himself conducted the funeral service. Five bishops and three archbishops sent their condolences, as did the abbots of Solesmes and Saint-Martin-de-Ligugé, and a long list of regular and secular clergy.[17]

But this far from exhausted the numbers of Catholic dignitaries who evinced admiration for Maurras. The venerable Cardinal Mercier, Archbishop of Malines, received him and complimented him in the most eulogistic terms, even writing him to say how much he enjoyed dipping from time to time in *Trois Idées politiques, L'Avenir de l'intelligence,* and *La Politique religieuse,* all of which had been condemned in 1914.[18]

In Rome, the director of the French Academy, the sculptor Denys Puech, whose brother was a Radical-Socialist deputy, told Robert Havard, the editor of an Action Française offspring, *Rome,* that his interest in the Action Française was due to the influence of his Rouergue compatriot, Archbishop Ernest Ricard of Auch. When in 1926 a young nationalist, Marcel Justinien,[19] lunched at his uncle's house and there met a friend of the family, Monseigneur Jean-Victor Chesnelong, Archbishop of Sens, he heard him confess that he was not only a royalist but a Maurrassian as well. A well-informed and hostile observer declared that by the early 'twenties most French cardinals and all the country's resident archbishops could be classed as friendly.[20] All of them, like Cardinal Andrieu—and like the Action Française, of course—agreed with Paul Bourget that "a liberal Catholic is a man who greatly loves liberalism, but who loves Catholicism very little."[21]

But the feud with the Catholic liberals which won the sympathies of a hierarchy trained and appointed in the days of Pius X also provided arguments against the growing power of the Action Française and its interference in Catholic affairs. After Daudet's failure to win a Senate seat in Maine-et-Loire, the Action Française had decided that liberals, who were responsible for the failure, should be refused all further electoral support. This hurt the liberals in the canton elections of July 1925, elections that were marked by successes of the Cartel and by a high proportion of abstentions.

The *Action française,* echoed by its provincial organs, had forbidden its friends to vote for liberal candidates, and it was able to claim a number of successes of a negative sort.[22] Liberals were defeated at Le Mans and Valence and in the Pas-de-Calais, the Haute-Loire, and the Haute-Saône. At Millau in the Aveyron, where the liberal candidate failed; in the Gironde, where most liberals went to a second ballot; in Anjou and in the Nord, Catholics had reason to deplore the numerous abstentions. The *Croix de l'Aveyron* and the *Dépêche du Nord* attributed them rightly to the intervention of the rue de Rome.[23]

Analyzing Gironde returns in the *Liberté du sud-ouest,* the Abbé Daniel Bergey, one of the Church's best political observers, noted that Action Française directives had played an important part in the elections throughout France. His conclusion was that Catholics could count only on themselves, "on their own organized and disciplined forces."[d] In so far as the Abbé's conclusion was heeded, this would mean that moderate Catholics, hitherto friendly, would be persuaded that dependence on the Action Française was to be avoided and that royalist influence was growing too strong for comfort.

It was, indeed, becoming increasingly clear that the "organized, disciplined forces" of Catholicism were often provided by the Camelots. Abbé Bergey's own Groups for Religious Defense and Action, formed in 1924, were frequently led by royalists, and at a meeting of the groups at Bordeaux on July 11, 1926, Camelots and *commissaires* were on hand to maintain order. As the Eleventh Action Française Congress was told, "Our influence has grown a good deal . . . because many of our friends distinguish themselves in helping Catholic undertakings."[e]

[d] In the *Nouvelle Guyenne,* Aug. 1, 1925, the Comte de Lur-Saluces answered Bergey that no necessary identity existed between liberals and Catholics, and that the Action Française had in the past supported Catholics and even republicans and would continue to do so, provided they were not liberals and took a patriotic anti-left-wing stand. For an opposite view, see Maurice Vaussard, *Politique religieuse et Action Française* (1927), p. 16, who affirms that the advice to abstain was not followed by Catholics. Whether or not this was the case, some Catholic politicians clearly believed that the instructions of the Action Française could and did influence Catholic voters.

[e] *AF,* Nov. 26, 1925. League directives encouraged section presidents to greater efforts at bringing young Catholics into the Action Française, especially members of patronages and Church groups. See F[7] 13198, July 28, 1926. Among the 76 royalist leaders who on October 5, 1926, signed an appeal of the Action Française Gironde Federation to Cardinal Andrieu, 21 were members of the Action Catholique, holding 96 distinguished Catholic offices among them.

The influence of integral nationalism was also apparent, in a disquieting manner, in Catholic organizations aimed at the working classes and at youth. The Catholic Association of French Youth (ACJF) found its members affected and its recruitment slowed by the strength of the royalists in the Catholic middle class. In March 1925, ACJF suburban delegates complained to the Association's committee of directors that Catholic workers were everywhere identified with "Fascists, royalists, and other enemies of the people." Jesuits preaching a mission at Rouen found it impossible to reach anyone in the working classes, and they attributed their failure to the fact that the Church and the Action Française had become one in the eyes of the workers. Other Jesuits engaged in popular missions, like those who acted as chaplains to the ACJF groups, found their work hindered by royalist activities, and they, too, began to be disturbed by the omnipresent influence with which they had to cope.[24]

On January 31, 1926, Georges Bidault, then a young teacher of history and the vice-president of the ACJF, read to the Federal Council of the Association his report concerning relations with political youth movements. It was a declaration of war:

> Their activity, their recruitment, affect the ACJF and compete with it. Their mere existence and the effects they have on the religious and moral attitudes of Catholic youth concern us. . . . It is our duty to see that Catholic youth should be neither compromised as a whole, nor led astray in detail, by political movements. . . . Their success is not simply great, it is immense . . . in certain milieus, especially in schools, a majority has adopted their attitudes. Young Catholics furnish almost all the membership of political movements founded on this basis. Many are those in ACJF ranks who agree with it; more numerous still those who bow before it; and there are already those who militate for it. . . . We must not let ourselves be invaded!

Bidault did not at first attack the Action Française specifically. He spoke against all movements based on the belief in a providential leader and hoped that "soon Boulanger's black stallion might follow Henry IV's white horse out of history and into legend." But as he progressed through his statement, it became clear that he had one particular group in mind, and finally two pages were entirely given over to an attack on Charles Maurras's "Politique d'abord"—"a slogan that has reached the height of its fortune." "Eprise à vrai dire de politiques très diverses, toute une génération répète: Politique d'abord." In whatever sense one wishes to interpret this, affirmed Bidault, the formula is not ours. The more specific he became, the more his audience approved. The only group attacked by name was the Action Française, and every attack brought applause.[25]

Shortly after this meeting, says Adrien Dansette, a confidential report of the ACJF chaplain-general supporting and documenting the Bidault position was sent off to Rome.[26] But by that time a more lively campaign from another quarter had already put the Action Française on the defensive and persuaded Rome that the reprieve of 1914 should be reconsidered.

Some of Maurras's warmest admirers were to be found in Belgium, where the great Catholic universities, especially that of Liège, were strongholds of integral nationalism. The Action Française had the prestige of a fashionable movement, of doctrines and ideas high in ecclesiastical favor, of a party and a publication that had never failed to support Belgium. Of King Albert's sympathy for Daudet and Maurras there are many stories. Daudet maintained—but perhaps with a sort of poetic license—that the King always kept the latest Daudet on the royal desk, putting it out of sight when he received the French Ambassador. A senior Belgian officer affirms that on hearing Maurras speak of Maurice Maeterlinck as a prince of poets, the King decided he should be made a prince in fact, and only lowered the honor to that of Count because of aristocratic opposition. However true all this may be, we may at any rate conclude that the King was well disposed toward the Action Française.

So, we have seen, was Cardinal Désiré Mercier, Archbishop of Malines. His biographer, Canon A. Simon, has indicated that, although the Cardinal was aware of dangerous elements in their thought, he appreciated integral nationalist ideas and looked upon the movement with interest and sympathy. A condemnation did not seem to him opportune, and, while he lived, ideological errors that could have been used against them were not so interpreted —or, at any rate, only benevolently, and in the hope that they would mend their ways.[27]

During the early 'twenties, no other foreign movement or idea, apart from Marxism, seems to have held quite the same position in Belgian thought, if only because for some years it went unattacked. Belgian patriots were favorable to integral nationalism; Belgian Catholics were too. The Christian Democrats, who, in France, were hostile, seem in Belgium to have remained either sympathetic or silent, at least for a time. The Demo-Christian *XXe Siècle* and Fernand Neuray's *Nation belge* recalled friendly relations of the great World War, and the latter newspaper was chief support of the Action Française in Belgium between the wars.

By 1925 paeans of praise were rising from most Belgian Catholic publications, especially to Maurras, who "followed in the footsteps of Bossuet and Louis Veuillot."[28] At the beginning of July 1925 the *Cahiers de la Jeunesse Belge,* the organ of the ACJB (Catholic Association of Belgian Youth, the Belgian equivalent of the French ACJF), which the Abbé J. Leclercq directed at the University of Louvain, published the results of a poll held among its readers. The question they had been asked was, "Among the writers of the last twenty-five years, whom do you consider to be your master?" The 443 replies gave 174 votes to Charles Maurras, 123 to Paul Bourget, 81 to Maurice Barrès, with Henry Bordeaux, Pierre Loti, and Cardinal Mercier far behind.

The extraordinary majorities of the first three names excited comment in Catholic circles. They furnished ammunition for those who, like their fellows in France, believed that the influence of the Action Française was growing beyond bounds. The ACJB had recently been joined by a movement of young Catholic workers, the Jeunesse Catholique Ouvrière, whose members might be alienated by such deliberately flaunted reactionary idols. In addition, the champions of the Maurrassian cause were shouting its new triumph from the housetops and almost forcing their more moderate opponents to react.

In the *XXe Siècle,* Maurras's warmest admirer, the Abbé Van den Hout, proclaimed his master's hold on the elite to be an excellent thing: "In the dark night where peoples and governments are struggling, only two beacons burn, though with unequal brightness: ROME . . . and MAURRAS." The world was going Left, but salvation was on the Right, and neither in Belgium nor in France was there another political master of the Right. Van den Hout saw the "urgent necessity of an ACTION BELGE which could secure for Belgium, too, the boon of Action Française ideas and methods."[29]

Abbé Leclercq asserted that he knew no other books than those of Maurras in which young Catholics could find a sound political philosophy. "In the void of contemporary thought, Maurras rises suddenly like a great oak in a ruined plain. . . . Over the plain devastated by the poison gases of liberal dogmatism, Maurras stands alone."[30]

Alerted by such adulation, and worried about those whom such rabid professions of Maurrassian faith would alienate, the moderate *Libre Belgique* entered the argument, observing that not all Catholics shared these opinions, which they could not but view with alarm. Elections were due in November, and Catholic moderates did not like the thought of being confused by the voters with the champions of reaction. On July 25, 1925, Fernand Passelecq, a lawyer and journalist close to Jesuit circles and to Cardinal Mercier, began a series of articles on the philosophy of Charles Maurras, which served to bring the issue out of the small circles of the University and the Catholic reviews into the general public view. And at Charleroi, another Catholic paper, the *Pays Wallon,* began a counterinquiry to that of the *Cahiers de la Jeunesse Belge,* directed at more distinguished representatives of Catholic opinion than the students had sought to sound.

Dismayed by the unexpected reaction to what had started as nothing more than a student publication stunt, the leaders of the ACJB tried to minimize the implications of their poll. In a letter to the *Libre Belgique,* the president of the organization, Giovanni Hoyois, declared that the nature of the poll had been purely literary. The term "writers" had been taken from the first to mean "masters of the pen," rather than masters of thought or life. This was a weak excuse, however, for, as the *Libre Belgique* noted, the *Cahiers* themselves hardly bore out Hoyois's argument when their publicity referred to "the doctrinal tendencies of Catholic youth," and their contributors to "masters whom youth wants to follow" and whose ideas were continually discussed.[31]

In any case, the debate was spreading. The *Pays Wallon* had publicized the sentiments of threescore public figures unfavorable to Maurras, among them two premiers, including the current one, the Minister of Justice, many Jesuits, and many university professors. Taking a leaf out of Maurras's own book, most of them expressed resentment at the intrusion of a foreign figure whose influence divided, hence weakened, the hitherto united Belgian Catholics, colonized the Catholic press, and imported strange excesses and polemics into an otherwise peaceful Belgian scene.

The *Libre Belgique* for its part presented its readers with a supplement, prepared by Passelecq, examining "this extraordinary enterprise of a declared anti-Christian presenting himself as the defender and almost sole social champion of Catholicism." Belgian Catholics, Passelecq concluded, could borrow selectively from Maurras, but never follow him as they would a master. The Maurrassian system was "radically vitiated by irremediable anti-Christianism." His works, those of an atheistic thinker inclined to paganism, were dangerous for young minds in the process of formation; and the reading of his newspaper should be advised against in the case of impressionable youth.[32] Professor Maurice Gand, of the Catholic University at Lille, concurred:

> With very rare exceptions, young people inspired by the Action Française stay resolutely away from Catholic works and from social action. . . . Their interests are elsewhere. Politics first is their slogan. And it is to politics—that is, to the propaganda of the Action Française—that they wholeheartedly devote themselves with all the passion of youth, and with admirable exuberance. All other forms of action seem to them vain.[f]

In the *Revue générale,* the *XXe Siècle,* and the *Revue catholique des idées et des faits* the defenders of integral nationalism countered that, far from corrupting, Maurras offered "a coordinated political system under which conservative ideas, freed once and for all from archaic bonds, could be expressed with the dynamic force they heretofore had lacked."[33] Yet, as the moderate liberal *Indépendence belge* warned, in defending Maurras against Passelecq and the *Libre Belgique,* Maurras's partisans were deluding themselves if they thought they could take his theory of the State and leave the rest.[34] *L'Indépendance belge* was right. Giovanni Hoyois might well insist that Maurras's influence had nothing to do with books of his that everyone ignored,[35] but the ideas nonetheless filtered down through the *Action française* to its reading public, coloring their judgment and their attitudes.

[f] Letter in *La Libre Belgique,* Oct. 2, 1925. Gand also condemns the royalists' execrable influence on Catholic electoral behavior, which went against the express policy of the hierarchy, and their disquieting intellectual influence.

As the approaching elections preoccupied the press in late autumn, the controversy died down. But the brief yet violent hassle had one significant effect. Cardinal Mercier had directed the Abbé Van den Hout to obtain explanations and reassurances from Action Française leaders about the nature of their doctrines. Given the opinions of the emissary, opinions his superiors had no occasion to ignore, it is not surprising the expected reassurance was forthcoming. There is no evidence that, before his death in January 1926, the Cardinal had backed or pressed accusations against men whom he might blame in theory but favor in fact. It was his death that opened the way to stronger representations in Rome, not some last-minute change of mind.

Meanwhile, echoes of the Belgian controversies were heard in France, and old criticisms of royalist irreligion returned to the surface. The Action Française found itself once more accused of letting politics take precedence over religion. In the *Action Française du dimanche,* the chief royalist commentator in Catholic Savoy, Pierre Bevillard, explained that religion and fatherland came first, politics second. "Politique d'abord" affirmed only a simple fact, not a system of values: political action must come first, as means come before the end, as the oxen come before the plough.[36]

Passelecq's special pages on the Action Française, a careless but striking compilation, were circulating in pamphlet form; so also were the answers received by the *Pays Wallon,* later published as a book under the title *Charles Maurras, maître de la jeunesse catholique.* "From various parts of the Gironde we hear that pamphlets representing the Action Française as a source of irreligion are circulating in Catholic circles," complained the *Nouvelle Guyenne.* "Where do these pamphlets come from? They come from Belgium."[37]

In Rome, by this time, the decision to censure the Action Française had already been taken. Late in 1925 or early in 1926 the Archbishop of Paris, Cardinal Louis Dubois, and the Papal Nuncio, Cardinal Bonaventura Ceretti, were instructed to find a prelate, preferably one of the integrist school, who could open what all assumed would be a reasonably dignified and short campaign against Maurrassism. Cardinal Alexis Charost of Rennes, who was approached in the spring of 1926, discussed the possibility with his suffragans, who confirmed his own feelings that the best of their Breton parishioners belonged to the Action Française, and judged any blame to be inopportune. Other prelates, including Louis-Henri Luçon of Reims and Touchet of Orléans, also shunned the task. Finally, Cardinal Andrieu agreed to take it.[38]

The Archbishop of Bordeaux had long been very close to the Action Française and had on more than one occasion praised it, as well as Maurras, whose pen, he once said, was worth a sword. His career, however, had been largely based on a responsive attitude to the wishes of the Holy See ("a weathercock," one appreciative parishioner called him), and of late he had begun speaking out against the Action Française, "the greatest heresy of modern times." To a group of Boy Scouts and their parents in his Cathedral in December 1925 he inveighed against unbelievers like Charles Maurras who would presume to lead the Catholics of France.[39] Now, urged on by the Vatican and fortified with Passelecq's compilation, he began repeating his earlier condemnations in greater detail and more resonant tones.

On August 27, 1926, *L'Aquitaine,* the religious bulletin of the diocese of Bordeaux, published what purported to be the reply of the Cardinal-Archbishop to a question asked by a group of young Catholics on the subject of the Action Française. In this reply—perhaps significantly dated August 25, the same date as that of Pius X's letter condemning the Sillon—Andrieu declared that nothing need prevent his young inquirers from following the Action Française if politics were its sole concern. As Leo XIII had said about the *ralliement* (an apt reminder in the context), Catholics were free to prefer one form of government to another. But the Action Française and its leaders dealt with other problems than politics alone, with religious, moral, and social problems—with God, with Church, with sociology, and there their treatment had gone counter to the teachings of the Church.

> Atheism, agnosticism, anti-Christianism, anti-Catholicism, anti-moralism both individual and social, the necessity (if one hopes to maintain order despite such subversive negations) of restoring paganism with all its violences and injustice—that, dear friends, is what the leaders of the Action Française teach their disciples, and what you must avoid listening to.

The neo-monarchists' much vaunted support of the Church was only the outcome of opportunism and of coincidence, the article continued: "The Church is a monarchy tempered by aristocracy, and such an organization in the religious sphere may well attract partisans of the similar organization that Action Française leaders seek to set up in the political sphere." But it was necessary to beware: "Catholics by calculation, not by conviction, the men who lead the Action Française use the Church, or hope, at least, to use it; but they serve it not, since they reject the divine message which it is the Church's mission to propagate."

The Cardinal was old and ailing, and his devotion outstripped his capacities. His arguments were feeble and ill-informed; Passelecq's somewhat casual journalistic allusions had been improved by some misquotations: the leaders of the Action Française were accused of an irreligiousness that applied to Maurras alone, and Maurras himself had ideas attributed to him (and even a title) that either were not his or else, more often, dated back to the nineteenth century. If Maurras's paganism had to be condemned and young men saved from the pernicious influence of works that were practically collector's items, it seemed a little late to be doing it. Furthermore, the attack appeared to come out of a blue sky, with no forewarning—on the contrary, after repeated praise from the most authoritative quarters. And when, at the beginning of September, a papal letter came to confirm and approve the Cardinal's judgment, it still failed to explain the suddenness of the condemnation.[g]

The *Action française,* remonstrating with unwonted mildness although with its customary length, published the papal letter along with a statement from its Catholic directors in which the leading figures of the movement (with the exception of non-Catholic Maurras) asked Cardinal Andrieu to reconsider charges, which, they explained, applied to them but little, if at all.[40] The tone was so blandly tactful that it disgusted Bernanos, who longed to make a real fight for what he believed was the most just of all just causes. But the general line was better reflected in *Candide,* which, though bristling at the attack, reaffirmed Maurras's respectful support of the Church. "It will be difficult to make the *Action française*'s editor an anti-clerical against his will. It is not likely in any case that the Church would prefer to have unbelievers as enemies rather than as friends, as if she had too many friends and not enough opponents."[41] Was there the veiled hint of a threat behind the friendly tone?[h]

While Camelots and students' organizations were busily sending protestations of loyalty to the Pope, the *Action française* continued outwardly confident and calm. On September 9, Maurras made a new appeal for money—this time for two million francs—and it quickly began to flow in, accompanied by the aggressive remarks of Catholics revolted, like Bernanos, by such rank injustice. "The morale of our troops is admirable," Bernanos wrote to Henri Massis. To his friends on a holiday in the country, the cool Bainville reported the same impression: "Despite the Pope, the Cardinal, the Nuncio, and the rest, everybody here is in excellent form. This will pass. The Action Française is like the Church itself. Persecutions do it good."[42] Cardinal Billot warmly congratulated Daudet and the others who had signed the statement to Andrieu, hoping that the Action Française would come out of the crisis more than ever admired by the good and feared by the wicked.[43]

During the preceding winter, Jacques Maritain had sketched out some chapters of a work in which he, Massis, and Maurras planned to answer the attacks of their Belgian critics. Rewritten in terms of the new situation, Maritain's pages were published in mid-September as *Une opinion sur Charles Maurras et le devoir des catholiques.* Maurras, said Maritain, had set out to

[g] As Louis de Saint-Martin commented a few months later in the hardly sympathetic *Libre Belgique,* February 25, 1927: "Il y a 25 ans qu'il [Maurras] a pris cette position, et après la lui avoir laissé prendre si longtemps on le condamne par un coup brusque et soudain: beaucoup de ces braves gens dont je parle en sont déroutés."

[h] Police reports suggest it. Behind the submissive addresses, ecclesiastical authorities scented the beginning of an underhand campaign against the hierarchy and its educational and philanthropic institutions. As early as September 11, Lucien Moreau was quoted as criticizing Andrieu and Pius XI at a private meeting of the League, and asking royalists to make no further contributions to Catholic causes. F[7] 13198, Sept. 11, 15, 1926.

analyze empirically the conditions of political stability and order. In the process, he had considered the Church in its social aspect rather than from the point of view of its higher spiritual end. It was quite possible that a movement whose political leader was an unbeliever needed to do more than merely affirm that its sentiment was Catholic. The worldly side should be offset by more specifically spiritual endeavors. His proposal to set up Catholic study groups within the League was welcomed by the royalist leaders, who at once requested the Archbishop of Paris to assign them chaplains who would "preserve their members against the dangers the Holy Father pointed out."[44]

But none of this good will made much impression on Rome's determination to cut the Action Française down to size. Before the end of September, Cardinal Andrieu had issued another pastoral letter explaining that the Action Française was not merely a political league but "a school" teaching a doctrine. Believer and renegade, he wrote, could not be one. A choice between the two was vital, and from the members of the Action Française, leaders or mere followers, an explicit disavowal of the false doctrines of their school was expected.[45]

Just what these false doctrines were had still not been made very clear. The Cardinal had spoken of paganism, of slavery, of State supremacy, of epicureanism, and of the refusal to permit God to interfere in purely natural conclusions. The Pope had noted a pagan renaissance connected with naturalism. But these were accusations that the *Action française* specifically denied, and until something more specific and more readily demonstrable could be named, the integral nationalists could hardly be expected to disavow anything.

In his reply to the Etudiants d'Action Française, the Papal Secretary of State, Cardinal Pietro Gasparri, was somewhat more explicit: It was quite insufficient, he wrote, to say that one accepted only the teaching of the Church in matters of morals and of faith, if one continued to follow the direction of leaders who, as their writings proved, were not masters of Christian doctrine and morality. To avoid the dangers inherent in non-Catholic influences, one must first of all shun them.[46]

A few days later, on October 17, the Pope himself, addressing the descendants of 191 martyrs who had refused to swear allegiance to the Civil Constitution of the Clergy in 1792, opposed the idea of integral obedience to that of integral nationalism. Many of his listeners belonged to the Action Française; he asked of them "the greatest of sacrifices, sacrifices of intelligence and of will."

These were the sacrifices that the men of the Action Française were least ready to make. They felt themselves unjustly attacked, and they replied with reasonable arguments where unquestioning submission was expected. In their resistance they were encouraged by the support and the more or less openly expressed sympathies of ecclesiastical friends. Throughout October the newspaper printed encouraging statements from the Archbishops of Auch, Lyon, and Albi and the Bishops of Aix and Montauban.[47] The last, one of its firmest friends, even attempted to view the Pope's remarks in a favorable light: "In fact, interpreted as it should be, the Pope's letter concerning the Action Française is a blessing."

A blessing, in disguise. The Pope, said Monseigneur Marty reassuringly, had been misrepresented by ill-intentioned men. In fact, he had declared that Catholics could read the paper and write in it, subscribe to it and join the League. The ill-intentioned elements, however, were still at work: the *Libre Belgique* and the Paris *Nonciature* denied Monseigneur Marty's news from Rome, but Marty reaffirmed it.[48]

The *Action française* continued to print episcopal declarations, both for and against, but confidence was waning; the tone of injured innocence was becoming gradually shriller, changing to the more familiar one of truculent aggression. From the beginning the paper had said that the condemnations were the result of a nefarious plot against the interests of the Church and of France itself.[49] When crowded meetings showed that popular support did not seem to be flagging, the Action Française was triumphant: "Here is the answer to all the maneuvers and all the betrayals by which it was hoped to bring us down." A week later, declaring that the *Osservatore romano* was not the voice of the papacy, the newspaper announced that it would no longer reprint news or official statements from the Vatican paper.[50] Instead it featured on three columns of the front page the friendly letter of the Archbishop of Rennes, Cardinal Charost, who declared that the Action Française represented the first vast and orderly counterrevolutionary movement to appear in France since the time of the *Encyclopédie*. He had no wish to disunite Catholic forces or to discourage the most valiant and hardworking of the defenders of the Church, and would therefore forbid neither the league nor the newspaper of the Action Française.[51]

Positions on both sides hardened, the tone of the argument became more heated, and on the principle of all good fights, onlookers began choosing sides. "Things have come to such a pass," reported the Paris correspondent of a Brussels paper, "that on social occasions one often begins with the stipulation that the Action Française must not be mentioned. Of course it always is, even in the most elegant and cosmopolitan drawing rooms."[52] On December 15, the *Action française,* firing from all six columns, replied to the Germanophiles of the *Osservatore romano* that the Action Française had nothing to do with the censure of Rome. It quoted Daniel O'Connell: "OUR FAITH FROM ROME. OUR POLICY FROM HOME." It gave the Pope his due, but it would not knuckle under.

This time, the Vatican's reply was immediate. In his consistorial allocution of December 20, Pius XI branded the men "who in their writings are alien to our dogma and morality." Catholics were specifically forbidden to follow the school of those who, setting the interests of party above the interests of religion, made religion servant to party; and they were equally forbidden to support or to read their publications.

To this, the neo-royalists found an answer which, for all that it was not original, was nonetheless apropos: "NON POSSUMUS," the headline in the paper ran. "It is no longer a matter of morals or of faith; it is a question of politics. . . . The safety of France would be in danger if the *Action française* were to disappear. To kill the *Action française* would be a betrayal. We shall not betray."

On December 29, 1926, the 1914 decree placing Maurras's books on the *Index* was promulgated; and to the books earlier prohibited was now added, on the initiative of the present Pope, the *Action française*.[i] It was the final condemnation, and by far the worst. To have had Maurras's books only on the *Index* would have been embarrassing, but the newspaper was crucial to the entire movement, and if Catholics obeyed the prohibition the Action Française would die. That it did not die is evidence of the extent to which Catholics, like royalists, had become Maurrassians—and evidence, too, perhaps, of the inherent justice of the condemnation.

The immediate reaction, however, saw no justice whatever. In *Cyrano,* Clément Vautel described the act as boorish and ungrateful. The Church always let its servants down, and in this respect the royalists' experience was one that could surprise only the victims. But it would do much to discourage recruits to a cause always lost because always defended in the midst of discord, and with the constant fear of being let down or disavowed: "On n'attire pas les mouches avec du vinaigre, pas même avec de l'eau bénite!" The two-million-strong Front National Catholique, which included many royalists, did not know quite where to turn. Even the hierarchy showed signs of restiveness. Archbishop Rivière of Aix calculated that eleven of France's seventeen cardinals and archbishops were favorable to the Action Française, but in their comments on the consistorial allocution most of them temporized: Cardinal Louis-Joseph Maurin of Lyon said nothing directly about the Action Francaise; Archbishop Ernest Ricard of Auch insisted upon the political liberty of Catholics rather than upon any incidental prohibitions: "Ce n'est pas nous qui chercherons des ennemis à droite."[53]

Dissatisfied with episcopal reactions, the Holy See demanded a collective declaration of all French ordinaries to show their disciplined obedience to orders. Different versions and projects were mooted through the winter and abandoned. On March 2, 1927, a brief address of loyalty to the Pope was made public, mentioning that 104 had signed it but bearing neither signatures nor date. On March 8 there appeared a longer and more explicit declaration stat-

[i] *Osservatore romano,* Dec. 21, 1926; *AF,* Dec. 24, 1926. The text of the decree was not printed in *AF* until January 9, 1927. Maurras replied that, although neither he nor the Action Française would cease to honor and venerate Catholicism because of a trifling error over a few books and their author, he had his duty to France.

ing that the distinction between political and spiritual authority was completely invalid and that to protest against the papal condemnation or to refuse to submit to it was open insurrection against the Roman pontiff's legitimate exercise of his sovereign authority. It was a wicked fancy to suggest that the Pope, ill-informed by bad advisers, did not really know what he was doing. Furthermore, it was a dangerous error to say that enemies of the Action Française were also the enemies of France, for no conflict in fact existed between submission to the Church and patriotic duty.[54]

This second declaration bore 118 names. In the end, only three ordinaries had failed to sign: Maurrass's old teacher Monseigneur Penon, who would end his life in exile at the Monastery of Frigolet; Monseigneur de Llobet, Archbishop Coadjutor of Avignon, who later attributed his not signing to a misunderstanding; and Monseigneur Marty, Bishop of Montauban. The case of Monseigneur Marty is not clear. He was said to have come round to the official position, signed, and apologized. But Rome remained dissatisfied, demanded his resignation on several occasions, and finally apprised him on his deathbed that his "resignation" was an accomplished fact.[55]

On the same day as the French prelates' declaration, March 8, the Holy Penitentiary promulgated a rescript concerning the sanctions against readers, members, and propagandists of the Action Française and, more especially, against such ecclesiastics as continued to tolerate or encourage the movement. The papal decree provided for severe reprimands and even suspension *a divinis* for clerics who remained frank partisans of the Action Française, gave theological opinions favorable to it, or gave absolution to impenitent readers and members of the League. Seminarists either openly or secretly attached to the condemned ideas were to be expelled as not fitted for an ecclesiastical calling. As for nonclerical sympathizers of the Action Française, they were to be excluded from the sacraments and from all Catholic organizations.

These instructions were published in the French press at the end of March, just close enough to Easter to make practicing Catholics uncomfortable.[56] And it is clear that the condemnation and prohibition of the *Action française* put good Catholics in a terrible quandary. One loyal subscriber, Comte Jean de Pontavice, sent Cardinal Charost his resignation from the post of Papal Chamberlain and from the order of St. Gregory the Great, although admitting that he had never read the works of either Maurras or Daudet.[57] Others reluctantly submitted—like Charles Journet, who quit the League, and Ambroise Rendu, who first gave up the economic page of the *Action française,* and then left the *Action française agricole*—despite their affirmations of continued belief in the political doctrines of the Action Française.[58] Still others, like the Marquis de Colbert and Emile Devaux, who were, respectively, president and secretary-treasurer of the royalist organization in the Cher, found in the condemnation an excuse to publicize their disagreement with the Action Française leaders, whose activity, wrote Colbert from Bourges, "served neither the Church, nor France, nor even the monarchist cause."[j]

Some Catholics, while literally obedient, sought the same fare somewhere else—in publications close to the Action Française like *Candide* and *Je suis partout,* in the conservative and chauvinistic *Gringoire,* and in a host of right-wing provincial papers which continued to echo the master's voice. A regretful and unfriendly witness, looking back in wartime to the years that followed the condemnation, found that the spirit of the Action Française had made enormous strides in the intervening years. The progress, he thought, was the work not simply of unbelievers and rebellious Catholics, but, in large measure, of Catholics who submitted to the *letter* of the condemnation, nothing more. This could be said of priests and prelates who were obliged to resign from the League but who remained faithful, and of all those who gave in to heavy ecclesiastical pressure but "continued to do their best to serve the Action Française and the royal cause, by discreet propaganda, by financial help."[59]

Inevitably, the condemnation gave rise to painful moral examinations. As Bernanos wrote to Francisque Gay:

> In sacrificing the Action Française or—what amounts to the same thing—letting its cadres be broken up or its troops dispersed, we think that we are losing the last chance for the country. But that is not all. Our thoughts and our actions are so closely linked to a certain critique of revolutionary ideology which Maurras has revived and refreshed, that it is impossible to deny it by halves. . . . If [Maurras's] doctrine of order is now considered the synthesis of all heresies, then we shall have to start our life all over again, from nothing.[60]

The problem was far from simple, but occasionally personal tragedy bordered on social comedy. In January 1928, for example, the friendly Bishop of Poitiers, Monseigneur de Durfort, approached the glowering president of the local Jeunes Filles Royalistes about the presence at the young ladies' meetings of men like the Marquis de Roux, with whom one could no longer have anything to do "on political grounds." Thus the president, Mlle Aubaret, described the scene in her diary:

> "One can meet them in drawing rooms, in society—they are not excommunicated. In short, one can be a royalist, and I am more a royalist than any one, so you can remain a royalist."
> "Without a paper to defend us?"
> "There are some being set up," said the Vicar-General.
> "I don't know of any," I answered in a glacial tone.
> "Neither do I," muttered Monseigneur Durfort.[61]

The stories in Jean de La Varende's *Les Manants du Roi* with their deep

[j] *La Vie catholique,* June 25, 1927; but cf. *ibid.,* July 9 and 23: Colbert had already been disowned by the Duc de Guise on this issue, and in July was removed from his presidency.

and grandiloquent passion, bear testimony to the dismay of Catholic *ligueurs* faced with the "irreparable divorce between the lilies and the cross."[62] How much more depressing the situation must have been for priests: random glances at *Action française* subscription lists show fifteen anonymous members of the clergy on February 3, 1927, seven on March 24, ten on May 12—and these were the ones who specified their profession. Contributions from wholly anonymous donors increased enormously. A typical sequence on February 3 reads: "Nous couchons sur les positions du Syllabus et l'anarchie chrétienne ne passera pas. Al. M., 50 fr.; Abbé J. C., 10 fr.; Une catholique, mais Française! 10 fr.; un curé de campagne, 100 fr." Some of the contributors undoubtedly felt sure the Pope himself had been ignobly misled: thus a Mlle D. of Le Vésinet, who wrote a stiff note to Francisque Gay asking that he discontinue sending her the *Vie Catholique,* until that weekly had learned to respect the truth. "No, it is not the Pope [who directs the persecution]. . . . He is deceived, and sooner or later the truth will out. . . . Your paper is fit to light the fire with."[63]

Denunciations on both sides shot up like headstrong weeds in some dioceses. Teachers in a Catholic girls' school denounced seventy confessor priests in Paris alone for being too lenient; priests were censored or suspended, like the Abbé Bouillon, of the Church of St. John the Baptist at Nice. A doctor of theology and laureate of the Académie Française, the Abbé had a few years before dedicated his *Politique de St. Thomas* to Charles Maurras, and he now refused to withdraw either the dedication or the book.[64] True to his name, Professor F. A. Guignon, of the Saint-Elme's school at Arcachon, was forced to resign from the League, in which he had held a local office, and died—of a broken heart, his friends said—a few days thereafter.[65]

In March 1928 an episcopal ordinance was issued to prohibit Action Française adherents from receiving religious marriages (except *in nigris*) or burials, from acting as godfathers, from participating in pious associations, and in every way enforcing the Penitentiary decrees of the previous year. A crop of major and minor scandals followed—broken engagements (some on the eve of marriage) and public scenes like that when the recalcitrant president of a local royalist league who had been refused communion followed the erstwhile-Maurrassian priest all over town shouting, "Monsieur l'abbé, vous êtes un imposteur et un Tartuffe!"

The refusal of the final sacraments or of religious burial was more serious. Quarrels erupted within families as within congregations, between those who were royalists and those who had been royalists, between those who were faithful to Rome and those who remained faithful to Maurras. The *Almanach* for the year 1929 cites thirteen cases in which marriage services had to be conducted in the sacristy, without a mass (eight of these concerned noble families); two cases in which members of the Action Française were prevented from acting as godfathers; six cases in which a religious burial was refused; and one case in which a young woman (in Bordeaux) broke her engagement rather than give up the *Action française*. It also lists thirteen local newspapers placed under interdict by their Bishops for being persistently sympathetic to the Action Française.[66]

Some years later, in May 1934, the little Picardy town of Humbercourt witnessed some of these troubles after the death of one of its municipal councilors, a local farmer named Tripet. M. Tripet was not a member of any royalist organization, but he had been a subscriber to the *Action française* for over twenty years, having stoutly refused to give it up to please a priest. When the Church denied him a religious burial, the sections of the Action Française rallied from all over Picardy to turn his funeral into a public demonstration against clerical intolerance and "the cynical exaltation of papal authority." They marched through the village, nearly broke into the church, and both amused and appalled the community.[k]

This was not the only time when the movement that had once disturbed the peace of the Republic turned its more riotous talents against the Church. Funerals were frequently the occasion for displays outside the church, or for spectacular attempts to evade the vigilance of local religious authorities by smuggling in a friendly priest willing to read the burial service over the grave. Dr. Pierre Mauriac, brother of the writer, who himself did not approach the communion table for something like four years, recalls a funeral in which the priest was flown over the grave in an airplane to give his blessing to the dead.

It was equally possible that devoted relatives would fake a deathbed repentance, either for the dead person's sake or, more probably, for their own. And this explains why a levelheaded man like Etienne de Resnes, the Pretender's regional delegate in the northern region, should write his friend Robert de Boisfleury to warn that on no account would he deny the Action Française on his deathbed, and that anything that might be said to the contrary could only be an error or a lie: "On m'enterrera comme un chien. Bien, j'y consens, mais comme un chien fidèle."[67]

It was becoming difficult even to put one's trust in God:

> —Le bon Dieu, le bon Dieu . . . fit Madame de la Huppe; au train où vont les choses je me demande s'il n'est pas papiste, lui aussi.
>
> —Sait-on jamais? . . . dit Monseigneur en levant les yeux au ciel.[68]

[k] Maurice Farcy, *La Terreur à Humbercourt* (Amiens, 1934), pp. 1–4. *Le Canard enchaîné*, Feb. 16, 1927, had foreseen the way things would develop when it pretended to advertise: "Lisez l'ACTION FRANÇAISE, seul journal anticlérical: Le scandale de l'abbé X et sa maîtresse; les hontes du Vatican; Un curé satyre; Etc. . . . etc. . . ." It did not exaggerate.

13

TRUTH AND CONSEQUENCES

FROM THE TIME of the papal condemnation in December 1926 to the eventual pardon or, one might say, reconciliation, almost thirteen years later, the attitude of the Action Française would be more or less acrimoniously to plead that an injustice had been perpetrated, which, as Catholics and as men, its members had a right to resist. They had appealed from the Cardinal to the Pope, from the Pope ill-informed to the Pope undeceived, from the Pope to the episcopate, and, finally, to natural law. On January 11, 1927, the paper publicized the ultimate argument against obeying Rome's present orders.

Suicide was not an act that could be imposed, the paper argued (on the advice, presumably, of theologian friends). A person could defend himself against unjust aggression. In this case, the newspaper could be considered a person, and natural law, which always had priority over positive law, permitted the Action Française to defend itself. It was no good to say that the only possible course was to submit. There was no arbitrary and omnipotent power in this world and a power that arrogated itself ends other than those that rightly belonged to it was wrong and could not expect to be obeyed. "On n'est légitimement obéi que dans son ressort." Powers established for spiritual ends need not be heeded on scientific or literary questions—one could properly disagree with their opinions and justifiably defend oneself if, in trying to enforce them, they exceeded their limits.

The concept of suicide could be further extended to France herself: for if the condemnation was the result of Briand's intrigues against France and the Action Française, the Pope's concession to a congeries of traitors, bankrupters, and assassins, then to surrender would be tantamount to betraying France.[a]

This being so, the Action Française felt that it could fight back honorably—at first with some real success, and never quite ineffectively; and though it suffered serious losses, it also inflicted losses in its turn. A cartoon in the *Canard enchaîné* of January 19, 1927, showed Maurras and Daudet standing dejected in the doorway of a shop marked "A l'Index," with signs in all the windows announcing a great clearance sale with lowest prices. The legend,

[a] *AF,* Jan. 10, 1927. Thus, when the ACJF declared that none of its members could be members, readers, or Camelots of the Action Française, the latter replied by calling the Catholic youth leaders "Les nouveaux sans-patrie." *La Croix,* Feb. 11, 1927; *AF,* Feb. 12, 1927.

"No doubt about it, business is bad," was somewhat premature for the times, but in many ways business was even worse just then in the *maison d'en face*.

When, following papal decisions, readers of the *Action française* were asked either to give up the newspaper or to withdraw from organizations like the ACJF and Catholic Action, the royalist leaders answered logically that if their presence was dangerous or corrupting in one respect, it was equally so in all, and they asked their followers to cease participation in every form of Catholic activity. The inevitable result can be seen from one early incident, in February 1927, when the *Revue mensuelle de la Ligue Dauphinoise d'Action Catholique* published a note from the Bishop of Grenoble explaining that one could not be a member of both the Action Catholique and the Action Française. Resigning from the Action Catholique and from the committees of numerous other Catholic groups in which he had long been interested, the president of the Action Française in Isère explained in an open letter:

> These works were founded by my family and I have done my best to help them live and prosper. . . . Submissive, like all Catholics of the Action Française, to the authority of the Holy See for all that concerns the spiritual domain of dogma and morals, I intend to remain sole judge of the political line I have to follow in order to aid with all my power the salvation of my country.

When the Bishop discovered to his distress that he could not have his cake and eat it, that royalist Catholics would not leave Catholic political leagues while maintaining their support of other works, he tried to draw a distinction between *ligues* like Action Catholique and benevolent organizations like the Society of St. Vincent de Paul. But this proved unacceptable, and in more departments than just Isère, the exclusion of a royalist from one Catholic group tended to precipitate a cascade of resignations and a sharp drop in the income of local charities.[1]

The issue here was the royalist attempt to hurt the Church by getting wealthy followers to withdraw their support, but another result of the policy was the progressive emancipation of the Catholic organizational apparatus from the strong Action Française influence of many years' standing. To begin with, however, the hierarchy felt the immediate losses, and it experienced great difficulty in making the faithful come to heel. The idea that reading the paper condemned a man to hell was not an easy one to stomach. When a supporter asked his priest if he thought he could go on reading the *Action française* without fear, the priest answered, "But of course! I read it myself and have no intention of being damned." And, from Albi, a bishop's relative described traveling to Toulouse to hear Admiral Antoine Schwerer and Paul Robain address a meeting of the Action Française. The Archbishop had forbidden Catholics to attend. Result: the immense hall of the Jardin-Royal at Toulouse was completely full.[2]

In June 1927, some six months after the condemnation had been effected, Francisque Gay of the *Vie catholique,* the royalists' most determined liberal foe, privately informed the Papal Nuncio that the Action Française still filled Catholic leaders with ridiculous terror. No one, he wrote, dared take the responsibility of applying the sanctions. It was generally known that the great majority of those who had really wanted to receive communion at Easter had found accommodating priests without having to give up the paper, or even open membership in the League. Every Sunday at mass, local personalities flaunted the *Action française* openly beside them on their prayer stools.

Where the *Action française* dolorously reported the zeal of those informing on its friends, Gay found that most Catholic colleges (not least the fashionable Collège Stanislas in Paris) deliberately closed their eyes to overt royalist propaganda in their classes. Monseigneur Henri Baudrillart, who almost resigned his rectorate of the Catholic Institute because he was unable to prevent most students from joining the Joan of Arc's Day parade as Etudiants d'Action Française, declared that in Catholic Faculties the papal orders met no greater obedience. No wonder, since the vice-rector, Monseigneur Louis Prunel, took little pains to hide his Action Française sympathies, and Lemaître, the general-secretary, made no secret at all of his.[3]

When at the end of June Gay tried to set up a committee to fight the Action Française, pleading that it was impossible that the Pope and the Church should not have the last word and be obeyed with alacrity, his friend, the Abbé Henri Brémond of the Académie Française, advised him to forget the idea. "Not that victory has been won," wrote Brémond; "Alas! that is not at all the case." But at the side, if not at the head, of the Action Française battle line one could distinguish almost in the open the presence of other personalities ("authorities," Brémond called them) too exalted for Catholic journalists to tackle. Thus, six months after the Pope had spoken, an eminent Catholic figure who was quite unsympathetic to Maurras had to consider "the possibility of the apparent triumph of the toughest, most formidable opponent that Rome had for a long time encountered."[b]

Who were the authorities who would intimidate the Abbé Brémond? There were, of course, some known supporters like the Archbishop of Rouen, Monsiegneur Dubois de la Villerabelle, and Cardinal Charost, who continued to stand by his friends, assuring them, it has been said, that they should not submit, that their position was impregnable. Most of the Breton clergy under Charost were sympathetic to the Action Française, and upon Charost's orders

[b] Gay, Circular No. 10 of June 26, 1927; Henri Brémond to Gay, June 1927 (Gay papers). Brémond, himself the son of a royalist *notaire* of Aix-en-Provence, was a childhood schoolfellow and rival of Maurras. In his *Lettres,* p. 271, Maurras recounts a story he claims to have heard from Brémond himself, that as the *notaire* lay dying in August 1883, he was told the news of the Comte de Chambord's death and, clasping the hands of his four sons, he murmured, "Vive le roi Philippe! Oui . . . Oui . . . C'est bien notre roi!"

several important Catholic colleges in the west refused to use any books published by Maurras's enemies in the great Catholic publishing firm of Bloud and Gay—a loss amounting to some 100,000 francs in 1928 alone, according to the publishers' own estimate.[c]

There were Father Le Floch and Cardinal Billot in Rome, trying to support the Action Française until they were both dismissed in the autumn of 1927, one from the directorship of the French Seminary, the other from the purple itself. There was the obstinately rebellious Bishop of Montauban, who, as late as September 1927, forced a priest of his diocese to retract a letter praising the *Vie catholique* for its support of the Pope and blaming Catholics who resisted the Pope's will.

At Montauban, where the Bishop's legal counsel continued to preside over the meetings of the Action Française, papal directives were almost ignored even a year after they had been issued. Diocesan authority had never informed the faithful, and the priests read only *L'Express du Midi* and *La Croix*. Those who wished to obey the Pope were intimidated and discouraged; and one of Gay's more timid correspondents even suggested that it might be prudent to carry on their epistolary exchanges under assumed names.[4] Monseigneur Marty had to appear in Rome and make excuses, but back in his diocese he still refused to toe the line. From darkest Tarn-et-Garonne a country priest declared that they were living under an Action Française terror.[5]

But it was not the integrists alone who could defend the Action Française and criticize its critics. It was not integrism that made Maurice Denis write his old friend Gay: "Discuter avec Charles Maurras, oui; discuter avec Tartuffe, non!" It was not the integrist public that caused the liberal *Vie catholique* to note that it was losing ground, and that throughout the summer of 1927 it lost more subscriptions than it gained.[6] It was not Cardinal Charost who made *La Croix* sluggish in following instructions from Rome. "*La Croix* ne marche que contrainte," a Catholic priest had noted; and nothing was more obvious than that. The letter of the *Aquitaine* published on August 27 took over a week to appear in its pages and it appeared only at the Pope's specific direction.[7]

For several months *La Croix* hedged, seeking to avoid both insubordination to the Pope and the ire of Maurras, finally retiring into noncommittal silence broken only by the publication of official documents and statements which it could not avoid. Even after January 1927, *La Croix* had done its best not to attack or blame the Action Française. Its director, the Abbé Bertois, was removed only after strong representations from Rome in mid-1927; Father Léon Mercklen, who succeeded him, was more cooperative, but the editor,

[c] Gay to Monseigneur Duthoit, Auxiliary Bishop of Lille, Nov. 29, 1930 (Gay papers). Shortly before his death in 1930 Charost renewed his assurances to his royalist friends. But then, cf., *cum grano salis*, *Les Nouvelles rennaises,* November 13, 1930, which suggests that the Cardinal's mind had been failing in the years preceding his death.

Jean Guiraud, a man of the traditionalist nationalistic Right, continued to support a policy of appeasement and used his pages to attack the intolerance of the royalists' persecutors.[d]

Equally hostile to the condemnation were most of the leaders of the National Catholic Federation—Groussau, Castelnau, and Vallat. Many local FNC leaders were royalists—some surreptitious, others open like the Comte d'Antin de Vaillac, who defended the Action Française in the friendly *Express du Midi*. And many more, like Castelnau himself, privately considered the condemnation unjust and did all they could to soften it.[8]

A good many people clearly shared this feeling. By October 1927 the "Yellow Book" of the Action Française, *L'Action Française et le Vatican,* which had been placed on the *Index* the previous month, had sold some forty thousand copies. On August 25 of the same year, the first anniversary of Cardinal Andrieu's letter, the Action Française had asked for financial aid; fifty days later over 700,000 francs had been received. An appeal for funds made by the *Vie catholique* on the same day brought only 31,000 francs. To an experienced journalist like Mermeix, the figures were a plebiscite showing where Catholic sympathies really lay.[9] The Sacred Penitentiary had to address yet one more note to remind French bishops of the prescriptions of March 8, and to point out these had remained a dead letter for many priests and monks who still continued to give absolution to readers and members of the Action Française.[10]

All this resistance seems to have come chiefly from a feeling widespread in most Catholic quarters, even in those least sympathetic to the Action Française, that coercion was no way of settling disagreements, at least among Catholics. Men like Georges Goyau, the permanent secretary of the Académie Française and president of the Catholic Society of French Publicists, a man much libeled by the royalists, opposed the deposition of Bernard de Vésins, vice-president of the Society, on the ground that it would be a mistake to adopt the intolerant methods of the integrists themselves. A host of charitable bishops opposed the condemnation of the Action Française, as they had formerly opposed that of the Sillon, disapproved ecclesiastical coercion, and agreed with Marc Sangnier that one should leave such work to time, not to anathemas.

Representative of this latter group was the Breton prelate who told an unrepentant nobleman of his diocese, "I am not intelligent enough to see anything bad in the Action Française. But I am the most humble of French bishops. I follow the Cardinals by discipline." And who, when his guest asked for absolution, replied, "I cannot give you absolution; I should be dis-

[d] Gay, *La Vie catholique,* Aug. 6, 1927, attacked the editors of *La Croix,* who published Vallat's letter against him simultaneously with the *Action française* (July 31). Guiraud, of whom Maurras approved, moved in circles of the Catholic Right not unsympathetic to the Action Française, although they were not of it. His son Paul, a professor of philosophy, was a close friend of ex-seminarist Marcel Bucard and became the editor of the violently anti-Semitic and collaborationist *Franciste.*

obedient in doing so. But my benediction is my own: I give you that with all my heart. Follow your conscience; you are on the right road."

Jean de La Varende has vividly described the cold despair of Catholics who could not bring themselves to submit, yet found the loss of the sacraments hard to bear. But in dioceses like Poitiers or Saint-Brieuc a Christian burial was never refused even to the most notorious members of the Action Française, and there were numerous instances of country gentlemen whose special privileges were maintained—the private family chapels, the privileged altars, the continued visit of parish processions, and marriages according to ancient custom, though (one cannot have everything) without the bells.[11]

How the prescribed sanctions were applied depended on individual priests and, above all, on the local bishop. At Lyon, where the archbishops were friendly or at least tolerant, no religious marriages or burials were denied. At Bordeaux, the new Bishop, the future Cardinal Feltin, who succeeded on the death of Andrieu, was much more tolerant. The recollections of royalists in Orléans confirm that the *Action française* exaggerated ecclesiastical harshness—that the Church tended to act only when action could not be avoided or when it wanted to make an example of a well-known person, and was in actual practice rather indulgent.[12]

The man who took the firmest stand was Cardinal Louis-Ernest Dubois, the Archbishop of Paris, who, as Bishop of Verdun, had been one of the first to speak out against the Sillon. Yet when he was criticized by fellow-prelates for his excessive harshness to Action Française priests, Dubois sent word to the Pope that (with one exception which had nothing to do with the Action Française) he had not in truth censored a single one among his priests: "No French bishop can penalize priests as long as bishops can brave the Pope without incurring censure."[e]

The integrists had sought the head of Cardinal Baudrillart, accused of modernism. Yet when, in 1928, Bloud and Gay tried to obtain his sermons for publication, Baudrillart refused, for, as he told one of the directors, the tone of Francisque Gay's campaigns had discredited the firm. The situation concerning the Action Française, wrote Father Ledochowski, General of the Jesuits, remained awkward. As Gay complained to the sympathetic but conciliatory Duthoit, the future Bishop of Arras, it was the first time in a century that so many bishops, even after the Pope had spoken, retained such obvious sympathies for a condemned movement.[13]

By the end of the 'twenties, however, the Action Française was beginning to feel the effects of the condemnation, far, far more than the Church. *Ligueurs* had resigned by the hundred from the very start. At the rue de Rome their index cards had been placed in separate files labeled "en sommeil," to be taken

[e] Francisque Gay, personal communication; the message, in March 1928, was delivered by him. When Dubois died in 1929 his funeral oration was pronounced in the most pejorative terms by—of all people—Cardinal Charost. This was held to be part of the Action Française feud.

out when, as it was hoped, they rejoined. Soon the sleeping files were more numerous than those of the active members. Some old militants who did not resign quietly edged away, like Baron Tristan Lambert, "doyen des Camelots du Roi." He continued to read the *Action française* himself on the strength of a papal dispensation, although he forbade his servant to do so, but he took no further part in the activities of the League.[14]

A petition of a group of Catholic professors for pardon and reconciliation got off to a good start in the summer of 1928 under the initiative of Henri Carteron of the University of Strasbourg and Pierre Mauriac of the Medical Faculty at Bordeaux. Under liberal attacks, however, it was quietly dropped. And in November of the same year one liberal observer concluded that the condemnation had "brutally mutilated" the movement.[15] At Easter 1929 a pilgrimage to Rome which Gay promoted as a challenge to the royalist supporters[f] proved extremely popular and marked the turning point.

In the meantime, the sales of the *Action française* reflected its loss in stature. In December 1925 newsstand and free circulation had been almost 60,000; twelve months later it was hardly 40,000, and by December 1927 it had fallen off even more. The Christmases of the next five years showed circulation figures wavering between 31,000 and 33,000, a startling contrast to the prosperity of previous years. If we assume that the proportion of unsold copies to total circulation remained the same throughout this period (somewhere near 30 percent), then between 1925 and 1928 the *Action française* had lost nearly half its readers—45 per cent of those in the provinces and 43 per cent of those in Paris.[g]

We shall have occasion to see the cumulative effects of ecclesiastical ire not only on the membership of the Action Française but on its resources and its activities. For the moment, it would be convenient to outline the subsequent development of the break with Rome, and its end in final reconciliation.

As the decade of the 'twenties drew to a close, the battle had reached something like a draw: the royalists were scarred but not weary, and if their activity was less, they were still of some significance on the national scene. The Church had not really made its point and thousands of Catholics still insisted on preferring the rue de Rome to Rome itself. The French episcopate still hoped for reconciliation rather than extermination, and after 1929, when both the Papal Secretary of State Cardinal Gasparri and Cardinal Dubois died, their attitude became one of increasingly open appeasement.

The policy of Cardinal Verdier, who replaced Dubois in the see of Paris, was to make friendly gestures, to avoid trouble, to obtain a semblance of

[f] Its stated object had been to repair the outrages inflicted on the head of the Church by "a fraction of French youth." The turnout exceeded the most optimistic predictions.

[g] These figures, concerning only free circulation and sales, totally ignore the solid core of subscribers. It might be mentioned that, even so, the circulation of the *Action française,* understandably less than that of the great popular dailies like *Le Quotidien* and *L'Echo de Paris,* compared favorably with that of papers like *Le Temps* and *Le Populaire.*

apology from the Action Française, and to save the Church's face. He was caught, however, between the quiet resolution of the Pope, to which steadfast opponents of the Action Française could always in the last resort appeal, and the intransigence of integral nationalist leaders. The best that could be hoped for was a cold war in which hostilities would progressively simmer down. By 1935 Robert de Boisfleury could report to the Twenty-second Congress of the Action Française that, although hostilities had not exactly ceased and nothing had changed officially, there was a new spirit in the air.[16]

The new spirit was strikingly displayed when, on Jacques Bainville's death in February 1936, old Canon Richard of the Church of Saint-Pierre-du-Gros-Caillou consented to give Bainville's remains the religious burial they should not by rights have received. Cardinal Verdier was not in Paris and the Archbishopric censored the unrepentant Canon, who quite refused to apologize. After an exchange of letters in which episcopal authority was publicly challenged, the old gentleman was placed under interdict. The *Action française* had publicized Canon Richard's stand; but when Gay decided to do as much by printing in his *Vie catholique* the correspondence that other Catholic publications had deliberately ignored, he was attacked from the most authoritative quarters as inviting trouble.

Monseigneur Chevrot, an honorary canon, and curé of the rich church of Saint-Francis-Xavier in the 7th Arrondissement, expressed a hearty wish that Gay might show less "inopportune zeal." *La Croix* and even the progressive *Sept,* said Monseigneur Chevrot, had kept the matter quiet, and the interdict against Richard had soon been lifted after a formal apology. The apology had been far more formal than regretful, but why publicize such "miserable polemics"? When Gay replied that Richard's letters should not have been published in the first place, and that the *Vie catholique* had done no more than follow others, Chevrot's rejoinder made clear what had for some time been the official policy in France. The matter should have been stifled on three counts, argued Chevrot: (1) To safeguard sacerdotal honor and hence limit scandal. It was obvious to all, he pointed out, that Canon Richard had been refusing to submit to the Church for nine years. Did one have to expose such wretchedness in public? (2) To spare the neglect of diocesan authority. The leaders of the Church in their desire for peace had chosen to close their eyes; should their disappointing behavior (which the more severe could call partial complicity) be held up to notice? (3) To obey the known wishes of Cardinal Verdier. The Church was in a very equivocal situation where the Action Française was concerned. Diocesan authorities applied disciplinary measures only when they could not do otherwise, but more and more public opinion was inclined to believe that the Action Française had been condemned for political reasons. In actual practice, it looked as if the authorities, regretting a condemnation that had proved ineffective, were trying to forget it: "L'autorité se tait: prenez comme *La Croix* et comme *Sept* le parti de vous taire." In any case, Cardinal Verdier had not endorsed his predecessor's orders to pursue the Action Française: "les ordres que vous avait donnés le Cardinal Dubois n'ayant pas été renouvelés . . . n'ont plus aucune valeur."[17]

By 1937, perceptive observers on the Left glimpsed the beginnings of reconciliation.[18] They were right. The Papal Secretary of State, Cardinal Eugenio Pacelli, visiting Paris and Lisieux for the feasts of Sainte-Thérèse, had been approached by Verdier, by the Catholic historian Georges Goyau, who wanted desperately to help patch up the rift with the Action Française, and by the Superior of the Carmelite convent in Lisieux, all interceding in favor of the condemned.

The most pressing interventions were being made on political grounds, where, as so often in Action Française history, sympathies were based on a similarity of views. Two years earlier, Pierre Laval, who occasionally met royalist personalities at the table of Maxime Réal del Sarte and who had seen Maurras and his friends in Réal del Sarte's house two days before his official journey to Italy and Russia, had broached the Action Française case with the Pope. It had been Laval, too, who as Premier and Foreign Minister facilitated Réal del Sarte's exploratory trip to Rome in July 1935, and who ordered the French Ambassador to the Vatican to afford the sculptor every aid in his attempts to obtain a pardon for the Action Française.[19]

But more influential and less casual aid would soon be forthcoming. The Abyssinian war, which divided Catholic opinion as it did that of other groups, provided the occasion for the first tentative *rapprochement.* In January 1936, an anti-Fascist observer discussing the division of Catholic opinion commented that, in the polemical confusion, the *Action française* line was nearest to that of the *Osservatore romano*—nearer to it than were the opinions of publications of the Catholic Left.[20] A few months later, Emmanuel Mounier learned from a very certain source in Rome that the Action Française, aware of the Vatican's fear of Communism, was conducting an intense campaign against everything that could be tarred with a left-wing brush, finding the stain of Communism in the French clergy and French Catholics high and low.

The chief agent of this campaign, Robert Havard, long editor of the *Action française*'s Roman offspring *Rome,* certainly based his argument on the right-wing influence that the Action Française had once brought and could still bring to bear in Catholic circles, which, without it, had shifted too far toward the Left.[21] The deviations of publications like *Sept, Esprit, L'Aube,* and *Le Temps présent* were, it was argued, due in part (and their influence even more) to a condemnation that had removed right-wing champions from Catholic ranks, thus leaving exponents of the Left—Mauriac, Mounier, Maritain, Madaule, Mercklen, Bidault, and Gay—a clear field for their corrupting activities.

The civil war in Spain pressed Rome into an even more determined anti-Communist position and hence into a more active right-wing policy. The most enthusiastic advocates on the Right were also, of course, the most earnest champions of the Action Française—like Cardinal Jean-Marie Rodrigue Villeneuve, Archbishop of Quebec, whose people had long held the twentieth century at bay, and Monsignor Gabriel Breynat, apostolic vicar of the Mackenzie district in Canada. The Spanish cardinals, whose country, so far as they were concerned, had scarcely got into the eighteenth century, were also favorably disposed. The Action Française was soon identified with the cause of Franco Spain; its enemies were also the enemies of Franco. The kind of argument that worked with the Spaniards was also used by a French prelate, Monseigneur Hérissé, in winning over Cardinal Lorenzo Lauri, to whom he was secretary. Cardinal Baudrillart, too, was by now manifestly friendly.

The campaigns to suppress the voices of the anti-Fascist Left in Catholic circles, temporarily halted in 1936, advanced with Franco's armies. A striking mark of their success came in August 1937 when the Dominican weekly *Sept,* born in 1934 under the auspices of the Pope himself, was suppressed on orders from the Vatican, reputedly for economic reasons, but practically for political ones. And the same Dominican Master-General, R. P. Gillet, who ordered *Sept* to scuttle could be found contributing two articles to the rabidly nationalist *Choc,* in August and September 1937. Official Catholic policy was moving openly to the Right.[22]

Meanwhile, a fairly lively correspondence had been established between the Vatican and the Action Française, mainly though not solely through the intermediary of the Carmelite sisters of Sainte-Thérèse of Lisieux, to whom Pius XI had officially entrusted the mediatory task as early as February 1929.[23] The first epistolary exchanges between Maurras and Pope Pius XI, which began in 1937 with the old nationalist's writing to express his pleasure and good wishes on the Pope's recovery from illness, reflected only their different positions. Maurras apprised the Pope that he had been wrongly advised in his decision to condemn the Action Française: "The enemies of the Action Française are the enemies of the party of order, of the fatherland, the Church, and the Papacy": it was they who had gained the first round in 1926. Not very surprisingly, the Pope sent word to Maurras, through an intermediary, that he was mistaken: "His Holiness categorically rejects this appreciation and says that in this affair he has himself, *seulement Lui et Lui seul,* decided, being informed, being well and personally acquainted with the works of Signore Maurras, whom he judges to be very far from Catholic thought." Only the sincere and total adhesion of Charles Maurras to the Church could change his mind about it. But he sent Maurras a message: *oportet semper orare et nunquam deficere.*[h]

[h] See *L'Observateur catholique,* II, No. 74 (November 1952), 3–6, for correspondence between the Pope, Maurras, Lisieux, and various intermediaries. Also Henry Bordeaux, *Charles Maurras et l'Académie Française* (1955), p. 37ff. When in January 1938 Bordeaux mentioned to the Pope the possibility of Maurras's being elected to the Académie, the Pope expressed dislike of

Other approaches throughout 1938 were equally fruitless. Goyau's request of Father Gillet that he intervene brought the answer that the time was not yet ripe, but that he had high hopes for the future.[24] Gillet knew whereof he spoke: in February 1939 Pope Pius XI died, and three weeks later Cardinal Pacelli, who was inclined toward a pardon, was elected to the Holy See. Havard had hastened to the Conclave to plead the Action Française case, and less than two months after Pacelli's election, in the last week of April 1939, an eminent prelate of the Secretariat of State, Monsignore Alfredo Ottaviani, arrived in Paris to arrange the details of the proposed submission. On a visit to Lisieux Ottaviani had, it seemed, told the prioress he would be glad to receive the royalist leaders in secret if they wished to see him. Apprised of this, Maurras and Boisfleury, while conducting open (though discreet) negotiations with the Archbishopric, were able to meet in private with the papal emissary they were supposed to ignore, and to work out with him and his secretary the details of the final agreement that he would carry back to Rome.[25]

This interview with Ottaviani certainly helped to bypass Cardinal Verdier and perhaps also to expedite the matter at the Vatican, where the Secretary of State, Monsignore Giovanni Montini, was not inclined to be favorable to the Action Française. Another private contact, at the Quai d'Orsay, skillfully bypassed the services of the Ambassador to the Vatican, Charles Roux. In the same month of April, following his gift of a statue of Joan of Arc to the United States, Maxime Réal del Sarte was invited to meet the Foreign Minister, Georges Bonnet. In the course of the interview Réal del Sarte asked Bonnet for a word which would persuade the Vatican that the French government would view a pardon without disfavor. The Action Française thought it knew that the General Secretary of the Quai, Alexis Léger, had been campaigning to convince Rome that a pardon would be interpreted as an unfriendly act, and that it might very likely result in the cutting off of subsidies to Catholic orders such as those with missions in the Orient.

Léger and also Champétier de Ribes, along with some others, including Monseigneur Bruno de Solages, rector of the Catholic Institute at Toulouse, apparently did attempt to persuade the Pope how inopportune a revision of the condemnation would be at that moment. Even Premier Edouard Daladier was moved to intervene. But Bonnet knew his own mind, and he went out of his way to give the Nuncio, Monsignore Valerio Valeri, all the reassurance he sought. When Valeri asked whether, as he had been informed, the government did indeed oppose the raising of sanctions against the Action Française and whether such an act would not cause hostile reactions in the country,

---

the idea but admitted that it would have no religious significance, a statement that was used to pacify the consciences of Catholic Academicians. Just a week before the election in June 1938, François Mauriac attacked Maurras's candidacy on Catholic grounds, but Cardinal Baudrillart made it clear that he, for one, had nothing against Maurras and viewed his candidacy as solely a literary one.

Bonnet insisted that any Roman decision concerning the Action Française was a religious matter and could in no sense be taken as a political act. The issue lay between the Pope and the Action Française: "J'estimais que cette affaire ne devait en aucun cas être examinée sous un jour politique." In a second conversation with the Nuncio, Bonnet, confident that his reassurances would result in a favorable decision, repeated that he saw nothing inconvenient about a pardon for the Action Française.[26]

In the second half of June the letter of submission that had been agreed upon with Ottaviani was signed by all the leaders of the Action Française[i] and forwarded to Rome by the Archbishopric of Paris. It seems doubtful that the signatories believed the formulas to which they had attached their names—that they really thought their condemnation "just" and truly regretted "that which appeared and was on [their] part disrespectful, injurious, and even unjust toward the person of the Pope and to the Holy See."[27] But the act of submission was a gesture, part of a compromise whose significance appeared quite clearly to those who could exclaim on hearing of the pardon, "Eh, bien! on reconnaît que nous avions raison."[28]

On July 7, 1939, the interdict on the *Action française* was lifted by the Holy Office. The official announcement appeared, appropriately enough, on July 15. Outside the jubilant Action Française circles, the general reaction was well summed up by Ambassador Roux, who, kept in the dark to the last, had learned of the decision from the pages of the *Osservatore romano*. To Substitute Secretary of State Montini, Roux declared (speaking without instructions, as he made clear) that the Holy See might at least have chosen for publication of its news another date than the morrow of the day on which France celebrated the birth of the Republic that the *Action française* daily covered with abuse. The Holy See, said Roux (not knowing what position Bonnet had chosen to adopt) could not ignore the fact that public opinion would look for the political motives in such a decision. It might easily be said that, after condemning the Action Française when it preached its integral nationalism, Rome had changed its mind as soon as that nationalism became somewhat indulgent to dictatorial regimes and when the Italian papers fed on its opinions.[j]

Why, indeed, was the Action Française condemned in the first place, and what did the condemnation achieve? The obvious reason is that the Action Française, a movement which had many Catholic members but was not under Catholic direction, was becoming much too strong in a sphere in which the Church wanted to be sole master: that of influencing Catholic opinion and

[i] Except for Colonel Larpent, whose refusal to sign fortunately went unnoticed.

[j] Telegram No. 565, July 18, 1939. There seems to be little doubt that the French Embassy was purposely left uninformed, both by the Quai d'Orsay and by Rome. How far the papal Secretariat of State itself was aware of what was happening is hard to say, since its head, Cardinal Maglione, was the same prelate whom, during his period as Nuncio in Paris, the Action Française had covered with the vilest abuse.

particularly the young. Catholic policy and Catholic organizations were being identified with a political movement that, whatever its professions, was independent and even alien. The identification, moreover, was being made on grounds that the new Pope, Pius XII, disapproved. Father Le Floch would one day declare that everything had been a matter of coincidence: "We [i.e., Le Floch and Billot] fought against liberalism, secularism, the principles of the revolution, from the doctrinal point of view. Now it so happened that the Action Française was fighting against the same plagues, but on the political plane."[29]

In his letter of August 25, 1910, Pius X had written:

> There is error and danger in linking, on principle, Catholicism to a form of government. The error and the danger are the greater when religion is identified with a form of democracy whose doctrines are erroneous. This is the case of the Sillon, which, in so identifying religion with a particular political idea, compromises the Church, divides Catholics, distracts youth and even seminarists and priests from forms of Catholic action, and profitlessly wastes the energies of a part of the nation. . . . The leaders of the Sillon allege that they move on ground that has no connection with the Church, that they pursue aims only of the temporal, not of the spiritual order.[30]

Despite their protestations, the Sillon had been condemned; and Maurras had jubilantly approved. Yet little change in the wording was needed to show that what was sauce for Sangnier was equally savory sauce for Maurras. The Action Française, too, identified religion with a political doctrine and a political form; it compromised the Church, divided Catholics, drew youth and clergy from mere Catholic action to political action. It, too, allied in one movement beyond clerical control believers and unbelievers. And, what is more, it, too, drew a distinction between temporal and spiritual aims, a distinction more precisely formulated as the debate of 1926–27 developed.

It has, of course, been argued that the condemnation was a political move, a sop to please the royalists' great enemy Briand, forming a part of Vatican foreign policy and affirming a new political line against the old integrist guard. There is some truth in this, and one has but to look at the declared policy of Benedict XV and Pius XI throughout the 1920's to see that it was in every respect different from the policy of the Action Française. Opposed to a harsh peace, the Vatican had condemned the occupation of the Ruhr and had approved the policy of conciliation and of peace, which was frequently in the hands of men whom the integrists and royalists had persecuted. In 1920, the Papal Secretary of State, Cardinal Gasparri, had expressed the confidence that the Holy See placed in Marc Sangnier; in 1923, the Nuncio, Monsignore Cerretti, had called for disarmament of spirit and of heart. The Vatican fully supported the Locarno policy, and it supported, as well, a policy of cooperation with the Republic even at the cost of concessions to Republican secularism: a policy that the Catholic Right—not least the Action Française—did everything to wreck and succeeded in hampering considerably.[k]

Hence it was that an old French prelate was only anticipating later views of Rome when he declared in 1921: "One thing the Pope must be asked for is energetic support against the clique that recruits our episcopate in conformity with the views of the Action Française. It is a hard but necessary campaign that must be fought. The justice of our case is evident. We cannot admit that Messrs. Daudet and Maurras might be qualified to select the leaders of the French clergy." This was the view clearly endorsed by Gasparri's "Pontifical Directions to French Catholics" a few years later: "The Church has a right to defend itself against parties that claim Catholic support in the interest, as they say, of the Church and that seek, in actual practice, to use the Church for the triumph of their cause."[31]

It was no good arguing, as the Action Française did, that politics simply came before religion as oxen came before a plough. Although they conceded the metaphysical importance of religion, in practice religious issues were useful in the immediate handling of political affairs. Maurras, who found the "Jewish Christ" distasteful, appreciated the value of Catholic doctrine in elevating man and society and saw in the Church a magnificent instrument of order, of progress, of civilization.[32] But his very praise condemned him; for, however flattering they might be as the opinion of an agnostic, such views had to be deprecated when coming from the most influential leader of Catholic youth. And by insisting upon avoiding matters of faith, he tended to put aside as non-essential those matters that were in the Church's eyes most essential.

When the *Action française* declared that it would take its faith from Rome, its politics from home, it entered an historical arena in which kings, emperors, popes, and sages had battled for over a thousand years. And Pius XI might not have been so hard had not the echoes of Anagni and Augsburg still sounded in the halls of the Vatican.

From the Catholic point of view, or from the Roman point of view, at least, the division between worldly and spiritual spheres, for all that it must sometimes in practice be allowed, can never in principle be admitted. The

[k] During January 1927, observers like Pierre Dominique in the *Rappel,* Maurice Muret in the *Gazette de Lausanne,* and Gonzague de Reynold in his private correspondence with Maritain interpreted the papal condemnation as a political move designed to facilitate Briand's foreign policy and Franco-German understanding. The royalists argued this from the first: See *AF,* Sept. 11, 1926, Aug. 5, 1932; *Gazette française,* Oct. 14, 1926; *RU,* XXVII, No. 17 (Dec. 1, 1926), 566. For the obstruction the French episcopate and the Catholic Right had made to conciliatory papal policies, see Jules Delahaye, *La Reprise des relations diplomatiques avec le Vatican* (1921), p. 161, explaining that he and his friends were not interested in the resumption of such relations, unless they were to carry "the appearance of a point scored by right-wing clericals." To the same point, see Monseigneur Chapon, *L'Eglise de France et la loi de 1905* (1921), pp. 3, 8; Canet-Fontaine, pp. 44–47; F^7 13198, Nov. 18, 1926.

authority of the Church cannot be excluded from any aspect of life; and the pretension to make such exclusions, even though it is backed by many years of Gallic tradition, comes close to heresy when there are no Concordats involved.

The Bishop of Nice, Monseigneur Ricard, was, it can be seen, very near the truth when he explained that the Church had condemned the Action Française "because in the Maurrassian concept of society, the Church, although it can give rules to individual life, is forbidden all authority over the social order, which is said to be subject to immutable laws, collected and defined in a sort of 'moral physiology.' Hence the Church that the Action Française dreams of would be one without the Scriptures, and if Maurras got his wish he would succeed in dechristianizing Catholicism."[33]

Thus, if the condemnation carried distinct political significance, its justification lay in a clear and increasingly present danger of the doctrinal sort. As Gillouin commented, "If there is anything surprising about it, it is not that the Action Française should be condemned, but that it was not condemned before."[34] But, added Gillouin, and here's the rub,

> It was thus inevitable that the Church should one day condemn Maurrassism. But was it inevitable that it should be condemned in quite the way it was, with such a pitiful mediocrity of language and of thought, with such an unpleasant appearance of prejudice and of bad faith, with such willful ignorance of services rendered to Catholicism and of the responsibilities Catholicism itself incurred by its tardy clairvoyance?

It was this clumsiness, this lack of finesse in handling a shift in policy, that made a wholly justifiable decision seem unjust and turned the royalists into martyrs in their own eyes and in the eyes of uncommitted observers. The things condemned in 1926 had been quite as dangerous and as censurable sixteen years before when the Sillon was condemned; the difference was that in 1910 it had not been considered politic to condemn the Action Française. But these were not things that could be said out loud. Unlike the Action Française, which took pride in its Machiavellian opportunism, the Church could not admit its own. It could not say that it suited its book to do now what might, on moral and doctrinal grounds, have been done before; and it cut rather a pitiable figure under the criticism of unrepentant victims who were able to cite repeated praises of the very things now suddenly, brutally, reproved.

It was a classic "dialogue de sourds": while the Action Française could only argue, the Church could only demand submission.[l] Both were right and both proved their opponents right: for if the Church had been unjust, the

[l] One may echo Maritain's remarks in *Primauté du spirituel*, p. 86: "C'est un grand sujet de méditation, quand on songe au prestige que l'Action Française aurait eu la chance d'acquérir si elle avait compris ces choses [the necessity for "filial submission"], de penser que Dieu a permis qu'elle ne les comprit pas."

Action Française was certainly not to be trusted, at least not from the point of view of the Church.

Perhaps the most significant effect of the condemnation was the freeing of the Church and Catholic organizations from the influence of the Action Française, which had been so strong in the early 'twenties. For better or for worse, the future lay with the champions of social Catholicism of one kind or another: the CFTC (Confederation of Christian Workers), founded in 1919 and growing slowly; the Equipes Sociales of Robert Garric; the Action Populaire, whose Jesuit leader Father Desbuquois was close to Cardinal Andrieu; the ACJF; and finally the JOC (Jeunesses Ouvrières Chrétiennes), founded in October 1926. A Christian Democratic Party (PDP) had been founded in 1924, and it played a certain part in interwar politics before it eventually, after the Second World War, became the MRP. None of these could have developed as they did had the Action Française not been effectively excluded from the Catholic field.

In September 1927, the *Croix* published one of the few positive reactions that the condemnation of the Action Française evoked—a letter from a group of Paris priests engaged in missionary work among the laboring class who thanked the Pope for his "acte libérateur": For over fifty years, the worker-priests wrote, the enemies of Catholicism in France had not ceased to represent the clergy as necessarily monarchist and opposed to the true interests of the people. The *Action française* began its action at the moment when these prejudices might possibly have been dispelled. Instead, it made them worse by insinuating itself into Catholic organizations, by pretending to furnish them its watchwords and its spirit, by trying to confer a political character on the celebrations of Joan of Arc, by blatantly selling its paper at the door of the church. By these and other means it had persuaded workers and clerks that Catholic aims and ideas were identical to those of the Action Française.

Now the JOC and the CFTC were free of this association, and they were free to act; and it was possible, too, for social Catholics and leaders of the Catholic intelligentsia to form some sort of alliance. In the middle 'twenties the leaders of the Catholic intellectual revival, with one or two exceptions like Claudel and Mauriac, were either of the Action Française or influenced by it. Now the situation had changed—not greatly, not all at once, but to a perceptible degree. And by 1937 Jacques Maritain, who had once been the coming theological sage of the Action Française, could address the International Congress of Christian Workers on "The Primacy of the Human"—not, as he might once have done, on the primacy of politics.[35]

PART IV: THE DOLDRUMS

Dans des temps comme les nôtres, l'ordre est aussi an idéal, plus fort et plus exaltant que la liberté.

—JACQUES BAINVILLE

14

THE MOVEMENT AND THE MEMBERSHIP

IT IS GENERALLY AGREED THAT, with the condemnation, the Action Française as a national movement aspiring to the kind of mass organization capable of a *coup d'état* entered a decline which, in spite of rebounds, it was never able to reverse. But it must be remembered that the Faisceau, so vigorous in 1926, was dead two years later, that the many citizens' defense groups of 1924 soon withered into nothing, whereas the Action Française not only survived this period but to some extent prospered. In 1931, a German journalist reviewing Waldemar Gurian's *Der Integrale Nationalismus in Frankreich* (itself a tribute to the enduring place of the movement), could only say that the hopes raised on the Left by the papal condemnation had not been realized. "Instead of crashing, the movement has, over the last five years, shown new development and new vigor."[1]

There was a measure of truth in this: the Action Française did adapt itself to the new circumstances better than the movements that had briefly mushroomed up around it; and the years after 1926 revealed a facet of its personality that was truly its own and yet had not previously been quite fulfilled. If the period from 1899 to 1914 was a time of affirmation, and the war and postwar years a time of exhilaration, the years from 1927 on gave scope for redefinition. The growing conservatism of the Action Française, replacing its earlier revolutionary character, had been reflected in its alliance with the Catholic Church. After 1926, its hopes of power dashed, it developed into the most outspoken representative of defeatist pessimism, and, in a series of violent breaks and starts, splintered off several highly articulate champions of a new nationalistic radicalism.

It was as if the spirit of the ardent revolutionary intellectuals so active in royalist ranks before 1914, the men who had been in good part lost in the war or, if they survived, expelled with Valois, had reappeared in the 1930's. And the disagreement between the fundamentally conservative leaders and their more untamed disciples, which had brought about the excommunication of men like Lagrange and of groups like those of the *Revue critique* and the Faisceau, reappeared after 1926 in the schisms of 1931 and 1934 and, finally, in the wartime excommunication of *Je suis partout.*

But although the condemnation provides an obvious and convenient breaking point in a story which up to that event seems like a long ascension and thereafter a gradual descent, it is important to define in greater detail the many stages of this second period, of which the break with Rome is only one incident among a multitude.

At first, as we have already seen, the results of the religious sanctions were scarcely noticed. The impetus gained in previous years seems, as a matter of fact, to have reached its high point in 1927. The various *Almanachs* list 89 sections of the League in 1923 (14 in Paris and two in the Paris region), 142 in 1927 (17 in Paris, six in the Paris region), and 173 in 1928 (16 in Paris and 14 in the Paris region). The circulation of the newspaper bore out the growth of sections: in the twelve months after the condemnation, circulation fell by less than 5 per cent. It was hardly surprising that, throughout 1927, the leaders insisted proudly that the papal altercation had left the Action Française unscathed, and even growing.[2] And even though some reports to the Fourteenth Congress in November 1927 mentioned difficulties (e.g., in Catholic Hérault, Ariège, and lower Brittany), others noted unexpected gains, particularly in less strongly Catholic areas like the Haute-Vienne and Bouches-du-Rhône, where anti-clericals may very possibly have made up the losses, like the Republican of the Oise who took to reading the *Action française* every morning when he heard that it had been condemned by Rome.[3]

But this was only the first reaction; by 1928 the Action Française had begun to feel the pinch. Circulation of the paper had fallen 17 per cent, and the Fifteenth Congress resounded with tales of woe. In the few places where positions held, it was at the expense of old friends: as at Saint-Laurent-de-la-Salanque in the Pyrénées-Orientales, where the section prospered while the number of communions in the parish dropped from 250 to 50.[4]

By 1929, all activity of the movement seemed to be focused on a desperate holding action. Some sections were surviving only in a state of suspended animation, like that of Romorantin in Loir-et-Cher which "dort un peu pour ne pas faire de la peine aux curés, qui sont si gentils."[5] Bernard de Vésins had to admit difficult circumstances and strong opposition, and soon the awkwardness of his position led him to resign on conscientious grounds.

The files of the Sûreté Générale reflect the movement's loss of impetus: bulging with reports until the end of 1926, they shrink thereafter, as local police find little to report and less to worry about. In Loire and Marne and Var, in Vienne and Ariège, throughout 1929 and 1930, the tale is much the same: no visible activity, no activity at all, serious difficulties, suspended animation. The numerous and active organizations in the Nord had fallen to pieces: in 1926, Lille alone had boasted six subdivisions, each with its own headquarters; by 1930, it counted only 110 members, no more *commissaires,* very few Camelots, only three of whom continued to sell the paper on Sundays. The ladies' group had shrunk to a score; where once the students had been 150, now they hardly mustered a dozen. The only royalist meeting of the year gathered 200 faithful from an invitation list of 1,800. The regional monthly, the *National de Flandres et d'Artois,* still printing 3,500 in 1928, had dropped to half that figure, and had not even appeared for several months.

Efforts to keep the sections on their toes by meetings, exercises, and secret plans for eventual action impressed neither the membership nor, apparently, the police. Reporting to his superiors on the royalist plan for a *coup d'état,* the Commissaire Spécial at Chalons-sur-Marne took his discovery calmly:

> L'activité des équipes de choc se manifeste, le plus souvent, à table, où, aux frais de quelques uns qui croient à leur mission royaliste, l'appétit et la soif des jeunes troupes trouvent à se satisfaire. On ne voit plus de démonstrations dans la rue, on n'entend plus crier le journal de M. Daudet.[6]

The fate of the movement in Gascony was symptomatic of the general trend: at the regional Action Française Congress at Bordeaux in June 1927, both at the meetings and at the final banquet, there was not enough room to accommodate the 1,500 persons who sought admission. The 1928 Congress was much less crowded. No figures were given, but, reading between the lines of the *Nouvelle Guyenne,* one sees that the best they could do was hold their ground.[a] Recruitment having come practically to a standstill, gaps caused by resignation and death were seldom filled. Attendance at meetings in rural areas also declined. Between 1925 and 1928, every issue of the *Nouvelle Guyenne* carried columns of announcements and reports; by 1930–31, there was almost no mention of meetings held outside Bordeaux itself. Even in Bordeaux, where formerly there had been active groups in every electoral canton, by 1932 only one lone group remained. During the winter of 1932–33, the resurgence of propaganda activity was confined to a few meetings around café tables.

The propaganda of the Ligue d'Action Française, once active on a national plane, had shrunk to pitiful dimensions, its budget, so the 1930 Congress was told, reduced to a bare minimum. Provincial propaganda meetings, 404 in 1926, fell to only 172 in 1929.[7] It is not clear whether the 151 meetings mentioned in 1932 are the total for the country or for the provinces alone,[8] but the stagnation was gaining ground. Plaintively, the head of the once-strong commercial travellers' group told the Twentieth Congress, "We ask our

[a] The decline of the movement in Bordeaux was slower than elsewhere. See F[7] 13203 (Gironde): a police report of December 11, 1929, expressed surprise at the fact that "to this day [the condemnation] has not caused any diminution of royalist members in the Gironde, as one might have expected." On January 23, 1930, more up-to-date information, assessing membership in the department at about 6,000 and sympathizers at 10,000 more, pronounced these figures clearly below those of preceding years. By November 4, "l'Action Française est depuis longs mois . . . à son point mort." By January 12, 1931, membership was estimated at 3,000 *ligueurs* and 250 Camelots, with some 8,000 sympathizers, whom only the papal condemnation kept from joining or rejoining. None of these reports inspires much confidence, and the figures should be considered as a sort of *ordre de grandeur.*

members to pay only two francs a year, but not everyone pays even that regularly." Worse still, too many members had quite forgotten the declaration that they had signed on joining. There was little zeal for fighting the Republic. The patriots were indifferent, lulled by conservative governments like that of André Tardieu; or simply reluctant for religious reasons to compromise themselves.[9] *Hora novissima, tempora pessima sunt . . .*

Outwardly, the *Action française* remained brash and cheerful: no one could tell quite what its sales or its subscribers were. Readers and Congresses were told that figures had increased or fallen by so much per cent, but they were never given the information to know the per cent of what. There is every indication that after 1927 subscriptions fell as street sales were to do somewhat later, and probably to an even greater extent. One source mentions a printing of 60,000-odd, about half what it had been in 1925–26. If the figure is true, that means about 20,000 subscribers (including those receiving the paper free) around 1930—somewhat fewer than those of the Socialist *Populaire,* which claimed 24,000 subscribers on May 24, 1930.[b]

Money, too, was sadly lacking. Numerous appeals were made for members to pay their outstanding dues, for sometimes at the end of a year a substantial proportion of the membership was in arrears; and meanwhile Maurras continued his now-traditional fund-raising campaigns, which brought in less and less, more and more slowly. At Christmas 1927, for example, a special subscription in the *Nouvelle Guyenne* brought in 150,000 francs in a few days, but the same call the following year brought in only a third as much. Soon, differences with Coty lost the Action Française even that source of income, and from then on the financial support of the movement came almost solely from small subscribers.

Of 200,000 francs donated between August and October 1931, 98 per cent came in gifts of less than 500 francs, 87 per cent in gifts of less than 100 francs. Anonymous windfalls occasionally appeared—250,000 francs from the industrialist and inventor Georges Claude, 200,000 from another industrialist—but these were exceptions to the rule that the really rich gave their money where it could bring them favors.[10] They had no desire to invest it where it would only stir up trouble. Respectable people were quite aware not only of the violence of royalist methods, or, at least, of their language, but also of their small numbers and the slim chance they seemed to have of a concrete success, and this was sufficient to make them take their trade elsewhere. But the small subscribers remained faithful and, as a police agent reported in 1934, "the permanent subscription lists sufficed for its needs."[11] They sufficed too, apparently, for the move in 1931 from the

[b] Carlton Hayes, *France, A Nation of Patriots* (New York, 1930), pp. 109, 431, attributes to the *Action française,* as of January 1, 1928, between 40,000 and 50,000 paid subscribers, and street sales of 100,000 copies or more. True figures at that date were less than half those obtained by Professor Hayes—an indication of how outsiders could be fooled concerning the state of the paper and of the movement as a whole.

rather shabby quarters in the rue de Rome to much finer ones at 1, rue du Boccador, where they remained until June 1940—a large four-storied building of noble proportions, with windows facing on the Avenue Montaigne, between the Théâtre des Champs-Elysées and the Hôtel Plaza-Athénée.[c]

Who were the small subscribers who made this possible? Who filled the subscription lists? Who, in other words, were the militants and the faithful? We have already seen that much Action Française support came from small local industrialists or landowners, to whom the corporatist movement was in the main directed. There was, for example, support from small textile manufacturers at Thizy and Cours in the Rhône; from manufacturers of agricultural implements in the Eure, around Evreux; from vineyard owners in the Bordelais-Médoc. All of these, still flourishing in the 'twenties, were beginning to decay in the 'thirties. The various château wines of the southwest, once owned by families many of which (like the Lur-Saluces, who still own Château-Yquem) were sympathetic to the Action Française, gradually passed into the hands of great distributors. The small factories around Evreux disappeared little by little as the manufacture of things like agricultural implements became the monopoly of a few large firms. At Saint-Etienne and elsewhere in the Rhône big enterprises pushed out the small and middling ones just as (a process to be completed after the war) department stores and Prisunics were squeezing out small, independent storekeepers.

As all these people began to feel the pinch, the professional classes that catered to their needs, especially doctors and men of law, not only their servitors but their kin, felt it too. The solid economic basis of Action Française support had been shrinking continually following the First World War, but the process was accelerated in the 'thirties. For in the depression, which hit France late in 1931, these were the people most affected. Nonetheless, these were also the people to whom the paper and the League would have to continue to look for support, whether they were the friends of H. Denys-Dunepveu of *Le Concierge* ("Organe corporatif hebdomadaire de la Chambre syndicale et de l'union professionnelle et d'Action sociale des concierges de Paris et du département de la Seine"), booksellers like M. Gans of Antibes, whose shop housed the local Action Française center, the four *batonniers* who, with others, attended the first banquet of the Paris group of the Avocats d'Action Française, or the old lady mentioned by Admiral Schwerer in his testimony before a Parliamentary commission, who, though in dire poverty, went with-

[c] After a number of proposals for a move from the rue de Rome, where the rent was being raised as their lease expired, a fifteen-year lease was finally signed for the building at 19, Avenue Montaigne and 1, rue du Boccador, to run from January 1, 1932, at a rent of 280,000 francs a year for the first four years and 300,000 a year thereafter. The move, which some militants disliked because the new headquarters were too far away from the center and from Saint-Lazare, was welcomed by the police, who noted that the royalist leaders no longer tapped the telephone calls of their political opponents. Police had kept a close eye on the installation of the new switchboard, See F[7] 13199, Oct. 25, 1931, Feb. 10, 1932.

out sugar in her coffee for a year in order to send the sum she thus saved to Maurras.[12]

In 1928, the Cercle Fustel de Coulanges was set up to sponsor the "collaboration of school, family, and great institutions of national life, regional and corporate, for the good of the child and the greatness of France." Its founder, Henri Boegner, a lanky, stooped philosopher and classicist, was the descendant of an old Protestant family of republican traditions, a nephew of Francis de Pressensé and a cousin of Pastor Marc Boegner, a leader of the Protestant church in France. Fascinated before 1914 by the syndicalist ideas of Sorel and the patriotism of Charles Péguy, he had moved on to Maurrassism because it offered a theory of the State, which he felt syndicalism lacked. After the war, as a teacher in the lycée at Mulhouse, where he led the local royalist section, he became inspired by Valois's theories of corporatism and decided that corporatist ideas could and should be applied to the teaching profession. But teachers, especially secondary school teachers, had liberal and individualistic tendencies which made an educational corporation within the UNC unlikely to succeed, and it was therefore decided to set up a separate body; its name was suggested by an interested student at the Ecole Normale Supérieure.

Never openly a part of the Action Française, the Cercle Fustel was dominated by Henri Boegner, who was now teaching in a lycée in Paris, and by such other Maurrassians as Pierre Heinrich, who taught history at Lyon, Pierre Dufrenne, a syndicalist *inspecteur primaire* converted by Maurras, and Serge Jeanneret, who headed the UNC's Union Corporative des Instituteurs before following Doriot into collaboration.

Within a narrower field than that of the Action Française, the new group set itself the task of doing the same kind of critical work and spreading the same ideas. It held monthly meetings for students of teacher-training colleges; it proselytized among the students of the Ecole Normale Supérieure; it sponsored works like Heinrich's and Antoinette de Beaucorp's *Historie de France* (1933), which was written in hopes of saving primary school pupils from antipatriotic demoralization;[d] and it sought to provide a focus for right-wing intellectuals in the University and in the services. Its annual banquets were attended by public figures like Léon Bérard, General Maxime Weygand, Daniel Halévy, Abel Bonnard, André Bellessort, and Albert Rivaud, some of whom, though unwilling to join an extremist organization, were ready to sympathize with many of its ideas. They applauded Professor L. Dunoyer when he asserted

[d] See *JSP*, Nov. 11, 1934; *Candide*, Aug. 13, 1936. The book contains some interesting views of history: for example, Louis XI was a politician without scruples—he was one of France's greatest kings (p. 92); Louis XIV completed French territorial unity by the conquest of natural frontiers (p. 114); the Third Republic dedicated itself primarily to the work of secularization—its colonial enterprises turned France away from the patriotic duty of reconquering Alsace-Lorraine and thus helped to bring about the war of 1914 (pp. 236, 240–42).

at the annual banquet in 1932, a banquet presided over by Marshal Lyautey and addressed by the Duke Pozzo di Borgo, "Au Cercle Fustel de Coulanges nous disons: la démocratie, voilà l'ennemi." Soon the Cercle boasted several hundred members, far more than were in the teachers' group, which had only fifteen in 1931 and one hundred in 1933.[e]

Like the secondary school teachers, many men of letters were also turning away from democracy—partly, so *Candide* saw it, because men of letters turn in the direction where they expect to find a public, and partly because "after all, men of letters are bourgeois. Why should they remain in the camp of those who want to take away their comfortable studies?"

More correctly, the men of letters seem to have hesitated at making a choice between those who wanted to rob them of their studies altogether, and those who would (apparently) preserve them from such a dreadful loss. As Daniel-Rops explained in the *Grande Revue,* most young intellectuals, disgusted by old ideologies, gravitated either toward the Communists or toward the Action Française. "The Action Française is incontestably the only great party of our day that has a place for intelligence in its program. . . . In the ranks of that party, an intellectual, far from feeling suspect as he would in the midst of the parties 'of order' will feel respected. Communism is less systematic about finding a place for intelligence."

It was perhaps, then, less interest that affected intellectuals than ideas. For young men in quest of ideas, the Action Française continued to be the great intellectual repository of the Right: the only uncompromising and consistent—because extreme—alternative to its equally extreme competitors on the Left. "Not only do the ideas of Maurras seem to me excellent nourishment for his disciples and friends," Daniel-Rops wrote in a letter to the *Action française*; "they are also fruitful for those who do not accept his doctrine."[13] The future Catholic historian was in good company.

The people to whom *Candide*'s analysis really did apply, who seemed to have moved en masse against those "who might want to take away their studies," were the doctors. Perhaps because of Daudet's acquaintances in medical circles and his frequent recourse to medical jargon, perhaps because of an authoritarian bent peculiar to medical men as a professional deformation, perhaps for simpler economic reasons in a profession affected as no other by overcrowding in a few urban centers, fierce competition for a scant number of clinical appointments, and the influx of foreign, frequently Jewish, col-

[e] Henri Boegner, personal communication; *AF,* May 21, 1928, June 1, 1932, Dec. 15, 1933; "Une expérience d'un quart de siècle," *Cahiers du Cercle Fustel de Coulanges,* nouvelle série, No. 1 (December 1953), Nos. 3–4 (December 1955). See No. 1, pp. 33–34, for the letter of Colonel de Gaulle to Henri Boegner (May 12, 1934) expressing delight at the suggestion of lecturing in a series sponsored by the Cercle at the Sorbonne. It was under its auspices that de Gaulle delivered his first lecture in those august halls.

leagues whom they bitterly resented, doctors had always been numerous in the ranks of the Action Française. Many professors at medical schools in Paris and the provinces figured prominently in the League's meetings, subscriptions, and even electoral lists.

In 1927, partly to make up for the loss of Catholic adherents—"by an appeal from obscurantism to science"—the Action Française began a serious effort to organize its medical friends. The organization expressed itself chiefly in a widely distributed review, *Le Médecin,* and in regular banquets which brought the nationalist doctors together—small ones in the provinces (40 at Strasbourg, 15 at Alençon, 100 at Toulouse and at Bordeaux, 200 at Lyon and at Marseille), and great ones in Paris (600 in 1931, 700 in 1932, more than twice as many in 1935).

By the middle 'thirties, the popularity of integral nationalism was greater in the medical profession than in any other. Members and sympathizers among doctors, students, interns, and druggists must have numbered several thousand, propagandists as useful in their way as were the commercial travelers, and apparently more faithful. Even today the medical profession of France still carries the mark of Action Française influence, and it was no real coincidence that when Maurras was sent from prison to Troyes in August 1951 for a medical examination, he found that both the nurse and the doctor who examined him, and with whom he spent an "enchanted hour," were of the Action Française.[14]

At the same time, the Action Française, chiefly by means of the newspaper, also exerted itself to attract the military, which had been of considerable importance to its early history and thought. Beginning in February 1928, the paper ran a special military page on the 10th and 25th of each month, which soon acquired a wide and attentive public throughout the officer corps. Young officers like Xavier de Hautecloque were sorry if they missed it just once, and (for a while) older ones were able to give full rein to their conviction that cavalry was the backbone of the Army and the horse essential to the proper cavalry spirit. (In any case, retired General Lavigne-Delville pointed out, if motorization was Radical-Socialist, the horse was conservative.)[f]

From the start, a discussion of the plight of the officer under the Republic set the rubric's tone: the Republic, a reign of mediocrity, was the enemy of every elite. It was therefore inevitable that the officer corps, which had always been an elite, should be the object of Republican jealousy. The argument was carried further in succeeding issues. In his regular column, General Lavigne-Delville argued first that officers had no reason to love or respect the regime they were supposed to serve; then, and more prophetically, that the Army should have its say in politics, in order to prevent politicians from harming

[f] "Les Dragons portés," *AF,* Dec. 10, 1930; "Cavalerie méconnue," *AF,* Nov. 25, 1931. This, however, was not quite typical, and the military page featured farsighted articles on the use of armor and mechanized warfare.

its interests and the interests of the nation. The enemies of France were Communists, Socialists, and those more moderate men who, although they recognized the danger from the Left, yet did not stir to stop it:

> All that is truly French is with us, and especially with the veterans. They are not numerous, and we are not many, either. But minorities, when active, impose their will. For over four years we were the country's *real* representatives, in the trenches and in battles, facing the foreign enemy. This gave us the right to speak up. If no one listens to us, we have the right and we have the duty to act, in order to save France a second time.[15]

But it hardly seemed, as the 'twenties drew to a close, as if the salvation of France were likely to come from the veterans, or from the rue de Rome either.

One interesting, though highly incomplete, picture of Action Française support in the 'twenties can be drawn from the occasional indications supplied by the yearly *Almanachs,* concerning the profession or origin of officials and representatives of the League. Like everything else the Action Française published, such details were not given either consistently or with certain accuracy. The best we have been able to find—and it is but an indifferent best—appeared in the *Almanach* for 1933, which listed 873 names of League officials and the occupations of just 212 among them. Of this quite random sample, almost a quarter (49) were doctors; 36 were shopkeepers, tradesmen, or artisans—to whom might be added the ten druggists; 32 gave military rank; 26 were farmers or landowners; 24 practiced the legal profession; and 16 could be classed as local industrialists of one sort or another. The seven public officials were very minor ones indeed—village mayors or their assistant *secrétaires de mairie.* Six clerks or shop assistants, three engineers, two insurance agents, and one banker complete the list. It is an almost perfect portrait of a pre-industrial society from which Julien Sorel might hope to escape or rise.

Many who listed no profession but whose address was Château de —— were probably landowners also. The same must apply to the nobles, of whom one can count 168 out of 873 names. Since the *particule* was not in every case printed, and since certain county families bear no *particule,* it can be assumed that about one-fifth of the officials of the League were nobles of one sort or other. This proportion, no more and perhaps less than would be expected of a royalist organization, is borne out by the long lists faithfully published by the *Action française* each January of those attending masses said on January 21 in memory of Louis XVI.[g]

[g] As we might expect, the reports of the provincial police show a great many names *à particule,* and in the Gironde, for instance, seven out of ten section presidents were titled. But not all the titles carried the same weight, and after clashes between royalists and Communists occurred in the little Berrichon town of Blanc (Indre) in August 1926, a letter in *L'Oeuvre* (September 3) signed Marie de Comines, denounced the assumed nobility of Action Française supporters, whose ancestors had enriched themselves at the expense of the native aristocracy, sometimes by buying up Church and emigrants' land in Revolutionary times: "Si ces gens aux louches antécédents sont

One thinks of certain old landed families of Touraine, somewhat impoverished, somewhat behind the times, like those described by Maurice Bedel in *Molinoff, Indre-et-Loire,* who relied on the *Action française* for news of the outside world, and who provided some of the most enthusiastic militants, catechizing their friends and collecting funds, and feeling about the movement, as one of the young ladies in the novel does: "It [the Action Française] is a great consolation for a young girl who knows herself destined to remain single [for lack of a dowry]. She finds there someone to whom she can give herself—the King."[16]

Where 1924, 1925, and 1926 were for France years of economic, and therefore of social, anxiety, the three—indeed the five—years that followed were years of prosperity and ease. On the home front, the change can best be indicated by the exchange rates, which everyone, fascinated by the fate of the franc and, hence, of his savings, followed carefully: in July 1926, the pound sterling had stood at 243 and the dollar at 50 francs; five months later these figures were almost exactly halved. Addressing the Financial Committee of the Chamber in January 1927, Premier Poincaré could report the Treasury in a comfortable way, the State repaying its obligations and successfully contracting more, the franc rising so fast that the Bank of France was having to buy foreign currency to counter dangerous speculation. Unemployment existed, and prices were high; but salaries were, in the main, keeping pace with prices, and unemployment was certainly less than in other European countries—indeed, France encouraged immigration.

Such obvious improvement in the state of the nation, although accompanied by the usual amount of grumbling, meant that the arguments of impending disaster which the Action Française still harped on were meeting with less attention. Its warnings and its riots reverberated less loudly in a relaxed atmosphere where governments were not always on the verge of toppling, economies on the verge of collapsing, and men on the verge of losing their jobs. But the lack of attention at first went unnoticed.

As 1927 opened, the old confidence still reigned, and Maritain, at work on his *Primauté du spirituel,* could still (and with no particular wish to boost the movement he had recently left) mention the paradox that "without having a single one of its members in Parliament, the Action Française enjoys among many the prestige of a virtual public authority or principate of opinion." Daudet agreed that the state of the movement had never been better. "It has welcomed thousands of new members, particularly in the last four months. It is the usual result of all agitation, of whatever kind, around a political group."[17]

à l'heure actuelle à la tête des turbulents d'action orléaniste, c'est qu'ils pensent gagner ainsi leurs quartiers de noblesse, et faire oublier leur roture. . . . Ce sont les arrière-petits-fils des profiteurs de la Révolution. . . . Eh bien, dites tout haut que les légitimistes les repoussent, comme le peuple les méprise." F^7 13200 ff; F^7 13203 (Gironde), July 7, 1931.

In the Joan of Arc's Day parade that May, the Action Française contingent, sole royalist group though it was, was generally thought to be the most impressive, especially since rival Catholic groups had been disorganized by false counterorders and fake last-minute changes invented by malicious Camelots and conveyed through their latest trick, wire-tapping. In the *Fortnightly Review* an enthusiastic English spectator marveled at the mass of royalist marchers. The Communists, always ready to discover reactionary influences lurking in the shadows around Poincaré, seemed equally impressed, despite their knowing quite well that relations between the old statesman and the Action Française were bad. Only *L'Ere nouvelle* perceived the significance of the many separate groups in the parade: "On ne renverse pas un régime avec des tronçons de faction."[18]

To defy the regime, however, was precisely what, for one brief and hopeless moment, Daudet tried to do not a month later. Summoned to serve the five-month sentence he had incurred in 1925 for slandering Bajot, he angrily refused. Then he barricaded himself in the *Action française* offices on the rue de Rome, along with the business manager, Joseph Delest, who would have preferred to go quietly to serve his own two-month sentence, and, defended by barbed wire and several score of determined Camelots, dared the police to come and get him. His stand was meant to arouse the sympathy of the French public, but it aroused their amusement far more, and the besieged took the matter more seriously than their besiegers did. The police, having no intention of breaking into a building they could easily reduce by flooding with hoses, busied themselves with easing the traffic jams caused by the many curious who converged on the area for a glimpse of Daudet's last stand. No one had any desire to intervene, and even the press showed little sympathy.[19]

With both police and Daudet apparently ready to let the days go by without overt action, rescue from what promised to become a very embarrassing situation for the self-styled martyrs turned up, oddly, in the person of the prefect of police himself, Jean Chiappe. There would have seemed to be small reason for this popular and efficient administrator to treat the royalists with forbearance, for he had himself endured Daudet's slander in 1917, when he was accused along with Malvy and others of being a spy.[20] But Chiappe, described by one contemporary as a sort of short-arsed opportunist,[21] liked to do favors and make friends. And, as Jules Lemaître had once remarked, it was very hard to hold a grudge against Léon. Through Horace de Carbuccia, the publisher of *Gringoire,* who knew the Chiappes well, and through Maxime Réal del Sarte, a satisfactory agreement with Daudet was arranged.[h]

[h] Later that year, in December, Carbuccia married the daughter of Mme Chiappe. But Réal del Sarte already knew the prefect of police, and his father-in-law, the surgeon Louis Renon, had saved the life of Carbuccia's future wife in an operation. Maxime was one of the negotiators of June 1927. See Glandy, *Réal del Sarte,* p. 175. For further details, see the contradictory assertions of Pujo and Dr. Paul Guérin in *AF,* November 6, 1932, the latter affirming that the terms of the surrender, including the preliminary show of force and the actors' speeches, had been completely prearranged.

At dawn on June 13, after three days of siege, with an impressive show of force behind him, Chiappe approached the barricaded building. He appealed to Daudet's high principles as a Frenchman to avoid the shedding of French blood; Daudet patriotically agreed. With honor safe, the makeshift barbed-wire barricades were disentangled, the locked and barred gates creaked open, and out into the pallid morning the unshaven Camelots marched two by two, free to go home and boast of having held the Republic at bay, while Daudet and Delest rode off in Chiappe's limousine to serve their prison terms in the Santé.

The two men's imprisonment was not of the harshest: they could receive visitors, write letters and articles, keep in touch with their offices, order whatever they wished to be bought for them by accommodating guards. Delest has described the excellent dinners brought in from the outside, the bottles of Chablis, the coffee and the newspapers fetched at breakfast time by obliging warders.[22] But even so, Daudet found the injustice of it all very hard to bear: he, a loving father, had been thrown into jail for protesting against the murder of his son and trying to see that justice was done. (It would never, of course, occur to him that in his rage he had maligned innocent people.) He and Mme Daudet even imagined there was a plot to poison him, most likely in the excellent meals provided by the restaurant close to the prison gates, the management of which had most suspiciously changed hands. His life was in danger—he must get out of prison or he would die there.

It is quite possible that their leader's life had little to do with it, that the Camelots could simply not resist the thought of a spectacular, first-class prank, but in any event, they arranged one. For some time they had been experimenting with various methods of tapping telephone lines, and they had been gleeful at the effective way in which they had made use of them to spoil the Joan of Arc's Day plans for their Catholic rivals. Now, they would employ them to obtain Daudet's release from prison.

On June 25, about noon, an urgent call from the Ministry of the Interior ordered the Director of the Santé to release three of his political prisoners—Daudet, Delest, and, for good measure, a Communist leader, Pierre Sémard. The government, said the voice on the telephone, wanted to improve the political climate and appease extremists on both the Right and the Left; but, to be effective, the gesture should be sudden. Written orders would follow in due course. The rather puzzled Director called back the Ministry, just to check, and was somewhat impatiently reassured: let him bestir himself. He did, and in a short time the three men, delighted and surprised, found themselves free.

History does not relate what happened to Sémard, but Daudet and Delest were handled with skillful expeditiousness. Picked up by a "cruising" taxi, they were passed from car to car, from hand to trusted hand, until they reached the fifteenth-century Château de Vigny, in Seine-et-Oise not very far from Paris. There, while police searched cars and trains and watched all borders, while enterprising Camelots swamped the Sûreté and local police with false tips about the escaped prisoners, the fugitives and Mme Daudet stayed quietly, unknown to all except their host and his wife. It was not until the first of August that they slipped across the border into Belgium, where, for two and a half years, they lived in a suburb of Brussels.[23]

The cleverly managed escape achieved what the farce in the rue de Rome had failed to do: made all France laugh. The public really cared little whether Daudet went to prison or not, but it was happy to see the authorities ridiculed and probably added, in the words of *Candide,* "Tout de même, cette Action Française, elle a du monde partout."

From a larger view, however, such a conclusion was not immediately apparent. Indeed, the Action Française was keeping remarkably quiet. Local quarrels with the clergy, discreet electoral agreements, efforts—also on a local scale—to reorganize depleted sections into regional groups and to drum up larger attendance at public meetings, seem to have kept the royalists busy, but out of the news. They crashed back into the headlines briefly in October 1928, when a gang of Camelots broke up a dedicatory ceremony for a bust of Emile Combes at Pons (Charente) and one of them, fired on for refusing to desist, was mortally wounded. But the young Camelot's death was not even a nine days' wonder. As André François-Poncet commented in an interview, the action of a mere Camelot could not have any political consequences: "C'est le geste d'un tout petit parti habitué à ce genre de manifestations."[24]

In December 1928, however, two resounding scandals afforded a chance for the royalists to renew their harangues. Clemenceau's former Minister of Finance, Louis Klotz, who had speculated and gambled himself into bankruptcy and ruin, was arrested for writing worthless checks, giving the antiparliamentary press a field day. At the same time, a remarkably able female speculator and crook, Marthe Hanau, whose financial sheet *Gazette du franc* had caused the ruin of many a small investor, was also arrested. The lady had numerous connections in political circles—mostly on the Left, said the Right; mostly in the middle, in fact; the *Gazette du franc* had supported all the right causes, and a special number of it devoted to the Kellogg-Briand Pact had been officially distributed to all French schools when Herriot was Minister of Education. It was Hanau money that had helped keep the once-honest left-wing *Quotidien* alive, and Hanau investment advice had cost many of its readers dearly. Here was a real-life parallel to the character of the corrupt and bearded windbag that Marcel Pagnol was portraying with much success in *Topaze.* And this was the moment when, perhaps to celebrate the revival of antiparliamentary sentiment that had been lying dormant for some years, the deputies decided to vote themselves a 33 per cent raise in salary—from 45,000 to 60,000 francs a year.

The Action Française had demonstrated alone in the Latin Quarter over the scandal of the *Gazette du franc,* and several dozen members had been held briefly under arrest just before Christmas.[25] But when Daudet, still writing from Brussels, now proclaimed that the regime was rotten, his voice was only one of many. There was ground for common understanding there, but also ground for jealousy and competition. Anti-parliamentary and anti-liberal ideas, so long a kind of private preserve of a small wing composed almost entirely of members of the Action Française, were spreading, and real royalists, real Maurrassians, were becoming difficult to identify. The press called all the participants in the Joan of Arc parade royalists,[26] and often tended to use royalist and Right as meaning the same thing.[27] Some members of the Right, like Charles Benoist, a former Ambassador to The Hague, Léon Mirman, who had represented the Republic in liberated Lorraine, and the millionaire chemist Georges Claude, followed their anti-democratic, anti-parliamentary beliefs to a logical conclusion and joined the Action Française, but more with a hope of destroying the Republic than of restoring the king. Benoist admitted to Henri de Kérillis that he did not believe a traditional monarchy could really be restored. "Then how can you be against something that exists," asked Kérillis, "and for something which, according to you, can never exist again?" "I do not know," answered Benoist. "All I know is that democracy in France shows itself more powerless every day to provide the country with a government."[28]

But if that was all the Action Française could offer now, why, necessarily, join it? Many others were expressing the same views—Taittinger and his rather Bonapartist but professedly "republican" Jeunesses Patriotes, Henry Bordeaux of the Académie Française, and numerous deputies, like Kerillis and Ybarnégaray. It was noteworthy, however, that few respectable men spoke strongly against the government while the balance of power remained in the hands of the moderates.

This may have been a consideration in finally obtaining a pardon for Daudet. Daudet's friends, especially those in the Société des Gens de Lettres, of which he was, of course, a member, had made repeated and fruitless efforts to persuade President Doumergue to allow him amnesty, but Daudet's venomous attacks on Poincaré and Louis Barthou, whom he held partly responsible for his misfortunes, cannot have helped their task. His articles accused Poincaré—*le nain Raymond, ce sinistre péteux*—of being involved in the shady affairs of his brother-in-law Lannes of the Sûreté; and they charged Barthou, the Minister of Justice, with depraved practices in a Left Bank brothel and a senile *penchant* for little girls.[29]

But in 1929, after Poincaré went on his way to illness and a lingering death, Daudet's great friend, the novelist Pierre Benoît, who had been elected to the presidency of the Société des Gens de Lettres, resumed the appeals, enlisted the support of the *Dépêche de Toulouse* and of sound republican politicians like Mandel, Marin, Herriot, and Daladier, and began to collect signatures for a petition asking that Daudet be pardoned.

More effective than the hundreds of signatures gathered on Benoît's petition may have been the fact that in November Barthou at last left the Ministry of Justice, where he had been for nearly three and a half years, and also the fact that the new Prime Minister, Tardieu, was inclined to be accommodating. At any rate, an arrangement was worked out which, it was hoped, would please both Left and Right. About the time of Daudet's condemnation another writer, Victor Margueritte, had horrified the antediluvian sections of the French reading public with a novel, *La Garçonne,* which today would scarcely cause a raised eyebrow in the *Saturday Evening Post,* and in the ensuing scandal had lost his rank as Commander of the sacrosanct Legion of Honor. The Société des Gens de Lettres now proposed, and the government agreed, that Margueritte should be restored to his rank in the Legion of Honor and Daudet should be allowed to return to France.[30]

On December 30, 1929, President Doumergue signed Daudet's pardon, and three days later the exile was back home again. In the train from Brussels, little girls begged for his autograph and adult passengers in the dining-car asked him to sign their menus. At the Gare du Nord crowds welcomed him: multitudes, said *Le Figaro,* several tens of thousands (*La Liberté*), 3,000–4,000 (*L'Intransigeant*), 2,000 (*L'Oeuvre*), 300 (*L'Echo de Paris*), about 200 Camelots (*Le Soir*).[31]

Daudet returned to find the League in the throes of serious internal dissensions. The leaders of the Paris federation, particularly those of the suburban groups, were battling with the directors of the Camelots and of the League itself. François de la Motte, the president of the Paris federation, and even more Henri Martin, the secretary, who was also assistant secretary of the League, and Dr. Paul Guérin, the vice-president, complained that the Camelots did nothing but waste time and energy playing games, when the real job was to organize the sections of the League into effective troops for a *coup d'état.*

They had been making some attempt to work up enthusiasm for an intensive program of drilling and night maneuvers, but against a lack of interest from many members who had no wish to spend their nights stumbling around suburban fields, and against bitter arguments with the Camelot leader, Pierre Lecoeur, and with Maurice Pujo. The question of whether the Action Française should try to carry out the intentions it had long professed, or whether it should devote itself to ideological propaganda centered upon the newspaper, was an important one. But it was never seriously debated, usually because personal motives entered in, and instead of exchanging arguments, the contenders exchanged accusations. Later in January 1930 Martin and Guérin recklessly accused Lecoeur of being a police spy—a favorite Action Française gambit, and perhaps not so wild, for the police seem to have had informers well placed in the organization. To those who called Lecoeur an agent of the police preventing active reorganization of a league that seemed to be relaxing into routine-ridden torpor, the accusation must have seemed at least objectively correct. But, whatever his responsibility for the organization's slackness, Lecoeur was no police spy; and when Martin and Guérin refused to apologize they were promptly drummed out of the League. Many of their friends left with them—most of the officials of the Paris federation, including de la Motte, followed by the president of the League himself, Bernard de Vésins.[32]

Vésins could see that, regardless of the rights and wrongs of the immediate situation, the men who left represented the active element of the League, at least in Paris, where the core of the movement was, and that those left behind were for the most part honest bureaucrats, devoted to the cause but with no imagination or initiative. Vésins had stuck with his friends after the papal condemnation at the cost of considerable personal anguish, and it is possible therefore that his resignation was simply an opportunity seized. But the big, horsy man with his polka-dotted cravats may also have felt that staying on at his post was hardly worth the trouble, if all it would bring would be the repetition of timeworn formulas.

What one of those who left in 1930 has called the *grande dissidence* is generally forgotten by historians of the Action Française. It made no great stir at the time, and Charlotte Montard alone, an unsympathetic chronicler, has bothered to describe the difficulties that beset the royalists as a sequel to the resignations. In the Paris area, she says, local headquarters were closed down one by one and sections were dissolved. Soon the difficulties spread to the provinces, where again personal rivalries entered in.[33] Such in truth may have been the state of things, but outwardly the *grande dissidence* seemed to make little difference. And that perhaps was the essential point of the crisis. Like the explusion of Valois, that of Martin and Guérin takes its place in the long list of historical "ifs." Had the activists triumphed, had they stayed, perhaps the Action Française would have taken another turning. As it was, it continued without change, only purged once more of its really active (or harebrained) elements.

The subsequent career of the rebels of 1930 is not without interest, and not without some bearing on the later fortunes of the Action Française. Their attempt to set up a rival organization in the Comités Royalistes de la Seine did not meet much success: a year after the break, the Comités, which never attracted more than two hundred or so members, remained an assembly of officers without troops. A move to join L'Oeillet Blanc—made up of survivors of the old royalist committees which had been supplanted by the Action Française before the war—seems to have fizzled out. At last, in September 1931, Vésins, de la Motte, René Calté, Pierre Chaboche, and a few others, joined the corporatist economist Pierre Lucius and Eugène Mathon, Valois's sometime supporter in the Nord, to set up the Société Française d'Edition et de Propagande, with offices in the Maison des Producteurs on the Boulevard

Haussmann.[34] To the corporatist ideas of their political past, they were now going to add a new doctrine of action.

Disappointed by Maurras's unwillingness to risk his *coup d'état* in the absence of a providential Monck, they found another source of inspiration in Curzio Malaparte's *Technique du coup d'état,* which appeared in a French translation in 1931. "We were all reading it and talking about it," one of them recalls. In this study, seminal in the thinking of the Extreme Right in Europe during the 'thirties, Malaparte pointed out—what was often at the time denied—that a *coup d'état* remained quite as possible in the highly organized and controlled modern state as it had ever been in the chaotic conditions of earlier societies. The political, economic, and social programs of the revolutionaries were of no particular importance, because the conquest of the state and its subsequent defense were not a political problem but a technical one. The circumstances favorable to a coup were not necessarily of a political or social nature, and so did not depend on the country's general situation. Mussolini had shown that a state had to defend itself not against the program of a revolution but against its tactics, and, given the right tactics, the present situation, Malaparte concluded, offered Catilinarians of both the Left and the Right great chances of success. "The modern state is more exposed to revolutionary danger than is usually believed."[35]

Martin and his friends derived from Malaparte's ideas the conviction that the doctrinal and didactic crusades of the Action Française would achieve nothing, as they had long since suspected, and that insurrectional organizations of a subversive and secret nature should be developed, for as Malaparte said, there was a good chance of getting somewhere even in a "free and organized" state, provided they went about it the right way. Henceforth, they concentrated on working out this right way, preparing their own *technique du coup d'état.* With like-minded friends who remained in the Action Française for several years more, with others in industry, in the Army, and in other leagues, these men were to provide the nucleus for the dangerous and determined secret organizations we shall eventually encounter under the label of the Cagoule.

15

FOREIGN AFFAIRS

The field in which the Action Française remained most active during its years of relative political stagnation was that of foreign affairs; and it was the newspaper's foreign policy that rallied a good many sympathies shaken or lost as a result of its other opinions. Three great related issues dominated foreign policy debates between the wars, all of them closely connected to the internal scene: Germany, Russia, and relations with the Western allies, specifically the British and the Italians.

Toward Germany, the royalist stand never varied: whatever its regime, by sheer bulk and geographic necessity, Germany was the enemy of France, and the first rule of any sound diplomacy must be to keep it down. The question was how this should be done without losing one's friends. A Russian alliance was out of the question: Russia in the grasp of Communism could be nothing but an agent of disintegration and a friend of France's enemies—never an ally of France. The British and Americans were allies by necessity, but their interests, too, often ran counter to those of France, particularly where German reparations and inter-Allied debts were concerned. Always ready to reduce Germany's reparations debts, they were uncompromising about France's duty to repay her allies. Only the Italians, with an efficient dictatorship to supplement their monarchy, allied to France by race and by a common interest in keeping the Germans down, could really be relied upon.

Between the wars these would be the dominant themes of nationalist policy in general and of the Action Française in particular. Their most effective protagonist was Jacques Bainville, a dry and dapper man of great acumen and prestige, director of the *Revue universelle* and a regular contributor to a multitude of other publications. His columns in *Candide,* the *Liberté,* the *Petit Journal,* the *Capital, L'Eclair du Midi,* and the *Nation belge* contributed to spread the point of view of the Action Française among a public and in circles where the journal might never penetrate. Bainville's prodigious journalistic influence was increased by the distribution of his books, all of which after the war sold at least fifty or sixty thousand copies, and many of which are still selling well today.[a]

[a] See Joseph de Pesquidoux's inaugural oration at the Académie Française, quoted in *AF,* May 28, 1937. According to figures furnished by Pierre Gaxotte, the up-to-date sales figures of Bainville's chief works at the beginning of 1961 were as follows: *Histoire de deux peuples,* 88,000;

In 1915, *L'Histoire de deux peuples* had presented Germany and France as eternal enemies, Germany always the threat and France always the threatened. Forty generations of French kings had known how to fight off the German enemy and how, by dividing it, to conquer. But in 1791 the royal protectors had been brushed away, and Germany had been taught a French-invented nationalism, which, with French help, she had soon learned to apply at her teacher's expense. Since then France had been paying for her mistake.

Bainville's next two historical works, which appeared in 1918 and in 1924, were *Histoire de trois générations* and *Histoire de France*. They argued the earlier thesis, but added an idea adapted to the growing public desire for an enduring peace: since the Revolution, the Left, which was the party of the Revolution, had stood for war and had caused it, the country reaping the whirlwind the ideologists had sown. The monarchy, on the contrary, had stood for peace. Late in the nineteenth century, republican politicians had adopted pacifism and anti-militarism as one more demagogic means of courting the peace-loving masses, but inevitably they had blundered into war, as into everything else. Peace and security could be ensured only by a stable central government, which no republican regime could, by its nature, furnish and which only the monarchy, acting according to the natural laws of the country's existence (of which it was itself a part) could provide.

Critics easily found the weaknesses in Bainville's argument, pointing out that there was nothing hereditary or eternal about Franco-German enmity, that Germany had often in the past been more sinned against than sinning, that the reputed superiority of forty royal generations ignored the messy record of most of them as well as their staggering cost to France.[1] Nonetheless, the simple thesis, brilliantly presented in a series of works more readable than scholarly and in a thousand articles, found a wide public avid for general explanations of particular situations. Fayard's yellow-covered series of *Grandes Etudes historiques* sold like hot cakes, but the critics never got beyond a narrow public, and their books gathered dust on library shelves.

The accuracy and foresight of Bainville's political analyses did a great deal to increase his influence. In 1919 he had warned against the writing of a peace too hard for Germany to accept and too soft to keep Germany from getting revenge. He had also warned against the possibility of losing Italy to the camp of the dissatisfied,[b] and had called for concrete pledges that Germany would fulfill the terms to which the treaties bound her. After Locarno, he kept himself busy pointing out the inconsistency of a policy of good understanding with Germany which ran parallel with a series of treaties designed to refuse her any satisfaction in the East. Realistically, he admitted the possi-

Histoire de trois générations, 60,000; *Histoire de France*, 340,000; *Histoire de la Troisième République*, 100,000; *Napoléon*, 180,000.

[b] Thus, commenting on the peace treaty with Bulgaria, *AF*, July 12, 1919: "Un syndicat de mécontents qui réunira Rome, Budapest et Sofia sera une des probabilités de l'avenir."

bility of reconciling the Germans at the expense of the new nationalities that had sprung up on her eastern borders; he did not like it, but it was a possibility. Briand, on the other hand, thought he could both have his cake and eat it—befriend the Germans and make Eastern alliances.

The crucial issue so far as Germany was concerned was Austria, which could be kept from an *Anschluss* only if the Italians were friendly. It followed that France should avoid all awkward and unproductive entanglements, for, just as one could not reassure both Germany and the Little Entente, so one could not easily be friends with both Italy and Yugoslavia. The important thing was perhaps less the choice itself (though Bainville knew what *he* would advise) than the awareness that choice was an element in the game—a realization that seemed to have escaped many pacifists and internationalists. Bainville quite understood that the dream of a United States of Europe, so dear to Briand's heart, was being advanced as one further device to avoid the necessary choice; and he opposed it not only, as others were to do twenty-five years later, on the grounds that it would hand over France with the rest of Europe to German domination, but as essentially a part of the mirage-policy, which, by public demand, seems to have been dominant in the postwar decade.[2]

It was natural that the Action Française should oppose the decision, taken largely under American pressure, to replace the 1924 Dawes plan of reparation payments, which had been working quite satisfactorily, with one that reduced reparations to a level more satisfactory to international financial interests and to the German government. The Young plan of 1929 confidently provided for annual German payments over a period of fifty-nine years; it transformed the political debt, directly collected by the creditor governments from German sources such as customs, railroads, and state monopolies, into a commercial one fed by loans and guaranteed by the German government; and it removed Allied economic and financial controls from German territory. What was more, once the German government had agreed to the scheme, it could pretend to have fulfilled the terms of the peace treaty and could ask, now that its reparations debt was taken care of, that the coercive measures supposed to ensure the treaty's execution be ended—in other words, that the Rhineland be fully evacuated.

Although very little of the Rhineland still remained under Allied occupation, such a request was tantamount to asking the Allies to give up what securities they had in return for promises as yet unfulfilled. But the British endorsed it, and the French government, eager to reassure the world of France's good intentions, followed suit. While the evacuation of the last Rhineland zone held by the French, that around Mainz, was being discussed in the Chamber, the Action Française made desperate efforts to defeat the measure: leaflets and broadsides were tossed all over Paris from monuments, from cinema balconies, and even from the visitors' gallery in the Palais Bourbon. On March 29, 1930, an airplane scattered 500,000 leaflets over the city, and sixty Camelots were arrested for demonstrating outside the Chamber. In spite of this activity, the Young plan was ratified and the evacuation of the Rhineland was approved by large majorities.

On April 5, 1930, the Senate in turn ratified the plan and approved the evacuation of Mainz by 248 votes to 8, with only 8 abstentions. All eight who voted against the measure were royalists, and all argued, as did the *Action française,* that France was abandoning concrete pledges in exchange for promises as yet quite unfulfilled. The following day Maurras acknowledged bitterly that all their warnings had been a failure:

> Complete failure, no doubt, and failure to which there is no remedy . . . failure whose responsibility falls upon the Republic and the Republican parties, all these parties without exception having approved the ratification, royalists alone, with a few honorable personal exceptions, having said clearly . . . what had to be said against this ruin of the fatherland.[3]

During the years that followed the evacuation of Mainz, the nationalists warned repeatedly, and always in vain, against the policy of peace and unpreparedness with which the Center bought the support of the Left and the approval of a misguided electorate which thought that security could be obtained at cut-rate prices. They criticized the interruption of the Maginot Line near Longwy, which left the border from Luxembourg to the sea unprotected.[4] They pointed out the menace implicit in the German election results, in which nationalist (and Communist) extremists showed ever greater strength, and in the bellicose demonstrations of the veteran-recruited Stahlhelm.[5] They pointed out the peculiarly dangerous nature of a German nationalism that would not be satisfied by territorial gains alone: "Germanism," wrote Bainville, "exists outside of 'history,' beyond borders or customs; it is an idea, an ideology, and may claim Riga as well as Strasbourg, Bohemia as easily as Austria. This idealistic nationalism tends to indefinite ambitions." They argued for a Franco-Italian *entente,* founded on a common awareness of menacing German irredentism, and they attacked the hospitality that France extended to anti-Fascists operating from French territory, which could only jeopardize Franco-Italian relations.[6]

"If we listened to the *Action française,*" the *Dépêche de Rouen* complained, "France would be in a permanent state of general mobilization. It would be too exhausting! M. Maurras thinks we never have enough generals, enough guns, enough troops."[7] Such observations were true but unfair: the royalists had wanted a peace that would have so weakened Germany as to permit France to rely on regular long-service troops, doing away altogether with the draft. Such a policy might, indeed, have been costly and exhausting, and it might have ended in a state of "permanent mobilization" but, since no one had wanted it, it had never been tried. And now the revival of German power, together with lively irredentist agitation, would yet call for the military effort everyone had wanted to avoid.

When the news broke in March 1931 that Germany and Austria were on the point of establishing a customs union, preliminary, as everyone had reason to fear, to a total *Anschluss,* the *Action française* cried woe. Germany had at Versailles undertaken to respect Austrian independence, and in 1922, in exchange for a Western loan which helped revive her economic situation, Austria had promised never to abuse her freedom. With Briand himself certain that an *Anschluss* would mean war, the *Action française* surprised no one by saying that none of this would have happened if French troops had stayed in Mainz. Having warned in vain, the royalists could not forbear to say "I told you so!"; and this became the leitmotiv of their growing exasperation.[c]

Bernanos commented in *Le Figaro*: "Since 1908, on every new occasion of misfortune to my unhappy land I have heard the voices of my friends whispering in my ear, 'We were right!' . . . Only, you see, in politics, just as in love, to *have been* right never did anyone any good. To *be* right, that is what matters." The *Action française,* said the former Camelot, was deluding young Frenchmen into thinking "that nothing is more heroic or more noble than to trace exactly, day after day, the graph of French humiliation."[8]

Yet what else could men do who, like Jeremiah, felt themselves to be calling in a heedless desert? "To whom shall I speak and give warning, that they may hear? . . . they cannot harken: behold the word of the Lord is unto them a reproach; they have no delight in it. Therefore I am full with the fury of the Lord; I am weary with holding in." Even so Daudet: "France, nous t'avons prévenue, comme il y a 18 ans. L'heure va sonner. Ouvre tes yeux tout grands et garde-toi!"[9]

As the depression worsened in Germany and unemployment soared to over four million, the brutal and impassioned figure of Adolf Hitler rose on the German political scene. From 800,000 votes won in the 1928 elections, his National-Socialist Party shot up to 6,400,000 in 1930, and to 13,700,000 (37.3 per cent of the total vote) in July 1932. Before these electoral successes had made the Nazis news, the *Action française* had already acquainted its readers with this movement, "one of the greatest dangers for France."[10] Hitler's party, which, like Mussolini's, combined anti-parliamentarianism and anti-Marxism, had a third, most effective, characteristic—anti-Semitism. It would bring war to France and Belgium, warned Maurras, and it would win, for France was in no way ready to meet the challenge. The Nazi majorities, which shocked the unprepared French public, were for Daudet's and Bainville's readers the simple confirmation of repeated and gloomy predictions, not only in the

[c] See *AF,* March 22, 24; *Journal des débats,* March 23, 1931; and the remainder of the Paris press for similar feelings. At the time of Hindenburg's election to the presidency of the Reich, *AF,* April 28, 1925, had quoted its epigraph of November 25, 1918: "Vous comprendrez et connaîtrez mieux la République allemande quand elle aura acclamé Hindenburg comme président."

Action française but in ancillary publications like the *Revue universelle* and *Je suis partout*.[11]

Few others had been quite so farsighted: in some business quarters there was complete unconcern as to whether France was to be ruled by Frenchmen or by conservative Germans. Anything was better than the hell of 1914–18 and the purgatory of the present time, wrote the middle-of-the-road financial rag *Le Parlement et la Bourse*. On the Left, in particular, pacifists and internationalists eager to minimize the menace of German nationalism, Communists trying hard to show the rise of their German cohorts as an encouraging phenomenon, had all ignored or underrated Nazism. Even after the Nazis' thumping electoral gains in 1932, Léon Blum still expressed a wishful hope that Hitler's charm was breaking, and Gabriel Péri found reason to report a brilliant Communist victory.[12] On the first day of January 1933, the *Populaire* predicted the disappearance of Hitler from German politics.[13] Thirty days later, Hitler was Chancellor of the Reich.

From the windows of the French Embassy in Berlin, André François-Poncet looked out upon the river of celebrating Brown Shirts that filled Unter den Linden, lighted by the flames of a monster torchlight parade. "With heavy heart and filled with foreboding" he watched the turbulent stream flow through the night, as many opponents must have done from the shadows. But in Paris the foreboding was less.

Political circles, preoccupied by the fall of one cabinet (Paul-Boncour's) and the formation of another, showed only faint understanding of the new developments in Germany. Socialist Suzanne Buisson, who a decade later would be put to death by Nazis, irritably warned her friends in the Seine Socialist Federation: "Mes petits amis, à force de crier au péril fasciste, vous allez le faire naître!" "Hitler in power or in the wings," said a Radical-Socialist deputy to the journalist Geneviève Tabouis, "what difference does it make?" And one patriotic Catholic remarked to Yves Simon that at least this way the issues were clear and Frenchmen would have less chance of being duped into concessions to men presented as safe conservatives. With an open nationalist in power, at any rate one knew where one stood.[14]

Some people on the Right even expressed satisfaction: Hitler was helping France by making Germany unpopular in England. In any case, said the eternally well-informed sources, he was no enemy of France. He was, in fact, only the enemy of Jews—a regrettable but minor aberration, and a much exaggerated one—and of the Communists, which made up for a very great deal. Gustave Hervé in his *Victoire* was pleased: Hitler would save Germany from the Red tide as Mussolini had saved Italy after the war. Hervé's Social-Nationalists, who had from the first followed the growth of Hitler's movement with sympathy—"toutes réserves faites sur son grossier anti-Sémitisme"—could only be glad.[15]

The position of the *Action française* was less clear-cut: beneath the unvarying hostility, one discerns a trace of respect for a worthy foe. Now that the danger they had warned against was upon them, the royalist leaders were divided between their consistent fear of Germany—more justified than ever, with a strong, determined group of men in power—their hatred of republican politicians who had stood by and allowed these things to happen, and their appreciation of the new German rulers' uninhibited anti-Marxism.[16] There was no particular sympathy for Nazi theory, let alone for the men who applied it; as Maurras's young protégé Thierry Maulnier explained, the Action Française could accept neither Nazi nor Fascist conceptions of national revival. The one postulated the primacy of race, the other the primacy of the state; yet neither of these was the real foundation of a nation: indeed, both race and state, the entity and the concept, were the creation and the result of the national process itself:

> *Racisme* and *étatisme* can result only in imperfect societies. A society in which civilization has attained its highest summit cannot content itself with such definitions; the structure of the rarest and most aristocratic values could not shelter these clumsy, coarse religions whose spiritual poverty is equaled only by their mischief and sterility. Opposed to racialism and statism, nationalism offers the only acceptable way of safeguarding true values, because it is the only social attitude equally free of abstraction and of mystery.[d]

But though it was not in the least friendly, the Action Française wanted to be realistic. In *Je suis partout,* Pierre Gaxotte explained: "The Third Reich is a threat to France: let us be strong, take our precautions, arm. But do not let us be abusive. All these gentlemen of the Left project their partisan hatreds onto the foreign plane."[17]

In this connection, the Action Française derided the widespread indignation at Hitler's anti-Semitism. It would not (at least, not yet) interfere with Bernard Lecache's newly founded International League Against Anti-Semitism (LICA).[e] But, Bainville told his readers, the Jews were still good Germans: a few more Jewish families would emigrate to France and spawn even more Germanophiles and Socialists on the banks of the Seine; meanwhile in *Candide,* Georges Blond criticized the exaggerated emphasis on German militarism and racial excesses in the newsreels: "This sentimental manipulation of newsreels can be dangerous," the future collaborator warned. During the summer of 1933, the *Revue universelle* published a long series of articles on the fate of German Jewry, in which Jérome and Jean Tharaud managed to combine confirmation of isolated acts of anti-Semitic brutality with a reassuring analysis of Hitler's wise moderation in limiting the fury of his followers and a

[d] *AF,* March 30, 1933; see also Maurras in *AF,* July 15, 1936: "L'entreprise raciste est certainement une folie pure et sans issue."

[e] Pujo in *AF,* April 8, 1933: "Nous ne fournirons à la mauvaise foi de nos adversaires aucun prétexte de nous accuser de défendre Hitler dont nous avons les premiers dénoncé le danger."

long historical account explaining the traditional grounds of German anti-Semitism and, as it seemed, almost justifying it.

And what if the Nazis were burning books? The books they burned were either in the line of Marx, or in that of André Gide. In France, reactionary works were quietly left to stifle; at least the German vandals were no hypocrites. As for the refugees, who, in any case, were these pitiable people whom humanitarians lamented over? *Je suis partout* published a cartoon, "The Exodus of Israel," showing a group of ugly-looking German Jews talking to an elderly Frenchwoman at the bottom of a staircase: "How do you know that I can put you up on the second floor?" the woman asks. "Because we pillaged the house in 1914."

There were also men like Einstein; and all branches of the Action Française went up in arms against the proposal to offer him a chair at the Collège de France. With unwonted consideration for the eternal enemy, *Candide* noted that all this could not be very pleasant for Hitler. The appointment of Einstein in France would be an insinuation that in Germany thought was enslaved, genius ignored, science and scientists threatened. Not the truth but the effects of such a step worried the popular weekly: "Vous verrez que les échauffés de la paix démocratique finiront par nous faire des histoires avec les voisins. Nous avons déjà eu la guerre de la justice et du droit. Pour la guerre de la 'liberté spirituelle,' merci beaucoup!"[18]

Now that the Left regretted its pusillanimity of the past, the royalists could be superior: "When we wanted to protect France against invasion," wrote Gaxotte in *Je suis partout,* "we were warmongers. But those who want to go to war with Germany for partisan reasons are called pacifists." Why should good Frenchmen go out of their way, or risk even one hair of their heads, to help the Communists suffering under Göring's tyranny? To the slogans of the Marxist international, suddenly turned warlike since its interests and its members' skins were threatened, French patriots must oppose their own: "Pas de guerre de propagande! Pas de guerre des démocraties!"[19]

The attitude Gaxotte expressed was not adopted for lack of knowledge of what Hitler was up to; it was simply that *sacro egoismo* had more weight than the realities of concentration camps. A front-page article in the *Action française* by a reserve officer, Georges Gaudy, described "the Horrible Life of Prisoners in Concentration Camps," leaving no doubt about the cruelty and degradation of the SS camps. But it pointed out that it was all Germany's affair, and besides, those who suffered were mostly Communists and Jews. "If the Communists had won, they would have furnished as many executioners and tormentors as Hitler's gang has done. What if one day the two were to join forces against us? Obviously, to safeguard herself against such an event, France must have a solid defense of well-oiled machine guns."[20]

This was to be the royalists' position for the next eleven years, often singularly restricting their opportunities of effective maneuver. When Blum proposed a spiritual and material boycott of Germany in August 1933, Daudet, in a lead article in the *Action française*, "Crusade for Israel," opposed the ideas as likely to lead to a war on behalf of Jewry.[21] Why should the French save the Communists, and why should they protect the Jews? Determined to avoid such calamitous coincidence, Daudet ignored the point that Blum and others were calling for precisely what the Action Française itself had so long demanded.

In actual fact, of course, Blum's ideas did differ from Action Française demands, for he was here concerned largely with moral sanctions, leaving rearmament tactfully aside as still unpalatable to important elements of the Left. The royalists could hardly find the source of French revival within a party whose members, like Jean Guéhenno, dreamed of peace and of "a France, modest and disarmed, but strong in her reasonable genius and her revolutionary tradition."[22] Diplomacy without arms, said Frederick the Great, is like music without instruments: Danton knew this much better than Guéhenno did. Hitler knew it, and so did Daudet. Pinpricks in the armor of German pride were senseless when effective measures of defense (at least a re-occupation of the Rhineland) were lacking.[23]

One could not fight the Germans with Jews as allies; even less with Reds. The *Action française* had already criticized the Franco-Russian Nonaggression Pact as something that could have been signed only in the throes of delirium tremens, and the social chronicler of *Candide*, André de Fouquières, a monument of vapid self-importance, set out singlehandedly to save Parisian society from "the snobbery of Bolshevism," praising the anti-Bolshevik Friday teas organized by Prince Golitsyn, Count Ostermann, and their International Committee of Anti-Bolshevik Initiative, criticizing "Bolshevik-lovers in evening dress," and advising his readers in best E. Phillips Oppenheim style to treat with suspicion the beautiful adventuresses, charming of manner and angelic of mien, whose wiles, sustained by Bolshevik generosity, served as a snare for the naïve and the easily inflamed.[f]

Before 1933 had ended, the Action Française was fully persuaded that Hitler hated France and was determined to crush her at the earliest opportunity. But this in no way justified the rapprochement with Russia that certain politicians extolled. "It is an idle fancy to believe that an alliance of any sort could be concluded with the Soviets," wrote Daudet. "The Soviet alliance is a snare and a delusion: if Hitler's Germany is our Scylla, Stalin's Russia is our Charybdis. Both of them desire our extermination."[24]

The antipathy, however, was rationalized: eccentric alliances were to be avoided, first for the ill-effect they might have on France's really reliable allies (Britain's suspicion of Russia was always brought up at this point), then for the adventures they might entail. It was her Eastern allies who had dragged

[f] See *AF*, Aug. 28, 1931; *Candide*, Jan. 21, Dec. 15, 1932. Fortunately, Fouquières added, if the men were an easy prey for Bolshevik temptresses, the ladies were on their guard.

France into war in 1914, and they would probably do so again if she once more became entangled with them. Let Hitler lead Germany eastward and fight the Russians for what he called their satellites. A Franco-Russian pact would only turn German attention to France, which the Nazis would have to liquidate before settling accounts with Russia. Again and again the spokesmen of the Action Française repeated that the Russian alliance could only lead to war.[25]

What, then, was the alternative? Gaudy's well-oiled machine guns: a policy of moral and military preparedness for France itself. It was only reasonable that France could never be truly healthy until the restoration swept away the debilitating corruption of democracy, but some restorative tonics could be administered in the interim. Those who persisted in ignoring the immediacy of the German peril had to be shown how true it was and how near—among other ways, by reading unexpurgated French translations of *Mein Kampf*. In the face of the inertia of a series of governments unwilling to risk Hitler's displeasure, Maurras campaigned untiringly to obtain such a translation.[26] Hitler's friends in France also had to be exposed, likewise the implications of a racism that might turn against Catholics and even against Latins, after it had liquidated the Jews. "But Hitler is of the Right!" someone objected. "Simple child," rejoined Maurras: "He is a German."[g]

When, in November 1934, *Le Matin* published the report of two important leaders of the veterans' movement, Jean Goy and Robert Mounier, of their reassuring interview with a responsive Hitler, Daudet and Maurras advised their readers not to let pacific words fool them, and they blamed Goy not only for meeting Hitler but for reporting his subtle arguments so uncritically.[h] Moreover, by its campaign throughout the winter of 1934–35 for military preparedness, and especially for the lengthening of military service from one year to two, the Action Française played no small part in the vote that, in March 1935, in effect introduced a military service of eighteen months immediately, and of two years beginning in October.[i]

[g] *AF,* Nov. 10, Dec. 29, 1934, April 6, 23, 1935. "Frenchmen must realize," Maurras wrote on the last date mentioned, "that the handful of society scribblers who preach Hitleromania are, for the most part, imbeciles." Among other scribblers the words referred to good friends like Louis Bertrand, with whom a break eventually occurred on this very issue.

[h] *Le Matin,* Nov. 18, 1934; *AF,* Nov. 19, 1934. In a debate between Jean Goy and Colonel Georges Larpent, reported in *AF,* May 11, 1935, Goy argued in favor of reaching an understanding with Germany, because if France defeated Germany in war this would simply bring Bolshevism to the shores of the Rhine. Although agreeing with Goy about the Soviet danger and the shameful deception of the Franco-Soviet pact, Larpent declined to find a solution in a Franco-German *rapprochement.* He changed his mind not long before his death in 1942 and followed Pierre Costantini into the Ligue Française, contributing to a number of anti-Bolshevik publications in occupied Paris.

[i] See Alfred Silbert, *L'Ordre,* March 16, 1935. A campaign against the two-year law followed, and Paris walls were covered with posters clamoring "A bas les deux ans." Alexander Werth tells the story of an old lady just over from England who said to him on seeing the inscriptions, "I suppose M. Laval is one of the donkeys, but who is the other?"

The best argument for the two-year law had come, of course, from the results of the Saar plebiscite of January 1935, when, after seventeen years of French occupation, 90 per cent of the voters in the Saar chose to return to Germany. Presumably because they were all that France had to put up alongside Brown Shirts and Hitler Youth, the Camelots of Lorraine were invited to help the French side on election day, January 13, and, given free transportation, they lent a hand to gendarmes and French authorities in the Saar.[27] But even their cooperation could not change the disheartening results: only 2,124 Saarlanders voted for incorporation into France, against the 477,119 who voted for Germany.

The lesson of this plebiscite was not lost on the Action Française, nor on the rest of France. The Socialists noted that this "victory of national sentiment over class consciousness" had come in a heavily industrialized region where one might have expected resentment over Hitler's treatment of Communists and Socialists at home. But apparently nation was more important to the Germans than class, prosperity and prestige more important than Marxist doctrine. It was easy for the Nationalists to argue that the French should long ago have made a similar choice.[28] But Bainville could draw a further lesson: Nazism, he wrote, had shown its ability to expand in the German world. It would not be content with the Saar. "Prague had better look out." And, warning liberal democrats against the delusion that they would ever be able to appease Germany's greed, he reminded them of Bismarck's dictum that he who seeks to buy his enemy's friendship with concessions will never be rich enough.[29]

What, then, was to be done? Arm, prepare, and secure really trustworthy alliances: Britain, Belgium, Italy. But how trustworthy were they? The British alliance was frequently mentioned—generally, as has been noted, to discourage overtures to Russia, which Whitehall was supposed to disapprove. But in effect, the Action Française had little confidence in British support. Their trust in Britain was clouded by old memories, as persistent in certain minds as they were in that of the woman in *Sodome et Gomorrhe* who refused to believe that it was not the hated English whom France had fought in 1870 and thought France should get her revenge on them. It may be of some significance that the most anti-British of Benoît's novels (*La Chaussée des géants* in 1922, *La Châtelaine du Liban* in 1924) were also the ones that sold the best.[30] Then, of course, British diplomacy in the postwar years, consistently taking the German side against a France too overweening in Whitehall's anxious eyes, had scarcely pleased the French, who had noted ironically that the much-talked-of British sense of justice tended to fade away when Britain's own interests were directly concerned. The British seemed to have a double standard, nationalists complained—one for themselves and one for France.[31]

But as the Action Française now saw it, Britain's behavior could elicit only admiration for a regime that protected its interests so well, and hopes that someday France would learn to do as much for herself. The strongest reason for distrusting the English was that, as Maurice Constantin-Weyer of the Croix de Feu remarked in a private letter to Daudet, their parliamentary system was no better than the French system. The only Allied head of state who knew what he wanted to do and had the energy to do it was Mussolini. And to Mussolini the sympathy and admiration of the Action Française went out most fully.

If England, then, was the necessary ally, Italy was the one for which royalists hankered. To Hitler's malignant racism, Maurras opposed another, desirable and beneficial: that of a Latin league. He treated Mussolini with unusual sympathy and understanding, and regarded lapses of Italian policy from the Maurrassian canon with lenience. Even the Italians' occasional Germanophilia had to be attributed entirely to the calculated insolence and insults of Briand's policy.[32]

As Hitler entrenched himself in power, the moderate French Right—papers like *L'Echo de Paris* and *La Croix*—discovered or rediscovered not only the convenience of Mussolini but also the convenience of his ideas. In October 1933 *Le Temps* published a long article suggesting in effect that it was necessary to move with one's times and that Mussolini's regime was a fine and "modern" one. Stressing French tendencies similar to Fascism which it had until that time studiously ignored, *Le Temps* quoted Barrès (of course), the dynamic yearnings of French youth, and, in addition, "the teachings of a philosopher who died in 1929, Jean Izoulet [an ardent admirer of Maurras], who had thousands of fervent auditors at the Collège de France."[j]

The oblique reference was significant. Here was ground on which the Action Française could agree (more or less discreetly) not only with immediate squabble-torn neighbors on the Extreme Right but also with the broad area of conservatism and with, as Yves Simon called it, "the most important fraction of the capitalist bourgeoisie."[33] Its opposition to any *rapprochement* with Soviet Communism and to any moves apt to alienate Italy supplied the Action Française of the 1930's with the audience it had progressively lost in the preceding decade. Once more the paper's closely reasoned articles began to provide a lead to those who wanted arguments to back their prejudices—in this instance for disliking Communism and liking Fascism.

The efficiency and martial spirit of the new Italian army were extolled, the regenerating effects of Fascist doctrines recommended: "Delicate souls," explained Jacques Delebecque, "are sometimes shocked by the violence that accompanies this immense operation of national revival . . . Too bad for delicate souls! . . . there's not much room left for them in the harsh world

[j] *Le Temps,* Oct. 7, 1933; see also the London *Morning Post,* Oct. 14, 1933, rejoicing over France's coming surrender to the "Fascist ferment in the political and spiritual restoration of the world," and predicting the dawn of a new civilization.

of today . . . The nobility of the end justifies the means that [Fascism] uses to achieve it."[34] In January 1935, Bainville greeted the accords signed by Laval and Mussolini in Rome as "The First Step" toward Franco-Italian understanding. Then, as the year drew on, as Italy's intentions toward Abyssinia became more obvious, and Britain's determination to withstand them became apparent, the *Action française* found itself in a quandary. If conflict between the two predestined allies became unavoidable, the best thing for France was to remain aloof, doing nothing to draw British chestnuts from the fire, but equally nothing to antagonize Whitehall. In any case, an England that had so easily given in to Hitler would not go very far in opposing the equally determined Mussolini.[35]

When, however, the British moved for sanctions and, at the end of August, the French government halfheartedly did the same, the *Action française* became a leading protagonist of the Italian party. It regarded the sanctions as part of a conspiracy against Mussolini, which included London, Moscow, and the Vatican, besides certain unspecified international oil interests. The League of Nations debate in September was reported by José Le Boucher entirely from the Italian point of view, and Professor Gaston Jèze, who had agreed to represent the Abyssinian side, was attacked for his treachery and his insolence to a friendly country.[36]

"Is the Salivary Society, alias the League of Nations, going to drag us into an European Masonic war?" asked Daudet. And *Je suis partout* undertook a wild campaign against Judeo-Masonic warmongers who were driving France into war at the behest of British colonialism and Russian Bolshevism, for the sake of cannibal Abyssinian slavers.[k]

The tension that had risen through the summer came to a head in September, as Italian troops moved up in ever greater force to Abyssinia's borders. Sanctions against Italian aggression, especially if they were effective, could lead to war. The Action Française launched the slogan "Les Sanctions, c'est la Guerre," and it was widely taken up; "Sanctions = war!" cried Léon Bailby in his *Jour*. "Frenchmen, will you fight for Cachin, Blum, and Stalin against Mussolini?" In *Candide,* Gaxotte explained that the war party had

[k] *AF,* Sept. 14, 1935; *JSP,* throughout September and October: see, e.g., Oct. 12, 1935. But cf. Louise Weiss, *Ce que femme veut. Souvenirs de la 3e République* (1946), pp. 153–54. Visiting Belfort at the height of the quarrel about sanctions, Mlle Weiss found the issue quite ignored in a city that had other, more pressing, concerns. Belfort cats had been eating the birds nesting in the trees around the Prefecture. The Prefect had announced he would set cat-traps to protect the birds. The president of the Belfort section of the S.P.C.A. had taken the side of the cats. The friends of birds (and of the Prefect), discovering that the cats' protector owned shares in a bullfighting enterprise, challenged him to ensure that there were no killings in the *corridas* his society organized. As a result, the *corridas* failed and the society went bankrupt. Hungry for revenge, the cat-and-bull man got a friend who was president of a veterans' organization to attack the Prefect, who was now worried about what this would do to his standing at the Ministry of the Interior. A settlement seems to have been arranged at last which involved replacing the traps by contraptions that would prevent the cats from climbing the trees but would not bite their legs off, and the birds were allowed to nest unmolested. Abyssinia was very far away.

three factions: Socialism, Communism, and Masonry. Tomorrow the gravestones would bear the inscriptions "Died for the Tcheka," "Died for the Grand Orient," "Died for the Negus."[l]

On September 22, going one better than either Bailby or Gaxotte, Maurras published a list of 140 members of Parliament alleged to be in favor of sanctions against Italy. These "murderers of peace, murderers of France," would expiate their crime on the day of mobilization. "In the absence of a national power capable of halting your treasonable enterprises, it is essential that supreme measures should be ordered. Your blood must be the first to flow. . . . The murderers of French youth shall be punished by death."[m] And Maurras advised his readers to keep the list tucked away in their wallets and proceed to execute his sentence if and when mobilization was decreed.

On October 3 the Abyssinian war began; and on October 7 the League of Nations declared Italy an aggressor. As Daudet reiterated "Down with sanctions, and down with war!" the Camelots began a series of demonstrations which lasted through the month. A subtler line of action was suggested by the "Manifesto of French Intellectuals for the Defense of the West and Peace in Europe."[37] The Manifesto, largely the work of Henri Massis, criticized England, whose colonial possessions occupied one-fifth of the world, for opposing the justifiable enterprises of young Italy, which were but one more expression of the great colonial achievements of a West fertile in humanitarian enterprises. The document reproved "the false juridical universalism of Geneva," which "placed superior and inferior, civilized and barbarian, on the same footing," and warned against the dangerous fiction that all nations are equal—an idea which had brought about the disastrous alliance of England with all the revolutionary forces that sought to install disorder in Europe.

> The results of this equalitarian madness, confusing everything and all, are before our eyes today: it is in its name that sanctions are formulated which, in order to prevent the civilizing conquest of one of the most backward countries in the world (where Christianity itself has had no effect), would not hesitate to unleash a universal war, to league together all anarchies and all ferment against a nation where in the last fifteen years some of the essential virtues of superior humanity have affirmed and fortified themselves. Such a fratricidal conflict would be not only a crime against peace, but an unforgivable outrage against Western civilization.

Endorsements flowed in—Cardinal Baudrillart, Henry Bordeaux, Maurice

[l] *L'Aube,* Sept. 29, 30, 1935; *Le Jour,* Sept. 22, 1935. *Candide,* September 26, 1935, featured a cartoon by Sennep, "Antifascisme," which showed Blum, Herriot, and Paul-Boncour in a brothel, saying to the Madam, "Donnez-nous la négresse!" Sennep's Jewish father owned the Pennès drugstore chain in Paris.

[m] *AF,* Sept. 22, 26, 1935. A note of September 28 added the names of Léon Blum and Francisque Gay. The list was probably compiled by Anatole de Monzie, a great friend of Italy and a good friend of Maurras.

Denis, Gabriel Marcel, all appended their signatures to a document that was soon taken as representing the cream of Catholic opinion.[38]

The document was followed by a countermanifesto of anti-Fascist intellectuals, and by another, less widely noticed, of Catholics, including Etienne Borne, Henri Guillemin, Jacques Madaule, Jacques Maritain, Emmanuel Mounier, and Pierre-Henri Simon, who did not want to be identified with what the *République* had called "an agglomeration of old academicians and *salonnards* around the Tartarins of the rue du Boccador." But this did not prevent most "respectable" people from applauding those who claimed that France had more to gain from friendship with Italy than from support of Abyssinia or of the League and ought therefore to act accordingly.[n]

Secure in its middle-class approval, the Action Française could join with fellow leagues (the Jeunesses Patriotes, the Solidarité Française, the Green Shirts, and even the Croix de Feu) in great meetings and demonstrations against republican warmongering. Prophetically, it asked "Voulez-vous mourir pour le Négus?" thus assuming the position it would not soon abandon. France, declared *Je suis partout,* was divided into two parties—that of War and that of Peace. The partisans of Peace (who were the partisans of France) were in a position of legitimate defense which justified the most desperate endeavors. The only course open to them, Maurras explained, was to *force* the government to do what it ought to do, and had so far refused to do —say "No" to England.[39]

On October 23, dismayed at the disorders caused by the pro-Italian campaign, the government sought to maintain public order by decree. All parades, demonstrations, and public meetings henceforth required three days' notice and the permission of local authorities; the numbers of the Garde Mobile were raised by one-third; and the procedure for dissolving political leagues was simplified. Pujo's characteristic comment on all this was "Et l'on s'en f——!"[40] but the idea that the Republic might have been stirred to defend itself at last, that measures for dissolution of the leagues were being contemplated, drew hortatory warnings from Action Française satellites in closer touch with other organizations: the leagues alone could bar the way to revolution, affirmed *Candide.* And that was why, added *Je suis partout,* since the next spring's elections would surely see the triumph of the Popular Front coalition, the Left sought to destroy the country's last best hope—the anti-parliamentary leagues.[41]

[n] See *La République,* Oct. 5, 1935; *La Vie catholique,* Oct. 19, 1935; *Esprit,* November 1935. In *AF,* October 24, 1935, Thierry Maulnier answered the signatories of the two manifestoes, "who, unable to choose explicitly between civilization and barbarism, vote instead for *morality.*" There is a serious confusion of thought, argued Maulnier, in treating the human sense of justice as the basis and principle of civilization, when it is only one of civilization's more precious results. Even if the Fascist conquerors of Abyssinia were not acting unselfishly, the results of their action would advance civilization, and human welfare too. Acts should be judged not only by their aims but also by their effects. See also Tabouis, *Vingt Ans de suspense diplomatique,* p. 252.

While Maurras returned over and over to threats which few beside Gay took seriously, Bainville, now seriously ill, pointed out the contradictory position in which partisans of Britain's anti-Italian policy must find themselves, since most of them also supported a Russian alliance that Britain opposed. To preserve British friendship, they sacrificed that of Italy; they then tried to counterbalance the loss of Italian support by seeking that of Russia, which, in turn, encouraged the British to move away from France and closer to Germany. In his last column for *Candide,* the dying historian warned once more against a Russian alliance which could only serve Bolshevik ends by precipitating France into a war with Germany that was alien to her own interests.

The logic of this position led him even further: as he had begun by pointing out after the First World War, all alliances could be awkward. France should, in general, avoid "Les Liaisons Dangereuses." His last article of all, which the *Eclair* of Montpellier printed the day after his death, reflected this evolution toward a new isolationism in which he questioned the usefulness of all the Eastern allies, as liable to end only in a German offensive upon France, while the help these allies furnished would always be less than the help they required. The only possible conclusion to this was drawn a few days later by Maurras: allies were fine, but armaments were better, he wrote: "Armons d'abord!"[42] Here was an *échappatoire* quite as logical, and quite as ineffective, as the internationalist project of a United States of Europe had once been. Consciously or unconsciously, both camps, uncertain what to do, avoided a positive choice by settling for the logical conclusion of their stand, empty though it would very likely, in the circumstances, prove to be.

Just how the new policy worked out soon became apparent, when, on March 7, 1936, Hitler denounced the remaining treaties binding Germany and sent his troops to reoccupy the Rhineland. France was just then immersed in a particularly bitter election campaign, and the government was in the hands of a moderately leftist coalition, headed by Sarraut, which had been chosen for its colorlessness. Two years earlier the German offense might still have met a positive reaction. But more than twelve months of unabated civil dissension had left the country gutless and spent, with hatred enough only for fellow-Frenchmen.

The news from Germany brought a wave of panic to Paris. In Auteuil and the Parc Monceau, humiliation seemed preferable to a military gesture which might threaten property and the social order. To the Palais Bourbon, no question of national security could possibly prevail over electoral concerns. To the working class it meant indignant declarations not backed by any concrete plan to arm. To much of the provincial mass, Germany and Russia seemed almost equally alien and almost equally remote. As a village mayor commented to a newspaper reporter, "Ce qu'il nous faut à nous autres, paysans, c'est qu'on nous foute la paix."[43] For that, however, he had to wait another four years.

Maurras, of course, and this time justifiably, blamed the government and Parliament for the humiliation that France had suffered. But he ignored the soldiers' share in the decision and he forgot that the utter division of French opinion at such a critical time was partly due to his campaigns and to those of his friends and imitators. When, in the 1890's, the republicans concluded an alliance with the Russian Tsar, whose tyranny violated every principle which France held dear, no such campaigns tore the country. Forgetting their own rule of *sacro egoismo,* French nationalists now went to bat against an alliance they detested on principle, and on behalf of a regime that equally on principle they favored. They refused to pick either British or Soviet chestnuts out of the fire, but they did not hesitate to reach into the flames on behalf of Mussolini. In their fear of social reverberations, they were prepared, indeed, to tolerate even the Nazis.

The national unity they exalted could be only of one kind—their kind. And in order to achieve it they would willingly destroy any cohesion of opinion, any basis of public support for *any* government to lean on. To some extent the same could also be said of the parties of the Left, but these do not concern us here. It is enough at this time to say that the men who criticized republicans for a kind of patriotism that said "France, but . . ." knew nothing else themselves. Although one may doubt the sincerity of some professional patriotic ranters, there is no reason and no evidence to doubt the profound love men like Maurras felt for their France. But *"their"* remains the operative word in a vision of France as hate-filled and as exclusive as that of the class warmongers they denounced.[o] "France, but . . ." was not the exclusive monopoly of the Left, or even of republicans.

All this was reflected in what the *Action française* wrote after the March disaster, but with a new note, which would soon become familiar. France, Maurras said, was not ready for war; it was useless to shout and vent one's gall when there was no force available to follow up the shouting. France must regain Italian friendship, drop the Soviet alliance, which had furnished Hitler the pretext for his move, restore the old alliance of the four "civilized" Western powers (France, Italy, Britain, and Belgium), and, above all, rearm in haste. But no republican government could be trusted to undertake the job, and the national union that the moment called for was impossible with republicans and with leftist traitors.

Thus, while inveighing against internal dissensions, the Action Française did a good deal to provoke them. The bitterness of having been right so long and yet ignored, at such a cost, was welling over. Just when it was essential for France to be united, Maurras and his friends insisted on the exclusion of what must have been at least a vast minority, and steadfastly refused the slightest

[o] *Le Crapouillot,* March 1936, p. 51, alleged that when the International Red Cross appealed to its member societies for aid for Abyssinia, the French Red Cross was the only one to refuse.

compromise with a political reality they rejected and denied. The allies that France could have, they did not want; the internal policies that France could try, they would not have; the only advice they could really give was, "First and above all, no war! Then, arm! arm! arm!"[44]

Along with *Figaro* and *Le Jour*, the *Action française* patronized the Comité National de Vigilance des Jeunes Français Mobilisables. Just as they had refused to fight against Italy, they and their friends new refused to march against Germany: the enemy counted less than the detested "friend." "Today, national union is being suggested; but one does not unite with traitors!" they proclaimed. "We are not available for the Jewish crusade."[45] Organized by Thierry Maulnier of the *Action française*, Jean-Pierre Maxence of *Gringoire*, Raymond Prince (a son of the briefly famous Judge Prince, late of the Stavisky affair) of the Solidarité Française, Robert Castille of the Etudiants d'Action Française, and Henry Charbonneau, a Camelot who had gone over to the more effective activities of the Cagoule, the Comité National held a huge meeting in the Magic City Music Hall, at which 4,000 determined young Frenchmen heard the professional anti-Semite Darquier de Pellepoix announce that he, for one, would not fight at the bidding of international plutocracy. No one should count on *them* for a Masonic and Soviet war, the organizers announced amid general enthusiasm.[46]

Only the day before, a left-wing pacifist, Pierre Bénard, had declared that he and his friends would not let themselves be caught by arguments that war was a means of fighting Fascism. Fascism or no Fascism, war was wrong, said the *Canard enchaîné*.[47] War or no war, Fascism was fine, said their opponents. The curious coincidence could not but be noted. The fire-eating Right had overnight adopted conscientious objection and begun to demand peace at all costs.[48] Against the excesses of such a policy, also, the *Action française* tried to exhort. A month earlier, when *Paris-Midi* published Bertrand de Jouvenel's interview of Hitler in which the temperamental dictator had suggested that Germany and France could be friends, José Le Boucher, who had taken over Bainville's foreign affairs column in the *Action française*, warned readers not to let themselves be lulled by soft words. Open Fascists like Marcel Bucard and his Francistes were denounced as *agents provocateurs*.[49] And when *Savez-vous* devoted a whole issue to Hitler and German might, in which René Jolivet argued in favor of a tripartite Franco-German-Italian alliance, Maurras countered, "Hold it!": France was far too weak and could only expect to be dominated in such company.[50]

In an important and closely argued article, Maurras had already admonished patriots against the grievous error of looking with favor on Hitler and on a Hitlerism which could only benefit Germany at the expense of France. He did not like the tendency of certain conservatives to bank on Hitler; international conservatism—the much-talked-about White International—was bound to end in the same divisive errors as the Red International.

> The call for property owners to unite justifies and verifies, absolves and consolidates the call for proletarians of every country to unite. . . . Our internationalists are making an effort to nationalize themselves. It would be a pity if at the same time our nationalists were to lose just what their opponents are after—their patriotic acropolis . . . for the ridiculous love of our chief enemy.

If conservative Hitler-lovers succeeded in giving Germany the upper hand, they would lose freedom, honor, *and* property, and become the slaves of their German masters.[51]

This was good advice, and it would have been well had it been more widely heeded. But whereas Maurras's words of hatred were lapped up by all and sundry, his wiser counsels seem to have been less closely followed, perhaps in part because he himself refused to accept the consequences of his observations. Never pro-German, Maurras could simply not bring himself to surmount his deep and fiery loathing of Germany's enemies, hence the negative quandary in which he would end his life. On the eve of the 1936 elections, all he could say to his votaries was "Vote against Revolution and against War."[52]

16

INTERNAL AFFAIRS

THE FOREIGN BACKGROUND against which internal affairs unfolded has perhaps helped a little to make sense of an otherwise muddled situation, or has at least given some indication of the uneasy state of the world. With the one exception of financial scandals heavy with political overtones, every internal issue of this time was in fact imported from abroad. The depression, the struggles over sanctions and a Franco-Soviet pact, the question of war or peace, the threat that foreign dictatorships constituted to national security and the growing temptation to imitate the efficiency of these regimes—all these were, in essence, imposed or suggested from without. It was at this time, indeed, that initiative slipped out of French hands. The French merely endured; they reacted to, or tried to cope with, situations not immediately of their making. No longer a great power, though with the responsibilities of one, they tried to keep up with the totalitarian Joneses, in itself a frustrating process, made worse under the nagging of smug Anglo-Saxon Smiths. In one sense, to look back to the 'thirties is to see the French, increasingly persuaded that they could not make democracy work, fumbling for some other kind of system, some other kind of rule.

In the growth of this persuasion, the steady propaganda of the Action Française must be allotted its important part. And if the French entered the war with only a mitigated dictatorship, it was perhaps less because of their lingering democratic faith than for a lack of men with sufficient character and ability to grasp the nettle that events held out, and that augmenting sections of the public half-hoped would find a taker.

Indecision and incoherence are the dominant characteristics of the whole decade. The 'thirties saw the disintegration of coherent public opinion, the abandonment and collapse of the policy of Versailles, the division of every political party (even, at last, of the Communists), the open admission by Parliament that the parliamentary system did not work, and the reversal of almost every traditional political slogan or position. Under stress, the pacifists turned warlike and the nationalists opposed war; the Communists turned moderate and the moderates looked for extreme solutions; professed revolutionaries legally in power shunned disturbing reforms, while the defenders of order planned nihilistic campaigns of destruction and revolt. All this occurred against a background of combined indifference and despair, enthusiasm, anger, tremendous intellectual challenge and activity, offering, as one might expect, plenty of scope for the Action Française in the exercise of its peculiar talents. Out of the doldrums of the late 'twenties, as things went increasingly wrong, as the depression crept in and Frenchmen despaired, certain once again that the country was going to the dogs, the Action Française would rise, a phoenix too frequent, and shaking the ashes out of its hair proceed to help turn dismay into despair, disillusion into anger, disaffection into revolt, and trouble into chaos.

Since 1926, cabinets of the Center Right, tending more and more to the real Right, had cajoled an increasingly unconcerned opinion. Moderation at home, pleasant to most of the Right, was rendered acceptable to much of the Left by good intentions abroad, incarnate in the figure of the perennial Foreign Minister, Aristide Briand. As Louis Lafon explained in *Le Temps,* most people, especially in the provinces, had given up trying to understand questions that were quite beyond them. Lacking any real confidence, even people who had once taken a lively interest in politics now left complex political problems to those who professed ability to solve them, and turned toward other, more pleasant or more immediate, concerns.[1]

What seemed surprising to Lafon as he looked back over years that had been full of crises may surprise us somewhat less. The complexity of such problems as those of reparations and exchange control would be unlikely to arouse much interest in a public capable of comprehending only fairly simple issues. Like most democratic publics, the French put their trust in men; and even though this trust was limited, so long as the men delivered the goods, they would be left alone. Only an issue couched in comprehensible terms of acts and personalities, of simple right and wrong, could hope to reach and move the listless mass.

The winter of 1930–31 furnished the beginnings of what anti-parliamentarians wanted—a good scandal, and a cabinet of the Left. The exposure of the *Gazette du franc* in 1928 had drawn the attention of the public to the activities of a financial world closely connected with certain political circles. Any doubts the electorate might entertain about the honesty of its representatives and rulers were reinforced when, in November 1930, three members of Tardieu's cabinet, including the Minister of Justice and former president of the Chamber, Raoul Péret, were implicated in a new financial scandal and thereupon resigned.

The scandal had its origins four years earlier. In 1926, while serving as Minister of Finance under Briand, Péret had done the banker and financier R. Oustric the favor of getting the stock of an Italian concern, the Snia Viscosa, accepted for quotation on the Paris Bourse. The screening services of the Finance Ministry had opposed the move, not because they suspected the company of being unsound, but because the banker had such an unsavory reputation; but with the support of the French Ambassador in Rome, René

Besnard, Péret had overriden the advice of his subordinates. As a reward, the eminent politician had soon thereafter become legal counsel of the Oustric Bank, with a handsome retainer; and Besnard later on had received a similar post with an Oustric subsidiary.

Things were quiet for a time, but in the autumn of 1930 the Oustric Bank and the stocks it sponsored found themselves in serious trouble and were forced to suspend payments. A judiciary inquiry into Oustric's affairs was ordered. Péret, now the Minister of Justice, once more intervened on behalf of his friend Oustric, and when his intervention was revealed, the scandal, which would otherwise have been simply a financial one, inevitably bespattered the political world. The *Action française* could once again exult over fresh proofs of parliamentary corruption.

At the beginning of December, with one minister, one ambassador, and three junior cabinet officers past or present involved in the Oustric affair, the Tardieu government was overthrown by a Senate vote.[a] And following Tardieu, after long days of laborious construction, there succeeded a cabinet much further to the Left, it seemed, than anything that France had known in years, led by the Protestant Radical-Socialist *bête noire* of the Action Française, Théodore Steeg. At last the paper could give itself full rein: when the German menace was at its worst and war might break out at any moment, the Minister of Defense was "mad, vicious, corrupt Barthou," and the Premier—"dit la Rançon de la Partouze," worse still, was the son and grandson of a Prussian:

> Les gens ricanent et clabaudent, mais ils supportent ça tranquillement! Cette charognade qui dure depuis quinze jours, . . . ce défilé d'obscènes, de tripoteurs, de puants, de traîtres, les intéresse sans les émouvoir. Ils ne doutent pas que leurs enfants, leurs biens, leurs vies dépendent de leur atonie, de leur impassibilité et que, sous cet amas de stupres, des centaines de milliers de tombes attendent, guettent leur malheureuse proie![2]

Despite some last-minute desertions (including that of Undersecretary of State for the Interior René Coty, who, four days before, had stoutly declared "One doesn't let people down in such circumstances"), Steeg managed to squeeze a majority of seven out of a Chamber impatient to prepare for Réveillon. The Action Française made the most of the uneasy situation. In January 1931 Camelots shouted down a filmed appeal from Steeg in Paris cinemas, demanded that the film be banned, tore the screen at the Aubert-Palace when the manager refused to follow their injunctions, and successfully intimidated other managers into deleting the offending reel.[3]

Before the end of January, Steeg was out, less than six weeks after taking office. He was replaced by Pierre Laval, a renegade Socialist agreeable to the

[a] The trial of the politicians involved in the Oustric affair ended several months later in their acquittal for lack of evidence.

Right, but the Camelots had liked the taste of action after so long and wanted more. They had had the approval of the moderate Right under a government that was left of Center, and now they could count on its sympathy in a government that was right of Center.

In February 1931 the Camelots discovered an excuse for action in a new play currently showing at the Ambigu, a theater on the Boulevard Saint-Martin. It was an adaptation by Jacques Richepin of a German play about the Dreyfus affair. First the Camelots interrupted loudly, then they threw stink bombs, and soon the fight had moved to the boulevard. Left-wing opponents retaliated a few days later, and soon there were nightly riots throughout most of the area between the Place de la République and the Porte Saint-Denis. As February drew to an end, other right-wing leagues began to join in: the Jeunesses Patriotes appeared, and the Croix de Feu, exchanging blows alongside the royalists and shouting along with them "Vive l'armée! A bas les Juifs!"[4]

The Action Française was attaining its goal: as usual, public sentiment was turning not against the disturbers of the peace but against the occasion of their ire. The play was declared ill-timed, provocative of passions and dissension; Tardieu's *Liberté* complained that the dignity of Paris was affronted by the bloody riots that broke out every evening; the committee of the Croix de Feu wrote Prefect of Police Chiappe asking that the play be banned.[5] And when the Prefect suspended *L'Affaire Dreyfus* on March 4, the *Action française* could claim that its Camelots had been victorious. "Again," crowed Daudet, "the infamous regime we have vowed to destroy has thrown in the sponge. It has bowed to our force." It had certainly bowed to their violence: The royalist blackmail had succeeded, commented the *Petite Gironde*. "They scare the government and it capitulates," wrote the *Populaire de Nantes*. To forestall a possible disturbance, Chiappe had also forbidden Felix Weingartner's scheduled appearances as conductor of the Concerts Pasdeloup. "Thus," angrily wrote the Socialist *Populaire,* "nationalism and Fascism, impudently flaunted, have won a double victory in a single day."[6]

The *Dreyfus* rioting had come just as the Oustric scandal was continuing its depressing way through inquiry committees of the Chamber, and on the eve of another scandal, this one concerning air-mail carrier contracts, and involving a leading figure of the Center parties, Pierre-Etienne Flandin. In mid-March, the matter of *L'Affaire Dreyfus* was broached in the Chamber, where the successful pressure of the Camelots was generally acknowledged and compared with similar shows of violence in Berlin. A week later, the play, freed of the prefectorial ban, attempted a comeback, but managed only two showings. Despite contingents of police and a heavy guard furnished by the Jeunesses Républicaines, more riots organized and led by Camelots forced it to give up. On March 30, the *Action française* could proclaim that its victory over the Ambigu was complete.[7]

In the right-wing weekly *Carrefour,* Léon Treich could see nothing but weakness and hypocrisy in a government that could not make up its mind either to ban a show or to put down those who disturbed it:

> These days, a handful of resolute, disciplined, well-led young men can scoff at the authorities and direct events. Theoretically, we cannot deplore this too much. Practically, given what we know of the weakness, the cowardice, sometimes the worthlessness of the authorities, and what we also know of the Camelots' national sentiments—practically, we conceive more than one hope.[b]

The Action Française was coming to life. In *L'Avenir de l'Oise,* Pierre-Louis Berthaud, later of the national council of the Gaullist RPF, counted up the Republic's enemies and found the Action Française to be the only open and official one: "But what an enemy! What an admirable fighting force! . . . A good part of the country's intelligentsia has enlisted in [it]—Daniel Halévy, Lucas-Dubreton, Farnoux-Reynaud sympathize." And, meaningfully: "If we cannot find balance and stability under the republicans, we shall have to seek it elsewhere." Henri Roux-Costadau's nationalist weekly *Libre-Opinion* said as much, more frankly: "If the Republic will not or cannot reform itself, we shall have to let it die, and we shall cry, Long live the King."[c]

Laval's was the sixth cabinet in the twenty months following Poincaré's resignation in July 1929. Once again, republican instability was becoming flagrant, and the devious parliamentary games which the country was ready to ignore in times of ease were beginning to jar as things got tighter. And things got ever tighter as the year went on. In May the Vienna Kreditanstalt closed its doors, ushering in the disintegration of Central European economy. In France, so far comparatively untouched, business began to feel the recession. Foreign markets shrank, then closed. Industrial production declined, and with it working hours, and with those take-home pay. Great banks like the Banque d'Alsace-Lorraine, the Banque Nationale de Crédit, and the Comptoir Lyon-Allemand managed to avoid bankruptcy, which could mean wider financial collapse, only with the discreet help of the Ministry of Finance. As the national revenue decreased, budget deficits rose, and economic problems became a parliamentary concern, resulting in even greater political instability.

But while these developments came slowly, the Action Française was fortifying its position, largely at the expense of internationalists and pacifists. Its first reason for self-congratulation was the part it played in preventing its old enemy, Aristide Briand, from becoming President of the Republic. Briand's candidacy, hastily and badly contrived, would probably have failed in any

[b] *Carrefour,* April 3, 1931. Treich was a regular contributor to *L'Ordre,* founded by Emile Buré in 1929 with the help of monarchist sympathizers to support the "national" cause.

[c] Quoted in *AF,* April 28, May 2, 1931. Roux-Costadau was deputy of the Drôme from 1910 to 1919.

case before the hostility of a Senate that backed his rival, Paul Doumer, and also of Clemenceau's old friends, who remembered how Briand sabotaged their leader's chances for the Presidency in 1919. But the Action Française nevertheless did its share to defeat him. It organized student demonstrations, and plastered Paris with posters proclaiming Briand the candidate of Germany and urging everyone to vote for the man who was backed by Blum, Malvy, and the Papal Nuncio.[d] Camelots were sent in groups of two and three to work on members of Parliament whose vote on May 13 seemed still in doubt. Their orders were to pursue them night and day, on the street, in Parliament, and at home (even to the bathroom if necessary, said Réal del Sarte), warning them of the dire consequences of voting for Briand. Georges Mandel is said to have estimated that these maneuvers achieved their convincing or intimidating purpose with about thirty of the men at whom they were directed.[8] Briand did lose by only forty-one votes—401 to Doumer's 442—but whether the Camelots actually swayed thirty of those votes one cannot be sure. Once more, however, and for immediate ends, the Action Française and "Clemencistes" seem to have been in touch, and although the latter cannot be denied their share of Briand's failure, the *Action française* could claim some of the kudos for itself. It did not fail to do so.[9]

Briand's defeat was a good point scored, and his death, less than a year later, "d'une injuste mort naturelle" was greeted with glee tempered only by regret that "his country's enemy" had thus escaped the punishment he deserved.[10] But the nationalists' real moment of glory came in November, when they broke up a great pacifist meeting at the Trocadéro.

On November 27, 1931, the International Disarmament Congress organized by Louise Weiss's Ecole de la Paix and by her anti-Fascist weekly *Europe nouvelle* held its final meeting in the great hall of the Trocadéro. The several thousand spectators, including officials and distinguished guests from some forty countries, were supposed to hear addresses by Painlevé, Salvador de Madariaga, and numerous other famous speakers. The Ambassadors of all the great powers were there, along with Jean Hennessy, Henry de Jouvenel, Pierre Cot, Lord Robert Cecil, Philip Noel-Baker, old uncle Tom Cobley, and all. The proceedings, presided over by Herriot with all the aplomb of an old *universitaire,* were being broadcast; and this meant that radio listeners were able to overhear the din that broke out almost from the very start.

Acting in concert, Camelots, members of the Croix de Feu, and Jeunesses Patriotes, drowned out the speakers' voices, overcame first the ushers and then the meager *service d'ordre.* Singing "La Madelon" and "Auprès de Ma Blonde," they took the platform by assault, drove away its eminent occupants, the police who tried to come to their rescue, and finally the public itself.

[d] When, on election eve, three Camelots arrested for putting up posters were found to be a plumber, a clerk, and a delivery boy, Maurras commented that this proved his was not a class party; see *AF,* May 14, 1931.

Startled radio listeners heard all the tumult in the hall, even Herriot's exasperated injunction to one of the inaudible speakers, "Speak up! Have a glass of water!" But in the final assault the microphone was broken, and no one heard a still little-known figure, Colonel Count de La Rocque of the Croix de Feu, attempting to read above the roar on the platform a statement on "our reasons for refusing to disarm."[11]

What the nationalist press on the following day described as the victory of the Trocadéro—and in fact, as at Cádiz in 1823, a *coup d'audace* had carried the night—marked for some observers of the diplomatic corps the end of an era. For France, it marked the re-emergence of the nationalist leagues.

No prosecution followed what *L'Oeuvre* called a Fascist coup. When the Chamber discussed the affair on December 8, Premier Laval brushed aside the protesting Left, and Maurras, marking the new governmental orientation, rejoiced that with their attack Camelots and other ligueurs had been the occasion of the debate in which Laval could take up position as the defender of order and of the fatherland. In *L'Ordre,* the former Camelot Jacques Debu-Bridel greeted the failure of "Anti-France."[e]

All the nationalist groups claimed the honors of the Trocadéro evening, and certainly de La Rocque had made his presence felt in a way the office-bound Action Française leaders seldom did. But, perhaps on the strength of their past record, royalists received most of the credit, or blame. The *Vie catholique* saw in Maurras and Daudet the leaders of "the nationalist conspiracy";[12] and some of the inspiration for the action may very likely have come from a similar breaking up of a great pacifist rally in the Bordeaux Athenaeum several months earlier. On that occasion Camelots chased away a brilliant gathering, including a Senator and a whole covey of academic figures.[13] At any rate, the idea now caught on, and in the ensuing months Camelots broke up pacifist lectures and meetings at every opportunity.[f] Once again it looked as if the nationalists were riding the crest of a still-rising wave, in more or less coincidental conjunction with a government group.

As the elections of 1932 approached, Laval's orientation became more clearly reactionary.[14] With Briand gone from the Foreign Office, the cabinet had lost the last tinge of what passed for progressivism; and Laval was doing his best to spur an electoral reform which, in doing away with the second ballot, might help the reasonably unified moderates to gain a clear majority over the undisciplined Left.

But Laval fell in February 1932, voted down by a hostile Senate, and the hopes of the Right seemed about to be dashed. It seemed more than a mere

[e] *JOC,* Dec. 8, 1931; *AF, L'Oeuvre, L'Ordre,* Dec. 9, 1931. Six years later, Ybarnégaray, who stood close to de La Rocque, testified in court that Minister of War André Maginot, and perhaps Laval himself, were not unconnected with the night's events. See his evidence in Pierre Dominique, *Vente et achat,* p. 53.

[f] In January 1932 alone they seem to have done this at Argenteuil, Béziers, Challans, Mazamet, Montpellier, Périgueux, and Toulouse; see F[7] 13203-5 for numerous reports.

coincidence that the Action Française, which had only two months before demonstrated its control of Left Bank student organizations at the cost of several hard clashes,[15] should foster wild student demonstrations around the Senate. Beginning on the day of Laval's fall to the strains of ditties like

Les sénateurs à Charenton
tontaine
Les sénateurs à Charenton
tonton

which alternated with

Les sénateurs sont des cochons
la faridondaine
la faridondon

the riots snowballed until, by the time Tardieu took office five days later, the Luxembourg gardens had been closed, the Latin Quarter was filled with police, the Senate was guarded by troops, and the Left Bank had been put in a state of joyous siege. Though not averse to molesting passing politicians like Senator Henry Chéron, against whom they held a grudge, the large student crowds were not in an ugly mood; they gathered daily after lecture hours, around eleven o'clock in the morning and four in the afternoon, but more or less dispersed for lunch and again for dinner, between seven and eight.

It was, it would seem, more a sport than a revolution. But their activities may well have hindered Painlevé's efforts to form a cabinet, which both the Center and the Right stubbornly refused to join. On February 20 Tardieu finally got together a cabinet remarkably like that of his predecessor, one that included Laval himself, and many observers felt that the Action Française had played an important part in his return to power.[g] The *Frankfurter Zeitung,* too, could not but remark that Tardieu and Laval had found in the Action Française an ally (though perhaps an undesirable one).

It is always difficult to tell the extent to which the Action Française was acting on its own initiative, but, as the *Frankfurter Zeitung* said, the Camelots' cries "Down with the Senate," "Vive Tardieu," and "Vive Laval," played their part in the tactics of Tardieu and Laval during the critical period of cabinet-making negotiations. Once again Camelot was being used as a generic term for much less definite and more inclusive groups. Most of the shouts probably came from unattached students or from followers of Taittinger, but it would seem that the Action Française was quite justifiably considered as being largely responsible.[16] As Nicolas Lerouge wrote in the *République,* "ça crevait les yeux."[17]

The Senate had not liked the electoral reform that Laval proposed; when,

[g] One of them was Albert Bayet, an important left-wing journalist who was a contributor to many republican publications and the editor of the anti-Fascist weekly *La Lumière.*

at the new cabinet's prompting, the Chamber adopted it nevertheless, it was Chéron, who had been kicked and manhandled by students the week before, who reported on the bill to his colleagues in the Senate:

> I fear for democracy: I fear the forces of money and of violence. [Hear! hear!] I do not understand why gilded youth should be allowed to make itself master of the streets [Hear! hear! Applause on the left. Exclamations on the right], apprentice itself to revolution, outrage Parliament [applause on the left, interruptions on the right]. In any case, it is not the moment, when universal suffrage will have to look out for all the traps set for it and for the collective aberrations produced by exasperated parties [Hear! hear!], to reduce the guarantees that election to Parliament requires.[18]

The question of electoral reform having been provisionally, hence finally, shelved, the riots around the Luxembourg Palace would appear to have had a twofold result: they kept the Left from power, but they also made an unfriendly Senate quite determined not to pass the measure on which the general elections would depend. This less desirable result could not have been predicted, however, except to the extent that Senate prejudice against the electoral bill was already strong.

The Action Française took little active part in the election battles of 1932, and then mainly in the second ballot. Of all the candidates to whom it lent support in the Paris area where it was traditionally strongest, only three out of thirteen survived, and, with but one exception, those it opposed (like Taittinger in the 1st Arrondissement and PDP [Christian Democrat] Vice-President Jean Lerolle in the 7th) got in. As always, electoral influence was its weak point. Strong appeals to royalists of Arles to vote for one of Maurras's fellow-*félibres,* Professor Emile Ripert, resulted in a gain of only 152 votes on the second ballot. Meanwhile, in places like Bordeaux, royalist interest seems to have leaned to solid right-wing Catholic or conservative candidates, even when, as in the case of Philippe Henriot, personal relations were far from good.[19]

Although open royalist support may have cost a candidate votes, as was apparently the case with Louis Marin, confidential orders were perhaps occasionally more effective, as certain unlucky candidates seem to have believed, and the paper's customary hostility to men of Taittinger's party sometimes gave way before personal appeals for help.[20]

Between the first and second ballots, on May 7, President Doumer had been assassinated by a deranged White Russian, Paul Gorgulov, who called himself the president of the Russian Nationalist Fascist Party.[21] At first, the Right had hoped the killing might help it in the second ballot to re-establish positions that had been shaken in the first. Being a Russian, Gorgulov must be a Communist. Unfortunately, the confusion could not be kept up very long,[h] and the second Sunday's voting confirmed the shift begun on May 1. The Socialists and the Radicals had turned the tables on the Right. "Brilliant victory of the Left," commented *L'Oeuvre,* dazzled. "In the new Chamber, the old opposition has the absolute majority." And *Le Temps* noted anxiously not only the Socialist successes but, what was worse, "l'affaiblissement du centre."[22]

Though badly galled, Daudet saw things more clearly when he described "L'Effroi des vainqueurs."[23] Four years of opposition had helped to reconcile Radicals and Socialists for electoral purposes but had not brought them close enough to rule together. The Radicals had voted with the rest of the National Assembly against Socialists and Communists to replace Doumer with moderate Albert Lebrun. In the same way, they would end by having to seek moderate support for the government they would form in June. It was not Herriot's fault alone: the Socialists refused to participate in a bourgeois government. But, blinded by the formulas they seemed to share, neither Socialists nor Radicals could see that their failure to agree reflected a much deeper division, in which Radicals, of necessity, stood with moderates, with whom they had much more in common than with would-be Marxist labor.

Whatever the causes, Herriot at any rate formed a cabinet in which, as Tardieu said, not only were there no Socialists, but from which even the left-wingers of the Radical-Socialist party were absent.[24] The inconsistencies that Tardieu pointed out would affect Herriot's entire short-lived government. The financial measures demanded by the deteriorating economic situation had to be either orthodox, involving strict economies, or drastic, involving taxation at one end and large-scale public spending at the other. All groups outside the Marxist Left favored orthodox measures, and so did Herriot's liberal Finance Minister, Germain Martin. The government's proposals, opposed by Socialists, were as strongly opposed by the Right and the Center, which valued political opposition above practical agreement. So, having lost a fraction of his own majority with whom he disagreed, Herriot could not make up for it with the support of Center parties whom his proposals suited. And, not to be outdone in inconsistency, the government itself, keener on holding office than on solving grave problems, dared not insist on measures it well knew to be necessary, in order not to rock a very leaky boat.

The so-called left-wing majority threatened to dissolve over every concrete economic issue. On the other hand, campaign slogans were still too fresh in people's minds to allow any sort of departure from them in the interests of cooperation with the conservative Right in introducing the moderate measures

[h] *JSP,* May 14, 1932, however, argued that, if not a Red, Gorgulov must have been put up to his crime by *agents provocateurs.* After seven months' reflection, Daudet had a better idea; in *AF,* Dec. 31, 1932, he announced that Doumer had been assassinated in an ambush, for having dared to oppose Briand in the Presidential election: "il fallait qu'il expiât ce crime de lèse-Allemagne. Gorgouloff n'a été qu'un instrument—déséquilibré—de cette police de Sûreté générale dont les crimes ne se comptent plus."

both sides favored. "The parliamentary machine has broken," rejoiced Daudet, somewhat prematurely.[25] But it would soon break down, under the power of a "Left" more inconsistent than the moderate Right that had governed France with hardly an interruption since 1926.

The Radicals, who, out of power, had found it reasonably easy to cooperate with the conservatives, found it much more difficult to construct, let alone to maintain, majorities of the Left. But they could not acknowledge, not even to themselves, that as a party they were now far removed in interests and make-up from the uncompromising Marxists, with whom they had little left in common besides memories. In this confusion, which spelled the end of a parliamentary system unable to function when too many participants could neither formulate their policies nor, if they succeeded in doing that much, stand by them, the uncompromising Right played as important a part as did the intransigent Left. If it was Blum who first refused a share of the left-wing coalition that Herriot had for a moment conceived, it was Tardieu who, rejecting Herriot's overtures toward the Center, rendered impossible the kind of moderate alliance that had succeeded under Poincaré. The Socialists had repulsed Herriot because they were aware that a coalition with the Radicals would probably be too conservative. But did Tardieu's friends of the Center reject Herriot's offers because they thought he would not be conservative enough? Is it not possible that certain sections of the Right—Tardieu himself, for one—would think a Radical alliance too conservative for *them*?

The confusion between Radicals and Marxists which helped to disintegrate the Left—a confusion, if we may use the terms unhampered by customary associations, between conservatives and radicals of the Left—had its counterpart on the Right. The Right, too, had its radicals and its conservatives. The many real conservatives in the ranks of the parliamentary Right were hampered in joining their true fellows in a coalition with Herriot by men who, like Tardieu, were not conservatives at all, who carried reform's babies on their arms, and whose aim was far from the moderate policy that Herriot and Germain Martin proposed.

What that aim was is hard to define; it was perhaps essentially a change in the form of the country's government, a change which moderate conservatives, just like their Radical counterparts, did not envisage. But in their work, the radicals of the Right were helped by the nationalist leagues, the most articulate among them being the Action Française, which, by continually harping on the difference between Right and Left, rendered the moderates' reconciliation far more difficult, artificially emphasized theoretical differences, and forced the confusion (as to who belonged on Left or Right) to continue indefinitely.

Clearly, the anti-republican, anti-parliamentary campaigns of the extreme Right would prove helpful to men who, like Tardieu, sought to keep political rivals apart and to prevent their possible cooperation. On the other hand, the work of the irreductible Right, carrying the conservatives with them, away from any effective cooperation in the Assemblies, and making for unstable majorities in an ineffective Chamber, created conditions most favorable to the development of anti-parliamentary leagues.

The first opportunity for these leagues to demonstrate, again largely under the impulse furnished by the Action Française, came when a payment of France's war debt to the United States fell due in December 1932. For years, France had tried to link inter-Allied debts to reparations payments, against the opposition of the United States. As the French gave in to successive measures designed to relieve the economic strain on Germany (which finally stopped all reparations payments under the Hoover Moratorium of June 1931), the impression grew in France that the United States had a moral if not a legal obligation not to demand payment of war debts, so long as reparations had not been resumed.

Since most of the French concessions had been made under American pressure, the feeling was easy to understand. But the Americans, persuaded that Europeans found no difficulty in raising money for murderous armaments which men like Senator Borah condemned as useless and costly, saw no reason why obligations that had been freely and knowingly incurred should not be discharged by solvent debtors. No French politician ever seriously questioned the Americans' legal right to demand that the debt be paid, but they all understood that public opinion was behind the slogan "Not a Cent to the States." As one of them said to Geneviève Tabouis, "I'm in the opposition, I've got to take advantage of the possibilities the situation offers."[26]

Clearly, the Action Française was not alone in its opinion, and it used it to advantage. The crucial debate on whether France would undertake her payments was scheduled to take place on Tuesday, December 13. On the preceding Saturday, students in the Latin Quarter began rioting at the *Action française*'s summons, and on Monday demonstrations and fights spread from the Boulevard Saint-Michel in the morning down the Boulevard Saint-Germain and even across to the Right Bank. On Tuesday the rioting continued from the Panthéon up to the Invalides. Police announced over two hundred arrests, the press six or seven hundred. By midnight, said the Paris *Herald Tribune*, the crowds around the Chamber numbered some thirty thousand, and the building was practically in a state of siege, some six thousand police and Gardes Républicaines having been brought out as a supplementary guard.[27]

That night, Herriot, whom a similarly irate crowd had nearly tossed into the Seine six years before, was voted down by a very large majority, and the payment of American debts with him. For once, as the *Journal des débats* declared, the demonstrations expressed public opinion pretty faithfully. As one of the riot's chief animators, Daudet once again exulted over "The Action Française's new victory."[28] There was little to justify his claim, except that the Action Française, too, had campaigned, in its usual, vigorous way. The measure it opposed, and the government with it, failed, but it is doubtful that in this instance its intervention was in any way decisive.

Few political commentators, however, questioned the importance of its interventions. Nicolas Lerouge in the *République* considered that it was the royalist solution that had won. Pierre Dominique, once president of a section of the Action Française but now an earnest critic of the royalist movement, also insisted on the royalists' role in Parliament's decision. The riots they had instigated had influenced eighty votes, affirmed Xavier de Magallon. In *L'Informateur,* Gaston Cagniard was equally convinced: "Once again the Action Française has shown itself the only true opposition force in France, the only organized force capable of energetic action in the national interest."[29]

Energetic action in the national interest was increasingly called for as the world depression began to invade France. Autarky and protection became the battle cries of anxious farmers and businessmen, like the manufacturers of the Grains Clérambourg, who boosted their product as "a French laxative adapted to French bowels." In the summer of 1932, hard times had forced a number of political papers to cut down or close shop altogether. Francisque Gay's *Aube* was temporarily suspended, Hervé's *Victoire* announced that it would appear only once a week during the summer months; *L'Homme libre* was reduced to two pages; in Toulouse, the liberal and democratic *Télégramme,* which had tried to compete with the royalist *Express du Midi,* had folded.[30] The *Action française,* however, continued, its newsstand circulation still around 33,000, its subscriptions still numerous. Then, in November, even it had to cut down; the Sports and Literature sections were cut in half, but the Military, Economic, and Social pages remained untouched.

If the depression that struck the rue du Boccador was fairly mild for the time, elsewhere it was becoming severe. Dropping produce prices were hard on farmers; small businessmen and investors had been suffering for months. During the winter of 1932–33, which ushered in the first really hard years for France, at the barracks gates in Paris, every freezing night, long lines of people who had never begged before waited, shivering, for scraps of food left by soldiers. The sight of members of Parliament voting to maintain their own fat salaries and then voting 350 millions' credit for an Austria that might join Germany against France any day, or threatening to pay American debts with money for which there seemed to be dire need at home—all this revolted more people than just the men of the Action Française. No wonder Colonel de La Rocque considered that La Patrie was in danger.[31] There was unlikely to be any improvement of its state under the cabinets that followed Herriot's. But, as always in a time of insecurity and fear, the state of the Action Française was getting better.

Herriot's fall had been followed by an attempt to reunite the left-wing majority of the Cartel des Gauches under the former Socialist, Paul-Boncour; but Paul-Boncour lasted hardly more than a month. The fiscal projects of

Finance Minister Chéron, who tried to cut budgetary expenses, aroused the wrath of everyone who was affected by his proposals, and indifference to politics became hostility. Taxpayers refused to pay their taxes; in Burgundy, Normandy, and Languedoc rebellious farmers and vintners ran tax inspectors out of towns and farmsteads; veterans met to cry down proposed pension cuts; students demonstrated against the suspension of competitions and examinations, burned fat Chéron in effigy, and clashed with the police. By mid-January 1933 the Latin Quarter was seething, and the Law Faculty, a stronghold of integral nationalism, was in something like a state of siege.

In the *Journée industrielle* economist Claude-Joseph Gignoux railed against governmental anarchy. By means of the students and the publications under its control, the Action Française did its best to spread the anarchy throughout France. *Je suis partout* criticized the Taxpayers' Federation for showing willingness to cooperate with the authorities and praised the veterans for organizing to oppose the Cartel. It cheered on the peasants of Florent Agricola's Agrarian Party who had flocked to Paris in such numbers to protest against hard times that even the Salle Wagram could not accommodate them. And it sent its Camelots and its *ligueurs* to lend a hand in the great meetings held by the Taxpayers' Federation at Magic City Hall, and at the Cirque Bullier.[32]

It was under the impulse of these active and alien elements, who furnished their *service d'ordre* and a good few of those who demonstrated in their name, that the taxpayers attempted, on the night of Paul-Boncour's fall, to march on the Elysée Palace and on the Chamber, clashing with police and stirring up the bourgeois residential quarters between the Pont de l'Alma and the Palais Bourbon.[i] While Daladier tried to form another cabinet, the student demonstrations continued, outside the Chamber and elsewhere in the city; and industrialists and businessmen meeting at the Salle Wagram criticized the mess that had resulted, they thought, from governmental impotence and party politics. In an epitaph on Paul-Boncour's short term in office, *Candide* noted that if his ill-fated government had done little else, at least it had witnessed the awakening of forces that had been asleep—taxpayers, peasants, businessmen had begun to stir.

During the month of February the agitation began spreading from Paris throughout France: every Sunday was the occasion for scores of protest meetings, increasingly vehement and sometimes even bloody. On February 12 alone, 3,000 taxpayers met at Niort, 2,000 farmers at Vervins, 4,000 others at Vienne, 3,000 veterans at Nîmes; taxpayers and farmers joined at Clermont-Ferrand, truck drivers at Saint-Brieuc, and so on. In the west, a brutal, energetic, hard-drinking and hard-hitting peasant agitator, Henri Dorgères, was

[i] Commission d'Enquête, *Rapport général,* Annexes, I, 10, 18, 117–18. The police authorities were persuaded that the Action Française was using and manipulating the Taxpayers' Federation. Behind the leader of the Taxpayers, Large, stood his secretary, Devauzelles, also known as Sainclair or St. Clair, who belonged to the Action Française.

mobilizing the farmers by the thousand and carrying his rabble-rousing talents out into other agricultural regions.

The *Quotidien* had to take notice of the fact that the small bourgeoisie was waking up: "petits fermiers, petits agriculteurs, petits bourgeois. Tout ce Tiers Etat aujourd'hui se dresse." In the *Journal,* Clément Vautel concurred: in the very circles where fatalism had been most apparent, opinion stirred and kicked.[33] It would be these forces of the Third Estate which, incoherently enough, would dominate the next eighteen months. And yet, even as the day-old Hitler cabinet was affirming its power in Berlin, the Bonapartist historian Louis Madelin, fascinated by socialism and by what he called the collectivist menace, could see only two alternatives: revolution or monarchy.[34]

It was this moment that the *Action française* considered opportune for publishing a manifesto of the Pretender, which the Duc de Guise addressed to his fellow Frenchmen in time of national concern. The royal recipe for dealing with depression was of the most orthodox kind. It attacked the internationalist State-centered system, which, so far as he was concerned, led straight to socialism, the tyranny of which must mean both economic ruin and a foreign yoke. The State should resolve to return to private enterprise the services which it itself ran badly and at great cost. Freed from bureaucratic control, education, social insurance, railroads, telephones, tobacco and match monopolies, all would function better and give better results. Thereafter, reassured by the presence of an *honest* and *national* State (presumably, a very unassuming one), capital now in hiding would reappear to enliven business and industrial activity.

But this return to prosperity was hampered by the selfishness of political parties, by the elective system they manipulated so cleverly, and, behind governmental factions, by the hidden hand of international finance. With these obstacles only a royal dictatorship could at the moment cope. Monarchy was not a party: its authority could rest on corporate and estate assemblies, cut through the confusion of red tape, and restore stability and national unity, of which it was the incarnation. The choice, said the Duc de Guise, lay between the authority and liberties of monarchy on the one hand and the oppression of inevitable socialist anarchy on the other.

The manifesto did not pass unnoticed. A complete version appeared in the *Petit Bleu, L'Ordre,* and the *Journal des débats,* and copious quotations or analyses were given by *Le Temps, La Liberté,* and *L'Echo de Paris.* To the Radical right's *République* it was "a symptom," and, significantly, its echoes could be heard even in union sheets like the postmen's *L'Action.*[35] In the *Gazette de Lausanne* friendly Maurice Muret reported that the offspring of a good many republicans had horrified their parents by becoming royalists. "Young men are royalists in 1933, as their grandfathers were republicans under the Second Empire."

But did this mean that they were really royalists, or that once again royalism was the symbol of anti-parliamentary opposition and disgust? One finds the belief that democracy was on the decline expressed in diverse quarters, along with an appreciation of the apparent successes of the methods of neighboring dictators. The shrewd Romanian Foreign Minister, Nicolaie Titulescu, in Paris to oppose the Four Power Pact, was struck by the impression that Hitler and Mussolini had made in parliamentary circles. An inquiry into the desirability of a dictator for France which was conducted by a great morning newspaper found that the idea met with general favor. Dictatorships did not seem to have worked out so badly for those who had tried them, and many Frenchmen, so the newspaper said, thought it would be worth a chance. Only the dictator himself was lacking.[36]

The Duc de Guise insisted that the potential and legitimate dictator was right there. In a letter to Le Provost de Launay, a Paris municipal councillor more Bonapartist than monarchist in inclination, the Pretender pointed out, not with any particular originality, that most Frenchmen were royalists without knowing it, and that the superior power, above factions and factional interests, could be wielded only by the traditional and hereditary leader of the nation—in other words, by himself. Reprinting the letter, the bien-pensant *Revue hebdomadaire* indicated that, although it was far from royalist, it could not help seeking, either in the Pretender or in someone else, some alternative to the existing regime.[37]

The older generation wanted to return to better days, the younger wanted to advance; anti-capitalism, anti-materialism—to so much young people on both the Right and the Left could generally agree.[38] And in the spring of 1933 a new party was founded with that in mind—the Social-National Party of Jean Hennessy and Alfred Fabre-Luce, very rich men, both tempted by ideas of "the Left," both dazzled by Hitler's success.[39] More significantly, while Hennessy and Fabre-Luce were trying, not very successfully, to copy Hitler, another tribute was paid dictatorship from more influential quarters. Addressing the Congress of the UNC (Union Nationale des Combattants) in late May 1933, Victor Beauregard, a former president of the great veterans' union, pointed out to loud applause the possibility that in a very short time France might find herself in a situation that called for intervention of "a young, powerful, solid force." This force, said Beauregard, could be none other than that of the veterans themselves. In Italy and Germany, it was undoubtedly the veterans who had saved the country and re-established order in a critical hour, when those two countries had seemed to be breaking into anarchy. Why should the same salutary intervention not re-establish things in France?[40]

Shortly thereafter, the Socialist Party found itself split between the solid mass of conservative Marxists and the young exponents of a new national socialism, no longer exclusive of the bourgeoisie, no longer looking for support to comrades in countries that accepted or endured dictatorship. Inspired by the Belgian Henri de Man, who had tried to adapt Socialist doctrines to the changed conditions of twentieth-century economy, by their own political ambitions, and by the example of successful national-socialist enterprise abroad, a handful of young critics shocked their hearers when the Thirtieth Congress of the SFIO met at the Mutualité hall in Paris in July.

Suggesting that from now on order and authority rather than calls for freedom should provide new slogans for Socialist action, Adrien Marquet, the deputy-mayor of Bordeaux, made plain what was already pretty evident to some: the Socialist previsions of the previous century were out of date, hopes of a harmonious and peaceful civilization were sentimental relics, and nations everywhere were succumbing to the most selfish national interests. "The tragedy, you see," explained Barthélémy Montagnon, a deputy of Paris, "is that we believed there was only one way of moving toward socialism; today the facts themselves make us realize that our way is not the only one, that there can be another—the Fascist way."[41]

The Neo-Socialist adventure, however, does not concern us here. The Action Française, which had said the same things a long time before, did not miss the radical tone of the Young Turks' ambitions, characterizing their movement as a sort of Boulangism without Boulanger. But the schismatic movement was symptomatic of the growing appeal of Fascism in a society in which long-accepted institutions and premises were collapsing.

The first to benefit from this interest in Fascism was the Croix de Feu, an association originally restricted to men decorated under fire, but broadened to admit any war veteran. Although generously subsidized by François Coty and by the industrial magnate Ernest Mercier, the Croix de Feu did not begin to grow until it was taken in hand by a retired Army officer, once on Foch's staff, Colonel Count François de La Rocque. Drawing subsidies from every possible source, including, it would seem, the government's own secret funds,[42] the Colonel had reorganized an exclusive war veterans' group into a mass movement with an enormous number of well-disciplined, hard-drilling sections.

Thousands of middle-class Frenchmen flocked to the Croix de Feu, attracted by the publicity it had received and hopeful that it might be the answer to the troubles of the depression. Thousands also of what a Croix de Feu official called young Fascist elements joined, hoping to find in de La Rocque a leader. To all these people the Colonel proposed a mystique, which, according to him, France lacked, of the heroes who had saved the country, the *anciens combattants,* heirs of the glorious dead, who would, who must, provide leadership for a strife-torn land.[43]

Perhaps because its program was beautifully vague, perhaps because the Colonel's personality was strong, his organizing ability impressive, and his aides devoted, the Croix de Feu prospered. It had already distinguished itself in the riots at the Ambigu theater and at the Trocadéro, and as it made itself known as a dependable defender of the Right, many royalists began joining, with the direct encouragement of the Action Française itself.[44] This calculated policy, quite different from that adopted toward other leagues, was perhaps inspired by a hope that the Croix de Feu could do for the Action Française what the Faisceau had failed to do. Also, although de La Rocque himself was noncommittal, there must have been some hope of his ultimate conversion, especially since his two brothers, Pierre and Edouard, were devoted royalists and had been close to the Action Française before entering the services of the Pretender's son Henri, Comte de Paris. The Pretender, at any rate, had such hopes. It is apparent, furthermore, that until the end of 1933 the Action Française underestimated the competition of the growing veterans' league.

Things were moving in France, and it must have seemed that there was room for all manner of leagues. In his *Intelligent Man's Review of Europe Today,* published in October 1933, G. D. H. Cole explained that "France, the traditional home of revolutionary movements since 1789, now seems by contrast the most stably organized of all nations of Continental Europe . . . the bourgeois Republic seems more stable in structure than any other continental state." On October 23, the Daladier cabinet, after nine months in office, bore out this judgment by falling, as a reporter put it, "under the menace of the street rumbling with corporatist demonstrations."[45]

Nobody believed that the Sarraut cabinet which succeeded Daladier would do much better. In their *Pamphlet,* Fabre-Luce and Pierre Dominique marked a fresh *crise de régime*; *Candide* drew a pitiful picture of the State rocking on its foundations; less grandiloquently, the man in the street was getting fed up with cabinets forever falling. Every day France had a new hand at the helm: Germany had only one, and it was there to stay. "Si on avait un roi on pourrait causer," a farmer at the Gintrac fair said to Maurice Colrat. "On n'a plus que des marionettes!"[46]

Like the farmer of Gintrac, though in more polished phrases, André Chaumeix welcomed François Mauriac into the Académie Française with a brief dissertation on political affairs:

> The government of the self, like that of people, calls for authority and for hierarchy. Every individual carries within himself a small republic which is only waiting to rebel and which needs an absolute monarchy to temper it. And this monarchy, for every one of us, is what was once known by the fine name of character.[47]

"One thing is certain," wrote the *Nation belge* on the day after Sarraut's twenty-eight-day-old cabinet had fallen, "Republican mystique no longer exists, and the Action Française alone manages to attract in Paris and in the provinces audiences as numerous as they are enthusiastic."[48]

Whether they approved the Action Française or not, more and more people were looking for an authoritarian government made in the German-Italian image, even if it had to be installed by a *coup de force*. As November ended, everyone from Left to Right agreed nervously that the structure of the whole regime was on the verge of collapse. In the *Bulletin du Redressement français* of December 1933, Marcel Champin, the president of the rich propaganda organization and an important figure in the steel and mining industries, predicted that the general discontent would soon bring about a clash whose first victims would be the members of Parliament. The January issue of the *Bulletin* warned politicians that they would be shortly swept away. "We French like to be led," it wrote, and the country should have a "gouvernement d'autorité." But no one need trouble much to do the sweeping, observed Bainville in *Candide*: "The regime is disintegrating by itself."[49]

On Sunday, November 26, the patriotic but moderately leftist council of the other great veterans' union, the UFC (Union Fédérale des Combattants), had voted a very strong monitory motion, reflecting the opinion of moderate well-intentioned men:

> [The UFC] in the presence of:
>
> The political disorder and lack of courage shown by Parliament;
>
> The anarchy of a Chamber where the multiplication of groups that disagree even within themselves serves only to conceal and satisfy personal ambitions contemptible as much for themselves as in the national interest;
>
> A Senate too many of whose members defend and represent powerful private interests from which they benefit;
>
> Warns Parliament for the last time that if the government about to be set up, whatever it may be, is overthrown before a budget has been speedily approved and sufficient measures of financial reform decided, a *crise du régime* will open whose responsibility will fall, individually and collectively, on the members of Parliament.

"The country awaits a leader," proclaimed Taittinger's *National* in an appeal distributed by the million. "The country hopes for revolution," intimated *Je suis partout*. By the time Camille Chautemps had appeared before the Chamber (on December 2) with a cabinet strikingly similar to the preceding one, and received the endorsement of 391 votes to 19, with 200 right-wing abstentions, Daudet could refer without undue exaggeration to the "Wind of Panic" blowing across the land. Five months earlier, Pierre Bernus, in the *Journal de Genève,* had expressed the view that before public opinion could wake up and impose the necessary changes, there had to be a general sense of panic to provide the necessary impetus. The *Action française* had taken careful note; now, it seemed, the moment had arrived. Public wrath skulked about the railings of the Palais Bourbon; it hovered over the regime night and day from every part of France.[50]

Into this heavy December atmosphere, the Comédie Française dropped its widow's mite by staging Shakespeare's *Coriolanus,* the tale of a soldier, brave, passionate, proud, and aristocratic, contemptuous not only of politicians but of the cowardly, belly-minded rabble and its assemblies

> where gentry, title, wisdom
> Cannot conclude but by the yea and no
> Of general ignorance,—it must omit
> Real necessities and give way the while
> To unstable slightness: purpose so barr'd, it follows
> Nothing is done to purpose.

To the audiences that nightly filled the Salle Richelieu, the play seemed to treat matters "of the most burning actuality." Henri Béraud, of *Gringoire,* agreed with the *Canard enchaîné* that the play came at the right moment. "On fêta les vérités que, d'une forte gueule et d'un visage écarlate, il jetait de notre part à nos gouvernants consternés."[51] Herriot came to see the play, and left before the end, embarrassed by the warrior's disdainful tirade as he hears the sentence of his banishment:

> You common cry of curs! whose breath I hate
> As reek o' the rotten fens, whose loves I prize
> As the dead carcasses of unburied men
> That do corrupt my air,—I banish you;
> And here remain with your uncertainty!
> Let every feeble rumour shake your hearts!
> Your enemies, with nodding of their plumes,
> Fan you into despair! Have the power still
> To banish your defenders; till at length
> Your ignorance, which finds not till it feels,
> Making not reservation of yourselves,
> Still your own foes, deliver you, as most
> Abated captives, to some nation
> That won you without blows! Despising,
> For you, the city, thus I turn my back:
> There is a world elsewhere.

The radical Léon Archimbaud denounced the play as Fascist propaganda and got the Finance Commission of the Chamber to cut the budget of the Comédie Française by a symbolic one thousand francs.[j]

As 1933 drew to an end in a climate more troubled than any since 1898–99,

[j] In the administrative shuffles of February 1934, Daladier got rid of the theater's Administrateur, Fabre, but he was later reinstated by Doumergue. *Coriolanus* was scheduled for Wednesday evening, February 7; unwilling to have it performed, but equally unwilling to cancel it at such a tense moment, the government closed all four national theaters for that night. On Friday, February 9, the government asked the Comédie Française to withdraw the play from its repertoire; the Company agreed, replacing it with *Le Malade imaginaire.* Ticket sales immediately fell from 32,000 to 5,000 francs per evening. See Lucien Dubech, *Candide,* Feb. 22, 1934, and other comments on Dec. 14 and 21, 1933.

the Action Française was once more on the upswing. The recruitment of Camelots and *commissaires,* as well as of League members, had picked up since 1932, though with a significant change. The comfortably well-off middle classes seemed to be staying out, held back by a social interdict more effective than the religious one—though perhaps based on it—and the new recruits were poorer. In small towns and villages particularly, the Action Française of the 'thirties was more pinched and less effective than of old, and funds for local action were not only more badly needed but less readily available than they had been prior to 1926. Yet this was less apparent than the enthusiasm of great open-air meetings, which reflected the movement's enduring, or revived, attraction. Early in July 1932, some 6,000 people had turned out to cheer Daudet at Saint-Martin-de-Crau one Sunday, twice as many Parisians at Noisy-le-Grand the next.[52] In January 1933, in Catholic Lorraine, despite a formal letter of the Bishop read from the pulpit of every church and prohibiting attendance on pain of mortal sin, a Sunday evening meeting at Nançy drew a crowd of 1,200, including a number of applauding priests, to hear Maurras, Daudet, and Paul Robain violently attack the Church as well as the Republic.[53] Another indication that the Catholic ban was breaking down was the good audience which came to a lecture by Daudet in the Black Mountains of central Brittany, despite the refusal of the local press to print a word of publicity.[54]

Subscriptions to the paper also increased: in 1931 the sales of the newspaper had risen in twenty-one departments, fallen in forty-three; in 1932, the proportion was reversed, with gains in fifty-one departments and losses in only eighteen; in 1933 losses outstripped gains in only eight departments. Even though such indications are extremely vague, Robert de Boisfleury's increasingly cheerful tone seems in itself revealing.[55] Similarly with propaganda lectures, where shrinking resources had allowed only 151 in 1932, in 1933 there were 700.[56]

In other less precisely reportable areas there was also progress—as when in October 1933 *Le Figaro* passed from Coty's hands into those of an editorial committee headed by the royalist-inclined Comte de Saint-Aulaire, a former Ambassador to London. When, on October 6, Daudet extended a warm welcome to the *Figaro*'s new team, Saint-Aulaire replied in a private letter that he intended to place his paper "immediately to the left of the *Action française* but in the same direction." He envisaged *Le Figaro* as an "apologiste du dehors"—a fellow-traveler, seconding Daudet's own campaigns and contributing to national salvation. The long, effusive letter was probably exaggerated, and Saint-Aulaire eventually came closer to de La Rocque than to Daudet; but flattery itself is revealing.

To B. M. E. Léger, preparing his classic account of political opinions in the French provinces, the Action Française in these years still appeared far more important than either Bonapartists or other "Fascist" groups. From an electoral point of view, the Action Francaise was very small fry indeed, but that was well known, and there was no pretense to the contrary. Léger nevertheless considered the League sufficiently influential to discuss it and its supporters in some detail, and at greater length not only than other groups on the Extreme Right, but even than the Communists.[57]

The Action Française was out of the doldrums, declaring once more with meridional enthusiasm: "Right now it is a question of being for France or against it, that is to say, of being for or against the Action Française."[58]

PART V: INDIAN SUMMER

Il y a des temps où l'on ne doit dépenser le mépris qu'avec économie, à cause du grand nombre de nécessiteux.

CHATEAUBRIAND

17

THE SIXTH OF FEBRUARY

CHRISTMAS 1933 was not a very joyous one in France. The idea of a putsch was in the air, bars carried signs "No Deputies Served Here," and in cinemas whistles and catcalls greeted the appearance of political leaders on the screen. Salaries had fallen by about a third since 1929, and the monthly average of bankruptcies had risen 70 per cent. In the country and in small towns, peasants and taxpayers, with occasional motorists and especially taxi drivers, disgruntled over the new government tax on gas, talked of rebellion. And in Paris, taxi drivers were furious, and civil servants were growing restless.

On the cold and foggy night of December 23 a terrible rail disaster occurred at Lagny, twenty-nine kilometers east of Paris, when the Paris-Strasbourg *rapide* crashed into a slower train, killing 219 people and badly injuring some 300 more. The disaster itself, the fumbling slowness with which help arrived, charges and countercharges, added up to the familiar theme: once more, someone had blundered. Who was to blame? Police questioned and held the engineer, the fireman, the signal agent; the public demanded that responsibility should be fixed on the real culprits higher up, the men who set timetables, neglected the equipment, and ignored adequate safety precautions. The Lagny disaster held the headlines to the end of the year, adding to the general malaise. It was evident, wrote a deputy and editor of *L'Intransigeant,* Colonel Jean Fabry, that Parisians had reached the end of their tether.[1]

On Christmas Eve the groundwork for another catastrophe was laid when a certain Tissier, manager of the Municipal Pawnshop at Bayonne, paid a call on the subprefect of the small southwestern port to confess that he had put on the market many million francs' worth of credit bonds, without any coverage worth speaking of. To do this he had used blank bonds previously signed by an *administrateur.* He had filled in the counterfoil and entered on the books small sums like 100 or 1,000 francs, while handing purchasers a bond showing 500,000 or 1,000,000 francs. In this way, the books showed no irregularities, and since the bonds did not fall due until two years from the date of issue, he and the others who were part of the scheme had time either to find the money to redeem the bonds by milking some other source, or to get away with the gains. In actual practice they had failed to do either of these things in time, and it was because the suspicions of creditors had been aroused—after a while, the mass of paper being issued at Bayonne could hardly be ignored—that Tissier lost his nerve and decided to confess.

His confession, however, showed him as only a cog in a larger machine whose presiding genius was one Serge Alexandre—or Sacha Stavisky—a good friend of the Bayonne deputy, Joseph Garat, a backer of Albert Dubarry's left-wing *La Volonté* (and of several other not very respectable sheets), the owner of the Empire theater in Paris and of a string of race horses, a well-known gambler and socialite moving in that shadowy half-world where fashionable people, crooks, adventurers, and politicians mixed without asking one another many questions except about current credit.

Stavisky was not a leading figure in this world, but his career, a tribute to free enterprise, showed the results of grit and perseverence. Starting as an immigrant from Eastern Europe and a small-time crook, he graduated from prison to writing worthless checks (which inexplicably disappeared from the official files), then to receiving stolen stocks and shares. He was arrested in 1926, released on parole eighteen months later, never to see the inside of a jail again. Faithful and hardworking lawyers, loyal friends, pleaded his case, obtained postponements, shifted his file from hand to hand, from desk to desk to pigeonhole. Any attempt to reopen his case was inevitably stalled. His trial, nineteen times scheduled, was nineteen times delayed.

The tactics were typical of what could be achieved by even a moderately able crook, given the opportunity. Stavisky never rose much above the lower ranks, but he grew rich, and rich along with him grew the blackmailers and the parasites who battened on his fortune. Like many bigger crooks, Stavisky could not have done so well, for so long a time, without some help from politicians, deputies, ex-ministers, and public officials in various departments, including police and magistrates, most of them corrupt only in the sense that a dinner or an appeal over the old-boy network could secure favors which they would not dream of selling. But Stavisky would pay the go-betweens, some of them more or less professional intermediaries like the publisher Dubarry, the reigning blackmailer of Paris, who was a particular enemy of the *Action française*; and he would pay others, of course, simply to be quiet. In this way he survived to construct his card castles of deception, and when they collapsed, to die.

The first newspaper in Paris to see the possibilities of a murky and involved affair in Tissier's confession was the *Action française*. "Another Republican Crash," the paper noted on December 28; "Another Republican Scandal," the next day. The other Paris papers were still too concerned with the Lagny disaster to heed the scent. Most people had never heard about Stavisky—even *Candide* did not think him worth a line. But as the case was investigated and the political ramifications began to emerge, other opposition papers showed interest. On December 30, the readers of the "information press" learned about the fraud, but, while the *Action française* continued to hammer at the case, in most other newspapers Stavisky's crimes had not yet become an "affair."

Then, on January 3, Pujo published two letters from Albert Dalimier, then Minister of Colonies in the Chautemps government and a former Minister of Justice under Sarraut. Most unwisely, Dalimier, in his official capacity, had once written two letters recommending Bayonne Municipal Pawnshop bonds. Pujo's article, with the text of the two letters, was a bombshell. The government had done its best to suppress the affair, and the press had hesitated about lending it too much importance, but now it was evident that a minister in office had gone out of his way to endorse a fraud. Pujo charged that there was even more to the case, that police officials were involved, and also certain magistrates, who, like the Premier's brother-in-law, Public Prosecutor Pressard, had allowed this swindle to occur. The first and least thing the *Action française* demanded, and now a good portion of the press with it, was the resignation of Dalimier and the appointment of a committee to investigate and clarify the responsibilities involved in the affair.[2]

By now, the Paris press had seized upon the scandal. Dalimier's stubborn refusal to resign under fire, and Chautemps's refusal to disavow him, were viciously criticized. On January 7 the *Action française* carried a front-page banner headline: "DOWN WITH THE THIEVES!" and an appeal "To the People of Paris," signed by Pujo:

> At a time when the Government and the Parliament of the Republic declare themselves incapable of balancing our budget, and continue to defend the topsy-turvy foundations of their regime; while they refuse to reduce the burden of taxation, and are actually inflicting more taxes on the French people, a scandal breaks out. This scandal shows that, far from protecting the savings of the people, the Republican authorities have given free course to the colossal rackets of an alien crook. A minister, M. Dalimier, by his letters of June 25 and September 23, 1932, deliberately provided an instrument which enabled the thief Stavisky to rob the insurance companies and the Social Insurance Fund of over half a billion francs. He has been urged to resign; but he has refused to do so. He should be imprisoned together with his pals, Stavisky and Dubarry; instead of which, he continues to be a member of the Government, whose duty it is to inquire into this affair. Dalimier is not alone; we can see behind him a crowd of other ministers and influential Members of Parliament, all of whom have, in one way or another, favored the adventurer's rackets, especially by instructing the police to leave him alone, and by suspending during many years the legal proceedings that should have been taken against him. There is no law and no justice in a country where magistrates and the police are the accomplices of criminals. *The honest people of France who want to protect their own interests, and who care for the cleanliness of public life, are forced to take the law into their own hands.*
>
> At the beginning of this week, Parliament will reassemble, and we urge

the people of Paris to come in large numbers before the Chamber of Deputies, to cry "Down with the Thieves," and to clamor for honesty and justice.[3]

The following day, by fortunate coincidence, brought the news that Stavisky, in hiding since Christmas, had been tracked by the police to a villa above Chamonix and there, unwilling to stand trial, had shot himself.

The French have great faith in their police: they think them more corrupt, more rough, more brutal than probably any other professional group; and for a long time they have attributed to them, not without reason, an uncanny talent for getting rid of awkward men. The idea that Stavisky had committed suicide was received with smiles, with shrugs, or with indignation, and the deaths of Syveton, Almereyda, and Philippe Daudet were alluded to, knowingly or angrily. For every person who might believe that Stavisky had died by his own hand, ten others were sure the police had murdered him because he knew too much. *L'Humanité* said so, likewise the *Populaire*; *L'Echo de Paris* wrote of "suicide," stressing the quotation marks. The *Quotidien* called it murder. So, of course, did the *Action française*.

In the furor, the news of Dalimier's resignation passed almost unnoticed, or was taken to confirm suspicions of more widespread guilt. To its call "Down with the Thieves!" the *Action française* of Tuesday, January 9, now added "Down with the Assassins!" and called for demonstrations that evening before the Chamber. By this time almost half the space of the six-page newspaper was devoted to the scandal.

That same evening there were Camelot demonstrations on the Boulevard Saint-Germain, between the Boulevard Raspail and the Place de Solférino, and also, to a somewhat lesser extent, in the Place de la Concorde, demonstrations described by a police witness as being "of a violence rare in recent years." The demonstrators used new tactics which involved scattering before the charges of police, converging to tear out benches and railings in their rear, stopping trams and traffic, even uprooting trees. But even though they turned the streets into a shambles, they were not able to get near the Palais Bourbon.

The press the following day did much to publicize the riots, although without specifically mentioning the Action Française;[4] and when on the Thursday the paper called again to arms, the crowd that answered its appeal was even greater than before. In the meantime, Dubarry of the left-wing *Volonté* and another newspaper publisher, Camille Aymard of the rightist *Liberté*, had been arrested for accepting money from Stavisky.

Thursday's demonstrations were of a serious kind: the Chamber, heavily guarded, was never threatened, but several hundred yards away the boulevard looked like 1848. Makeshift barricades halted trams and buses, causing vast, hooting traffic jams; the gates of the Ministry of Public Works were nearly broken in; trees and railings were torn out and dragged across the street, and kiosks were overturned and set on fire. Fierce fights developed between the rioters and the police, and many were very badly injured (one unfortunate newspaperman lost an eye); some four hundred arrests were made.

On Friday, January 12, the royalist paper's headlines were promising: "LA REVOLTE DE PARIS: CONTRE LES VOLEURS! POUR L'HONNEUR FRANÇAIS! EN AVANT! JUSQU'AU BOUT!" That evening, in a steady rain, the opposing sides gathered again, ready to do battle. But before any moves could be made, Pujo sought out Chiappe, the Prefect of Police, to suggest that both sides disperse. And that is what was done, avoiding a very wet and uncomfortable brawl. In the *Action française* the next day, Pujo explained that the League had nothing against its "temporary opponents," fine Frenchmen all, and that the mutual confidence displayed the previous night bore witness to a common courtesy and fraternity.

The move was odd. It almost looked as if the rain had furnished a convenient pretext for breaking off hostilities that were getting out of hand. Since the Action Française did not mind messy fights, it appears that they wanted to avoid antagonizing the police and turning men against them with whom they would prefer to cooperate.

On January 11 and 12, the Chamber had discussed the scandal. Few of the speeches went much beyond the same sort of reckless taunts and denunciations that filled the press, but Chautemps clearly did not appreciate to what extent the partisan mudslinging in Parliament and press was indicative of a confused and outraged public opinion. To him, the troubles in the street were the work of insignificant rabble rousers, and to appoint a committee of inquiry would be merely to publicize a "fait divers banal" and to envenom a political atmosphere that needed to be calmed; the press, rather than being given more information, ought to be muzzled, in order to prevent the indiscriminate slander of honorable men without in many cases a shred of proof. Chautemps therefore proposed that the judiciary be allowed to continue investigating the Stavisky case without extraneous meddling, that police services be reorganized, influence peddling penalized, and legislation concerning libel and slander stiffened. In the midst of a howling scandal with wide ramifications, all he saw fit to propose was to leave the investigation to magistrates whose honesty was highly questionable, to penalize police who, if they had failed in their duties, had clearly done so under influential pressures, and to shut up those who might denounce real responsibilities for such corruption.

No doubt, like any seasoned politician, Chautemps accepted corruption as a fact of politics and shrugged off criticism as little more than a reflection of right-wing hostility, which in great measure it was. The men who criticized the Chautemps government would have been more indulgent to their own; they found it convenient to rise in anger and point with scorn at actions of the enemy which they had condoned and would condone in friends. As for the press, it was little more than the opportunistic echo of the interests it served, and it pursued its often innocent and helpless quarries with poisonous persistence. Chautemps and his friends felt as Chéron did when he remarked that one thing was worse than the scandals themselves, and that was the way the scandals were exploited.

There was a lot of truth in such an attitude, and a good deal of self-righteousness, too. But beyond that, Chautemps's stand reflected a more general professional deformation. Most men in Parliament, and especially the leaders, were inclined to think that reality was what went on inside the Chamber walls. Obsessed by petty corridor intrigues, they heeded the opinion of their constituents mainly at election time, and could not believe that their distorted values did not apply to the world outside. From a certain cynical point of view, Chautemps was right: public opinion was quite sufficiently aroused, and instead of being further excited by the revelations that a parliamentary commission would dig up, it needed to be soothed. The press could also be calmed, and the furor of the hostile Right used as a means of strengthening the unity of the Left; after a while, the storm would be forgotten.

But what Chautemps was not perceptive enough to realize was that this time the criticism expressed the feelings of a great many average people who did not take the same sophisticated view. To them, the government's indifference, feigned or true, and Chautemps's mild behavior seemed to indicate either a lack of moral fiber or a deliberate maneuver to hide the awkward truth. After the Socialists and the Radicals had given the government the vote of confidence it asked for, the *Action française* was, indeed, not far wrong when it declared "The Stavisky Affair Begins."[5]

The Premier had also overlooked two other important elements—first of all, that in reforging the majority of 1932 and gaining Socialist support, he had roused the ire of powerful financial interests, which, broadminded where corruption was concerned, would never tolerate a coalition that sought to enact measures unfavorable to them.[6] Second, and of more immediate importance, talk of police reorganization was a hint that the powerful Prefect of Police, Jean Chiappe, might have to go.[7] This would be the first price to pay for Socialist support. And it would mean that, while ignoring troubles in the street, the government might find itself deserted by the very force that gave it the confidence to ignore such troubles.

Since this second matter was to play such an important part in the events of the next few weeks, a closer look at its central figure would be in order here. Chiappe, a Corsican, was doubly implicated in these fresh troubles: for one thing, he was known to have maintained friendly relations with Dubarry and, at his request, to have received Stavisky. On January 10, the *Canard enchaîné* printed a cartoon showing Chiappe and Stavisky, dressed in evening clothes, grinning affably at each other in a theater box, Chiappe's arm around Stavisky's shoulders. The caption was "M. Jean Chiappe mettant la main au collet de Stavisky." All the police services had shown grave lapses in the course of the affair, and it seemed obvious that the responsible officials would in some way or other have to pay.

Another fact, more troubling to the Left, was that Chiappe was in the enemy camp. Most of his friends belonged to the Center Right, and his name had recently been mentioned among the possible leaders of an authoritarian coup. The Paris Prefect of Police, like the Praetorian Prefect in Imperial Rome, had and still has enormous power, and seven years in this post had given Chiappe time to make sure of the forces upon whose trust and devotion he relied. He had consistently used these forces to keep the Communists down, at the same time being fairly lenient toward rioters of a more moderate complexion.

In his term in office, Chiappe had made himself popular by introducing pedestrian crossings, cutting down the number of traffic accidents, vigorously suppressing open prostitution, and redesigning the shape of Paris *pissotières*. He was a public figure, always recognized in his top hat and white silk scarf, and his agents were personally devoted to him. The Paris bourgeoisie appreciated his respectable reign, and his relations with the Extreme Right, which dominated the Paris Municipal Council, were excellent. None of these things endeared him to the Left, of course. As long ago as March 1933 the Left had bitterly accused Chiappe of favoring the Action Française, and the *Canard* had suggested that, just as the Berlin police wore Hitler's swastika, the police might well begin to wear the fleur-de-lis. Their resentment even gave rise to talk of a possible transfer either to a North African governorship, in Tunis or Morocco, or to an Embassy.[8] But Premier Daladier was friendly, the majority far too weak for bold gestures that risked a fight, and rumors of Chiappe's removal had died down.

Yet gossip of Chiappe's collusion with the Action Française was rife in every quarter,[a] and it seemed to be borne out by the relative mildness with which police treated the Camelots in January, turning with far more violence on members of the press than on the demonstrators. And when police had got their tempers up, had it not been advice from the Prefecture that made the royalists suggest an end to the fighting; or was it even a wish to spare their friends (or friends-to-be) against the day when they should be side by side?

True or not, the thought must have occurred to Chiappe's enemies, as it occurred to Beau de Loménie who, amused by the *mise-en-scène* of the rainy 12th, called up Pujo two days later, pretending to speak from the Prefect's office: "Je tiens à vous dire que la pluie a cessé, et demander pour quand est-ce qu'il faut rétablir le service d'ordre." Nonplussed, Pujo, a rather humorless

[a] The Prefect's censors did not know that in answer to discreet inquiries as to how he could be of service to Maurras, Chiappe had learned that Maurras was much concerned over the fate of a fine old plane tree on the right bank of the Seine just east of the Pont Royal, which the river threatened to bring down. The tree still stands today, on a slight projection that mars the otherwise straight line of the quay, an enduring tribute to the old royalist's affections for Paris, and to his credit no less.

type, had taken a little while to comprehend the joke. But he had not seemed surprised by the idea of a personal call from Chiappe's office—and no more, had they but known it, would members of the Left have been.

It was in these circumstances that public turmoil boiled anew after a few days' lull, both in the Chamber, where Minister of Justice Eugène Raynaldy was accused of being involved in another shady deal, and in the streets, where, after a week of silence, the Camelots renewed their action, this time on both banks of the Seine. Thereafter, every day the Chamber was in session there were violent fights and police charges, arrests and the sound of warning bells of ambulances careening through the crowds, and boisterous singing:

> Ça ira, ça ira, ça ira
> Les députés à la lanterne
> Ça ira, ça ira, ça ira,
> Les députés on les pendra!

Rowdy crowds battered police, upset newspaper stands, and created monster traffic jams on the boulevards and near the Chamber. The public seemed to view it all with considerable pleasure, and the growing exasperation of the police force itself no longer seems to have concerned organizers, who now had one immediate aim—to overthrow Chautemps.

"Welcome reactions are near," trumpeted *Je suis partout.* In the *Petit Journal* Maurice Colrat found all the violence reassuring: only this sort of thing might help to clear the air. *La Ville de Paris,* the organ of the Paris Municipal Council, thought the demonstrations reflected the indignation of honest citizens against the creeping rot. "Until now only the Camelots du Roi have dared to act: 1,500 strong the first day they came out, they were 4,000 on January 11; tomorrow they will gather round themselves all honest men who want to throw out government profiteers."[9] As Coriolanus declaimed to wild applause from the royalist claque that had noisily ensconced itself at the Comédie Française:

> What should the people do with these bald tribunes?
> On whom depending, their obedience fails
> To the greater bench: in a rebellion,
> When what's not meet, but what must be, was law,
> Then were they chosen: in a better hour,
> Let what it meet be said it must be meet,
> And throw their power i' the dust!

On Saturday, January 27, the Action Française called out its troops in full force; joined by other nationalists, and probably by a good many incidental rowdies, the mob successfully broke through police cordons, slashed firemen's hoses, smashed café chairs and tables, stopped traffic, brushed even horse guards out of its way (with firecrackers), and was only halted before the Place de la Concorde by a wall of heavy police vans that could not be overturned. Deputies and newspapermen on the terrace of the Palais Bourbon could see the crowd milling across the square, and into the rue Royale, and could hear the words of their singing:

> Les députés on les pendra
> Et si on ne les pend pas
> On leur cassera la gueule
> La gueule on leur cassera!

The rioting continued through the late afternoon and evening, but by five o'clock Chautemps had already resigned on the heels of Raynaldy. Although he had received Socialist support and had the necessary majority, Raynaldy's resignation and the rioting made the government's position impossible. The official statement of the resigning cabinet pointed out that, with a large majority in both houses of Parliament, the government was "master of its own decisions." But "public life is at the present time dominated by the unrest arising from a judiciary scandal, and by a political agitation for which this scandal serves as an excuse." The country needed calm, and so Chautemps would go.

"For the first time in the history of the Third Republic," wrote Socialist Compère-Morel, "a parliamentary majority has capitulated and its government has abandoned power under the menace of the street and under the jeers of demonstrators mobilized by its opponents." For a few hours that Saturday evening something like insurrection had become master in the streets, partly—as the Left indignantly pointed out—because police handled the rioters with indulgence.[10]

Everyone agreed that the Action Française had been the hero of the day. To Socialists like Camille Benassy, deputy of the Creuse, and opportunists like Emile Buré, to Parisian, foreign, and provincial newspapers, the royalists had originated the riots and crystallized public opinion round them. There was no doubt, Chiappe later testified before a parliamentary committee, that, especially on the 27th, people came into the streets to demonstrate for the Action Française.[11]

With Chautemps gone, bids for the next cabinet were open. President Albert Lebrun tried to find a soothing figure to replace him: former President Gaston Doumergue, President of the Senate Jules Jeanneney, President of the Chamber Albert Bouisson, all refused. On Jeanneney's advice, Lebrun then fell back on the one Radical leader on whom there was so far no muddy splotch, Edouard Daladier, a former history teacher from the Vaucluse, respected for his firmness and solid taciturnity, and still free from the disfavor even of the *Action française*.

Daladier wanted to arrange a government "above the party fight," running from Socialists to the Right. Unable to make up his mind, however, to give men like Adrien Marquet or Ybarnégaray the power to administer anything that smacked of ruthless justice, he wound up with a government composed mainly of political lightweights. It did include some representatives of the Center Right (which promptly disowned them), some bright young Radicals like Jean Mistler and Pierre Cot, and one reputed tough politician, the Minister of the Interior, Eugène Frot.

The fate of the new cabinet hinged from the start on Prefect Chiappe.[12] No left-wing majority would allow him to remain at the prefecture, no right-wing deputies wanted him to go. The government, which had promised to act "firmly and fast," was being watched by a nation that seemed to have suspended all private quarrels. Only severe measures against everyone involved in the corruption could satisfy the public and put an end to the rioting. But most attempts at sanctions would stir up a hornet's nest in Parliament. Daladier's predicament was very difficult indeed.

Daladier's first idea seems to have been to leave Chiappe where he was. A commission of inquiry would be appointed to trace down responsibilities, a few administrative reprimands would throw the public some expendable scapegoats, and with luck the scandal would join its predecessors in the limbo of history. Reassured of his position, Chiappe returned the favor by persuading the veterans to cancel a mass demonstration they were planning for Sunday, February 4. But by Sunday, left-wing pressure had become so great that Chiappe was out, after all.

Daladier later explained his change of mind by saying that on Friday night (February 2), he had for the first time studied a file known as the Mossé report, which showed that at the very least Chiappe had been extremely negligent in not taking steps against Stavisky, or in not giving warning about a man whose police file bulged with reports of shady activities. But faithful service over many years deserved better than a curt dismissal, and so the Premier had decided to remove Chiappe by sending him as Resident-General to Rabat.

When Daladier telephoned Chiappe on Saturday morning, he found him laid up with an attack of sciatica that seemed to have all the symptoms of a diplomatic illness. Chiappe absolutely refused to accept the Moroccan post, the plum of the French colonial service, and, becoming increasingly violent, finally threatened that if he were removed from the prefecture, he would be found that evening in the street—presumably demonstrating with the rest. Faced with such open insubordination, the Premier had no choice: he dismissed the Prefect, knowing that Chiappe's Center Right supporters in the cabinet and all hopes of coalition would go with him.

Daladier's version of the facts did not go unchallenged. Chiappe and his friends claimed that the Premier either misunderstood or lied about the words exchanged. The Prefect had never said he would be *dans la rue*—rioting in the street—but *à la rue,* out of a job, ruined, and homeless.[13] In light of Colonel Fabry's personal evidence (though at second hand), even the skeptic Alexander Werth felt that Daladier's version might be wrong, particularly since the Prefect could hardly have expected to lead a riot when he was crippled with sciatica.

Daladier probably did not tell the truth when he said that the Mossé report, which he examined late Friday night, had caused him to change his mind about Chiappe. The cabinet meeting on Saturday had been scheduled early Friday evening, and it seems probable that by then Daladier's mind was made up. But his telephone conversation with Chiappe took place in the presence of Eugène Frot, and it is hard to think that, laying down the receiver after a heated argument, the stolid Premier would have had sufficient quickness of mind to invent the clinching argument of Chiappe's threat. Nor is it likely that he and Frot, between whom there was mutual dislike and envy, would have worked out the story together.

The possibility that in the heat of the exchange Daladier may have heard Chiappe incorrectly can hardly be excluded, especially if one recalls the way Paris telephones functioned before the war. But Chiappe's own account rather argues against this possibility, for, when the quarrel between the two men was first talked about, there was not a single mention of the soon-current *à la rue*. On Sunday *Le Matin,* whose publisher was a close friend of the Chiappes, quoted the Prefect as declaring that he had not said "qu'il serait ce soir dans la rue," but "qu'il se promenerait le soir en rentier dans la rue." And even two weeks later, Stéphane Lauzanne wrote that Chiappe's exact words had been, "Je serai, ce soir, en veston, dans la rue." All other friendly versions amounted to the same thing: no longer an official, the discharged Prefect would be strolling the streets that evening as a private citizen.[14]

It seems quite clear that at this early stage Chiappe's friends had not yet taken up the story of "je serai à la rue"—broke or ruined—that has since gained credit. This version was adopted later, quite possibly because it was soon pointed out[15] that at the time Chiappe claimed to have talked of promenades, he was also supposed to be bedridden with sciatica.

What probably happened was this: Daladier had given Chiappe every reason to believe he was secure, but had then realized that he could not expect a working majority if the Prefect were to stay. Chiappe's friends in the cabinet, Piétri and Fabry, did not ensure the votes of the Center Right, still obstinately hostile, and could not compensate for Socialist defections. So the left-wing majority had to be preserved by letting Chiappe and his friends go. But since Chiappe was too powerful to risk offending, it was necessary to buy him off with a promotion, using the Mossé report as an excuse for the decision. Daladier's telephone conversation with Chiappe had soon deteriorated into a heated argument, as Chiappe clung grimly to his post, knowing that for him to lose it would certainly imply his connection with the Stavisky case. In his temper, Chiappe made threats that Daladier, who did not look for trouble, would probably have discounted; but at the moment, with Frot beside him, the Premier repeated the threats, and Frot referred to them in the cabinet meeting on Saturday, where, out of context, they assumed more significance than either Chiappe or Daladier would have given them. Piétri and Fabry at once, of course, hurried off to learn Chiappe's side of the story.

Chiappe, meanwhile, had had time to think over his outburst and to regret it, though not to change his stand. When Piétri and Fabry arrived he gave a different version, though based on what he remembered having said. His version—and this seems crucial—included the words *dans la rue,* and this was the substance of his published defense. Later, when the explosion of February 6 brought renewed inquiries, this version had to be reconsidered. Its inconsistency seemed too obvious, and so, by means of the subtleties of the French language, instead of promenades, poverty was implied.

The argument of *à la rue* was no doubt suggested by Chiappe's letter to Daladier, following his dismissal, in which he pathetically presented his side of the case, saying, among other things, "Je suis entré riche dans la maison que vous m'obligez à quitter; j'en sors pauvre." The phrase, of course, was largely rhetoric. Everyone knew that Chiappe's wife was very rich and Chiappe was a wealthy man in his own right. If his worldly estate had shrunk of late, it was because, like everybody else, he had been hit by the slump at the Bourse and had also made some unwise speculations on the advice of a close friend.[16] But public memory is short, and public perceptions are not acute, and the later version, which was the one offered to the Parliamentary Commission, is the one that has been quoted ever since.[b]

At any rate, Chiappe's dismissal, which made the Sunday papers, showed how firmly and quickly Daladier could act: not only the Prefect and two ministers had left, and had already been replaced, but a second prefect, of the department of the Seine, had resigned in sympathy. Emile Fabre, director of the Comédie Française, had been "allowed to retire," and had been replaced by Thomé, the former head of the Sûreté Générale. As for Pressard, the lax Public Prosecutor, he had been transferred to another job, no less desirable, in the judicial world. After so many promises and so much hope, it was very little indeed, and very muddled and ridiculous.

The Sunday-evening performance of *Coriolanus* was thrown into chaos by the Camelots, and an old gentleman whose moustache and red rosette had led him to be taken for Thomé was almost lynched. Ironic stories went the rounds. The Director of the Opéra, called to the telephone while dining with Jean Mistler, remarked to his host, "It must be to tell me Chiappe has been appointed in my place"; and to a lady who asked how the new film version of *Les Misérables* ended, Tristan Bernard answered, "Javert [the policeman] becomes director of the Odéon."

[b] The *Canard,* March 14, 1934, had a third version of its own. Chiappe was supposed to have said: "Je dînerai ce soir en veston chez Larue"—a threat far more shocking, since Larue's was a fashionable restaurant where a black tie was *de rigueur.* No wonder Chiappe had to go!

That Sunday, Chiappe became the martyr of the Right. The UNC,[c] which at Chiappe's request had just abandoned one plan for a mass demonstration, announced on Monday evening that it was organizing for the following day "a great protest demonstration against the measures taken concerning Chiappe." The Croix de Feu, which had violently been protesting Chiappe's dismissal all day, also called out their members for Tuesday, "to demonstrate in the street against the government and the shelving of Chiappe." Other groups —the Action Française, the Jeunesses Patriotes, the Solidarité Française, the Corsican Veterans, and the Taxpayers' Federation—published statements of their own and called their followers to protest against Chiappe's disgraceful treatment.[d]

A concerted campaign was preparing the ground for something more serious. The regime, Daudet had written on February 3, could defend itself only with machine guns. "I know from an absolutely unquestionable source that twelve of these, dismounted, were transported in great secret to the Palais Bourbon four days ago." Another article in the same issue predicted that orders would be given to shoot the people down. "We know that tanks have been ordered up from Compiègne," affirmed the *Jour* and the *Liberté*.[17] On the morning of the 6th the front page of *L'Echo de Paris* carried the photo of a machine-gun detachment on the street, with the caption: "A machine-gun detachment from the provinces, making its way yesterday to a Paris *mairie* in readiness for today's demonstrations." In a letter to the President of the Republic carried by nearly all the papers that day, the Taxpayers' Federation spoke of "those black troops backed by tanks, by cannon, by machine guns, which a government that has not even been confirmed by Parliament expects to throw against the people of Paris who are considered the enemy." Many believed that the cellars of the Grand Palais were being filled with Algerian *spahis* who would be called out to fall upon the helpless crowd.

In a monograph written before the war and familiar to the royalists, Augustin Cochin discussed the different ways of creating the *inquiétude* necessary for effective revolutionary action: "The favorite means of creating and using this uneasiness," Cochin wrote, "are elastic 'reasons' impossible to define: the (ineffective) power, the (supposed) projects of reaction, the ire of the people against traitors, or, when this popular anger is too obviously lacking, the true interests of the people."[18] The formula was sound, and the Action Française followed it carefully.

[c] The UNC president, Henri Rossignol, turned out to be on the board of Stavisky's last and most magnificent swindle, the Caisse Autonome de Règlements des Grands Travaux Internationaux.

[d] See *AF, Le Flambeau, Le Matin,* Feb. 5, 6, 1934; *Les Documents politiques,* XV, Nos. 2–3, 106–7. Léon Bailby, *Pourquoi je me suis battu* (1951), p. 208, provides evidence that a man with his ear to the ground had good reason to expect serious trouble. On Saturday morning, Bailby gave orders to cancel arrangements for the Bal des Petits Lits Blancs which was to be held on the night of the sixth.

Machine guns, tanks, Senegalese troops, artillery, one after another the imagined elements of a monstrous plot were being spoken of as facts. By February 5 the Action Française had already called for vengeance against those about to spill French blood. Such men, specifically Frot and certain police officials, said the *Action française,* would be killed without mercy. "Des gens qui n'ont pas froid aux yeux vengeront leurs frères"—it was making sure that there would be brothers to revenge. These threats, clearly an incitement to violence, followed a simply reasoned argument: the enemy (that is, the authorities) would not hesitate to use harsh means to quell patriotic violence; this made them criminals, and justified preventive action of the most extreme kind.

On Monday evening, Lucien Rebatet glanced at a note lying on Pujo's desk: "Je sors de chez vous savez qui," it said. "La voie est libre pour demain soir." *Si non e vero* . . . the way seemed clear. For what?

The events of February 6, 1934, have been described in great detail, in a great many articles and books, not least the thirteen volumes of the Inquiry Commission set up to cut some kind of path through the maze of charges and countercharges that immediately thereafter filled the air. Fourteen French citizens died that day, thirteen more in events arising directly from it, on February 7, 9 and 12, and at least fifty-seven others were seriously injured. The impact of the events of that Tuesday affected the country for many years to come, and most specifically it affected the history of the Action Française.

We shall come later on to a detailed account of all that happened, but it suffices at this point to say that all the right-wing leagues, the UNC, and also the Communist veterans' organization, ARAC (Association Républicaine des Anciens Combattants), called on their followers to demonstrate as a means of exerting pressure on the cabinet and on the Chamber, which were meeting at three that afternoon to hear the declaration of the new Daladier government. When the deputies dispersed, some six hours later, shots were being exchanged in the fierce and confused fighting that had developed at the entrance of the bridge leading from the Place de la Concorde to the Palais Bourbon. Daladier had got his majority, not because a majority really supported him but because a majority refused to give in to mob intimidation. But the fighting, which continued for some hours into the night, with casualties on every side, made certain that the government endorsed under fire would shortly resign, to be replaced by a conservative coalition "of national union," under the reassuring leadership of former President Doumergue, coaxed out of retirement "to preserve the peace of the country."

Undoubtedly, the hard core of that day's rioters had hoped for more than just another patched-up coalition, and rumors persist of plots that would have brushed away Parliament to set up a Fascist government backed by activist groups. All available evidence proves, however, that, although such a coup was certainly thought of in certain quarters, and to some extent prepared for, there was no plan of united action among the different leagues, and there was no single group that could seriously have hoped to take power by itself. What happened to the Action Française provides a case in point.

When the Stavisky scandal broke at the beginning of the year, Maurras, Pujo, and Admiral Schwerer visited the royal family in Brussels, at the Manoir d'Anjou.[19] They discussed the situation with the Duc de Guise, head of the Orléans branch and Pretender to the throne of France, with the Duchesse, a great friend of theirs, and with the Comte de Paris, the heir. In 1932, the Comte de Paris, at the age of twenty-four, had assumed charge of political affairs, which his father always tended to ignore. Now, at twenty-six, very keen, he was convinced that the Action Française "n'avait absolument pas la volonté d'aboutir."

The Comte de Paris believed that matters would soon come to a head when judicial irregularities in the Paris Parquet were exposed; he thought he could count on the support of farm leaders (like Dorgères) and men like Charles Nicolle, who as general secretary of the Comité de Salut Economique was the spokesman for many Paris shopkeepers. Pierre de La Rocque, his close adviser, seems to have thought that his brother the Colonel, head of the Croix de Feu, would support the Prince. It was important to take advantage of the moment when new revelations would cause an upsurge of public sentiment and create a situation propitious for overthrowing the Republic. A serious effort had to be made to organize for the opportunity that would soon arise; even if it were to fail, said the Prince, at least it would be worth trying. The veterans, particularly, should be stirred up; a committee might be named, to include also friendly nationalist and veteran leaders on the Paris Municipal Council, men like Taittinger, Ferrandi, Charles Trochu, and Jean Goy, to plan an uprising or a coup. And the Prince himself would like to be in charge.

The leaders of the Action Française must have been taken aback by the directness of the proposal. They knew that the Prince was inclined to be impatient and not very friendly, considering them too slow and cautious. Furthermore, they were sure that what the Prince counted as reliable support was no more than amiable good will on the part of leaders whose troops, whether veterans, Jeunesses Patriotes, or small businessmen, were not a bit interested in monarchy or in its restoration. They felt more certain than ever that a coup could succeed only with the support of a General Monck, willing to risk his national reputation and at least a section of the armed forces.

But it was a delicate situation. "You failed to do anything in 1926," the Prince said. "This time you have the opportunity to do something. Will you take it?" They could not answer No without admitting that the Action Française had abandoned all hope of achieving a restoration through its own efforts, that for a long time it had been mouthing empty platitudes, and that the royal interest had come to nothing in its hands. And so they answered

Yes. They would take charge of the planning and would have things ready when the moment come.

It was on the day after this interview that Camelot demonstrations first began, and the project discussed at the Manoir d'Anjou was apparently under way. The demonstrations attracted the most lively elements of other right-wing leagues,[20] aroused the public, and created an almost insurrectionist climate in Paris. But this success of the Action Française operated against it in the equally important matter of enlisting the cooperation of other movements.

The Prince had been under the impression that the Jeunesses Patriotes and the Paris Municipal Council would follow him: but the leaders of the former and nationalists in the latter (often the same persons) were somewhat Bonapartist and but little interested in an Orléanist restoration. The leaders of the veterans, despite certain anti-parliamentary leanings, showed no particular interest in royalism. No more did François de La Rocque. The first result of the successful royalist-organized demonstrations, therefore, was to convince the leaders of the other leagues that they must take their troops in hand if they did not want to lose the initiative to the Camelots. Members of the Croix de Feu were strictly enjoined to keep apart, and when Taittinger returned on February 1 from a long journey to West and North Africa he, too, took steps to mark the differences between his league and the Action Française.

The instructions issued to their members by the leagues for the Tuesday mobilization show that they went into action in the most scattered order. The Jeunesses Patriotes were told to meet at the Hôtel de Ville, about a mile from the Chamber; the veterans on the Champs-Elysées, between the Rond-Point and the Grand Palais; the Solidarité Française on the boulevards, not far from the Opéra; the nationalist Front Universitaire on the Boulevard Saint-Michel, about two miles away; the Taxpayers' League in the Place de la Concorde; the Croix de Feu, which had staged its own demonstration in the Faubourg Saint-Honoré the night before, behind the Chamber, near the Invalides. All the rallies were fixed for different hours, starting in the late afternoon and extending until after the dinner hour for the veterans, who did not want to miss their dinner.

This wide dispersal shows rather more a mutual desire to keep apart from one another than to operate in a strategically deployed plan. Of this the Action Française was quite aware. Its leaders were resigned to the fact that nothing had been arranged for common action, and that the day would turn out to be just a repetition on a larger scale of what had happened on January 27, with the important difference that their nationalist fellows had decided to prevent the royalists from taking the lead again and emerging once more the seeming victors and beneficiaries of the day.

The leaders of the Action Française also knew that the Jeunesses Patriotes thought that if the trouble went far enough they might hark back to the city's Communal traditions and try to proclaim a government at the Hôtel de Ville.[21]

They had taken their precautions against the possibility by seeing that two of their men, Réal del Sarte and Binet-Valmer, were invited to serve as liaison at the Hôtel de Ville, and by discreetly posting a body of Camelots on the quay near by, to lend them a hand should the need arise.

On Tuesday morning, the *Action française* called on "the people of France" to rise against a government that would give free rein to socialistic anarchy and allow Masonic crooks to go unpunished. It sneered at the kind of public order that incited dissatisfied citizens to match their bare fists with tanks, their canes with the machine guns of Senegalese troops, which it alleged, had hastily been poured into the city. Contrary to Frot's lies, every kind of weapon was being mobilized "against the victims of crooks who acquired fortunes with the political complicities of Parliament." Let Frenchmen meet in front of the Chamber when offices and factories had closed, to "tell the government and its parliamentary supporters that they had had enough of this putrid regime."

Along with the open invitation to gather on the Place de la Concorde, the Camelots were given verbal orders to meet in the usual gathering place on the Boulevard Saint-Germain, near the Boulevard Raspail, thence to move, if all went well, toward the War Office on the rue Saint-Dominique. The royalist tacticians realized that the Chamber would be more difficult to reach from the Right Bank than from the Left Bank on which it stood, where there were more possibilities of maneuver. They may also have known of the secret plan for sealing off the Place de la Concorde—a plan which, in the end, for one reason or another, was not used.[e]

When it became clear that the Concorde formed the focus of attraction and that, indeed, many Camelots, disregarding their instructions, had gone straight there at once, any ideas of advancing down the boulevard were abandoned and the young men went off to join the crowd in the vast square. It is very likely that the energetic people mentioned by reports as particularly active on the terrace of the Tuileries between five and six that evening came from their ranks. They broke up garden chairs, collected stones, and tore out the curved iron edgings around the flower beds to use as weapons against the police and the Gardes Républicaines. The Croix de Feu contingent was somewhere else, the Solidarité Française did not arrive upon the scene until seven-thirty, and the Jeunesses Patriotes were posted near the Hôtel de Ville.

This is not to imply that the Camelots were everywhere and did everything. As usual in such situations, the crowd was extremely mixed. Apart from the great mass of independent citizens, there were among it elements of every other league. Not all the members of the Croix de Feu or Solidarité

[e] Maurice Pujo, "Le Vrai 6 février," *AF*, Feb. 5, 1944; Guillain de Benouville, *Le Sacrifice du matin* (1946), pp. 65–66; Georges Gaudy, personal communication. But royalist plans went further. They had hoped to try and occupy the Palais Bourbon around noon on Tuesday, before the guard increased and the deputies assembled, and to barricade a force of Camelots inside the building, thus encouraging the rioters to a real goal. The plan had to be abandoned when other nationalist movements refused to cooperate.

Française were at their assigned places (any more than all royalists were in theirs), and when the first bus was set on fire, around six-thirty, the flames were started with a copy of the *National,* the organ of the Jeunesses Patriotes. But whereas the major part of these leagues was somewhere else, that of the Action Française was right on the Concorde. And it was Réal del Sarte who, tired of waiting at the Hôtel de Ville, persuaded the Jeunesses Patriotes gathered there to march on to the Chamber, led by a mixed group of nationalist councilors and deputies including followers of Maurras like Henri du Moulin de la Barthète and Darquier de Pellepoix.[f] The column crossed the Seine, advanced along the Quai d'Orsay, encountered the police at Pont de Solférino, and was repulsed just one long block from the Palais Bourbon.

The fight at the Solférino was a hard one, in which Réal del Sarte was one of fifty people injured. Among the leaders of the column, only the municipal councilors were allowed to pass and talk to Daladier. The conversation seems to have been brief: according to Paul-Boncour, the angry Premier got to the point at once: "What do you want? To avenge morality? There must be about ten corrupt people here. How many have you got?"[g] Meanwhile, the column had broken up. Most of its members crossed the Seine (it must have been around eight o'clock) to swell the mob in the Concorde.

By then the most dynamic actors were on stage and the fury of the onslaught had already forced the frightened guards to fire on the rioters in self-defense. Following the failure of an assault on the bridge by the Solidarité Française around seven-thirty, all pretense of order and leadership had vanished. People milled around, ran forward to hurl whatever was in their hands, ran back before charges of police and guards. Some had obviously come prepared, with canes to which razor blades were fastened and marbles or roller bearings to throw under the horses' hoofs. But most of them used the raw materials of revolt—stones, broken bits of pavement, lead pipes, railings, and so on.

Meanwhile, halfway up the Champs-Elysées, between the Rond-Point and the statue of Clemenceau, the veterans were assembling: blind men and invalids in front, the rest behind them, many middle-aged, their medals jingling on their chests, with great banners overhead proclaiming "United as at the Front." Their neat column came marching down into the Place de la Concorde about eight-forty-five, turned to the bridge, then turned back again (*they* had no desire to fight their way into the Chamber), and marched on up the rue Royale, past the Ministry of Marine, where firemen were still trying to put out a fire started by the rioters earlier in the evening.

[f] Pujo in *AF,* Feb. 5, 1944, asserts that in the absence of Réal del Sarte a municipal councilor offered Binet-Valmer, who had remained behind at the Hôtel de Ville, a place in the provisional cabinet then being considered there.

[g] Joseph Paul-Boncour, *Entre deux guerres* (1945), II, 304. It is well to remember that several members of the Municipal Council who had accepted large bribes from a mysterious publicity account of the Paris Métro were afraid of being involved in a scandal of their own.

This early departure of the veterans' column is interesting, because, after a number of clashes with police, both on the rue Royale and on the boulevards, it later doubled back on its tracks and returned to the Concorde in a less detached mood, to help attack the bridge. Well-handled, the veterans might have been led away from the scene for good. Their leaders were not looking for trouble. But a protest march needs some kind of aim: they had agreed to ignore the Chamber; then, when they turned away, had intended to march up the rue du Faubourg Saint-Honoré to present a petition to President Lebrun. The police interfered with that plan, however, turning them back into the rue Royale after a violent skirmish, so they continued on up the boulevards, toward the rue Richelieu. But there was nothing there, the march seemed increasingly to be only for marching's sake, and, with Camelots on bicycles and on foot shouting slogans and directives, the meandering and resentful column soon acquired a clear direction and turned back toward the Place de la Concorde where it could do some good.[22]

When the veterans reached the Place the second time, around ten o'clock, the crowd was milling around in almost total darkness, save for two smoldering buses, one near the Obelisk, the other near the American Embassy, and some illumination from the windows of the Hôtel Crillon, jammed with spectators cheering on the rioters and throwing things down on the police.

In the meantime, what had happened to the leaders?[23]

Daudet had been in Brussels that morning with his wife, had lunched at the Manoir d'Anjou, and, according to some accounts, had intended to spend the night there at the home of friends. He knew that demonstrations had been planned for that evening, but he had no real idea how far they would go. When a telephone call from Paris informed him that trouble was brewing, he changed his plans at once and returned to Paris by a late-afternoon train. He was just sitting down to dinner, at about eight o'clock, when he got news, by phone, that Réal del Sarte was dead. He rushed to the rue du Boccador, where he found only Maurras, Paul Robain, Pierre Lecoeur, Marie de Roux, and two or three reporters. Everyone else had gone to dinner and then, presumably, off to the fray.

Until reassurance arrived several hours later that Réal del Sarte was only injured, Daudet was in a fury of vengeance. At first he wanted to lead the Camelots in a wild charge on the police barricades at the Place de la Concorde, but he was dissuaded finally by Maurras, who felt that the best weapon was the newspaper and that they should all get busy on the next day's edition. The group dissolved, to rejoin at the printing shop on the other side of the city, where all soon became frenzied: fantastic rumors flew of several hundred dead; friends and reporters came and went bringing the latest word from the riot. Pujo and Georges Calzant were nowhere to be found, it was reported, and Daudet insisted that something should be done, even if only with the hundred or so Camelots who could be rounded up. But once again he was dissuaded, and, like Maurras, sat down to write his column for Wednesday.

No action would be attempted. Young men fretted and fumed while the leaders went off to bed. Maurras spent the small hours of the night writing Provençal verse destined for Daudet's wife, Pampille. Around eleven o'clock, a few enthusiasts, including Lucien Rebatet and Guillain de Benouville, convinced themselves that a small but determined force might yet be decisive, for the guards on the Pont de la Concorde seemed near to breaking point; but the last assaults on the bridge, at eleven and eleven-thirty, failed, and by midnight the police had succeeded in clearing out the square.

The Sixth of February was over, and the chance to take the Chamber, perhaps, some thought, even to overthrow the Republic, had certainly been missed. How had this happened?

The first and certainly the most important reason for the failure was that the nationalist leagues never came to an agreement at the top. Although their members worked together in the streets whenever they were left free and readily followed the lead of whoever initiated action, the leaders squabbled among themselves. Pujo has accused the other leagues, notably the Croix de Feu and the Jeunesses Patriotes, of having mobilized on February 6 less against Parliament than against the Action Française, with the aim of destroying their hold on Paris crowds.[24]

Taittinger tried to keep his men from mixing with the royalists, who, of course, had to devote part of their energy to seeing that their friends at the Hôtel de Ville did not steal a march on them. As for Colonel de La Rocque, he did his best to keep the Croix de Feu out of the fighting, and seemed to be far more concerned with preserving discipline than with taking an effective part in the riot.

When everyone denied that there had been a plot to overthrow the Republic, this was true. There had been much talk, and some plans, but several separate ones, which hardly came to a real conspiracy. All the groups involved had declared that they would turn against any single contender for the role of dictator.[25] Relations between the Action Française and the Jeunesses Patriotes did not go far beyond polite mistrust, but those between the royalists and de La Rocque had deteriorated considerably.[h] No one but the Action Française was interested in restoring the monarchy, and the royalists had no intention of working for just another set of parliamentary debaters.

This probably explains why the Action Française, as well as all the other groups, was caught unprepared by the explosion on Tuesday evening. They had expected a medium-sized riot like all the others, and planned no special tactics or follow-through. When things did not turn out as expected, they had

[h] The Action Française and the Croix de Feu had clashed on the Left Bank on January 31, when the latter tried to poach on royalist preserves by holding a meeting, and Gaudy had accused La Rocque of attacking the nationalist groups.

no alternative plan to follow; they just gave up. Georges Gaudy, the president of the royalist veterans' organization, the Association Marius Plateau, tried to use his men for some concerted action on the veterans' column of which they were a part, and other individuals often led scattered attacks, but these were certainly not part of any general plan.

"The Action Française is and has been the most active and decided element, the one with a precise aim," Frot later told the Committee of Inquiry: "They have provided the active elements, in some way the nucleus of the turbulence . . . the Action Française has been one of the slogans of the day."[26]

Casualty figures bore this out: among the fourteen who were killed, four were royalists, two were Jeunesses Patriotes, one was a member of the Solidarité Française. Of civilians wounded by gunfire that night, twenty-six belonged to the Action Française, two to the Jeunesses Patriotes, eight to the Solidarité Française, two to the Croix de Feu, and two to the Communist Party. The proportions are revealing: of total casualties, the various leagues accounted for 63 per cent, including 42 per cent for the Action Française alone—or two out of every three casualties among the leagues. This indicates a majority in numbers on the spot, but, even more, superior combativeness, the tendency to lead attacks, to bring up the rear in retreat, to look for trouble or create it, all characteristic of the Camelot.[27]

But if the troops were valiant, the leadership was poor. The more or less careful planning that preceded the street battles of the previous month was oddly missing in this instance. Little or nothing was done to alert friends in the provinces, although the January riots had also been without imitators except for Camelot action in cities like Marseille and Bordeaux. Of nine provincial cities where demonstrations in sympathy occurred on the night of February 6 following news of the riots in Paris, only in Lille did the royalists seem to take the initiative alone. In all the others they acted as one element in an almost automatic coalition of nationalist forces, and often in a secondary role, as in Cherbourg, where the lead seems to have been taken by the Croix de Feu.[28] A police alert from Toulouse warned that the Action Française was mobilizing its provincial sections to converge on Paris in its support,[29] but I have found no evidence to confirm the truth of the alarm, and responsible royalist leaders in Bordeaux, Lyon, Orléans, and other centers seem to have had no inkling of such orders, or, for that matter, of any general plan whatever. This can explain why Yves O'Mahony, the son of the regional secretary at Orléans, after attending afternoon lectures at the Law Faculty in Paris, caught the train home for dinner instead of staying in Paris for a demonstration he assumed would be no different from those he had taken part in during the previous few weeks.

In Paris, too, no serious attempt was made to mobilize the sections or to keep them in readiness. Like Yves O'Mahony, members who had turned out in January were given no indication that February 6 would be particularly different, except, perhaps, in scale. And for the Camelots, too, no concrete effort at organization seems to have been made. Pujo and Georges Calzant, finding the Boulevard Saint-Germain quiet and useless as a battlefield, did not transfer their efforts where they could have been effective—say, to the terrace of the Tuileries—they simply left. Lacking the initiative to keep their men in hand, they allowed them to leave and then took themselves off out of harm's way—Pujo, at any rate, could not be found, even by his friends, for the next two days.

One need not attribute this to personal cowardice; rather, it illustrates the kind of negligence and lack of forethought that no would-be revolutionary leader should permit himself. It was this kind of remissness that set the tone of the Action Française. As Admiral Schwerer said, with unquestionable sincerity, the Action Française strategists had never dreamed the rioters would take the Chamber. Perhaps they were right, but their cautiousness was nothing to be proud of, for when an insurrectionist situation arose, the professed insurrectionist organization was wholly unprepared. This was what shocked the energetic young men who, having been taught to regard Maurras, especially, as omniscient and to think that their movement was determined to take advantage of the first chance to carry out a coup, were offered instead the same old arguments about the situation's not being exactly propitious.

Pujo's comment, "Dira-t-on que nous envisagions le renversement du régime? Eh! nous ne cessons jamais de l'envisager!"[30] no longer could be taken either as a promise or as a threat; it was only the facile excuse of men who knew they were incapable of living up to their word.

Convinced that the Republic could have been overthrown that day, young men like Guillain de Benouville and Jacques Renouvin, both of whom soon drifted to the Cagoule before finding their way into the Resistance, left the Action Française persuaded that Maurras did not really believe in the revolution, or even want it, and talked about it only to satisfy his young followers' desire for a change.[31] And there were a good many others who would have agreed with the solid provincial bourgeois who, two days later, wrote to his son in the Action Française: "Our sixth of February lacked a Danton. I know the reasons given for not pressing the adventure further, but it seems to me that, however high the price, circumstances were so favorable that one ought to have gone on to the end. The game was worth the candle."[32]

18

1934-1936

THE SIXTH OF FEBRUARY was a victory lost; but one, perhaps, that was fated to be lost. It was the moment of truth which showed up the emptiness of almost everyone's position. A parliamentary majority was shown to be the meaningless thing it is when it does not represent positive public opinion; the forces of law and order had managed to hold out against the rioters, but just barely, and they would probably not hold much longer; the authoritarian pretensions of the leagues appeared so many grandiose threats; and the leaders of the Action Française were exposed as a lot of theorists capable enough of exchanging blows with the police or trading insults with rival pamphleteers but sorely lacking the capacity to carry out their dreams.

It is characteristic that the only one who benefited from the events of the day was Colonel de La Rocque, simply because he did not move at all. Although it took some time for the movements to grasp it, the sense of failure was overwhelming. The government's supporters had not really held their ground, the government's opponents had not really succeeded. And so, the man who had deliberately remained aloof reaped the reward of discretion—the respect of the authorities, whom he had not antagonized, and the trust of the middle classes. A conservative league was something very useful when more ambitious and adventurous bodies had failed to reach their goals.

The future course of the Croix de Feu is not our main concern, but their increasing popularity following their behavior on February 6 was significant in two ways. First of all, it cut into the public and the funds of all the other nationalist leagues, most seriously into the public of the Action Française. And, further, it reflected the nature of middle-class opinion, increasingly aware that there was something radically wrong, increasingly desirous of order, honesty, and strength, but loath to achieve it by means of violently obtained radical measures.

To the extent that the other leagues had national-socialist overtones of sorts, to the extent that they were associated in the public mind with hooligan engagements in the streets or with the lunatic fringe, these movements would not do. Nor would the older parties, much too familiar not to be despised. The Croix de Feu were serious: well-organized, disciplined, and active (though seldom rowdy), usually for a specific purpose. In this sense, their inaction on the fateful night and their cooperation with various governments, their apparent moderation and robust concern with legality, do much to explain their popularity.

The success of the Croix de Feu was not greatly different from that of the conservatives who quickly moved in to take advantage of the events of February 6. Men had stampeded, fought, and died so that a coalition government, yet one more, could reassure the country. Perhaps the country really did not want more than such reassurance; it welcomed tin soldiers painted to look like steel, clay senators painted to look like marble, and soft words disguised to look like facts. All sides competed in the make-believe, and the aftermath of that bloody Tuesday reflects this very well.

The cabinet, so much of it as met, discussed the possibilities of the situation throughout the night of the riot. They considered appealing to the unions for help, but feared they might inadvertently start a civil war, or throw too much credit to the Left. They knew that the rioters would be back, this time, as some had threatened, better armed. The police and guards had suffered heavy casualties, and their morale was low. No one really wanted to call in the Army, of uncertain loyalty, particularly, as it became apparent the next morning, in the core of generals. The President of the Republic, dismayed by the events of the night, considered resignation. He, like Daladier, was the target for numerous interventions all arguing that the government had no choice but to go.

The public mood was, of course, aggravated by the press. The headlines of most papers were similar to those of the *Action française*: "PARIS COVERED WITH BLOOD. To stifle the revolt of decent people the guards fire on crowd. Fifty dead, thousands wounded." Daudet was more extreme: "A government of whores and scoundrels has had the Paris people fired on, shot down savagely with automatic arms." *Le Jour* published fake photographs of troops entering Paris, and of the Chamber guarded by guns.[a]

All over the capital hostile demonstrations against the government and Parliament broke out like fires in dry brush. A senator was dragged out of a bus and beaten, policemen were stoned, brokers demonstrated outside the Bourse, singing the Camelot song about hanging the deputies. That morning, writes Bertrand de Jouvenel, when he met a deputy in the street and said, "Bonjour, monsieur le deputé," the poor man answered, looking furtively about, "Shush! Shush!" His host at luncheon that day, a Radical deputy, declared that only monarchy could save the country from the rising tide of Fascism, violence, and blood.[1]

[a] Such reports were not confined to Paris or to France. The French Canadian press of Montreal and Québec, staunchly behind the Action Française, gave frightful accounts of a crumbling government of murderers and crooks and expressed grave misgivings about the fate of Maurras and his friends; see *Le Soleil, L'Evénement, Le Canada,* Feb. 7–8, 1934. The latter reported that the Army had machine-gunned rioters and that attempts to get in touch with the editors of the *Action française* had proved unavailing—hardly surprising, since the offices of the newspaper had closed as usual on the evening of the 6th.

With the exception of the Socialists, the portion of opinion that expressed itself seemed to feel that justice was on the side of the rioters, who, cruelly mowed down by the brutal forces of law and government, should be rewarded at least by the resignation of the cabinet.

Soon after noon Daladier made up his mind to go, and news of the resignation reached the public shortly after three o'clock that afternoon, along with the information that former President Doumergue, past seventy, had consented to undertake the formation of the next government. What had happened during the crucial hours when it was still possible to think the rioting might be resumed? What concrete measures had been planned against a government that might be so stubborn as not to depart? What had the nationalists done during the interval from midnight to early afternoon, when they might have been expected to finish off the job started for them the previous evening?

In a last flurry of self-preservation, the police, on Frot's direction, had issued orders for the preventive arrest of several nationalist leaders, including those of the Action Française. The police missed Pujo, who had not been home since the evening of the 5th. Daudet refused to go without a warrant, and the policemen retreated in dismay under the storm of Mme Daudet, who declared she would not let them murder her husband as they had done her son. Maurras's door stayed closed under their knocking; exhausted from his night's labors at writing poetry, Maurras was sound asleep. He did not awake until mid-afternoon, and by then no one was after him, not even his friends.

In the rue du Boccador, the police managed to pick up twenty-one persons who entered or left the royalist headquarters before noon, including a member of the directorial committee, Robert de Boisfleury (who was soon released).[b] But the blockade of their offices need not have prevented the direct action that many still envisaged. The morning edition of the *Action française* reflected the League's indignant, excited mood—a mood prevalent among the Parisian middle class that day.

Since early morning, groups had been gathering in the Place de la Concorde, examining the bullet holes and the bloodstains on the pavement. Pierre Lecoeur, whose job included gathering information, had been out to smell the temper of the town and had seen a mounted detachment of the Garde Républicaine clatter by under a hail of insults and a good few stones without making any reply. He also knew from several sources, including a friend in the police detachment sent to arrest Daudet, that both the Garde and the police were uncertain, exasperated on account of the recent troubles as much against the authorities as against the crowds.

[b] The Action Française naturally protested against such practices. Yet it had always advocated the preventive arrest of the enemies of order, and it never thought to object when, on the eve of May 1, 1929, Chiappe ordered the preventive arrest of a great many syndicalists and Communists.

There was new talk of a provisional government at the Hôtel de Ville, and Gaston Le Provost de Launay had been sounding out royalist leaders in this connection. League officials met in the morning at Paul-Robain's apartment, and again in the early afternoon at Admiral Schwerer's. A dense, expectant crowd filled the boulevards between the Opéra and the Place de la Concorde, and it was proposed that Daudet should rally the people outside the Opéra and lead them on to the Elysée Palace. Conditions were propitious, and this time they might win.

The leaders talked but could not make up their minds. Pujo was still not to be found, and Maurras was asleep. The moment slipped by, and soon special editions were being shouted in the street with news that Doumergue was taking over. It must have been a relief. That evening at the printing shop Lecoeur told Maurras about the ideas they had entertained and asked him what he thought. The old man was surprised: "But I have not had time to see the papers yet!"[2]

That night, while the leagues stayed home, reassured by the announcement of an honest government to come, the gangs came down into the center of Paris. From the Champs-Elysées and the rue de Rivoli to the Gare Saint-Lazare they smashed shop windows, stole everything they could lay hands on, and for the most part got away. Several people were killed that night, several more buses were set on fire, and in many ways things were as bad or worse in the central area as they had been the night before. But there was no political significance to what went on, except to those who actually believed the thieves and looters to be Communists.

To the property-owning middle class, the equation between Communism and crime was obvious and natural. The gangs that came down from other arrondissements into the rue de Rivoli and the rue de la Paix, the Faubourg Saint-Honoré and the rue Tronchet behind the Madeleine, to vandalize shops, pretended to be Communists; the press and the police, who were in a position to know better, pretended to believe them; and to the great mass of the public, that was that.

The Communists, in fact, were in a state of confusion. They had sent their men to demonstrate both with the veterans and in the Place de la Concorde. They had attacked the government and the regime as ardently as had the other leagues, and they laid the blame at their door that morning with the rest. The Party Committee knew where it stood: it hated everybody—the other parts of the Left, for their moderation; the doomed regime for its nature; and the reactionary or Fascist leagues simply for being their enemies. It really wanted to fight them all at once, alone, with no contaminating allies. This explains why the Communists staged their own demonstration two days later, on February 9, in the working-class quarter around the Place de la République, the Gare de l'Est, and the Gare du Nord. No looting occurred then, only hard fighting with half a dozen deaths and several hundred injured.

Like the right-wing leagues, the movements of the Left had great difficulty in working together. At the end of January, the Central Committee of the French Communist Party had declared, "We do not seek in any case an accord with the leaders of the Socialist Party, or with the Party itself, which we consider an enemy." The Communists, like the Action Française, welcomed cooperation with many other groups, but *à la base,* which meant in actual practice under Communist leadership. When they said, "we want to organize the common struggle with Socialist workers, in spite of and against Socialist leaders and organizations,"[3] their formula could have applied just as well to the practice, if not the stated theory, of every right-wing league.

But the division on the Left went even deeper than among the nationalists, since the Communists insisted on openly attacking Socialists and brutally rejecting their offers of cooperation. According to *L'Humanité* on February 8, Socialists as much as Radicals were working only for the benefit of French Fascism, and it was impossible to think of cooperating with such class criminals. On February 12, however, the Communists had to follow the lead of the Socialists and organize a simultaneous demonstration also "against the Fascist peril"; the two parades soon became one, expressing the reaction of the working class and of the nonconservative Left in general to an apparent triumph of the Right. A widespread, almost general, strike on the same day effectively proved the capacity of unions to act concretely if they chose. The bourgeois press somewhat inconsistently described the strike not only as extremely dangerous but also as a conspicuous failure,[4] but the general public knew it had been successful.

The Action Française, too, was in a good position to know it, for theirs was the only newspaper to appear in Paris that day. Printed in a non-union shop and distributed by the Camelots, the *Action française* was snapped up in unprecedented numbers. It appeared in two editions, and sold, its leaders claimed, about 800,000 copies.

Nothing came of this demonstration of left-wing strength, however. The union did not last beyond the symbolic gestures of the day, and soon *L'Humanité* had renewed its attacks upon the flunkeys of the bourgeoisie, upon the social-fascists of the *Populaire.*[5] So, for the moment, the politics of Communists and Socialists can be left aside: irrelevant to our story, their own divisions made them irrelevant for some time longer to that of France as well, and left the country under the domination of the heirs and beneficiaries of February 6.

On the morning of February 8 Doumergue arrived in Paris to begin discussions for the forming of his cabinet. The press was busy rehashing the events of the last few days. Most of the press agreed that the Sixth had been an attempted *coup d'état*—but on the part of a parliamentary majority and a government that desired to install a revolutionary dictatorship of their own and did not hesitate to have their forces fire on the innocent, unarmed people who tried to show their disapproval.[6] The only demonstrators who had carried weapons on Tuesday night had been the Communists, who used both crowbars and razor blades without compunction; the members of the patriotic leagues had not been armed, and it was only by an infamous trick that the two sections of the rioting throng had become confused.[7]

The theories varied in detail, but the essentials were the same: what happened at the Place de la Concorde was in no way the work of the leagues. Tardieu declared that Communists and Socialists led the assailants on the bridge; Flandin convinced himself that the people had been drawn into an ambush prepared by unscrupulous politicians.[8] As for *Candide,* its readers knew that honest citizens asking for justice had been killed instead. "They" had used machine guns. Not content with being thieves, they had turned murderers, too.[c]

The *Action française* published an appeal of the Duc de Guise calling on Frenchmen to rally to the monarchy, but in the next column suspended its verdict on Doumergue.[d] The general tone was hardly that of a publication determined to see that monarchy was restored "by any means," and Maurras sounded faintly sympathetic though hardly optimistic. On February 10, however, the list of Doumergue's cabinet, including every party in the Chamber except Socialists and Communists, was naturally received by the royalists with more than skepticism.[e] There would be no more sympathy for these conservatives than for any other parliamentary combination.

The cabinet, indeed, offered the classic image of French conservative coalitions: both Herriot and Tardieu were Ministers of State, Saurraut was at the Place Beauvau—thus letting Radicals have the Interior strings they always liked to hold and giving satisfaction, too, to those who remembered his anti-Communism. Pétain was Minister of War, and everybody trusted the hero of Verdun. A dull, safe professor of economics, Germain Martin, was Minister of Finance, and veterans were satisfied to have their representative at the Ministry of Pensions, Georges Rivollet. All the important posts were in the hands of very reliable old men; "Why is France ruled by seventy-five-year-olds?" some people asked. The answer was that the men of eighty were dead.

The new watchword, however, was that the country was not ready for more, that Daladier's resignation was "the first step" and that the next one would need more preparation.[9] Hence, the *Action française* concentrated on calling for the punishment of those responsible for the massacre of the innocents—Daladier, Frot, Cot, Blum, and their underlings, whose dreams of a *coup d'état* had foundered in the blood they helped to shed.[10] And, like its fellow-publications on the Extreme Right, the paper indicated that "decent

[c] *Candide,* Feb. 8, 1934. The myth of the machine guns has been slow to die. Only a few years ago it reappeared in Pierre de Boisdeffre's *Les Fins dernières* (1952), p. 25.

[d] *AF,* Feb. 8, 1934. The paper had in the past treated Doumergue mildly, calling him nothing much worse than a fool, a filcher, and a mediocrity; see, e.g., *A.F.,* Feb. 26, Sept. 22, 1920.

[e] The Action Française had some reason for concern; Foreign Minister Louis Barthou was by now its uncompromising enemy. See Glandy, *Réal del Sarte,* pp. 131–32.

Frenchmen," heretofore unable to reach agreement, were being united by their common sacrifices in blood. Pathetically, *Candide* provided the new note of the day:

> To the processions of wrath, the processions of mourning have succeeded. The last rites of murdered patriots have been a part of last week's rhythm. . . . [In the Church of Saint-François-Xavier] among the somber colors, two brighter notes stood out in every rank: the bandages of the wounded and the blue shirts of the young men of the Solidarité Française giving the Roman salute at the church door. The again-united cluster of flags—yesterday's rivals, today as one in mourning and in victory—fluttered under the fleur-de-lis of the Action Française, the escutcheon of the Jeunesses Patriotes, the devices of the veterans and of the Croix de Feu. . . . In this martial and civic communion there was no room left for grief. Funerals of warriors, noble and grave, they have impressed us more than a procession of vengeance and clamor. France, awakened, watches.[11]

It was pretty obvious that France was watching—watching other Frenchmen. French people were eyeing one another warily, all staunchly persuaded their enemies were plotting their destruction. Not since the Dreyfus affair had politics extended so far into everyday life. Drawing rooms buzzed with talk of valor and of woe. In the sixth and seventh forms of the Lycée Pasteur, in residential, middle-class Neuilly, where Roger Nimier and Daladier's son were students, ten-year-old boys played the game of demonstrators fighting *gardes mobiles*.[12] In some schools, the children of leftist parents, notably of teachers and other subversive intellectuals, were shunned or insulted as the children of murderers or accessories to murder. The bourgeoisie felt it had been wronged and sought revenge against the evil-doers on all fronts.

Reverberations in social circles throughout the next few months reached almost incredible proportions, affecting not only leftists but also those who thoughtlessly, or stubbornly, maintained relations with leftists. No one in society dared question that the young men who had won their battle honors at the Concorde were any less valiant than the knights of old. The slightest sign of doubt could mean social ostracism. Invitation lists were purged of all embarrassing names. Ministers in Daladier's cabinet who, like Guy La Chambre and Jean Mistler, had been darlings of the Paris drawing rooms were banished for a good long while. And they were even liable to unexpected attacks in public places—Frot, who was constantly described as a killer by the *Action française,* had to face attacks both in the street and in the law courts. Public incidents sometimes led to clandestine duels, as when a Camelot, Roger Detours, gave Jean Mistler a box on the ear in a Carcassonne café, or when barrister Jacques Renouvin slapped Guy La Chambre. In the latter duel, Renouvin was only slightly wounded, but one of La Chambre's seconds, General Barthélémy, had to resign the presidency of his local reserve officers' association for keeping such bad company.

Jean Fayard, heir to the great publishing house and a close friend both of the royalists and of the Croix de Feu, claimed that a society in which progressive talk had been fashionable now had moved firmly to the Right. Mme Chautemps's receptions went unattended; and even a young woman of the publisher's acquaintance switched her flirtations from the Radical-Socialists exclusively to the nationalists.[13]

But the most fascinating reflections of this change appear in the regular *Candide* column of the would-be society arbiter André de Fouquières, which for a while became an open attempt to intimidate nonconformists and rid society of anybody even faintly sympathetic to the Left. There could be no excuse in Fouquières's eyes for "those who spread subversive ideas by extolling discredited individuals and books of an internationalist nature." "The discipline of decent people is indispensable to rid the drawing rooms of their anarchic and Bolshevik elements."[f]

The domination of public opinion on which the Right imposed its views and where dissenters would be largely silenced (except within their own restricted circles), became very apparent when, at the end of February, a judge of the Parquet, Councilor Albert Prince, was found dead—tied and drugged—on the railroad track not far from Dijon, where he had gone that day in answer to a mysterious summons. The judge had been accused of a certain negligence and in an attempt to clear himself had promised sensational revelations about the responsibility of his chief, Pressard, in not bringing charges against Stavisky sooner. His revelations were never heard, the damning papers he had taken to Dijon were missing, but the memory of his allegations was enough.

His death was immediately likened to those of other persons who had got in the way of the dark and powerful forces of the Sûreté. To the *Action française,* this was "Un Crime Maçonnique et Policier." The respectable *Journal des débats* asserted that "public opinion feels that there exists a gangster organization, driven insane with fear, capable of anything, and ready to do anything to hide the truth and thwart justice." Within a few days, the nature of the organization had become clear: Chautemps and his brother-in-law Pressard, Daudet informed his readers, had instigated the crime. The Sûreté was a *maffia.* It had successively done in General Mangin and the Russian General Koutiepov, André Maginot and Paul Doumer, as it had killed Marius Plateau, Philippe Daudet, Ernest Berger, and Jean Guiraud, all of the Action Française. Now the *maffia* had got poor Prince: "Doumergue will soon have cause to

[f] André de Fouquières, "L'Epuration des Salons," *Candide,* March 1, 1934: "Certaines femmes du monde, même aujourd'hui, se croient assez indépendantes et assez haut juchées pour manifester un esprit quelque peu frondeur, en voulant à tout prix soutenir des snobinettes d'extrême-gauche qu'elles connaissent depuis longtemps. . . . Nous les engageons à ne pas continuer ce petit jeu dangereux! L'excuse de certaines fautes est de la complicité ou de la bassesse; et il se pourrait bien que ces dames huppées ne sombrent avec leurs petites protégées." See also *ibid.,* Feb. 15, April 26, 1934.

regret his failure to call on my services. In calling me to help he would have spared France great trials."[14]

Although few other publications went quite so far, none but the Left dared to suggest that Prince might not actually have been murdered. If the investigations were slow and ineffectual, it was a result of the Sûreté's inherent rottenness. But newspapers that hired their own detectives, including Georges Simenon and several gentlemen from Scotland Yard, did not get much further than the Sûreté, and investigations that had started with great hullabaloo were quietly dropped when the free-lance investigators, like the maligned detectives of the State, seemed to conclude that Prince had committed suicide. As Jean Prouvost, the "progressive-minded" millionaire director of *Paris Soir,* was reported to have complained, "A suicide means the loss of two hundred thousand readers. I have to have a murder!"[15]

The mystery of Prince's death was never solved: it is hard to believe that a man, even in a frenzy of worry, would choose to take his life in so complicated and horrible a manner. But the evidence for murder is even slighter than the evidence for suicide, and, without going into various theories, the significant fact appears that the reigning Right not only stood by the quite unproved murder theory but insisted that the murder had been the work of the mysterious *maffia* with which Chautemps and Pressard were supposed to be connected, presumably through their Masonic ties.[g] Not only, Daudet claimed, did papers that denied the possibility lose readers while "the *Action française,* which accused, saw its circulation rise," but it seemed clear that any open denial of a murder, any official statement indicating doubt, could bring a renewal of the riots of the Sixth. "It is not possible to resist popular pressure when it reaches such proportions," Daudet proclaimed.[16]

While personal pressures of this sort were being applied, the broader reform programs envisaged by the Right were held in abeyance. Two separate parliamentary commissions had been established to investigate the Stavisky scandals and the riots. But the evidence that they uncovered was far too controversial to please the royalists, and, worse still, it failed to bear out some of their fundamental charges. In a short while Maurras noted the disillusion of those who had received Doumergue with such high hopes only six weeks before. To Paul Courcoural, the Premier had always been a poultice which had no chance at all of curing the regime. The national-conservatives had always failed to act according to royalist recipes, unable to make up their minds to the radical measures that alone could put the country right. And now, again, they were falling into their compromising half-measures. Georges Bernanos, no longer of the Action Française, nevertheless in a sense expressed its views when, in a

[g] Chautemps prided himself on his Masonic affiliations, but it was unfair to connect him so persistently with Pressard when it was common knowledge in Parisian society that the Premier's relations with his wife, who was the sister of the Public Prosecutor, had been distant for some time. Chautemps was at this time in love with another woman, whom he married in 1936.

private letter, he denounced the movement that carried all these well-meaning people to serve the ends of a collapsing bourgeois order: "They think to restore France, and will only restore M. Guizot. *Merde*!"[17]

The fact was that no one knew quite what he wanted to restore. All the Right talked about constitutional reforms that would give France a strong executive and an independent judiciary. But no one could agree on how reforms were to be made. When Philippe Henriot expressed his views, the definite suggestions came down to suppressing Masonic societies, abolishing the right of civil servants to vote and to strike, and restricting membership in the Legion of Honor solely to those who had performed acts of military valor. The Comité des Forges talked about administrative, fiscal, and social reforms that aimed to "free the Executive from the Legislative, and the latter from the electoral power." Tardieu, too, spoke of "subtracting the Executive from the joint domination of Chamber and Senate."[18]

None of this amounted to much in royalist eyes, which looked beyond the possibilities of merely revamping the regime by strengthening the Executive and trying to lessen parliamentary instability. They knew that only the sweeping change they advocated could do the country good, but since their calls for a royal restoration went unheeded, they concentrated on issuing warning of the Left's revival, exhorting friends and members not to imagine that they had won.[19]

The royalists themselves were disturbed by the rise of the Croix de Feu. Provincial sections of the veterans' organization still had members of the Action Française at their head in April, when Admiral Schwerer testified before the Chamber, but royalist members of the Croix de Feu were increasingly being forced to choose between the two organizations. It was not easy, but the Paris *Herald Tribune,* which was sensitive to trends, tended to emphasize de La Rocque's doings and to ignore the royalists as being no longer newsworthy.[h] It was the sort of portent that the publicity-conscious men in the rue du Boccador could only with difficulty ignore.

The other leagues, too, were organizing: with the Jeunesses Patriotes and the Solidarité Française, the Action Française joined a coordinating committee entitled L'Ordre Français, from which the Croix de Feu officially abstained.[i] It also helped to set up the Front National, whose general secretary was Charles Trochu, a descendant of the great General Kléber and a grandson of the military commander of besieged Paris in 1870–71. Though a Bonapartist and a sympathizer of the Jeunesses Patriotes, Trochu was a good friend of Georges Gaudy and from that time on was friendly with Maurrassians.

[h] Thus, on May 14, 1934, its account of the Joan of Arc parade, in which both organizations had impressive contingents, boosted the Croix de Feu at the expense of the Action Française.

[i] At a mass meeting organized by L'Ordre Français at the Salle Wagram on May 30 details from all three leagues were on hand to ensure order. The two principal speakers, René Dommange and Philippe Henriot, introduced as the most anti-parliamentary of parliamentarians, called for authoritarian and corporatist reforms. See *JSP,* June 2, 1934.

The Front National included the Jeunesses Patriotes, the Solidarité Française, the Taxpayers' Federation, the Ligue des Chefs de Section (a veterans' organization headed by the Maurrassian Binet-Valmer), and several lesser bodies. It did not openly include the Action Française, whose royalist policy remained officially indigestible, but it kept in close touch with it, organized joint meetings, and always regarded Maurras as its leading doctrinaire.

The Front National served as the coordinating body of all the movements of the Extreme Right during the prewar years, excluding only the uncooperative Croix de Feu and openly Nazi movements like Marcel Bucard's Francistes. It is important to bear in mind how powerful the influence of integral nationalism was in it, even after the Front had been joined by strong individualists like Jacques Doriot.[20]

Although paradoxically condemned to stand alone, the Action Française found itself by now almost the embodiment of what might seem the spirit of the time. Its enemies considered it the epitome of everything they fought against;[21] its friends thought it commanded the most hopeful intellectual credit.[22] Abroad, its role was in a sense exaggerated, sometimes by men who appreciated it, sometimes by those who feared it, sometimes by those who simply understood the advantage of being quoted in the "Revue de la Presse."[23] French writers addressing foreign readers sometimes overemphasized possibilities that seemed very slender to the French themslves.[24]

The vigilant Catholic *Vie intellectuelle* warned against the revived influence and attraction of the paper and the league that Rome had banned. "Too many Catholics, concerned about the future of France, are returning to the movement they think will have the best chance of bringing about the national revival they seek."[25] Maurras could well boast, too, that the most important polemical publication of the time was the work of young men whom he had inspired: *Demain la France,* which appeared in 1934, seemed a satisfyingly tangible result of all his years of work. As Pierre Chardon remarked in a review, integral nationalism had "invaded young Frenchmen's hearts and brains; the Action Française ideas had become an unconscious influence whose distant sources were ignored, but to which more people than were aware of it and more than would admit it unconsciously responded." *L'Illustration,* which no right-thinking family would want to be without, published the photograph of an open-air royalist meeting, with "resolute Camelots in berets keeping order." Daudet, "with his proconsul's face," was speaking. "He flagellates the Republic," said the caption. "But does the Republic really mind? She is a woman, and, like certain women, no doubt does not dislike being manhandled occasionally."[26]

An interesting instance of the effective use made by the Action Française of its considerable hold on a broad reading public, not only of its own newspaper but of other satellite publications, appeared in the autumn of 1934 at Marseille, when King Alexander of Yugoslavia, arriving in France on a state visit, French Foreign Minister Louis Barthou, and an accompanying general were all assassinated as they were being driven from the port to the station. Security arrangements for the King's reception had been woefully lax, and there was ample reason to charge the Minister of the Interior, Albert Sarraut, and his subordinates, with extraordinary neglect. The *Action française,* however, found it an occasion not simply to attack Sarraut but to deplore the shocking laxity of the whole government—overlooking, of course, the equally murderous laxity of the Bourbons and the House of Orléans, including the murder of the Duc de Berry.

In any case, the attack on Sarraut was secondary to a more complicated argument. Barthou, an old-fashioned patriot who had played his part in France's preparation for the 1914 conflict, had been fond of traditional remedies for traditional problems. At the time of his assassination he had been engaged in promoting agreements with eastern Europe, including a Franco-Soviet pact designed to combat the growing might and menace of Hitler's Germany. The idea had met with strenuous opposition in certain right-wing quarters—not least, as we have seen, from the Action Française. The League therefore took Barthou's death as an excuse for recalling the misguided Russian *rapprochement.*

As headlines cried the murders of Marseille, Maurras could not forbear expressing his bitterness against the dead Barthou, who had dragged the country into alliance with common criminals. The first account of the tragedy printed in the *Action française* hinted at Communist responsibility, and probably also that of the execrable Sûreté. *Candide,* the following day, was even more explicit: the murderers were foreign, and foreigners could only mean Reds. The national territory should be cleared of foreign trash; the Communist Party, protector of all aliens, responsible for their being brought to France, dealers in individual and collective murder, should be dissolved and banned. In a bitter article in *Je suis partout,* Gaxotte spoke of "France Invaded" by foreigners and Bolsheviks, and attributed the assassinations to Communists whom a shortsighted policy first tolerated, then befriended. Maurras, too, was specific: the King had been the victim of a vast international plot hatched together by the Germans and the Russians. And there is the implication that even if his suggestion were not factually true, it must nevertheless be true in a symbolic sense: whoever the real murderer might be, "objectively" this was the only sound explanation for the reading public as well as for the members of the Action Française.

At any rate, no other explanation was given them. As in the case of Gorgulov, the first assumption had soon been proved wrong: the murder had been planned and executed by Fascist Croat thugs whose most honorable description would be "nationalists." But the true facts were never printed in the three royalist papers. *Candide* simply let the matter drop. *Je suis partout* stubbornly continued to insist on the guilt of Reds. Gaxotte, more sensible, and unable to ignore the evidence altogether, used language that by indirection attributed responsibility to foreign refugees, implying that these were Communists and Jews, and to the governmental weakness concerning them.[27] People who got their information solely from such sources—and there were hundreds of thousands who did—may well have gone on all their lives unaware that the King of Yugoslavia was murdered by the Ustashi, trained in Hungary and paid with Italian funds.

In general, however, despite their show of brash confidence, the Action Française and its fellow-leagues faced serious difficulties. Unlike their counterparts on the Left, the organizations of the Extreme Right in France tend to lose their influence under a conservative government, because their public is also a conservative public, ready to approve action against the Left but not against the status quo. Doumergue was doing little, but he did it in a way that moderates approved, and all in all the government seemed to them in sound hands. They had no desire for violent action, or even for any reform of a regime that seemed to be very much their own. The nationalists, of course, not least the Action Française, disapproved of Doumergue because of his faniente. But it is interesting to see that even the nationalist crowds, which always cheered the usual general criticisms and familiar denunciations, lost their enthusiasm as soon as concrete measures were proposed.[28]

And so, for a little while, the leagues marked time. In October 1934 a cartoon in *Je suis partout* showed the nationalists behind their banners on the Place de la Concorde, with the legend: "M. le Président, we have been waiting since February 6!"[29] A few weeks later, deserted by his Radical ministers, the good Doumergue resigned and the moment seemed right for action, but a new government quite as conservative as the old one was hastily got together, and so the moment slipped away. Indeed, from 1934 to early 1936, while the Left was working to recoup its power in the coming elections, the leagues were hamstrung by reassuringly conservative governments, which made it impossible to convince the upper and middle classes that there was any need for action. Throughout these years the most powerful league of all, the Croix de Feu, reflected this middle-class quiescence, showing no insurrectional notions whatever. Relations between Doumergue and de La Rocque were always good, and after Doumergue's death his daughter retained a faithful interest in de La Rocque's league for several years. But even following Doumergue's resignation, de La Rocque refused to cooperate with the other leagues. He refused specifically to participate in Armistice Day plans for 1934, and it is small wonder that the Action Française and its papers loathed him.[30] With Flandin, who succeeded Doumergue, he probably bore the chief responsibility for seeing that there was no repetition of the February riots either in November 1934, or in February 1935, on the first anniversary of the Place de la Concorde episode.

The nationalists tried their best to honor the anniversary of what Pierre

Gaxotte described as "the sacrifice of those heroic Frenchmen whose death prevented the *coup d'état* of Blum and Daladier, marked the end of the dictatorship of the Masonic lodges, and destroyed an attempt at tyranny that would have plunged the country into ruin and grief."[31] The Action Française point of view, which was also that of the Front National, was well expressed by a regular contributor to *Je suis partout,* Pierre Villette, writing under the pen name Dorsay, when he described February 6, 1934, as one of the happiest revolutions of all time—"the victory of honesty, good sense, and civic courage over corruption, imbecile vanity, and funk." The best hopes for the future lay in extra-, indeed anti-, parliamentary action, inspired by the spirit of that day. The trouble, Dorsay intimated, was in the lack of provocation. Nothing was happening now that could occasion the same kind of public stir. The new left-wing Front Commun offered no provocation and would not show its hand in any open action, especially in the street. Meanwhile, behind this hypocritical façade, this pretence of doing nothing, the leftists were once more infiltrating the structure of the State: "Attendre pour agir une attaque en fanfare du Front social-communiste serait faire preuve d'un bien inopportun esprit opportuniste. Répétons que ce serait bien mal connaître la Maçonnerie."[32]

There was not much attempt to veil the obvious implication that the Left was quietly preparing its own revolution, planning the country's ruin and its doom. There was no evidence of such intentions because the Left, especially the Masons, was far too hypocritical and cunning to show its hand. Its talent for concealment heightened the danger and provided still further reason for scotching such nefarious plans by carrying out a right-wing revolution first.

There is no evidence that there were definite plans for February 6, 1935, any more than there had been in 1934. The Action Française tried to create an inflammatory climate by calling a student strike to protest the number of foreigners in the schools. The strike, which was announced at a student meeting addressed by Daudet on January 29, began on February 1 and spread to the Faculties of Medicine and Law, but it does not seem to have had much significance.[33] Clearly, the mood of the country, even in Paris, was far different from what it had been the previous year, although many people were nervous about what might happen on February 6 and the authorities considered banning all public demonstrations for the day. It soon appeared, however, that such a step might very likely cause trouble instead of preventing it.

Instead, Flandin preferred a quiet understanding with certain nationalist municipal councilors most likely to give the Front National a lead. As bait, he used a bill designed to reapportion the municipal bailiwicks of Paris, which were (and still are) notoriously favorable to the more prosperous districts, that is, to the Right. The Premier offered the bill, which had passed the Chamber and was about to come before the Senate, in exchange for the cooperation of the councilors. Then, so fortified, he forbade all demonstrations for February 6 save those controlled by the Municipality of Paris.[34]

On February 6, while attending an official ceremony at Notre Dame in honor of the fallen, Flandin was slapped by a young nationalist, Alain de la Rochefordière, who was enraged at not having got a chance to riot in celebration of the victorious past. Sentenced to a year in prison, the young gentleman received a pardon before the month was out; Flandin wanted to keep the nationalists quiet, not incite them.

Within the limits of the law, nationalist ideas seemed fashionable. Even *Le Temps,* whose conservatism generally stopped at the boundary of the republican field, henceforth expressed its appreciation of all the leagues, including the royalists. It was a royalist, and great admirer of Maurras, Simon Arbellot de Vacqueur, to whom *Le Temps* entrusted a series of articles on the nationalist leagues, in which the Action Française, quite naturally, came out very well. In general, *Le Temps* felt glad to have the leagues around, representing "an elite of present-day youth." It urged the alliance of all national-republicans (why could not the Action Française drop that ridiculous king?) to oppose the Front Commun, which incorporated the enemies of the nation and of the Republic. One could not very well include the professed royalist enemies of the Republic among the latter, since they were so obviously the nation's friends, but one could be discreet about their cooperation and encouraging about their performance, and one could praise the royalist-inspired National Teachers' Federation for its "national and French" tone, opposed to "Communist, Socialist and Sillonist" excesses. In quarters less exalted than the noble *Temps—L'Humanité, Le Populaire,* the Demo-Catholic *Aube* and the conservative *Jour*—the movement was constantly in the news, the Right ever more often echoing its ideas, the Left admitting its power and deploring its influence.[35]

A tribute altogether pleasing to the League came in March 1935 when Bainville was elected to the Académie Française, to take the seat left empty by the death of Raymond Poincaré. With him there entered also André Bellessort, the literary and drama critic of the *Journal des débats* and a regular lecturer of the Institut d'Action Française, and Claude Farrère, in no way connected with the organization, but friendly, and strongly approved by it as president of the patriotic Association des Ecrivains Combattants. Georges Bidault's comment reflected the general impression in the country: "Three votes, three results, three men elected, whose chief merit is their sympathy for the Action Française."[36] It was unfair to put it quite that way: "characteristic" might be a better word than merit, and Bainville, at least, had other things to recommend him than his royalism. But this was the impression that the election gave to many; and the Action Française would not argue.

France was now entering an open power struggle between the Left and the Right, in which, once more, extremes began to count. If institutions as representative of conservative interests as *Le Temps* and the Académie Française were openly endorsing what had for a long time been regarded as a well-meaning but excessive, sometimes almost lunatic, fringe, it was because they were convinced that the order for which they stood was being dangerously challenged by the reorganization and advances of the "revolutionary" Left.

In the country-wide municipal elections early in May 1935, the conservative groups that had held power since February 6 lost ground everywhere. Both Radicals and the classic Center parties lost votes and seats. In urban and industrial centers the Socialists and Communists made gains, and in rural areas and small towns the candidates endorsed by the Agrarian Party and by the Croix de Feu showed surprising strength.

In Paris, where it was expected that the Communists would win the industrial suburbs and the nationalists the bourgeois center of the city, the traditional division was underscored when candidates of both extremes made important gains. The "Sixth of February candidates" found their majorities heavily increased, as did the Communists in the "Red belt" around the capital.[37] Under political stress, and hard-hit by the deepening economic crisis, the electorate was being polarized even beyond its usual division: the middle class abandoned traditional moderation and chose between the deliberate representatives of radical extremes.

For a few days at the beginning of June a clash between moderation and extremes seemed almost imminent. On May 30, Flandin, unable to secure the plenary powers he wanted to deal with financial problems, submitted his resignation. A man of moderate complexion but of the Radical camp, Fernand Buisson, tried to set up a cabinet to succeed him. He failed to gain a majority in the Chamber, and while new arrangements were being made the Camelots staged a series of demonstrations. They broke the windows of the *Petit Journal* building and of the Masonic Grand Orient headquarters; they demonstrated in and around the Bourse, shouting that it was the Cartel that was ruining the franc, and paraded through their Left Bank strongholds around the Boulevard Saint-Michel.[38]

But again a moderate stepped in—Pierre Laval, who formed a cabinet not signally different from the several preceding ones. The Radicals decided to support him: their party was "resolved not to expose the country to difficulties that could be exploited by the enemies of the Republic."[39] By now, Parliament was so discredited in the country that a parliamentary majority meant nothing against a display of public indignation. And Paris was full of men who would be glad to organize such a display, for which they could expect only approval from the general public.

For over a year now, the names of the deputies had been worthless, and men even used the title as a form of insult. Two brawling taxi drivers came to court because one called the other "Espèce de député!"[40] When Laval was forming his cabinet to succeed Buisson, the well-known nationalist Jean Goy, who had led the veterans' column on February sixth, was booed at a great veterans' rally simply because he was a member of Parliament. The veterans agreed that Parliament was "a collection of old crocks who would never do anything worthwhile except under the pressure of the street."[41]

This view was widespread. But whatever its justification, it was true only to the extent that the right-wing leagues could carry the conservative mass with them, and this they could not do as long as conservative governments were in control. A government that was considered to be of the Left, whatever its true nature, permitted them to maneuver, even when its policies and make-up differed little from those of the Center Right. Thus, a Chamber whose center of gravity was on the classic Left was forced to support governments that, if perhaps more representative of the public mood, were not, however, representative of its own proportions. And nationalists who despised moderates both of the Right and the Left were responsible for moderate cabinets, which without them could not have reached power or maintained themselves in it even as long as they did.[42]

This pressure, against which the Constitution offered no safeguard, was but one more element in the confusion of motives and positions that afflicted the country and its Parliament during a time when classic political labels were concealing profound changes in political attitudes.[43] But it was important, and was recognized as such by Parliament.

What would evolve into the Popular Front was busy organizing its forces, and nationalists argued that revolution might come from its activities. Others, on the contrary, interpreted the left-wing movement as a conservative force, defending Republican institutions and providing some sort of counterbalance to the irresponsible pressures of the leagues. The nationalists blamed Laval for trying to keep an even balance between extremists of the Left and Right.[44] If he did this, and he did not overdo it, the reason was that even the Communists were gradually abandoning their revolutionary chatter, turning to the defensive and, at least in some respects, to conservatism. Henceforth, in one way or another, the revolutionary role in France would be assumed by the Extreme Right.

The language of the leaders of the nationalist leagues was reminiscent of the aspirations of social royalists before the war. Everywhere, Thierry Maulnier noted with his unusually perceptive sense of political contingencies, parties and leagues were trying to adapt to new circumstances, those of the Left by incorporating some form of nationalism into Socialist and Communist ideology, those on the Right by seeking a broader popular basis and a more comprehensive social program. True, Maulnier pointed out, there were essential contradictions between "democratic and Jacobin nationalism" and his own more empirical sort, just as there were between the corporation and planned economy. But similar efforts to change in all quarters reflected similar anxieties, and were symptoms of a more or less general public demand.[45]

Like Maulnier, Pierre Dominique, himself a sometime Maurrassian, envisaged a new party, social like the Left and national like the Right, a social-national party animated by a revolutionary spirit. The leader of the Solidarité Française, Jean Renaud, felt much the same: "Tomorrow belongs to the movement that can synthesize the social and the national." And his resident ideologist, Jean-Pierre Maxence, said: "Knock down the money power first, then Parliament, and the national and social revolution will be more than half accomplished."[j]

A situation had arisen in which economic confusion and distress had caused old supporters of the existing order to turn against it. And though neither the men nor the situation was yet so dangerous as to threaten the country, their troubles sparked the activity of the leagues by throwing discredit on the old parties and established institutions which had done nothing to prevent the ruin. They also helped the Left, of course, as 1936 would show. But the Left proposed radical changes which only a minority of the French people would seriously entertain. The Right proposed reaction: the changes it wanted were represented as turning the country back toward a happier time and made a natural appeal to widespread conservative instincts and dreams of happy days gone by. To this extent, it was the royalist doctrine, though very often without the royalism, that generally inspired the movements of reaction. As Bailby declared, apart from the Action Française, right-wing reform ideas were nothing more than vague, incoherent projects.[46] It was in the *Action française* and, even more, in the proposals of men who had grown up on it, that the opposition to the Popular Front found its ideas.

The situation was hopelessly confused. Most people in the country wanted change. But some wanted radical changes running the gamut of political, social, and economic reform, while others merely wanted a change in institutions or in political methods that did not seem to function satisfactorily. As economic distress and political confusion grew worse, the advocates of change became more insistent, their spokesmen more strident. But the nature of the changes they desired did not become any clearer, partly because even within long-established political groups radicals and moderates could not agree on what they really wanted, or coherently express their positions.

Roughly, the situation seemed to be one in which the great conservative mass was becoming increasingly beguiled by extreme solutions to its troubles as these troubles became more severe. But though it lent an increasingly attentive ear to radical appeals, even in its anxiety, a majority of the public still turned to those who proposed to maintain or restore familiar conditions, and wanted to return the country to an even keel by reforms of a merely institutional sort.

[j] *La République,* Aug. 2, 3, 1935. In the course of an inquiry conducted among rising young politicians the *République* found a striking agreement among representatives of all sides that, in the words of Georges Izard (a future deputy of Bergery's Frontist Party and later still an active member of the Resistance), France needed a national-socialist, anti-Communist, and anti-bourgeois movement.

More extreme panaceas, offered by both the Left and the Right, met with less favor. The social revolution that not only the Communists but even some right-wing leagues proposed was not nearly so attractive as the limited modifications suggested by the moderates.[k] Not revolution but restoration was in the public mind. The Communist Party reflected this awareness when it adopted what was effectively a conservative position within the Popular Front. So did the Croix de Feu. And it was not by chance that the most popular and probably the most impressive of the leagues was also the most moderate and most vague.[47] People scoffed at what had been found wanting and liked hearing promises of change, but at the same time they did not want to plunge into anything either too specific or too extreme. Essentially, all that many looked for was somebody or something to reassure them with promises they could believe.

What was the place of the extremist nationalists in all this—what was the place of the Action Française? Clinging to royalism, the movement stoutly affirmed its inflexible opposition to the prevailing order, which Communists and Croix de Feu alike endorsed. The radical point of view represented by the Action Française did profit from the radical tenor of the times, but it was not on the whole favored by a public that far preferred legerdemain to revolution and soothing panaceas to any root-and-branch approach.

Neither the Action Française nor its allies in the Front National could, therefore, claim to represent the masses. But in a country in which there were so many conservatives, the language they spoke could at least be understood, and they used all the symbols and slogans of the Right more precisely and more aggressively than any other group, and in such a way that even moderates could sympathize, if not endorse them. The excesses of the nationalists were excused in light of the excesses that seemed to be threatened from the other side.

Here we may be close to the crux of the confusion. Conservative-minded people might occasionally, or even regularly, vote together, but they remained divided by party slogans which they continued to intone even when they had lost practically all connection with reality. There is no doubt that the Radical and Radical-Socialist electorate was not on economic matters much more than moderate. And since economic issues were crucial at this time, the practical indifference with which this Radical hostility to radical economics was treated caused more chaos in Parliament than any other single matter. In fact, no majority ever existed in the Chamber for any but the most orthodox economic measures; but this was concealed by ideological arguments and dissensions. The inadequacy of timid economic solutions was compounded by a political

[k] See Jean Lhomme, "La Société française et son histoire," *Aspects de la société française* (1954), pp. 86–87: farmers and the bourgeoisie joined the *political* movement but took no part in the *social* one; they voted in 1936 for the Popular Front, but more out of ill-humor and contrariness than for any common program.

instability caused less by the repeated failure of these weak solutions than by an inability, or unwillingness, to recognize the real lines of division in the Chamber.

The enduring coalitions of the interwar years were those that catered to the conservative majority—the Frenchmen who preferred governments that did little or nothing to governments that did anything at all. Yet coalitions that tended to group all Center parties, excluding only the Socialists, were wrecked time and again on ideological issues and on simple party issues alike, which really implied no serious differences but were sufficiently important to conceal their basic unity. And as long as this real unity remained concealed, political unity was impossible. Pretended radicals were forced into uneasy partnership with real ones, while across the ideological divide acknowledged conservatives had to fight this "Left" with weapons furnished by their own radical wing, the stubborn, unrelenting, sometimes imaginative doctrinaires of the Extreme Right.

Among the latter, the position of Maurras was unequaled and unchallenged.[l] His patriotic logic quite naturally appealed to men who were in need of arguments to counter the theories of the Left. On most points, though not on all, the theses of the *Action Française,* extreme though they might be, anticipated the needs of more conservative groups: they were more logical, more striking, and also more consistent than those that other groups could formulate or, indeed, wish to follow; but they were available when there was nothing else. This was why, the nationalist leagues, deprived of power because of their excesses at a time when political polarization reached its peak, managed nonetheless to assume much greater influence and significance than before.

For, fearful of the growing danger of a Left proposing collectivist solutions at least in theory if not in fact, the mass of those whom the threat repelled turned not to revolutionary reaction but to some kind of (probably authoritarian) conservatism—which, paradoxically, drew much of its logic and its inspiration from the extremists whom it helped keep down. Whenever conservative interests seemed in danger, the extremists reappeared with special force, released like jack-in-the-boxes to scare the enemy and give their own

[l] See tributes and confirmation in, e.g., Yves Simon, *La Campagne d'Ethiopie et la pensée politique française* (1936), p. 74; Pierre Taittinger, *Notre Dernière Chance* (1937), p. 121; Ernest Roussel, *Les Nuées Maurrassiennes* (1938), p. 195 and *passim*; Pierre Cot, *Le Procès de la République* (New York, 1944), I, 133; Jean Zay, *Souvenirs et solitude* (1945), p. 75. At the Sixteenth Congress of the UNC, held at Brest in 1935, the report on intellectual action among young people concluded with a brief list of recommended books, including many by Maurras, Bainville, Gaxotte, Charles Benoist, and the Marquis de Roux; see *Congrès National de l'UNC* (1935), pp. 278–79. One recalls the words of Roger Priouret, *Journal du Parlement,* quoted in *Rivarol,* Jan. 6, 1955: "Il y a 20 ans j'ai eu à la Faculté des camarades qui militaient à l'extrême-droite. Je les ai vu lire Montherlant pour se distraire. Drieu les intéressait comme un homme en quête de la vérité, non pas comme un maître. Ils n'ouvraient pas Barrès. Quand ils allaient donner des coups ou en recevoir, c'était pour Charles Maurras. Le chef intellectuel de la droite, le seul, le vrai, le voilà."

side heart by assuring it that their violence was ready in the event of serious trouble.

Thus, when the Left began to show its teeth during the summer of 1935, especially on July 14, when a Popular Front parade rolled like a jaunty but unruly river between the Bastille and the Place de la Nation, a similar parade of the Croix de Feu across the city at the Etoile in straight and serried ranks comforted and encouraged the Right. In the words of *Je suis partout,* their strength was an assurance that "Ils ne passeront pas."[48]

That leagues were thought of as armies may seem less odd if we remember that they were armed. After the February 6 riot, France became caught up in a great game of Fascists against anti-Fascists. So far, mainly the strategic background of this game has been told, but the daily press related all the less articulate scrimmages, the grim and bloody fights between newspaper sellers of the Extreme Left and the Extreme Right, the attacks on rival meetings, the gang battles over disputed streets. Beginning in the spring of 1934, the two forces clashed throughout the country, and the right-wing press had frequent occasion to complain about the methods of their enemy. They were no longer dealing with timid bourgeois or with police forces held in check by cautious governments, but with opponents at least as tough as they and as aggressive. Skirmishes grew fiercer during the summer and autumn of 1935, and the climate ever more oppressive. In the Jesuit journal *Etudes* Father Henri du Passage remarked on the almost physical impression of a brewing storm. For the *Courrier royal,* the weekly organ of the Comte de Paris, not since the Dreyfus affair had the division of France into two camps been so profound or so apparent: "We are on the eve of a civil war," it declared.[49]

The royalists, of course, sought to bolster this impression and to encourage the conviction of many people that an electoral victory of the Popular Front would, at the least, bring economic ruin, and probably civil and foreign war soon after.[50] With such a prospect before them, it was vital that the leagues should continue to exist. Ybarnégaray and de La Rocque were blamed for letting the side down when, in December 1935, they agreed to a dissolution of armed leagues, which, the Action Française argued, would leave the Right vulnerable. The government, concerned with public order, and the Left, maintained that the right-wing leagues exerted undue pressure on Parliament, introduced an unhealthy element of discontent, and were liable to cause trouble any time. Quite reasonably, the royalists rejoined that only governmental impotence was responsible for these private ventures which stepped in to fill a power void. Most of the Right agreed. It was not the leagues that made the government weak, wrote Jean Guiraud, editor of *La Croix.* The inefficiency and timidity of public authorities forced private individuals to organize as a means of defending themselves against the aggressive bodies that rose from the anarchy promoted by governmental weakness.[51]

Meanwhile, the Action Française showed that it still had strength in the

Faculties, by organizing strikes and riots against Professor Gaston Jèze of the School of Law, who had betrayed civilization by serving as adviser to the Negus in the League of Nations and had thereby disqualified himself for teaching French students.[m] They also showed their power in the law courts, where they operated through a body known as the Avocats du 6 Février—a group that was chiefly devoted to preventing "the murderer" Frot from exercising his calling at the bar. Fights started whenever Frot tried to set foot in the Palais de Justice, but, as arrests on these occasions showed, the men who began them were recruited not among lawyers but among the Camelots du Roi.[52]

In spite of these demonstrations of how efficiently the leagues could be used to defend society against aggression, the Chamber concluded that it would be well to ban armed political formations. Then, in a sanguine mood, it also, on January 10, 1936, passed a law transferring certain press offenses from the indulgent juries of the Assizes to the jurisdiction of the judges in the Correctional Courts. Since the direct occasion of the measure had been Maurras's threats against those favoring sanctions against Italy, it soon became known as the Loi Maurras. Undaunted, the cause and object of the measure replied on January 13 with an article repeating his threats of death to the 142 men whom he had previously listed, "if they should dare provoke a Franco-Italian war." In time, all this would lead to trial and imprisonment, but such an outcome was now among the least of Maurras's worries.

Then, in late January, Laval fell when the overtures that he and Sir Samuel Hoare had made to Mussolini were revealed. While a makeshift cabinet headed by Sarraut was being contrived to hold the fort until the forthcoming elections, the Camelots demonstrated and rained handbills over the Opéra and the Comédie Française. In *Candide* Gaxotte gave a gloomy analysis of the situation, a curious combination of insight and invective typical of the Action Française.

Laval's fall, according to Gaxotte, had come from a stab in the back by Herriot, the stated reasons for voting against the Premier being no more than camouflage of a Popular Front conspiracy, whose program was one of devalu-

[m] An eminent teacher but a ferocious examiner, Jèze was if anything a man of the Right. He contributed articles to respectable financial periodicals, was rumored to sit on the board of several companies, and had signed (in 1925) a protest against Georges Scelle's appointment to the Faculty of Law. Attacked for his anti-Italian position, he was forced by student demonstrators to suspend his courses in November 1935. The following January, an attempt to resume his teaching caused rioting which led to the temporary closing of the Law Faculty, and to protest strikes by students in other faculties, both in Paris and in the provinces. The violence, involving casualties among faculty, students, and police, continued until March, when the offending courses were transferred to the premises of the Musée Pédagogique in the rue d'Ulm. Everybody took this as a nationalist success. See *AF,* Nov. 14, 15, 1935, January 1936 *passim,* Feb. 2, 12, 13, 18, 26, March 5, 6, 1936; *L'Ordre, L'Oeuvre, La République,* Feb. 2, 1936. After one lecture had been stink-bombed to a premature end, the *Canard enchaîné,* February 5, commented: "Voilà qui sentait bon la vieille France."

ation of the franc and war. France was antagonizing Italy. Next, its insistence on the Franco-Soviet Pact would anger England. The Germans would take the Franco-Russian Pact as a provocation and react by remilitarizing the Rhineland. France, alone and isolated, would be left to face the results of her inept policies. War with Germany was dictated by Stalin, by Socialists, by Masons, and by "obscure powers." This whole infamous band had found accomplices among the Radicals and among "millionaires without a fatherland." The Laval cabinet had succumbed, undermined by a disgusting coalition of profiteers, warmongers, racketeers, speculators, and visionaries. The end of the national union that it represented, willed by Stalin, prepared by Blum, announced by Herriot, marked the beginnings of disastrous times.[53]

Just how disastrous the times might be was implied in Maxence's determined words at a meeting of the Solidarité Française (now, on account of anti-league legislation, rechristened the National Corporatist and Republican Party): "If ever we take power, this is what will happen: at six, suppression of the Socialist press; at seven, suppression of Freemasons; at eight, M. Blum will be shot."[54]

Some of the real hate behind such statements was vented in an ugly incident at the funeral of Jacques Bainville, who died on February 9. On February 13, as the last of the long cortege, moving from the rue de l'Université to the Church of Saint-Pierre-du-Gros-Caillou, crossed the Boulevard Saint-Germain, an automobile carrying Socialist Deputy Georges Monnet, Mme Monnet, and Léon Blum tried to pass. The car was immediately surrounded by a group of men, who mobbed and mauled the Socialist leader and his fellow-passengers, injuring Blum and Monnet slightly. The incident might have been even worse had not some workers from the near-by Ministry of War (whose sentries did not bother to intervene) come to the rescue.

When the news reached the Palais Bourbon early in the afternoon, the politicians rose in apparent unison against Blum's attackers. The extreme anger expressed by such usually mild men as Sarraut and Herriot was evidence of the general feeling that they had been lenient quite long enough. As Herriot put it, "a situation intolerable for the honor of the Republic and the honor of France," was coming to an end.[55] Maurras's threats had been ignored so long as they seemed only empty ones, but now that it appeared possible that they might be carried out, the deputies lost patience. Within a few hours, at six-thirty, a cabinet meeting at the Elysée decreed the dissolution of the Action Française, the Camelots, and the Etudiants d'Action Française. They had lasted, respectively, 37, 28, and 31 years, and were never going to be reconstituted.

The blow was totally unexpected, and the royalists were the more outraged because the men who attacked Blum were part of a group that had been expelled from the League not long before, who followed the funeral unattached to any Action Française delegation. Although the extent of responsibility was never altogether clarified, the Action Française was held accountable for having created the kind of situation in which violence of this sort could happen in the street. But even though the accusation was probably justified, the suddenness of the decision after such a long period of forbearance inevitably recalled the condemnation incurred ten years before.

While Socialists, Communists, and left-wing Catholics rejoiced at the dissolution of "the most dangerous of the leagues,"[n] there were many on the Right who bemoaned Blum's escape. Privately, Maxence congratulated members of the Action Française for clobbering Blum and expressed regret that they had not finished him off.[56] And in at least one aristocratic drawing room, similar sentiments were expressed.[57] In any case, as the *Journal des débats* said the next day, Blum's injuries had been no more than a superficial scalp wound, hardly enough to make a fuss about.

The conservative press adopted a tone that was at most deprecating of rash blows directed at old men, but the Action Française and its friends were, as usual, outspoken. The incident on February 13 had been a put-up job, a deliberate provocation, a plot of the police, the Bolsheviks, and the British. England had insisted on the suppression of the royalists because the *Action française* had led the campaign against sanctions. The government was bent on revenge for the royalist campaigns against the Staviskyites. The field was being cleared for the invasion of the Soviets. Here indeed was a portent of dreadful things to come.[58]

The vitriolic response of the Action Française press was taken up in some measure by publications as far apart as the *Informateur* of Château-Thierry and *Le Temps*. On February 16, when the members of the Popular Front organized a mass demonstration in support of Blum, *Le Temps* turned on them a reserve of disapproval it never tapped against the royalists. The article, by Joseph Barthélémy, the future Minister of Justice under Marshal Pétain, denounced them as "the supporters of revolution, the adepts of social confusion, the enemies of the best French traditions," whose violence could create incidents of the most damaging nature.[59] Before a week had passed, the *Canard enchaîné* was moved to announce with righteous satisfaction that the frightful attack of M. Blum against M. Maurras had pitifully failed.[60]

Others thought it had succeeded only too well, and did not hide where their sympathies lay. As a good republican could remark in a provincial sheet: "Between M. Charles Maurras, an eminent writer and sincere patriot, and Léon Blum, this Hebrew full of hatred . . . our choice is made."[61]

[n] See *Marseille socialiste,* quoted in *AF,* Feb. 21, 1936: Socialist Deputy Ray Vidal declared, "I have always said that [the Action Française] is the most dangerous league; beside it the Croix de Feu are nothing but a lot of loudmouths."

19

THE LEAGUE AND THE LEAGUES

Unlike the condemnation of 1926, the dissolution of the League, of the Camelots, and of the student organization came when all these bodies were losing ground. It may even have permitted them to end with a flourish careers that otherwise would have dragged on in a slow, gradual decline. Precise figures are, as always, lacking; but the League had never managed to regain the strong position it held in 1926. Recruitment had picked up with the depression, and local activity had to some extent revived. But, more than ever, the newspaper had become the crucial thing. What had been an important means had become the acknowledged end. The League organized meetings and carried on propaganda and recruiting; the royalist ladies and Jeunes Filles met for tea and gossip and canvassed their friends for gifts; the Camelots sold the paper, fought and demonstrated, and broke up rival meetings or lectures at the Sorbonne. But the main activity of all these groups was to raise funds for a newspaper whose losses between 1930 and 1935 averaged about 1,154,800 francs a year.[1] It was a job that was difficult, as the Congress of 1935 was told,[2] because the most reliable friends of the Action Française were people with small or middling incomes particularly affected by a depression from which France, even by the late 'thirties, had not markedly recovered.

The subscription lists of the *Action française* are not wholly reliable sources of information, because the accounting was sometimes slipshod and at other times deliberately manipulated to leave a false impression. But if we assume these elements of error to be constant, the lists reflect the movement's measure

	1928	1930	1934	1936
Zone 1 (North)	12,809.00	12,941.80	10,671.25	11,293.85
Zone 2 (Normandy)	31,588.00	3,297.55	90.00	4,662.00
Zone 3 (Brittany)	12,320.05	8,953.50	7,309.00	8,927.00
Zone 4 (East)	12,249.00	42,820.05	2,865.00	5,267.00
Zone 5 (Loire)	9,942.00	7,420.00	1,190.00	2,572.60
Zone 6—North (West-Rochefort)	11,332.00	5,584.00	413.00	4,363.85
Zone 6—South (Bordeaux)	118,302.00	17,344.10	5,933.00	10,164.75
Zone 7 (Center)	6,440.85	983.00	0	5,076.00
Zone 8 (Lyon)	39,093.50	31,216.10	8,375.10	34,308.20
Zone 9 (Toulouse)	16,785.00	8,140.50	4,381.85	12,721.75
Zone 10 (Midi)	41,898.70	21,160.25	14,559.20	48,210.05
Total, francs	312,760.10	159,860.85	55,787.40	147,567.05

of success, and also the enthusiasm and the potential of its members. A glance at such subscriptions, by zone, reported during the first quarters of 1928, 1930, 1934, and 1936 will show the straits in which the Action Française found itself. The totals are striking. The income in 1928, itself less than half what it had been in the same period in 1925, was almost double that of 1930. Because of understandable delays, the figures published by the paper during the first quarter of a year reflect for the most part sums collected in the last quarter of the previous year. The disastrous drop of 1934 therefore reflects the very bad days of late 1933 which helped to create the mood on which the rioters of February 6 capitalized.[3] In 1936 a recovery is apparent, but of a mild sort. The general effect remains one of decline.

Several witnesses before the parliamentary Committee of Inquiry in 1934 cited membership figures that sound reasonably accurate. A police official estimated that there were about 60,000 members in the League; this figure was seemingly borne out by Admiral Schwerer, the president of the League, who gave a membership figure of 70,000 as of January 1934 (but, he added, increasing fast since then). The same police witness estimated that the Jeunesses Patriotes numbered 90,000, and the Solidarité Française twice that many. Since the Sûreté took most of its figures from statements made by the organizations themselves, which naturally wanted to make a good showing, all figures of this sort will tend to be inflated. It is impossible to know whether the Action Française exaggerated as much, or more, or less, than the other leagues. In any case, however, membership figures as such do little to reflect a party's national position: available figures for 1934 show that SFIO Socialists had only twice as many members as the Action Française (about 130,000), and the Communist Party, with 30,000 or 40,000, had a great deal fewer. On the other hand, the Solidarité Française, a movement of little strength or influence, but very boastful, was credited with 150 or even 180,000 members—about as many as the Croix de Feu and its ancillary organizations. How significant is it to know that the Jeunes Filles Royalistes were more numerous than members of the Communist Party? What counted more was how many people an organization could get on the street when it wanted to, and in that respect the Action Française could compare favorably with rivals like the Jeunesses Patriotes and the Solidarité Française, which, according to the police and other expert witnesses, could marshal between 1,500 and 2,000 men each.[4]

The active royalist troops, as always, were Camelots, *commissaires,* and students, whom the police estimated in 1934 as numbering altogether no more than 1,200 in the Paris region. Other estimates for the same area have varied between 1,000 and 6,000-odd.[5] This wide range stems to some extent from the confusion between the three categories, sometimes lumped together under the term Camelot, sometimes cited in terms of practical effectives, sometimes again as only paper figures to brag about but hardly to consider useful. The sixty-eight-year-old Camelot[6] who could afford to donate a sum equal to well over

$350 in the autumn of 1935 might perhaps have lent a hand in selling the paper, but he would not have been much use in a street fight.

The Camelots' vitality made them appear more numerous than they really were. A stubborn enemy like Bernard Lecache, the sworn opponent of anti-Semites, whose men often traded blows with Camelots in the street, estimated their numbers at 16,000 or 17,000, a manifest exaggeration. One must in fact agree with Guillain de Benouville's opinion that in the Paris region this turbulent association never numbered over 1,500, remembering that in the provinces, where even in the most favored region they counted no more than several hundred,[7] they could give an impression of considerable strength by concentrating small forces at any given time.

All this contributed to their reputation, to a widespread belief that royalists could count on solid troops—"dynamic, alert, and resolute," as an envious republican saw them[8]—and, in police opinion, unusually well disciplined. Before the Committee of Inquiry, an appreciative policeman commented on their technique in the 1934 riots: "Those in the Action Française cried 'Down with the thieves!' because they were told to do so. Everything is organized and ordered in Action Française demonstrations. Here and there a few may have cried 'Long live the King!' but generally it was 'Down with the thieves!' "[9] But even though the February 6 riots created enthusiasm and raised newspaper sales, the results were not so great as might have been expected because of the competition from the numerous other leagues that had sprung up in the few years before 1934. Not unsurprisingly, some of them had drawn potential recruits away from the Action Française, and by December 1935, at the time of the Twenty-second, and last, Congress, recruitment to the League had fallen off badly, primarily because of "the extraordinary vogue of the Croix de Feu."[10]

Another cause of trouble was the disillusion suffered by many of the most aggressive members when their hopes of January 1934 were dashed by prolonged inaction. Many men, like the republican professor who wrote to Maurras in 1930, had joined the movement because they saw in the Action Française a party of action, and they remained in it as long as it acted.[11] But the action of the 'thirties was far from satisfying for true activists, who could now find something more to their taste in other, more rigorous leagues.

Small local fights merely repelled respectable members, who had no desire to attend meetings likely to deteriorate into near-brawls when anti-Fascists intervened. And the general loss of verve in turn depressed those who wanted to do more than just sell the paper and collect funds. Some of the leaders of the movement knew this, and were worried about losing their liveliest members, to whom activity was indispensable.[12] Many Camelot exploits were no more than deliberate attempts to keep them busy.

Certain recurring items listed as contributions from Camelot sources give a good idea of Camelot activities. On one list, although some gifts, even substantial ones, come from strangers—as, for example, two donations from the bourgeois 17th Arrondissement (Ternes, Wagram) amounting to 1,000 francs ($67)—the large part of the revenue is derived from the old custom, begun in 1908, of taking impromptu collections after a tour of duty, or an arrest, or a beating up, more or less to celebrate the event. The list shows donations made by Camelot squads on various assignments, chiefly guard duty at the Action Française printing shop; from one group which held a banquet before demonstrating in the street; and from many young enthusiasts spending the night in jail. Nor are royalists the sole contributors: some of the Jeunesses Patriotes chipped in; and one interesting entry shows 65 francs ($4.30) collected at the police station of the Opéra, among five Camelots, one Croix de Feu member, and sixty members of the Solidarité Française, all under arrest.[13]

But those who looked beyond the immediate fun of minor pranks and scuffles were aware that a policy had been adopted which, since 1930, and obviously in 1934, made effective action most unlikely, and less and less popular at the top.

The last symptom of this division between the membership and the leaders appeared in 1935 when fresh ideas of action within the Paris Federation led to a clash between a group of Camelots and Leaguers headed by Jean Filliol on the one side and, on the other, Pujo, Calzant, and Réal del Sarte. Ninety-seven signatories of a long memorandum charging the three leaders with letting the movement down were promptly expelled, and a new hegira started of one more faction which had found the hierarchy too firmly installed to budge. It was members of this band who were responsible for the attack on Blum, and who later on furnished a good many recruits, not least Filliol himself, to the underground organizations of the Cagoule, bent on the kind of action they could no longer find in the rue du Boccador.

So, people left, and others were expelled. A few months before the dissolution, Maurras boasted that the League was a thousand sections strong. The 1936 *Almanach* tells another tale: it lists 469 sections, 427 centers, groups, or correspondents, and 30 sections more in Paris and its suburbs. Thus, the organizational rules established by Plateau in 1920 were met in 500 sections at the most; no more than that could muster the forty dues-paying members technically required, and, since the rule was often ignored, probably fewer.

We have seen that by the end of 1933 the *Action française* had a circulation of around 30,000. In January and February 1934 there was a tremendous upswing, but because of careless distribution methods and generally poor organization—much of it owing to Maurras's own habitual sloth—sales were not maintained. Few readers outside Paris were ever able to count on finding the paper at their usual kiosk each morning, and within six months, newsstand circulation, which had risen to over 130,000 in January 1934, was back to around 56,000. This was a good deal higher than in preceding years, but certainly nothing to brag about in view of the opportunities there had been for permanent gains.

The jagged rise and fall of circulation in 1934 contrasts noticeably with the record of comparable papers, which, although making less sensational strides, nevertheless overtook the royalists. The Paris circulation of *Le Figaro* and *Le Populaire* in 1933, 1934, and 1935, according to the figures of an important distributor, was for the most part higher than that of the *Action française*:

	Action française	*Le Figaro*	*Le Populaire*
January 1933	8,935	9,730	16,280
January 1934	40,000	8,090	13,495
January 1935	16,000	26,000	21,350
February 1935	15,850	12,550	21,270

In the first quarter of 1936, however, the average circulation of the *Action française* in Paris and the provinces was still holding its own in comparison with competitors like *Le Temps* and *Le Figaro*:

	Action française	*Le Figaro*	*Le Temps*
Sales in Paris..........	20,266	12,970	17,480
Sales in the provinces...	37,593	17,922	19,408
Subscribers	13,889[14]	18,705	36,700
Total	71,748	49,597	73,588

These considerations may have been behind the fairly philosophical acceptance with which the official dissolution was greeted by some royalists: "It is the newspaper that always made for the strength and unity of the League. Suppress the latter, it is no more than a detail. Keep the paper, it is the principle, it is all."[15] Not that the royalists really meant to respect the dissolution: the *Action française* always spoke of "dissolved" Camelots and "dissolved" Leaguers, ironically implying that the decree had not actually done anything to prevent their existence.[16]

By Joan of Arc's Day in 1936, the "dissolved" militants had regrouped themselves in several royalist organizations: the Marius Plateau Association of Veterans; the Action Française Institute; the newspaper; the once-separate royalist Oeillet Blanc now pressed back into service; the organizations of royalist nurses and social assistants, royalist ladies and the Jeunes Filles; the Royalist Railwaymen, whose section in the League had now assumed autonomous existence; the odorous Halles Françaises; and, most numerous of all since the addition of members of the dissolved League, the Union of French Corporations, the old creation of Georges Valois, which had been vegetating for over a decade.

Press observers for the most part agreed that dissolution had not made much difference to the Action Française. *Le Matin, Le Figaro, Le Journal,* and *Le Petit Parisien* concurred in noting the numbers and the discipline of the royalist column, all of whose participants carried the paper in lieu of the forbidden badge. *L'Humanité* was predictably revolted to see how freely royalist leaders paraded with their "disbanded" leagues.[17]

Despite this favorable publicity in May, the spring had been full of disappointments for the Action Française, which were only a foretaste of more to come. On April 4, the highest legal body, the Conseil d'Etat, rejected the royalist appeal of the decree of dissolution, despite their plea that the Action Française was not a party but a doctrine, hence hardly to be considered under the terms of the law as an organization aiming to overthrow the Republic by force.[18] For once, Maurras's statements were fated to be taken at face value and turned against him by representatives of an order which had for so long failed to defend itself that, when it did, the change seemed an unjust attack.

This was not the only legal blow to Maurras: on March 21, he had been sentenced to four months in jail for incitements to murder contained in his articles of September 23, 1935, and January 13, 1936, against the proponents of sanctions. Even as his appeal was on file, however, he made new threats, against Léon Blum. The Socialist leader, wrote Maurras on May 16, would be the first victim of his own policy if it should lead to fratricidal war between the Latin allies of 1915: "Il ne faudra abattre physiquement M. Blum que le jour où sa politique nous aura amené la guerre impie qu'il rêve contre nos compagnons d'armes italiens. Ce jour-là, il est vrai, il ne faudra pas le manquer." For this, seven days later, another court sentenced the indomitable old royalist to another eight months in jail and a small fine. On May 26 Maurras's appeal of the first sentence came to court, with the result of a slightly milder verdict than the original one—the four months were cut down to three, to be served in addition to the other eight.

While all this was happening, France was in the throes of general elections, which both sides regarded as crucial, akin to a revolutionary experience. The Action Française, aware of how much was at stake, no longer attempted to pretend detachment from the elections and was battling with the rest. Early in April, the paper advised its readers what their attitude should be. They were told to take no official sides for any candidate and to accept no seats on any electoral committee. They were to concentrate upon opposing the enemies of France, the tools of the foreigner, which could be classed under three categories: the friends of Russia, of Hitler, or of Britain; "Red Christians" and supporters of the Popular Front; members of Daladier's cabinet on February 6, and those appearing on the famous list of 140—which actually numbered 142.

Royalists were told to follow certain simple rules: when a "National" candidate opposed the Popular Front, they were to vote for him; when National candidates opposed each other, they were to secure from one of them formal and public declarations "in the sense of the national and economic policy we serve"; when Popular Front candidates opposed one another, they were to vote for none.[19]

The three main arguments brought against the Left followed in general the right-wing platform: Spain, where a Popular Front was ruling, was cited as an awful warning of what might come from a victory of the Reds; such a victory would be sure to cost France her British allies, with the ensuing collapse of the Entente Cordiale; and, third, a government of the Popular Front would cause financial panic and send the franc plummeting.[20]

The *Action française* actually endorsed a good many candidates of the National Republican coalition—Chiappe, Trochu, Frédéric-Dupont, and others—but approvals were, on the whole, less frequent than attacks. When the paper mentioned the names of candidates it was either noncommittally or damningly. It opposed Paul Reynaud, Chappedelaine, Raymond Patenôtre, Jean Mistler, Henri Ducos, Guy La Chambre, and Marcel Déat, all of whom, except Déat, were elected.[21]

It must be said at once that, as always, the Action Française played almost no real part in the election or in its results. The campaign was fought in a strange confusion, in which Thorez offered the hand of friendship to Catholics and to the Croix de Feu, and *L'Humanité* called on those who wanted order to vote Communist.[22] Both sides argued that the victory of the other side meant war: "Whoever is against the Popular Front is for Hitler, whoever is with Hitler is for war," the Communists explained; "If you vote for the Popular Front supported by Moscow, it is WAR," countered the posters for the National Republican Entente.[23] Each side emphasized the most extreme aspect of the other: in one case the fight was against Fascism, in the other against Communism. The arguments in every case were calculated to drive the uncommitted voter toward a positive stand, to persuade him that in order to make his vote effective he must cast it at one extreme or the other.

Inevitably, when dreadful outcomes were predicted as following upon what had hitherto been no more than the exercise of a rather empty right, people everywhere were nervous, and many spoke out who had in past elections always kept their opinions to themselves. Just before the first ballot, Pierre Benoît welcomed Claude Farrère into the Académie Française with a hortatory oration that came as a clap of thunder on the Quai Conti:

> We have laws to banish the heirs of our kings, the kings of France! But we have none to put down the hideous scum of international thuggery that come to France to play just as they like with knives and bombs . . . And there is something more horrible than our responsibility [in letting them run free], it is the excuse we have to use: our disorganization, our anarchy. We ask ourselves in anguish if there is not someone just as badly defended as King Alexander of Yugoslavia . . . or President Doumer . . . and if that is not France: the France of 1914, and of 1936.

The press recorded the success of this peroration, and of other similar political allusions in the speeches of both Benoît and Farrère. Maurice Noël in *Le Figaro* pointed out that they were mere echoes of Charles Maurras, for that was where the two speakers drew their ideas. "It was the themes of Maurras's daily struggle, the lessons of his beliefs, that shone out yesterday under the dome of the Académie."[24] There was even an echo of Maurras just before the second ballot in *Le Temps,* in a call on all patriotic Frenchmen to unite in one gigantic counterrevolutionary party.[25]

The first ballot of the election was held on April 26. With five and a half million votes, the Popular Front gained what seemed a spectacular victory over its opponents, for whom only 4,233,928 ballots were cast. After the second ballot, on May 3, there were 72 Communist deputies where only eleven had sat before, 198 Socialists (SFIO and dissident groups) where the last Chamber had had 168. Moderates in both camps were the great losers, 51 fewer Radical-Socialists sitting in the new assembly and 44 fewer representatives of various center Left groups opposed to the Popular Front.

Between the 25th and the 29th of April, quotations on the Paris Bourse fell alarmingly; government 4.5% bonds reached the lowest rate since the reconversion of 1932; those of the Bank of France, the lowest in eleven years. And though events were to show how indecisive, in reality, the election returns were, they seemed ominous enough to many at the time. The trends of the past years were coming to a head. Political polarization was completed as the conservative mass was herded by its press into the reactionary camp. Like less notorious papers, the *Action française* and its satellites simply concentrated on recruiting the counterrevolutionary party to which *Le Temps* referred, by persuading people that no alternative existed any longer between reaction and Bolshevism.[a] The great working-class demonstrations that followed the election seemed to bear this out; and the widespread sit-in strikes that began at the end of May were taken by many property owners as signs that the worst predictions of their political guides were coming true.

In the near-panic that gripped conservatives about the time the Popular Front cabinet took office on June 2, the stand adopted by the nationalists, for which the Action Française had shown the way, was largely that of anti-Semitism directed against the leader of the left-wing coalition, Léon Blum, and against all his people. There was in these outbursts some sheer anti-Semitic prejudice of the most brutish kind. There was also some puerile resentment, of the sort that drove the novelists Louis-Ferdinand Céline and Marcel Jouhandeau, the latter of whom found the Popular Front "inopportune" and its policies fatal for France.[b] But the idea, or the intuition, behind the campaign

[a] See, e.g., *Le Matin,* May 5, 1936; *JSP,* June 13, 1936; *Candide,* May 21, 1936; *AF,* June 5–12, 1936. The image that royalists wished to create was reflected in *Candide*'s report of May 21, that the great Communist meeting at the Salle Wagram on May 18 had broken up to cries of "Maurras en prison."

[b] In the case of Céline, whose *Bagatelles pour un massacre* appeared late in 1937 and received an ecstatic review from Rebatet in *JSP,* January 21, 1938, the cause seems to have been that a ballet project he had submitted for the Exhibition of 1937 had been rejected by the Jewish Minister of Education, Jean Zay. After that, the Jewish conspiracy could not be gainsaid. Jouhandeau's conversion had come at an earlier date. *AF,* October 8, 1936, published a long article by him, "Comment je suis devenu anti-sémite," in which he spewed forth his dislike of Maurice Sachs, Léon Pollès, and Julien Benda of the *Nouvelle Revue française,* and also of Léon Blum, denounced Jewish oppression, hatred, and contempt of Frenchmen and the Frenchmen's God, and ended by vowing he would not cease to denounce Jews while a single one remained in France without

went deeper: it was a deliberate attempt to emphasize national unity at the expense of aliens, or of those who were declared to be such.

The nationalists did not want to oppose French workmen, or even to give full support to capitalism, about whose virtues they were, at best, divided. They solved their problem by arguing that workmen were deluded by foreign agents and doctrines, and that the representatives of capital could be divided between wicked aliens and well-intentioned but unfortunately ignorant natives. With the blame for misery and dissension thrown on outsiders, the principle of unity was at any rate preserved and the theory, as usual, helped to rationalize the practice.

Anti-Semitism is inherent in national-socialist argument wherever there are Jews, because without it the working class would run the risk of being excluded from the national community, when unity and social justice are on the nationalist's tongue—and sometimes on his mind. But Jews are a group excluded to begin with, and attacks against them can theoretically replace attacks against opponents who as compatriots are beyond reach, and perhaps eventual converts to national-socialism. When *L'Etudiant français* declared, on April 10, 1937, that being anti-Marxist implied being anti-Semitic, it meant, among other things, that this way it did not have to be explicitly against anybody else, opposition to whom might prove doctrinally embarrassing. The Jews were wicked, their dupes merely misled.

If employers were unjust, if workers were unruly, if the government was, to say the least, unwise, it was more convenient to attribute all this to aliens than to fellow-Frenchmen, especially when a symbol of the alien already existed in the person of a man who was both a Jew and head of the "revolutionary" coalition.

The Action Française and Henry Coston's Francistes were the two nationalist movements that stood outspokenly against Jews. The Jeunesses Patriotes and the Croix de Feu had never shared these views, and the snobbish anti-Semitism of certain right-wing circles did not express itself in doctrines or in political terms. The royalists had to some extent restrained their pragmatic anti-Semitism until the depression brought a wave of immigration of German Jews, disturbing a country already struggling with dire unemployment problems. Even then, however, they had left anti-Semitism incidental, an occasional diatribe rather than the central theme.

In February 1936, however, dissolution of the League following the attack on Blum brought the royalists to a paroxysm of fury. They transferred their resentment at the crucial blow to the man who had unwittingly furnished its occasion, and then to his people as a whole. As Maurras put it, the excessive

control by special statute. He also published a book, *Le Saladier* (1936), on similar lines, comment on which can be found in *AF,* October 12, 1936. See *AF,* October 22, for Sachs's excellent answer, followed by further Jouhandoesque lucubrations. In a letter of December 1, 1960, Jouhandeau attributes what he now considers an aberration to the fact that "l'inopportunité du Front Populaire m'avait fait me hérisser contre les responsables."

furor over Blum's petty bruises proved only the overweening power and vanity of the Jews, whose tyranny was no longer to be borne:

> Our patience is at an end. Ah, no! Ah, no! These Jewish masters forget the indulgence with which they have been treated of late. Sleeping justice shall awaken, and if it does not wake of its own accord then it will be awakened. *Down with the Jews!* Those whom we made the mistake of treating as if they were our equals display a ridiculous ambition to dominate us. They shall be put in their place, and it will be a pleasure to do so.[c]

The campaign that began in February continued into April. Election results encouraged it to persist and amplified its tone. There was no denying "the Jewish fact," argued Maurras. France was held in thrall by Jews who were a foreign power and ran the country for their profit.[26] Evidently, this did not prevent them from seeking its ruin as well. A tract the royalists published at this time had the title, *"Where Does Revolution Come From? Revolution Comes From Jews."*

Darquier de Pellepoix, once a member of the League but now a municipal councilor with an anti-Semitic organization of his own, presented to the General Council of the Seine a "Project against Jewish tyranny and foreign invasion," which called for the immediate annulment of all naturalizations granted since 1918 and the promulgation of a statute regulating the Jew's right to vote and to hold public office. He had to wait a few years before he could get his wish, but his relations with the Action Française remained good until the eve of war.[d]

It was an even closer friend of the Action Française, *blanc du midi* Xavier Vallat, who intervened in Blum's investiture debate on June 6 to call his premiership an historic occasion: for the first time this old Gallo-Roman country was to be governed by a Jew.[27] Henceforth, the paper's anti-Blum campaign was to be conducted in violently anti-Semitic terms, soon applied to the Popular Front regime as a whole: "The kike's riposte," "The Jewish ship adrift," "The Jewish revolution sings its victory." The cabinet became "The cabinet of the Talmud."[28] Blum was subjected to a torrent of insults, frequently from the pen of Maurras.[e] In one article only fifty lines long the royalist whom Albert Thibaudet had described as "An Ambassador of France to the French" managed to call the Premier of his country a camel sixteen times. The rest of the cabinet he described as idiots, fanatics, deserters,

[c] *AF*, Feb. 19, 1936; see also Daudet's threats on Feb. 17, and those in *JSP*, Feb. 22. This did not prevent the Action Française from backing a Jewish patriot, a veterans' leader named Edmond Bloch, in the 4th Arrondissement of Paris.

[d] The Action Française's quarrel with Darquier came about as a result of his publishing, some years later, an article by Urbain Gohier, who in the course of a slanging match, had called Daudet and Maurras Jews. "Our enemies' friends cannot be our friends," declared Maurras in February 1939.

[e] See *Le Voltaire*, Dec. 12, 1936, pp. 12–13; in this connection, one may recall Paul Marion, *La République*, Sept. 21, 1935: "Charles Maurras est le Léon Blum du royalisme, m'a dit un ancien camelot."

crooks, pederasts, traitors, prostitutes, and assorted species of the animal kingdom.

These attempts to discredit the Premier eventually stuck, even though they were shrugged off by people with intelligence. It is always shrewd to underestimate the intelligence of the public, as the success of most political slander has proved, and repeated innuendoes and outright assertions that Blum was a rich, hypocritical millionaire leading a movement of expropriation were not ignored by all who heard them. There was, in particular, the story about his splendid household silver. In 1937, when Blum was leading President Lebrun round the great retrospective exhibition of French Art, he stopped before a particularly magnificent set of silver objects from the Louvre, commenting, "Here is my famous collection of silver." Jean Zay noted that night that the President, who had remained discreetly silent, later asked a guard to see if this were true.[29]

Another story had even more impact. In June 1936 a rather obscure satirical weekly printed the information that Blum had been born in Bessarabia, with the name Karfunkelstein. Within two days the *Action française,* delighted by such manna, repeated the story, and often thereafter in its pages hyphenated the two names. Two years later Blum made it clear in an article in *Le Populaire* that he was French, born of French parents and grandparents in Paris, in the rue Saint-Denis.[30] And yet in 1959 the new edition of the *Petit Larousse Illustré* appeared with a biographical notice on the late Léon Blum repeating the old nonsense, long since exploded, and had to be withdrawn under the threat of legal action.

Although they freely attacked Blum, the royalists were far from wanting to oppose head-on the working masses who had voted him into power. The strikes were revolutionary movements, and bad as such; but they were symptoms of a profound malaise. The problem was to harness the revolutionary spirit, to seduce the working masses back from Communism, and to enlist them in a "national revolution."[31] *Je suis partout* expressed this point of view:

> Recent strikes have revealed great misery in the working class, insufficient salaries, terrible instances of exploitation. It is too simple to denounce Communist intervention in popular movements, without recognizing at the same time, when this is the case, the valid reasons of the workers' claims. The mass of workers will never be recovered for patriotism and the fatherland if the task and the honor of defending the legitimate interests of the proletariat are left to the Communists. The only solution to the present malaise lies in the creation of French unions that will defend the workers' interests within the order of the French fatherland.[32]

As Gaxotte insisted, the unions had to be purged of Communism, which poisoned and killed them, and a free, national, French unionism must be established to oppose the unionism enslaved to Kremlin bureaucrats. "The working class is part of the nation," he wrote; "the misery of workers is that of the fatherland. The misery of the fatherland is the misery of workers."[33] In other words, the insurgency of workers had been transferred to ground that was theoretically safe: it could be dealt with by appealing to well-meaning workers, by approving unionism in principle as long as the unions were in the right hands, by implying that existing unions were under foreign domination and suggesting that they should be directed by Frenchmen and freed from foreign interests.

There was no hope of persuading the French workers, who were well ahead of their own unions, that their activities and their demands were being directed from abroad; but this detail did not matter. The qualified sympathy to laboring men that royalist theorists evolved coped with the problem of proletarian violence in such a way as to avoid the open opposition of the working class, and so the essential theory was safe.

More important from the nationalist point of view was the fact that the Radical public was becoming uneasy under the impact of the sit-in strikes. Fear of the workers' soviets was teaching Radicals some wisdom, the *Action française* noted only three weeks after Blum had assumed power. Maurras urged the Radicals to realize how important it was that the Communists be sent back to Russia, by the Radicals in cooperation with the Action Française and with all other good Frenchmen.[34] This was somewhat premature. The middle-class reaction against working-class excesses was essentially a fear of social and economic revolution, but it had to express itself in respectable, patriotic terms. The opportunity to do this would be afforded by a government decision, even before the crashing impact of international affairs.

On June 18, following violent clashes between strikers and nationalists at Marseille, which perhaps encouraged the decision, the government dissolved the nationalist leagues and banned the wearing of their emblems and the display of their banners. Not surprisingly, the action drew a torrent of abuse from the nationalists, who, bitterly protesting that the move must have been dictated by Moscow,[35] called upon their friends to wear the tricolor rosettes and to hang tricolor flags from their windows, in answer to the red flags of the Left. The red-white-and-blue was now flaunted in all the bourgeois sections of Paris; in some suburbs like Auteuil flags appeared at almost every window, and nationalists demonstrated in the Latin Quarter and on the Champs-Elysées wearing tricolor emblems and singing the "Marseillaise."[36]

Here was the ideal cause to rally conservatives, and it is significant that nationalist demonstrators were henceforth described mainly as "patriots."[37] The patriots were defending the national colors against the alien followers of the red flag. "No one is going to turn us into slaves after the Russian model!" the *Croix* declared self-righteously. "We shall impose the French flag in the street," announced the *République,* "if the police will do nothing to impose it;

we shall tear down the other, if the police do not tear it down; in a word, we shall play the role the government does not dare to play."[38]

The *Action française* professed itself shocked and disgusted by the cries of hatred that the display of the national colors excited from the Left, even though on further research the only concrete example of left-wing anarchy that they seemed able to find was "Les fascistes à Charenton / On en f'ra du saucisson," a form of vulgar jingling to which Camelots never abased themselves.

But here was the ideal situation in which provocation and counterprovocation became impossible to separate. By taking the national colors for their own, the nationalists had turned attacks against themselves into attacks on national honor. The gangs of demonstrators met head on, singing the "Marseillaise" on the one side, answering with the "Internationale" on the other; wearing the tricolor on the one side, sporting red on the other. In all the mix-up, the instigators and the retaliators were not always certain, but clearly it was the tricolor that was the winning trick. The Left had allowed itself to be caught in an idiotic position, for supposedly neutral persons would in the end, inevitably, sympathize with the defenders of simple patriotism. The reactions of such persons were reflected in a letter read aloud in the Chamber, in which the daughter of a Radical-Socialist senator protested against what seemed to her the anti-militaristic demonstrations of the Left:

> I am a Republican and in no way hostile to the Popular Front; but if this front turns out to be Communist and anti-French, there will be many of us who will turn to the national parties, whichever they may be. They are trying to foist the red flag and the "Internationale" upon us. We want to know only the red-white-and-blue and the "Marseillaise."[39]

This was precisely the effect that the men with the tricolor had hoped for, and every major riot in which the Left attacked the flag of France served to drive home their point that they were fighting foreigners, not Frenchmen.

It is not easy to know what part the *Action française* played in this campaign, except that it seems to have been the first to launch the tricolor idea. The *République,* perhaps too generously, attributed to it the whole responsibility, and ascribed what it considered the great recent effectiveness of the royalists to the dissolution of the other leagues.

Discussing the dissolution of the leagues, Vallat had remarked in the Chamber that it had always been a matter of chance what league one joined: essentially they all were much the same. One joined them "by the accident of personal relations, of circumstances, and of time and place." But although the members of the leagues were united by mutual aspirations, the leaders saw that they should stay apart. "In dissolving the separate organizations," Vallat warned Minister of the Interior Roger Salengro, who had signed the dissolution order (and would soon pay for the act with his life), "you have suppressed the artificial division of their members and facilitated the rise of a *ligue unique*."[40]

Only a few weeks later, Vallat's gloomy predictions seemed to be coming true. "Who led last Sunday's fighting?" asked the *République*.[41] "There is no question that it was the men of the Action Française. They are the only ones who have experience of the streets and a taste for street fighting."

> The dissolution of the leagues has practically turned their members into a single mass, and the yeast of this mass today is the Action Française. Since the dissolution, with a minimum of its own troops, the Action Française wields a considerable force because it surreptitiously manipulates masses far superior in number to anything the old League ever managed to recruit.

The Action Française leaders themselves were not so sure of their effectiveness. Throughout July, while fighting the good fight against the Jews, the Communists, the government, and the Republic, the royalist leaders were casting anxious eyes on troops difficult to hold in hand now that the structure of the old leagues no longer existed. They issued dire warnings against listening to the siren calls of rival organizations, against dispersing and joining other movements.[42] Any advantage to be reaped from the dissolution of the other leagues could be enjoyed only so long as they stayed dissolved. In such a case a newspaper and a small active group could hope for great effect.

But two new movements were growing, which would inherit most of what was left of the other leagues: the PPF (Parti Populaire Français), founded by Jacques Doriot on June 28, and the PSF (Parti Social Français), formed on July 11 by de La Rocque to replace the now-dissolved Croix de Feu. Both new parties tried to suggest in their titles as in their policies the aspirations of most young nationalist thinkers for a "national revolution" or national socialism. But it would still always be the Action Française that launched the slogans. On July 18, 1936, *Je suis partout* carried a stern headline: "The Popular Front Means War." The same day, in the Spanish Republic, an insurrection led by a general set off the civil war that might well bear this out.

20

SPAIN

FRENCH ROYALISTS had always been in close touch with sympathetic friends south of the Pyrenees, to whom, as for José Martinez Ruiz, Conservative deputy to the Spanish Cortes and a contributor to the great Madrid daily *ABC,* love for the Action Française and love for France meant one and the same thing.[1] In 1931, royalists in France marked the abdication of Alfonso XIII as a day of mourning, shadowing forth the rise on its southern border of a republican government "notoriously Germanophile, if not Russophile." After that April, the *Action française* could only predict the worst for a republic in which Communism was making the most disquieting gains.[2]

In February 1936, its worst fears were realized when the Spanish elected a Popular Front coalition—obviously the harbinger of Red revolution. Disorder and anarchy of the worst kind were being installed at the French back door, with convicts set free to perpetrate the most iniquitous crimes, street murders a common occurrence, the desecration or burning of churches and convents a matter of course. The record of the left-wing coalition was summed up by the *Action française,* and by the rest of France's "proper" press, as "Riots, Arson, Expropriations, and Murder." And when the Red terror disappointingly proved milder than first reported, the explanation was that Moscow had ordered it toned down until general elections in France were over.[a]

The influence of Maurras and the Action Française had played its part in inspiring one of the most intellectually active groups of the Spanish Right, the men centered round the Cultura Española and its review, entitled *Acción Española* after the *Action française.* The leaders of this Spanish group, all of whom died in or on the eve of the Civil War, were three: Ramiro de Maeztu, sometime anarchist son of a Cuban and an Englishwoman, a "theologian in politics"; Victor Pradera, the traditionalist philosopher; and José Calvo Sotelo, a politician and financier.[3] But it was Eugenio Vegas Latapié, won over to Maurrassian ideas as a student in Paris, who had been instrumental in bringing them to Calvo Sotelo's attention. It is unlikely that the *Acción Española* was founded simply to spread the doctrines of the Action Française, as a member

[a] *AF,* Feb. 21, April 16, 1936. On July 14 and 15, the *Action française* reported that Calvo Sotelo had been murdered by government Assault Guards, but, hastening to present his killing as being of Muscovite inspiration, made no mention of its having been done in retaliation for the murder of a Guards officer by a right-wing military organization.

of the latter organization has suggested, but it nevertheless did its best in this direction.

It published translations of *L'Enquête sur la monarchie,* of Gaxotte's *French Revolution,* of Benoist's *Lois de la politique française,* and even, at the beginning of 1936, of La Tour du Pin's *Vers un ordre social chrétien*; and to Spanish intellectuals it presented Maurras, Daudet, Benoist, Gaxotte, Louis Bertrand, Abel Bonnard, Robert Vallery-Radot, and other nationalist writers of or close to the Action Française, as the ideal of French culture and political thought. Other well-known members of the Spanish Right were interested in these ideas or openly sympathized: Antonio Goicoechea, leader of the Traditionalist (or Carlist) Party, the Marquis de las Mirasmas, director of the daily *Epoca,* the poet José M. Peman, José Felix de Lequerica, future Ambassador to France (and later to the United Nations). Late in 1936, Eduardo Aunós asserted that the reaction against the social-democratic Republic crystallized around French counterrevolutionary thinking, led by Maurras.[4]

French nationalists greeted news of the Army uprisings in Spanish Morocco, then in Spain itself, with rejoicing, mingled with the hope that a similar escape might be in store for France. The *pronunciamento* issued by the insurgent generals was taken from the first not as a rebellion against the country's legal government but as counterrevolution.[5] The Insurgents became almost at once the "Nationals" or "Nationalist forces." Within three days, borrowing a formula launched by Edouard Helsey in the *Journal,* the *Action française* affirmed that this was a "guerre de religion" between the revolution of the Left and the social order represented by the Insurrectionists. The issue, wrote Maurras, lay between individualists, with their anarchic tendencies, and the "others who believe that man counts only as part of a natural group—his family or his profession. The struggle will be without mercy."[6]

A Fascist insurrection south of the Pyrenees seemed not only to threaten the security of a professed democratic regime, which had to give serious attention to the possibility of war with Fascist powers on another border, but also to represent a direct challenge to the new Popular Front. Quite apart from this, however, the Spanish government had the money as well as the right to buy foreign arms to defend itself. Even if one did not choose to regard the Republican government as the only one, or want to help because of sympathy, the only reasonable attitude, as Winston Churchill, no friend of Communism, wrote,[7] was to recognize the belligerency of both sides and sell to both whatever goods they could afford to buy.

Yet when the Madrid government, desperately in need of arms after the defection of most of its regular Army troops, attempted to buy them abroad, it found the market unexpectedly tight. France, as the only major power sharing a common frontier with Spain, was immediately approached about the acquisition of arms, ammunition, and especially planes. But here, perhaps, the Action Française made its greatest contribution to the victory of the

Nationalists, for its denunciation of all aid to Spain effectively prevented any sizable shipments to the Republican forces.

On July 22 Pujo reported that a Spanish mission had arrived in Paris to negotiate for aid: "What do the Madrid envoys want? Money, guns, planes? Whatever it is, the French forbid the government of the Jew Blum to give it. Not because the Spanish insurgents are 'Facists.' But because these 'insurgents,' if they win, will be Spain's next government and would not forgive France for what she did." Pursuing the subject the next day, Pujo explained that such a deal would constitute an odious and dangerous intervention in the internal affairs of Spain—a dangerous and dishonorable adventure that could only lead to war.

On July 24, Maurras himself expressed his opposition to furnishing military aid of any sort. Such help would bring German and Italian intervention, and an internal Spanish conflict would develop into a general war. Fear of war in France had reached proportions the country had never known before, and the nationalist campaign against "intervention," like the campaign against sanctions in the preceding year, took advantage of the general apprehension. Meanwhile, Pujo, kept supplied with information by friends at the Spanish Embassy and in the French government, was denouncing in precise detail the arrangements being concluded for the sale and delivery of planes and ammunition.[b]

After the first salvo by the *Action française,* the other right-wing papers had followed suit. Within twenty-four hours of Pujo's first article, *L'Echo de Paris* expressed vague but decided opposition to the idea of arming the Spanish Republicans, and on July 24 Henri de Kerillis denounced in greater detail the plans for delivering material to government forces, while in the Chamber Pierre Taittinger and René Dommange embarrassed the cabinet with their questions. By now, the right-wing press had been mobilized, and a violent campaign was under way, fed by information from pro-Insurrectionists in both Spain and France, to prevent the French government from intervening in any way, even by allowing private firms to conclude deals with the Frente Popular.[8]

The president of the Senate Foreign Affairs Commission, Henry Bérenger, intervened with Lebrun to ask that all scheduled shipments to Spain be prevented, and a special cabinet meeting held at the Elysée on July 25 decided to comply with the request. A brief communiqué after the meeting stated that "the French Government was resolved not to practice a policy of intervention." The *Action française* was jubilant: "Blum-la-guerre a dû reculer!"[9] Thereafter, friends and militants of the Action Française kept a tight check on ports, border stations, and airfields to see that no supplies left the country, and all attempts to get around this were denounced.[10]

[b] *AF,* July 22–24, 1936. As the Communists were well aware (see Lucien Sampaix's articles in *L'Humanité,* March–April 1936, and especially April 2), royalist information services continued to operate remarkably well; friendships with Air Force officers proved particularly useful.

It has been claimed that the British threatened to suspend the treaty of Locarno if Blum agreed to supply the Frente Popular with arms.[11] In a letter to his wife, written during the war, the Premier stated very clearly, however, that his reason for not helping Spain in 1936 was to avoid a civil war in France: "As soon as the situation became more dangerously tense, we should have had in France the counterpart of Franco's *coup de force.* Before any foreign war, France would have had civil war—with few chances of victory for the Republic."[12] In the end, the arms issue and the government's indecision served to aggravate the growing moral upheaval in France and to hasten the disintegration not only of the Popular Front but of the morale of the entire nation.

The Spanish war was an ulcer for the French; and Blum's decision not to intervene was more symbolic of the resignation of the country, and especially of the Left, than any other official act could be. There were good moral reasons to dislike the Frente Popular, but every actual reason that influenced the cabinet's decision was the reflection of timidity, of weakness, of a national climate of surrender. To the layman, the immediate cause of the cabinet's statement of position was certainly the wild barrage of the conservatives and the Right, a press campaign which mobilized national opinion and set in motion the parliamentary interventions that resulted in the statement of the 25th.

The origin of this campaign was to be found in the *Action française.* As *Charivari* declared:

> It must be said because it is the truth: a French newspaperman has this week rendered a signal service to his country: Maurice Pujo. It was Pujo who first, with proofs and details in support, denounced the odious deal . . . It was Pujo who first put a stop to execution of the bargain, who provoked the intervention of M. Henry Bérenger . . . and the special cabinet council of Saturday afternoon.[13]

The royalist argument had been from the start that if France refused to lend the Spanish Republicans a hand, no other power would have cause to intervene in the peninsular war. And, so the argument ran, all trade with the Spanish government, though quite justified under international law, was intervention, and "intervention" was bound to lead straight to a European war.[14] Consistency not being a hampering consideration in such matters, however, when Pujo, on July 30, reported deliveries of German Junker and Italian Caproni aircraft to Franco's forces, he laid responsibility for this on Blum and on Air Minister Pierre Cot, whose "imbecile obstinacy" in wanting to help the Spanish Republicans had given the waiting Fascists the justification for helping their friends the Insurgents.

From then on, the *Action française,* like Pertinax in *L'Echo de Paris,* Jacques Doriot in *L'Emancipation nationale,* Saint-Brice in *Le Journal,* and

Leon Bailby in *Le Jour,* abandoned the line that aid to Madrid would justify widespread foreign intervention and argued instead that, even if it were proved, Italian intervention could never justify the risk of war.[15] This view was ultimately expressed by Maurras in a formula which had the advantage of being clear, when he declared on August 10, 1936, that France must under no pretext intervene in Spain, whatever anybody else might do.[c]

By then, Blum's government had announced that all exports to Spain had been suspended pending the negotiation of a nonintervention agreement, which would enable it to give in altogether but with a seeming appearance of initiative. But it did continue to give the Republicans a trickle of aid in secret,[16] accompanied by repeated denunciations from the royalist press. Even the nonintervention proposals could not find favor with Maurras, who, deploring the subjection of the French people to such a company of idiots and scoundrels, denounced Blum's cabinet for being the first to break the policy that it itself proposed.[17]

And in *Je suis partout,* in the purplest of purple prose, Robert Brasillach predicted to his appalled readers the fate of innocent Spaniards, women and children, churchmen and lay, who had been butchered by Bolshevik killers or forced to flee their homes in cars identified with foreign flags to secure a minimum of safety:

> Par la grâce d'un gouvernement de pleutres et de bandits, les cyniques, les marchands d'armes, les sadiques comme ce petit Pierre Cot (il suffit de regarder son portrait pour deviner chez lui on ne sait quel érotisme du sang et de la mort), font la loi à ces pauvres gueules de pions chahutés que montrent Blum et Salengro. Le jour viendra, le jour n'est pas loin, où nous confectionnerons . . . quelque bannière étoilée, quelque étendard de l'Union Jack. Où nous apprendrons que Paris, ou Lyon, ou Marseille ont envoyé dans les petites villes leurs camions de tueurs. Où les évêques rouges seront pendus dans leurs chiffons de pourpre et les curés démocrates éventrés avec leurs enfants de choeur, au pied des croix renversées et des ciboires souillés d'excréments.[18]

To the readers of the *Action française* and its fellow-publications, foreign intervention must have appeared in a peculiar light. The title of an article by Pierre Varillon in the *Action française* was characteristic: "German Concentration in Spanish Waters. Will Our Crews Be Defended Against the Agents

[c] Not all royalists shared this point of view. Although Bernanos's *Les Grands Cimetières sous la lune* (Paris, 1938) is in no way representative, other than moral indignation inspired men like the French Military Attaché in Madrid, Lt. Col. Morel, who made no bones about his sympathies for the Action Française. Recalled for consultation by Blum in the spring of 1937, he expressed in his advice a tone more familiar to nationalists than Maurras's opportunistic comment: "Monsieur le Président du Conseil, je n'ai qu'un mot à vous dire, un roi de France ferait la guerre." *Les Evénements survenus en France de 1933 à 1945,* Témoignages et Documents (Paris, 1947), I, 254.

of Moscow?[d] When Insurgent bombers destroyed Guernica in April 1937 and even the staid *Croix* protested the cruelty to which the Basque people were subjected, the *Action française* was there to set things straight. An article in the May 6 edition told how Red lies had been exposed by the inquiries of honest French reporters who found that not Nationalist planes and bombs but fires set by Russians had destroyed the town. And when this version proved slow to gain acceptance, both Frédéric Delebecque and Maurras attacked the dirty tactics of those who spread their lies about this and other matters in hope that some of the mud they threw so irresponsibly would stick. It was a good thing, wrote Delebecque, a Protestant renowned for his high moral tone, that there were still a few people in France who were ready and willing to brand the ignominy of such methods and shout it from the housetops.[19]

In September 1937 the sinking of the British destroyer *Havoc* by an unknown submarine was also attributed to the Russians. *Je suis partout* called "piracy in the Mediterranean the supreme resource of the Reds." Beaten in Spain, the Soviets sought war elsewhere; only they could have torpedoed the British destroyer, hoping thereby to set off a conflict which alone could save them from ultimate destruction. Conclusion: "European peace could be founded only on the destruction of Communism."[20]

The Times appreciated the consistent way in which the *Action française* was showing up French intervention in Spain, and the articles and illustrations in the royalist paper were taken up eagerly by many elements of the foreign press, especially by the Germans.[21] No better justification could be hoped for by the Fascist powers than the articles of the royalist paper, in which the French government appeared as the most thoughtless warmonger of all.[e] It is small wonder that the reputation of the Action Française stood high in Franco's Spain.

When Franco was proclaimed Head of State in Burgos, the Action Française was quick to wire congratulations expressing its admiration of his work.[22] In January 1937, Maxime Réal del Sarte was given a warm reception at San Sebastián, where he reviewed units of the Falange and was invited to address the radio audience. French-language broadcasts from San Sebastián devoted a good deal of time to excerpts from the paper, and sometimes began and ended by playing the Action Française hymn "La Royale." One Nationalist aviator, Major Juan Antonio Ansaldo, who had organized Falangist terrorism before the war, confided to an *Action française* correspondent that he

[d] *AF,* Aug. 15, 1936. The article said that German gold was pouring into Spain to encourage the anarchy there, the implication being that it went to support the activities of the Reds.

[e] There was no mention in the press of the fact that it was royalist General Paul-Louis-Alexandre Lavigne-Delville, a regular contributor to the *Action française* military columns, an original member of Deloncle's MSR and a future sponsor of the Milice, who, with Charles Trochu and Jacques Percheron of the Front National, recruited French volunteers for Franco's Bandera Jeanne D'Arc. See Emile Decroix, *Complot contre la France* (1938), p. 21.

was almost deaf, but proud to be so, because that made him "a little like the great Maurras."[23]

In May 1938 Maurras and a group of friends made a visit to Nationalist-held Spain. The old man was welcomed with semi-official honors, was officially fêted at Burgos and elsewhere, received the personal thanks of Franco, and was elected a corresponding member of the Royal Academy of Spain. For Maurras the trip was something like a dream come true—the new Monck that he had envisioned had at last arrived—but, alas, not in his own country. He bewailed the mistakes that had prevented his own government from realizing the importance of siding with Franco from the first; and when, in February 1939, the Chamber voted to recognize Franco as the Caudillo of Spain, he regretted that the official gesture came too late to secure the friendship of the Spanish leader, who had been antagonized but not defeated by so many unsympathetic pinpricks.

21

THE CAGOULE

THE SPANISH CANKER was only one of the dissensions that disrupted France in general and affected the Action Française in particular. Before surveying the foreign issues upon whose tide the country let itself be carried into war, we must pause for a look at the role of the Action Française in the internal scene.

With the summer and autumn of 1936 came the brief fruition of the Popular Front and its disintegration. Bitter about their election losses, the Radical partners of the victorious coalition were being gradually alienated from their confederates by the fear that Blum, unable to hold his troops in check, would lead the country into revolution, war, and ruin. Some of the right-wing extremists who had been briefly eliminated by the polls or invalidated by the Chamber were being re-elected. In August Jean Chiappe, in September Philippe Henriot and Jean-Louis Tixier-Vignancour[a] were returned to the Chamber. Jean Fabry, who had been defeated by a Communist in April, was returned to the Senate in November from the Franche-Comté, on a platform of national defense.

Led by Emile Roche, president of their Federation of the North and a director of the *République* as well as of several big industrial concerns, the Radicals, whom Henriot had as early as 1934 described as the most conservative and bourgeois of French parties, were digging in their heels.[1]

Addressing the Radical Congress at Biarritz that summer, César Campinchi had made a telling slip: "In the last legislative elections," the Corsican deputy told the delegates, "we suffered a partial defeat. We lost 300,000 francs."[2] Everyone knew he meant not francs but votes; but though the audience roared, the mistake was revealing. The Radical public and the Party backers were losing money, and they were afraid of losing more. In the circumstances, the talk of social reform by the Popular Front was hardly reassuring. As Maurras pointed out, there was nothing really to separate them from any right-wing Republican, besides the old suspicions. The evolution of the Radicals was only a matter of time.[3]

The most popular play in Paris during that winter season, *La Fessée*, by

[a] Jean-Louis Tixier, not yet hyphenated, Camelot of the 6th Arrondissement, was charged with assault against the forces of order when the Etudiants d'Action Française attacked a Communist meeting on March 9, 1926; see F[7] 13198.

Jean de Letraz, offers an excellent *raccourci* of what was taking place. The farcical plot concerns a husband who, while imprudently giving his wife a spanking in front of an open window, is photographed by an indiscreet amateur. Sent to be developed in Paris, the negative falls into the hands of striking workers, who use it for a poster supposed to represent first an example of capitalist turpitude, then the symbol of reaction being scourged by the proletariat. The storm of publicity proves highly embarrassing to the couple until a shrewd newspaperwoman reinterprets the picture to show it no longer as the image of long-stifled revolt but rather of order aroused into giving anarchy its due. The husband, who had been scorned by his friends, now becomes a national hero because of his magnificent gesture, the inspiration of national opinion finally aroused against disorder. And the play ends on the happiest of notes, with the husband marrying the charming female reporter, the wife the interfering photographer, and both being taken up by the very best society.

It was against this background that more mundane affairs continued on their way. On October 29, the Cour de Cassation having rejected his appeals, Maurras was arrested to serve the sentences he had received that spring. "Maurras imprisoned for having saved the peace," lamented the *Action française,* while thirty municipal councilors and general councilors of Paris and the Seine signed a "respectful homage to the man whose thought honored France."[4] *Candide* was tearfully indignant at the thought of his being jailed by the rogues and nincompoops who pretended to rule France: never had there been a man more helpful to others, himself more preoccupied with all that could affect his people, readier to sacrifice his time and effort to help those struck by adversity. Young at heart and goldenhearted, he was rewarded for his devotion to his fatherland for over fifty years by being arrested under conditions that made even policemen blush. The ministers who ordered this could only be tyrants, liars, traitors, and cowards.[5]

The conditions of Maurras's imprisonment seem not, however, to have been severe. Maurras was the only inhabitant of the political detention quarters at the Santé; his cell was heated, and he could read, write, receive mail, and pass his time much as he pleased. Since the government did not prohibit journalism, Maurras continued to write for publication, though under a pseudonym. In memory of a secretary of Nicholas Fouquet who during a five-year prison sentence had completed a history of Louis XIV, Maurras took as his pen name Pellisson, and articles so signed appeared in the *Action française* almost daily. After a short time, the prisoner was permitted to receive visitors in his cell, and it became one of the favorite haunts of literary society, to the delight of Henry Bordeaux, who likened it to a drawing room where one could always get good talk.[6]

While Maurras was thus occupying himself in his cell, his enemies outside were being slanderously and repeatedly attacked by the nationalist press;

and in November, one of the victims, Minister of the Interior Roger Salengro, committed suicide. As the Socialist mayor of Lille, then as a deputy and the Minister of Interior, Salengro had provided a prime target for the leagues. It was Salengro who had signed the order for their dissolution, and since the outbreak of the Spanish war he, along with Pierre Cot, had been one of the warmest advocates of serious aid to the Republicans. Naturally, his enemies were determined to get back at him in any way they could.

In 1915, as a battalion cyclist in an infantry regiment, Salengro had been captured by the Germans while carrying a message in No Man's Land. The French procedure in such cases was to court-martial the missing soldier, and then attempt to establish whether he could be held guilty of desertion. This had been done in Salengro's case, with the result that he had been completely cleared; and at the end of the war, like thousands of other prisoners released, Salengro had received an honorable discharge. There the incident had dropped, save for one occasion when Communist opponents in the north tried to make political capital out of it.

On July 14, 1936, however, the *Action française* accused the Socialist Minister of having been condemned to death by default by a Divisional Court-Martial, for having abandoned his post and deserted to the enemy. Within a few days, *Gringoire* had taken up the charges and challenged Salengro to reply. Horace de Carbuccia's weekly review was not bound to the Action Française as *Candide* and *Je suis partout* were. There were friendly relations, there was community of views, but there was no organic connection. *Gringoire,* however, had the biggest sales of any national weekly and must have reached at least 500,000 families. Relentlessly it kept up its charges against Salengro, and they were fed by what seemed crushing personal evidence provided by his former company commander and by another wartime comrade.

The *Action française,* although it had been the first to accuse Salengro, observed a certain circumspection in continuing the charges. For some time, it did little more than echo weakly the poisonous and detailed allegations of *Gringoire.*[7] By October, the accusations had by the sheer power of accumulation become one more political "affair," and at the request of the harassed Minister a Court of Honor was appointed to investigate the charges and denials. General Gamelin and two well-known veterans' leaders completely cleared Salengro of all charges; but by that time it was not enough. In France, especially, these days, no one believed sufficiently in anybody's honor not to think that the conclusions even of a Court of Honor had been rigged. The right-wing press had suggested that there would be fraud even before the Court met; in its eyes, any conclusions drawn by Gamelin and his two colleagues would necessarily be tainted with deceit.[8] The Court of Honor was as if it had never been. Salengro's enemies would not abandon their angry allegations that the Minister of the Interior was a deserter, a coward, and a fraud, and evidently nothing that anybody could say or do to the contrary was likely to make them change their mind.

There could be no defense against such campaigning except a thick skin and sufficient self-confidence to last out the bombardment, shrugging off the slander so as to survive with the least amount of damage to character and nerves. Unfortunately, Salengro was without the stamina that might have enabled him to do this; his wife had died the year before, his mother was gravely ill, he was beset with grave self-doubts about his fitness for the ministry he held. One night in mid-November he returned to his empty and unheated apartment in Lille to find the cold supper the maid had left upon the kitchen table. Depression must have overcome him, weariness at battling against a slander impossible to live down, and loneliness of season and of heart: he turned on the gas and killed himself.

His death was, of course, attributed to the savage attacks to which he had been subjected. "They Have Killed Him" headlined the *Populaire*; and *The Times* published an indignant article on the campaigns of the *Action française* and *Gringoire,* too absurd to be taken seriously, yet exercising dismayingly serious influence.[9]

The opinion of the *Action française,* needless to say, was different. When Colonel Henry and Gabriel Syveton died, the paper argued, their opponents took the suicide as clear evidence of guilt. Why should this not be true also in the Salengro case? Perhaps in committing suicide Salengro had deserted for a second time. That this seemed reasonable to others appears from the story told by Yves Simon about the headmistress of a Catholic girls' school and her charges, who were fascinated by the Salengro case. All these good Christian ladies, young and old, were jubilant over the news of Salengro's suicide: "C'est l'aveu," they crowed, bristling at any suggestion that judgment on the matter might prudently be reserved.[10]

To some degree or other, this seems to have been the attitude of most Catholics of the Right, who argued, like *L'Echo de Paris*—and also like *Gringoire*—that it was no one's fault but Salengro's if his nerves were too feeble and his moral fiber too weak for him to save himself from the sin of suicide, even if by chance he had not been guilty of desertion. As for *Candide,* the detail of Salengro's suicide was secondary to an irritation at Blum's unnecessary "exploitation" of a "mysterious" death.[11]

One must conclude with Cardinal Liénart, Archbishop of Lille, that regardless of what other factors may have determined Salengro's suicide, the responsibility of the muckraking press was grave. To the *Osservatore romano* their libelous campaign had been "the determining cause of this tragic end."[b] The Catholic intellectuals who criticized this sort of reckless behavior in the democratic *Aube,* emphasized, without naming names, "the crushing responsibility of those who dare to speak without proof against a man's honor, of those who accuse opponents in such a manner that no refutation can ever

[b] *L'Aube,* Nov. 20, 1936; *Osservatore romano,* Jan. 9, 1937. A well-informed witness who lived through these events in the inner circles of *Candide* and *Je suis partout* declares that the Salengro affair was rigged in retaliation for Maurras's imprisonment.

dispel the doubt introduced in passionately prejudiced minds."[c] Paul Faure, at least, had very little doubt where the responsibility belonged. At a great Socialist meeting in the Vélodrome d'Hiver, where Popular Front tenors gathered to pay homage to the dead man, the second-in-command of the Socialist Party concluded his speech with a direct attack on the Action Française: "There is not a country in the world," said Faure, "where the *Action française* could appear; not one where such defamation would be tolerated . . . We must put an end to this scandal. In that way we shall have avenged Salengro." And out of the great round hall, above the answering roar, a voice rang out, "A mort l'Action Française!"[12]

But if the Action Française was to be put to death, it was sure to put up a vigorous fight. Indeed, future events might show that not the royalists but their opponents were riding for a fall.

The winter of 1936–37 was devoted to awakening the people of France to the menace of Red revolution. From November 1936 to January 1937, the military page of the *Action française* featured a series of articles on self-defense in a civil war against the Reds. When, in January, *L'Echo de Paris* published, with a guarantee of authenticity, "Instructions to the Red militia on how to neutralize the Army," Daudet repeated the revelations under the promising headline "A Plan for Collective Murder." The Spanish civil war was inspiring both the Extreme Right and the Extreme Left, and each saw its own position as a defensive one. It was important, however, to win over the masses of the public that were not usually politically active or alive, to make them consider the idea of Communist revolution as a matter of course, to persuade them of the necessity of preparing for that moment, and of the wisdom of acting before the Communists did.

"Will the Communists try their insurrection soon?" asked *L'Insurgé*, beseeching the middle classes to organize their own defense. *Candide* devoted its front page for two weeks running to an imaginative description by Pierre Dominique of what would happen after the *coup d'état* which, one dawn, would enforce on the country a Red dictatorship giving free rein to lower-class hostility against the bourgeoisie.[d] Cassandra had always been the patron saint of the Action Française; but now the readers of *Candide* were being treated to a view in which the monotony of a dismal present was relieved only by promises of an even more dreadful future. The subjects of a few articles from one issue at random concern the Communist tyranny over workingmen, the decadence of French economy, the fact that France had become a country where

[c] *L'Aube*, Nov. 21, 1936. Among those who signed the text were Georges Bidault, Charles Dullin, Francisque Gay, Jacques Madaule, Jacques Maritain, Maurice Merleau-Ponty, Brice Parain, and André Thérive.

[d] *L'Echo de Paris*, Jan. 14, 1937; *AF*, Jan. 15, 1937; *L'Insurgé*, Feb. 17, 1937; *Candide*, Feb. 11, 18, 1937: "Le Matin du grand soir." One of the tragedies of the revolutionary upset occurs when a respected political figure who has been keeping two tarts in an apartment is held for ransom and humiliated by them and their pimp at the news of the coup.

no one worked any longer, where laziness had become the supreme law (there was no reference to insolence in *this* number), where inflation was creeping up, and, with inflation, misery; and where the government, here mildly described as ineffectual and unjust, busied itself with schemes designed to deprive conservative, patriotic Frenchmen of their civic rights.[13]

These dangers were soon illustrated, when, on March 16, police forces trying to maintain order as Socialists and Communists turned out to demonstrate against a PSF rally in a Clichy hall were forced to open fire. Five of the demonstrators were killed, and some 150 were injured. The right-wing press was delighted, the Popular Front appalled. Socialist and Communist papers attributed the trouble to provocations of the PSF. More to the point, the rival left-wing agitators seem to have raised the tone in meetings and in print to keep ahead each of the other's overbidding. It is also possible, though it was not at the time suspected, that the riot was instigated by a group of Cagoulards led by a certain Jacques Corrèze, the righthand man of Eugène Deloncle, head of the Cagoule.[e] Clearly, said the Right, the fault lay with a government that not only was unable to keep its putative supporters out of trouble but even had to shoot them down. Cartoonist Ralph Soupault drew an enormous cartoon for *L'Insurgé,* showing Blum, dripping with gore, standing in a great pool of red and asking, "Who said I had no French blood?"—under a headline that clamored "MURDERERS! RESIGN!"[f]

The Clichy riots fitted into the pattern of the long alarmist campaign against the Communist Party and the left-wing leagues which carried on undisturbed when those of the Right had been outlawed. The fighting at Clichy was represented as having been the work of the Communist paramilitary organization, the Autodéfense Ouvrière. The danger from the Jeunes Gardes Socialistes was also emphasized in a way obviously meant to alarm conservatives. *Candide* readers were given the impression that they had been left defenseless while the Communists and the Socialists were preparing for a coup.[14]

If the men who were behind this campaign really felt uneasy, it was less on account of the imagined Red menace than because their own activities were not going so well as they could wish. As usual, they had high hopes of achieving national unity and founding a majority party of the Right. And also as usual, their hopes were being ruined by the unwillingness of nationalist leaders to collaborate. Everyone professed himself ready to work with the others, provided he was the one to say who would do what. In May 1937 there

[e] See René Maublanc, *La France en péril* (1938), p. 18; Fernand Fontenay, *La Cagoule contre la France* (1938), *passim*. Corrèze's father, an important figure in provincial banking circles, was one of the leaders of the PSF at Auxerre.

[f] *L'Insurgé,* March 24, 1937. Soupault, whose ferocious cartoons appeared in most Action Française publications, later, during the Occupation, lent his talents to the Milice, and thereafter to *Rivarol.*

was published an open letter from former President Doumergue to Jacques Bardoux deploring the fact that the enemies of the Popular Front "do not manage to join in a single, disciplined and active group." Jacques Doriot suggested such a coalition in a "Freedom Front," but with the PSF naturally excluded, because most nationalist leaders were at dagger's point with Colonel de La Rocque; and the Action Française replied that it, for one, though friendly, preferred to work alone.[g]

But if they were incapable of showing a united front, the nationalists could take up the fight against one another. From spring to fall of 1937, the Action Française joined several other groups in trying to crush de La Rocque, who was spoiling the hopes of anti-parliamentary action by sucking into his PSF too great a share of the funds and the men on which the Right could draw. On July 15, 1937, *Choc,* financed by Duc Pozzo di Borgo, a sometime leader of the Croix de Feu who had refused to join the PSF, denounced de La Rocque for having solicited and received payments out of secret funds from Tardieu and Pierre Laval during their terms in office. The allegations were taken up by Doriot's *Liberté, Le Jour,* and *Gringoire,* as well as by the left-wing press. They were also pressed with great enthusiasm by the *Action française.* De La Rocque quickly brought charges against his accusers, accusing them in turn of insults and slander. The cases were tried in October and November, and, after the crushing evidence given by Tardieu, they ended badly for de La Rocque, who lost his case of slander and won only slight damages for insults from *Choc, L'Humanité,* the *Populaire,* and the *Action française.*[15]

The thing to note here is the different motives of de La Rocque's enemies: the left-wing press, of course, welcomed any dissension of the Right and gladly repeated charges and countercharges. Pozzo di Borgo wanted to destroy the PSF for the benefit of the more active subversive underground with which he was connected. Doriot had similar motives, but on behalf of his own Popular Party (PPF). As for Tardieu, he presumably welcomed the chance to damage a league and to expose one of the men whom he despised. Out of the depths of his own pessimism, he probably loathed the men with whom chance allied him equally; all the advice that the retired Premier vouchsafed was "Upset everything!"[16]

The Action Française, for its part, had from the start taken up a position strongly opposing de La Rocque, not out of any sympathy for Tardieu or for the Cagoulards but, in the main, out of hatred for the man who had refused to act with them on February 6, who was now a dangerous competitor syphoning off funds and manpower that it coveted. The *Courrier de Genève* reported that the *Action française* "was the heart of the campaign against the president of the PSF in which it distinguished itself by a flood of malignant passion,"[17]

[g] *Choc,* May 13, 1937; *AF,* May 24, 1937; Alfred Fabre-Luce, *Journal intime, 1937* (1938), p. 122. Actually, personal relations were excellent, and a good many of the younger members of the Action Française contributed regularly to *Liberté.*

but the opinion was exaggerated. For once the *Action française* did not lead but follow. Its language was no more excessive than what it generally used in such cases, although it was bad enough to shock the Genevese.

In the end, the Action Française drew little profit from all this; and no more did the Right, which had insisted on washing its dirty linen in public while the whole country, fascinated, watched.[18] All parties to the de La Rocque trials displayed as much capacity for corrupt dealings, mutual denunciations, and internal dissensions as the Left, which they liked to scold for all these things. If de La Rocque's good name was besmirched, his hold on his own party hardly suffered. His adherents got their own version of the affair from the *Flambeau* and the *Petit Journal,* as did the Communists from *L'Humanité* and the royalists from the *Action française.* French society lived and thought in separate compartments, with a different idiom and different truths for each.

Hopes may have existed among Action Française leaders that if the offensive against de La Rocque succeeded, Maurras would be recognized at last as the only possible leader of the nationalist cause. The old royalist's imprisonment had inspired his friends to exuberant heights of admiration for him. Beginning on November 1, 1936, the *Action française* published lists of the messages of sympathy that had been received. Among those mentioned were 43 *khâgneux* (students of the superior rhetoric class) of the Lycée Henri-IV, the editors and staff of numerous publications, aristocrats like Baron Henry d'Astier de la Vigerie, the Comte and Comtesse de Bertier de Sauvigny, the Marquise de Saint-Exupéry, the Comte and Comtesse de Lusignan, Toulouse-Lautrec, and a host of artistic, literary and political figures: Francis de Miomandre, Marcel Jouhandeau, Robert Puvis de Chavannes, Henri Ghéon, Victor Giraud, Jacques Bardoux, Claude Farrère, Camille Barrère, and Victor Rivoire.

In January 1937 the *Revue universelle* had published a special number to celebrate the fiftieth anniversary of the start of its master's literary career,[19] to which the following had lent their names: Henry Bordeaux, Pierre Benoît, André Bellessort, Jacques Bardoux, Emile Baumann, René Benjamin, Jacques Boulanger, Robert Bourget-Pailleron, G. Brunet, André Chaumeix, P. Camo, Jacques Charpentier, Maurice Constantin-Weyer, Lucien Corpechot, Paul Dresse, Alfred Droin, Lucien Dubech, Claude Farrère, Jean Fayard, Ramon Fernandez, Henri Ghéon, René Gillouin, Bernard Grasset, Daniel Halévy, Edmond Jaloux, Marcel Jouhandeau, Georges Lecomte, Pierre Lafue, G. Le Cardonnel, Xavier de Magallon, Jean Martet, Henri Martineau, Henri Massis, Guy Mazeline, Mario Meunier, Francis de Miomandre, Joseph de Pesquidoux, Edmond Pilon, Henri Rambaud, Marie de Roux, the Comte de Saint-Aulaire, Saint-Georges de Bouhelier, Gaëtan Sanvoisin, Jérôme and Jean Tharaud, and Gonzague Truc.

In England there had been protests against the scandalous arrest of a man who, as Professor Yvon Eccles of London University said, represented the greatest intellectual force of contemporary France.[20] A few months later, an inter-university committee was set up to nominate Maurras for the Nobel Peace Prize, as one who, by his campaigns against sanctions, had done more than anyone else to avoid a European war. The president of the committee was Professor Fernand Desnonay of the University of Liège, and the other members were the Honorary Rector Zdziekowski and Professor Francis Brossowski of Wilno University, Jean Bruchesi of Montreal, Francis Yvon Eccles of London, and Colonel Gilly of the Belgian Colonial University at Antwerp. When their petition was submitted to the Nobel Prize Commission of the Norwegian Storting, it bore the signatures of professors from thirty-three universities in fourteen countries, including seven deans or former deans, seven members of the Institut or the Academy of Medicine of France, ten members of different national Academies, and two holders of the Nobel Prize.[21]

By the end of June 1937, as the historian Jérôme Carcopino told Count Ciano, the Popular Front was a matter of the past. Blum had resigned, to be succeeded by the Radical Camille Chautemps, the coloring of whose cabinet was symbolized less by the presence of Blum himself than by that of Georges Bonnet, a well-known opponent of Popular Front policies, as Minister of Finance. The situation was strikingly reflected in the election of a new president for the General Council of the Seine, which previously had been led by a Communist. The Socialist candidate, André Le Troquer, had been favored for election, but he lost by 66 votes to the 69 cast in favor of "National" Victor Constant, one of the councilors who had been active on February 6, and whom the *Action française* triumphantly described as "a fierce defender of the middle class and of small businessmen, scorned and ruined by the Popular Front."[22]

This was the climate of affairs when Maurras emerged from prison, a hero of the Right. His release on July 6, after 250 days in jail, was as triumphant as his friends and followers could make it. On July 5, 6, and 7 the great "information" press treated it as front-page news, and published interviews with the man who had suffered for his ideas.[23] On July 8 a great meeting at the Vélodrome d'Hiver attracted 30,000 people, gathered, under the honorary presidency of Marshal Joffre's widow, to honor "the greatest political writer of our time, the purest, least debatable of patriots."[24] The meeting was organized by the Republican Federation of Louis Marin, Xavier Vallat, and Philippe Henriot, by the Republican National and Social Party (the old JP) of Taittinger, by the French Popular Rally (the old SF) of Jean Renaud, and, of course, by the Action Française. Lucien Romier, the political editor of *Le Figaro,* Bailby, publisher of *Le Jour,* as well as Chaumeix, Bellessort, and Abel Bonnard of the Académie Française, were there to pay public homage to their friend. It was, as *Candide* commented, a sort of apotheosis.[25]

The *Charivari* devoted its center section to a great "Tribute to Maurras," in which twenty deputies, nine of them from Paris, waxed lyrical about his talents and the injustice of throwing such a man in jail: "Il a menacé! . . . La guerre n'a pas eu lieu! . . . Au lieu de lui tresser des couronnes de reconnaissance, on l'a emprisonné."[26] To republican observers, "the quasi-spontaneous conjunction of all national or nationalist forces" at the Vel d'Hiv meeting seemed ominous. As the political chronicler of the Radical *Petit Havre* put it, this sort of "crystallization" around Maurras would not have occurred the year before. But now the champion of integral nationalism could appear "as the living symbol of opposition to the Popular Front," and some of the incense burned to him was also for his doctrine. "La cristallisation Maurras est un fait politique qu'un chroniqueur politique doit enregistrer."[27]

Another political observer, and a very perceptive one, noted the same phenomenon. In two articles published that July, Albert Bayet suggested that with Doriot discredited by his failure to win re-election as mayor of Saint-Denis, with de La Rocque discredited by the revelations of Pozzo di Borgo and Tardieu, with Jean Chiappe discredited by his unsavory and notorious underworld contacts, a union of the Right was being contemplated around Maurras, whose imprisonment had given him the aura of martyrdom. But such a union could be achieved only if Maurras gave up his royalism and made peace with the Church. This was why, Bayet pointed out, at the Vel d'Hiv meeting royalism was for the most part ignored and the praise was all of Maurras as "the leader," "the savior of peace," the man in whose hands "the destinies of the Fatherland" should rest. Not the "Royale" but the "Marseillaise" was sung by those who celebrated his merits, and without protest from the hero himself.

> The way seems open for Maurras, and the idea of making him sole chief of the right-wing factions, provided he declares himself loyal to Republic and to Church, seems perfectly feasible. "Well-informed sources" are sketching the scenario in advance: first Maurras's conversion by the grace of Sainte-Theresa of Lisieux, then his election to the Académie Française by the grace of M. Bellessort, then grand national assizes and the proclamation of Maurras as *Duce* to the strains of the "Marseillaise."[28]

All this, in truth, would be asking far too much not only of Maurras, who remained faithful both to royalism and to agnosticism, but also of his fellow-nationalists, who were incapable of working together for any long period. One cannot doubt, however, that Bayet had wind of plans and expectations, for he obviously had detailed information. Maurras's stature now seemed sufficiently great to lend credence to such hopes, and several times after the Vel d'Hiv meeting Daudet called for "Maurras au pouvoir,"[29] and fellow-nationalists—Taittinger, Chiappe, Trochu—treated Maurras as a sort of banner, the grand old symbol of their fight.[30]

But if they did, it may have been because by then Maurras was in fact little more than a symbolic figure; and though his followers were willing to make him an honored figurehead—even if it should be a *figure de proue*—they would probably have been slower to accept him as a captain. But Maurras was showing himself much more broad-minded: one could refer to him from an amazing variety of positions. His disciples could now express views which a decade before would have led to excommunication. A constellation of young men who were far more Maurrassian than royalist now filled the pages of *Combat, L'Insurgé, France réelle, Pays réel, Réaction, Frontières,* not to mention the most important of all, *Je suis partout.* Their royalism, to the extent that it existed, was directed more against the Republic than toward the king, and their old master had little interest in showing them their error. He had always appreciated incense more than the reasons for it; but now he perhaps reflected that he had already lost enough disciples to staff most of the other movements of the Right and hesitated to disown any more.

Before the year was out, however, some of these disciples, disowned or not, properly appalled the country and also the Action Française, plaguing the League with some ticklish problems in discipline. On September 11, 1937, two buildings belonging to the Employers' Federations, in the heart of Paris, one on the rue de Presbourg, the other on the rue Boissière, were dynamited; severe damage was done, though, fortunately, there was no loss of life. The question of who planted the bombs was, to begin with, baffling in the extreme. Pujo suggested that it was the work of *agents provocateurs* preparing the way to war. But were they the agents of Germany or of Russia? Perhaps, said Pujo, of both.[31] His doubts seem to have been quickly resolved, for while most of the daily papers forbore throwing the blame on the Left, and even *Le Journal* attributed the crimes to madmen, the *Action française* was certain that those responsible were Soviet agents.

During the next few days newspapers made all sorts of wild speculations. *L'Insurgé* was going to place the blame fairly and squarely: "Bombes de police," its headline said, and then, less certainly, "Un crime de police, mi-français, mi-russe?" The *Candide* editorial was more pointed: proceeding from innuendo to supposition, from supposition to assumption, and from assumption to affirmation, it concluded that responsibility for the explosions must rest with Trotskyites and/or terroristic anarchists, both of whom were evidently close to Communist circles and Communist counsels.[32]

Le Matin, straddling the different interpretations, had a Solomonesque position of its own. Under the title "France for the French," it said: "The bombs come from abroad and serve a foreign cause. It makes no difference what flag is behind them. We may disagree among ourselves on this point, but we are as one in claiming that France must be for the French."[33]

It was not clear whether *Le Matin* would have been happier to learn that the bombs had been made in France by Frenchmen, but this appeared to be the case when, on September 16, the police made several arrests indicating the existence of a secret anti-Communist organization. Such an idea must be nonsense, exploded the nationalists: the bombs, *Je suis partout* asserted, had been planted by agents in the service of the Comintern, and Marx Dormoy, the new Minister of the Interior (who a few years later would be murdered by sometime Cagoulards), was either a fool or a knave to insist on a non-existent Fascist plot, thereby allowing the real criminals to escape across the Pyrenees into Red Spain. To the *Action française,* the arrests were nothing more than a maneuver designed to distract attention from the political failures of the government, or simply to hide the fact that the police had not managed to find those who were really guilty.[34]

Ironically analyzing the suggestion that the bombing outrage could be the work of Cagoulards and that the existence of such a secret body was to be taken seriously, *Candide* agreed with fellow-Maurrassians. The sudden discovery and exposure of a Cagoulard conspiracy was nothing more or less than a put-up job designed by the Sûreté to please a government a-sniffing out the *fashists.* Looked at more closely, the sinister Cagoulards were seen to be merely wild young men, or else old lags and double agents. The whole affair crumbled to a vast hoax conjured up to make people forget that those who were actually responsible for the bombings were still at large. Abel Faivre's cartoon showed Marianne with a soapy smile welcoming a nasty-looking bunch of foreign immigrants: "Sont-ils gentils de venir faire la bombe chez moi!" This was the point on which all could agree. As *L'Insurgent* put it, whether the crimes were Fascist or anti-Fascist, they had been committed by foreigners, *chez nous*![35]

By the end of September, the hoax of the Cagoule had been all but forgotten by the public of the right-wing press. Placed in its proper perspective, it had been shrugged off for what it was—at best, a feeble attempt to hide the inefficiency of the secret service and the police, at worst the camouflage for an impending left-wing insurrection. *Candide* could afford to drop the story and, in its stead, regale its readers with horrifying revelations of how the Soviets were at that moment preparing the Red Terror.[36]

Eight years later, in an official deposition made in July 1945, Maurras would speak another language about the various crimes attributed to the Cagoule:

> Everybody on the morrow [of one of their outrages] knew who was really responsible . . . The authors were easy to discover . . . In effect, after every Cagoule crime, authors, circumstances, and the least little details were so well known and widely talked about that, at the Action Française, the youngest Camelots knew and discussed them among themselves.[37]

It had been the Action Française that first raised the alarm against the secret organizations whose very existence it would now scoff at. Since many of the leading members of the Cagoule had been *ligueurs* and Camelots, the royalists were in a good position to know what they were up to. The Action Française had disapproved the activists' tendencies when they were in its ranks; it disapproved even more when they set up on their own. Beginning in the summer of 1936, the royalist leaders had issued a series of private and public warnings against hasty and irresponsible action. Maurras had told his friends to disregard solicitations "anonymous or personal, open or undercover, public or hidden," and, in a column whose title was explicit, "Petite Intrigue—Gros Danger," had denied having any part in plots in which former members of the Action Française were now involved:

> To our friends we say: Beware! Beware of recruiters. Beware of canvassers. Beware the ludicrous oaths of a pretended white or gray Masonic order which might not be unconnected with the Masonry of the Reds. Beware especially of gross liars who say that I belong to it when actually I do not, and neither does any of the other Action Française leaders. Take no chances with the Cause and with the Fatherland!

Obviously, his exhortations were not heeded. That winter Pujo again found it necessary to warn readers against the men to whom he now applied the sobriquet Cagoulards, comic-opera conspirators who claimed Action Française support when they did not have it in any way.[38]

Thus the Action Française not only had full knowledge of the so-called Cagoule but was itself responsible for the name under which it would pass into history. Like Whigs or Tories, the nickname Pujo invented to ridicule the group stuck, and was adopted as a generic term.

There were, in fact, a number of secret societies and gangs, most of which were never discovered by the police, or were at least not brought into the open. Most of them were founded in 1936, by men who had left the right-wing leagues at one time or another, disgusted with their unwillingness or inability to act effectively. The dissolution of the Action Française in February 1936 and of the other leagues a few months later permitted these secret organizations to recruit among old comrades who were looking around for new leaders and new organizations. Cagoulards came from all quarters: Robert Jurquet de la Salle, the general-secretary of one society, was a Franciste; Jean-Pierre Locuty, who helped to make the bombs, confessed to Trotskyist sympathies; Pozzo di Borgo had been in the Croix de Feu; the Jeantet brothers belonged to the PPF. But a remarkable number of them had been involved at some point with the Action Française—Corrèze, Filliol, Martin, Jacques de Bernonville, Joseph Darnand, the Jeantet brothers, to mention only those who were in the news, had left the Action Française in the successive banishments of unruly activists. Even Pozzo di Borgo, whose forebears had been royalists, had moved in Action Française circles, particularly those of the Cercle Fustel, to whose *Cahiers* he had contributed. Another Pozzo di Borgo, who fell in action in 1915, had been a member of the Action Française section of Toulouse.

In March 1936 a group of integral nationalists actually set up a National and Social Revolutionary Party, which seems never to have been active at all. But most of them joined either the openly declared UCAD (Union of Defensive Action Committees), led by retired Air Force General Duseigneur and Pozzo di Borgo, or the CSAR (Secret Committee for Revolutionary

Action), headed by a naval engineer and sometime *Polytechnicien,* Eugène Deloncle.

Deloncle, who was on the board of several shipbuilding and financial enterprises, had been vice-president of the Action Française section in the 16th Arrondissement but had broken with the royalist leaders before the dissolution. He decided that to found another political party would be useless: the only effective action had to be carried on underground. Separate and secret societies must be set up, based on isolated cells, which ignored one another so as to avoid detection and increase conspiratorial efficacy. "An explosive force had to be accumulated, which could explode, and explode effectively, at a time of peril."[39]

Soon, Deloncle's CSAR, although not organically connected with the UCAD, was said to have infiltrated the latter organization and obtained control. Its chief purpose was to provoke Communists to action and then to strike back after having assembled around itself the forces of anti-Communist reaction. The aim might well be advanced by creating a situation in which the Communist revolution supposed to provide the justification for counterrevolutionary action could be provoked or, failing provocation, simulated.[40] After Deloncle's offices were searched by the police in November 1937 and some of his papers seized, the Minister of the Interior announced that the aim of the conspiracy had been to substitute for republican order "a dictatorial regime which would prepare for the restoration of the monarchy."

It is difficult to know what part the royalist ideals still played in the thinking of the Cagoule. Since many of them had come from royalism, it may have seemed a logical conclusion, if perhaps not an immediate one, to any successful coup. It is also true that their investigations led the police to search the offices of the *Courrier royal* and to question, though not to hold, Pierre Longone, one of the heads of the Secretariat of the Comte de Paris. But it was more their royalist origins than any royalist plans which then connected the Cagoulards with the Orléans pretenders. In May 1942, Deloncle tried to explain his motives and those of his fellow-Cagoulards in the *Révolution,* the organ of his party at the time. There had been a conspiracy, Deloncle said, but "a conspiracy for the security of France":

> the peril to the country had become so serious, so imminent, that one solution only remained possible: recourse to arms. . . . What distinguished us from other parties that existed then was that we had no political ambition whatever, that we did not want to use either paper or words, because the time was one in which one had to fall back on VIRILE ACTIONS. What distinguished us from contemporary politicians was that we shunned the platform and all public places where one could reap advantages and applause, and took our stand solely in action and in preparing the National Revolution, where one found in one's way only *blows, struggles,* and *jail.*

Although the denunciations of political action and political oratory, the denial of political ambitions, and the overwhelming concern for the safety of France are strongly reminiscent of the Action Française, the statement as a whole could not be further from Maurras's determined intellectualism, his insistence on the written word and on didactic propaganda of every sort, nor from the endless temporizing and lack of self-reliance of the Action Française.

Pujo has told how, at the time when sit-in strikes were alarming industrial leaders and fights between rival gangs wearing the red and the tricolor were outraging honest patriots, a man who represented "important material interests" and who had been disillusioned by the Croix de Feu came to ask if the Action Française could "organize the necessary counter force." Certainly it could, Pujo told him, but at the moment all that one could do was to remain on guard, preparing for action when a propitious situation arose. Apparently deciding that Pujo lacked the right spirit, the visitor departed to find somebody else who wanted arms and money, and, Pujo said, got them.[41]

By 1936 the Action Française was too inert, too verbalistic to be of use in this sort of scheme. Its three surviving leaders were in their sixties: Daudet was sixty-nine, Maurras sixty-eight, Pujo sixty-four. Their most active elements had left them the way Joseph Darnand had done, calling them "Une bande de cons!" Darnand's friend Dominican Father R. L. Bruckberger explained that he had used the phrase because they were incapable of carrying out their promises. "Il a bien vu que ces vieillards éreintés ne feraient jamais aucun coup de force et il les a quittés en crachant son mépris."[42]

However, although relations between the older royalist leaders and the Cagoule were fiercely competitive, many of the younger royalists belonged to one of the secret groups, or were at any rate sympathetic. When the Cagoulards got into trouble with the police, the royalists did their best to ridicule the charges brought against them and to press for their release.

In November and December 1937, following the discovery by the police of important caches of arms, including machine guns, grenades, and radio sets, many Cagoulard leaders were arrested. The country was agog with talk of plots, but the *Action française, Candide,* and *Je suis partout* treated the idea of an armed conspiracy of the Right with sarcasm. According to them, the Cagoule was pure nonsense: the really serious danger was a Communist conspiracy, and it had been averted only by the speedy intervention of military intelligence. The false conspiracy of the Cagoule was merely a red herring brought up to confuse the issue.

At the same time, however, and in the very number of *Je suis partout* in which Gaxotte and Dorsay denounced "le truc des cagoulards," Jean Meillonas (whose real name was Camille Fégy), who had left the Communist Party for Doriot's PPF (previous to editing Chateaubriant's *La Gerbe*), explained that the Cagoule recruited those who on the morrow of the Popular Front sought to revive the flames of national honor. Communists were taking over the State, preparing to hand France over to the enemy. The patriots joined together unselfishly, readying themselves for the time when the enemy would act, when they would stop him or die in the attempt.[43]

Out of all this, the careful reader might be able to conclude that brave, patriotic Frenchmen wished to halt the progress of the Reds in France. Infiltrated by police, their harmless, virile, and well-meaning groups had then been strung along by *agents provocateurs* and, in the end, denounced to cover up the plotting of the Left. The conservative's image of the activist has always been that of the man betrayed; but in this case Cagoulards were endowed with naïveté amounting almost to dimwittedness. Now these dimwitted patriots were lingering in jail, paying for their good intentions, and the whole Right could take their cause to heart. *Candide* lamented "the martyrdom of heroes" like General Duseigneur, Pozzo di Borgo, and Deloncle, hounded by police spies and by enemies with Semitic names. By January 1938, a committee had been set up to defend the "glorious accused"; among the first to join it were members of the Action Française, like General Clément-Grandcourt, and friends of it like Abel Bonnard, Henry Bordeaux, and the surgeon Thierry de Martel, who did not share the aversion of his mother (Gyp) for Maurras.[44]

Even when in January 1938 Locuty confessed to making and planting the bombs in the rue de Presbourg, naming his accomplices and incriminating the CSAR, when the Sûreté arrested some of the men who had murdered the anti-Fascist Rosselli brothers in June 1936, and when they themselves had very good reason to know that a Filliol in flight was closely connected with these and other murders, the skepticism of *Candide* and *Je suis partout* held firm. No doubt the deeds of certain Cagoulards were dark, but those of other factions were darker still. To Fascist crimes, Communist horrors, either past or future, were opposed, and it was insisted that the Red Cagoule was the one to bear in mind.[45] As Simon Arbellot, a faithful Maurrassian, told readers of *Le Document,*[46] it had been fear of a left-wing putsch that convinced the patriots they had to organize and drove them to conspiracies.

But this was just what another disciple of Maurras, Maulnier, reproached them for not having done. Calling in *Combat,* in December 1937, for a conspiracy against the security of the State that would be worthy of the name, Maulnier blamed the Cagoule not for having stocked arms but for having failed to use them effectively and in time. As in the Croix de Feu, their secret codes, their arms, and their disguises were nothing more than a swaggering form of *waiting,* a blustering show of really doing nothing much. "Thus," wrote Maulnier in a sentence applicable to his friends as well, "for action was substituted the romanticism of action."

The charge was just. Despite its determined-sounding aims, the Cagoule, which the Left feared far more than the leagues,[47] had not overcome the inclination to talk instead of act, the very weakness of the movements it wished to supersede. It drew up plans for striking, as the Action Française had done, but it got no nearer executing them than had the tired old men whom it decried. Though disavowed by the Action Française, the Cagoulards could claim that when the royalists were lagging and exhausted and other leagues seemed impotent, Deloncle and his friends had proposed to carry Maurras's ideas to their practical conclusion, which must consist of applying them. The only criticism they deserved—as Maulnier said—both from the point of view of integral nationalism and from their own, was that their attempts failed.

Looking back now, however, one can add another. The revelation of the conspiracies of men like Deloncle, who would appropriately die under Gestapo bullets after serving the Germans during most of the war, struck a last blow at the confidence and the unity of the country they purported to serve. No evidence has ever been unearthed of the Red plot on which Cagoulard efforts were always predicated, but the campaigns designed to convince the public that such a plot existed made their point. The French were persuaded that any appearance of order was deceptive, that below the surface lurked threats from both the Left and the Right. What had been ordinary divisions that one could discuss sensibly while leaning on the *zinc* became sinister problems involving an enemy bent on extermination.

A dirty stream of undifferentiated hate distorted human and social realities. Myths of pervading evil turned superficial disagreements into haunting fears and political differences into vendettas, and the French body politic became incapable of any kind of unity because all foundation for mutual trust had been shattered during these ruthless and bitter fights, which no one carried on with more envenomed shrillness than the Right. Serious or childish, the plots of the Cagoule helped to convince both sides that all such plots were real, with real arms and bloodcurdling threats that one had to believe. And the result of it all, as one epigone of integral nationalism wrote, was what nationalists least wanted:

> Troubled by the increase in social agitation, bewildered by press campaigns suggesting the probability of civil war, fearing "Cagoulards" as much as it did "Communists," weary of economic crisis, a fraction of French opinion, losing all national sense, began to seek its savior beyond the country's borders.[h]

[h] Debu-Bridel, *L'Agonie de la 3e République*, p. 403. See also, e.g., Louis Bertrand, *Courrier royal*, Sept. 28, 1935. Simone Weil, *L'Enracinement* (1949), p. 132, mentions an article by a young French girl in a student publication, expressing the hope that among his many concerns Mussolini would find time to restore order in France. And *AF*, Jan. 1, 1938, quoted Gustave Hervé: "Tout plutôt que l'immonde anarchie! . . . Combien, tous ces jours-ci, doivent murmurer entre leurs dents: 'Ah! Vive Mussolini et vive Hitler!' "

22

THE BREAK WITH ROYALTY

WHILE MOST FRENCHMEN were beset with anxieties about the Cagoule, the Action Française was face to face with a serious crisis of its own. On November 11, 1937, the paper printed a manifesto written by the Pretender, the Duc de Guise, and read by his son before a delegation of royalists at the Hôtel Beaurivage in Geneva.

The document was long, and most of it contained little to account for the explosive effect it had on French royalist circles. The sting was carried in the tail. Following a passage addressed to the Catholics of France, there came the affirmation that no identity existed between the Action Française and the royal house. Members of the Action Française had defended the royal house, but "the Action Française, which is a party, has always acted under its own responsibility and in complete independence," and it was a serious confusion that had tended to turn it into the official interpreter of the royal cause. "If its political doctrine postulates the monarchical principle, the teachings of its school, on the contrary, have revealed themselves incompatible with the traditions of the House of France."[1]

To this unequivocal statement, the Action Française replied with protestations of complete devotion and the suggestion that it was largely the influence of bad advisers on the Pretender's staff that explained the blow. Here, it said, was one more maneuver of the wily de La Rocques. Reviving tactics it had used in 1910 and 1926, the newspaper appealed from the ill-advised Pretender to the better-counseled one, hoping that a show of equanimity combined with power would produce a change of tone (if not of mind) at the Manoir d'Anjou.

Since royalism, in practice, meant the royalism of the Action Française, the League could count on a certain amount of support. The paper publicized expressions of indignant sympathy ranging from Clément Vautel's in the *Journal* to that of a "Liberal Republican" in the *Progrès de la Charente-Inférieure*. All blamed the princes for forgetting that without the Action Française there would not be threescore royalists in France; and all were more or less disgusted that "just when, without becoming royalists, all nationalists . . . were gathering around the upright Maurras, his Prince simply drops him cold!"[2]

The Duc de Guise cared little for controversy, and his very detachment made him fairly impervious to such campaigns. As for the Comte de Paris, his heir, he was made of sterner stuff than the skirt-chasing uncle who had backed down in 1911. On December 3, the *Action française* published his statement "To Set Things Straight," in which, using arguments strongly reminiscent of papal ones in 1926, he answered criticisms of his father's manifesto.

The leaders of the Action Française, the Comte de Paris declared, had developed a doctrine the dangerous consequences of which had been shown by experience. By integrating monarchism in nationalism, which was a Jacobin creation, they had created an equivocal situation that must be clarified. The French nationalist places his fatherland above all else, said the young prince. But the Monarchy does not consider nationalism as the sole means of securing the spiritual and moral perfection of the individual person. "By turning the proper concern for national interest and the just love of country into an absolute cult, a focus of all political preoccupation, the Action Française has caused the tradition of French monarchism to deviate. Theoretically, its teaching concludes in rational royalism; practically, it leads to Cesarism and to autocracy."

The aims that Maurras preached, the "Mise au Point" went on, were foreign to the temperament of the French and to monarchic aims of ensuring the spiritual, moral, and material happiness of the people of France. The polemical methods of the Action Française had alienated many Frenchmen from the monarchy; but since the leaders of the rue du Boccador were at the head of an independent movement, there would have been no justification for intervention in their affairs had they not presumed to represent and monopolize all royalist activity in France. Yet every time the Pretender, who never obstructed the independence of the Action Française, tried to act independently himself, he met the bitter opposition of the Action Française.

The Action Française leadership never took the Pretender's suggestions into account, they slandered the members of his entourage—to insult whom, the "Mise au Point" said, was to attack the princes—and they spread malicious rumors about the princes themselves. "We have been forced to conclude," explained the Comte de Paris in almost the same phrases that ecclesiastical authorities had used eleven years earlier, "that, instead of serving the princes, the directors of the Action Française have tried to use them for their own ends."[3]

The break had been in the offing for a long time.[a] With his lively political interests, the Comte de Paris had always coveted the leadership of the royalist

[a] A flutter in royalist dovecotes had already been caused by the death of the Duc d'Orléans in 1926. The Action Française was said to view the new Pretender without enthusiasm, a sentiment the Duc de Guise returned toward a movement too overbearing for his tastes. In July 1926 a police informant reported: "Il se confirme dans les milieux royalistes que les relations entre le nouveau prétendant au trône de France et les grands Chefs de l'Action Française sont de plus en plus froides"; see F[7] 13198, April–July 1926. The Duchesse, however, seems to have worked to improve relations.

activity that the Action Française had arrogated to itself, a leadership which, by his position, he felt he had a right to claim. His early ambitions had not got very far before the dictatorial opposition of Maurras, and, furthermore, he was faced with the real problem of how to try to direct a political movement while maintaining residence abroad. His most trusted adviser was Count Pierre de La Rocque, who in his youth had been a Camelot. In 1933, in order to have a personal platform, he had founded a quarterly, *Questions du jour,* naming as editor the youngest of the de La Rocque brothers, Edouard. Less than a year later, after trying unsuccessfully to persuade the Action Française leaders to entrust him with a page of their newspaper, he decided to launch a new publication, the *Courrier royal.*

Following the disappointment of February 6, which he attributed to the failure of the royalist leaders to "sense the air" and to collaborate with others, the Comte was convinced that no successful action could be expected from the Action Française. That summer in Brussels, Maurras, Pujo, and Admiral Schwerer were told of the Comte's plans for the new publication; and understandably, they opposed it vigorously. An inconclusive discussion on the subject came to an unhopeful end in the small hours of the morning. Then, showing Maurras to the room where he was to spend the night, the Comte de Paris recalled Maurras's triumph over the Duc d'Orléans and Larègle, many years before: "You were young then; I am young now. The future is with me. Think it over." Apparently Maurras did, for in the morning a compromise was reached. The *Courrier royal* would be an unaggressive periodical, and the Action Française would give it its support.[4]

The first number of the new review, at first a monthly, appeared on December 10, 1934. Within three months it had around 40,000 subscribers, most of them, according to its editor, Pierre Longone, members or readers of the Action Française. There was at first little enough to set the new review apart from the general run of integral nationalist fare. In its first number it proclaimed the slogan "La Monarchie n'est pas un parti," but this was hardly different from what the Action Française had been saying since 1899. The contributors being for the most part drawn from the Action Française stable or from its pastures, the royalist leaders were treated with respect and admiration and Maurras got his full share of honeyed words.

During the years 1935–37 the contributors included Abel Bonnard, Henry Bordeaux, Louis Bertrand, Georges Bernanos, Emile Baumann, Pierre Chardon, Marcel Chaminade, R. Costa de Beauregard, General Duval, Lucien Dubech, Jean de Fabrègues, Bernard Faÿ, C.-J. Gignoux, Jean Héritier, René Jolivet, G. de Montfort, André Maurois, Gabriel Marcel, Thierry Maulnier, Jacques Ploncard d'Assac, Marcel Péguy, Lucien Rebatet (using the pen name François Vinneuil), Gaëtan Sanvoisin, Georges Simenon, and Louis Salleron, and the cartoonists Ralph Soupault and Hermann-Paul. It was not surprising that the Romanian Georges Téfas, preparing a study of the economic ideas of the Action Française, viewed the *Courrier royal,* along with *Combat* and *Je suis partout,* as a doctrinal satellite of the Action Française. All three, said Téfas, "found their line in the columns of Maurras's paper, drew their principles from the *Enquête sur la monarchie,* that bible of French counterrevolutionary royalism."[5]

There was sufficient reason for such an interpretation. The Comte's *Essai sur le gouvernement de demain: Faillite d'un régime,* published in 1936, reads like a résumé of Maurras's ideas—almost a textbook for the Action Française: corporatism, decentralization, reference to traditions, criticism of liberalism and of democracy, all are there. And yet the Prince was far less conservative than Maurras had become. The monarchy that he envisaged had little of the middle-class elitism contributed by the intellectuals of the Action Française. As the slogan of the *Courrier royal* and the Prince's public statements liked to emphasize, the new monarchy looked hopefully to workers and to peasants. Where Maurras saw the king as an authoritarian figure best represented by Louis XIV, the Comte de Paris looked to the Capetians for a symbol. As he explained to Bertrand de Jouvenel, "Il faut que les travailleurs, comme au temps de Louis XI, désirent à nouveau un justicier auprès duquel ils peuvent faire appel de l'arbitraire féodal."

Less obsessed than the Action Française leadership by questions of social discipline, he could praise the Jeunesses Patriotes and the Croix de Feu for attempting to re-establish order in the land, but sympathize at the same time with the sense of social injustice nursed by their opponents. The Prince, who showed no friendliness for modern capitalism, had learned his corporatist doctrine from Valois, which meant that, although his thought was similar to that of the Action Française, his sympathies were somewhat different.[6] Even a slight difference at the start can end, when paths diverge, in positions very wide apart. So, the *Courrier royal* avoided the violence and slander of the *Action française,* and, with a few exceptions immediately after the elections of 1936,[7] avoided also the anti-Semitism and the virulent nastiness of the cartoons relished by other royalist publications.

In September 1935, the *Courrier royal* turned from a monthly to a weekly publication, handsome and well-illustrated. The Prince was gaining confidence in his ability to assert himself against the masters of the Action Française, and his staff pressed ahead with a network of propaganda and distribution centers (the Propagande Monarchique) designed to outflank the Maurrassian monopoly of royalist action. A point of view that had until now been only hinted at was expressed in an interview granted by the Comte de Paris to the *Petite Gironde*:

> The Action Française has always worked under its own responsibility, without committing the princes of the house of France. . . . Today, the royal intention is not to divide but to unite, and, to this end, we have contacts in every quarter of French politics. It is equally to this end that the

Courrier royal was created, which allows royalty to express FREELY its position toward all problems of the moment.[8]

In his pre-election manifesto of March 1936, the Duc de Guise put the issue just as clearly, but from a different angle: "It is around the princes that all the royalists must gather."[9] The implication was clear. Not independent organizations, but the direct and unhampered direction of the royal house itself was considered desirable.

Although friction threatened, relations still seemed good on the surface. The *Courrier royal* criticized democracy, as did the rue du Boccador; the Pretender echoed the doctrines of the Action Française, and the dissolution of the League, as well as Maurras's prison sentence later on, evoked indignant protests.[10] But knowledgeable sources—the Jesuits, the *Canard enchaîné*—sensed that the wind was changing. At the end of 1936, when old Ernest Renauld, once a director of the royalist *Soleil,* brought out his *L'Action Française contre l'Eglise catholique et contre la Monarchie,* denouncing "this heresy that poisoned the Capetian cause," the knowledge spread that the Manoir d'Anjou was not only impressed but was engaged in discreet propaganda in favor of Renauld's book.[11]

Meanwhile, the Action Française had abandoned its position of reserve for one of covert but determined hostility. As the *Courrier royal* and the Propagande Monarchiste enlarged their network, setting up some sixty "sellers' groups" after the Camelot pattern in forty departments, establishing their own corporatist group, the Métiers Français, and even advertising their own insignia, a small shield with three fleurs-de-lis, to compete with the single lily of the Action Française, the rue du Boccador passed the word that readers should cancel their subscriptions to the *Courrier royal* and refuse support to the Propagande Monarchiste. By the beginning of 1937, this campaign had been so successful that the *Courrier,* two-thirds of its subscribers lost, had to cut its pages and soon after that reduce its format.[12]

Rival teams of speakers sought to attract provincial royalists, but despite Lucien Lacour's decision to join the Prince, despite accusations of treachery by his friends, Maurras's hold on the royalist public was too strong to be effectively challenged. While the *Action française* maintained absolute silence, the *Courrier royal,* down to about 30,000 subscribers, hovered between compliments to Maurras, "great patriot, glory of French letters," and stern warnings that "the absolute duty of every monarchist . . . is to subscribe or resubscribe to the *Courrier royal*."[13]

This preliminary skirmishing had been useful not only in that it permitted the Comte de Paris to affirm a position, which, weak though it was in 1937, had been nonexistent three years before, but also in preparing for the break, so that when it came it did not seem so hard as it might otherwise have been. The sour grapes had long ago been abandoned. Since the *Courrier royal* had already lost most of its Maurrassian readers, there were only some four or five thousand of them left to cancel their subscriptions in the weeks after the "Mise au Point." Twenty-five thousand was the lowest figure the *Courrier royal* would reach, and it was gradually able to make good its losses, until by 1939 it had risen to about 31,000 or 32,000 subscribers. But it never again came close to attaining the high point of 1935.[14]

The royal excommunication of 1937 hurt the Pretender far more than it did the Action Française. Five out of ten regional delegates and twenty-seven presidents of royalist committees were relieved of their duties, generally at their own request. Most of the royalist press sided with the Action Française: the *Nouvelle Guyenne,* the *République lyonnaise,* the *Union royaliste* (also of Lyon), the *Roussillon,* the *Journal du Jura,* the *Provincial,* the *Courrier de Lorraine, France réelle,* the *Clairon de l'Ardêche,* the *Salut national,* the *Courrier du Midi,* the *Action algérienne,* the *Maine,* the *Observateur de Ruffec,* the *Réveil de Grasse,* as well as the *Canada* of Montreal and Léon Degrelle's *Pays réel.* All, according to their messages and statements quoted in the *Action française* of December 1937 and January 1938, were opposed to the princes.

Most old royalists were indignant that the Comte de Paris should dare to treat Maurras this way. The young ones, many of whom had joined in recent years when loyalty to the crown seemed an increasingly spurious decoration to far more serious matters, were indifferent or contemptuous. Out of a Paris section of two hundred, Samuel Osgood tells us, only two Camelots left the Action Française.[15]

The royal condemnation was approved by those who condemned Maurras already, not all of them friends of royalism. Some of them had left the Action Française because they did not like its manners or its irreligion; and even some of those survived whom royal expediency had denied in 1911. It followed that, although the field was narrow, the Comte de Paris could still, as he had hoped, recruit royalists who gave undivided allegiance to the tradition for which he stood. But the Action Française was little affected by this. A sort of natural selection had purged both movements of their uncertain elements before the break took place. For the young prince it now remained to take advantage of the future, and to make quite clear wherein he differed from the group that he had disavowed.

He did this by denouncing violence, the *coup de force,* and anti-Semitism; by taking his stand for moderation but against defeatism, and by asserting his refusal to aggravate the disunion of his land. As the Jesuit Yves de la Brière remarked in *Les Etudes,* the difference between the Action Française and the Comte de Paris lay largely in the accent with which they treated things: "The spirit of concord, of charity, of cordial collaboration, is not an unimportant detail," he said.[16]

As for the Action Française, it, too, could now stand more clearly for what it really was: it had abandoned Catholic trappings and lost most of its pretended activism; its royalism had steadily been waning, becoming more an article of faith or invocation than one of real belief. As Beau de Loménie would describe it, if one said "I am not a royalist, but Charles Maurras is a great man," one could pass muster. If one said "I am a convinced royalist, but Maurras's doctrines are debatable," one became suspect, and likely soon to be excluded.[17] And why not? Maurras's doctrines, as he himself pointed out in an article for *Je suis partout,* had never been shaken or even seriously contested, despite repeated demonstrations:

> The state of the discussions, the factors of the experiment, its regular confirmations, thus give us the right, the absolute right, to call the object of our teaching *the political truth*—like the *Quid inconcussum* of History and Reason. In these conditions how could a trial, any given trial, ever affect us?[18]

And now, God gone, king gone, and dangerous rivals gone, Maurras was left alone in the center of the movement he had made and then remade in his hardening image—intolerant, exclusive, clever, and doctrinaire, the incarnation of criticism and opposition, a phenomenon which, healthy in a sound body, could be almost mortal in one which, like France then, was sick. What by that time the Action Française and its leader had come to symbolize was expressed in Léon Bérard's remark when Maurras was elected to the Académie Française: "Of course I voted for him. One does not often have the chance to vote against the Republic, against the King, and against the Pope, all at one and the same time!"

23

THE EVE OF WAR, 1937-1939

THE WINTER OF 1937–38 brought the return of hard times, both moral and material. A new depression which had hit the economy of the West late in 1937 had resulted in an increase in unemployment throughout the world and a drop in production everywhere except in Germany. In France, the industrial production index, briefly higher in 1936, had fallen back by 1938, and the growl of numerous unemployed both cheered and alarmed the rancorous employers. Any gains labor might have made from higher wages were quickly lost by higher prices. The clumsy financial maneuvers of uncertain and economically ignorant politicians did nothing to improve matters. Although the French economy trod water it failed to keep up with that of its neighbors: where between 1930 and 1939 the productivity of other European countries rose by about a quarter per head, that of France declined 14 per cent. So did its investment level, leaving the productive plant, worn and ill-equipped, in no position to compete with foreign challenges or be much help in the national effort that the times demanded. The country, economically insecure, seemed in the grip of irresistible inflation, the result of governments too feeble for any firm decision, unable to impose either a socialist economic plan of taxation and investment, or one that was thoroughly liberal.

As early as February 1937 Blum had called a halt to the reforms of the Popular Front—reforms that had been crumbling, with the movement, since that time. The working class, aware that it had lost, was increasingly grim, and, as if in response, the rest of the nation assumed a similarly harsh countenance. People and classes feared, hated, and annoyed one another, a strained mood that was apparent in all public activities, from buying bus tickets to mustering votes in Parliament. One scored and counted points, inflicted pain or, at the least, discomfort, in one long running battle in which all the French were at the same time the hurting and the hurt, in which, in national terms at least, no one could ever win.

Led by its press, goaded by its fears, induced to refuse all credit to its adversary and to turn political opponents into enemies, the Right was the aggressor in this siege of hate. Since 1936, it had known no rest, and its resentment festered until it corrupted all contending groups and, indeed, the whole atmosphere of France. One is tempted to agree with Simone Weil that self-esteem, even more than fear, was the cause of this vindictive fretfulness:

"No one had done them harm; but they had been afraid; they had been humiliated and, what was an unpardonable crime, humiliated by those whom they regarded as their inferiors."[1]

During the early months of 1938, while Chautemps's all-Radical cabinet tacked round to find a way of keeping out of trouble, while Hitler armed, while the franc dropped and unions snarled, the Right staged an outburst calling for a dictatorship or for, at least, a strong government "de salut public."[2] Their rage grew more frantic when, on March 10, unable to resolve the country's problems without dissolving the moribund coalition of the Left, Chautemps resigned. His departure was well timed: on March 9 Chancellor Schuschnigg had announced the Austrian plebiscite; on March 11, German troops entered Austria. On March 12, *Le Matin,* while violently attacking the Communists, announced that the hour for national unity had struck and class war should now be forgotten; *Le Figaro* called for a small cabinet of public safety gathered around "an incontestable national figure." In speeches at Saintes on March 12 and in Paris on the 14th, Taittinger argued that this figure could only be Pétain, the only one of France's World War marshals who could still serve. Jacques Bardoux, the officious representative of powerful financial interests, endorsed the suggestion in a letter to President Lebrun, calling for a Government of "National Safety" around Pétain, or, if not Pétain, Daladier.[3]

Blum tried to arrange a government of "National Union," running from Maurice Thorez to Louis Marin, far on the nationalist Right; but encouraged by the Radicals, the Right and the Right Center rejected Blum's offers, chiefly on the ground that they would not and could not collaborate with the Communists, whatever danger there might be to the country from the outside. "There is only one danger—the Communist danger," Flandin declared; and Joseph Lémery, a good friend of Maurras whose Society of the Friends of National Russia included seventy-two members of Parliament, insisted, "The true danger of war for Europe lies in the Soviets!" Emile Roche affirmed the same view in the *République*: "National Union? YES! With the Communists? NO! They no longer represent anything in France."[4]

Fascinated by the Russian peril, most conservatives ignored the threat of Hitler and continued to sympathize with Mussolini. For Blum himself they had no time at all, except to disparage him, and they found the most articulate expressions of their mounting exasperation in the publications of the Extreme Right. *Candide* described Blum's cabinet as "the same heap of imbeciles, incompetents, bankrupts, hypocrites, fops, and incorrigibles [as in 1936], an insult to good sense, an insult to the nation." "Never," said *Candide*—and its respectable readers could not but agree—"has the necessity of a national revolution been so evident."[5] Nor did Gaxotte mince words. To him, Blum was "A Man Accursed." "He incarnates all that revolts our blood and makes our flesh creep. He is evil. He is death."[6]

In less than a month, with this inspired prompting, the Senate had voted Blum's defeat. On April 10, Daladier, coaxed out of retirement for the occasion, formed a new cabinet reassuring both to the Radicals and to the Right. The presence of Bonnet at the Foreign Office established the victory of moderate appeasement over the "warmongering" Left.

Spring brought new evidence of how the wind was blowing in a series of ballots and public meetings which showed the momentum of the Right. On the day Daladier took power, Victor Constant, a nationalist candidate, favored by the Action Française, was elected Senator of the Seine, narrowly defeating his Communist opponent. On May 8, while the Joan of Arc's Day parade, forbidden the year before, was taking place in Paris with official blessing and giving the "dissolved" Action Française a chance to preen,[7] Jean Goy, whose victory in the 1937 election had been invalidated, was re-elected in Normandy with practically the same number of votes he had received before, while his Radical-Socialist opponent got nearly 1,200 less than in 1937. *Candide* was right in remarking, "Le radicalisme a changé de front." Soon at a Saintes by-election the Radical would be elected against a Socialist, with the support of all the right-wing parties.[8] Meanwhile, the left-wing contingents at the traditional memorial ceremonies of the Mur des Fédérés (where Montherlant had counted some 600,000 only two years before) were noticeably sparse and lacking in enthusiasm.[9]

There was no lack of enthusiasm in Action Française circles that summer, however, for they had a success that brushed away both the *Anschluss* and the threat of war. On June 9, Maurras was elected a member of the Académie Française, the only public honor he had ever sought. The project had been mooted while he was in prison, and this time it was handled with discretion and tact. Rival contenders like Jérôme Tharaud, who might have split the vote of the Right, privately consented to withdraw. In contrast to its usual habits, the *Action française* mentioned the candidacy only on June 5, after other papers got wind of it.

The vote, which Maurras won on the first ballot over his poetic rival, Fernand Gregh, seems to have been largely on party lines. Twenty Academicians voted for him—probably André Bellessort, Pierre Benoît, Léon Bérard, Louis Bertrand, Abel Bonnard, Henry Bordeaux, Paul Cambon, André Chaumeix, Maurice Donnay, Edouard Estaunié, Claude Farrère, the Duc de la Force, Franchet d'Esperey, Abel Hermant, Jacques de Lacretelle, Georges Lecomte, Maurice Paléologue, Joseph de Pesquidoux, Philippe Pétain, and Maxime Weygand. The Duc de Broglie, whom Jean de La Varende had not succeeded in convincing, voted against him, along with eleven others, largely for a combination of political, religious, and literary reasons—probably Joseph Bédier, André Chevrillon, Louis Doumic, Georges Duhamel, Louis Gillet, Lacaze, Louis Madelin, François Mauriac, André Picard, Marcel Prévost, and Paul Valéry. The Bishops, Baudrillart and Grente, abstained, although they would have cast their vote for Maurras in twelve months' time, and so did two other Catholics torn between their allegiance to the Church and their sympathies, Emile Mâle and Georges Goyau, although Goyau let it be known that if Maurras lost on the first ballot he would vote for him on the second.[a]

Even more than Bainville's election, the election of Maurras not only was a tribute to lasting literary power and production but also carried political implications which every side was quick to analyze. The comments of the Christian-Democratic *Politique* showed the reaction in the enemy camp, shocked by the victory but not surprised:

> Maurras's talent may be debatable, the hold of his dialectic may be surprising. The fact is there: he has marked, marked terribly, a whole generation . . . The tragedy of M. Maurras . . . is that he has corrupted the traditions he pretends to serve . . . To the extent that [he and his friends] have succeeded, they have debased the tenor of royalist society, perverted that of young literature, created a peculiar and anarchic mood which operates against the Pope and the King, and against the hereditary and chivalrous virtues traditional to France.[10]

More matter of fact, *Le Temps*[11] recalled the unsuccessful try of 1926 and felt that if the Académie now welcomed Maurras so gladly it was because it contained more of his attentive readers than it had fifteen years before.[b] Faithful *Candide* devoted its editorial and almost the entire literary page to celebrating the Maurras election.[12] As for Maurras's loyal friends, they could but echo the sentiments Albert Pestour had expressed shortly before, on the thirtieth anniversary of the *Action française,* when he lauded Maurras as "The Pilot":

> Maurras, Prince des pilotes,
> Vieux Martégal aux yeux clairs,
> Malgré l'écueil, elle flotte
> Ta barque, sous les éclairs.
>
> . . . .
>
> Car au devant de toi roule
> Comme un tonnerre d'espoir,
> Couvrant les voix de la houle,
> Ce cri: MAURRAS AU POUVOIR!

If the crises of late summer 1938 did not bring Maurras to power as his faithful thought they should, they did see the general expression of ideas on

[a] Opinions on how the votes were cast differed little. The only exception to the suggestion given here appeared in *AF,* September 3, 1938, when, after the death of Bédier, who had been Daudet's schoolmate, a correspondent reported that the republican Medievalist had told him that, turning royalist at the end of his life, he had voted for Maurras.

[b] A few months later one of his attentive readers in another quarter, Professor Gaillard de Champris of the Catholic Institute, read a paper on Vauvenargues to the Académie des Sciences Morales et Politiques, comparing that worthy's mentality to that of Maurras. See *Le Temps,* Oct. 11, 1938.

which he had for years insisted. In a long interview in *Candide,* Flandin unconsciously echoed Maurras's assumption that the political system was incapable of performing its function and that France could reform herself only above and outside the party structure. Tardieu had reached the same conclusion several years before, and now, from Left to Right, this seemed to be the consensus. Even *Le Temps* reflected it, in an anonymous front-page article entitled "Politique d'abord." In *Combat,* Louis Salleron expressed views even more radical than those of the integral nationalists when he called for the suspension of Parliament and of electoral institutions in order to build a hierarchic France based on the family and on the organized professions. "Everything is ready for this," the Catholic corporatist declared; "only the best men's will is needed."[13] He had to wait a little longer before German arms would supply the deficiencies of good men's will.

The general opinion outside the largely Marxist, anti-Fascist camp had become that Communists constituted the greatest threat to peace. At the Radical Party Congress held that October at Marseille, Daladier's attack on Communists for their sabotage of peace and production received enthusiastic applause. The Action Française likewise directed its sharpest shafts against those whom, with a nice sense of nuances, it described as the Hitlerites of the Left: Communists, Socialists, warmongers, and Jews. While not averse to sometimes blaming the conservative or moderate conciliators of Hitler, it seldom turned against the increasingly vocal Germanophiles of the Extreme Right, where it had many friends. When Darquier de Pellepoix in his *France enchaînée* protested against French anti-Semites like himself being connected with Hitler, the *Action française* quoted with approval his assurance that for the friends of Hitler one really had to look "on the side of disorder and corruption, of politicians, Masons, Jew-lovers, and Jews."[14]

Its arguments remained ingenious; when Reynaud took over the Ministry of Finance in November, Daudet warned that his installation in the rue de Rivoli was very dangerous because he wanted war. Reynaud, whom the paper had at times variously described as avid, vain, ambitious, a blinking rat, a nothing, a pretentious little mussel, a little slubberdegullion, and a new Tom Thumb, was head of France's war clan because he was the puppet of Moscow. He was the puppet of Moscow, Daudet explained, because he had big investments in Mexico where the forty-hour week already existed and Communism advanced with giant steps.[c]

Small wonder that Bidault had come to feel that the *Action française* had ceased to be a nationalist, let alone royalist, paper, and had become completely Fascist.[15] Small wonder, too, that Mauriac could write to Kerillis (who, disgusted by the pusillanimity of his appeasing friends, had joined the "war-

[c] *AF,* Nov. 6, 1938. As a matter of fact, Reynaud's Egeria, Hélène de Portes, was reported to have royalist sympathies; Pierre Lazareff, *De Munich à Vichy* (New York, 1944), p. 105, suggests that the more Reynaud tended to the Left, the more she inclined to the Right.

mongering" party), "When the history of nationalism comes to be written, it will be curious to study this strange evolution which creates in the nationalists of today an unconscious hatred of their country."[16]

When, in November, the unions tried to strike against the paring of the social legislation of 1936 and to disown the capitulation before Germany at Munich, the *Action française* presented it as a revolutionary move intended to wreck the country which earlier left-wing plots had failed to drag to war. The strike was a miserable failure, and nationalists could celebrate their score. Now with the whip hand over the workers, they urged the government to sterner blows. As the *Action française* put it, "Et maintenant, il faut payer!" *Candide,* glad that France had defeated Moscow (as if France had not defeated France!), editorially demanded the dissolution of the Communist Party. *Je suis partout* went further: not only the Communists should be banned, but warmongers of Left and Right should be arrested. Why were they waiting to throw into jail the leaders of the Moscow gang and all their allies both of the Left and Right?[17]

Sadly, Blum had to concede defeat: reaction had won at last. In March 1939, under the shock of Germany's having broken her word once more, the Chamber voted full powers to Premier Daladier, whom only a few years before Daudet had mildly described as "aspirant à une dictature de W.-C. de gare." Returning to his seat, Blum was heard to mutter, "There is nothing to be done with this Chamber. It has turned Fascist!"[18]

As the United States Ambassador remarked at the ceremonial commemoration of Joan of Arc, "the unity and serenity of France today are the honor of the human race." President Lebrun, quoting this perceptive tribute on June 4, said, yes, "France is united and serene." The human race could look after itself. Lucien Corpechot—Robert de Flers's *Torchepot*—wrote to Daudet, "Vous avez raison. Nous sommes gouvernés par des cochons!"[19] But the pigs at the helm were swine of the Center Right. Maurras could approve Colonel, now Senator, Jean Fabry expressing sentiments shared by a good many of the middle-class: "When France is in danger, one must not pretend that the Republic is the endangered one. And when the government has the responsibility of saving France, one must not undertake to save the Constitution against it."[20]

As usual when political power rested in reassuringly conservative hands, the Action Française discovered that things were stagnant. Now Communists could hold their meetings almost undisturbed, and need worry only about trouble from the police, not from the once-pugnacious legions of the Action Française. And in *Candide* Lucien Rebatet expressed his indignation that no one had been found to break up a Communist meeting in the Mutualité hall. In his day, Rebatet recalled, it was the Action Française that laid down the law in the Latin Quarter. Where were the Camelots of yesteryear?[21]

The handiest indicator of the movement's effectiveness now rested more than ever in the newspaper; and the newsstand circulation, though stable, showed little sign of rising. With a brief pause in September 1938, it had fallen steadily from the high levels last reached in 1934 until in 1939 it stood around 37,000, with subscribers counting for perhaps half again as much. Police estimates gave the paper 40,000 subscribers and a total circulation of 125,000.[22] This seems a gross exaggeration. A well-informed source has indicated that during March 1939 actual sales averaged just under 29,000 copies a day, in addition to subscription copies. Even if one stretched these figures, they remain a far cry from those of the police.

The dissolution had seriously affected both funds and numbers of the Action Française, and great efforts had been made to keep the League alive: the Camelots had become *vendeurs volontaires,* the Etudiants had kept the premises of the Institute, the Directorial Committees of the League had continued to meet. The sections had mostly been reformed under different names: Le Bouclier and Cadoudal at Nantes, Alliance Fabert at Metz, Lys et Chardon at Nancy, Lugdunum at Lyon, Cercle François-I at Geneva, Politica at Rueil-Malmaison, Blanche de Castille at Pontoise, Jeanne d'Arc at Raincy, Colbert at Cluzes, Joseph de Maistre at Chambéry, the Alliance Monarchiste du Bassin de l'Escaut at Lille, the Alliance Nationale et Civique du Poitou at Poitiers; the 6th Arrondissement adopted Mabillon, the 14th a dead patriotic *chansonnier,* Maxime Brienne. A series of Cercles Jacques Bainville founded after the historian's death in Paris, Nantes, Bordeaux, Marseille, New York, and other cities grouped intellectual aspirants of the Right, not all necessarily members of the Action Française. In Paris, the honorary president of the Cercle, who after 1937 was a regular contributor to the monthly foreign affairs magazine *Frontières,* was Marshal Franchet d'Esperey. On its committee sat five other Academicians—Bonnard, Bordeaux, Donnay, Georges Lecomte, and Valéry—and names like those of Maeterlinck, René Gillouin, and Maurice Colrat de Montrozies appeared beside the expected ones of Maurras, Daudet, Dubech, and Georges Claude. The same "nonpartisan" illusion was maintained in the provinces. Thus, the address sent by the Cercle Jacques Bainville of Nancy to Maurras while he was in prison was signed by the local royalist leader Charles Berlet and by the editor of the royalist *Courrier de Lorraine,* but also by a colonel, who was the president of the Cercle, by a professor of the Nancy Science Faculty, and by the assistant principal of the Catholic Académie Stanislas. A banquet of the Marseille Cercle was attended by some one hundred guests, under the chairmanship of the vice-president of the Marseille Chamber of Commerce. The guests included the president of the local ACJF; the president of the local PNP (the new name of the Jeunesses Patriotes); two municipal councilors; Canon Armand d'Aguel, president of the society L'Art Religieux; Léon Bancal, editor of the *Petit Marseillais*; and Paul Barlatier, publisher of the *Sémaphore.* The main speakers were Henri Massis and Pierre Varillon, who had traveled down from Paris for the occasion.[23]

The ingenuity and multiplicity of means for getting round the dissolution of the League appeared in the organizations listed by the *Action française* on May 8, 1937, as having planned to march in the forbidden Joan of Arc's Day parade: the Solution (a study center of the 7th Arrondissement), the Avocats du 6 et 7 Février, Les Halles Françaises, the Groupe des Infirmières et Assistantes Sociales Royalistes, the Cercle Centre Paris Rive Droite, the Cercle Fustel de Coulanges, the Cause, the Comité Robert-le-Fort, the Comité Vauban, the Tradition, the Union Corporatiste des Instituteurs, the Cercle Charles Le Goffic, the Alliance André Chénier, the Association Geneviève Lecomte, the Association Madeleine Ageron, the Association Sully (of nationalist Protestants), the Comité Maréchal Bugeaud, and a good many more.

But no amount of ingenuity and of devotion could really halt the gradual decline. From jail, Pellisson-Maurras expressed his concern about the lack of numbers and of funds.[24] In all parts of France, royalist friends were slim. In Bordeaux, the *Nouvelle Guyenne* appealed for help in both the spring and the fall of 1937. It tried to economize by suspending publication during the summer months, and when it reappeared in October it was as a monthly. In 1938, propagandists tried to regroup old friends and recruit new ones into the Action Française-surrogate Union Girondine d'Action Politique et Sociale, which had been founded in June 1936. Of those approached, all of whom were thought to be sympathetic, 18 per cent joined, 46 per cent contributed money, and 36 per cent did neither.[25]

The organizers obstinately did their best; and yet inevitably nothing was the same. The Sûreté estimated that some 60,000 adherents still held fast, about a tenth of them in Paris,[26] but now that they had abandoned brawling for sedate and rather dull meetings and discussions they retained little if any practical significance. After 1936, however hard they tried, in public matters the reorganized groups of the Action Française were as if they had never been. And this had a very serious bearing on all possibilities of the movement that tried to advocate Maurras as an effective leader of the Right.

After being retired from the Army in 1938 because of his Cagoulard activities, Pétain's sometime aide, Major Georges Loustaunau-Lacau, sought a platform in the Paris press from which he could warn against military unpreparedness. He was disgusted with de La Rocque and therefore attempted to join the *Action française*. Since his impression was that Pujo always tried to use Maurras's deafness as an excuse for isolating him from possible competitors, Loustaunau-Lacau paid a visit to the old warrior at Martigues, where they spent a splendid evening writing out their conversation. Still looking for a General Monck to save the country, Maurras thought Pétain might be that Monck. Loustaunau-Lacau, however, thought Pétain was too old, and kept repeating "80"; and though he was at first fascinated by Maurras's skillful logic, he at last concluded that "reason denied by facts is error all the same."

The two men parted friends, but no understanding between them was possible because Maurras continued to insist on Monarchy as the essential end. For Loustaunau-Lacau, "la position de flanquement irréductible qu'avait prise l'Action Française me paraîssait frappée de stérilité." A similar conclusion was reached by another old friend, Joseph Lahille, who wrote to his daughter-in-law, "His doctrines, rigorously true in the domain of the Absolute, cease to be true in that of reality. They always make me think of experiments in physics that we used to conduct in college with the pneumatic machine. Phenomena noted in the container once the air had been pumped out could not be repeated in the atmosphere."[27]

Whether out of unwillingness or out of impotence, Maurras's incapacity to reconcile theory and practice, so evident in internal policy, appeared even more plainly in the foreign field. In foreign affairs, the Action Française position was still dominated by fear of Germany, hostility to whom was and remained the leader's cankerworm of care. This overriding concern, however, was sometimes overshadowed by what was regarded a more immediate threat—the conspiracy of evil leaders, ready to come to terms with Communism, who hurt the country by their chaotic policies, promoted class conflict, and were ready to plunge it into war, unarmed and unprepared, to serve the interests of their friends abroad, primarily those of the Comintern. Maurras made the distinction plain when he presented the two issues as that of Enemy No. 1 and No. 1, *Bis*:

> Among the readers of the *Action française* not one ignores or can possibly ignore that their country's Enemy No. 1 is Germany . . . After Hitler, or, who knows, before him on quite another plane, there is another enemy. It is the democratic Republic, the elective and parliamentary regime legally superimposed like a grotesque and repugnant mask on the true essence of France.[28]

Within these terms of reference, the policy of the Action Française was consistent: it did not trust a Left that, in all conscience, was wavering enough. True, it tended to forget that the sympathy Socialists had shown for democratic Germany had waned after 1933. But then there was some reason for doubting the determination of a Socialist Party that was deeply split between the primarily anti-Fascist followers of Blum and the primarily pacifist followers of Blum's second-in-command, Paul Faure, in whose *Populaire,*[29] more than three years after the Reichstag fire, Marceau Pivert declared, "Not a man, not a cent for national defence." There was equally good reason for suspecting the Communists, who changed their song on orders from abroad and could change it again if Moscow's policy should change; and also for looking askance at the "progressive" Left, which throughout this time showed extraordinary persistence in trying to satisfy insatiable Germany with snacks.[30]

The conviction that the Left was weak and liable to the control of both Communists and Jews implied, of course, that any policy to which the Left inclined was thereby damned as likely to be that of the foreigner. Such policies had to be exposed for what they were, and the French public had to be taught to recognize the ways in which an alien faction was leading it to what was ultimately war not in its own interests but in those of the international conspiracy which planned the ruin of France and of other countries as well. Equally important, the public had to be warned that offers of national union were a delusion if alien-dominated groups were included, for they would be certain to corrupt it. Before France could play an effective part in international affairs, it had to put its own house in order by removing the harmful alien forces and rearming itself both physically and morally.

So far as armament was concerned, the royalists, as usual, allowed prejudice to obscure a view that had originally been clear. Although they were wholly aware that France needed to arm and seemed progressive and well-informed in their military opinions, they so distrusted most of the leaders of the country that they consistently tried to block rearmament plans. Forgetting that to secure arms credits in a democratic society one must emphasize the threat of war, they damned the ministers as warmongers when they appealed to workers for the sake of national defense.[31]

So persuaded were they that France was weak (because under a republican government it could not be otherwise), that they constantly underrated national strength. Unable to secure the Latin, authoritarian allies whom they trusted, unwilling to trust Soviet or democratic ones, they came to feel that the only hope for France lay in deliberate isolation, even at the loss of all her remaining friends.

French nationalists had never in the past century shown particularly imperialistic leanings; but now they led the purely defensive camp in arguing that their country should remain aloof. There was about this point of view something like a confession of failure: as a result of disregarding their advice and warnings, France had become too weak to risk a hazardous war. Given time, it might recover and hold its own, perhaps assert its will. But, fundamentally, just as Maurras renounced action on February 6, the writer-leaders of the Action Française wished to renounce action on behalf of France and put their hope in a policy of talk and equivocation, articulate but sterile.

Like the members of other movements, the followers of Maurras took widely varying positions at this time. While men like Jean Héritier, Georges Blond, and Bernard Faÿ supported Fernand de Brinon's efforts to reach an understanding with Germany, others, like Dumoulin de La Barthète, resigned from pro-German clubs as soon as they understood their positions clearly. The general public to which these men appealed was equally varied in mood and in awareness. Many read their usual journals or frequented their usual circles simply out of habit. Men of good family and social position joined the Club du Grand Pavois, a pro-German front similar to the Cercle France-Allemagne, not out of sympathy with its point of view but because they liked its terrace overlooking the Champs-Elysées. At the same time they might well be reading *Candide,* hardly a Nazi paper, for its excellent literary page, and *Je suis partout* for its devastating cartoons.

Nevertheless, most readers of these publications shared some characteristics—a wounded self-esteem rubbed raw by constant friction with the lower orders which had abandoned deference for taunts; a fear of revolution, Communism, and Russia, to them the several aspects of a single theme; a distrust of the Republic, of democracy, and of all politicians whom they could not buy. It was thus possible to reach most readers by a judicious appeal to these mutual prejudices and fears.

One wonders how far those who condemned the class politics of the Marxists realized the extent to which class prejudices influenced their own. Opposition to Communism and sympathy for Italy and Spain were not based simply on political opportunism; they reflected a social philosophy in which allies were selected in the image of what France herself should be, but a philosophy which remained inarticulate in almost all right-wing quarters except those where the Action Française gave voice.

While breathing ritual sympathy for the laboring masses, after 1936 the theorists of the Action Française represented more than ever a movement of middle-class intellectuals, who, like most of their sort, had certain aristocratic pretensions. Their France, the France they loved, was one in which nineteenth-century bourgeois ideals could prevail unthreatened by dark dissatisfactions which they faced perplexed. They did not like the present because it was not sufficiently like their cozy image of the past; they did not like the future, because it might be even worse. They had no sympathy for developments growing out of economic changes they could not understand, looked upon both capital and labor as almost equally vexing, and thought that by digging in their heels they could hold back time. To hold back France and let the rest of the world slip by might be a fair expression of their attitude. But of course they forgot that France could not be separated and would whirl with all of Europe into the maelstrom.

Here again, Maurras's faniente attitude lost him the most aggressive of his followers. Authoritarian revolution having always been a part of the Action Française creed, it seemed logical to approve the regimes of Mussolini, Franco, and Salazar, wise statesmen who appeared to forge ahead in the proper ways. Why then, some members argued, withhold approval from the effective authoritarian regime par excellence, that of the Nazis? The *Action française* never softened its disgust with "the Hitleromaniacs of the Right," whom it described as dolts and imbeciles,[32] but some of its friends were less relentless, and some of them became leading supporters of Hitler.

As early as 1908, the Abbé Brémond had chided Maurras with being too ready to make every allowance for his own supporters; it was a characteristic that he always had. Until the war, dissensions within the Action Française were always the result of personal rather than doctrinal issues, and members were dropped ultimately on some challenge to the wisdom of the leader or of his lieutenants. At the same time, there was great latitude for disagreement so long as loyalty to Maurras was not in question.

Thus it was that, although the *Action française* repeatedly attacked Hitler and Hitlerites in France, sometimes standing alone on the Right in doing so,[33] its friends, especially on *Je suis partout,* followed an altogether different line without incurring any blame at all until they made the final decision to collaborate. Pellisson-Maurras admonished the *Journal des débats* for publishing extracts from *La Gerbe des forces,* but he breathed not a word of reproach about *Je suis partout*'s long interview with Alphonse de Chateaubriant.[34]

Apart from Maurras's natural indulgence, some explanation of such inconsistent positions lies in the superficial coincidence of their policies. When the *Action française* declared on July 13, 1936, that no one in its pages ever made a concession to Hitlerism, this could not be gainsaid. But at that very time it quite refused to censor or break with the blatant Alsatian semi-Nazi Joseph Bilger or with his newssheet *Volk,* which, in its anti-Semitic nationalism, stood close to the royalists' own *Province d'Alsace.*[35] It did not find fault with Claude Jeantet when, in a long article on the Nürnberg Congress, he defended Hitler and his party as the determined opponents of Bolshevism and concluded that talk of a German menace was no more than a red herring to remove attention from what should be a French patriot's true concern; "The German menace is one thing," he wrote, "the Communist danger is another, and the fact that Germans denounce the latter in no way makes it any less."[36]

Je suis partout frequently argued that France must be strong, so that it could talk to Hitler from strength; the implication that strength would come from applying Hitler's methods was not so clear as to be obvious, and the *Action française* chose to ignore it, while accepting the other point. Similarly, in March 1938, Maurras warned "conservatives and ex-nationalists who grovel before Hitler" that only slavery and ruin could come from Germany to France: "Look out! No anti-democratism or anti-Semitism is worth it!" Three weeks later *Je suis partout* featured a special number on the Jews which rivaled Julius Streicher's virulent *Stürmer,* without evoking a single word of stricture from the censor generally so quick to attack the world.[37]

In a sense, of course, one can argue that the Action Française could hardly be responsible for the policies of publications that it did not control. But the men who ran these publications were the professed followers of Maurras, and during these years they were never reproached by the man who was their acknowledged master. The moment came when he finally disowned them, but it was because of open treachery, not for their prewar policies. Also, merely by disowning them when he did, Maurras indicated that he might have disowned them sooner had he wanted to do so. He wasted little time in getting rid of the men on the *Revue critique* years before when they embarrassed him. That he waited so long to turn on the men of *Je suis partout* must be attributed, when all is said and done, to the fact that, at bottom, he believed their sentiments to be essentially right.

Where *Candide* spoke in the more sedate and bourgeois voice of integral nationalism, *Je suis partout* was its more radical expression—more coarse, more gross, more brutal, more aggressive, sparkling with the translucent brilliance of flies that gather on a rubbish heap, but ultimately very much the same as the *Action française.* Altogether, these three publications came as close as any in the later 'thirties to being the voice of the noninterventionist Right.

True, this would imply a certain incoherence, as different points were stressed at different times to a different degree. But the total impression was as one—that if the German threat had now become serious, it was the fault of the French government, and most immediately of the Communists. Thus when, in August 1936, Hitler increased the period of German military service from one year to two, the *Action française* attributed his decision to the anti-Fascist attacks of the Popular Front in France. In answer to inquiries of the magazine *Futur,* Maurras asserted, "Hitler is still our enemy No. 1; Moscow is a good deal less dangerous"; and as if in reply, Daudet clamored a few days later, "Ecrasons l'infâme—l'infâme communisme!" This gave the first hint of the sustained campaign against aid to Republican Spain, as being nothing else than aid to Moscow and to Bolshevism, which eventually got to the point of blaming France even for the signing of the Berlin-Rome-Tokyo pact against Russia.[38]

Far from wanting France to become involved in a Red-willed war, the Action Française seemed to think it would be much better if France would withdraw even from its own obligations, if any of them threatened to bring it into conflict with militant anti-Communism. Where intervention in Spain had been blamed as stupidly naïve, it was found to be unnecessarily heroic in the case of Austria. "We prefer a slap in the face to bullets in our skin," the pacifist Union of Teachers declared, to the horror of patriots. But when Flandin rose in Parliament to plead "Let us not go into heroics about Austria, let us take refuge behind our Maginot Line," respectable men approved. *Candide* declared, "To preach war is to will invasion, and this is what the Soviets want us to do."[39]

When, in the midst of a French cabinet crisis, the Germans entered Austria, political recriminations were the main reaction of the royalist paper—that and the refusal to accept the broad union proposed by Léon Blum, including dire predictions about the criminal madmen he finally managed to gather in a catastrophic cabinet defined as one of provocation and of ruin. What was important now, with Austria gone, was to make sure that France would not have to fight for the Czechs. On March 12, the Paris *Herald Tribune* quoted Charles Corbin, Ambassador to the Court of St. James, as saying that France would fight if her ally, Czechoslovakia, were to be attacked by Germany. If France must fight, Maurras declared sensibly, she must prepare for war. But first she must get rid of those responsible for the present situation: "Pas la guerre, ou pas ceux qui ont passé leur vie à crier que la guerre était impossible et qu'il fallait d'abord désarmer!"[40] More artlessly, Daudet, in an article entitled "C'est pou les Tchéques," set forth a simple argument which appealed to many Frenchmen, and became familiar in other countries as well:

> It is no longer Jack Everyman, but, peasant or worker, Jack Clod, the guinea pig of bloody Democracy, who has to go to his slaughter at the nod of a Jew he hates in some obscure, faraway dump about which he hasn't the least notion. That's what the Republic asks, and our beloved freedom![41]

Ambassador Corbin's words, brought up in the Senate Foreign Affairs Commission, were soon given a polite official denial. "It continues to be understood," the statement said, "that on the Czech question France will do nothing except what is in accord with England." Maurras took care to cross the t's: "It is of the highest importance that the world should know that France remains free to act—or not to act. . . . If one does not say this, what illusions might not continue to be entertained in Central Europe!" No illusions could, at any rate, be warranted on his behalf, when two days later the paper proclaimed its new isolationism: "NOTHING FOR A WAR OF DOCTRINE. ALL FOR THE DEFENSE OF OUR SACRED SOIL!"[42]

From that moment on, the *Action française* battled in the vanguard of a concerted offensive to disengage France from Prague, pointing out that there were no bonds entailing French support if the Czechs should be attacked by any foreign power, and that French interests would surely suffer if France became involved in a discreditable Central European roughhouse. The weakness and the racial disunity of a country far too close to the Communists had for some time been an accepted fact of the right-wing press.[43] Now the attacks began against the pernicious warmongering ogres unwilling to cease their oppression of minorities. "Must Frenchmen die for F∴ Benes?" asked François Dauture (Henri Lèbre, once a catechumen of Maurras), who would soon show himself reluctant to die for F∴ France; and in *Candide* Gaxotte explained how silly it would be to lay down one's life for an awkward jigsaw of nationalities.[d]

The campaign was well organized and even better financed. In *L'Epoque,* Kerillis revealed the existence of a large company "with headquarters in Marseille" which had sent out a sumptuous illustrated pamphlet to all the notables of the 2,800 communes in nine departments of southeastern France, "all mayors, assistant mayors, village councilors, priests, teachers, doctors, veteri-

[d] *JSP,* March 25, 1938; *Candide,* March 31, 1938. The article attracted much criticism, which Gaxotte answered on May 26 by saying that Premier Hodža's proposed nationalities statute proved his point.

narians, barbers, stationmasters, and tradesmen"—the pamphlet's object, to show that Czechoslovakia was an artificial country, unfit to be defended or to exist, open to Germany's grasp at any time, with which, in consequence, it would be madness to become involved.[44]

In May 1938, the *Action française* began a series of front-page articles by Video (Colonel Bouvet), one of its regular military contributors, under the title "The Gory Gamble." It was perhaps an indication of the view of "the highest personalities in the French Army," whom Bouvet was often said to represent: "The time has come to understand and say that the French Army cannot lend itself to gambles which it has been rendered unfit to win. Strictly 'defensive,' our Army is incapable of attack, and hence of going to anybody's help. Would that it might, at least, be able to protect us!"[45] Why, in any case, should France exert herself for those who spurned her? As Salleron eloquently put it, why should the French exhaust themselves carrying the responsibilities of a stupid Europe that detested them? "Rentrons dans notre pré carré et barricadons-nous-y."[46]

As Hitler's tone kept rising, so, equally, did that of the nationalist press, but not defiantly, as in 1912: the Czechs were playing with fire, the Czechs wanted "their" war, and, if not the Czechs, then the leaders of the Popular Front. Whatever happened, the country must be kept out of war.[47] While the nationalists were condemning the "alarmists" of the Left, they either echoed or ignored those of the Right. *Je suis partout* was becoming increasingly nasty as the danger of war deepened. On September 16 it called on all six columns for the gallows as the portion of French warmongers. A special page on Germany extolled the dynamism and youth on show at Nürnberg, and portrayed Hitler, as usual, in the most favorable light, while Cousteau, on another page, enjoined, "Not a widow, not an orphan for the Czechs," and Gaxotte insisted that before it mobilized, France had better clean up the rear.

The *Action française,* in the meantime, which welcomed Chamberlain's initiatives and gladly lent its pages to an address of French Mothers extolling the British Premier as Defender of the Peace, lambasted all warlike moves—that is, any suggestion that a firmer stand might bring better results than capitulation. The war, Maurras repeated, was either for the men of Moscow or for Jews. Both Daudet and Maurras took up Barthélémy's argument in *Le Temps,* to the effect that the Franco-Czech treaty of 1925 was part of the Locarno Pact, which, having lapsed, was in no way binding on France or France's honor. How could anyone be blamed for violating nonexisting treaties, asked Maurras. The real tragedy was that the balance of power had been too markedly altered as a result of disregarding his advice. These were the arguments, as Voltaire once said, of people who reason very well, destined for people who do not reason at all.

When for a moment, after September 23, Hitler's intractability made war seem likely, the nationalists' exasperation led them to run amuck. That day, with small white posters calling the reserves to arms, great yellow and red handbills appeared on Paris hoardings: FRANÇAIS ON VOUS TROMPE. PAS DE CHANTAGE AU PATRIOTISME! The headlines on the 24th were all of a kind: In the *Action française,* "A bas la guerre! Les Français ne veulent se battre ni pour les Juifs, ni pour les Russes, ni pour les francs-maçons de Prague"; in *L'Oeuvre,* "Faisons donc la paix avant la guerre!"; in *Le Jour,* "Va-t-on faire la guerre pour une question de procédure?"; in *L'Eclair de Nice,* "Tous les Tchécoslovaques du monde ne valent pas les os d'un petit soldat français!"

The following day, news of Chamberlain's departure from Bad Godesberg in circumstances which made it seem that negotiations had broken down sent Daudet off into a frenzy: "The trouble in Czechoslovakia is no business and no interest of ours. Our bargain with M. Benes, who bought Berthelot like a pig at a fair, was part of the sinister farce of Locarno and disappeared with that baroque and jigsaw treaty."[48]

In the *Action française* of September 27, "A BAS LA GUERRE" ran the width of a particularly vicious front page. The general impression it conveyed was that the country was entering a conflict unprepared, with her cities open to devastation from the air, her borders poorly defended against German forces immensely stronger than her own. The next issue maintained the tone, and Maurras, reverting to an old tactic, listed the names of the cabinet members, with a veiled threat of vengeance should they lead France into a war. On the 29th, news that Chamberlain, Daladier, Hitler, and Mussolini were meeting at Munich was greeted with joy: "HONNEUR À CHAMBERLAIN," said the headline; but the slogan of the day was an adaptation of the "Internationale":

> S'ils s'obstinent ces cannibales
> A faire de nous des héros,
> Il faut que nos premières balles
> Soient pour Mandel, Blum et Reynaud.

Paul Reynaud, the Minister of Justice, had the issue of the paper seized, but by the time his order had been carried out, rather late in the day, most of the copies had already been sold. The charges Reynaud ordered for incitement to murder were soon lost in the sands of slow-moving judicial procedure. *Je suit partout,* which had missed the Munich story on the 29th because of its early press deadline, was apoplectic: "It is the war of the Jews!" it headlined; "We shall not fight it, but we shall make them pay." "War for liars? For forgers? For traitors? NO, NO, AND NO!" To reservists who were gathering to defend their country while France still considered carrying out the agreements that bound it, Gaxotte declared that their only valid duty was to prevent the suicide of their country at the behest of Russians, Jews, aliens, the traitors and the corrupt. Whatever its issue, war would be the end of France: "If we lose, there will be no more France. If we win, there will be no more Frenchmen!"[49]

But, blessed relief, the threats of *Je suis partout,* it seemed, were for the moment unnecessary. "La Paix! La Paix! La Paix!" cried the *Action française* of September 30. The news of the West's most abject retreat was interpreted as a victory—which, of course, to some extent it was, for the conscious and unconscious auxiliaries of Hitler, whose virulent and persistent hammering had forced or had permitted Western statesmen to back down. On October 4, the *Action française* announced a generous tribute to the hero of the hour: Maurras had withdrawn his candidacy to the Nobel Prize for Peace in favor of Chamberlain, "benefactor to the peace of the world."

The brief moment of relief ended, the *Action française* once again reflected the characteristic incapacity of the movement to choose between its several hates. Maurras admitted that Munich was a defeat for France, though one that had to be accepted to avoid the worst consequences of past errors. Appeasement was far from the paper's line, and Delebecque soon took Chamberlain to task for thinking he could secure peace from Germany by a policy of concessions, while Maurras attacked straightforward pacifist Flandin for wiring Hitler his congratulations after Munich: "Is the man an imbecile? Has he understood nothing of Munich's implications?"[50]

Rearmament was foremost in Maurras's thought, and yet, knowing now that war was near and that soon France would have to call on all her resources, he and his friends persisted in violently rejecting the possibility of cooperation with Hitler's worst enemies. While *Candide* exulted that Moscow's war would not take place, *Je suis partout* cried out for vengeance against the warmongers whom they would in no way consider even as members of the national community of France.

Stubborn and quasi-suicidal tendencies like these might seem too strange even for *Je suis partout,* did we not have a straightforward explanation of them from Thierry Maulnier. In the November issue of *Combat,* Maulnier attacked critics of the Munich agreement while he explained its merits with his customary lucidity: the parties of the Right, he said, believed that German defeat would mean the collapse of authoritarian systems which constituted the main rampart against the Bolshevik revolution and, perhaps, against the Bolshevization of the whole of Europe. A French defeat would be a French defeat all right, but a French victory would be less the victory of France than the victory of principles rightly considered as leading straight to the ruin of France, and of all civilization. It was a pity that men and parties that entertained this idea would not admit it. There was nothing about it that could not be expressed. For here, for people of a certain mind, was one of the soundest reasons—if not *the* soundest—for not going to war in September 1938.

Then, on November 7, a seventeen-year-old German-Jewish refugee, Herschel Grinszpan, driven to despair by all that he and his family had suffered at the hands of the Nazis, shot and killed the third secretary of the German

Embassy in Paris, Ernst vom Rath. Daudet at once concluded that the Jewish boy had been put up to the job. The *Action française* had often warned against the danger of giving shelter in Paris to all the scum of Europe, and now the expected had happened. The bloody German pogroms which followed on the murder evoked only one reaction from the paper: "Let us hope that no one takes them as a pretext for gushing over Jews at a time when their latest arrivals constitute a mortal peril for France."

A significant exchange took place at this time between Emile Buré in *L'Ordre* and his erstwhile friends of the *Action française*: "No ideological crusade—agreed," remarked Buré; "but do you think that by deliberately ignoring the sufferings of minorities subject to Nazi law, and especially by basely kowtowing to those who made and who apply the law, France and England do not risk incurring, in their turn, the evils which, because of their indifference, their accommodating complacency, overwhelm so many nations and so many persons who share their principles? In any case, their miserable policy threatens the rapid loss of any prestige they might as yet retain." "No," answered the *Action française*: "The prestige of France is not affected when a synagogue is burned somewhere. They can all be burned; it is no concern of ours and does not affect us in any way. No diplomatic intervention, no war for the Jews!"[51]

France, it is true, did not have to fight or suffer for the Jews, any more than it had to suffer for Spaniards, Austrians, or Czechs, and one might well have wondered, considering the mire of mutual hatred in which the country wallowed, how many would be ready to fight for France itself when the day for that should come. Not many, as it turned out. But it should be noted that the *Action française* in those days only expressed more frankly what many Frenchmen were thinking.[52] *Candide,* however, was fairly restrained. After expressing shock and horror at the pogroms in Germany, it suggested a possible cause: "One would incline to suspect that a sort of Communist rabble, not yet assimilated into the Third Reich, had staged this impromptu manifestation to the sole end of creating difficulties for the Führer and his ministers, and in order to lower the prestige of the country."[53]

By November 18, after a determined campaign under the slogan "let's keep out of this," Maurras noted with pleasure that "nationalist papers seemed to be coming to their senses," as shown in part by an article in *Echos de Paris,* from which he quoted, which made the point that Jews and Reds were only suffering what they themselves in the old days of Weimar had inflicted on Francophile Rhenish separatists.[54]

One always knew the Germans were barbarians, but this did not mean that one had to go to war, especially when Hitler was offering to guarantee France's existing borders. And so, on December 6, the field was clear for the Von Ribbentrop-Bonnet accords in Paris, which helped to persuade both

Hitlerites and Russians that, as Maulnier had hoped, the Munich accord implied a free hand for Germany in the East. Certainly *Candide* thought so, and early in 1939 even believed the Germans to be sparing France beyond and contrary to the spirit of the Axis. Either the Russians could not defend their lands against the Germans, in which case their alliance was no good anyway, or else they could, and Hitler would be involved in a perilous adventure which, in its own safe position, the West could watch.

This attitude was the one Maurras held in March 1939 when Germany took over what was left of Czechoslovakia. Everybody, he said, knew that Munich opened Germany's road to the East. This was unfortunate, but it would have been sadder still to let her gain certain victory over a West that was unarmed and unprepared. For France, the only prospect was "Arm! Rearm! Fight like the plague anything that will come at all close to a declaration of war! Gain time—our positions are strong, with time they will get stronger."

This cogent point of view was perfectly expressed by Daudet when he addressed a thousand doctors and pharmacists of the Action Française at a banquet at the Trocadéro. Germany's economy, Daudet explained, was overextended and needed tremendous resources, the acquisition of which demanded constant expansion, invasion, and extortion. "Whatever happens and under no pretext, we must not declare war and thus favor her tactics. We must let her entangle herself more deeply in them." If these remarks expressed anything beyond the pious hope that the Reich might die of indigestion, it was the open invitation for Germany to grab at will. As if to answer it, Germany's rulers seized Memel from Lithuania on the very day Daudet's speech appeared in the *Action française*.[55]

Je suis partout, which had welcomed the fall of Czechoslovakia as proof of what madness it would have been to fight for a country incapable of standing on her own, and in which Brasillach expressed his romantic humor by trampling with zest over "the ignoble human excrement called Benes (have you noticed in his speeches the voluptuous thrill at the thought of possible carrion and corpses?)," now emphasized that there could be no question of a "sacred union" with the rabble. In the hour of danger, wrote Brasillach, all support is welcome. But one must not ask too much. Reasonable tolerance must end somewhere, and even Brasillach could not be asked to join with people whose goals were alien to his—Soviets, Jews, Czechs, trade unionists, Communists, Socialists, the USR,[e] and so on down the line. Not only must this rabble be excluded, but a dire fate awaited their leaders. That André Marty should be expeditiously eliminated for his part in the Spanish war furnished no matter for debate, "Mais le petit matin frais où l'on conduira Blum à Vincennes sera un jour de fête dans les familles françaises, et on pourra boire le champagne à

[e] The Union Socialiste et Républicaine of Frossard, Ramadier, Violette, and Paul-Boncour.

l'occasion. Alors, oui, on saurait que le pays est gouverné, car, pour repousser l'invasion étrangère, il faut supprimer les traîtres de l'intérieur."[56]

The curious thing is that these people much preferred Paul Faure, the pacifist, to Blum, who actively supported rearmament. What, above all, they wanted to avoid was no longer a particular war for the wrong cause, at the wrong time, but war itself—the war, as Cousteau said, that would turn Europe into a Soviet colony.[57]

That spring, relations with Italy became cooler and more strained. The Italian campaigns for French territories in Europe and in Africa were met first with persiflage, then with less delicate criticism.[58] The occupation of Albania on Good Friday (April 7) drew criticism even from *Je suis partout,* which found it "odious and burlesque." Strangely enough, in the wake of these events, Maurras, who that Easter turned the Duce's portrait in his study with its face to the wall, welcomed the Franco-British guarantees of Romania, Greece, and Poland against attack.[59] By now, even *Candide* could see that the country stood on the brink of war. And it stood there, all the evidence shows, more deeply and unhappily divided than it had been since 1848.

Looking back in later years at the state of things on the eve of war, Flandin drew a picture that comes as close as anything we have to a capsule analysis of the situation. Partly because they were jealous of the urban workers who were not called to fight, and partly because foreign affairs seemed very far away, the peasantry of France was stoutly pacifist. The workers were divided: the Communists were at Moscow's beck and call, the Socialists, though anti-Fascist, were still strongly pacifist. The great unions, of teachers, postmen, and civil servants, supported Faure, who represented the majority of the Socialist Party, while most of the intellectuals gave their support to Blum.

The bourgeois parties, likewise, were divided: the upper middle class was torn between its fear of war as endangering capital and capital investments, and an avidity for profits from armament; the middle middle class was torn between its desire for a *rapprochement* with Germany and Italy against Russia, and the yearning to have done with it all, to teach Germany a lesson and bring the present uncertainty to an end; the lower middle class had on the whole accepted the formula of resistance without arms and victory without struggle. Where the upper and middle middle class were more concerned with weakening the State and its institutions than with what the French position in Europe and world politics might be, the lower middle class thought France invincible and so, although not warlike, was quite chauvinistic enough to approve steps that could bring war. It wanted France to speak loudly, but refused to pay for a stick, and it bitterly resented the results of its own attitude when, soon, they appeared.

The judgment of the conservative statesman was to be borne out by events. But the inept Machiavellianism of those who hoped that Germany could be sicked onto the Soviet foe and the two enemies fixed at each other's throats while Western Europe watched, was dashed by news that Stalin had made his own bargain first and that, unwanted by those he had courted for so long, he had come to terms with his most dangerous foe.

To the Action Française, the German-Soviet pact was one more proof of Moscow's treachery. As the paper wrote on the day the Pact was announced,[60] the event was hardly a surprise: it was Rapallo all over again, and only what Maurras had always predicted. Thereafter, while struggling against the growing certainty of war, the *Action française* reflected the near-panic taking hold all around. Maurras, who had approved the guarantee to Poland, now censored Daladier for identifying Danzig, Poland, and France. His strictures against Chamberlain were even stronger: Chamberlain, who had woken up rather late, had said that Britain would not be fighting for Danzig but for a principle, the abandonment of which would imply the end of peace and security for all peoples everywhere. This, for Maurras, was not the moment for visionary talk. Hitler "had his eye on other enemies than us." Why, then, send Frenchmen to be killed for the sake of the sempiternal Jews or, more specifically, that of the English-speaking powers?

> Qu'on se hérisse de défense, qu'on mobilise et qu'on remobilise! Qu'on se couvre sur tous les points! C'est naturel, c'est nécessaire! Il serait criminel de ne pas faire, là-dessus, tout . . . Mais marcher avant que l'on ait marché sur nous, c'est une autre affaire.

He, unlike Chamberlain, would not change his tune. War was not inevitable. Peace could be had, and must be had; for France, Maurras was sure, lacked all means of fighting a war for the kind of principles that suddenly inspired Chamberlain. After hamstringing France for years, after refusing to move when the moment was as propitious as the cause was just, the British now wanted to rush into war for principles which they had made quite certain they would be incapable of carrying out: "Foncer maintenant parce que l'Angleterre y fonce ou parce que les principes anglais exigent de foncer, est une politique romantique, révolutionnaire et sacrificielle."[f]

That day, August 28, the head of the Police Judiciaire in Paris called in Maurice Pujo to ask on Daladier's behalf that the paper's anti-war campaign be stopped or, at least, toned down. Pujo refused. The *Action française* accepted its responsibilities—let the government accept its own. If Daladier did not like what the paper published, let censorship of the press be imposed.[61]

It was. And on August 29 most of Maurras's political article, five and a half columns on the front page, appeared in blank. Four years later, the *Action française* gave the text of the censored article in full: in essence, it

[f] *AF,* Aug. 26, 28, 1939. On August 26, Maurras's editorial was reproduced in full by a German dispatch from Paris, triumphantly illustrating the anti-war sentiment on which Hitler could rely: see *German Diplomatic Documents,* series D, VII, 308. But *L'Epoque,* on August 27, complained that the *Action française* was alone in all the press to criticize Daladier's firmness as being too bellicose.

repeated the determination not to wage war and called for a national government that would include the Action Française. But the argument was typical of the dream and the thought of Charles Maurras:

> We are told, so you will let Poland down? We will not. But we note that Poland is a fragile structure, which needs help to stay alive . . . True friends of Poland, those who are really wise, know that the country's greatest interest is the survival of France. Anything compromising this would be worse than a death blow to Poland, since it would prevent its revival. Poland has died before and it has revived. It will revive again as long as France survives . . . When in doubt, save the mother . . . Save France to save the Polish future.[62]

The thinking of the Action Française was at this point divided. In the hands of its Fayard publishers, *Candide* could not continue to hold out: on the eve of war it adopted the grave and patriotic line its public would traditionally expect. *Je suis partout* appeared on September 1 with headlines that summed up *its* attitude: "A Bas la Guerre! Vive la France!" Maurras himself, now rather dimmed by censorship, insisted again on the possibility and necessity for France to bide her time and keep the peace, but he lost his way in long, repetitive reminders of how right he had been in the past, and never quite managed to explain just how the peace could be maintained in the present circumstances.

That was the day when German troops invaded Poland, when France and Britain decreed general mobilization, when what might be called a new Thirty Years' War began. When Pierre Varillon came to Maurras with the news of general mobilization, Maurras clenched his fists: "What folly!" he said; then, "What a crime!" Then he added, "Poor, poor children!" The following day, his editorial rang through with resignation: "The enemy is here . . . There is only one thing to do: Forward! . . . since we are at war, forward to victory."[63]

PART VI: LA FRANCE SEULE

"Thinkers," muttered the major absently, "prepare the Revolution; bandits carry it out. At the moment no one can say with any assurance, 'So-and-so is a revolutionary and What's-his-name is a bandit.' Tomorrow, perhaps, it will be clearer."

MARIANO AZUELA, "THE FLIES"

24

THE WINTER AND THE SUMMER WARS

IF THE FIRST WORLD WAR was one that the Action Française desired, enjoyed, and understood, the Second was one it hated. Jean Cocteau's quip in 1918 about Barrès, that he would have to secure German naturalization in order to go on calling for Alsace-Lorraine, struck close to home. All the demanding justice of *revanchard* campaigns was taken over by the Germans after 1918, and French nationalists, still properly worried, were deprived of their most effective hold on the general public. Patriots, on the defensive, as most Frenchmen were, lost impetus when their wounds were salved; the burning sense of grievance, the pretext and spur of unabashed aggression, was now on the other side, not just because the French, exhausted and bled white, regarded any quarrel with extreme reluctance, but because, with Alsace-Lorraine returned, there was no longer anything worth fighting about.

The nationalists had called for war before 1914 to make France whole; before 1939 they called for peace to keep her that way and safe from harm. If they were belligerent in the 'twenties, when France was relatively strong, this was to keep her out of danger; it was with the same end in mind that they turned isolationist once enemies they feared too much appeared. In both decades their aim was constant—to take no chances with what was far too precious for mere gambles. With peasant doggedness, having secured the family land, they refused to risk losing it in foreign adventures. No reason could be strong enough to tempt them from this French hexagon, the sum of their ambitions and their hopes; and when one did appear to shake their resolute isolationism, they did their best to rationalize it away, as we have seen Maurras doing at every crisis in the 'thirties—even when, as in the case of Austria and Poland, his left-wing enemies in no way stood to gain.

Where 1914–18 had been an Action Française dream (marred only by too much bloodshed), 1939–44 would be a horrible nightmare. From the start, it saw things in black: Claude Roy, called up to a War Office job, reported to his friends that Nancy had been bombed until not a stone was left; Alain Laubreaux hoped that the conflict would be disastrous and brief.[1] As for Maurras, to whom General Gaston Prételat had said, "Guerre offensive, guerre défensive, désastre pour la France," the whole experience was a calamity. He could cope with it only by attributing it all to a malignant foe who had led France unaware into disasters with which she was not concerned. Shortly before his death he declared: "The barbarous occupation of 1940 would not have taken place without the Jews of 1939, without their filthy war, the war they undertook and they declared; our occupiers were introduced by them, it was the Jews who launched us into catastrophe."[2] This was his way of rejecting responsibility. Just as on soldiers' tongues some blasphemies recur with incantatory monotony, so would this charge come repeatedly from Maurras's pen after 1940. First peace, then war, then even the slender chances of the Armistice, were to be lost for France by alien bunglers and traitors who paid no heed to the advice of which he was so prodigal. Unable to agree with his fellow-Frenchmen, critical of what he considered their repeated errors and failures, Maurras simply barred them from the national community, instead of withdrawing from it himself, as others were inclined to do. The position he finally adopted was so rigid that it excluded practically all Frenchmen who fought and thought.

At first, however, whatever Maurras's pessimism, the *Action française* did its patriotic best. Like General Clément-Grandcourt, who at the age of seventy rejoined the Army in 1939 as a lowly private, like the president of the League, Baron François de Lassus Saint-Geniès, who rejoined the artillery regiment he had once commanded and died near Tergnier (Aisne) in June 1940, all members of the Action Française willingly answered the call of duty. Maurras and Daudet, like cavalry horses responding to the sound of the bugle, recalled their training and took up the cry of victory. When Hitler offered peace to the West after the debacle in Poland, Maurras rejected the offer with disgust. No peace was possible without return to the *status quo ante* 1936, and *ante* Hitler too, no peace while the twenty-six German states remained unified within one Reich. The newspaper reminded its readers that this time victory must be total, and it criticized the British and Socialist notion that the war was against Hitler, not against the German people. Hitler was only one of the manifold expressions of secular and brutal Germanism, and the defeat of Hitler, if it were not also the defeat of the Germans, would solve no problems, just as the 1919 treaties had failed to do. Nor was it reasonable to think that Hitler's Germany should be spared in order that it might serve as a shield against the Communists, to whom, indeed, it had just opened wide the gates of Europe. The war was to be hard, and all that one could hope was that it might at least settle the German problem once and for all.[3]

Maurras's arguments found ready support, in both Paris and the provinces. As Robert Kemp, of Doriot's *Liberté,* wrote in *Le Temps*: "Bainville predicted everything that has been happening . . . I wanted to believe that he was having a nightmare, that he was wrong . . . But here we are."[4] Within a few months, most French publications standing to the right of the Socialists had more or less accepted the Action Française point of view, in which Germany and Hitlerism were seen as one; and the German radio, advised by men who, like Ferdonnet and Jean Hérold-Paquis, knew their Maurras well, made no mistake when, on several occasions, it referred to Maurras's ideas as representative of France's war aims.[5]

On November 22, Maurras had some sensible remarks to make concerning the war. He warned against putting all faith in the Allied blockade, which, he hoped, might weaken Germany but could not be decisive. True hope lay in the Army. The barbarians were getting ready to hurl themselves at France, and the means to resist and counterattack successfully had to be prepared. Thoughtless and hurried offensives were dangerous, but a serious military offensive had to be planned with every means the Allies could command.

Within a few days of these remarks, however, all talk of offensives disappeared from the pages of the *Action française*. The issue of December 1 contained news of the aggression against Finland by the "Judeo-Slavic hordes." Thereafter, news of the Franco-German war was severely reduced; reports from the French Army were relegated to the second or third page, as was news of the war at sea. "The War" on the front page was the Russo-Finnish conflict.

Here was an issue the Right could grasp in terms of black and white. Unable or unwilling to cope with Germany, it found a war on Russia much to its taste. The possibility of Anglo-French intervention was mooted from the first, and the *Action française,* of course, promoted the idea.[6] On December 9, Delebecque called for a break with Russia—"Le Geste attendu." Moscow and Berlin were clearly one, and therefore to intervene in Finland was to hurt the Germans. *Je suis partout* took up the call immediately, and *Candide* in turn. It was ridiculous, its editorial argued on December 13, to make war on the Germans over Poland, rather than on Russia, which had just bitten off half of it. It was impossible to let aggression against helpless neutrals like Finland occur without stepping in to stop it.

At last the anti-Communists had found their cause. The war with Germany, which they had never liked, almost forgotten, they concentrated on something closer to their hearts. The men who had cried about the shortage of equipment, who had protested against giving precious arms to foreigners when first needs were at home, forgot their concern now that it came to Finland: "True, the chief theater of operations is on our border," wrote Delebecque on December 14. "Is this a reason for denying ourselves diversions which, without weakening us or compromising our safety, would have (not to mention their moral value) the certain effect of sharply thwarting the free development of the enemy's plans?"

By now just who the enemy was no longer seemed quite clear. "At last," rejoiced the *Action française* on the first day of 1940, "the enemy is getting walloped." Who was the enemy? "Both Germany and Russia."

The paper had no patience for the "imbeciles" who wanted France to choose between Hitler and Stalin. Both men were enemies, both regimes were evil. But, clearly, although Frenchmen who preferred the first against the second were fools, those who preferred the latter against the former were much worse. Franco-German understanding was still a mug's game to the *Action française*; but it had not been treason—at least not when it was advocated by old friends. Treason it was, right now, the *Action française* of January 5 proclaimed, "to try to prevent France from taking against the ally of her enemy the urgent and vital action that circumstances called for."

The fate of Finland took on an aspect which that of Czechs and Poles had never had. Poland's fall had evoked no suggestion from the *Action française* of diversionary intervention, and those who criticized the Army leadership for doing nothing had quickly been slapped down,[7] but now it appeared that the Allies had not a day to lose in intervening.[8] This, Maulnier said, was a war to defend civilization against barbarism, small nations against big. Here "a miraculous chance" was offered to strike, at very little cost, what might be a decisive blow. "A cette chaîne de diamant, à ce clou d'or pourpré," wrote Maurras, letting his pen run riot, "les destins de l'Europe et de la planète sont suspendus . . . Vous voulez vivre? Mieux: vous ne voulez pas mourir? Alors, secourez la Finlande!"[9]

This should be done even if Finland did not officially request French help, even if neutrals refused to permit troops and aid to cross their boundaries. Other things were more important than international law or having to fight one's way through Norwegian territory: "Our honor is in Finland. If Finland is defeated, no civilized nation can still consider its honor unblemished." Maulnier was more than right in saying this; he also gave a useful indication why his and his friends' honor had been so hard to find in 1938: it had been in Finland all the time, and here it was, at stake. The Verdun of this war, Maulnier advised his readers, lay in the Finnish snow.[10]

There were sound reasons for sympathizing with Finland against Russia, but the reasons of French nationalists were clearly very special ones: for the first time since the 'twenties the Right had found a cause it could embrace wholeheartedly, where no injustice was involved as in Abyssinia, and where nothing was the least muddled as it had been in Spain. Now it could be converted to somewhat more doubtful use in the great anti-Communist witch hunt safely behind the front. After dealing with its own Communists, wrote *Candide* in an article entitled "The Nest of Vipers," France should be cleared of German Communists, defined as those who spoke in the name of the exiled Catholics, liberals, and democrats. In other words, like other right-wing publications, *Candide* envisaged the war effort largely in terms of helping Finland and clearing French territory of Communists, Socialists, and foreign refugees. The Germans could be taken care of by blockade and by jibes in French cartoons.[11]

To what extent could they have hoped that Finland's German friends might be induced at last to turn against Red Russia, or even that a common cause might put an end to fighting in the West? Nothing was said about Finnish hopes of aid not from the democracies but from Hitler, in whom, with little justification, some Finns put their trust. At any rate, while fighting raged in Finland, Maurras could characterize the West as a peninsula of peace: "Thanks to a solid wall, to two fine armies and two sovereign fleets commanding sky and ocean, a relative calm, not unworthy of being called peace, is enjoyed by our peoples thus covered and defended."[12]

Enthusiasm and anger were followed by dismay when, in mid-March, the Finns, "whose destiny was bound to that of France," had to accept Russian peace terms.[13] The demand for more vigorous leadership than Daladier could furnish was heeded at last, and on March 20 his cabinet was replaced by one headed by Reynaud which far from satisfied the desires of the Right.[14] Less than three weeks after Reynaud took over, German troops were attacking Denmark and Norway; just four weeks later, what General Edward Spears has called the slimy mess of disastrous incompetence in France brought the new cabinet to collapse on the eve of Germany's major offensive on the West.

Addressing the French colony in Madrid on New Year's Day, Marshal Pétain had assured them that the Allies fulfilled all the conditions that victory required. "We can await the great clash without fear."[15] Now the *Action française,* which had been most sanguine throughout the Norwegian battles,[16] was glad: "The war of nerves is ended: the other one begins. All France, glimpsing the moment of victory, cries out: AT LAST!"[17] Daudet, who, unlike all his colleagues, had predicted a short, sharp war, was delighted that events now bore him out: Hitler's hysterical impatience and the high morale of the French troops made German disaster certain.[18]

Within a week after the attack, the French lines had crumpled near Sedan, much of the northern army as a fighting force was gone, and German armor, having cut the Allied troops in two, was herding off one lot toward Dunkerque, while desperate efforts were being made in Paris to regroup the rest. Like most of the Paris press, the *Action française* showed stubborn hope bolstered by increasingly desperate affirmations of faith in French arms. On May 19 it welcomed the news of General Weygand's promotion to Commander-in-Chief, and of cabinet changes in which Pétain became the second man.[19] On June 5, Maurras commented approvingly on Churchill's assurance to his countrymen after Dunkerque—"We shall never surrender; and even if, which I do not for a moment believe, this Island or a large part of it were subjugated and starving, then our Empire beyond the seas, armed and guarded by the British Fleet, would carry on the struggle"—expressing only doubts that Churchill might be dramatizing things: "Nous avons aussi de belles portes de sortie du côté de l'Algérie et de toute l'Afrique du Nord,—mais, diable! diable! diable! comment peut-on penser qu'on en puisse venir là! Tout le monde est résolu à se défendre. Personne ne se rendra. Personne n'acceptera aucune paix des Boches."

On Saturday, June 8, Brasillach, who had been held by the police for questioning about his pro-Nazi sentiments, dropped in on Maurras at the printing plant and found the master and his staff full of a naïve optimism. On Monday, June 10, the Action Française staff left Paris for the South. The newspaper would never appear in the capital again.

They traveled by auto, slowly, but in no discomfort, for they had friends in almost every town; one member of the group remembers that Pujo's chief concern was who, since every member of the little party was a person of a certain social standing, would carry in the suitcases when they stopped for the night. The first halt of consequence was made at Poitiers, where six issues of the paper were printed between June 13 and 18. The Prefect of Poitiers, arriving at the print shop to pay a courtesy call on Maurras just as the Germans began their first air raid on the town, found Maurras writing his lead article in the cellar. When he gave him news of the raid, which he could not hear, Maurras hardly looked up: "Que voulez-vous, Monsieur le Préfet, 70 ans de démocratie . . . ça s'expie! Au revoir, Monsieur." And that was that.[20]

On June 18, as advancing German forces were threatening Poitiers, the Action Française caravan took to the road again, planning to head for Toulouse, but changing its direction on hearing that the Government intended to move from Bordeaux to a more central city. They were in Villefranche-de-Rouergue, in Pujo's Aveyron, when they got the news of the Armistice, signed on June 22, and it was from there that they wired Pétain their warm approval of his call for national unity. There was no talk now of carrying on the struggle in the Empire beyond the seas, which, three weeks earlier, Maurras had thought would certainly be done if things were to get that far. One had to be stark, raving mad, he declared to the Agence Havas, to try to substitute one's judgment for the military acumen of Pétain and Weygand. Continuing the war would mean taking refuge in the colonies and leaving France. And when would one see France again? Perhaps never. Dreams such as these were too far-fetched: the only thing to do now was to work together for national recovery under the leadership of Pétain.

The endorsement, detailed and emphatic, which the news agency carried on its wires reflected the dominant national mood. In France and overseas it was quoted as part of the great optimism-in-pessimism campaign of support for the grand old savior, Marshal Pétain. Who had more right to speak up at this hour than the tireless Cassandra of the rue du Boccador? Welcoming the statement, *L'Orient* of Beirut added, on June 29:

> Quelle voix s'impose davantage ajourd'hui à l'audience et au respect de tous les Français que celle de Charles Maurras? Quel nom plus pur, quelle plus haute et plus forte autorité peut opérer les ralliements nécessaires . . . Si des Français, dans la cruelle soumission qui vient de leur être imposée, conservaient encore quelque doute ou quelque scrupule, le seul témoignage de Maurras doit suffire à les libérer.

A doctrine the essence of which was the division between the real France and the legal structure of gimcrack institutions stifling it, now came to aid a statesman who was determined to preserve all that he could of France, regardless of what happened to the human values that the Action Française, too, had never ceased to belittle.

As Pujo said in the *Action française,* on July 1, when, installed for a while on the premises of the *Courrier du Centre* in France's dreariest city, Limoges, it got out a special issue covering the period since June 19, continuing the fight from overseas would mean abandoning the *patrie réelle* to its fate as a German protectorate, for the sake of an ideal *patrie* which would inevitably be blown away. This sort of concept could satisfy idealists who had no feeling for the soil of France, and it might allow real responsibilities for defeat to be ignored, but it would not satisfy Pujo. Where the responsibilities lay, Maurras expressed in the same issue of the paper when he inaugurated the now time-honored practice of celebrating defeats by honoring the soldiers who incurred them, calling on the Army to assume power and, presumably, make the same mess of things in office as it had already done in the field.[21]

When the National Assembly, meeting appropriately in the Casino at Vichy, granted full powers to Pétain by a vote of 569 to 80, the *Action française* expressed its "joy and hope," but it warned sternly that hopes of revival would be in vain without an exemplary requital for those who had brought the country to this pass.[22] The June-July issue of the *Nouvelle Guyenne,* which Paul Courcoural continued to publish in German-occupied Bordeaux, sang the paean that most Frenchmen sang at this time, to the old soldier savior:

> Une grande fortune nous est venue dans notre immense misère. Dieu nous avait préparé un grand chef. Le Maréchal Pétain a recueilli la France au jour même de sa détresse . . . Ce qui se réalise, du fait des décisions prises à Vichy . . . c'est la Contre-Révolution. Avec Charles Maurras et tous ses amis nous en saluons les premiers actes avec une émotion, une fierté et une espérance qui s'expliquent par toute notre vie depuis 50 ans dévouée à ces principes . . . On ne fera donc plus, en France, que de l'action française.

25

THE DIVINE SURPRISE

Courcoural's happy pun must have seemed to describe reality to some of those who lived under or observed the Vichy regime from afar; and even to the leaders of the Action Française there must have been at first a hope that it might come true. In several ways it did. When Maurras and Pujo were tried at Lyon in January 1945, part of the indictment concerned the "preponderant" influence Maurras had exercised over French thought during the preceding few years: "Maurras's articles are quoted on the radio every day, reprinted in all the papers, circulated abroad, to the extent that a great many people who have never bought a single copy of the *Action française* know every day what Maurras, who reflects the Marshal's thought, is thinking."[1]

One wonders to what extent this last assertion should not be inverted to say that Pétain reflected a great deal of Maurras's thought. In one of the innumerable articles in his praise which were published about this time, Paul Barlatier, director of the Marseille *Sémaphore,* voiced what many seemed to think: "If Maurras has no part in Pétain's government, it does seem on the other hand that his thought inspires it; and it is not one of the least reasons for the confidence we place in the great Marshal to know that he acts and governs in a manner that is distinctly Maurrassian."[2]

In January 1941, the *Almanach de la France nouvelle,* edited by the Vichy Information Services, listed the writers whose influence on current thought had, in approved opinion, been most important: De Maistre, Taine, La Tour du Pin, Sorel, Péguy, Barrès, and, last in time, Maurras. "Tomorrow," said the paragraph on Maurras, written by Gaxotte, "Maurras will be read in all the schools, and children will recite the pages he has written as they recite Racine or Bossuet. He will remain for us the master who rediscovered the great laws that make states prosperous and powerful: it is in [his] principles that France seeks her salvation today."

Particularly during the honeymoon period of Vichy, the first twelve months or so, tributes of this order were frequent. Moreover, sales of Maurras's books, as of Bainville's and Gaxotte's, increased as the public sought an explanation for what had happened and what was to be done. Anatole de Monzie and Ludovic Frossard, at odds about most things, agreed on the profound influence of Charles Maurras, and even Mauriac held that Maurras and Bainville were the only writers who ever influenced politics or government in their own time—"with profound effects even on those they fought with passionate logic." Otto Abetz attested to the credit given to the Action Française, and he seemed to regard the National Revolution as something attempted under its influence.[a]

Because of the nature of integral nationalism, it is difficult to estimate its part in the counsels and decisions of the Vichy regime. The Action Française was, especially by this time, a doctrine, a newspaper, a set of books, a kind of attitude, the influence of a man. There were individuals who were imbued by its spirit and who represented its views, even though they themselves never belonged to any of its organized bodies—Massis and Gaxotte are good examples. One was "a friend," one thought the way it did, at least on general lines, one could become its champion and interpreter, without carrying a card, attending meetings, paying a contribution or a fee. One could "belong" without joining—and certainly many joined who never belonged at all.

This very vagueness, in which there was no question of membership but only that of sympathy, made the Action Française particularly effective in what was never anything like a party regime, but was instead a gathering of men united by similarity of outlook or ambition around the central figure of Philippe Pétain. In a regime whose outstanding characteristic was that it was extremely personal, the equally personal and almost, one might say, intimate nature of Maurrassian influence could fit in very well. As Xavier Vallat has put it, a great many politicians were Maurrassian without being royalists. One might go further and say that a good many also were Maurrassian without being aware of it. Maurras's ideas had illuminated all right-wing thought for so long that men had assimilated them on every side, frequently without knowing that they did so. Thus, even though actual members of the Action Française were never very numerous at Vichy, the place was pervaded with a strong, though diffuse, Maurrassism.

Although national-socialism or its equivalent was dominant in Paris, Pierre Dominique has declared, looking back on that time, that "what ruled at Vichy was nationalism, a right-wing nationalism of which Maurras was the expression." The sharpest-eyed observers have testified to this: Vallat, Fabre-Luce, Loustaunau-Lacau, Maurice Martin du Gard, and Robert Aron have all been

[a] *Le Jour-Echo,* Sept. 28, 1940, Jan. 20, Oct. 13, 1941; Firmin Roz, *RU,* January 1942, February 1944; Frossard, *Le Mot d'ordre,* quoted in *AF,* July 6, 1943; Mauriac, *Figaro littéraire,* Jan. 25, 1941. Abetz, *Histoire d'une politique franco-allemande* (1953), p. 183, cites the Action Française as foremost among preponderant influences in Pétain's entourage, and Maurras as "without question the intellectual leader of the French Right, who for thirty years had the strongest political and intellectual influence in France and abroad . . . Even de Gaulle and Giraud . . . passed through the Action Française school." See also J.-J. Alméras, *Thèses pour la Révolution nationale* (1942), p. 23 and final section entitled "Politique d'abord." On July 19, 1942, the German occupation authorities in Belgium placed the works of Bainville, Daudet, and Maurras on their list of banned books. Paul Delandsheere and Alphonse Ooms, *La Belgique sous les Nazis* (Brussels, n.d.), II, 303.

impressed with the integral nationalist preponderance in the Marshal's entourage.[3] General Bernard de Sérigny found his old friend surrounded by men whom he considered to be Action Française militants—Henri Dumoulin de La Barthète, Raphaël Alibert, Paul Baudoin, General Brécard—none of whom had ever belonged to an Action Française formation, bar Dumoulin, who had been an Etudiant d'Action Française. So had Yves Bouthillier, who was Minister of Finance from 1940 to 1942. The others were just "friends," like Minister of Agriculture Pierre Caziot, Dr. Huard, Minister of Health in 1941, and Admiral Jean Fernet, general secretary of the Presidency of the Council, whose brother had been one of the royalists' young hopes.[4]

Not only were friends of the Action Française foremost among the Marshal's personal collaborators, ghostwriting his speeches or directing public relations—men like Massis, René Benjamin, René Gillouin, Fernet, and Dumoulin—they were even more numerous in secondary positions in the Vichy structure. Such leaders of the Légion des Combattants as General Nadal were also members of the Action Française. The censorship and information services (Pierre Héricourt, for instance, was director of the radio news service before being sent as consul to Barcelona) had been heavily colonized. So had the services of education, and, most of all, Pétain's own cabinet, in which even those who, like Roger de Saivre or Dr. Ménétrel, had belonged to the Jeunesses Patriotes were strongly influenced by Maurrassian thought, and in which, while he lasted, a man like Dumoulin was considered by his colleagues as the primary inspiration of the group.[5]

Among the military, Maurras had always counted numerous sympathizers. Now that the government was dominated by soldiers, the friends his doctrine made in military circles carried its influence into effective action, as, for instance, in the military courts. Thus, two of the principal military judges whom Mendès-France had to endure during his prison term were great admirers of the Action Française, which did not make the fate of a Jewish politician of the Third Republic any easier.[6]

Another province in which Action Française influence was strong was the Institute of Corporatist and Social Studies (IECS), which, although dating from well before the war, was taken up by Vichy after 1940 and henceforth became important in helping to establish professional corporatist movements and in training their local leaders and organizers. The IECS committees and the faculties of the schools set up by the Institute were studded with names familiar in Action Française annals, like those of Pesquidoux, Pierre Lucius, Firmin Baconnier, Louis Le Fur, Achille Mestre, and Maurice Bouvier-Ajam. André Voisin directed the College of Syndical and Corporatist Studies, Louis Salleron both the Collège Paysan and the advanced work of the Cours Supérieur de L'Institut d'Etudes Corporatives.

An area where the inspiration of integral nationalism was strong was in the youth movement, on which Massis at Vichy kept an eye—both in the

Chantiers de la Jeunesse set up by General de La Porte du Theil and in the famous Ecole Nationale des Cadres at Uriage, set up by Catholic cavalry officers inspired by the social Christianity of Albert de Mun and by the authoritarian ideas of Maurras to train the elements of a new Christian knighthood. It would be a mistake to think Uriage Maurrassian; but leading figures like P.-D. Dunoyer de Segonzac and P.-H. Chombart de Lauwe started from the terrain of the Action Française, their first friend at court being probably Massis. All these movements which aimed at remaking France needed a doctrine, and that of the Action Française was among the most obvious choices. At Uriage the study program allotted a week to study of "the masters of French politics"—Proudhon, Péguy, and Maurras.

It may indeed have been under the influence of such ideas, and not only of those introduced by Emmanuel Mounier and Hubert Beuve-Méry, that the spirit of the school began to turn against its original doctrinal heroes seen to be misapplying the ideals for which they were supposed to stand. The school at Uriage became increasingly nationalistic against the compromising retired nationalists of Lyon and Vichy, and was at last dissolved in 1942; its staff and pupils furnished a good number of Resistance leaders in southeastern France,[7] and its premises became a training school for the cadres of Darnand's Milice.

What happened at Uriage reflects what happened to the Action Française: 1940 and to some extent 1941 witnessed the height of a love affair in which Pétain's policy seemed to reflect ideas that Maurras had spent his life trying to teach the French. For instance, in his message of October 11, 1940, the Head of State rejected "the false notion of the natural equality of men" and promised that the new regime would be "a social hierarchy." On June 4, 1941, he declared that the State, "hierarchic and authoritarian," had to be founded on responsible leadership exercised downward from the top. A few weeks earlier, on the first of May, which had been taken over as the feast of Saint Philippe, he had for the umpteenth time denounced "the practice of worker or employer coalitions rising one against the other" and spoken of the new corporatist order including all members of the same métier.

In practice, too, the law of July 17, 1940, forbidding the public service and the legal profession to anyone born of a foreign father, the law of July 22 ordering revision of all naturalizations since 1927, the law of July 30 that set up a Supreme Court of Justice to try ministers of the Third Republic accused of having failed in or betrayed their duties, the law of August 13 prohibiting secret associations, especially Masonic ones, and requiring public servants to affirm that they belonged to none, the measures of August 24 and September 3 facilitating the arrest and trial of anyone "endangering the safety of the State," the Statute of the Jews on October 3 forbidding them most public and a good many private offices, and the ancillary measures withdrawing citizenship from Algerian Jews and providing for the internment of all foreign ones—even the replacement of the old motto, "Liberté, Egalité, Fraternité" by an Alibert-devised "Travail, Famille, Patrie," and the botched-up Labor Charter of 1941—all were evidence of the triumph of the Action Française. The drafting and the application of these measures were in the hands of men who, like Alibert, Vallat, and Darquier de Pellepoix, owed most of their ideas to the Action Française.

Even though Maurras was seldom at Vichy, and though his meetings with Pétain were few and far between,[b] his advice reached the provincial capital not only by his articles but by word of mouth. Dumoulin's aide, André Lavagne, who was deputy director of the Civil Cabinet, has testified that at regular intervals Georges Calzant would arrive as messenger to carry Maurras's opinions straight into the Marshal's inner sanctum.[8] Pétain's personal regard for his colleague of the Académie was high: in 1941 he sent him his *Paroles aux français,* with the inscription "Au plus Français des Français"; and when in 1942 Maurras fell ill while lecturing at Pau in the Pyrenees, he ordered a special railroad car to be put at his disposal. On the eve of Pétain's treason trial in 1945, while Pétain was discussing with his counsel, Jacques Isorni, the phrasing of the declaration he would make before the High Court of Justice, the question arose whether at a particular point "liberty" or "liberties" would be the *mot juste.* "What is the difference?" asked Pétain. "'Liberty' sounds more republican; 'our liberties' has a more Maurrassian sound," Isorni explained. The Marshal thought for a moment: "Put 'our liberties,'" he said.[c]

All this the Action Française repaid with interest. Of all the bodies and publications that were quick to praise Pétain in 1940, it always remained his steadiest supporter. Without its ever being actually said, Pétain took the place of a king, and to Pétain the royalists transferred the loyalty they had heretofore reserved for the Pretender. When the economist and social geographer Jean-François Gravier lectured at Uriage, his advocacy of the hierarchic State, strong but not "Statist," ended in arguments for what was in effect monarchy redefined as "le gouvernement d'un seul"—"the only formula possible in France." What was Vichy, "cet Etat incarné par un pouvoir personnel devant être entouré de conseils," but a fulfillment, somewhat altered, of Maurrassian dreams? Jean Guitton saw very well that to look upon Pétain as the concrete image of the fatherland, the man who incarnates the nation, was to endow

[b] Anon., *Le Patriotisme ne doit pas tuer la patrie* (1947), p. 10, declares that Maurras was twice consulted by Pétain on specific questions, the first time whether he should call the Chambers to affirm his authority against Germany (Maurras affirmative), the second time concerning some suggestions for peace intervention (Maurras negative). The two men met on several other occasions, three public, six private. During one of the latter, in October 1940, Maurras denounced Laval and his truckling to the Germans.

[c] Jacques Isorni, *Souffrance et mort du Maréchal,* p. 91, quoted in *Libertés françaises,* No. 10, May 1956, p. 95. See also Jean-Albert Boucher, "Le Testament Politique du Maréchal Pétain," *ibid.,* pp. 109–10, for Pétain's declaration of July 31, 1944, in which the fundamental law and authority of the State seems to be based upon "historical heredity—that is the designation provided by birth in a family whose authority has been consecrated by history."

him with the characteristics of a king. And, reading him, Havard de la Montagne could share the feeling that perhaps in the present time the king might appear in a form other than that of hereditary and dynastic royalty. In a most revealing essay, "L'Immédiat," the old legitimist Jean de La Varende has focused on the hero of Verdun all the emotion his earlier writings had lavished on the king.[9] "Aimer c'est croire et croire c'est agir," wrote de La Varende; he and his friends loved Pétain and they believed in him. That was the essence of their position, and they would pay for it.

The most notorious instance of this Pétainist exaltation is the oft-misrepresented article published by Maurras himself under the title "The Divine Surprise," in the *Petit Marseillais* of February 9, 1941. In it, Maurras set out the reasons why Pétain embodied all the hopes of France. Far from being a paean over the defeat of France, or even on the end of the loathed Third Republic, the surprise referred to in the title was that of the old Marshal's miraculous political capacities. There is no doubt that for Maurras the fall of the Republic offered some consolation for the fall of France; but this is not what he alludes to here; and although one may find his praise of the old man excessive, nothing he says smacks of treachery:

> Un poète . . . a dit que—lorsque la Poésie vient d'atteindre tous les points de sa perfection consommée—quand elle a touché même le sublime, quelque chose lui manque encore si elle n'a produit ce qu'on peut appeler *La Divine Surprise,* celle précisément qui submerge tous les espoirs de l'admiration la mieux disposée.
>
> C'est dans le même sens qu'il a été parlé de la "partie divine" de l'art de la guerre.
>
> Eh bien! la partie divine de l'art politique est touchée par les extraordinaires surprises que nous a faites le Maréchal.
>
> On attendait tant de lui, on pouvait et on devait tout attendre. A cette attente naturelle il a su ajouter quelque chose. Il n'y manque plus rien désormais.

The essay was no more eulogistic than others written at the time and for a long time thereafter, when men like Claudel, Valéry, Herriot, Jeanneney, Wladimir d'Ormesson and Mauriac went out of their way to laud the man whom Emile Henriot as late as 1943 described as "Le chef et le père."[10]

In July 1941, when the battle for Syria was a source of worry to the French public, the Comte de Paris, now in Morocco, circulated a "Message to French Monarchists"[11] which also backed the Marshal to the hilt:

> This man of Providence has managed to accomplish a triple miracle: he has prevented the total disappearance of the fatherland; he has by his sole presence enabled the country to stay alive; and, last, he has set France on the path of its great traditional destinies by breaking with the principles of the fallen regime. . . . The beliefs of the Marshal proceed from the same sources as ours do. It is right to aid their dissemination and their defense. *There lies our duty as Frenchmen.*

While Pétain was on one of his triumphal tours a month later, this time in the southwest, Monseigneur Béguin, Archbishop of Auch, told him: "One must be with you or against you. The Catholics and their clergy, M. le Maréchal, are with you with all their heart." Why, with such praise so common, should the Action Française withhold its approval?

The true difference appeared after 1941, when many, for patriotic or opportunistic motives, left Pétain, whereas the Action Française never altered its position. From first to last, rejecting both Resistance and Collaboration, its leaders remained loyal to the Marshal; and it was Massis who, at the end of August 1944, on the eve of Pétain's deportation to Germany, helped the old man to prepare his last message to the French people.[d]

But the effect of this stubborn loyalty was disastrous for what was left of the Action Française as a movement. For, as the war went on, the necessity of choice became more urgent. Some chose to join the Germans, to fight either against values they hated or for a new order in which they could believe. Others chose resistance, to the Germans, but also to Vichy, whose authorities were becoming increasingly subservient to the occupant. And those who refused to make either choice found themselves deserted on both sides, attacked as German lovers by resistants and as Anglophiles by the collaborators.

In effect, despite an almost equal hatred of both sides, the Action Française contributed to both in similar proportions. As in the late 'thirties, Maurras's creed was isolationist, determined by a dream of keeping France, or what was left of it, free of entanglements, united, and at peace. As in the late 'thirties, this was to prove impossible: defeated France would not be left alone any more than she had been when she was a power; Frenchmen would not resign themselves to cowed insignificance, but sought to play a part in world affairs even at the risk of their own lives and the lives of others. Before long, doing something became easier than doing nothing, and under the impact of such pressures the Action Française split, leaving only a small hard core.

Naturally, most of the publicity received by the Action Française has concerned the collaboration of sometime friends and members with the German enemy. Years after the events had passed, a Belgian journalist who had paid for *his* collaboration explained that if so many followers of Maurras in France and Belgium decided to collaborate with the occupying enemy, it was not because of some ideological affinity, but because of their taste for political realism. "Those who had so lucidly foreseen the disaster were not surprised when it came about. Like blindness and neglect, obstinate hope was democratic. The readers of the *Action française* had long known that one day, save for a miracle, they would have to look facts in the face and come to terms with

[d] Massis sent a copy of Pétain's message to Maurras by secret messenger, and when Maurras was interviewed by American journalists at Lyon on September 4, 1944, he released the text, which had been suppressed both by the Germans and by the Resistance. It was following this interview that Maurras was arrested.

things. After the disasters of 1940, they were the first to bestir themselves and to take steps to cope with what had happened." In one way or another.[12]

All this is as it might be. In some cases collaboration was much more enthusiastic than resigned. The men who had been national-socialists before the war and who were strongly anti-Masonic and anti-Semitic remained true to themselves when they cooperated with the Nazis. Considering the broad influence of the *Action française,* it was inevitable that among the most lively and enthusiastic collaborators of the Right a good many should have come from Maurrassism. The interwar years, particularly the 'thirties, had seen the nationalists playing musical chairs with leagues and parties, moving from one to another and occasionally sitting in several at once. In their search for effectiveness, or merely for an opportunity to assert themselves, Maurrassians tried every other movement, wrote for practically every publication that the Extreme Right brought out. And when the chance came to express their views under the patronage of the Germans, some hesitated no more than they had done before Coty's money, or that of the Italians.

Though never of the Action Française, men like Ferdonnet, Jean Hérold-Paquis, and Henri Lèbre had served their apprenticeship in Maurrassian circles. It was Bainville who helped Ferdonnet get to Berlin as foreign correspondent for *Liberté,* and the traitor's last book before the war, inspired by *Je suis partout,* was dedicated to Gaxotte and to "those who are for France."[13] The entire staff of *Je suis partout* came straight from the Action Française, and when Lesca and Laubreaux were arrested in June 1940 for intelligence with the enemy, Maurras was alone in taking—and effectively taking—their defense.[14]

It was understandable that some should find it impossible to embrace both anti-Germanism and anti-Communism with equal heartiness. The journalists who, before the war, had in the pages of *Je suis partout* and *Combat* been moving toward a national-socialism *à la française,* the conspirators who had followed Deloncle in his CSAR, were merely carrying their ideas to a logical conclusion which Maurras shunned. But even lesser men found that the logic of their prejudices forced them to join the German anti-Communist crusade. To many in Vichy, it seemed reasonable to think that collaboration with the victorious Germans offered the only hope of French revival. When the German forces invaded Russia in the summer of 1941, others who had been hesitating were drawn first to approval, then to espousal of the German cause.

Men like Georges Claude, starting from simple support of Pétain's policy and opposition to those who, in looking for Allied help, were risking the loss of French unity, became more strongly pro-German as the Germans became more openly anti-Communist.[15] Count François de Puységur, once a leader of the Action Française in the Lot, rejoiced over the German invasion of Russia: like Saint Louis, who sought to deliver the tomb of Christ, Hitler was out to save Western civilization from its most determined foe—Communism. General Lavigne-Delville, before the war a regular contributor to the *Action française,* agreed with his friend Puységur: to both, the Resistance was a coalition of the Jew-lovers, the Mason-lovers, and the Communist-lovers of France, essentially the same malignant forces they had always fought. By 1943, both men looked to the Nazis to help reform a France that seventy-one years of an evil Republic had rotted to the core.[e]

Most characteristic of this development in which true patriots became the implacable enemies and hunters of the French is the story of the Milice, which was officially established on January 30, 1943, by Pierre Laval to "assemble Frenchmen who are resolved to take an active part in the political, social, economic, intellectual, and moral revival of France." But the foundation of the Milice had been laid a long time before by Joseph Darnand, sometime Camelot, sometime member of the Croix de Feu and of the PPF, a sympathizer of the Cagoule, and an undoubted hero of two wars. Demobilized in 1940 and hoping (as he talked things over with his Dominican friend Father Bruckberger) to get the country out of politicians' hands and rouse it sufficiently to re-enter the war, this time to win, Darnand became president of the Légion des Combattants in the Alpes-Maritimes. When rumors reached Nice that the Italians might occupy the region, Darnand and his friends began to prepare arms depots and fighting groups within the Legion to oppose them. The rumor faded, but the groups that had been formed remained to grow into what became the SOL (Service d'Ordre Légionnaire), which soon spread from Nice all over the Unoccupied Zone.

In 1941, the SOL became officially a branch of the Légion des Combattants. After England and Russia joined against the Germans, its orientation gradually changed to favor an understanding with Hitler, who fought the Communists. Relations between the strictly *Pétainiste* and anti-German Légion and Darnand's SOL, which favored action even with Germany against the enemies of the Germans, became more and more strained until finally Darnand decided to break the restraining affiliation and turn the SOL into a *Milice française.* Darnand was sick of doing nothing but parading and drilling with no concrete objective, but the message in which he outlined his ideas, on October 4, 1942, was no more specific than the plans of other activists. Darnand declared that his organization would enter the "revolutionary struggle" on both the internal and the international fronts. Opposed to bourgeois selfishness and capitalist injustice just as they were to Marxism, they would not hinder "the European reality, which some still hold to be incompatible with French greatness," but "conquer for our country a place worthy of its past" in the new Europe "enfin solide."

There is no doubt that at first Darnand was surrounded by men who were

[e] Comte de Puységur, *Lettres, 1941–1944,* Bibliothèque Nationale, MS. Rés. 4° Lb[58]. 156, June 28, 1941, Feb. 5, 1943. On July 7, 1944, Puységur bewailed the murder of Philippe Henriot as the last in a series that began with Marius Plateau. It was a strange but revealing *rapprochement.*

for the most part, all witnesses agree, imbued "with the purest Maurrassian spirit."[16] His SOL and thereafter his Milice drew heavily upon Maurras's ideas, and many men joined after being told that they would be "purely national and in no way contaminated by the foreigner."[17] The special school set up at Uriage after the Ecole Nationale des Cadres was closed was run by Maurrassians like Alfred Giaume and the French-Canadian La Noue du Vair, and it taught Maurras's ideas along with those of the counterrevolutionary masters whom he had publicized. The weekly review *Combats* was edited, first at Vichy, then in Paris, by Henry Charbonneau, who had been Camelot before following Deloncle to the CSAR.

Most of these men were good Frenchmen by their own standards, and often virulently anti-German; Darnand himself loathed the Boche. But they were drawn into ever closer cooperation with the occupying enemy. To fulfill its avowed purpose of being "a force of order to serve *La France Seule,*"[18] to fight "the hidden powers" that menaced the safety of the Vichy regime and above all the Communism with which all Resistance activities were equated, the Milice needed arms: it could get these only from the Germans, and only in return for service. And so, as a kind of pledge of good faith, Darnand's militiamen were encouraged to join a French SS unit to fight the Communists on the Russian Front. *Devenir,* the newspaper of the French SS, declared: "The French volunteers of the SS are fighting for their country; while waiting to help the leader of France carry out the French revolution tomorrow, they are the Führer's soldiers. They are the fanatical and loyal soldiers of Adolf Hitler."[19] There, under the command of French Army officers like Jean de Vaugelas and Henri de Bourmont and former Camelots like Jacques de Bernonville, they paradoxically found "the last refuge of Germanophobe Maurrassians fighting against the soldiers of the workers' international."[f]

Service on the Russian Front was the most striking activity of the Milice, but far more important after it had obtained some arms in the autumn of 1943 were its operations against the Resistance and against Jews, in which it proved itself a useful auxiliary of Nazi power.

Late in 1943 the Action Française leaders realized what had happened to the Milice, from which they hoped so much, and they did their utmost to warn their friends to leave it. They did not object to its hunting Communists, and every kind of resistant whom they objectively identified with Communism, but they could not abide a movement that came to terms with the Waffen-SS and with the national-socialist clan of Marcel Déat. Unable to print or circulate open disavowals, they tried by word of mouth to counteract the influence of the Milice, and thus brought down on themselves the hatred of the militiamen.[20] By then, however, Darnand's position was much stronger than that of

[f] From Lucien Combelle, *Prisons de l'espérance* (1952), pp. 36–48, in a description of meeting in prison the son of a Limoges shopkeeper who, starting as a Camelot and Christian monarchist, entered the Milice only to end in the SS.

the old and ineffective journalists in Lyon, who were not even able to take a very clear or forceful stand; and, although some Maurrassians did leave the Milice, there were probably more who left the Action Française—which, as Maurras explained at his trial, "came down to the same thing."[21]

The opposition to Darnand, as soon as Darnand made the mistake of becoming an out-and-out collaborator, was typical of a stand that never swerved into the dangerous bypaths of collaboration, be it in the cause of anti-Communism.[22] Maurras would have absolutely nothing to do with old friends or disciples who drifted in that slippery direction. When Vichy authorities asked newspapermen to publicize Paul Chacq's traveling anti-Soviet propaganda exhibit, Maurras replied, "It is not the Russians who occupy France. If you organize an anti-German exhibit, I shall talk about it."[g] And when Georges Claude visited Lyon to lecture on the new order in Europe, the *Action française* refused to print any announcements of the lectures and made it as plain as possible that relations with their erstwhile friend had been broken.[23]

Dominique Sordet, who had been the music critic of the *Action française,* had set up the news agency Inter-France, before the war; after 1940 this became the news center of the collaborationist press. As soon as Maurras saw a copy of the agency's news bulletin, *Inter-France,* in August 1940, he wrote Sordet to tell him that his name would never stain the pages of the *Action française* again.[24] The same applied to *Je suis partout,* which Maurras had advised should not be published in the German zone. In February 1941 Maurras prepared the following note to express the Action Française position toward its erring offspring:

> The publishers and collaborators of *Je suis partout* consulted Charles Maurras on whether to reappear or not. Charles Maurras advised against it most strongly, and Lesca's messenger, Nicolas, who returned to Paris with this advice, left the *Je suis partout* staff. But the review did reappear, and now Maurras obeys his duty, which is to warn our old friends that they are being rash. The political error is a flagrant one. I can say no more.

He could not even say that much, for the statement never got past the censors and was made public only at his trial, in January 1945.[25]

Brasillach, at least, had been publicly disowned,[26] and Maurras thereafter refused ever to see him again, even when his plump disciple requested an interview. When, in a conversation with Vallat, Maurras violently denied the imputation that he could have been the master of Brasillach or of Georges Suarez, he obviously did not mean that it was untrue in fact, but that he had cut himself off from the Germanophile heretics they had become.[27]

Just how completely he severed connections was indicated by the bitter attacks directed against him by the Paris press, for which "all that is against Germany and against the European revolution" was to be found in the Maur-

[g] Kléber Haedens, personal communication. Paul Chacq was shot after the Liberation.

rassian camp.[h] A special number of *Notre Combat* examined "the enigma of Maurras,"[28] "one of the most sinister scoundrels and cretins" the world had ever known. Using on the old man his own technique of guilt by association, his rebellious disciples accused him of "rejoining the clan of the Jewish war, of unleashed democracy, of gory Jacobinism, of Masonry, of liberalism that opens its arms to Stalin." And, shortly before D-Day, *Inter-France* pointed out again that for the past four years Maurras and his paper had been the center of active resistance "to the unification of Europe under German direction," and concluded: "L'attentisme français, le refus de la France à une politique de rapprochement franco-allemand, a trouvé dans *l'Action française* son expression quotidienne la plus habile."[29]

It was ironic that the *Action française,* which did not mind such attacks but hated the Vichy censorship's interdiction to reply, should have to defend itself against charges of being only pseudo-anti-Semitic, or not sufficiently anti-British.[30] The argument that who is not with us is against us was turned against the old beards in the Lyon office who would not make up their minds to accept the necessity of a new international order. How could they, in view of the situation as outlined by Nel Ariès in the last number of the *Nouvelle Guyenne*:

> At last we hold what we had been asking for; things are not quite the way we had foreseen, but we do have for the moment the leader that we wanted —alone and singlehanded, at one with national interest, independent of election and master of his own decisions: all the essentials of our doctrine. Are we to take all this as nothing just when it moves from theory into practice?[31]

Not at all! And this was why Professor Pierre Mauriac, dean of the Medical Faculty at Bordeaux, told his hearers at commencement exercises in 1942, "How well I understand the profound words of Bossuet: *The heretic is the one who has an opinion.*"[32]

The world was full of heretics, alas, and no one would let the state of France remain as it was. But they did not all come from this most publicized extreme. In testifying on Maurras's behalf, Georges Gaudy, who had fought through Italy and the south of France in units that included many ardent sympathizers of Maurras, pointed out with some reason that although the accused was blamed for nurturing collaborators, he was never praised for having influenced Resistance figures like Jacques Debu-Bridel or André Rousseaux. This

[h] *L'Oeuvre,* March 21, April 9, 1941. Marcel Déat, no disciple of course, was particularly hostile to an influence whose discretion masked the most determined opposition to his hopes of collaboration and revolutionary reform. In *L'Oeuvre,* December 2, 1940, an editorial, "Il faut les chasser," attacked the anonymous clique of "monarchists on principle, ultraconservatives by definition," who had been running things since the Armistice and on whose advice Pétain relied. Further attacks appeared in *Nouveau départ, nouveaux combats* (1941), pp. 11–13, and *Le parti unique* (1942), as well as in many numbers of *L'Oeuvre.*

touched an aspect of royalist disintegration that has received little notice. Members of the Action Française were represented in all the different sections of Resistance, both in France and overseas: Colette, who unsuccessfully shot at Laval, had once been a member of the Action Française; so had Henri d'Astier de la Vigerie, the inspiration of North African resistance; so had Fernand Bonnier de la Chapelle, whose father was a militant in Constantine and who, for his part, did shoot successfully at Darlan. Guillain de Benouville, now editor of *Jours de France,* Jacques Renouvin, who died in a concentration camp, Honoré d'Estienne d'Orves, one of the first to be shot by the Gestapo, and a great many others were among the earliest members of the Resistance.[33]

So was the man now known as Colonel Rémy, who has attributed the feelings that made him leave for England in June 1940 to the ideas that twenty years' daily reading of the *Action française* had instilled in him: "Nourished on the *Action française,* it was not possible for me to recognize the French defeat as final."[34] The same motives clearly inspired Alain Cordier, the aide of Jean Moulin, who, says Georges Bidault, came to the Resistance from the Action Française. They help explain the Gaullist agent whom Socialist Deputy Pierre Bloch, just escaped from jail, met in 1941 carrying a book by Charles Maurras under his arm: he had once been a Camelot, Jacques de Guélis told Bloch, and though he had broken with the Action Française he had not given up a good deal of its thought.[35]

Pierre Boutang, one of the most brilliant among the younger generation, who never agreed to join the Paris press, has told the story of two friends from the Ecole Normale Supérieure whom he had converted to the Action Française, the one from Fascism, the other from socialism: while the former went through the *Pétainiste* Compagnons de France to Resistance and Gaullism, the latter turned to Catholicism and entered a Franciscan monastery.[i] A less drastic evolution was that of writers like André Rousseaux, who in the last period of peace moved from effusive praise of Maurras to thoughtful coolness which deepened as the war drew on, and Claude Roy, whose relations with the Action Française remained good until, some time in 1943, he decided to transfer his enthusiasms to the Communists.[36]

But although young men could follow their patriotic instincts—and probably their love of adventure—into Underground action without feeling many qualms about the break with a master venerated as long as he could suit their mood, and intellectuals could follow their reasons, their rationalizations, or their interests, in one direction or another, the choice of collaboration or resistance could be very painful for men to whom the Action Française had

[i] Pierre Boutang, "Reconnaissance à Charles Maurras" in *Les Abeilles de Delphes* (1952). The young *normalien,* exiled for his uncompromising views to a school in the Algerian south, took part in the confused conspiracies that surrounded the Allied landings in North Africa. This was a moment in which royalists played an important role and even enjoyed a brief moment of power. Boutang was Chef de Cabinet to Jean Rigault while the latter was in charge of the Algerian Secretariat of Political Affairs after the landings.

symbolized a supreme love for France—men like the Duc de Choiseul-Praslin, who remained true to Maurras when Pope and King condemned him, yet could not bring himself to accept collaboration. Shocked by the pro-German arguments of Maurrassians like Lesca and Maubourguet, the Duc tried to write Maurras, with whom his relations had been "confident and cordial." Once his critical senses were aroused, however, he found Maurras's way of arguing by reiteration and calling people names less convincing, and when Maurras realized that he was no longer persuading, the letters stopped.

When the Duc made up his mind to join the Resistance, his friends and neighbors, who were still loyal to Maurras and to order, denounced him and his son as British agents. But even after this, he found the final break with the Action Française difficult, and it was not until January 1942 that he sent his old friends a long letter telling of his disgust with them, and adding some significant remarks:

> The time is gone when you could repudiate the opinion of the idiots who read you because their insignificant number did not count. Today, you have the ear of the masters of France; it follows that the immense number of Frenchmen who always want to know what their masters think and what they propose to do looks daily in your pages to find out what one should think and what one should foresee; . . . you are responsible, History will take note, for the reactions that you provoke.[37]

Many years before, in a strangely prophetic passage, Bernanos had predicted that in the coming war Maurras would be a vain and powerless Cassandra, "un homme dont je souhaite de toutes mes forces que la vieillesse ne soit pas une immense déception pour mon pays!"[38] But Maurras was, as he saw it, wholly consistent: he did not put Resistance fighters in a class with the "unworthy and depraved" pro-Germans; but he would go to any lengths to eliminate "anarchy" from the land. What de Gaulle was doing, his "dissidence," Maurras explained in a private letter he wrote from prison to Colonel Rémy after the end of the war, was a capital error, an enormous political mistake, which was inflicting terrible wounds on France. Just when defeat led one to hope that the difference between "real" and "legal" country would vanish in a new-found unity, de Gaulle's initiative created a new division, between two separate groups of patriots accusing each other of not being patriotic. Worst of all, said Maurras, Catholic public opinion, until then healthy and sane, would also be affected by de Gaulle's appeal and split in turn, reflecting the new divisions of the nation.[39] This was what the old nationalist could not abide. As he wrote Gaxotte in 1942, about the current nonsense being published: "All this will be swept away. But the errors will remain. And if we give ourselves the luxury of a revolution instead of uniting for serious things, Europe will be organized without us or against us."[40]

Here was the crux, in "Do not rock the boat!" Regardless of who won the war, France had to be united. She had a head of State; and anything that disturbed his position lessened the authority with which he could speak for France. But Maurras forgot that, to use another simile, France was less like a boat than like a bicycle whose stability is dependent on movement, not immobility—or that, to return to the nautical figure, while hurricanes were raging, salvation lay not in riding at anchor but in running with the storm.

Maurras objected to collaboration, and he objected to resistance, because they weakened and endangered a cohesion which he would have preferred to be monolithic. But this was all part of his insistence that reality should conform with the models he never ceased constructing *in vacuo*. De Gaulle is reported to have commented that Maurras was so right that it would drive him mad. The disciples who left Maurras to throw in their lot with one side or another did more than he to see that Europe should not, as he feared, be reorganized without France.

26

FRANCE, ONLY FRANCE

THE OCCUPATION BROUGHT serious difficulties for the Action Française; both the newspaper and the League were banned in the Occupied Zone, and in Vichy France most of the groups, deprived of the firm basis provided by the League, disintegrated into incoherence and decay. With communications difficult in the South and illegal in the Northern Zone, it was hard to re-establish contact after the defeat, let alone to maintain any sort of activity. Instructions from headquarters, first at Limoges, then after the end of September 1940 at Lyon, were carried largely by word of mouth, sometimes through the services of the veterans' legion, sometimes through friendly travelers of every kind.

The leadership had changed over the past few years: Admiral Schwerer had died in 1936, and his successor, François de Lassus, was killed in the Battle of France. Robert de Boisfleury died in April 1940. Lucien Lacour, long head of the Camelots, had left during the royalist squabbles of 1937–38 to join the party of the *Courrier royal.* Daudet, greatly depressed by the fall of France and weakened by a lingering illness, retired to the family property at Saint-Rémy, whence he continued to contribute articles, but he had less and less to do with the management of the paper or its policies in the months preceding his death from a cerebral hemorrhage on July 2, 1942. Gaxotte, who had become a regular contributor in 1939, decided soon after the fall of France not to compromise himself and temporarily retired from public writing. Maxime Réal del Sarte, not in the best of health, was living in his Pyrenean home, not far from Saint-Jean-de-Luz.

Maurras was left alone, relying more and more on Pujo, who, tall, big-footed, bearded and slightly bent, sleepy, and so careless of his appearance that his trousers sometimes went unbuttoned, was the only man to have the master's ear. There were several younger men—François Daudet, Léon's son, soft-spoken, dark, and tense; Thierry Maulnier, gangling and clever; Roger Joseph, who came from Orléans to act as editorial secretary and the most devoted of amanuenses; the sports-loving literary critic and historian Kléber Haedens—but the leading figure was the broad-shouldered, heavy-handed lawyer Georges Calzant, perennial president of the Etudiants, who now helped Pujo to run what was left of the movement.

In the Occupied Zone the task of keeping up was far from easy. At Nantes, for instance, where the local section had carried on after 1936 in the guise of a club called Le Bouclier, the *Action française* arrived only rarely, when some obliging railwayman smuggled a package over the interzonal boundary. The circle received mimeographed bulletins from League headquarters in Paris, but only infrequently, and most people subscribed either to the *Nouvelle Guyenne* (which, since Bordeaux was also occupied by Germans, could circulate within the Occupied Zone) or to the *Courrier de Saint-Nazaire,* for which the president of the Action Française section, Georges Paquet, was political editor for a while.

Late in September 1940, the first direct word from Maurras reached Nantes by way of a Breton officer, who, demobilized in the Free Zone, carried back news and instructions from Action Française headquarters, which he had made a point of visiting at Limoges. On his journey home he stopped here and there to address private meetings of Action Française members who had been cut off by the Occupation and were hungry for information. At Nantes, one who heard him noted at the time,[1] he explained how the defeat of France as well as the capitulation of the Belgians was a result of Great Britain's refusal to take its responsibilities in the war. Laval, "who had demolished the Third Republic," was looked on as a friend and described as indispensable. De Gaulle's appeal had caused some wavering, but his republicanism had made the leadership decide against him in the end. De Gaulle's messages were addressed too blatantly to French republicans, and his calls for the revolt of the Army had rallied Communists to him. Pétain, on the other hand, had declared himself in favor of monarchy in France, and not a liberal monarchy either. And so the sympathy of the Action Française for Pétain and its hostility to de Gaulle and the British had stemmed in part, the royalists of Nantes were told, from the fact that British propaganda insisted on republican solidarity and traditions. The present duty of the royalists was to hold firm, ignoring all the blandishments of alien camps and of their several allies among the French.

The leaders of Le Bouclier did their best to hold their group together as headquarters wished. When section meetings ceased, the section library was made a lending library, thus permitting the section secretariat to carry on undercover, keeping in touch with members and trying to dissuade its people from becoming either collaborationists or Gaullists. During the winter of 1941–42, Paul Courcoural traveled from Bordeaux throughout the German-occupied areas of the west and southwest, addressing groups of thirty or forty persons gathered in private homes. But after 1942 things went from bad to worse: the *Nouvelle Guyenne* folded in August, and when the *Courrier de Saint-Nazaire* became more and more collaborationist in tone, Paquet ceased writing his column for it. The private groups that met in drawing rooms began to express doubts about Pétain's wisdom and to criticize the Germans more bitterly and loudly, until, in 1943, a series of arrests extinguished even this little flicker of activity.

In Paris, too, where most of the records of the League were lost when the big building on the rue du Boccador was requisitioned by the Germans for a service club, where former members of the Action Française now in German pay sometimes spied on old comrades who had chosen the other camp, the royalists held meetings in private homes, including that of Laval's dentist on Boulevard Haussman; and some of them were arrested for their underground activity and eventually were deported to die in German concentration camps.[2]

In Bordeaux the activities of the Légion were at first dominated by Maurrassians, and so, too, was the youth movement there. The first meeting of the Légion d'Aquitaine de la Jeunesse Française, held on August 11, 1941, at the Athénée, was honored by the presence of Professor Pierre Mauriac; of the four speakers, two were well-known members of the Action Française, and the other two were friends. The first lecture delivered at the "Intellectual and Artistic Center" of the Légion (on August 2) was on the subject of Charles Maurras.

In Vichy territory, the Action Française was active in centers like Marseille and Montpellier, among the students whose meetings had resumed, and in most of the new youth movements launched to support the Marshal, especially Philippe d'Elbée's Equipes du Bulletin des Jeunes, and in the Compagnons, in which Roy and Haedens took some part, but many of whose members would before long join the Resistance.

The newspaper, more than ever, remained the focus of activity. It had moved from Limoges to Lyon late in September 1940 in order to be near the center of things and to tap a big-city public, but its circulation had nevertheless been cut by half. Beginning in 1941, it printed about 60,000 copies daily; between October 1943 and August 1944, a period for which precise figures exist, the average run was 38,000 for the first edition, and 25,000 for the second, five-o'clock, edition.[3]

Its ideas, however, enjoyed a wider circulation than these figures would suggest since they continued to be spread by other publications, including old friends like the *Revue universelle, Frontières,* and *Candide,* and several new ones run by younger men. At Clermont-Ferrand, Gustave Thibon, Gilbert Maire, and Maurice Bouvier-Ajam published the *Cahiers de Formation politique*; at Angoulême, Jean Arfel (better known today as Jean Madiran) and Jean Roche-Boiteaud brought out a series of Maurrassian-Pétainist reviews which, under different titles (*France, La Grande France, Nouveaux Cahiers de France*) mirrored integrist views. The old *Etudiant français* was reborn at Marseille; and at Montpellier a local publication, *L'Echo des étudiants,* founded in 1910 as an intellectual and academic weekly, was taken over by a group with strong Action Française overtones, under the editorship of René Barjavel and Jean Renon, a well-known royalist. The same familiar names—Gillouin, Challais, Roy, Bouvier-Ajam, Michel Mohrt, Jean Rivain, Louis de Gérin-Ricard—tended to recur in most of the publications of the Free Zone and, most of all, in doctrinaire reviews like *France* and *Idées,* set up at Vichy to work out the ideology of national revolution.

When in 1941 the Ministry of Information extended offers of a regular subsidy to all the Paris papers that had taken refuge in the Free Zone and had therefore lost their public in the capital, the *Action française* was one of only two to refuse the offer, replying that it supported Pétain but needed its independence to defend him. The *Action française,* therefore, never received any financial aid from Vichy, let alone from the Germans; moreover, although it accepted the publicity given by the government, it refused all advertisements for collaborationist books, for collaborationist publications like *Gringoire,* or for German-sponsored ones like the *Signal.*[a]

Unhampered by a government subsidy, helped by the rather more stable economic situation in which almost as many copies sold as could be printed and no costly returns of unsold copies weighed on the budget, primed by the contributions that faithful friends continued to maintain, the *Action française* refused for a long time to publish the official handouts of the OFI (French Information Office) which other papers printed. It gave space to communiqués of both sides (British and Germans, Italians and Greeks), and rejected stories that government censorship attempted to impose. Thus, in a private letter of June 9, 1941, Pujo reminded a Vichy official that he had no right to require the publication of any text that the paper did not wish to print:

> Even when we support the government with all our power, we do not write to please it and to obtain its favors. I remind you that the Action Française has refused all subsidies and that no one has the right to address it in this way. We shall continue to write only what we think. We should be curious to know if the *Censure* presumes to limit or modify the articles of Charles Maurras.[4]

This happy situation lasted some two years. It began to alter several months before the Germans occupied the Free Zone; but even then the paper did its best to show the flag. Thus Haedens remembers that, while he was temporarily in charge of the Press Review, Maurras passed him a note referring to the shooting of nineteen Jewish hostages by the Germans with the request that it be mentioned in the Press Review and criticized. When Haedens pointed out that it would be sure to fall under the censor's scissors, Maurras replied, "Yes, but the censors will read it first."

[a] See Pujo's declarations and Admiral Auphan's evidence in *Procès de Charles Maurras,* pp. 164–67, 200, and a letter of December 27, 1944, from the Agence Havas, OFI, Lyon branch, quoted by Pujo, *L'Action Française contre l'Allemagne,* p. 25, testifying that the Action Française "a toujours refusé les ordres de publicité que l'Agence Havas s'était vue dans l'obligation de transmettre sur l'ordre des autorités d'occupation ou des services annexes en ressortissant." When Yves Bonnefoy, General Secretary of Information, proposed in 1942 that the press could cease publishing the obligatory bulletins of his office if they undertook to express their tenor in two or three weekly editorials, all but the *Montagne* (Clermont), *Paris-Soir* (Toulouse), and the *Action française* accepted the bargain and signed contracts to this effect. Chambrun collection, No. 65.

To what use did the *Action française* put this relative independence? How, aside from such gratuitous gestures as the one just mentioned, did it advise or lead its Vichy readers?

In July 1941, Maurras devoted a long article in *Candide* (to which he was a frequent contributor during this time) to advocating that France should have a social policy at last: but what he wrote made it clear that, although it might reflect prevailing Vichy views faithfully enough, it was not his corner that would provide a "social" lead. "L'inégalité des biens," said Maurras, "est un bien." One cannot reconstruct a country without powerful elites, and these elites would be powerless without the stability that only property can bring. The disquisition ended with a hymn to the best tool of progress—"capital, capital divin."[5] This was what one might expect from the man who, in answer to Pétain's question in July 1940 of what France needed most at that time, told him succinctly, "A good officer corps and a good clergy!"[6]

Equally predictable was the newspaper's attitude to the measures of the national revolution, in which, as Havard thought, "daring, initiative, and vast schemes went hand in hand with order and authority," and which Maurras welcomed as offering a chance to turn the defeat of France's armies into a victory of peace, indeed, perhaps something rather on the lines of the Prussian *Tugendbund* of 1813.[7] The Action Française welcomed all Vichy measures to punish traitors and incompetents responsible for the defeat, to expose and expel Masons and foreigners, to purge the professions and the public service of aliens (defined as all those not born of a French father), and to mete out punishment to the followers of de Gaulle. It exulted when its long campaigns bore fruit in the measures of 1940, and it led a long and at last successful campaign to change street names: in Carpentras, the Boulevard Daladier became the Boulevard du Musée, and in Algiers *rues* Jean Jaurès, Camille Pelletan, Jules Guesde, and Emile Zola became *rues* Jean Chiappe, Charles Péguy, Edouard Drumont, and General Marchand, and the Boulevard de la République was changed to the Boulevard Philippe Pétain.[b]

While members of the Cercle Fustel de Coulanges and of its northern offshoot, L'Education Française, supported Rector, later Minister of Education, Jérome Carcopino in his reforms and in his attempts to calm the ardor of young people in the schools, the paper in Lyon went further and espoused the cause of (unsuccessful) educational reformers who sought to do away with a system of free education, which, they claimed, tempted mediocre students to leave the land and/or their father's trade, where they would be better off.[8] The *Action française* approved Bernard Faÿ's anti-Masonic crusade and reiterated its belief that Masons, who had plotted to take over the Third Republic, were now conspiring to sabotage Vichy;[9] and it insisted tirelessly that past responsibilities must never be forgotten, attacking those who spread the

[b] The *Action française* had special reasons for the campaigns: in Limoges its offices had been 12, Place de la République, and in Lyon they were 66, rue de la République.

dangerous and unjust rumor that all Frenchmen shared the responsibility for national disaster.[10] In October 1941, Maurras welcomed Pétain's decision to condemn Blum, Daladier, and Gamelin *before* a trial, as an act of justice and high policy "carried out with simple and majestic tranquillity which will honor France in everybody's eyes."[11]

The trial at Riom did little to back up the vast, vague charges brought against the accused. What had begun with bold affirmations[12] ended in the embarrassed silence of abandonment. But if the higher criminals, incarcerated, could not be shown up as they deserved, one could at least get rid of those who failed to carry out their duty to Vichy. In a prophetic phrase Jean Arfel called for "le nettoyage des cerveaux français et de la société française," and Jacques Delebecque stated the opinion of the *Action française*: "The duty of public servants is clear: they have to serve the cause of national revolution *actively*. The government's duty is equally clear: it must punish ruthlessly those among its agents who fail or falter in their mission."[13]

Even more than faltering public servants, the Jews were a prime object of *Action française* concern, against whom even Ronsard and Malherbe had to be mobilized. The paper applauded and praised the Statut des Juifs but demanded that it needed perfecting: there should be an early census of Jews, with the names made public; all names changed in the past fifty years should be revoked; a *numerus clausus* should be introduced in all professions except the law, which no Jews except war veterans should be allowed to enter at all; and severe penalties should be established to enforce the rules.[c]

Soon, Maurras and his collaborators were criticizing the laxity with which the anti-Semitic legislation was enforced. While noting with satisfaction that Jews had been excluded from the Army, the Navy, the Air Force, the universities, the public services, and numerous professions, and that 2,000 Jewish firms in the Free Zone and about 23,000 in the North were in an administrator's hands, Maurras called for more serious efforts to rid the land of Jewish refugees who fed the Black Market and Gaullist propaganda, and who continued to corrupt the country as they had done before the war. Jews were growing fat in the Pyrenees and on the Côte d'Azur, ranging the countryside in search of opportunities to debauch honest peasants with their tempting gold, always thinking of themselves first at the expense of Frenchmen—and of good manners, too. The Jews and their Christian protectors should be punished, and to this end the Commissariat aux Questions Juives should be granted wider and more effective powers.[14]

Robert Havard, who had long been the Vatican adviser to the League, deplored the men of little faith who disguised their opposition to Marshal

[c] See, e.g., *AF*, Oct. 31, Dec. 1, 1940. In *Le Procureur et l'habitant*, p. 52, Maurras asserts: "La législation défensive contre les Juifs, élaborée à Vichy, avait été expressément soumise au Vatican, qui n'y vit rien de contraire à la loi chrétienne."

Pétain behind attacks on Vichy's Jewish policies. Too many stories were being circulated that came from British sources and that the credulous continued to believe: "Ils ont crié à la barbarie sans se demander ce qu'il y avait de véridique dans les récits complaisamment répandus. Aucune preuve n'a été fournie de ces prétendus 'excès.'" In the circumstances, Havard could not but welcome the telegram in which the Bishops of Nice, Fréjus, and Monaco and the Abbots of Lérins and Frigolet reaffirmed their loyalty to Pétain as a disavowal of certain unpatriotic Christians whose marked concern for Jews concealed their disloyalty to the regime.[15]

More patriotic Christians, heeding the newspaper's "appeals to common sense" and its protests at the inordinate fuss over the fate of Jews and the exaggerated fables circulated by the enemies of France, expressed sounder feelings by demanding that concentration camps should be set up for Jews "like those in Germany."[16] The venom poured by Delebecque, Calzant, and Maurras himself on the Jewish people does not bear detail in its repetitiousness. Here was one clear instance in which the coincidence of hatreds with the Germans left the Action Française untroubled. Even though, unlike some of its followers, its leaders took no concrete steps to harm any of those whom they so loathed, even though, as someone later testified, Maurras was quite incapable of harming a hair of anybody's head, nonetheless their ideas, endlessly repeated, furnished justification for the vilest acts, for which one could not even plead the marginal usefulness that they might have for France.

Having filled in the general lines, let us now see how the *Action française* reflected the fortunes of France during the next few years. First, Mers-el-Kebir revealed the true colors of perfidious Albion, just as Dakar marked the treachery of de Gaulle. Old griefs rose up like a sour taste in the throat—griefs against an England that had always behaved badly toward France, had always opposed a sensible German policy, supported the injudicious Left, destroyed the possibility of Italian alliance, and—not least valid of all—entertained only left-wing newspapermen and politicians in a den of intrigue which Noël Coward, notorious in the cavalry of Saint George, had lately kept in Paris. Where could such manners lead but to Mers-el-Kebir![d]

"L'Allemagne ne s'est jamais fait tant de bien que ne lui en a fait l'Angleterre en ces 3 et 6 juillet," Maurras wrote angrily in the issue dated July 6–9. By such odious aggressions, Delebecque explained, the British had forced their French friends to choose between servitude to their will or independent action to save French freedom and French honor. "Their choice is made." That the

[d] *AF*, July 17, 1940, also *AF*, July 9, 14, 25, 1940. Cf. François Mauriac in *Le Figaro*, July 15, 1940: "et tout à coup ce suprême malheur . . . Les corps de ces marins que chacun de nous veille dans son coeur. M. Churchill a dressé pour combien d'années, contre l'Angleterre, une France unanime . . . Nous ne nous étions pas attendu à voir cet ignoble visage de Gorgone penché sur elle."

choice might be less definite than Delebecque implied was suggested when a month later Pierre Varillon attacked bad Frenchmen who persisted in their friendliness and indulgence for England even after her aggression, her treacheries, and murders: "Murderers of our sailors, responsible in great part for our defeat and now, moreover, the starvers of the French people, [the English] have their accomplices among us and seek still more who should be ready to accept their infamous bargain."[17]

The British and their accomplices had turned out even worse than it had seemed at first. Not satisfied with applying Nelsonian (or Maurrassian *sacro egoismo*) tactics at Oran, the Royal Navy encouraged the colonies of equatorial Africa to join de Gaulle, while French metropolitan territory was placed under blockade, prohibiting exchanges with territories overseas except with British sanction and threatening the starvation of French economy and French population. The *Action française* could only record the series of aggressions, beginning with Dakar, in which the treacherous de Gaulle helped his British masters to dismember the Empire and divide the French.

By the summer of 1941, if perplexity ever existed, it had gone. The alliance of Britain and Russia, *de facto* in 1941, *de jure* in 1942, instead of recalling a similar opportunism on the part of Christian kings allied with Mohammedans or with Protestant heretics, merely furnished the ultimate reason for damning both. Those who might have kept a spark of sympathy for the enemies of Germany could preserve none for the friends of the Soviets, who (unlike Frenchmen) "tied their fate to that of the worst enemies of religion, of society, of civilization, and of liberty."[18] This reflected upon the Resistance, too: by 1941, Maurras, who had appreciated the ideas and the personality of de Gaulle (whose father was a legitimist), was boasting that "the toughest and most enduring anti-Gaullist campaigns are ours."[19]

His boast was quite justified: no mercy was shown in the Action Française press for those who disturbed the order of the State. The "terrorists," whose refractoriness brought down reprisals on civilian heads, especially those who, by killing Germans, endangered the lives of numerous hostages, were denounced as agents of London and of Moscow: "Pour ce troupeau sanglant de la vieille invasion métèque, on ne peut former d'autres voeux que de le voir châtié vite et dur." This applied not simply to active terrorists, but also to the theorists, the planners, the real subversives: "No mercy for the leaders is the first principle of true justice," Havard wrote in the *Revue universelle*: "Forced labor and death are not too rigorous penalties to inflict when the question is one of public safety."[20]

"A sort of martial law was proclaimed yesterday," wrote Maurras on December 13, 1941. "It was difficult to ignore the urgent necessity of one. It was called for a good long time before the war." He welcomed the government's announcement that to the 11,000 prisoners of the last six weeks the last three days had added nearly 2,000 more. "Mais il y a lieu de redoubler de surveillance."

In a speech he made in 1919 before an enthusiastic public at the Salle Wagram, Léon Daudet told his listeners:

> If the Germans had won, do you know what would have happened? France would have been split into two parties, and I do not want to know which would have been the greater. On one side we should have had the resistance: those who under the German heel would have gone on protesting, crying out, who would have laid down their lives, believe you me, as ransom for lost honor! The second part of the unfortunate French nation would have been made up of cowards, temporizers, poltroons of every kind, who would have accepted the German yoke.[21]

This merely goes to show how hazardous it is to make assumptions based on prejudice, how dangerous to attribute disreputable motives to actions that may stem from perfectly innocuous or worthy ones. The remaining public of the Action Française considered itself far from cowardly, and although its position was one of temporization, and although the passage of time would make it increasingly wrongheaded, it was not perhaps based on motives any more unworthy than those from which most human attitudes and actions spring.

When one excluded all the possible allies, the necessary conclusion was that France must stand alone. But that was not the essence of the slogan which the paper carried like a banner from August 1940 to the end. "La France, La France seule" did not mean "France alone." It meant, as Marcel Déat was the first to see, refusal to enter into the new order extolled by the Parisians: "a patriotic pretext to refuse all European cooperation."[22] It meant, above all else, that far from thinking of France in terms of someone else's "order," as so many partisans did, one had to think of France first, of France alone, of France before and above all else, and to approach all problems and all situations with only this in mind.

That the formula might also mean more than that was seldom actually suggested by the Action Française. But in July 1941 a two-page mimeographed sheet, published clandestinely, afforded a hint that there might be more to say if one could say it. *Les Documents nationalistes français,* as the two pages were grandly called, violently opposed the Germans and their European schemes, at the same time pledging support of the national revolution. Although it echoed Maurras's isolationist patriotism, *Les Documents* went beyond it to preach French reconquest of lost territory and grandeur:

> We used to be anti-Republican, anti-Semitic, anti-Masonic; there is no reason why we should cease to be these things. But we have always fought against Germanism, and in this, too, we intend to continue . . . Before the triumph of Germanism we intend, beginning now, to maintain the traditional positions of French nationalism . . . To wipe out the humili-

ation of 1940, to deliver Alsace and Lorraine, to regain the grandeur of past time, these are the aims and slogans to which, openly or in secret, all French consciences must cling.[e]

Hence, it was natural that, although accepting Pétain's policy of collaboration after the Hitler interview at Montoire-sur-le-Loir in October 1940,[23] the Action Française should have a hand in plotting to remove Laval, who seemed too much the Germans' man, too little that of France. How much of a hand, exactly, it is still hard to say. The Ministers who were involved in removing Laval were not "d'Action Française," but the actual steps on December 13, 1940, were taken by men like Dumoulin and Alibert, and the Groupes de Protection which stood watch at the Hôtel du Parc were recruited among Cagoulards, themselves sometime Maurrassians, and led by Henri Martin. So far as Otto Abetz was concerned, the Action Française was "the moving element behind the scenes"; it was, he reported in his telegram No. 1556 of December 18, 1940, the Action Française that "acted logically [in terms of its anti-German policy] when it had Laval arrested."[24]

Judging from the available evidence, it is apparent that Abetz was giving too much credit to a talking shop. Laval's sudden removal from the premiership and his arrest, from which he was delivered only by German intervention, came as the result of palace intrigues, in which patriotic and personal motives were inextricably entangled, but in which the hand of the Action Française, hidden though it may have been, seems far from paramount. On the other hand, Abetz could well have said that many of the actors in the plot reflected something of the Action Française spirit, which had touched them to a greater or lesser degree in the past. The Action Française did not always hold its men, but it marked them. Bouthillier did not want France dragged into war again, this time as the battered second of the Germans; and no more did Maurras. Laval seemed to be doing everything to bring such a thing about, and Maurras therefore considered him a traitor. He said so in public and in private, although, of course, never in print, and the same view was shared more or less by those who organized the events of December 13.[f] This

[e] Note that this reproduces exactly the slogans of pre-1914 nationalism, with 1940 taking the place of 1871. *Les Documents* is the only Action Française or monarchist publication listed among the 1,106 that appear in the Bibliothèque Nationale's *Catalogue des périodiques clandestins diffusés en France de 1939 à 1945* (1954).

[f] *Au Grand Juge de France,* p. 46; Robert Aron, *Histoire de Vichy,* chap. 6. For another view, see René Chateau, Chambrun collection, No. 80. Chateau, a Popular Front deputy of Charente-Inférieure and editor of *France socialiste,* felt that Laval was blamed chiefly for remaining republican and "parliamentary." Dominique Sordet came close to the truth when he described the conspiracy as "une conjuration hétéroclite où étaient représentés pêle-mêle les intérêts anglo-américains, l'armée, la cagoule, le grand capitalisme, la juiverie, la maçonnerie, l'Action française," against "le négociateur français . . . qui s'efforçait de réaliser le rapprochement franco-allemand." *Le Coup du 13 décembre* (1943), p. 6.

seems to have been the essence of the *coup de barre* which temporarily got Laval out of the way and perhaps saved France from becoming deeply entangled with the Germans.

This, clearly, was what counted for Maurras. In a world in turmoil, France offered the deceptive spectacle of a land at peace. Her colonies might fall or be endangered, one country after another might be drawn into the conflict, but France was safe behind the screen of an armistice "whose benefits could never be sufficiently praised." For this, the collaboration that Pétain proposed was a small price to pay and one, moreover, in which all the responsibility was the Marshal's. The rest of Frenchmen had only to obey: "We owe the leader absolute and total confidence, without giving our opinion, even approbative, about what he decides . . . For if we approved, that might permit others to disapprove."[25]

This fragile state of peace for which so many moral sacrifices would be made, this isolationism which insisted that France could withdraw from international struggles and let others fight, was broken once and for all by news of the Anglo-American landings in North Africa on November 8, 1942, and, three days later, by the German occupation of the Free Zone. Both Maurras and *Candide* blamed the disaster on the mad appetites of Americans who listened only to London and Jerusalem, of Englishmen who listened only to the voices of greed and ambition, of traitors who listened only to their vanity and to the clink of foreign gold, all of which resulted simply in more trouble for the French and in their occupation by an enemy who, because of the Allied offense, was compelled to tighten its defenses.[26] As Pujo declared in a speech that New Year's Eve, "It was not Pétain's France that gave up what was left of France after the Armistice. It was not the Germans, either, who wished to take it from us: it was the Americans and the English, helped by the treason of bad Frenchmen whom thoughtless French believed." As matters stood, he said, this meant that if the Germans won the war these idiots would have deprived Pétain of his remaining trumps.[27]

Pétain shared the same feeling; after receiving the news of the scuttling of the French fleet at Toulon, he remarked to his aides, "Messieurs, il n'y a plus qu'à faire oraison . . . Si la France pouvait le comprendre et devenir un grand monastère?"[28] To Maurras as well, the loss of the French fleet came as a dreadful blow, only three days after he had praised the loyal relations between France and the occupying Germans which could still spare the French some trying experiences.[29] But also like Pétain, his overriding concern was for peace in France, which, it appeared, must be maintained at any cost. There is a strange air of unreality about René Benjamin's account of the two old men meeting at dinner, one month after the landings in Africa, two weeks after the scuttling of the fleet: "The first words of the Marshal were, 'There's nothing desperate about the situation.' At this, Maurras, eternally young, caught fire. The conversation took off between Heaven and Earth. By the end of the evening, they were both trying to find a definition of Honor."[30]

As Maurras told friends gathered to hear him on February 3, 1943, at a banquet in Lyon given by André Nicolas's *Frontières*:[g] "The only area where we can foresee or legislate with independence and operate freely is exactly and almost solely the ideal area where our ideas, our sentiments, our wills, can move in pride and honor." The statement seems to mean that, whatever happened on the ideal plane, the *Action française* would be in favor of giving in to the Germans and would oppose all attempts to resist them. Whatever reservations it may have held in private, the outward tone of the newspaper was one of resigned cooperation. In June 1942, while incoherently opposing Laval's opinion that France must take sides in a war he hoped Germany would win, Maurras supported the plan of sending French workers to Germany in return for the release of French prisoners.[31] And a year later, when Gauleiter Sauckel declared that Germany was entitled to claim French aid to defeat Bolshevism, Maurras maintained that it was no good discussing the principle Sauckel affirmed; France had to do what the Germans asked, and French youth must be persuaded to do their duty to France by performing the tasks demanded by the Germans: "Nous avons été battus, nous nous devons de ne pas rendre plus amères encore les conséquences de la défaite. Nous devons consentir tout sacrifice pour cela."[32]

No hope should be entertained of possible liberation. The discomfort and humiliation of occupation were preferable to any "illusions funestes." A German victory, with Communism crushed and British domination broken, could be regarded with a certain equanimity, whereas "if the Anglo-Americans were to win, this would mean the re-emergence of Masons, Jews, and all the political personnel eliminated in 1940." To hope for assistance from the Anglo-Americans was to take sides and, furthermore, "the wrong side," Maurras said.[33]

It was a position he maintained from the outset. When, after seeing Hitler at Montoire, Pétain announced that he accepted the principle of collaboration between France and Germany, Maurras, in a dialogue with himself, asserted that the matter was beyond discussion:

> Are you in favor of this collaboration?
> I do not have to favor it.
> Do you oppose it, then?
> I do not.
> Are you neutral?
> No, not that, either.
> Then, you admit it?
> I have neither to admit, nor to discuss it . . .

[g] Besides the staff of the *Action française,* Jean de Fabrègues, Louis Jasseron, the industrialist Jean Berliet, and many others attended the dinner, at which Maurras presided. The Vichy Secretary for Propaganda, Paul Creyssel, sent his regrets.

The greatest misfortune for France, he thought, would be for people to take sides, for or against collaboration, and for opposing factions to be formed around that issue; the dispersal, the division, would be fatal. The Marshal was responsible; he had admirably expressed his mind, and the people of France must understand.[34]

Quieta non movere was the *Action française* ideal, but it was not a question of letting sleeping dogs lie; the dogs were up, barking and scrapping for dear life. "A plague on both their houses," muttered under one's breath, was not enough to put an end to the divisive factions. The *Action française* therefore voiced its disapproval of the factions—but its criticism of the one was hardly audible, because the pro-German faction was pretty well protected, and little that was said against it ever got even close to print, while criticism of the other stood out as unilateral. This was the great mistake.

In December 1942, when Roger Stéphane met Maulnier, whose recent book, *La France, la guerre, et la paix,* he had admired, he asked him how a man as intelligent as he was could continue to stand by the Action Française. Maulnier was well aware of the disapproval attached to writing in the paper: "Mais je veux écrire, et il n'y a pas de mauvaise tribune." From the outside, he told Stéphane, the Action Française seemed Germanophile. But this was the effect of censorship; many articles were suppressed which, if published, would have given a different impression. The fault of Maurras, Resistant and Pétainist agreed, was that he did not respect the balance. It was impossible for the *Action française* to publish what it thought about the Germans, but, at the same time, it was not forced to express what under the circumstances could not but seem to be unqualified hatred for the other side. Since he was not permitted to express his dislike of Germany, he could at least temper his dislike of England.[35]

But this was asking too much, or too little, of the Action Française. The paper could have stopped publication, which was what Gaxotte advised and what some publications (e.g., *Le Figaro*) actually did, especially after November 1942. It could have turned itself into an innocuous literary or gastronomic journal, but that would have been tantamount to suspending publication; and for Maurras political writing was the staff of life. As Rebatet once said to Laubréaux, he could no more cease writing than he could cease his physical functions. He had to give his opinion on events, especially now when it seemed that his opinion counted. What his paper printed *was* what he wanted to say—a part of it, at least, if not all, or even, to take him at his word, if not the essential. More literally than most public figures, Maurras was the man of his word; his printed statements forged his image, guided the faithful, expressed his stand. He chose to let half of his thought be known rather than none at all. No one could be blamed for judging him upon that half alone.

In several of the articles in which, after the Liberation, he castigated the Action Française, Mauriac marveled at how the doctrines of integral nationalism ended "in those daily copies of the *Action française* published under German control, in the daily articles of Maurras approved by the Kommandatur," and he laid to these doctrines responsibility for the fact that an important section of the bourgeoisie, under their influence, took the side of the occupying enemy, of the torturers, and allowed itself to be mobilized against the Resistance, under the banner of Vichy:

> Il est remarquable que la doctrine, chez trop de maurrassiens, a dominé et bridé l'instinct profond de la race qui les eut jetés dans la résistance à l'envahisseur . . . de sorte que, dans bien des cas, la patrie aura été défendue par des "sans-patrie," et abandonnée par des "patriotes."[36]

But Maurrassian doctrine, like every other doctrine, is capable of a variety of interpretations. What made Maurras and the rest abandon all resistance was neither theory nor obvious villainy, but a hierarchy of values, a hierarchy of fears, in which, often unconsciously, their interests, immediate and particular, were equated with those of the fatherland. The upholders of principle and ideals fell back upon a blind love for a patch of soil ("La Provence, la Provence seule," jeered *Je suis partout*), which they never realized was far, far less than the "pays réel" that they professed to love. The practitioners of an empirical realism, or so they thought, became frozen in the most inflexible position of all. Those who had fulminated against the crass materialism of their republican enemies were soon reduced to defending an ever shrinking area of material interests. Those who had started by denouncing lies were driven to humiliating hypocrisy.

Step by step, by the remorseless logic of the position they had taken, the once-incorruptible enemies of the Germans became the servants of German will. Obsessed by the maintenance of an order that it was impossible to maintain, exasperated by the activities of those whose patriotism demanded more than isolation, they turned ever more furiously upon the forces of resistance. No newspaper, apart from those of Paris, denounced the "terrorists" more fiercely; and as more friends of the Action Française fell under the bullets of the Underground, calls for revenge became thirsty calls for blood.[h]

Maurras's passionate language, excessive under normal circumstances, now seemed appropriate. Maurras was in the position of a man who suddenly finds that his words, heretofore inapplicable to any concrete situation, can turn to deeds; for over half a century he had denounced his foes, invoked the plagues upon them, condemned them to various forms of humiliation or death. But what had been empty threats before could now be condemnations, directing upon the objects of his wrath the deadly attentions of Gestapo or militiamen.

Most of the "incitements to murder" with which Maurras was charged at

[h] See Maurras, "Justice! Justice!" *AF,* Nov. 2, 1943. In the last published number of his paper, issued on August 24, 1944, Maurras was still lamenting the deaths of members and friends killed or executed by the Resistance.

his trial were made in general terms, as was his habit. He called for hostages and for killing without mercy, he advised that captured Gaullists might be shot out of hand, he declared that "if the death penalty is not sufficient to put a stop to the Gaullists, members of their families should be seized as hostages and executed."[37] No penalties were strong enough:

> We repeat that there must be . . . heads of well-known Communists and Gaullists. Can they not be made to roll? We add that it is not enough to make sure of people as, apparently, is being done since we are flattering ourselves about a few thousand arrests. The main thing is to sort out, to judge, to condemn, to execute. A shadow of security will be re-established only at this price . . . Nothing, in fact, will be too much to put an end to the growing terror.[38]

It was pleaded at Maurras's trial that no evidence existed to link any of his denunciations with actual murders, and certainly none of the charges of this nature leveled against him got very far. But such a defense not only narrows the possible influence of a political mentor to limits that Maurras himself would not accept, but also overrates the capacity of Maurras's readers to follow him in fine distinctions about what to do. Maurras's task, though he sometimes forgot it, was not to say "do this," "do that," but to create a climate of opinion that would arouse others to action. He did this very effectively, for instance, by glorifying political denunciation not only in the difficult days when the Resistance may have endangered the lives of peaceful citizens, but from the very first, against the opponents of Pétain and of the national revolution. Choiseul-Praslin felt the effects of this in 1940,[39] and Maurras's practice of nominal denunciation, applied to Gay, Claudel, Bidault, and other lesser figures in times when open and illegal murder was rife, if not deliberately meant to do them harm, could only be explained by utter callousness or an infantile lack of self-control.

One instance of how Maurras's influence made itself felt, despite his determination to separate cause and effect, appears in the murder, in February 1944, of the Jewish banker Pierre Worms. On February 2, Maurras referred in his column to Worms's son Roger (Roger Stéphane) a prewar pillar of the LICA, who had attracted his venomous attention by suggesting that French demographic shortcomings might be remedied by settlement in France of Jewish refugees from German persecution:

> On serait curieux de savoir si la noble famille est dans un camp de concentration, ou en Angleterre, ou en Amérique ou en Afrique,—ou si par hasard elle a gardé le droit d'épanouir ses beaux restes de prospérité dans quelque coin, favorisé ou non, de notre Côte d'Azur? Dans la plupart des cas, la voilà hors d'atteinte et de portée sauf en un seul, celui que nous mentionnons en dernier lieu: si la tribu nomade était restée en France, il faudrait faire cesser à tout prix une hospitalité scandaleuse et une tolérance qui touche à la folie. Nous disons plusieurs fois par semaine que la meilleure

> manière de répondre aux menaces des terroristes est de leur imposer une légitime contre-terreur. L'axiome est applicable aux violences de parole et d'attitude dont se rendent coupables les hordes juives: le talion.

Four days after this appeared, armed men in search of Roger Worms and of the Worms millions broke into the family villa on the Côte d'Azur and, after stealing what they could, kidnapped Pierre Worms, whom they killed and abandoned shortly after.

Brought up at Maurras's trial by the son, who believed that the article had played its part in his father's death, the accusation got short shrift, after evoking from Maurras some revealing comments:

> When you say, as you do, M. le Président, that in February 1944 drawing public attention to a Jew was to point him out, his family and himself, to the reprisals of the Germans, to spoliation, to concentration camps, perhaps to torture and to death, not only did I ignore these fine things, but I knew the contrary: that there were lots of places [in France] where Jewish colonies were flourishing, where they got everything on the black market, where they profoundly corrupted the peasant proprietors . . . At the beginning of 1944, Jews in a lot of places were becoming very arrogant, they were saying—"See, the Allies are coming and they will show you!"[40]

This was the sort of information Maurras got, the sort of thing he heard, the sort of thing he was prepared to believe. Against the continued threat of the Jews, the French had still, perhaps more than ever, to defend themselves. Hence his warnings, hence his murderous advice. But, as he insisted at his trial, and at greater length in *Le Procureur et l'habitant,* drawn up before his death, his advice for counterterrorist activity was not the same as his advice for counter-Jewish activity. A careful reading of the incriminating article will show that, in effect, for the Wormses he demands not death but an end of tolerance and hospitality; for Jewish violence in attitude and words he demands the talion—an eye for an eye, a tooth for a tooth. But the juxtaposition of calls to counterterror and to what one might call mere countermanifestations, facilitated a confusion, which we may concede to have been absent from Maurras's mind but which will be readily apparent to every reader. The minds of Maurras's readers were like a fluid solution ready to crystallize according to his word. Were they likely to pause to meditate and see the difference between variants of retaliation, or would they simply grasp the obvious conclusion and, hearing "eye for eye," jump up to tear one out?

Maurras, of course, accepted no responsibility for such folly. Nor, certainly, would he have allowed the argument that, in the circumstances of the time, even the call to end hospitality and tolerance, if heeded, was bound to mean either death or something very close to it. To Maurras, only ignorance or spite could explain any other interpretation of his words than that which, with great logic, he presented in the 108 pages of the pamphlet published after his death, in 1953; and one would be inclined to grant that he was sincere, but for his habit of distorting the words of his enemies to suit his own interpretation.[41]

With Maurras all argument became quite literally *un dialogue de sourds,* the *mot* in this case being not only *bon* but *juste*. Maurras's deafness undoubtedly isolated him more and more,[42] until by 1940 it had left him open only to the opinions and influence of a very small group of men, chief among them Pujo, who selected both his relationships and his information. If one bears in mind the poverty of printed news during the Occupation, the necessity of relying for the most part on word of mouth and on the BBC, together with Maurras's dependence on his advisers, all of them prejudiced and many of them of mediocre intelligence, one can understand that the loneliness of the old man at war with almost everyone around him except his band of postulants was a fundamental element in the demise of the Action Française—as, for that matter, it must have been throughout its liveliest days.

The last months of the Action Française, like those of the Vichy regime, were troubled and confused. In June, the Allied landings brought back to the soil of France the war that Maurras had so dreaded. It was the eighth foreign invasion since 1789, Maurras reminded his readers on August 23, 1944, ten days before the liberation of Lyon. All that Liberation meant, it seemed, was blood and ruins; they had been wished on France by bad Frenchmen who masqueraded as patriots. But the Action Française leaders were accustomed to fearing for their lives: they had had reason to fear the murderers of the MSR (Social Revolutionary Movement), the wartime successor of Deloncle and Filliol's Cagoulard CSAR. After these had blown up Marx Dormoy, Pujo got the Prefect of Lyon to provide a police guard for Maurras, Calzant, and himself. Then, in June 1944, Pujo and Calzant were imprisoned by the Germans in Fort Montluc, possibly because of some Milice intrigue, and were released only after pressing interventions on the part of Maurras (June 22–July 10).

Lyon—the Resistance capital of France, as Robert Aron calls it—was also, especially in July and August, the capital of terror and counterterror. The Germans themselves were not likely to harm the paper or its staff, except perhaps in one of the many street incidents where, on account of a shot or sometimes at the sound of a blown-out tire, whole blocks were set on fire and their inhabitants prevented from escaping; but the city was full of rival and almost equally murderous bands of militia and resistants, none of which had much sympathy for the Action Française.

On August 24, while to the south the battle for the Rhône Valley was raging, the last, small issue of the paper appeared, with two and a half columns by Maurras about André Chénier and a strange article by François Daudet, "Le Destin de la France seule," lamenting that many who opposed the formula now rallied to it when it was too late: the many conversions to patriotism and common sense came, Daudet wrote, just too late, when they could no longer be of any help. But what were these conversions if not regrets of the bourgeois in the street that Lyon was in the grip of terror and soon would be in the path of war, the voice of timid prudence, which, glad to be saved from Communism by Germans, resented German demands, and happy to be liberated from the occupant, wished war to pass it by. The article was the eternal "if only," the oft-repeated "I told you so" of the Action Française, under the pen of a younger generation appropriately signing off under a misapprehension.

Arrested at Lyon on September 8, six days after the liberation of the city, Maurras was on the following day taken to Fort Montluc, then to the Hôpital de l'Antiquaille and thence to the prison of Saint-Paul and Saint-Joseph, where he and Pujo remained until their trial in January 1945. Maurras's friends, certain that he would be condemned to death, made desperate efforts to save him by having the case transferred to Paris, where, they thought, the old Academician might stand a better chance, and by enlisting those whose reputation had survived the last few years and who could be induced to testify on his behalf. Not many could be found who were not compromised in the eyes of Liberation courts.

In both Lyon and Paris, where the heat of partisan passions had to make up for lack of fuel during that grim and dreary winter, the press campaign around the trial raged vindictive and fierce: "With his disciple Pétain, Maurras bears the chief responsibility [for collaboration]," the judges were reminded.[43] "On s'attend à une condamnation à mort," wrote André Réal del Sarte to Captain Georges Gaudy: "Vous êtes le seul autour de nous que son passé et ses récents états de service autorisent à parler haut devant un tribunal comme celui qui jugera Charles." "Si vous ne venez pas à son secours," wrote another friend, "il est perdu."[44]

At their last meeting in Lyon, Pétain had asked Maurras: "Vous avez des amis, vous?" and Maurras, who saw the despair of loneliness in the other's eyes, had answered: "La vie m'a gâté en amis."[45] Not all of them turned up in his hour of need, but many did—if not enough to convince a court that would not be convinced, at least enough to make him feel that they were true.

It was not the evidence of witnesses that would decide the verdict, in any case. As Dr. Ernst Nolte, a sensitive German student of the Maurras saga, has remarked, the trial of Maurras was in one sense a re-enactment of the Dreyfus trial which provided the start of his political career. Here, too, the Court was of an exceptional kind, far from respectful of juridical niceties; here, too, guilt was presupposed, condemnation a foregone conclusion; here, too, important documents were withheld; even the charge of which the accused was declared guilty—the crime of intelligence with the enemy—was much the same as that leveled at Dreyfus and, legally, with as much justice as in the earlier case.

The difference between the two cases, half a century apart, lay in two directions: for one thing, and it is most important, Dreyfus was condemned by an authority he respected, and he suffered mentally; Maurras considered his whole trial a vindictive farce. Wearing Pétain's Francisque, Number 2068, in his buttonhole, the seventy-six-year-old defendant demolished practically all the prosecution charges, addressed the government prosecutor as "M. le procureur de la femme sans tête," and held the floor for six tedious hours, reading an interminable memorandum which no one, he least of all, could hear. The long autobiographical-political testament was one more indictment of the Republic.

The second difference between the two cases, as Dr. Nolte points out, is that although the verdict in both was one of circumstance and expediency, from a metajuristical point of view the charges in the latter case were really justified. "Objectively" if not intentionally, Maurras betrayed his country; he did work on what became the enemy's side, and he was guilty in a sense higher than the letter of the law. The verdict he received simply expelled him from a France and from a French society which he himself had rejected and denied.[46]

Perhaps he was right in crying when he was told the verdict—imprisonment for life and national degradation—"C'est la revanche de Dreyfus!"

Pujo, condemned to five years in prison, national degradation, and a heavy fine, shouted only "Vive la France!" But Pujo was a subordinate. For Maurras the battle was a personal one, the sentence only the end of one more round in his long struggle against the Republic—that Republic of which the symbol incarnate in his eyes was Alfred Dreyfus. Like Rastignac with Paris, Maurras had challenged the Republic to a fight. For the moment, the enemy had won the fifty-year conflict. Detained first at Riom, then at Clairvaux, the doughty warrior never ceased to defend himself by continuing to attack.

In August 1951, he was transferred to the Hôtel-Dieu at Troyes, and in March 1952 to a private clinic near Tours, from which he wrote to President Vincent Auriol: "La liberté physique m'est rendue. C'est grâce à vous, Monsieur. Je vous en remercie. Je tiens même à vous en féliciter, car elle m'était due." The next step, said the indomitable patient, was to appease those who had been wronged since 1944 by executing François de Menthon, the Minister of Justice responsible for the purges of the Liberation.

The letter, published in *Aspects de la France,* provoked a debate in the National Assembly.[i] But Maurras had lost his power to create a national crisis. Despite the chalk signs "Libérez Maurras" on walls and hoardings, the furor quickly died, until the news of Maurras's death on November 16, 1952, reminded the French public that he had been with them until then.

In France, although Jules Romains in the Académie Française praised the

[i] *Aspects,* March 28, 1952; *JOC,* April 11, 1952. During the debate, there were half a dozen references to Maurras's responsibility for the murder of Jaurès.

man "who exercised a real influence in our country's thought, precisely at a time when France needed it in order to take herself in hand," the government prohibited a meeting at the Salle Pleyel called by Henry Bordeaux to honor the dead man's memory. But the radios of Geneva, Montreal, and Spain paid tribute to Maurras, as did the Spanish and the Portuguese Academies and the Madrid Municipal Council, which renamed a street Paseo Charles Maurras.

Lying in the family vault at Roquevaire, Maurras[j] was bearing out what André Malraux had said in 1944, "One cannot practice Bainville's policies and condemn Maurras to death."[47] The France of today is too heavily impregnated by the ideas for which Maurras and Bainville stood, by the ideas of the Action Française, which modeled a whole generation of French nationalists, including those who never professed them, for them to die; if only because, as Bernanos wrote in 1932, Maurras and Bainville, even while they were still alive, became a part of the history of their country. "It will only be realized at a later date," Gonzague de Reynold wrote of Maurras in March 1953, "when time has appeased the passions he raised around himself, how deeply his thought has penetrated, since one discovers it already in the thinking of his opponents, indeed in that of his enemies."[k]

[j] Maurras had died reconciled with God. Chanoine Aristide Cormier, who was delegated by the Archbishop of Tours to attempt his conversion and succeeded when Maurras was on his deathbed, has recounted their interviews in *Mes entretiens de prêtre avec Charles Maurras* (1953), in which the conversion is attributed to Maurras's desire to believe and to the weariness of a long and fruitless search (see p. 41: "Je suis las de raisonner . . ."). The plain and pious little book received a prize of the Académie Française, and the gentle Canon was encouraged to publish a study of *La Vie intérieure de Charles Maurras* (1956), a man whom he had long admired.

[k] Gonzague de Reynold, in the unpublished draft of a study on Maurras; see also Pierre Boutang's *Nation française,* Nov. 4, 1959: "How right J.J.S.S. [Jean-Jacques Servan Schreiber, editor of *L'Express*] is in thinking that General de Gaulle is a disciple of Maurras." The *Nation française,* which enjoyed government subsidies during a good part of the Fifth Republic, was in a good position to know what it was saying.

PART VII: THE LAMBENT FLAME

Mais il s'en faut que le rayonnement d'une Pensée, les contre-coups d'un mouvement, restent circonscrits à la sphère des disciples reconnus et des filiations avouées. Il pourrait être intéressant et non inutile de rechercher dans les milieux dirigeants de notre opinion ou de nos affaires nationales, les hommes qui ont reçu quelque empreinte du nationalisme d'Action Française . . . Parce que l'audience accordée . . . aux écrivains de l'Action Française, considérés comme les interprètes du patriotisme, ne se traduit pas par des adhésions en règle, on aurait tort de croire qu'une telle influence soit négligeable.

GEORGES BIDAULT

27

FOREIGN FRIENDS

SAINTE-BEUVE SAYS SOMEWHERE that it would not be just to a man to take into account only what he did and not also what he caused to be done by others. This is particularly appropriate in the case of the Action Française in general and of Maurras in particular. What was this influence, how was it manifested, where did the authority of the Action Française hold sway?

In their monumental *Biblio-iconographie générale de Charles Maurras,* published in 1953, Roger Joseph and Jean Forges list 103 works devoted specifically to their subject, the first dated 1900 and the last 1953, and 84 others attacking either him or the Action Française. *Le Chapon* of Gyp (later his sworn enemy), published in 1902, was the first of 42 books and songs dedicated to Maurras, to which one might add 48 stories, articles, poems, and other fragments, including one in Anatole France's *Etui de nacre* and Edouard Herriot's "Pour un Milésien," which appeared in *La Revue Parisienne* of May 1894.

Before the Second World War, several important works published abroad examined integral nationalism—particularly those of Waldemar Gurian, Charlotte Muret, Walter Frank, Hugo Friedrich, Hans Naumann, and William Buthman[1]—and Alphonse V. Roche's *Idées traditionalistes en France de Rivarol à Charles Maurras* (Urbana, Ill., 1937) was in itself a tribute to the interest awakened in an American literary historian by the many allusions to Maurras made by his friends and by university professors like Régis Michaud, whose courses, Roche declares, convinced him of the important place Maurras's ideas had assumed in all domains of contemporary thought.

On the whole, however, in Germany and in the English-speaking countries, the Action Française seems to have attracted the attention of few outside limited academic circles. What the French call "des atomes crochus" seem to have been in slightest evidence with the Germans. Young Otto Abetz, in Paris with the best intentions of making friends, felt at ease in certain Bonapartist circles, as he did in those of the enlightened Left, but he was never able to establish good relations with the royalists of the Action Française.[2] Their anti-German feelings were too intransigent for a normal—and even for a persevering—German to overcome. There must have been few Germans indeed who, like the man who later broadcast on Radio Stuttgart and on the radio in Occupied Paris as Dr. Friedrich, imbibed French monarchist culture in the course of selling the *Action française* at church doors and on the boulevards.[3]

It was a rare Englishman, too, who was acquainted with the paper, much less read it regularly; Charles Strachey, Hilaire Belloc, Montgomery Belgion, and Yvon Eccles were among the few who knew it well. Particular students of France like D. W. Brogan and Ronald Balfour, both of Cambridge, were quite aware of the importance of the movement, but Action Française ideas were too alien to British tradition and too foreign to Britain's twentieth-century interests to be regarded as more than curiosities even by most of those who knew that they existed.

North America was less behindhand in this respect. In French Canada, of course, many leaders maintained personal ties with the royalists in France,[4] and both the Catholic hierarchy and the press were sympathetic.[5] In the United States there was an important measure of literary and academic interest among historians and political scientists and in departments of Romance languages (Irving Babbitt, Carlton Hayes, Nickerson, Michaud), which was eventually reflected in doctoral dissertations in the 'thirties but which even in the 'twenties showed up in the conversations of some New York intellectuals who turned to the *Action française* for indications of trends in French public opinion.[6]

Significantly, it was an American poet who came to the conclusion that the political and social thought of Charles Maurras could be fused with British ideas in a new political philosophy. To T. S. Eliot, then editor of the *New Criterion* in London, the only alternative that could be found to Fascism was to oppose Maurras's thought to that of the Communists and, by infusing this authoritarian stimulant into political arguments, give Toryism a new vigor.[7]

In 1911 Eliot, then studying in Paris, picked up a copy of *L'Avenir de l'intelligence* and thus became acquainted for the first time with Maurras's thought. Affected by the opinions of Irving Babbitt, who found Maurras's work romantically anti-romantic, the young American thought Maurras "a sort of Virgil who leads them to the temple gate," and liked his doctrinaire concept of monarchy and hierarchy. The sympathy he acquired before the First World War never left him, and thirty-seven years later he was still ready to declare it in a letter to *Aspects de la France*.[a] But this, as we have seen, was an exceptional case; a few unrepresentative persons apart, Lucien Dubech was right in stating in 1938 that the country in which the Action Française was least known was England.[8]

The effect of Action Française doctrines was strongest of all in the Latin countries, which sent many students to Paris, and in which Maurras's traditionalist political elitism and the literary prestige of a conformist and accessible school suited their upper-class aspirations better than anything else they could find in France. Out of ignorance, I have not taken into account Latin American countries, although in Mexico and Argentina Maurrassian influence was

[a] *Aspects,* April 25, 1948. Another regular reader, at least of the literary page, was Wyndham Lewis. See his letter in *AF,* Nov. 1, 1930.

lively and is worthy of special study. The remarks that follow refer only to European countries.

We have already seen that Maurrassian ideas and prestige were reflected by the Italian nationalists before the First World War, not only by *Idea Nazionale* and *Il Regno* in northern Italy but also by such important papers as *Il Mattino* in Naples.[9] Born in 1911, a year after the Associatione Nazionalista Italina had been set up in Florence by Enrico Corradini, Luigi Federzoni, Francesco Coppola, and R. Forges-Davanzati, *Idea Nazionale* shared almost every idea of the Action Française. It opposed parliament, democracy, individualism, socialism, Freemasonry, internationalism, and political factionalism; it honored the Monarchy and the Church as glorious symbols of order and national tradition; it proposed to free national culture of foreign influences and reaffirm the secular traditions of Rome and of the Empire.

By 1914, the followers of Corradini, who had always hoped to fuse nationalist and syndicalist revolution, just as the friends of Berth and Georges Valois were doing at the time, were proclaiming that nationalism and liberalism were incompatible. They found no difficulty after the war in making common front with Mussolini, whose Fascist legions, similarly revolutionary, similarly nationalist, anti-Communist, anti-Masonic, and anti-democratic, were likewise the proclaimed defenders of "order" and of the social hierarchy whose name Mussolini gave to the doctrinal review *Gerarchia,* which he founded in 1922.

But Mussolini, who seems to have retained a bad impression of the Action Française from his syndicalist days,[10] would have nothing to do with foreign imports. His system, in any case, had little of the doctrinaire character typical both of the *Idea Nazionale* and the Action Française; and he had learned his lessons from quite different sources. Significantly, it was Valois rather than Maurras or any of the others who saw in Mussolini the fulfillment of his dreams.

And so, although relations were good to excellent, and although the Action Française happily recognized many of its ideas in the regime that installed itself in Rome, there was in this case no doctrinal dependence. There was, indeed, a fundamental difference, which, if Maurras saw it, he never would admit. The world view of the Action Française, as of Corradini, was colored by conservative pessimism, whereas the views of Fascism, though no less fundamentally pessimistic, were of a revolutionary sort. The Action Française rid itself of its revolutionaries, or it tamed them, but the Associatione Nazionalista joined the revolutionaries, and thus the fundamental differences came out in the end. For the Action Française came close to fulfilling its aims within a conservative regime which could hardly have been more pessimistic, while Mussolini, whose Fascist revolution bogged down in compromise and corruption, remembered in defeat his early socialist hopes and dreams, and tried to realize them in the doomed Socialist Republic he set up at Salo in 1943.

We have also seen that integral nationalism enjoyed some prestige in nationalist circles of the Spanish intelligentsia. It is hard to say much more than that. The whole history of Hispanidad still awaits objective investigation which can probe beyond the superficial national fundamentalism of the doctrine to its actual intellectual origins. The movement that Ramiro de Maeztu, shifting from youthful anarchist sympathies to Catholic and monarchist convictions, launched with his *Defensa de Hispanidad,* does not lightly betray its foreign inspiration. By its very nature, Hispanidad, first developed in the pages of the reputedly Maurrassian *Acción Española,* which Maeztu edited from 1931 to 1937, can claim only Spanish sources;[b] and the Catholicism of its leaders led them to reject the possible influence of men in bad odor with the Church. It is characteristic that Maeztu cites Maurras at some length only to disagree with him. But it is perhaps equally significant that in the Mexico of today a man as steadfast in his Hispanism as Jésus Guisa de Azevedo, once known to his countrymen as "nuestro Maurrassito," refuses to acknowledge or discuss his Maurrassian roots.

It might be hazarded that perhaps more than any others, the Spanish-speaking intellectuals who were exposed to some of Maurras's ideas in their youth—often indirectly, like Maeztu in the English circle of Belloc and Chesterton, or like Guisa de Azevedo at Louvain—assimilated them, but reworked them to suit their particular circumstances and problems, applying them within another frame of reference that lost sight of their origin. But this remains to be seen, and I advance the suggestion here only tentatively.

After 1936, Maurrassism, fated to lose favor in a climate of newly triumphant nativist principles, was bolstered, on the other hand, by recognition of the support given by the Action Française to Franco. As the Duke of Alba, Franco's first Ambassador to London, wrote to Léon Daudet:

> Nous autres espagnols, nous n'oublierons jamais ce que vous et les votres ont fait pour notre cause, qui est en même temps la cause du Christianisme et de la Civilization. Vous avez été dans l'Action Française le porte-voix de la vraie France, et heureusement en Espagne on a bien compris la différence entre la voix de la France et les actes de son Gouvernement.[11]

One of the enduring relations forged at the time was that between Maurras and General Moscardo, the hero of the Alcazar siege in Toledo, who kept the old man supplied with honey while he was imprisoned in Clairvaux.

But the greatest acknowledged successes of the Action Française were in countries in which the influence of French culture was traditionally strongest.

[b] At least in public. In any case, Maeztu represented only one side of *Acción Española.* See Pierre Félix, "Le Mouvement de l'Action Espagnole," *Revue du siècle,* I, No. 2 (May 1933), 81–85: "Comme le libéralisme espagnol est venu de la Révolution française, la nouvelle école nationaliste n'a pas de fausse honte à déclarer qu'elle prend le remède en France . . . Maurras, Daudet, La Tour du Pin, etc. Cela suffit pour montrer l'orientation de ce mouvement de jeunes nationalistes espagnols."

To Romanians ("all good Romanians go to Paris when they die!") France has always appeared as the great Latin sister. Political and cultural allegiance meant the same thing for the Romanian upper and middle classes, which took their reading, their manners, their fashions, and often their governesses from Paris, and for whom French was a second language in current use. Isolated among restless neighbors of Slavic or Asiatic race, ruled by a small aristocracy of land and money and by an ambitious and pretentious bureaucracy, threatened by national claims without and social claims within, the Romanians grabbed at integral nationalism with both hands.

It is fair to say that all the French nationalist Right had followers in Romania, but as the most articulate representative of this Right, the Action Française was by far the best known. A monarchist doctrine was bound to be welcomed in a country where the monarchy was identified with independence and freedom from foreign rule, and even before the First World War, reviews like *Românul* were considering the possible applications of Maurrassian thought to Romania.[12] After the war, Action Française activities became the current knowledge of certain Romanian circles, usually influential ones. It was not surprising, therefore, that when, during the 'twenties, the Illinois Association of Romanian Jews protested to the Romanian Premier, General Alexandru Averescu, about the unpunished murder of a Jewish student by a Romanian one, the General's reply referred to an affair that must have drawn blank looks in Illinois but was familiar enough to Romanian readers of the *Action française*: Germaine Berton's acquittal after the murder of Marius Plateau.[13]

By the 'thirties, as George Téfas pointed out in his *Conceptions économiques de l'Action Française*,[14] Romania was a colony of the French Right; the *Action française, Candide, Gringoire,* and *Je suis partout* sold well, especially in Bucharest and Iasi; books by Maurras and Bainville were in the libraries of all intellectuals,[c] and Action Française ideas appeared in university lectures, in newspapers, and in literary and political reviews. *Curentul, România, Gândirea,* the weekly *Sfarmă Piatră,* the daily *Calendarul,* not to mention the *Stürmer*-like *Porunca Vremei,* were strongly Maurrassian, or, by the late 'thirties, in the line of *Je suis partout.* When Maurras was released from prison, the whole conservative press rejoiced, and Professor Iorga's *Neamul Românesc* praised him as "a pillar of Europe."[15] The short-lived Fascia Naţională Româna of 1923, though modeled on Italian Fascism, sought its inspiration in Maurras as well as in Mussolini; the anti-Semitic League of National Christian Defense, also founded in 1923, was led by a great admirer

[c] "*L'Enquête sur la monarchie* was to be found on the shelves of every contemporary Romanian politician," affirms a Romanian correspondent. Even Hegelian traditionalists like Nikifor Crainic could not ignore the import of a Maurras, whom Crainic described in his review *Gândirea* (Thought) as "the greatest French thinker of our day." Toma Vlădescu, "Nikifor Crainic," *Revue du siècle,* I, No. 2 (May 1933), 93.

and student of integral nationalism, Professor Alexander Cuza. Nor did the Iron Guard's Corneliu Codreanu, though more a mystic than Cuza, ignore it. And in 1938 a Romanian student, Mihail Fârcăşanu, passed his doctoral examination in Berlin with a thesis on "The Spiritual Development of the Monarchic Idea Throughout History," which he dedicated to Maurras, from whom (along with Daudet, Bainville, and the remainder of the Action Française pantheon) his ideas seem to have been culled.

Relations with the royalists were frequently personal as well as intellectual. Romanians studying in Paris often became "foreign members" and even Action Française militants. Some stayed. It was a Romanian, Bernard Simionesco (who during the Occupation worked for *Inter-France* as Bernard Simiot), who reported King Alfonso XIII's visit to Paris in 1926 for the *Action française*;[16] and it was the Romanians who, next to the French, furnished the greatest number of signers of Maurras's Nobel Peace Prize petition. Friends of the Action Française visited Romania on journalistic investigations or lecture tours; some, like Rebatet, even found wives there.

In Romania, more than anywhere else, *Candide* and the *Action française* seemed designed for the mentality and the tastes of the established order, echoing the anti-democratic and anti-Semitic beliefs and the Latin-culture yearnings of the ruling classes. The doctrine of these papers did not challenge the established order in Romania so much as it seemed to conservatives to do in France itself; rather, it reinforced existing prejudices and positions. But if Maurrassian thought was popular with such conservatives as Iorga and Averescu, the Romanian right-wing extremists preferred the social mysticism exacerbated by racism which they got in *Je suis partout* (and also in *Gringoire*), and sought more effective help from National-Socialists and Fascists.

Another country in which the Action Française was much appreciated—and is still highly regarded today—was Portugal. Even more than the Spanish, the Portuguese intelligentsia before the First World War were marked by their discovery of the authoritarian, traditionalist, and royalist ideas of the Action Française. Portuguese exiles, travelers, and students, disgusted with the democratic liberalism and apparent chaos of the republican regime installed in 1910 and in search of some countersystem, were overwhelmed when they stumbled upon the new political school so popular among Parisian students.

Hipolito Raposo has related how, on a visit to Paris some years before the war, he was amazed to hear a French student tell him that nothing good would come of the recently established Portuguese Republic. Back in Coimbra, Raposo told his friends that counterrevolutionary ideas were currently accepted on the banks of the Seine, that one could be a royalist in spite of the adverse current then prevalent in Portugal, and that, indeed, in Paris student circles royalism was a fashionable idea.[17] His message was bolstered by that of Father

Amadeu de Vasconcelos, who in 1913, from Paris, began to publish his weekly *Os meus Cadernos. Cadernos,* which carried as its slogan a phrase of Charles Maurras—"Ah! que l'Intelligence use vite de ce qui lui reste de temps!"—claimed, like Maurras, that the first and essential task for Portugal was one of intellectual purification. Vasconcelos, under the pen name Mariotte, lauded Maurras as "his eminent master and friend,"[18] and wrote appreciatively of the fact that at last in Maurras's thought the monarchy had been drawn out of the liberal, constitutionalist, and democratic byways in which it had been floundering far too long.

Meanwhile, in Lisbon and Coimbra people read the *Action française* as well. The results began to appear in 1914, in Antonio Sardinha's *Naçao Portuguesa* and in the movement of Lusitanian Integralism which centered around it. Proof enough that Lusitanian Integralism was inspired by the Action Française lies in its name; the essence of its thought was to present monarchy as the *integral* realization of nationalist aspirations. Other similarities were so great that in 1915 Sardinha and Raposo were forced to deny publicly that Integralism was a French import. Later on, however, Raposo himself outlined, in great detail, just how many lessons had been learned in France; and Dr. Julio Evangelista, in his excellent account of Maurrassian influence in Portugal which appeared in 1955, feels that Integralism took from the Action Française "its example, its suggestions, and its ways of acting":

> And if we consider that the main doctrinal line is similar in both movements, both being monarchist, nationalist, and traditionalist, that it is common to see Portuguese theorists cite men of the Action Française, and that one cannot deny the influence which, e.g., Maurras, Bourget, and Bainville have had on a great part of Integralist youth who read them, one must admit that this influence went well beyond [mere example].[19]

The works of the Action Française masters have not been translated into Portuguese, largely because Portuguese intellectuals can easily read them in the original French; but books and articles about them in Portuguese are not lacking. In 1914 Ayres d'Ornellas published *As Doutrinas politicas de Charles Maurras,* and now the official information service is preparing an anthology of selected passages from the monarchist thinker. Between the wars, the *Action française* was read daily by many intellectual and politically inclined men, some of whom, as a contributor to *A Voz* noted, had read Maurras's books in their student days. The direct influence of the paper was supplemented by the works of Portuguese theorists sympathetic to Maurras, so that when the newspaper disappeared, although it left a gap, its ideas did not vanish altogether.[20]

The persistence of the influence is due in no small part also to the fact that Salazar's Estado Novo, established after 1926, has intimately recognized its close relationship with Maurrassian philosophy. Indeed, as Dr. Evangelista observes, Portugal owes some measure of "the peace and order that it has enjoyed for the last two decades to the application of certain principles of the Action Française, assimilated through the movement of Lusitanian Integralism."

There is no knowing, of course, to what extent Salazar himself has assimilated these principles. A number of writers, from Bainville to Mme Christine Garnier, have claimed that Maurras's influence on Salazar is strong, that Salazar admits he owes Maurras the notion of "politique d'abord," the idea of the strong State in a decentralized society, and the distinction between demophilism and democracy. "Quel accord de conscience entre ces deux hommes," says Henri Massis, through whom in 1952 Salazar expressed to Maurras his "profound respect and admiration"; what essential agreement there is between "their certainties, their fears, and their desires!"[d]

Based on this firm foundation, the mutual admiration between Maurras and Salazar remained lively until Maurras's death. While Maurras was in prison, the two men corresponded, and on one occasion Salazar sent his friend a case of port.[21] Veterans like Marcel Wiriath (now a director of the Crédit Lyonnais), Massis, and Vallat never failed to visit Salazar whenever they were in Lisbon in order to convey Maurras's messages and good wishes. But Maurras's crucial intervention came at the end of May 1951, in a letter delivered by Massis.

Marshal Carmona, President of the Portuguese Republic since 1928, had died in April; the question then arose whether Salazar would choose to succeed him or would continue to hold in his strong hands, as Maurras phrased it, the governmental power of which he was the head. No doubt the Portuguese dictator had reached his own decision, but Maurras's intervention seems to have helped confirm it in his mind. "Restez! Tenez!" Maurras entreated; on June 5, Salazar (who read the letter out to his cabinet colleagues) announced that he had decided to remain Premier. On July 19, in the vast hall of the Sports Palace in Lisbon, in Salazar's presence, one of the masters of the Integralist movement, Dr. Joao do Amaral, read Maurras's letter aloud, partly in explanation of the dictator's political decision, and partly in homage to the man who signed "Charles Maurras, No. 8321"—"the master of my mind, who taught my generation and many others what Monarchy was, and what should be its doctrine."[22]

The traditionalist and Latin ideas so much appreciated in Portugal were reinforced by the bond of language in the case of two of France's neighbors,

[d] Jacques Bainville, *The Dictators* (London, 1937) p. 236; Christine Garnier, *Vacances avec Salazar* (1952), p. 177; Henri Massis, *Maurras et notre temps* (1961), pp. 419–20. See also Salazar's speeches of May 28, 1930, and Jan. 26, 1934, in *Une révolution dans la paix* (1937), especially pp. 78–79, 210–22. That Salazar does not mind a measure of identification with the French sage was made clear when his confidential secretary, Dr. José Solari Allegro, who left him in 1960 to take up an important government post after thirteen years of service, did not hesitate in print to draw a close comparison of the two men's moral and intellectual qualities; see *Diario da Manha,* Feb. 2, 1960.

Belgium and Switzerland. In Belgium, where the foreign influence of the Action Française probably reached its height around the middle 'twenties, the young members of a society that still tends to get much of its culture from Paris, who, in the days before the First World War wanted to look beyond Anatole France and *La Vie Parisienne,* discovered Bourget, Barrès, and the school of the Action Française, which, says Paul Dresse,[23] appeared as the vanguard of French political and cultural nationalism.

At this time, the Action Française's most effective propagandists seem to have been recruited in the ranks of the religious orders—some of whom, like Dom Besse, had been expelled from France with other Benedictines and had settled in the abbey of Saint-Martin-de-Ligugé, near Namur, others of whom were teaching in Catholic colleges and universities, especially those of Louvain and Liège.[e] As for the Belgians themselves, the chief center of Action Française ideas seems to have been the Jesuit college of Saint-Servais at Liège. Before 1914, Valois's *Le Père* and Maurras's *L'Enquête sur la monarchie* were studied in the seminars of the "Rhetoric" sections; and the professor of poetry was described as being "equally a fanatic of Léon Bloy and of the *Action française*."

Jesuits in general were among the great propounders of the doctrine. Father de Smet, a noted preacher, led the way at Liège, and in Brussels the Collège Saint-Michel had its enthusiasts, led by Father Deharvenz, Professor of Rhetoric, and by Carlos Lefèvre, Professor of Science. They were attracted above all by the literary and aesthetic views of the Action Française and tended particularly to cite passages that confirmed their own ideas about classical letters. But, as Dresse points out, it was inevitable that young men at an age when ideas can be fascinating (especially when they are skillfully set forth) should be fired by the thought that violence might be employed in the service of reason. The exciting stories of Camelot pranks for the violent, the echoes of new and enticing ideas for the bookish, helped to create a great deal of interest and even enthusiasm for the Action Française among Belgian Catholic students and intellectuals.

On the eve of the First World War, the successes of the early 'twenties were already being foreshadowed by a first wave of Maurrassian authoritarianism. As Jacques Serruys remembered, looking back in 1935, "On voyait déjà poindre les tendances de la Jeunesse de 1919": in 1914, in the public lecture series organized by the Jeune Barreau de Bruxelles, a whole covey of young barristers—Pierre Nothomb, Henri Goffinet, André Puttemans, Alfred Dorff—reflected in their lectures the Maurrassian ideas in which they had

[e] Dom Besse himself did his best to spread the good word in lectures like the series delivered at Louvain in 1908, attended by "the flower of Catholic youth" (Charles d'Aspremont-Lynden, Louis de Lichtervelde, Paul Gérard, etc.), and in letters to students who showed any interest, such as Paul Nève de Mévergnies, later Professor of Philosophy in the University of Liège, to whom he recommended the *Action française* as a source of ideas for articles and studies for "young men of an inquiring mind." Dresse MS, I, 11–11 bis; see also Fabricius, *Revue de l'ordre corporatif,* October 1939.

been steeped. "Ces conférenciers dénonçaient déjà le parlementarisme, la politique de parti, pronaient la restauration du pouvoir dans l'Etat, analysaient les tendances de Maurras et ses positions vis-à-vis de Rome."[24]

The war eclipsed this intellectual radiance. Belgians at home were cut off from all French contacts for four years, and those intellectuals who found refuge in France or pursued the battle there were too busy to pay much attention to a movement that was not directly concerned with their own country. When Paul Nève tried to sound out the officers of the Belgian Ronarch Brigade, in whose mess he was dining, he was disappointed to get only non-committal replies.

Some of Maurras's former admirers who found themselves in France during the war did, however, keep up their reading of the paper, always favorable to Belgium and to its Soldier King, who seemed to represent most of the virtues of Maurras's ideal monarch. Young Pierre Nothomb (today a Senator and Baron of the Kingdom, then Chef de Cabinet of Premier Carton de Wiart) could get the cooperation of the paper when it was needed, and we have seen that on occasion he could instill his own, frequently Maurrassian, ideas into the policy statements of his chief. Relations were excellent, too, with Fernand Neuray's *Nation belge,* which had been set up largely with French funds to serve as a mouthpiece of Belgian patriotism.

After the Armistice, Belgian universities were filled with a strange, conglomerate horde of students, some of them still in uniform. A few, as in the good old days, came straight from the lycées, but others were just out of the Army or prison camps. As Professor Marcel de Corte has remarked, Belgian students have never been particularly interested in ideas or intellectual problems: "Belgae amant scientias grossas et palpabile." But there was then a general eagerness in the air, a feeling of impatience and an odd excitement about commonplace situations which a lapse of years had rendered unfamiliar.

There were many among the students who had a vague but restless desire to rebuild, to reorder, to plan something for the future and to tackle it at once. One such group, small to begin with, was that of the *Jeunesse nouvelle,* which, founded at Easter 1919, soon became the center of Maurrassian thought in the University of Louvain. For two or three years it remained chiefly a literary review, while Maurrassian ideas slowly jelled, but in March 1923 it became frankly political and simultaneously launched a new Ligue de la Jeunesse Nouvelle, authoritarian and anti-democratic. Within a year, in January 1924, the Ligue de la Jeunesse Nouvelle issued the first number of *Pour L'Autorité,* an openly political bimonthly dedicated to the crusade of order, to a revival of local traditions, to the subordination of the individual to the family and the family to the general good, to the restoration of hierarchy in society and values, to the reinforcement of the executive power of the State, and to the reduction of the "exorbitant role" of the legislative. The spirit of the magazine, proclaimed its opening manifesto, was "a reaction against the predominance of democratic incompetence, against the passion for political equality, against the electoralism which results from this, and against the overbidding it provokes."

Pour L'Autorité lasted some six or seven years, but faded away after the condemnation of the Action Française. According to Dresse, the movement was a training ground for numerous well-known Belgians: Luc Hommel and Carlo de Mey went on to win distinction at the bar, Geoffroy d'Aspremont-Wilden and Hubert Carton de Wiart entered the diplomatic service, Charles du Bus de Warnaffe and Paul Van Zeeland sought political careers, Fernand Baud'hoin became a distinguished professor and financial journalist; but most of the writers continued their literary pursuits, even when, like poets Jean Tengels and Hugues Lecocq, it was not their profession.

Of them, Dresse makes this comment:

> Ces catholiques de *l'Autorité* gardèrent presque tous, de leur première attitude devant la vie, de leur quête d'une doctrine qu'ils allèrent chercher en France faute de la trouver en Belgique, de l'emprise de Maurras qu'ils avouèrent tous pour leur Maître en certaines matières, un souci de la culture, un goût des idées générales qu'on ne décèle pas plus chez leurs devanciers immédiats que chez leurs successeurs directs. Florissants aux beaux jours du maurrassisme, ils en restèrent marqués.

And Serruys agrees: "From this passing contact with Maurrassian doctrine, the team that worked together in *L'Autorité* has kept not only a similar political vocabulary, but even a certain parallelism of positions and conceptions"[25] —as, for instance, in their stand against liberalism.

But this was only one of several such groups. By the mid-1920's, the *Action française* was selling some five hundred copies daily at Louvain, and more than that at Liège: "une véritable frénésie d'Action Française avait saisi des milliers de jeunes gens."[f] Not only student reviews but practically all right-wing Catholic publications were at least tinged with Maurrassism and generally dominated by Maurrassians. The clergy, eager to find a strong opponent to militant anticlericalism, encouraged them. We have seen the culmination of this enthusiasm in the debates of 1925–26, and in the condemnation that followed.

The Roman condemnation killed the Action Française, but not its indirect influence. The students, like their clerical advisers, had been interested less in the League than in Maurrassism, and although most of them gave up Maurras's works as well as the newspaper after 1927, what they had learned stayed

[f] Léon Degrelle, *Jeunes Plumes et vieilles barbes de Belgique,* mentions 325 copies sold in one day by the leading Louvain bookshop alone; *Pourquoi pas?* April 17, 1931, gives a total of 500 a day, which is perhaps an exaggeration. For purposes of comparison, we might remember that at about the same time, according to information supplied by Roger Joseph, Orléans had some 150 subscribers, and newspaper vendors there sold another 60 to 80 copies a day. But Orléans, of course, had no university.

with them in their historical and cultural attitudes. Less "Catholic" than other Belgian papers, and still close to its wartime friends, Fernand Neuray's *Nation belge* continued to publish Bainville's articles, and, in a broad sense, to reflect the views of the *Action française*. During his Brussels exile, Daudet became a regular contributor, and he did his best to keep interest alive throughout the country by numerous private contacts and by lecture tours. The condemned ideas also remained alive, especially in the universities, in certain groups gathered around small literary reviews. At Liège these sympathies found expression in the *Vaillant*, the *Quartier Latin*,[g] and most particularly in *Cahiers Mosans*, to which Dresse, Albert Fassbender, and Raymond Janne contributed. And the Catholic Students' Union, of which Fassbender was several times president, was purged of integral nationalism only to turn to Rexism.

The "young Catholic elite" which José Streel described in *Les Jeunes Gens et la politique*, published in 1932, was left politically lost and divided by the condemnation. There seemed to be no alternative for Maurrassism—all parties, socialist or conservative, Catholic or liberal, seemed inert and corrupt. Many students left the country in disgust—Dresse went to Africa, Pierre Daye to France, Léon Degrelle to Mexico. But they returned, and in a few years a fresh lead was offered by an unexpected person, Degrelle.

It was at the college of Notre-Dame-de-la-Paix at Namur that Degrelle was first introduced by a Jesuit instructor to the works of Maurras and La Tour du Pin and to the *Action française*. He read the poems of Louis Boumal (whose statue stands in Liège), an early admirer of Maurras and of the paper, who was consecrated after his death in 1918 one of the masters of the young monarchist school. At the University of Louvain, Degrelle grew to be an ardent Maurrassian, but he gave up the Action Française in 1927 along with most of his fellows. Maurras, however, and France, remained for him "tout de même un morceau de notre âme." In 1930, with the help of clerical friends, Degrelle became the director of a Catholic publishing house in Louvain, Christus-Rex, soon shortened to the more striking Rex. The offices of the firm were on the premises of the Belgian Catholic Youth Association, and gradually the loud and aggressive publicist and orator gathered around him the young men whom the papal condemnation of the Action Française had left at loose ends.[26]

By 1935, when his movement shot into the public eye, the *Action française, Candide, Je suis partout*, and their friends were giving Degrelle all the publicity they could.[27] Rexist deputies like Streel and Daye were frequent con-

[g] Founded by recalcitrant Catholics from the *Vaillant*, the *Quartier Latin* lived only a few months, after which its staff members went their separate ways: Dresse remained steadfastly Maurrassian and monarchist; Curvers, who had been the editor, became a novelist and found success with *Tempo di Roma*; Janne took up law at Liège; Jules Van Erck, after working for the Catholic *Gazette de Liège*, followed Robert Poulet into collaboration and has lived in France since 1945.

tributors to *Je suis partout,* and Brasillach was one of the first to introduce Degrelle to the French public. As Brasillach understood them, the ideas of Rex were far more closely related to the Action Française and to La Tour du Pin, to the Comte de Paris and to Salazar, than they were to National-Socialism or Fascism.[28] But this was not quite so. Although it was full of integral nationalist alumni who frankly acknowledged their debt to Maurras, Rex was much more Fascist than the Action Française. Its emphasis was corporatist and activist, more on the order of Valois and of the current line of *Je suis partout,* and it soon alienated more conservative nationalists.

Like its French friends, Rex, which fell on hard times after its flash-in-the-pan success of 1936–37, welcomed the opportunity of collaboration; and a number of its members, including Poulet and Streel, received severe sentences, even the death penalty, after the war.[h] Meanwhile, more conformist Maurrassians carried on. In Brussels, a group of them formed a study circle which met periodically to hear papers from its members. When Maurras was elected to the Académie Française in 1938, they organized a banquet in his honor. He was unable to attend, but in February 1940 he did go to Brussels for a "causerie littéraire." The great hall of the Palais des Académies was full for the occasion, and even though only the first few rows could hear what Maurras said in his low, hollow voice, "on venait surtout pour voir le maître de la réaction française."

The most patriotic among Maurras's Belgian admirers were, however, alienated by the "collaborationist" policies of the *Action française* during the Occupation. A senior officer in the Belgian Army, an old admirer of Maurras, who happened to meet Maurras and Pujo in the office of the Prefect of Vienne at Poitiers during the great retreat, remembers Maurras grumbling to him, "Oui, tout ça c'est bien mérité. Nous sommes un régime pourri. Je l'avais toujours dit. Maintenant nous devons tirer partie de la défaite. Il faudra nous entendre avec les Allemands." The officer still shudders at the memory of hearing the words spoken "with relish when people were crying in the street." We are not here concerned with the question of the accuracy of the recollection, which is no doubt, in part at least, essentially correct; what is significant is that it reflects an impression that became general, of defeatism and even, for some, of treachery. And so, because of war, it has been in Belgium, where the Action Française in its several forms was at one time the strongest, that it has least endured.[29]

The influence of the Action Française in Switzerland—in Neuchâtel, Fribourg, Geneva, and the Canton de Vaud—is less well known but, in a small way, perhaps more enduring.

It was in 1904 that a group of young Lausanne intellectuals, led by two brothers, Charles-Albert and Alexandre Cingria-Vaneyre, brought out the

[h] Not all the sentences were carried out. Robert Poulet was pardoned and now lives in France, where he is an active contributor to *Rivarol* and other publications.

Voile latine, whose title alone was intended as a manifesto and was recognized as such by the *Journal de Genève,*[30] which spoke of it as "a manifestation of the Latin spirit, both Catholic and ancient." *Suisse romande* literature was dozing at the time, deep "in a state of localism, Calvinist moralism, and contempt of art."[31] It was Alexandre Cingria who first introduced his friends to Maurras and Maurras's ideas, and who worked with Ramuz and Adrien Bovy, Gonzague de Reynold, and the poet Henri Spiess to adapt these ideas to Swiss circumstances. Cingria was republican in the sense of wanting to reestablish in Switzerland "nos anciennes républiques aristocratiques," but he declared himself anti-democratic, anti-Protestant (because Protestantism existed in terms of anti-Catholicism, and this implied a denial of the whole Latin heritage he cherished), and, of course, reactionary. Within a few years, the original group had been joined by several others, including Gonzague de Reynold's cousin, the poet Robert de Traz, who had arrived from Paris trailing all the prestige of the boulevards: "He knows who Charles Maurras is. He is well aware of the favor that reactionary ideas enjoy with the enlightened public."[32]

At the time of the squabble between the *Action française,* Arthur Meyer's *Gaulois,* and the conservative royalists, Alexandre Cingria wanted the *Voile* to take a stand, but De Traz, as editor,[i] refused, and shortly thereafter the Cingrias resigned to publish their own review, the *Voix Clémentine.* Like Vasconcellos's *Cadernos* two years later, the *Voix Clémentine* carried a slogan taken from Maurras (from the *Dilemme de Marc Sangnier*): "Je suis Romain, je suis humain, deux propositions identiques," and it affirmed that "our ideal conforms to the program summarized in Maurras's splendid statement. . . . Our particular purpose, however, has been to define a *Lemanic* modality of this Latin, human, universal idea of which Maurras, by the statement of his nationalism, has expressed for himself and his friends only a French modality." What this Lemanic modality might be, Alexandre Cingria explained, was "a cultivated Switzerland, organic in its constitution, and hence aristocratic, military, conservative, and Latin, speaking clearly, thinking straight, cherishing its *true* past and the awareness of what made its *true* glory."[33]

The *Voix Clémentine* did not live long, nor did the *Feuillets* that Traz and Gonzague brought out, but by 1912, when both parties had established close relations with the Action Française in Paris, the work of the little groups was done: "Direct or indirect, the influence of Charles Maurras is there. It prevents a whole generation of the *Suisse romande* from losing all interest in their community, it helps them to connect action and thought." All over Switzerland, young men, or at least the thoughtful and imaginative ones, felt that a war was coming; at its approach, and also in reaction to internal social pressures similar to those flaring up around their borders, "a movement of

[i] Not only was De Traz too critical of Maurras to suit the Cingrias, he was also a Protestant.

national union" was organized under the name Nouvelle Société Helvétique. Maurras's influence on this was not noticeable, but, says Gonzague de Reynold, its leaders had acquired from him, at first or second hand, a desire for "a return to national traditions, the will to defend themselves against foreign influences and to draw nothing except from our own tradition."[34]

All this is reminiscent of the Portuguese nationalists: the same fascination with the latest Paris fashion, at first literary; the same aristocratic reaction; the same small reviews, and eventually the same declarations that, although the Action Française provided an example, the tradition they drew on was their own, and that far from wanting to imitate the French they sought no more than the return of their own society "to the natural conditions of its formation and development."[35]

Only one of Maurras's Swiss admirers actually chose to fight for France during the war. Born in Geneva of a family of French Protestant refugees, Jean Binet-Valmer (who in 1902 had joined Gabriel Hanotaux, José María de Heredia, Pierre Louÿs, Edmond Jaloux, and Claude Farrère in founding *La Renaissance latine* and made his contribution to the renascence with a series of rather daring third-rate novels of which *Les Métèques,* 1906, was the most successful) volunteered in 1914. He was commissioned in the field, and given French citizenship, and he emerged from four years of war with a splendid record: the Legion of Honor, three wounds, four mentions in dispatches. After his discharge he founded a reserve-officers' association, the Ligue des Chefs de Section, and, as a journalist, worked hard for various worthy causes —the children of the devastated regions, the tomb of the unknown soldier at the Arc de Triomphe, and the Armistice monument at Rethondes, the inscription for which he himself drew up.

A Republican, a monarchist, a Maurrassian, and a Camelot, the swashbuckling, bemonocled Swiss was looked at somewhat askance by the leaders of the Action Française, but he was nevertheless useful to them at times. "Je n'aime pas beaucoup ce Suisse protestant," said Bernard de Vésins, "qui joue au patriote français et qui boit comme un polonais." And yet it was the Swiss Protestant who effected the *rapprochement* of the Action Française and the old-line royalist Oeillet Blanc; and it was he also who, especially after Plateau's death, served as an intermediary between the League and other leagues and veterans' groups.[36]

Maurrassism suffered something of an eclipse in Switzerland during the war, the work of the Cingrias and of Ramuz becoming increasingly self-centered and unpolitical. Yet in reaction to the climate of cozy security in the mountain fortress, a few young people, chiefly in western Switzerland, turned to integral nationalism, usually in direct proportion to their desire for order, discipline, and firm authority.[37]

The first and most effective of the movements started by these young integral nationalists was Ordre et Tradition, which was founded in Lausanne in

1919 by five schoolboys, including Albert Morel and Marcel Regamey, who were interested in studying history, genealogy, and heraldry. The boys soon became preoccupied with a search for some more convincing political philosophy than the one embodied in the optimistic and facile idealism prevailing at the time, and their historical studies eventually led them to adopt the principle of dynastic heredity as an essential element in the political development of nations—a conclusion they arrived at in complete ignorance of any French royalist movement. In an account written in 1929, Regamey tells how unaware he and his friends were in 1919 of the Action Française:

> We were sure that there was no royalist group in France; the names of Maurras and Daudet were completely unknown to us. It was only one year later that a friend came to tell us his extraordinary discovery; he brought us a copy of the *Action française*. So there existed a royalist newspaper in Paris . . . With enthusiasm we noted the identity of principles, the identity of conclusions in detail.[38]

The Action Française served partly to confirm their own conclusions, and partly also to save them from an error they had been tempted to make—sympathizing with the idea of a "White International."[j] "To the revolutionary international it seemed logical to oppose an international league of partisans of the traditional order. The Action Française made us see the dangers of this seductive idea." Guided by the French, Ordre et Tradition saw that a truly orderly regime must be a national one, and that such a regime could not rely on foreign support without endangering its very existence. Furthermore, they reasoned, since every people had the kind of regime that best suited it, determined by circumstances and by history, a White International would have to take its stand on the most general principles, whose abstraction might lead to adopting a phraseology similar to that of the Revolution and just as bad, "for vague ideas do more harm than ideas that are obviously false."

Abandoning the idea of an international league, Ordre et Tradition decided that within the Swiss Confederation itself a reactionary federalism should be based on cantonal nationalism—"moderate because national, but integral." Though Protestant, the group insisted on its common patrimony with Catholicism and on the formula "Pas d'ennemis à droite." Within a few years, it was joined by some members of the Cercle Fédéraliste in Lausanne, which had been plodding along with a somewhat similar program. In 1926, when it had gained a measure of public attention, it launched a series of pamphlets which attempted to work out an acceptable definition of what the

[j] See Hipolito Raposo, *Dois Nacionalismos,* p. 143, for a 1921 initiative concerning an international league to defend Latin countries against Masonic influences and democratic slavery. Gonzague de Reynold mentions the same "Internationale de Droite" in a private letter to Maurras, dated January 20, 1927, in which he laments the fact that the condemnation of the Action Française would prevent it from taking the leading role which would be its own in such a movement. But Maurras never cared for the idea and always advised against it.

national interest of the Canton de Vaud might be, and to furnish proof that democracy was not a necessary condition of Helvetic existence, as it had not been in the past.

The group made an effort to spread its ideas beyond the limits of its own canton by establishing an affiliation with the Cercle Fédéraliste in Geneva and by helping Bern and Neuchâtel to set up autonomous nationalist circles of their own, and in February 1928 all these groups founded the Swiss Nationalist Federation, whose stated purpose was to "restore the Swiss Confederation to institutions in conformity with the sovereignty and interests of its Cantons," to oppose parties, anticlerical activity, state and federal centralization; and which, considering the army "the only real guarantee of Swiss independence," affirmed the dignity of military service against the vain theories of Communists and humanitarians.

Who were the other members of this grandly named Nationalist Federation? The Groupe Nationaliste de Berne was founded in 1923 by a few young Bernese, who had been meeting regularly to discuss art, literature, and politics. In their Declaration of Principles they deplored the threat to civilization implied in a growing intellectual disorder, with firm doctrines lacking in every realm, everywhere ill-defined terms, vague and imprecise ideas, creating extreme confusion in all minds, while the invasion of foreign ideologies contrary to local traditions was sapping the foundations of national life. They proposed a return to the principles of authority and of Greco-Latin civilization, instead of the mediocre leveling influences of democracy, and urged the reconstitution of intellectual and social elites, by opposing "Statism" and centralization and rediscovering the political and social principles upon which Switzerland had been founded.

The program was grandiose, and so were their plans. They established a League, intended to be nation-wide, and prepared a plan of campaign which, drawing much of its inspiration from Action Française ideas, declared in Point Number 8: "the movement must be presented to the public as a *national movement,* inspired by the most authentic Helvetic traditions . . . and completely devoid of all foreign influence. To appear in the public eye as an annex of the Action Française or of Fascism would condemn the movement to absolutely certain failure."[39] Even such astuteness availed them nothing. All attempts to establish the nationalist league throughout Switzerland proved fruitless, and the original impetus began to flag, until in 1928 the group was reconstituted under the influence of Ordre et Tradition and joined the Nationalist Federation.

In contrast to so much hope, the Genevan Cercle Fédéraliste made but a poor showing. Founded late in 1924 by a score or two of Genevese intellectuals, and including a good contingent of artists, the Cercle was simply a glorified discussion group under direct Maurrassian influence, whose aim was to oppose on Christian, regionalist, and traditionalist grounds "the revolutionary principles undermining a European civilization which, since Latin days, has always been directed by Rome." Its statutes proclaimed the struggle against Pan-Germanism, Bolshevism, theosophy, anthroposophy, and Anglo-Saxon pluralism, and also against plutocracy, which "enslaves our civilization and our intelligence by means of the press and of international finance," but they proposed to tolerate the Jews and to oppose only "that which in their attitude is offensive to our civilization and tends to dominate it."[40]

The publication of the Cercle's "Thèses doctrinales" in Gonzague de Reynold's *La Démocratie et la Suisse* in 1929 went unnoticed. By then, membership in the Cercle was small and unenthusiastic; recruitment had fallen off, and the group's sour report to the Nationalist Federation admitted that most intellectuals, whether active or not, were not yet philosophically liberated to the point of accepting a distinctly reactionary political doctrine.

Although Geneva still honors each year on August 10 its soldiers murdered by the revolutionary mob at Versailles, it has not been fertile ground for reactionary initiatives. Neuchâtel, on the other hand, has a strong reactionary tradition; and the Cercle Nationaliste Neuchâtelois (CNN) followed in a long series of reactionary movements which, throughout the nineteenth century, tried to return Neuchâtel to Hohenzollern rule. From these, of course, the pro-French CNN dissociated itself, but it harked back to other movements, like the short-lived Ordre et Liberté and the Union Helvétique, which had joined in a Parti Progressiste National before collapsing and disappearing altogether. An Association of Young Neuchâtel Liberals, under Action Française inspiration, had been active in the postwar years but was in a state of decay by the time the new Cercle was organized. The Young Liberals were anti-democratic and cantonal nationalists who wanted a sort of dictatorship of the Neuchâtel Conseil d'Etat, that could cope with the canton's economic problems, which had been aggravated by the coming of peace. By 1926, their program openly imitated the ideas of Valois's *Nouveau Siècle,* but at Neuchâtel they could not even draw on the sort of veteran sentiment that briefly backed the Faisceau.

The CNN appeared about 1926, when the Young Liberal movement was failing, to pick up the banner of Neuchâtel reaction. Their program was one of reaction pure and simple: against democratic stupidities, against the myth of popular sovereignty, against the reign of factions and a regime which, according to them, corrupted the national sentiment.[41] It came almost, in one sense, as a conservative "Maurrassian" reaction against the simili-Fascist deviations of the so-called Liberals. Thus, Neuchâtel showed not only the Maurrassian influence apparent in the other groups but also an internal division comparable to that in the Action Française itself.

The interesting thing about these Swiss experiments, all but one of which had little enough importance, and very little effect, even on a local scale, is how, in a whole series of separate communities, nationalists looked to Paris, to the Action Française specifically, for ideas, and found in its doctrines the answer to their needs.

The different members of the Swiss Nationalist Federation had different fortunes: the lack of documents about the group at Bern seems to indicate eventual demise. The spirit of the CNN, which existed until the mid-1930's, persists today around Eddy Bauer and Claude-Philippe Bodinier in the *Feuille d'Avis de Neuchâtel,* which is generally considered the mouthpiece of influential circles in the Army. The Genevan Federalists, attracted by publications like the *Nouvelle Revue Romande* and *Res Helvetica,* died out as a group, although, after 1932, some of them, under the influence of Geneva Deputy Georges Oltramare, drifted toward Nazi-inspired Frontisme.[42] The only group that still exists today is Ordre et Tradition, under the name Ligue Vaudoise, which it adopted in 1933.

The Ligue Vaudoise is not a political party but operates in terms of direct democracy by launching occasional initiatives. Among these was the one which after the last war brought to an end the extraordinary powers granted the Swiss Federal Council during the crisis and returned constitutional rights to cantonal authority. The Ligue achieved a good deal of influence during the last war, when both the Army and the Federal Council were dominated by citizens of Vaud, with whom it sympathized. The social security system in the canton, built on corporatist lines inspired by La Tour du Pin, is largely a monument to its labors, as are the strong employers' federations (Groupements Patronaux Vaudois) and Bertil Galland's Fédération Ouvrière Vaudoise. It also publishes a weekly paper, the *Nation.*

Marcel Regamey, one of the schoolboy founders, today holds a position similar to that of Maurras (whose photograph hangs over his desk) in that he has enormous personal influence and prestige and in that the Ligue Vaudoise tends to be equated with him.[k] He has been described as a Fascist, but he has shown no sympathy for the "caporalist" side of Fascism, or, as a good Maurrassian, for its "religion of the State," and has managed to adapt a working version of nationalist doctrine to his own small *patrie.* Vaud has this particularity, that it is one of the few political entities left today still small enough to allow effective personal intervention, yet large and diversified enough to have more than a narrow parochial significance. This is the fatherland to which the Ligue dedicates itself and in which Regamey tries to apply his thinking.

Regamey's thought is close to that of Maurras, who between 1932 and 1942 paid yearly visits to Lausanne to address his followers and admirers. Like the *Voix Clémentine,* the propaganda pamphlets of the Ligue Vaudoise begin

[k] See "Der Eremit von Epalinges," *National Zeitung* (Basel), Aug. 16, 1956, which decribes Regamey as an influential idealist of Fascist-Maurrassian inspiration, highly regarded in all serious political and industrial circles.

with a quotation from Maurras[43] (one from Ramuz follows), and emphasize that union, liberty, and "the sense of the State" must be sought in the traditional institutions of the land. In a canton commonly credited with less cohesion or "national tradition" than most Swiss cantons, Regamey stresses—almost "invents"—a local history. Beyond it, he offers what might be termed a "service conservatism."

For the false dogma of popular sovereignty he would substitute the more empirical approach of a personal regime which took account of essential traditions but adapted them always to the circumstances of the time. There is no idealism about such a system: it takes men as it finds them, most often selfish and narrow, and does its best to make them live together with the least amount of friction and hate. Since equality is a myth, a society founded on such myths as democracy is bound to result in disorder, because it permits inequalities to exist without providing any compensating solutions. A positive regime, as Regamey conceives it, would acknowledge the real diversities that exist among men, instead of pretending that the law should be the same for everyone. But it would also connect privilege and function, so that the one should only exist when justified by the other. This, says Regamey, would be the realism that recognizes facts and makes the best possible use of them for the public good. Liberal, democratic, or revolutionary ideals are not to be condemned because they are intrinsically bad, but because, being ideals, they are unreal. Doctrines that are concerned only with ideals will deliberately ignore facts that do not fit into their model of reality, and thus will provide worse government by failing to cope with problems for which they are usually unprepared.

This is in good part why "an enlightened demophile detests democracy, for to confer upon people a pretended sovereignty it cannot exercise is to betray it." To act effectively, "one must resolutely give up the title of democrat, even if this renunciation should cost one public favor to begin with." Regamey advocates establishing an elite "not of masters and profiteers of the State, but of servants of the public good."[44] Unlike the other Swiss theorists, however, who are all aristocratic and would interpret these ideas as justifying a "natural" elite, he makes it clear that his "reactionaries" in no way favor "aristocracy, patriciate, nobility, an intellectual or money elite," but simply a functional one under a single leader.

As early as 1931 Regamey stressed the importance of adapting one's policies to times and circumstances instead of keeping them frozen in an unchanging mold. If I have devoted some space to outlining his ideas, it is because he offers one of the few instances in which Maurrassian doctrine has actually managed to survive without completely losing its identity. Fated to lose impetus in France and to be reduced to the most stubborn conservatism, fated to disappear behind the vigorous front of native Fascist movements in Romania, Italy, and Spain, or to contribute little more than the national-syndicalism that it had itself discarded to groups like that of Rex and *Je suis partout,* surviving in the thought of conservative, aristocratic-minded intellectuals of talent but little influence in other Swiss cantons and in Belgium, the Action Française has made essential contributions to applied experiments only in Portugal and in the Canton of Vaud.

In one case the experiment has affected a whole state, in the other only a small society, but in each case it has lasted so far only by applying the empirical flexibility which the young Maurras advocated—"positivisme, empirisme organizateur"—and which the old Maurras forgot, as did his less imaginative, more servile imitators in France and elsewhere.

This may help to explain the success of the two exceptions. All the movements we have considered were the inspiration of bright, upper-class students and dilettantes who lighted upon the Action Française at a time when, dissatisfied with certain conditions obtaining around them, they were looking for an intellectual guide. These people who went to Paris, started small reviews, or subscribed to foreign papers were generally unrepresentative. Conceiving their way of life to be of value, they sought not only to preserve it but also to justify it, to themselves as well as to others. In this respect, the Action Française provided a doctrinal foundation for revindication movements of the dispossessed or for the defensive movements of peoples, classes, or institutions threatened either passively or actually by national, social, and ideological pressures. Where no such pressure existed, as it existed in the case of monarchists in France, Portugal, and later on in Spain, and in the case of Romanians, Walloons, and French-speaking Swiss, and of the Catholic upper class in France and Belgium, the ideas of the Action Française were occasionally examined with curiosity, but they never acquired political significance.

Aristocrats and reactionary intellectuals took up Maurrassian doctrines; so, until 1926, did the Catholic clergy, alarmed by irreligion and anti-clerical campaigns. But what the Action Française provided was talking points, the theoretical confirmation of a state of mind, and hardly very effective in concrete terms of political action in a crisis. When events grew serious, the bookish ruthlessness of Action Française doctrinaires and the thoughtless violence of Action Française troops tended to be disregarded while more brutal, less thoughtful, men and movements took the field. The doctrinaires could teach an order of the intellect and of the spirit, but they could hardly apply or enforce it.

Even in Pétain's Vichy and Salazar's Portugal, something like Maurrassism triumphed only by abandoning essential tenets—the noninterfering State, the self-regulated regions and professional corporations, and, above all, the king. Not less but more centralization accompanied both regimes. Only in Switzerland, where the origin of power is local and communal, could talk of decentralization ever amount to anything more than a political gambit for out-of-office politicians. Only in Switzerland, where social and political pressures are kept at a minimum, could Maurrassian ideas be sensibly adapted and, losing their pungency but none of their essentials, turn into ideals of culture and service which do not exist simply on an imaginary plane.

But Portugal does share one trait with Switzerland: whereas in every other case the nationalist groups began by adopting an idea from outside, Salazar and Regamey developed their ideas by themselves. Maurras was welcomed, as one always welcomes confirmation of one's thought, and he was used; but the essentials would have been there without him. Hence the superior adaptability, the closer correspondence with immediate needs, and the greater capacity for empirical adjustment which others, too insistently theorist, lacked almost entirely.

But, when all this is said, it means no more than that the influence of the Action Française was modified by the minds of men on which it was exercised, by the circumstances of its introduction, and by the changing times, which brought new social and political problems for men of Maurrassian grounding to grapple with. That a variety of situations resulted in a variety of solutions, and that the same situation should bring different reactions from Maurrassism filtered through different minds, need hardly surprise us. And we shall see later how the variety of Maurrassian vehicles and voices merely increased the scope of the doctrine.

If, as Gonzague de Reynold declares,[45] Maurras crystallized the anxiety of a whole generation and made it a diagnostic, then the prescription that followed differed not only from case to case but, as often happens, from one physician to another. Nonetheless, the medical school left its mark on all its students, however varied their practices might be.

28

THE PRINTED WORD

BEGINNING WITH PRE-1914 PUBLICATIONS like the *Revue critique* and Jean-Marc Bernard's *Guêpes,* ideas of the Action Française readily found expression in journals, pamphlets, and reviews derived more or less directly from the parent magazine. Some of these were chiefly literary, like Pierre d'Espezel's *Cahiers de la République des lettres,* Jacques Raynaud's *Muses* and *Latinité,* and Pierre Pascal's *Eurydice*; others, like *Cérès,* published by the glovemakers of Millau (Aveyron), were traditionalist and local; and still others, like René Hener's *Cahiers de points et contrepoints* and René de Planhol's *Nouvelle Lanterne,* were small literary and political periodicals created mainly to allow the founder to express his own views.[a]

Whether they proclaimed it openly or not, more general reviews—the *Gazette française,* the *Pensée française,* the *Révolution du siècle,* and even, especially after 1926, *Charivari*—were soaked in an Action Française solution, and were recognized, if not always by their readers, at least by their contributors, and by those in the know, as being under Maurras's influence. Several major publications among the many lesser ones made an important contribution in interpreting the thought of the Action Française and carrying it into circles much wider than those touched by the books and publications that openly professed allegiance. In this class should be placed the *Revue universelle, Candide,* and *Je suis partout,* and two *sui generis* periodicals, *Combat* and *L'Insurgé.* The first two in date of founding, the *Revue universelle* and *Candide,* were also the most sedate and broadly influential, as well as the closest editorially to the Action Française.

On July 19, 1919, *Le Figaro,* and several other papers, printed the Manifesto of the Parti de l'Intelligence, which proposed the organization of an intellectual defense of the humanistic, Christian West against intellectual Bolshe-

[a] This did not necessarily mean a short life. Planhol, who brought out his monthly in 1927, after losing his job as court reporter for *L'Echo de Paris* over the Philippe Daudet affair, kept the *Nouvelle Lanterne* afloat for ten years. In other instances, the same enterprise survived under a variety of titles. This was notably the case of *Réaction pour l'ordre,* which Jean de Fabrègues brought out in 1930, and whose manifesto was signed, among others, by Robert Buron, future minister of the MRP and of de Gaulle. Catholic, corporatist, and strongly tinged with Maurrassism, the team of *Réaction,* which included Bernanos, Pierre Lucius, Thierry Maulnier, and René Vincent, passed almost en bloc to the *Revue du siècle* when it was founded in 1933, and then, in 1934, to the *Revue du XX*[e] *siècle.*

vism. "Dans cette grande réforme sociale qu'on nous prépare, c'est un attentat contre la culture qui s'apprête." Since modern industrialism ignored moral realities, not simply material reform was important, but the reform of man's spiritual being.

The document, drawn up by Henri Massis, called for the enlivening of French public spirit by means of an intellectual federation of Europe and the world under the aegis of victorious France, the guardian of all civilization. As the work of a young man who before the war had been an interested but skeptical observer of the Action Française, the Manifesto contained some remarkably Maurrassian statements that seemed to bear out Jacques Rivière's opinion that "le parti de l'intelligence c'est, camouflée pour la circonstance, l'éternelle Action Française."[1] "Believers, we hold the Catholic Church to be the only legitimate moral power; unbelievers, we judge its alliance to be indispensable." The poor and powerless were mentioned with paternal concern as in need of defense against plutocracy, "which presents itself as the party of ignorance"; and the document, which, Massis wrote later, plainly followed the Maurrassian idea of an organizing empiricism, concluded: "*Le parti de l'intelligence,* c'est celui que nous prétendons servir pour l'opposer [au] bolchevisme."[b]

The Manifesto met with great success and was endorsed by an impressive cross section of the conservative intelligentsia. When a carper in the *Pays* objected that no country had the kind of intellectual monopoly or supremacy Massis assumed, *Paris-Midi* retorted "No! no! M——, do not blaspheme the eternal supremacy of French thought!" and the *Action française* pointed out the objection as a clear instance of what separates patriots from left-wing intellectuals: the latter had no confidence in the fatherland.[2] In addition to the expected signatures of the Action Française contingent, endorsements by Juliette Adam, Pierre Benoît, Gaston Baty, Maurice Denis, Joachim Gasquet, Henry Ghéon, Daniel Halévy, Francis Jammes, Edmond Jaloux, Louis Le Cardonnel, Guy de Lamarzelle, Camille Mauclair, Jean Psichari, Joseph de Pesquidoux, Firmin Roz, René Salomé, and Jean-Louis Vaudoyer were proof that many others lacked no such confidence at all.

Then, Massis told the Eighth Action Française Congress two years later, came the idea of sounding out, beyond the ranks of acknowledged royalists, a "second zone"—"dans des milieux fort bien préparés par eux-mêmes." Money was found (or most of it) when Maurras and Jacques Maritain diverted to the new publication a portion of the million francs left to them on the death of the rich royalist Pierre Villard. Other contributions were collected from some of the signers of the 1919 Manifesto, which, in perspective, "apparaît maintenant comme l'appel où se comptèrent les troupes de la future *Revue universelle*."[3] On April 1, 1920, the first number of the *Revue* appeared, with

[b] Massis, *Maurras et notre temps* (1961), p. 95, explains that, of course, he did not mean to found a political party, but to take sides with "intelligence" ("prendre parti pour").

Bainville as publisher and Massis as editor. Its orientation, eclectic but definite, was reflected in the table of contents, which listed, in this order, articles by Cardinal Mercier, Maurras, Maurois, Cochin, and that strange, mystical Catholic Emile Baumann; and in the program, which, emphasizing the inspiration of the Manifesto, called right-wing intellectuals to arms. Against the international of revolution, the *Revue universelle* proposed to gather all "who took sides against destruction."

By 1921, the new review had established itself as a serious periodical. It reached some 5,000 subscribers, a good many of whom had been won away from other publications of the same complexion, notably from the *Correspondant,* and it was generally looked upon as one of the most significant publications of the Catholic Right.[4] Maritain, the editor of the philosophy section, resigned after the 1926 condemnation, but aside from that the review was little touched by religious questions. By the 'thirties the circulation had grown to around 9,000, a quite respectable figure for a serious monthly.

The *Revue universelle* opened a window onto England which most other nationalist publications tended to ignore, printing translations from English authors as well as critical discussions of them. But its selections reflected its tastes: apart from a solitary appearance by D. H. Lawrence it favored G. K. Chesterton, Kipling, and Hilaire Belloc. The sections devoted to literature, art, and philosophy, edited by Daudet, Maulnier, André Rousseaux, and Brasillach, were often brilliant; the political articles, as might be expected, reflected the views of the Action Française. The cover of one number (July 15, 1938) chosen at random lists eighteen names, of which only six are not obviously connected with the royalists. The contributors numbered not only Charles Benoist, regularly (and, after his death in 1936, Marie de Roux and Havard de la Montagne) but all the other chief figures of integral nationalism —Johannet, Valois, Bacconier, Pierre-Antoine Cousteau, Gaudy, Gustave Thibon, Gaxotte, Roy, Gonzague de Reynold, and, after 1941, Pierre Boutang and Raoul Girardet.

Occasionally anti-Semitic and always chauvinist,[5] the *Revue universelle* was naturally sympathetic to Mussolini and to the "moderate legalism" of Fascism, which, at least by 1933, it hoped France might be persuaded to adopt.[6] It publicized the horrors of Red terror in Bolshevik and atheistic Spain,[7] and warned against plans of Hitlerite expansion, publishing in 1934, at the particular request of Daudet and Maurras, the alarming impressions brought back by the Comtesse de Dreux-Brézé from a stay with Austrians who turned out to be Nazis.[8] But by 1937 the tone of the *Revue universelle,* like that of the *Action française,* had become one of pessimistic isolationism, and when Brasillach returned from Nürnberg drunk with the romance and *strangeness* of what he described as "the new religion" of National-Socialism, he was rather quickly dropped.[9] The *Revue universelle* was steadfastly anti-German. After 1941, when it reappeared at Vichy under government subsidy, it became increasingly Catholic[10] and increasingly "*Maréchaliste,*" sometimes violent against the troublemakers of the Resistance. It ceased publication in August 1944 with an appeal to support Pétain's sole and supreme authority, its members uncompromised by any truck with Germans.

A similar but less sedate career, and a much wider public, were enjoyed by *Candide,* which was started when, after a few years of publishing the *Revue universelle,* Bainville persuaded his friend Arthème Fayard to publish a weekly directed toward a similar public but in a somewhat less serious, less long-winded way.[11] The first number, in March 1924, featured contributions by Paul Morand, Sacha Guitry, René Boylesve, René Benjamin, Claude Farrère, and Tristan Bernard: clearly not weightiness but sophistication was to be the tone. Throughout its twenty-year history, *Candide* was distinguished both by its light touch and by its high literary quality. Readers were wooed with big names—Bordeaux, Maurice Dekobra, Henry de Montherlant, Thibaudet, Jules Romains, Georges Mandel, and Francis de Miomandre—and were evidently pleased, for the circulation, which was 80,000 the first year, had reached about 600,000 ten years later and remained steady for the next decade.[12]

Regular writers for the *Action française* were often welcomed in *Candide.* Lucien Dubech was the drama critic for both papers, and Bainville contributed a weekly political commentary, although it was printed unsigned until a few months before his death. Gaxotte, Blond, René Bizet, Rousseaux, Manouvriez, Johannet, Bernard de Vaulx, Louis Bertrand, Dr. Charles Fiessinger, and Dominique Sordet appeared frequently in its pages. Never "monarchist," the weekly specialized from the beginning in satirizing the Republic and other pet aversions. Short stories and a regular column by Pierre Veber mocked Parliament and the government in general.[13] Although the cartoons to which the back page was devoted came largely from English and American publications, particularly from *Punch,* the political cartoons throughout the paper were not only anti-Communist, anti-Socialist, anti-Radical, and sometimes anti-French,[c] but often, and increasingly, as time went on, anti-Semitic.

Over the years, anti-Semitism, which had started mildly enough, combined with xenophobia to become a pervasive attitude, more effective for being less blatant than that of some of the frankly political publications. Bankers in short stories usually bore Jewish names;[14] foreigners, unless they were gentlemen or Fascists,[15] were dangerous; "Jeunes filles, n'aimez que les hommes de votre pays!" warned Veber, appalled by the number of "petites Françaises massacrées par leurs amants métèques." Reviewing the revival of *Retour de Jérusalem,* written by Maurice Donnay when he was close to the Ligue de la Patrie Française, Dubech reminded his readers that the anti-Dreyfusard con-

[c] G. Tabouis, *Vingt Ans de suspense diplomatique,* p. 130, mentions that the *Candide* of November 2, 1932, sold with great success in all departments of the League of Nations, although its front-page cartoon showed a skinny Marianne placing a vast funeral wreath on a gravestone marked "victory."

clusions of the play were still valid: where the Jew has been, "order and morality are disturbed and anarchy spontaneously appears."[16] It was not surprising that after Hitler's coming to power in Germany, *Candide* objected to the refugees who sought to flee to France. Georges Imann chided the French State for the foolish naïveté that let in the dregs of German Jewry to set up a "Chanaan sur Seine." P.-A. Cousteau exposed the danger of foreigners and Jews in the Faculty of Law and championed the "anti-*métèque*" campaigns at the Sorbonne. Dr. Paul Guérin, not yet an avowed Nazi, predicted the difficulties the French medical profession would face as a result of the foreign influx. Lucien Rebatet contributed a poisonous article on those who fled the Saar after the Nazi victory in the Plebiscite.[17]

Candide presented its readers a deplorable picture—of mounting crime, political and social disorder, threats against property, capital, savings, even against their personal safety. It denounced public school teachers—"apôtres du désordre et du bolchevisme" carrying on propaganda among their helpless charges—as well as the ineffective Parliamentary system, the weak-kneed muddles of most governments in power, and the efforts that were being made to abolish armed nationalist leagues.[18] By 1938, although the articles on Germany were aimed at intensifying public dislike, suspicion, and fear of the neighboring ogre, the review had reached a firm policy of agreement with what we now know as the party of Munich; and though, as we have seen, it accepted the war with less constraint than the Action Française, it accepted Pétain, the "symbol of salvation," from the very first.[19]

The first issue in exile was printed in Clermont-Ferrand on June 12, 1940; after a three-week break, the journal appeared regularly for the next four years. Despite occasional tributes to members of the royal family, and especially to the Duc d'Orléans for so perspicaciously denouncing anonymous and vagabond Jewish wealth,[20] *Candide* had not been royalist. But it had been Maurrassian, and its leading political commentators (Gaxotte had stepped into Bainville's place after the latter's death) drew their inspiration from Maurras. There had been bouquets for the old royalist's wisdom,[21] and Maurras himself (though less often than Daudet) had written articles from time to time.[22] With the defeat, however, *Candide* pointed out that Maurras was the one man who had seen clearly all along,[23] and henceforth he was a frequent contributor.

Increasingly anti-Semitic, anti-métèque, and anti-Masonic, *Candide* stood equally against Communism and against the horrors of democratic and republican parliamentary government; it inveighed against rich Jews who were regularly displaying their wealth in the Occupied Zone, and it warned against the dangers of the "Judeo-Russo-English" alliance, which could mobilize the enormous resources of Anglo-Jewish wealth in the service of a secret anarchist movement that aimed to conquer the world. It also campaigned to change street names from those of the republican mythology to those of more edifying patrons like Marshal Fayolle, Paul Bourget, and Pierre de Nolhac, although it refrained from violent criticism of the Resistance.[24]

This was not the case of *Je suis partout,* which was founded in 1930 as a weekly review of international news and comment. In view of later developments, it is worth mentioning that the original purpose of the magazine launched by Fayard under Gaxotte supervision was not explicitly polemical and was far from anti-Semitic. Indeed, the first man to be considered as editor was a Jew, André Levinsohn, the dance critic of *Candide,* who, as it turned out, became editor of British affairs instead. The first number, lyrically welcomed by Léon Daudet,[25] appeared on November 29, 1930, with Gaxotte and Pierre Villette (Dorsay) as front-page editors and with contributions from several writers of quite another feather like Camille Mallarmé, Miguel Zamacois, and the well-known anti-Fascist Benjamin Crémieux, whose left-wing sympathies seemed to promise a balanced editorial policy.[d]

Gradually, however, *Je suis partout* became the home of an extremely active group of young Action Française *epigoni* gathered around Gaxotte and, later, when the historian proved too slow, around Brasillach. The most important of these were Maurice Bardèche, Cousteau, François Dauture (H. Lèbre), Pierre Daye, Paul Guérin, Claude Jeantet, Alain Laubreaux, Jean Meillonas (C. Fégy), André Nicolas, Jacques Perret, Georges Roux, Claude Roy, and Lucien Rebatet. Of the contributors, four (Gaxotte, Rebatet, Louis Michaut, and Bernard de Vaulx) had at one time or another served as secretaries to Maurras; and two, Ralph Soupault and Hermann-Paul, were among the most brilliantly vicious cartoonists in France.

Beginning in 1933, *Je suis partout* became more and more anti-Semitic, and by 1934 it was openly and deliberately so, although it still accepted advertisements for Dr. Magnus Hirschfeld's "Titus Pills" against impotence, senility, and sexual decay, with their explicit illustrations.[e] Its well-informed and well-written foreign and political pages pointed out the advantage of better understanding between Germany and France, the successes of Italian Fascism, and the dangers of Bolshevik corruption. A typical number, chosen at random (August 17, 1935), featured the following titles: page 1: "Il faut rompre l'alliance russe," "Les instituteurs révolutionnaires contre la nation"; page 3: "Il est encore temps . . . mais tout juste"; page 4: "Le mouvement d'Action Française" (review); page 5: "L'humour italien et le conflit abyssin"; page 6: (Bourse et finances) "L'oeuvre de protection de l'épargne n'est pas achevée"; page 7: (Germany) "Grande enquête par Henri Claudet—Un français moyen à la découverte de l'Allemagne hitlérienne: La question juive"; page 9: (U.S.A.) "Grand reportage par P.-A. Cousteau—Les Gangsters," which con-

[d] On May 30, 1931, *JSP* published excerpts from André Maurois's forthcoming life of Lyautey. Maurois's signature appeared in many "rightist" publications, from *Réaction* to *Courrier royal.*

[e] Other faithful advertisers were Persil, Byrrh, and the Samaritaine.

cludes: "American immigration regulations may stop honest Scandinavian farmers, but not Italian anti-Fascists, the Judeo-Marxists of whom Germany has rid itself, and the refuse of Mediterranean thievery. That is the true American tragedy."

Apparently this fare was not enough to attract the reading public, and on May 9, 1936, the journal, whose circulation had not managed to top 100,000 but stagnated at around 80,000 or so, sadly announced that financial problems no longer permitted the continuation of the publication, which had been carried on so far to serve the national cause, but which had not been helped by election results. The following week, however, *Je suis partout* made a new announcement: it would not go under after all. Its staff had given up one-third of their salaries to help out, and "friends had come to its aid during the reorganization period."[26]

The details of the operation that saved the life of the weekly are not entirely clear, but the outline can be traced. In 1936 *Je suis partout* was owned by the Fayard family (Arthème and then Jean Fayard, and the latter's brother-in-law Fernand Brouty), who wanted to get rid of it, partly for political reasons (they did not like its increasingly pro-German tone), and partly because they wanted to concentrate on *Candide,* which was doing well.[27] Their shares were taken over by three persons, though not, apparently, all at once: André Nicolas, a wealthy Lyon industrialist and an admirer of Maurras; Charles Lesca, another friend of Maurras, who had inherited a South American meat-packing fortune; and the great Paris printer Georges Lang, an Alsatian Jew of royalist sympathies who was married to a Catholic.[28]

Both Nicolas, who took 40 per cent of the shares, and Lang, who took 20 per cent, were favorable to the Comte de Paris and had hopes of making *Je suis partout* a royalist publication. The review had hinted at royalist sympathies before this,[29] but now, with royalists holding a majority of the shares, its line could be more firm. Nicolas, however, along with Lesca, was a Maurrassian more than a royalist, and with relations between the rue du Boccador and the Manoir d'Anjou almost at a breaking point, the two men were hardly inclined to hand the Pretender a tribune of his own. Actually, the new owners had very little control over policy, and the energetic editorial staff, now free of financial worry, was already going ahead with an out-and-out Nazi and anti-Semitic line.[f]

The growing excesses of what one contributor to the *Action française* described as the gang of *Je suis partout* alarmed and angered most integral nationalists. Both José Le Boucher and Colonel Larpent, warned Maurras, "ils

[f] An attempt was made in 1938, under the influence of the Comte de Paris, to combine Lang's and Nicolas's shares against Lesca and change the direction of the paper both in ideology and in fact, but it failed. Nicolas held on to his shares until 1940, when he sold them to Jeantet. Lang, who had ignored royal advice to withdraw in 1938, also ceded his shares about this time, thus ending the paradoxical situation of a Jewish shareholder in France's most virulent anti-Semitic publication of the 'thirties.

vous débordent, ils vous échappent," but Maurras would not admit that he himself was being left behind. Early in 1938 the *Action française* still offered support and sympathy,[30] and in the Munich crisis they fought side by side. According to an old militant, it was Georges Bonnet himself who provided *Je suis partout* with funds for a special number to be sent to all the mayors and vicars in France. History does not record what Bonnet thought of Cousteau's advice, after Czechoslovakia had been traded away for a skimpy pottage of peace, that the next thing to do was to destroy democracy in France.[g] Even after January 1939, when Gaxotte at last severed connections with a review whose tone he and his friends now thought excessive,[31] Brasillach lauded his master, "Maurras, c'est la Paix!" and Daudet in the *Action française* referred to *Je suis partout* as "our brother in arms."[32]

The war somewhat altered the Nazi line, but it did not affect the success of a publication that had by now built itself a solid corner in the Areopagus of nationalist reviews. By May 1940, three hundred soldiers' clubs subscribed to it and two hundred others had applied for subscriptions. In spite of the denunciations thundered by Kerillis in *L'Epoque,* its readers seem to have considered it "décidément un journal pour vrais mobilisés."[33] That French Intelligence services did not concur appeared when, on June 3, 1940, with French troops in full retreat, Lesca and Laubreaux were arrested for intelligence with the enemy and Rebatet was detained for questioning. While the *Action française* protested against the injustice of the move, Pierre Varillon, Pierre Lucius, and Maulnier brought out one last issue of *Je suis partout,*[h] which contained not a word about the arrest of their colleagues.

When the new *Je suis partout* appeared in Paris on February 7, 1941, connection with the Action Française had been shed: the Comte de Paris was now nothing but a "comte bloqué," and the national-socialist tendencies of prewar years were freely expressed in unreserved support of the new and revolutionary German order. In two long articles in May 1941, Abel Bonnard invited reactionaries like him to throw off their immobility, to reject their old notions of an endless struggle between France and Germany, to abandon their petulant isolationism and their pursuit of impossible causes (a reference to royalism), and to be grateful for the fact that what they had been unable to do in prewar France (ridding the country of Jews, for example) was now being accomplished throughout Europe. For the first time, pleaded Bonnard, once a good friend of the Action Française, reactionaries had a chance to be really affirma-

[g] Henry Jamet, personal communication; *JSP,* Sept. 23, 1938. Jamet and his able and enterprising wife were responsible for organizing a lecture series called "Rive Gauche," which afforded speakers from *Je suis partout* an opportunity to air their opinions and to meet those who were uncommitted but perhaps sympathetic. In 1937–38, the program of Rive Gauche featured the names of Montherlant, Henriot, Paul Creyssel, Tixier-Vignancour, Marc Chadourne, Maurras, Abetz, Marinetti, Maulnier, Camille Fegy, Benda, Robert Vallery-Radot, Helsey and A. t'Serstevens, Massis, Bertrand de Jouvenel, Gaxotte, Brasillach, Blond, Jeantet, Cousteau, Rebatet, Charles Plisnier, Mme Janine-Weill, Louis Hourticq, Martial-Piéchaud, Ghéon, Francis Poulenc, Dubech.

[h] *JSP,* June 7, 1940. These "traitors to friendship" were denounced in the first number of *Je suis partout* published under the Occupation.

tive rather than contradictory, to act in the direction of the future, to be carried by the current of history, not rejected by it. But for this they must first break off from those "who remain stuck in the cramped, grimacing positions of the past": "Il ne s'agit plus de s'enfermer dans un fanatisme étroit et pur. Un monde se fait, et il faut en être."[34]

This appeal—or challenge—to the Action Française and to its Vichy friends marked the open break. Maurras never saw Bonnard again, nor any of the staff of *Je suis partout.* Although it pretended for some time longer to be close to the Action Française,[35] a pretense that deceived many in the Occupied Zone, who were unaware of Maurras's disavowals, *Je suis partout* now had free rein. Massis became a "revanchard de couloirs ministériels et de salons académiques," Benjamin "un va-t'en guerre, un prussophobe maniaque," Maulnier "an Englishman." Cousteau reviled "les synarques paternalistes et les badernes revanchardes qui ont noyé la Révolution nationale dans un flot de rhétorique vertueuse," but Maurras himself was never denounced by name.[36]

In September 1943, when German fortunes had begun to wane, the staff, united in support of a new order which, as Cousteau said, was only the application of what they always thought,[37] became divided on the question of whether German war communiqués should be embellished as the Germans demanded. Blond, Brasillach, and Dorsay, who had opposed *bourrage de crâne* in 1939 and 1940, continued to object to it in 1943; Lesca and Jeantet, now the owners of the weekly, accused them of defeatism. Brasillach, who but a month before had written, "Je suis germanophile et Français, Français plus que national-socialiste, pour le dire," and had called for a Franco-German entente, refused to cooperate in fooling a public which, he knew, could not be fooled anyway, left *Je suis partout,* and henceforth confined his writing to the new *Chronique de Paris* and to Jean Fontenoy's "Doriotist" and "social" *Révolution nationale.*[38]

This break was not, of course, the result of any fundamental political disagreement. Brasillach, who in 1941 had wanted resistants treated with utmost ruthlessness, whether they were terrorists, distributors of tracts, or "*grands bourgeois* who cut up Métro tickets into the shape of a cross of Lorraine," continued in this vein to the end. Nor did his sympathy for Germany diminish: the defeat had thrown the French and Germans into each other's arms. There was no way in which this could, no reason why it should, be undone. In January 1944 he expressed his sentiments in a significant comment: "Les Français de quelque reflexion durant ces années, auront plus ou moins couché avec l'Allemagne, non sans querelles, et le souvenir leur en restera doux."[39]

With all this, as Rebatet declared, the hope of France, as of *Je suis partout,* was Fascist.[i] The bourgeoisie was almost as loathsome as "terrorists" or Jews.[40] As for the latter, their mass extermination was hopefully demanded.[41] Like Brasillach, Cousteau, who became editor in 1943, had found the embrace of Germany sweet: "We feel solidarity with Germany, whose soldiers constitute

[i] *JSP,* Sept. 10, 1943. The number bearing a headline to this effect was in print when news arrived of Premier Badoglio's request for an armistice.

the last protective rampart of civilized Europe," wrote the man who wanted one hundred Jews picked at random to be executed for every militiaman killed by the Resistance.[42] And as Allied troops rushed toward Paris, Rebatet called for loyalty to National-Socialism,[j] and Lesca joined Doriot and Déat to proclaim "The union of revolutionaries, hope of France."[43]

One might be justified in saying that by this time the men who five years earlier had still agreed with Laubreaux that they had arrived at their opinions thanks to Maurras, Bainville, and Gaxotte,[44] had gone a long way beyond their masters. This is perfectly true, but it would at the same time be wrong to underestimate the influence of those masters. French Fascists had to refer to Maurras, if only, like Lucien Combelle, to deny him.[45] The fairest judgment seems that of the Belgian Robert Poulet, looking back on those exciting years from the cushioned comfort of the *Parisienne*.[46] The masters of French Fascist youth, he writes, were La Tour du Pin, Sorel, and Maurras. The first was reasonable, but old-fashioned; the second was vigorously realistic in his thinking, but contradictory and imprecise in his formulas:

> Pour en finir, nous acceptions les principes généraux dégagés par l'école d'Action française; nous les acceptions sous la forme suivante: "C'est, *grosso modo,* dans cette direction qu'il faut marcher. Et d'un bon pas: assez allègrement pour que les hobereaux fatigués, les traîneurs de sabres, les manieurs d'argent et les bonnes jeunes gens de patronage soient semés sur la route." Le premier point était de reprendre et de garder le contact du peuple.

Maurras, between the wars, had enlisted these young men on a crusade which, earnest in concept, was in fact a great romantic adventure, a children's crusade. He had tamed them a little, he had taught them some things, he had endowed them with a revolution of their own—that of counterrevolution. Now they were fulfilling what they thought they had derived from him, carrying his teachings to what seemed to them their logical conclusion when actually it was only one of several possible conclusions. No wonder they were as disillusioned in him as he was in them; no wonder they felt like the angry disciples in Browning's "Lost Leader":

> We that had loved him so, followed him, honored him,
> Lived in his mild and magnificent eye,
> Learned his great language, caught his clear accents,
> Made him our pattern to live and to die!

let down and alone:

> We shall march prospering—not through his presence;
> Songs may inspirit us—not from his lyre;
> Deeds will be done—while he boasts his quiescence,
> Still bidding crouch whom the rest bade aspire . . .

[j] *JSP,* July 28, 1944. This resulted in brief suspension of the review by the Germans at Laval's request.

To understand more easily how such a parting of the ways should have occurred, we must turn back to two publications that never knew either the success of *Candide* or the notoriety of *Je suis partout*—*L'Insurgé* and *Combat*. The first, a "political and social weekly," began publication on January 13, 1937, financed, apparently, by Jacques Lemaigre-Dubreuil, of Cagoule fame and Huiles Lesieur fortune, who was involved in a good many adventures until his murder in Morocco after the war. Maxence and Maulnier were joint editors, and under them was a young, energetic, and clever staff—Haedens, Blond, Maurice Blanchot, François Gravier, Jean Héritier, Louis Salleron, Maurice-Yvan Sicard, and, as the jazz expert, Hugues Panassié. Among the contributors to the review during its short life of ten months, there was a striking number with social and corporatist interests: André Voisin and Max Graincourt of the royalist Métiers Français, Jean Fontenoy and Sicard of the PPF, Paul Specklin of the Peasant Unions, Henri Lauridan, who had been a member of the French delegation to the 1922 Congress of the Communist International in Moscow, Jean Loisy, Salleron, and Serge Jeanneret, the last three active and rising in corporatist circles.

L'Insurgé represented the most deliberate nationalist attempt before the Second World War to appeal to workers as well as to the middle classes. Anti-Semitic, anti-democratic, more xenophobic than chauvinistic, it quoted Edouard Drumont and Jules Vallès in its first number, later Proudhon. Its friends were the Fascist-style activists of the moment—Henri Dorgères, Léon Degrelle, Darquier de Pellepoix; its enemies—politicians, trusts, and the petty bourgeoisie, all as cowardly as they were rotten. "L'avenir, on ne l'espère pas, on le fait," Maulnier wrote; and Dominique Bertin, "Nous voulons des agitateurs." *L'Insurgé,* they said, must find its influence and its expression "in the street." The existing order could not be demolished with theoretical arms: "*L'Insurgé* will devote itself above all to the street, because it will devote itself above all to *agitation*." It will fight the present masters and exploiters of France "on all grounds, by all means, with all arms."[47]

And for what? The aims, amplifying the slogan "National-syndicalists of all France, unite!" were expressed by Bertin: (1) Suppress the proletariat by giving everyone a professional status, property, and a place in the nation. (2) Abolish the dictatorship of money over labor, without putting the State in its place. (3) Make capital the paid servant of labor, instead of continuing to allow labor to be the servant of capital. (4) As the end of capitalism is profit and the end of socialism is the service of a bureaucratic state and an anonymous collectivity, show labor that its end lies in the well-being, happiness, and dignity of the worker. (5) Assure each worker his independence by giving him the intangible right to exercise his trade, to receive full pay for his work, to control his savings, and to enjoy the benefits of technical progress.[48]

This list of aims helps but little to define *L'Insurgé*'s real purpose, however. Even assuming them to be more than extravagant phrases, all that they really amount to is a hope of seasoning corporatism—a moderate, bourgeois plaything as a rule—with a dash of violence. In the pages of the review, nationalism and the quest for social justice were combined. "France is in the thrall of bankers, of foreigners, of England"; "Politiciens, bas les pattes devant le premier Mai, Fête Nationale du Travail!" "No valid nationalism without social justice."[49]

But the unions were infested with Soviet agents, and the political parties were controlled by secret funds and maneuvered by *agents provocateurs*; even the leagues were conservative, without strong doctrine, talking instead of acting as they should.[k] Maxence called upon "insurgents of all parties" to join "the front of a united youth, for bread, grandeur, and freedom, in profound loathing of capitalist democracy."[50] What was to come after insurrection, they dreamed, was an elitist, corporatist state,[51] which, as the last number on October 27, 1937, declared, would reject all of capitalist democracy in the name of a Maurrassian "pays réel."

This was where the extreme violence of the newspaper lapsed into the truer accents of a conservative frame of mind: "L'Etat nouveau doit se fonder sur les réalitiés naturelles du sol, du sang, de l'histoire; une de ses tâches essentielles sera de protéger libéralement mais fermement la race et l'esprit français contre l'envahissement d'éléments étrangers inassimilables et susceptibles de corrompre les caractères nationaux."[52] What is noteworthy here is the idea that French national character is something "given" once and for all, static, and apt to change only for the worse in the sense of corruption. This is not racism, but the same static view of history which refers to "the forty kings who in a thousand years made France," implicitly recognizing an evolution under their regime, but nothing valid thereafter. There could be no real hope of revolution or of effective action, so long as the mentality revealed by such views lay behind the high-mettled language. This was the difficulty that Maulnier recognized and that he and his friends set out to overcome in a doctrinal monthly named *Combat,* whose thirty-seven issues spanned the last three prewar years.

As Maulnier wrote in his influential *Au-delà du nationalisme,* published in 1938,[53] the wish to stabilize in its present form a society that was being driven to change by all the forces of its organic destiny, and the hope of mastering these forces by restoring an order that had been previously defeated by similar forces, were anti-historical and blind. "A new social balance is possible only in so far as it will be different from the old."

But how could this awareness be reconciled with a public which, if it could be persuaded to give up clinging to the old order, would accept a new order only if it were as little different from the old one as possible? *L'Insurgé* tried to do it by inviting the forces of change to accept agitation as a substitute for

[k] The Action Française, which has a clear doctrine and a clear position, says Louis Guesclin, *L'Insurgé,* March 3, 1937, is not a league and is not affected by this criticism.

change. It failed. In the best Maurrassian tradition, the theorists of *Combat* (some of them the same men) attempted to work out *their* answer by intellectual means: "Intelligence," their opening manifesto declared, "must not put itself in the service of the masses, but must inform and lead them; it must not follow the evolution of history, but make it." The proper function of intelligence was "to govern the social world without submitting to it, to dominate without despising it. . . . Before the bankruptcy of idealism, before the threat of materialism, the time has come to restore a new realism."[54]

If these declarations meant anything, it was that far from wooing the dangerous masses with the phony attractions of violent action, those who denied the solutions of left-wing revolution while sensing the problems of which they were the fruit were expressing a new determination to give intellect its due—which was essentially a rephrasing of Maurras's old theme that ideas came first, and then *political* action inspired by an intellectual elite.[l]

But this was not clear at first, and the pages of *Combat* mirror the differences between those who, like Brasillach, sought action above all else and those who, like Maulnier, wanted to "free nationalism from febrile sterility" and define the necessary revolution before embarking upon it.[55] To begin with, however, the confusion between the two aims existed even in the advocates of the latter view: "Pour la subversion nécessaire," Maulnier wrote in February 1936, "les élites du désintéressement se complèteront assez bien par les élites du désespoir. . . . Il y faut les deux violences: c'est à nous de les unir." And in July 1936 Maurice Blanchot praised terrorism as a method of *salut public*: "We are not of those who prefer to avoid a revolution, or refer hypocritically to a peaceful, spiritual revolution. . . . A revolution is necessary."

Within a year, however, the diverse points of view began falling into place. Jean de Fabrègues denounced National-Socialism as a "materialist mystique"; Jean Le Marchand attacked "nationalist barbarism" and the "ridiculous xenophobia of the French petty bourgeoisie"; Blanchot opposed the undiscriminating violence of Fascism; Maulnier himself warned against the diversionary uses of anti-Semitism, "the mask of a reformism as violent as it is ineffective," which ends "by leaving the political organization and the social structure standing, while partially changing their masters."[56]

Thus, the dilemma, unsolved in *L'Insurgé,* answered by commitment to violence in the pages of *Je suis partout,* was being resolved in *Combat* by an open choice against formulas and passions indulged in as a substitute for something more difficult and more effective: thought. "The recourse to Action, to Race, to Blood, to the predestined Leader, to the superior mission of a people, all the suspicious garb of modern nationalism, are nothing more than substitutes for failure of intelligence, man's appeal to the forces of darkness to regain mastery of a world where reason is powerless to help him."[57] Fabrègues,

[l] In March 1936, Blond asserted that no syndical action was possible at the moment by any but political means.

Blanchot, and Maulnier were not *against* Fascism, nationalism, National-Socialism, or anti-Semitism, but only against their use as easy panaceas prescribed for wooden legs. But this was enough to put off Brasillach's friends of *Je suis partout* who cared more for febrility than they did about sterility.

Pol Vandromme was right when he compared Fascism to a cry in the night which promises unknown excitements and untold adventure. For Brasillach, Fascism was not a doctrine but a fevered excitement, "un mouvement non de la raison, mais du sentiment, la recherche d'une atmosphère enfiévrée."[58] In lieu of something solid, it proposed a mood, exaltation, banners, the tingling stimulation of being part of an emotional power-mass, with only the vaguest hint of direction and purpose.

"L'action, l'action, il y a 30 ans que Maurras fait de l'action," Maulnier exclaimed to a Canadian journalist. "As long as he is beside us, we shall be in action, but in the essence of action. . . . *Doctrine* is our true politics."[59] The danger, as Maurras's own evolution showed, was that while disowning action without clear and definite ends, one might insist on the formulation of these ends to the exclusion of action altogether. In this respect, Maulnier's words to the Canadian journalist in the spring of 1940 are revealing. When he was asked whether French youth was ready for the good fight, whether the Action Française had decided the time and the direction of the attack that would implant its ideas and place its men in the seats of power, Maulnier (whose nearsightedness had kept him out of the Army) replied: "The duty of French youth is, above all, to perpetuate tradition, that is, to reintroduce dignity into the life of France by giving intellectual, moral, and spiritual values their true place; it is to believe that cultural values dominate political and economic values which are no more than their application, their tangible reflection." "In that case," the Canadian pursued, "you do not believe in a *revolution* in France?" "Yes, yes, we do," Maulnier answered; "but not in a noisy, blatant revolution, not in a destructive revolution. We believe . . . in the *revolution of the spirit*."[60]

It was this revolution of the spirit that *Combat* was thinking of when it chose to support the National Revolution of Vichy. It is interesting to see how many of its contributors, and especially the hard Maurrassian core, gravitated toward Vichy: Gravier, Salleron, Loisy, Roy, all found their way into its corporatist or propaganda services, and the three editors of *Combat* were among the doctrinal leaders of the regime: Vincent founded *Idées,* Fabrègues *Demain,* and Maulnier, in the *Action française* and the *Revue universelle,* tried to redefine the principles he had asserted over the past few years.

The articles that Maulnier published in 1942 under the title *La France, la guerre et la paix* reflect both the difficulties of such a task and the fundamental causes of the dissension emphasized by the break between Paris and Vichy. There is in Maulnier's writings no sympathy for anti-Semitism, for racism, for foreign myths, for collaboration in itself, or for his erstwhile comrades riding the revolutionary bandwagon in the capital. Faced with the crucial choice, those who had picked Maurras as teacher of revolutionary action abandoned him for the action that they craved. Jean Azéma, the friend of Hérold-Paquis, "violent, bagarreur, Don Quichotte du royalisme, puis du nationalisme le plus intransigeant," and ex-Camelot Robert Jullien-Courtine, both of whom had left the Action Française in the 'thirties for more exciting fields, ended by broadcasting on the ironically named Radio-Patrie at Baden-Baden; Jacques de Bernonville became one of Darnand's lieutenants, and Darnand himself an auxiliary of the Gestapo and the Waffen-SS. Like Pierre de Boisdeffre's hero in *Les Fins dernières,* "De ce que j'écrivais dans *l'Action,* je me foutais pas mal. La révolte me suffisait."[61]

But those who appreciated Maurras's lucidity stuck with the principles, which counted more than deeds. "The salvation of France is not to be found in National-Socialism or in Fascism," Maulnier wrote, "but in *its own* national revolution. A national revolution that comes from abroad is a contradiction in terms, and Frenchmen who, in the Occupied Zone, are trying to carry out this revolution according to foreign principles are coming up against this insoluble contradiction."[62] Maulnier himself had taken his stand quite a long time before. In an article written in 1935 and published the following year, an article expressing ideas similar to those that Bertrand de Jouvenel later developed in two works, *Power* and *Sovereignty,* he explained very clearly why Fascism was not the answer to French problems, or not, at any rate, an answer that a Maurrassian could accept.

Fascism, wrote the young Maulnier, is the logical conclusion of the democratic principle of mass sovereignty. The idea that all legitimate power stems from the collectivity justifies all oppressions because it implies that the individual, when he obeys, obeys only himself. Fascism, born of democracy, remains democratic in that it substitutes for real liberties (consisting of an autonomous realm, respected and guaranteed) the idea of a part of sovereignty and glory, of an active participation in the collective destiny, whether expressed by votes or by some plebiscitary means. To the principle of a political and social community which Fascism raises up against the present anarchy, another principle must be opposed—that of political and social *liberties,* affirmed and defended by the institutions themselves. Man's participation in the material and spiritual destiny of his group, which Fascism confuses with the exercise of personal activity, must be separated anew from this kind of gratuitous pretense. "To totalitarian societies, built on continuous exchanges between man and collectivity, man giving society everything and expecting everything from it, we must oppose a dualistic society, in which State and individual will be, in their respective activities, independent, protected, and respectively guaranteed."[63]

For those alarmed by collectivism, Fascism appeared as its epitome. For those concerned with stable and enduring order, Fascism (especially in

France) appeared as its contradiction. Fascism was the opposite of order: it was not a discipline but a force, not a hierarchy but a revolution, not the rule of an elite surrounding the king but that of a climate of opinion around a charismatic leader. Maurras had proposed revolution against what seemed to him the anarchy of the established order; he had attracted those who rebelled against the established order itself and against all its beneficiaries. It was a grave misunderstanding.

But what, then, did Maulnier have to offer in place of the collectivistic doctrines of the Left or Right which he was adept at criticizing? His collaborationist friends had chosen a revolution of deeds; he chose one of words, less harmful, but also less effective than theirs. Too clearsighted to make the same mistakes as they, he was nonetheless isolated, like his master Maurras, on an analytic promontory, high above the reality that he had hoped to grasp. France, he said, must react to foreign challenges not by imitation but by finding its own way according to its peculiar nature and traditions. It must avoid the errors of democracy and collectivism, of vulgar capitalism and nationalism. French civilization was in its principle aristocratic, as the historical vocation of France was an aristocratic one. The hope of man lay not in the cult of production, of society, of work, but in that of higher and more important things which would enable him to be himself, to live and think as he should."[illegible]

Whatever we may think of these views, which were more or less typical of the faithful Maurrassian core, it is clear that there was little about them that could serve as a basis for a working policy in any country that was not completely isolated. And if old comrades in Paris had been much given to looking back, they could have reminded François Gravier, a loyal follower of Pétain, of his words in *Combat* of December 1937: "The will to Revolution has been deflected toward the putrid marshes of the old Right. What in 1937 is generally known as nationalism, is a capitalism with a Boulangist superstructure." The reasons for struggling, Gravier had then complained, had been stifled beneath all sorts of inhibitions about honor. But, one could well remark in 1943 or 1944, these men had long forgotten any reason for struggling, except the most purely intellectual, and this condemned them to ineffectiveness.

29

THE CREED, THE VASSALS, AND THE THRALLS

ONE MAY WELL ASK HOW A MOVEMENT whose history abounds in failures and frustrations could have been so influential in such wide areas of opinion, literature, and politics, not only in France but in neighboring countries as well. That it was can by this point, it would seem, hardly be gainsaid. In 1927, one of its staunch enemies who today confesses appreciation of its ideas and its role explained to his friends that the failures the Action Française encountered in political *practice* should not lead them to underrate its constant gains in the realm of political *thought.* "It would be difficult," wrote Georges Bidault, "to exaggerate these advances; the attitude of important sections of opinion, especially Catholic opinion, on international questions is often incontestably the conscious or unconscious copy of the Action Française attitude. Thus Maurras's success, which will never take the form of his coming to power, will be realized under another aspect, by the conquest of ever more numerous minds." And, looking back from quite another perspective, fourteen years later, another Catholic intellectual, Yves Simon, asserted that one could never sufficiently insist upon the part the Action Française played in the political life of contemporary France: it dominated—indeed, sometimes it was—the political horizon of French intellectuals.[1]

Between the two wars, every sort of observer backed up this view. Acute republican observers like Roger Martin du Gard and Alphonse Séché acknowledged Maurras's part in forging the political outlook of men who had been youths in 1912 and 1914. Before the 'twenties were over a hostile critic had declared:

> the Action Française has drained to its profit all the forces that should be marshaled in the service of the Pope and of legitimate authority . . . all the right-wing press, even great popular newspapers, are more or less imbued with its spirit and more or less accept its theses. . . . Even where the Action Française has not been able to implant its monarchist doctrine, it has created, in the conservative world, a common way of thinking. And the circumstances of our political life are such that its influence is felt as far as the ranks of national radicals, perhaps even farther afield.

More than a decade later, in 1938, a writer in the *NRF* made use of the identical phrase: "l'Action Française a drainé les plus ardents des patriotes."[2]

Enemies—enemies all: republicans, Catholics, socialists, heads of the Sûreté, collaborators—before the bar they could agree on the influence of the newspaper and of its theorists. Regretfully, resentfully, they admitted the extent of the influence—all the right-wing press, according to Charles André; all the critical publications, said Ducloux; the schools and the professions, said Tissier; "tous les grands corps publics," said Guéhenno: "Generals, judges, ambassadors, they served the Republic, of course, but they despised it."[3]

This last had been true enough before Maurras came; but until then the declining upper classes had felt that they were fighting against historical laws which they could not hold back any more than they could hold back the tides. The *ralliement* had been the symbol not of conversion but of acceptance of what seemed an inexorable fate. Maurras's intervention provided intellectual reassurance that time and tide could be challenged. The Action Française doctrine of reaction presented this as a healthy and natural phenomenon with hopeful implications. Against an apparently relentless historical progress, it raised the arguments of equally relentless logic, pointing necessity the other way. Maurras's arguments may not have seemed convincing to those who did not need them, but for those who had lost hope they came as a refreshing breeze. Against the arguments of historical inevitability and economic determinism, they now could pit necessities and arguments of their own.

The influence was first of all a literary one, but literature is not an isolated field; in France, especially, it is a way of life. Thus, to say that many of the literary greats and even more of the lesser greats were at one time or another fascinated by Maurras is to establish one of the royal roads by which the Action Française invaded the republican citadel.

When, after the First World War, the *Revue hebdomadaire* asked of promising young writers (among them Carco, Béraud, Dorgelès, MacOrlan, Maurois, and Tristan Derème) the question "who are the great contemporary French writers who have influenced you most, in whom you recognize your masters?" three names were offered with striking regularity—Maurras, Bourget, and Barrès.[4] Two years later, when young Belgian Catholics put Maurras at the head of their own poll, they were probably unaware that *L'Eclair* had just asked 150 writers what three books they would recommend to carry the banner of France throughout the world: "The works of Charles Maurras and Bainville's *History of France* come out *en tête*," reported Marcel Espiau, "then Victor Hugo's *Légende des siècles,* which got as many votes as Dorgelès's moving *Croix de bois*."[5]

It was not the infantry of Grub Street who cast such votes. In 1923 André Malraux, who began as an ardent admirer of Barrès and at twenty had discovered Maurras and read him through, affirmed that "Maurras is one of the great intellectual forces of today." "Aller de l'anarchie intellectuelle à l'Action

Française," wrote Malraux in the Introduction he contributed to one of Maurras's works, "n'est pas se contredire, mais construire":

> Je l'imagine surtout au Moyen-Age, prêtre fervent, confesseur de grands, architecte de cathédrales et organisateur de croisades . . . son système est formé de théories dont la force que représente leur application fait une partie de la valeur. Son oeuvre est une suite de constructions destinées à créer ou à maintenir une harmonie. Il prise par dessus tout et fait admirer l'ordre, parce que tout ordre représente de la beauté et de la force.[6]

"Three men have formed our generation," Tristan Derème told *Le Nouveau Mercure*: "They are Barrès, Bourget, and Maurras." But Bourget was getting old and Barrès's influence was on the wane; Maurras was holding fast: "Why deny it?" asked Pierre Dominique, "Ma jeunesse et la tienne, Français de moins de 40 ans, intelligent, lettré et soucieux de politique ou simplement de l'existence de ta Patrie, s'en vinrent choquer contre Maurras comme un fleuve contre une montagne."[7] And Montherlant, who, with his friend Drieu, had followed Plateau's funeral and whiled away the funeral service walking up and down before the church: "Mon maître! . . . Beaucoup sursautent au nom de Maurras, qui sont venus, persuadés qu'ils y venaient librement, sur un terrain choisi par Maurras et où Maurras les conduisait. Et c'est pourquoi son influence réelle est plus grande encore que ce qui en est reconnu."[8]

Montherlant was more perceptive than he perhaps realized: in Plateau's funeral procession was another man who never acknowledged his interest in the Action Française in such effusive terms—François Mauriac. During the war he, like Gide, found occasion to approve a movement that he more often criticized; in 1928 he admitted to his Maurrassian brother that he found the Action Française "sympathique," and in answer to *Candide* in 1933 he described Maurras, with Péguy and Barrès, as his master in politics.[9]

"J'ai toujours reconnu, ce qui est indéniable, que Maurras a été un des maîtres de notre génération, mais un maître auquel je me suis toujours opposé, violemment ou mollement selon les époques," declares Mauriac today.[10] But Mauriac has had to battle constantly against a latent sympathy for the royalist movement, which will no doubt appear more obvious on the day when his letters to his brother Pierre, and his brother's memoirs are published. The man whom Paul Souday described in 1926 as "Catholic and Monarchist,"[11] the patriot who never hid his anti-parliamentarian scorn and his belief in strong government, who quietly slipped into the crowd behind the coffin of Plateau, who spent sleepless nights when the Action Française was condemned, and who, by some accounts, continued to read the newspaper even after that, would find it hard to deny what he himself has said: "The marks of man on man are eternal, and no destiny has ever crossed our own with impunity."[12]

Others were less reluctant to express their debt: "Maurras has taught me to think properly" (Claude Farrère); "genius of French reason" (André

Chaumeix); "a Counselor of State" (Saint-Aulaire); "The leader of national union" (Darquier de Pellepoix); "One cannot but admire him" (Henry Bordeaux); "Dans tous les pays, même les plus éloignés de la civilization française, les bons esprits qu'on interroge sur les sommets de l'esprit humain, répondent 'Maurras' " (Lucien Romier).[13] "What would be left to us if we lost Daudet and Maurras?" asked Maeterlinck in 1937, who in 1926 had written to Daudet from Nice, "Que vos enemis deviennent les miens, c'est l'honneur que je me souhaite."[14]

In his contribution to Simon Arbellot's account of the Action Française in 1935, Maulnier commented that Maurrassism never completely leaves those whom it has touched: "It marks them in their literary, technical, and political activity; and one may say that beside its real, visible, measurable force, the Action Française disposes of another force composed of all those who have left it."[15] This is remarkably true, and when estimating the reach of the movement one should always bear in mind the individuals and the groups that transferred aspects of its doctrine into far-flung circles.

There is, of course, above all, the more or less obvious influence that we have followed through this book, which should allow us to conclude with Régis de Vibraye (not wholly sympathetic to the Action Française) that "Tout le nationalisme en France se rattache en effet avec des atténuations plus ou moins considérables, mais aucune différence essentielle, à celui de l'Action Française."[16] There was, in addition, the literary influence, a result largely of the fact that until the late 'twenties the Action Française was alone among Catholic and right-wing groups in creating not only an important literary forum but a literary *doctrine,* thus making a noteworthy contribution to an "aesthetic of the Right." And when the vogue of neoclassicism had begun to fade, the Action Française had on hand a new class of young writers who had been schooled in its pages or in those of the *Etudiant français,* whose distinction was that they wore their culture lightly and with an air, exuding what Michel Déon (representative of a still younger generation) recognizes in himself today: "un certain anarchisme de droite, un pessimisme foncier qui vise à la lucidité."[a]

Alive to everything that happened on or below the surface, the *Canard* noted in 1937 that the young men of the *Action française* were making their way into practically all the offices of so-called "Parisian" journalism—in the literary, theatrical, and news and comment sections of *Paris-Midi* and *Paris-Soir,* in *L'Assaut* and *Le Figaro,* and even in the *Temps* press review, not to mention most of the periodicals. "They are," said the *Canard enchaîné,* "charming, polite, agreeable young men—*mais qui se tiennent les coudes.*"[17] Just how they worked can be seen from an unimportant instance, the publication in

[a] Letter from Michel Déon, dated Dec. 26, 1960. Others of this "Young Right" group are Jacques Laurent (Cecil Saint-Laurent), Roland Laudenbach (Michel Braspart), Roger Nimier, Antoine Blondin, Michel Mourre, and Félicien Marceau.

1936 of Blond's *Journal d'un imprudent.* Within some weeks, Brasillach in the *Action française* had compared it with *Le Rouge et le noir* and, to be safe, with Bourget's *Le Disciple*; Laubreaux in the *Dépêche* had found it admirable and masterly; André Rousseaux in *Figaro* thought it authoritative (in *Candide,* he commented that Blond was following in Péguy's footsteps); Louis de Gérin-Ricard in the *Petit Marseillais* praised it as having a high order of excellence; and Gabriel Brunet in *Je suis partout* declared it striking, exciting, and human.[18]

The clique—one might almost say the claque[b]—of Action Française alumni could hold its own against any on the Left; and because of the large number of publications at their disposal, their public was much broader than that of the Left. Even Eugène Dabit, the friend of Guéhenno and Gide, spending four months in the new Republican Spain of 1934, read *Candide* and *Je suis partout* in order, he said, to get back into the swim of things before returning to Paris—and perhaps also because they were no doubt the only serious French periodicals on sale in Madrid.[c]

But what about those who forsook the Action Française? How much did they forget? I have been unable to determine to what degree, if at all, men like Mitterand, Robert Buron, and René Pléven were affected by their brief acquaintances with Action Française circles. Catholics like Maritain and Louis-Martin Chauffier have not shown noticeable traces of their earlier association with, or admiration for, Maurras; but many of the rank-and-file who left the movement as long ago as the days of the Faisceau profess themselves to have been marked forever. It cannot be mere coincidence that one of these should have published the first and most significant postwar attack on French centralization and the scheme of regional revival, and that another should be responsible for the most perceptive inquiry into Maurras's ideas since Thibaudet. "One might say that, for a period of forty years, the history of the Action Française has been one of successive dissidences, ending sometimes in resounding quarrels," writes Beau de Loménie, who was among the first to suffer for the crime of lèse-Maurras.[19] But here we must remember Maulnier's observation, and none provides a better illustration of the truth of it than Bernanos, in whose work Maurras continually recurs as the symbol of the Biblical father who when his son asked for bread gave him a serpent.[20]

Like the Sturel of *Leurs Figures* who pursued his old philosophy teacher not with a simple hatred but from the depths of a sort of love betrayed,[21] Bernanos acknowledged that Maurras had become a part of his life and soul. He

[b] Sometimes quite literally, as we see in a police report, F7 13199, October 31, 1931: "Une dizaine de camelots du roi ont été désignés par Roulland pour venir applaudir cet après-midi, vers 15 heures, la seconde représentation du 'Désir,' au Théâtre du Grand Guignol. Cette pièce est l'oeuvre de M. Binet-Valmer qui fait ses débuts au théâtre et que l'Action Française classe comme étant le 'premier dramaturge d'aujourd'hui.' "

[c] Eugène Dabit, *Journal intime, 1928–1936* (1939), p. 255. *Candide* alone had a circulation three times greater than that of its most popular left-wing rival *Marianne.*

was the man for whom he had allowed himself to be deprived of the Sacraments for years, the man whose person and whose criticism of the democratic error had become a part of the national heritage, the man with whom, even when prematurely aged and dying of a liver ailment, he never ceased to argue while talking to himself.[22] In the Action Française and outside it, Bernanos remained what André Thérive has called him, the Ezekiel of the Action Française,[23] burning with the passion of one dedicated to arousing his countrymen to their historical destiny. But the revelation that Israel was and should be one people, following one king, worshiping one God, that France should no longer be two nations and the Lord's sanctuary in the midst of them for evermore, he owed to Maurras and to the days before 1914 when he and his friends had heeded the prophet's injunction.

For Bernanos as for other French nationalists, the ideas that Maurras and the Action Française had expounded for half a century had become an entrenched ideological framework, incorporating criticism of democracy, criticism of liberalism, opposition to the money interest (however lost it might be in the stinking marshes of anti-Semitism), championship of a corporate order, acceptance of illegal action, above all the principle of a supreme authority not dictated by universal suffrage. The ideas were not new, but now they were classified and analyzed. Moods, opinions, and tendencies were drawn together into a great body of doctrine, where those in whom similar ideas had sprung independently could find not only confirmation but inspiration.

If it is not clear how Marxist the French Left was between the wars, it is at any rate certain that the Right was more or less Maurrassian. But what of Maurras himself? The minimum program that he outlined in the *Gazette de France* in 1900, which is often cited as the essential program of reform, listed five aims: reconstitute the provinces, grant the universities their freedom, suppress equal division of property among heirs, recreate powerful industrial and landed patrimonies, and give syndicates and denominations their autonomy.[24] Where is the royalism? Where is the concern for order in this jungle of traditionalist reaction? What would the kings say, those forty generations of whom had forged France by bending every energy and every effort to humbling the powerful opposition in the provinces, the guilds, the nobility, and the Church?

Two generations later, Maurras was still writing in the same vein, denying the State's "economic and even administrative competence": "One should not fear to deny it all virtue outside foreign affairs, army, navy, high finance, and high justice—everything else to the collectives, to [independent] bodies, not just the nationalized industries, but public education, all of it, and even the postal services—à l'Etat le simple contrôle."[25] Such a program might very well, he knew, hand the country over "to autonomous groups and autocracies themselves exposed to anarchy and communism," but clearly he anticipated no worries once the "natural social authorities" had come into their own.

Such an analysis is helpful in clarifying the nature of Maurras's doctrine, the nature of its support, and its eventual fate. The famous authoritarianism of the Action Française was there, true enough,[d] but the real authority envisaged was not that of the king. The royalism was far from that of Louis XIV, or of any of his successors, always excepting Charles X; it was an idealized, philosophical seventeenth-century variety, in which the ruler was a kind of King Log reigning among a virile, reconstituted aristocracy of function, birth, and service.

It is perhaps excessive to speak of King Log when Maurras's king is one who can keep all his vassals in their appointed places with one hand. But the appointed places are so numerous that it is hard to see how conflict between the various interests can be arbitrated by a royal power so unassuming, or how a royal power strong enough to keep presumptuous interests in their place could forbear from further self-assertion.

Questions like these arise when reading the histories of France by Bainville and Gaxotte, both of whom show rather more brilliance than veracity. In both, the business of King and State is largely foreign; and Richelieu (highly approved) is nonetheless given a light rap on the knuckles for allowing great nobles and Protestants to distract him from his essential business with Germany. The monarchy has to dominate and discipline the internal power over which it rules. It is the great protector of corporate and local liberties, yet it is blamed for weakness when it fails to suppress them, and inevitably falls. Obviously, all this is based on a belief in a natural order of things, the upsetting of which leads to disaster. This is precisely the thesis of Eugène Cavaignac's *Esquisse d'une histoire de France,*[e] in which the discussion of the period 1715–1815 is given the general heading "Trafalgar," that on 1789–99 "Aboukir," the Napoleonic Empire "Waterloo," and the entire nineteenth century "Sedan."

Clearing one's way through the thickets of apparent contradiction, through the inevitable confusion arising when one applies the term royalism to what is actually traditionalism harking back to a multiple-elitist past consecrated by historical mythology, we find that more and more the king appears as a symbol, a symbol above all of the relentless logic that stops at nothing in order to be true to itself. The Pretenders showed understanding of the truth when they complained that their restoration was not really the end of Maurras's politics—it was only the end of his argument. Like politics, kings were a

[d] In *Revue de l'Action Française,* February 1, 1900, Vaugeois wrote that only "the taste for authority as a condition of social welfare" provided the common principle on which nationalists of different tendencies could agree.

[e] Published in 1910, the book was still being recommended by the *Action française* in 1920 (April 23), along with the works of Taine, Fustel, Auguste Longnon, Funck-Brentano, and P. de la Gorce. The current historians of the Action Française school are much more respectable from a scholarly point of view, to judge by the work of Raoul Girardet and, especially, of Philippe Ariès, both former Camelots and professed Maurrassians.

means to a higher goal—the order and the unity of France. But an Orléanist publicist was in a good position to know that kings need not be born—just made. Bereft of his king in 1937, Maurras consoled himself quite easily with a much better royal figure at Vichy.

There were two sides to Action Française doctrine, both in philosophy and in politics. On one hand, a reaction against eclecticism and relativistic multiplicity led to demands for greater discipline and purity and to the assertion that reason provides only one right answer to any given problem. This neoclassical position was linked with a protest against all monopoly of power, whether in the university or in the State, a protest by the "outs" against the "ins" reflected in arguments for regionalism and decentralization which seem a long way from the former point of view. How can one reconcile nationalism and regionalism, an insistence on general order and on particular freedom, a desire for a less interfering yet essentially stronger State?

Maurras solved the problem by an appeal to "natural" law and reason, which exchanged class divisions for natural professional unities, the power of the State or great financial interests for regional and corporate bodies, the anarchy of irresponsible electorates or State teachers for the disciplined hierarchy of right-thinking elites and Church, all under a strong central authority and ultimate arbiter—the king—backed by tradition, interest, and logic to enforce his position yet control his hand. The ultimate authority was not the king so much as the tradition, the natural order that everyone was to obey, reinforced by an artificially fostered balance of great social powers. This reasoning seemed to reconcile unity and diversity by assigning each its role; but by overlooking or misinterpreting historical developments it made the mistake of failing to offer a working program of practical politics, which is necessary if a conclusive set of logical deductions is ever to go beyond the classroom.

Maurras persuaded many people that his whole analysis of the existing order was well-founded, and he probably persuaded a good many more on special points; for after 1900 he was never exposed to scrutiny all in one place, which could have revealed all the contradictions of his thought. By writing mainly articles and essays he forced his public to garner his ideas piecemeal, and thus perhaps to be unaware of inconsistencies. "Politique d'abord," for instance, was fair prescription. But when one asked "Politics, for what?" the answer was usually expressed in a negative way. So far as it hazarded any specific directions, culminating in the restoration of "natural" representative bodies and a strong but restricted monarchy, Maurrassian doctrine was essentially anti-historical: it assumed, that is, that an order which could by reasoning be proved the best should therefore reign even if this meant ignoring the developments of more than a century and every force and pressure of the present. Before a scheme of order so desirable as his own, reality had either to adapt itself or be ignored. And by reality I mean quite simply the administrative, economic, and technical developments which make size and quantity such important factors in modern political calculations.

In the stand it took, the Action Française drew support from those who were threatened by a new economic and social order. *Rentiers* hard hit by inflation, landowners whose tenants paid in depreciated currency, owners of urban real estate whose rents were frozen or controlled at very low levels readily found in its political criticisms the explanation of unjust and incomprehensible disasters. These people, in particularly bad straits after the First World War, joined others who had begun to drift toward it earlier: the landed aristocracy and local notables whose political decline had long since caught up with their economic insignificance, officers and magistrates whose allegiance to king or Church had caused them to break with the secular Republic, antimodernist integrist clerics, also yearning for their conception of the good old days. Gradually, they recruited others: small industrialists menaced by larger, more modern enterprises, uncompetitive businessmen, shopkeepers and professional men like Poujade's father, artisans, even political journalists whose importance was diminishing in an age of press trusts and vulgar mass appeals.

Like predestination, which seems to imbue Calvinists with a strange confidence that they are certain to be among the saved, Maurras's theory of social order seems to have cheered marginal social groups greatly. When Maurras told his followers in the medical profession that the only governmental principle worthy of France would substitute the predominance of elites for the ridiculous reign of majorities,[26] they clearly felt that their importance had been recognized at last, and it must have comforted them a good deal.

It is possible that Action Française elitism was a middle-class reaction to changes that were threatening their property and position. Just as the aristocracy once reacted to bourgeois claims and pressures by stressing anachronistic reasons for its privileges and exaggerating its culture and abilities, so now the bourgeoisie in turn pleaded a higher appreciation of its habits and values, a qualitative reason for survival that the corrupting chaos of democracy ignored.

It may be also that the thought that superior men were kept down by the existing order could console men and groups who knew they were losing ground. For self-excluded noblemen, marginal businessmen, second-rate journalists and intellectuals, for a whole class on the way down, the affirmation that failure was a proof of *merit* came as a consolation and almost as a promise of revenge. Even to those who did not want to grow up—perennial students, brawlers, and barflies—the notion was a welcome rationale. In his review of Roger Vercel's *Capitaine Conan,*[27] Brasillach presents Conan as a victim not of war but of peace, of a *democratic* conception of society, whereas Conan is (unconsciously) an *aristocrat* of war. This view of things explains the mutual sympathy between the Action Française and Camelot Peter Pans like Pujo, Calzant, and Darnand, who could pursue their "aristocratic" inclinations within its ranks.

Again and again, the appeal of the Action Française was directed, it appears, to the unadaptable and the unadapted. "There are few today," wrote the *Gazette de Liège,* "who [like Maurras] give their readers such a feeling of security."[28] There were few papers, too. The strong draughts of calls to action that readers of the *Action française* imbibed gave those who wanted either to move backward or not to move at all the dizzy feeling that they were actually doing something, or—since they had in the end to admit it—that they certainly would someday. Like the chorus in *Faust,* they sang "We march," and thought they were doing more than standing still; like the Egyptian army in *Aïda,* they crossed the stage and came round to re-enter on the other side. But though they walked a long way before the show was over, they were no farther advanced when the curtain fell.

Criticizing Action Française ideas in *L'Enracinement,*[29] Simone Weil makes the just remark that the French bourgeoisie which was so ready to accept Maurras's ideas envisaged politics as an attempt to get others to install them into a power they had lost. In saying this, she puts her finger on a fault apparent not only in a Maurrassism condemned to stumble in the wilderness until it finds a Monck, but in much of the French right-wing thought of the 'thirties and early 'forties, in which salvation is expected from outside. When Daudet promised his readers that the Republic would fall like a rotten peach,[30] he excused them from any effort to bring about something that was bound to happen of its own accord. It was a promissory note on dreams, henceforth attainable by simple wishing, no longer calling for exertions on their part.

"Nous devons être intellectuels et violents," Maurras once said, and Vaugeois echoed him in the brash, early days when those in the Action Française were both.[31] Gradually, however, the Action Française became less violent and more intellectual; and those who wanted to be both moved further and further away from it to express what once had been the ideas of integral nationalism in national-socialist terms. They took Maurras's ideas about national unity and order and converted them into social and political programs that were condemned as Fascist. To protect the little man they found it necessary to increase the functions and power of the State, not diminish them. To restore a semblance of "natural" order, they fell back on coercion that contradicted their ends, imposing "natural" elites by means of the monolithic central authority they professed to abhor.

In the free economy advocated by the Action Française, the social-economic basis of its support disappeared. The petty bourgeoisie who had liked its language could not abide its panaceas: they had to be forcibly guarded, artificially restored, or otherwise pacified and enrolled in the new world they were fighting tooth and nail. The great financial and industrial interests whom the Action Française was torn between approving and opposing, backed other movements that also mobilized the little man, but with more tolerable slogans that did not threaten them or the order in which their interests were vested. And thus the Action Française was left with diminished resources to compete with rival groups of similar but less uncompromisingly awkward doctrine for the support of a shrinking public whose interests it was in no position to defend. Rejecting the ugly compromises of its hungrier alumni, unable to speak the language of the crowd or to accept working arrangements that would dim its logic, it was happy to settle for the isolated elitism and intellectualism inherent in its first pronouncements.

Like Metternich in exile, Maurras could boast that error had never even approached his mind. But, unlike Metternich, he would never admit that he was dead.

30

CONCLUSION

AFTER WHAT HAS BEEN SAID ALREADY, a conclusion can only be an anti-climax. Indeed, this is less a conclusion than an attempt to sum up some of my impressions in a sort of progress report. The Action Française is still remembered, its *epigoni* still survive, and so does a vestige of its influence, in the discussions and attitudes current in France today.[1] Its influence in French politics, literature, and journalism between the last two wars cannot be gainsaid, nor can its failure to use this influence to grasp the levers of power or, barring a brief and barren period, to apply the ideas it professed. Why should this be so?

One cannot overlook what has been stressed in the preceding pages: the fanciful or deteriorating character of the leadership, especially of that element which survived the Second World War; the deliberate concentration on theory rather than practice, with its concomitant of sporadic and rather puerile activity which only emphasized the movement's lack of "seriousness"; and the inherent inconsistency of a doctrine that sought to reconcile revolutionary changes with traditionalist arguments.

In addition—and this is important in an age when organization is an essential of power—the Action Française was never a party. If we follow Professor Friedrich in defining a party as a group stably organized "with the objective of securing or maintaining for its leaders control of the government, and with the further objective of giving its members, through such control, ideal and material benefits and advantages,"[2] the Action Française no more qualifies as a party than does the Ligue des Droits de l'Homme. Indeed, comparison with the latter organization (also a stably organized group, and a very influential one), is more appropriate than with the Communist Party, with the PSF, or with the PPF. However strong their ideological inspiration, these parties wanted to seize power. The Action Française wanted to affect power and influence society, but only indirectly, in the role not of executive but of teacher. This was both a modest and an ambitious aim—one predicated on the belief that the accidents of power mattered less than the structure within which these accidents took place, and underrating the opportunities that power has to modify such structures. But politics is the art of improvisation, a limited and opportunistic enterprise alien to the systematic rationalism of Maurras, and the ability to make piecemeal decisions can be more important than the general lines within which these decisions are made.

The Action Française was also too old-fashioned to be truly autocratic—even to the extent that some "democratic" parties are autocratic. The paranoiac ends and means of modern totalitarianism were even further removed from its ken. If Hannah Arendt is right in suggesting that the *Protocols of Zion* provides an excellent outline of, for example, Nazi purposes and plans,[3] then we can understand more easily how, shocked by the methods and measures the *Protocols* proposed, royalist intellectuals would not envisage, let alone approve, their being carried into practice.

Viewed in the light of recent experience, the threats and fierce exclusions of Maurras and Daudet seem to bear more resemblance to the petty rages of nineteenth-century pedagogues than to the coldly efficient extermination policies of modern political technicians.[a] Unable to admit the totalitarian implications of the changes they advocated, unwilling to accept the *étatisme* modern conditions impose, and most especially on radical reformers, they camped on the barren plains of increasingly academic purism, excommunicating one by one those of their followers who wished to apply one aspect of the doctrine at the expense of another, or who declared themselves willing to pay the destructive price of political effectiveness. In the end, by neglecting the politics of power, the Action Française lost out on the power of politics.

The fundamental explanation, however, of its failure—if failure it be, or of success limited to an abstract, ideological area beyond which it never managed to go—seems to lie in the nature of the society in which Vaugeois and Maurras and their followers preached the doctrine of integral nationalism.

Unlike their counterparts in neighboring countries, where the existing order either collapsed or seemed always on the verge of doing so, the French middle or property-owning classes were never seriously threatened by revolution of any sort, and they were never obliged to take more than formal steps to defend the economic and social order. In moments of apparent danger, superficial defensive gestures, small-scale riots and parliamentary pressures, were sufficient to re-establish some kind of conventional regime which reassured them that no drastic change would alter the status quo.

After the turn of the century, the Third Republic was dominated by conservative forces, and by a conservative frame of mind, which either stifled or assimilated all opposition movements. Action was taken not to secure change but to prevent it. The privilege of "movement" passed to the camp of reaction. And political parties, like the Socialists or the Communists, reached formal

[a] Maurras always indulged in bloodcurdling wishful thinking. In a letter to Barrès (Dec. 2, 1898, Maurras papers) he affirms: "Le parti de Dreyfus mériterait qu'on le fusillât tout entier comme insurgé . . . Une nation qui enveloppe de si grandes diversités ne s'unifie et ne se réforme que dans le sang. Il faudra venir à l'épée . . . Ne me croyez pas le moins du monde exalté. C'est seulement mon dégoût physique qui crève." Tout Maurras est là!

"power" by adapting themselves to a conservative climate. When a crisis occurred, often as a result of the moderation of self-professed radicals, the country would appeal to moderate saviors like Poincaré or Doumergue, who brought reassurance and calm but did very little indeed.

In such circumstances, a movement that advocated change—even though in a reactionary direction—had small chance of success. The arguments it furnished were useful in opposing the advocates of change on the other side, but that was all. The great conservative mass had no more thought of acting on Maurras's ideas than of allowing the Left to achieve its reforms. Gradually, as its more perceptive members realized, the Action Française toned down and then abandoned its radical, reformist views, developing instead those conservative aspects of its doctrine that suited the conservative public (if not its own following) to which it could most logically appeal.

Reactionary, but radically so, in 1899, forty years later it had become a leading advocate of *quieta non movere*. And when the events of 1940 offered an unexpected opportunity of applying some of its cherished ideas, it was not the Action Française itself but second- or third-hand students who represented the doctrines in the offices of Vichy. Thus the history of Vichy, especially at the start, can be viewed either as a tribute to the influence of the Action Française or as a mournful reflection on its inability to carry out its dream.

By then, of course, the Action Française as a movement was dead, having fulfilled what was apparently its sole historic function—not (as Maurras continued to pretend) to usher in the monarchy, but to furnish the Right with an ideology with which it could mask its lack of a positive program or purpose in what was largely an obstinate—and often effective—holding action against change.

The truly significant aspect of Maurrassian thought was its attempt to restore a unanimously accepted principle of authority as firm base for French society. Guglielmo Ferrero has referred to destructive revolutions, when legitimate authority collapses and another authority to replace it is lacking. For a hundred years before the Action Française was founded, one system after another had claimed the loyalty of all Frenchmen, obtained that of a faction, and collapsed before it could secure any general acceptance. The Dreyfus affair, coming on the heels of several public scandals which seemed to justify every suspicion of parliamentary qualifications for ultimate political authority, the foreign crises which followed on its heels, and the aggravation of both these problems in political discredit and national danger after 1914, all seemed to call for an alternative which Maurras sought to provide. But the early activistic gestures of the Action Française were soon replaced by a more coherent theory of authority based on history, the analysis of France's past leading to a criticism of France's present, and to a prescription for France's future.

Convincing enough to those who wanted to be convinced, Maurras's historical interpretation was, however, tendentious. It suffered less from a complete disregard of most recent chapters of French history than from a misinterpretation of them, and, especially, from deliberately ignoring the repeated defeats of Maurras's candidates to ultimate authority—the kings of 1792, 1830, 1848, and 1873—defeats that lowered them from the class of self-evident authorities into the crowded ranks of mere postulants for power, no different from the others. This, of course, was precisely what Maurras denied, when he prescribed the monarchic order as most suitable for France. "Chaque peuple a le sien, conforme à sa nature / Q'on ne saurait changer sans lui faire une injure," declares Corneille in *Cinna*. But it may be argued that a successful change will alter the character of a people in such a way that what suited it before will not suit it again, will not fit it as *spontaneously* as the lesson of a different epoch may suggest.

Maurras was right in believing that stable authority must have its roots in the past, not in the shifting moods of an ill-defined democracy, but he persisted in ignoring the damage that had been done to those roots, which cast doubt on the authority of "authority" itself. The monarchy he desired to restore was the unquestioned, apparently natural, growth whose existence had seemed to its subjects quite as God-willed and inevitable as the shape of Mont Ventoux. But the only monarchy he could possibly have restored would have been an institution as artificial and questionable from the historical and the utilitarian points of view as the other political institutions that he never ceased to attack. "No está en la mano de cualquier pueblo tener una Monarquia, pero sí tener una República," wrote José María Pemán in 1931.[b] "Una revolucíon se hace en veinticuatro horas; una Monarquia, no."

The only way to make royalist historical arguments effective would have been by a totalitarian indoctrination into Action Française historiography, which would justify the rule of kings in France as similar methods have justified the rule of a class or of a race. And this method, of course, the Action Française refused to accept. In any case, totalitarian methods would have rendered the doctrines redundant: for such methods are their own justification, and theory provides only the anthem of their struggle, not its motivation. Maurras sought a rational way out of the dilemma in which he found the French state, and he believed in the solution he evolved. Much as he disliked them, he followed in the tradition of Enlightened Jacobins, envisaging coercion not as a crux but as an incidental means of clearing the ground and thus introducing his ideas to minds that were cluttered but not incapable of appreciating the truth when given the chance. Hence, although his historical opportunism was too unhistorical to convince any but the converted, it was neither opportunistic enough nor ruthless enough to succeed in spite of it.

[b] *Cartas a un escéptico ante la Monarquia* (Madrid, 1956) p. 100. Written in 1931, this is one of the best available defenses of monarchist traditionalism, very close to the thought of Maurras and Benoist. But both Pemán and Maurras should have realized that the remark quoted applied to their own countries as well.

We must, all the same, give him credit for trying, for tackling the question as he saw it and going straight to its most essential aspect. The crux of Maurrassian doctrine is not legitimate authority alone but its continuity: the problem of regulating the succession and thus ensuring order untroubled by the seismic effects of political change is solved by the hereditary system, hence by monarchy.[c] In insisting on this, Maurras may have been anachronistic, or deliberately indifferent to contemporary realities, but he put his finger on one crucial difficulty that plagues the increasingly total (even when they are not totalitarian) regimes of today, subjecting them (whether in France, the United States, or the U.S.S.R.) to long stretches of uncertainty and incoherence. Maurras's solution may have been an impossible one, and its form was certainly unpopular; but he came face to face with a question that others continue to ignore. His statement of the question, however, was typical of his unreconstructed traditionalism, which he refused to adapt to modern situations.

Traditionalism is not *ipso facto* anachronistic, and as an element in political thought it is better acknowledged than ignored. But as a political method, it can be effective only when combined, as in the British—and Burkeian—manner, with a pragmatic and empirical approach supple enough to allow for change and to adopt it *before* resistance becomes useless. Action Française doctrine could have lent itself to such an approach. Its original principles were empirical enough. But as it developed, the nature of the support it attracted and the prejudices of the surviving leadership combined to produce a conservatism that verged on immobility. The Action Française, never moderate, shed its radicalism, and was left with a reactionary dogma that amounted in the end to nothing more than standing pat. Many of its admirers were not interested in putting theory into practice, or were not capable of combining the two; and so what counted was the *existence* of the doctrine and its, so to speak, "inspirational" possibilities. Such a problem is not uncommon in the history of religion or philosophy and need not surprise us. Like advocates of Christianity, or of democracy, the disciples of integral nationalism respected it more in the breach than in the observance. *C'était, tout de même, ça.*

This is all to say again that the position of the Action Française was an anomalous one—a traditionalist movement preaching violent change, a minority movement in a mass age, an intellectual movement tackling a demagogic task.

Elitism is one way of reconciling ideas of radical change with the intellectual's distrust of the mob. Although Daudet's boisterous approach may give us pause,[d] one has only to read Maulnier to know that the revolution of

[c] It should be noted particularly that Vichy, too, was actively concerned with the problem of ensuring a smooth succession after the disappearance of an authoritarian leader, and that it sought to solve it in a symbolically monarchic vein by inventing the Dauphin.

[d] Maurras took it in his stride. To Barrès he wrote: "Je doute que Daudet ait jamais rien compris profondément. Il est ivre de mots et aussi de quelques images" (undated letter, 1898 or 99). Years later, in a letter of May 25, 1913, commenting on an overstatement of his own, he would add: "Exagération à la Léon Daudet" (Maurras papers).

the intellectuals need not be the revolt of the masses. Both the intellectual aristocratism of Maulnier and the social racism of *Je suis partout*—another, less restrained, form of the same thing—were attempts to modify the thought of Maurras, who had ignored the masses, by putting the masses in their place and allotting a special role to the creative interpreter and leader, an aim that young French intellectuals of the 'thirties shared with their Bolshevik and Fascist predecessors. Their impact on the French public was small, because the undifferentiated "masses" had not yet come to play a really significant role: property owners still in a majority were not yet united in a common slough of despond; workers and left-wing intellectuals were still fascinated by particularistic class doctrines. Only in the dreary urban conditions of the German occupation, especially in Paris, could this modified national-socialism catch on, and then only at the sacrifice of the classic virtues integral nationalism had wanted to defend. Thus, the misadventures of those who deserted him bore out Maurras's severe warnings to those who wanted to adapt his theories to new circumstances, that compromise threatened not only the integrity of Maurrassian thought but the very values it hoped to restore. But they reflected, too, the impossible dilemma of those who sought to treat Maurrassism as more than an intellectual exercise or an incantation, and defined the system for what it was: an interpretation of history, not a basis for political action.

It is noticeable that, as the history of the movement progresses, the nationalism which had been a dominant note of royalist argument and public purpose recedes. The Action Française had settled on royalism for nationalistic reasons. In time, both these characteristics became altered. The necessities of an ever more conservative attitude, while continuing to make use of nationalist phraseology, sometimes clashed with the implications of a truly nationalistic stand, which is not calculating but impetuous.

Too old-fashioned for the unruly 'thirties, nationalism nevertheless continued to hold the interests of France as the highest good. No amount of rationalization could change that. And, since the old leaders of integral nationalism were sincere, they could not temporize in the 'forties as they had been able to do in the previous decade. In any case, they would not accept the concomitants of what now came to pass as nationalism—the racism, the terror, the totalitarian ambitions of new orders in which they recognized their old and familiar enemies of imperialism, universalism, and *étatisme*. Too conservative to preserve their nationalism intact when its reckless application might have shattered the society they pretended to spurn, they were also too nationalistic to accept a foreign solution, especially one presented in such alien and revolutionary terms. In this they were more clearsighted than other "nationalist" and "conservative" collaborators, who, blinded by the Red glare in the East, blundered into the arms of a national-socialism as revolutionary, and perhaps even more nihilistic, than the Bolshevism from which they hoped it would preserve them.

Among these blunderers, the Action Française, of course, had its eminent representatives. We have seen how, in the explosion brought on by the pressures of the 'thirties, men and ideas of the Action Française had, so to speak, fertilized a number of truly revolutionary groups which developed those national-socialist strains that the main body wanted to ignore. And we have seen the difficulties and frictions arising out of this. But the division became apparent only when the Occupation forced men to choose explicitly among a variety of allegiances. True, the determination to resist the occupant helped to confuse the issues as well as to clarify them. But, just as in 1914 nationalism drove the Action Française into a temporary acceptance of the Republic that it opposed in principle, so in 1940 national-socialism drove some of its adherents into collaboration with a similar-thinking occupying nation that, as nationalists, they mistrusted.

In both cases, the decision (at least on the rational plane) reflected the values uppermost in the minds of those who made it. In both cases, those who made the decision betrayed one aspect of their creed to be true to another which they considered of greater importance. In both cases, not so much the choice as the necessity of choice between apparently irreconcilable alternatives betrayed the basic inconsistency of a system of thought that tried to encompass too much.

This, however, is the fate of every doctrine. Ideas are advanced by their betrayals, progress by their failures; they live on in their vulgarizations, misinterpretations, and misapplications. The pure idea is a sterile thing. It is when men take from it what they choose, and make of it what they can, that it affects not only thought but life.

In so far as it is not the history of all thought, the history of vulgarization remains to be written. The later influence of the Action Française remains to be traced. If this is ever done, it should reveal variants and deviations as curious, vagaries as unpredictable, alliances as unsuspected, as those that we have observed in the history of the movement itself.

NOTES

NOTES

Unless otherwise indicated, all books mentioned are published in Paris.
The following abbreviations are used:

AF	*L'Action française*
AFD	*L'Action française du dimanche*
JOC	*Journal officiel de la République française, Débats, Chambre*
JOS	*Journal officiel de la République française, Débats, Sénat*
JSP	*Je suis partout*
NG	*La Nouvelle Guyenne*
RAF	*Revue de l'Action Française*
RU	*Revue universelle*

CHAPTER I

1. *Gazette de France,* Sept. 6, 7, 1898; *RAF,* III, 744–64.
2. Quoted in *RAF,* III, 753.
3. *Le Figaro,* Sept. 14, 1891.
4. Roger Joseph and Jean Forges, *Biblio-iconographie générale de Charles Maurras,* 2 vols. (Paris, 1953); Charles Maurras, *Pour un jeune français* (1949); Alphonse Séché, *Dans la mêlée littéraire: Souvenirs et correspondance, 1900–1930* (1935), pp. 190–91; Xavier Vallat, *Charles Maurras, No. d'écrou 8321* (1953), pp. 64–65.
5. *Mont de Saturne* (1950), pp. 25, 187.
6. Maurras, *RAF,* I, 316; and Preface to *Chemin de paradis* (1895), pp. xxviii–xxx.
7. *Mont de Saturne,* p. 230; Maurice Martin du Gard, *Les Mémorables* (1960), II, 357; Roger Stéphane, *Chaque Homme est lié au monde* (1946), p. 249.
8. Robert Rouquette, "Charles Maurras et la Papauté," *Etudes,* June 1953, pp. 392–400; Vallat, *Maurras,* pp. 79, 274, 238, 271.
9. Marchand to Léon Daudet, July 26, 1906 (in the papers of Dr. François Daudet).
10. *AF,* April 10, 1913, and Sept. 10, 1920; see also Maurice Clavière, *Léon Daudet* (1943), p. 13: "C'est par amour de la beauté que M. Maurras s'est appliqué à la restauration de l'ordre. Cette recherche l'a fait pénétrer dans le divin secret des hiérarchies."
11. "Prologue d'un essai sur la critique," *Revue encyclopédique Larousse,* Dec. 26, 1896; *RU,* May 15, 1927; *Oeuvres capitales* (1954), III, 7–34.
12. *Oeuvres capitales,* I, 357.
13. This was written in the early 'nineties, and is quoted in *Au signe de Flore* (1933), p. 27.
14. *Ibid.,* pp. 44–49; *Les Idées royalistes sur les partis, l'état, la nation* (1919), pp. 22–23.
15. "Les intérêts royalistes," *Gazette de France,* Oct. 15, 1897.
16. Quoted by Maurras from the memoirs of Aymée de Coigny, in *Mademoiselle Monk* (1923), p. 41.
17. See Maurras and Henri Dutrait-Crozon, *Si le coup de force est possible* (1910),

and Colonel Jacques Milleret's comments upon it in *Aunis-Saintonge-Angoumois,* May 15, 1910.

18. *Instruction publique,* July 21, 1888, p. 459; "Aristocratie intellectuelle?" *Le Soleil,* July 6, 1898, quoted in Léon Roudiez, *Maurras jusqu'à l'Action Française* (1957), pp. 129, 326–27.

19. E. Goichon, *A la mémoire d'Ernest Psichari* (1946), p. 254; Société des Amis de Georges Bernanos, *Bulletin périodique,* No. 11 (July 1952): letter to Dom Besse.

20. *Le Soleil,* Oct. 23, 1896; *Gazette de France,* Dec. 2, 1897; Roudiez, pp. 319–20.

21. Louis Dimier, *Vingt Ans d'Action Française* (1926), p. 9.

22. *RAF,* July 1, 1899, pp. 14, 19, 27–29, and *passim.*

23. *RAF,* Aug. 1, 1899, p. 9, Aug. 15, 1899, pp. 92–94.

24. Achille Dauphin-Meunier in *RAF,* Oct. 15, 1899; also Nov. 15, 1899: "Sortir de la légalité pour rentrer dans le droit."

25. See J. Caplain-Cortambert in *RAF,* July 1, 1899.

26. "Dictateur et Roi," in *Petit Manuel de l'enquête sur la monarchie* (1928), pp. 203–4.

27. Maurras to Barrès, undated letter, 1899 (Maurras papers); Caplain-Cortambert, *Le Colonel de Villebois-Mareuil* (1902), pp. iii–iv; *RAF,* June 15, 1901, p. 979; Maurras, *Au signe de Flore,* pp. 289–90.

28. Archives Nationales, Action Française, F^7 12853, 3/228; F^7 12440 of Nov. 29, 1904; F^7 12862, 1/24 of March 12, 1905.

29. F^7 12862, 1/30, 1/34 of Nov. 26, 1905, and May 10, 1906; F^7 12564 of Nov. 26, 1905.

30. Maurice Barrès, *Le Journal,* Oct. 30, 1899.

31. *L'Enquête sur la monarchie,* p. 118, quoted in Lazare de Gérin-Ricard and Louis Truc, *Histoire de L'Action Française* (1949), p. 46.

32. Dimier, *Vingt Ans,* p. 25.

33. *Ibid.,* p. 20.

34. *Ibid.,* p. 23.

35. F^7 12862, 1/24 of March 12, 1905.

36. F^7 12440 of Nov. 29, 1904; F^7 12564 of March 1 and Aug. 1, 1906.

37. F^7 12862, 1/35–38 of June 18, 1906.

38. Adrien Dansette, *Histoire religieuse de la France contemporaine* (1951), II, 281.

39. *Ibid.,* p. 276. Reinach, one of the editors of *Le Siècle,* was a leading revisionist.

40. *Ibid.,* p. 277.

41. *Ibid.,* pp. 299, 302.

42. *RAF,* Feb. 15, 1902, p. 299; Abbé Appert, quoted in André Mirambel, *La Comédie du Nationalisme intégral* (1947), p. 79.

43. Nicolas Fontaine (pseud. of Louis Canet, subsequently referred to as Canet-Fontaine), *Saint-Siège, Action Française et Catholiques intégraux* (1928), pp. 42–44; Dimier, *Vingt Ans,* p. 208.

44. Canet-Fontaine, p. 43.

45. *Vingt Ans,* pp. 85ff.

46. *JOC,* May 22, 28, 1900. The vote was 425 to 60.

47. Société des Amis de Georges Bernanos, *Bulletin périodique,* No. 14 (February 1953), pp. 2–3; *Dépêche de Toulouse,* Oct. 9, 1906.

CHAPTER 2

1. *AF,* Jan. 11, 1936; J.-H. Rosny, *Torches et lumignons* (1921), quoted in Paul Dresse, *Léon Daudet vivant* (1947), p. 97; cf. Daudet's own recollection of the scene in *La Nation belge,* Oct. 31, 1930.

2. See Georges Bernanos, "Léon Daudet," *L'Avant-garde de Normandie,* June 6, 1914, and *Crépuscule des vieux* (1956), pp. 145–65; Goncourt, quoted in Dresse, p. 65.

3. See André Gaucher, *L'Obsédé* (1925), pp. ix–x.

4. Ernest Renauld, *L'Action Française contre l'église catholique* (1937), p. 89; Daudet, *AF*, Jan. 13, 1918; Arthur Meyer, *Ce que je peux dire* (1912); Vallat, *Maurras*, pp. 26, 86.

5. *Ibid.*, and testimony of Michel Missoffe.

6. *AF*, March 21, 1913; F^7 12862 of Aug. 13, 1913; also Gaucher, *L'Honorable Léon Daudet* (n.d.), pp. 189–98; F^7 12862, 2/110–11 of Dec. 15, 1908; Renauld, p. 89, may have drawn his information from Gaucher.

7. F^7 12440 of June 7, 1907; and the Paris press at the end of May 1907.

8. F^7 12862, No. 2/4–5 of Jan. 10, 1908, and No. 5 of April 19, 1909; for higher estimates, see Renauld, p. 89.

9. Arthur Raffalovitch, *L'Abominable Vénalité de la presse* (1931), p. 216; Jean Drault, *Drumont, la France juive et La Libre Parole* (1935), p. 298; F^7 12862, of May 2 and Sept. 25, 1909.

10. *Les Camelots du Roi* (1933), p. xvi.

11. *Le Progrès de Lyon*, March 4, 1908; *JOC*, March 19, 1908; *AF*, March 30, 1908.

12. *AF*, April 1, 1908.

13. Jules Renard, *Correspondance* (1928), p. 375; Jacques Rivière and Alain-Fournier, *Correspondance, 1905–1914* (1926), II, 206.

14. See Eugen Weber, *The Nationalist Revival in France, 1905–1914* (Berkeley, 1959), *passim*; *L'Aurore*, March 30, 1908; *La Lanterne*, March 30, June 6, 1908; *Le Progrès de Lyon*, March 4, April 1, 1908; *Dépêche de Toulouse*, May 17, 1908.

15. F^7 12862, 2/62–65 of Sept. 13, 1908; 2/66 of Sept. 17, 1908; 2/74 of Sept. 27, 1908.

16. See Henri Tilliette, "Bernanos en Artois," in Société des Amis de Georges Bernanos, *Bulletin périodique*, No. 14 (February 1953), p. 15. Tilliette was a Camelot with Bernanos in pre-1914 days. In his opinion, Bernanos was sincere in his allegiance to the Action Française, but seemed to care little about its theoretical side. For the early days of the Camelots, see Pujo, *Les Camelots du Roi*, pp. 32ff and *passim*; Pujo in *AF*, Dec. 2, 1925.

17. *AF*, Dec. 10, 11, 1908; Barrès in *L'Echo de Paris*, Jan. 13, 20, 30, 1909.

18. Aulard in *Dépêche de Toulouse*, Jan. 28, 1909.

19. F^7 12862, 3/17 of Feb. 3, 1909; 2/106–7 of Dec. 12, 1908.

20. F^7 12862, 2/126–29 of Dec. 21, 1908.

21. F^7 12862, 4/11 of Feb. 8, 1909; 4/33 of March 4, 1909; 4/117 ff of Aug. 21, 1909; and F^7 12862, No. 5.

22. See *La Démocratie sociale*, Dec. 11, 1909; F^7 12862, 4/46 of April 18, 1909; 4/158–65 of Dec. 23, 1909.

23. The background and incidents of the affair are to be found in file F^7 12853, No. 5, of March 30, 1910; its polemics in the *Gaulois* and the *Action française*, March 20–28, 1910.

24. F^7 12853, No. 5.

25. F^7 12862, 5/45–47 of June 12, 21, 1910.

26. F^7 12862, 5/53 of July 10, 1910; *AF*, July 12, Oct. 20, 21, 25, 1910.

27. *L'Eclair*, Dec. 4, 1910; *L'Intransigeant*, Dec. 17, 1910; Dimier, *Vingt Ans*, pp. 197ff.

28. F^7 12862, 5/147 of Dec. 21, 1910.

29. Cellerier to Gonzague de Reynold, Dec. 16, 1910; from the latter's papers.

30. F^7 12862, 7/59 of May 19, 1911; 7/73 of June 14, 1911.

31. F^7 12862, 7/121–22 of Nov. 6, 1911.

32. *AF*, Dec. 21, 1911.

33. F^7 12862, 5/131–34 of Dec. 6, 1910; *AF*, Dec. 2–4, 1910; *Almanach de l'Action Française*, 1910 and 1911.

34. See the letters and messages in the *AF*, December 1910–January 1911, where out of over 800 correspondents the proportion of nobility is about 18 per cent. Edward R. Tannenbaum, *The Action Française* (New York, 1962), pp. 125–26, is more precise.

35. Maurras, "Le Monarchisme et les grands," *AF,* Aug. 5, 1922; Dimier, *Vingt Ans,* p. 321.

36. F[7] 12864 of Nov. 16, 1909, and April 7, 1910.

37. *Le Journal,* July 15, 1911.

38. Dom J.-M. Besse, *Ce qu'est la monarchie* (1910), p. 16.

39. Jacques Rocafort, *Les Résistances à la politique de Pie X* (1920), p. 11.

40. Canet-Fontaine, p. 48.

41. F[7] 12862, 4/128–29, 121–24 of September 1909; Emmanuel Barbier, *Histoire du Catholicisme libéral,* V, 220, quoted in Canet-Fontaine, p. 49.

42. The letter was addressed to the Abbé Jules Pierre, to thank him for the gift of a pamphlet attacking Maurras and the Action Franaçise: *Avec Nietzsche à l'assaut du Christianisme* (Limoges, 1910); Pierre reprinted it in *Comment l'abbé Emmanuel Barbier fabriquait l'histoire de l'Eglise de France contemporaine* (1926), pp. 39–40.

43. Cardinal Eugène Tisserand to Francisque Gay, May 31, 1950 (F. Gay papers).

44. Marc Sangnier, *Autrefois* (1937), pp. 170–81.

45. See, e.g., F[7] 12862 of Jan. 26, 1907, and April 11, 1908.

CHAPTER 3

1. Dimier, *Vingt Ans,* p. 94.

2. Auguste Pawlowski, *Les Syndicats jaunes* (1911); Pierre Bietry, *Le socialisme et les Jaunes* (1906); *Les Jaunes de France* (1907); F[7] 12863, No. 1 (1912).

3. *La Cocarde,* Jan. 17, 1895; Henri Clouard, *La Cocarde* (1910), p. 23.

4. F[7] 12862 of April 9, 1906, April 22, 1908, Nov. 10, 1908, Dec. 17, 1908, March 3, 1912.

5. Georges Valois, *L'Homme contre l'argent* (1928), pp. 61–62; Jacques de Coursac in *Aunis-Saintonge-Angoumois,* Nov. 15, 1910; and a great many police reports concerning the cooperation of the Action Française with groups of the Extreme Left: e.g., F[7] 12862, 2/1 of Jan. 6, 1908; 2/40 of June 5, 1908; 4/46 of April 18, 1909; 4/61 of June 16, 21, 1909; 5/72–73 of Oct. 17, 1910, and Jan. 27, 1911; 7/32 of March 19, 1911. A report of March 15, 1912, indicates that some 1,200 people attended an anti-parliamentary meeting for workers at the Hall of the Sociétés Savantes; but only about fifty of them were Socialists.

6. Edouard Drumont, *La Fin d'un monde* (1888), quoted in *Combat,* January 1938. The history of nineteenth-century French anti-Semitism is masterfully treated in Robert F. Byrnes, *Antisemitism in Modern France* (New Brunswick, N.J., 1950).

7. Dimier, *Vingt Ans,* p. 124.

8. "Le Fascisme et son avenir en France," *RU,* Jan. 1, 1936.

9. See Thierry Maulnier, "Charles Maurras et le socialisme," *RU,* Jan. 1, 1937.

10. See his remarks in *La Cocarde,* March 7, 1895; *Gazette de France,* March 2, 1900; letter to Jacques Maurras of Aug. 4, 1947; the Postface to *Mont de Saturne* (1950); and Roger Joseph, *Les Faux Maurras* (1958), pp. 45–46. These provide a relevant commentary to Reino Virtanen, "Nietzsche and the Action Française," *Journal of the History of Ideas,* XI (1950), 191–214.

11. "La Déroute des mufles," *Divenire sociale,* July 16, 1909, translated in *Aspects de la France,* Dec. 1, 1949.

12. "Urbain Gohier," *L'Indépendance,* Jan. 1, 1912, pp. 305–20.

13. Maxime Brienne in *Les Essaims nouveaux,* September-October 1917; *Combat,* February 1936; see also Jean Saillenfest, "Fascisme et syndicalisme," *Combat,* October 1936.

14. Henri Lagrange, "Proudhon critique littéraire," in *Introduction aux femmelins,* p. 15.

15. Barrès, *Adieu à Moréas* (1910), quoted in Maurras, *Lettres de prison* (1958), p. 152.

16. Barrès, *Scènes et doctrines du nationalisme,* quoted in Clouard, *La Cocarde,* p. 48.

17. Henri Massis, "De Barrès à Maurras," *Ecrits de Paris,* April 1951.

18. Clouard, *La Cocarde,* p. 45 and *passim*; see also his *Les Disciplines,* published in 1913 by Sorel's publisher Marcel Rivière and written, as Massis has put it, in a Maurrassian corset.

19. Quoted in *Aunis-Saintonge-Angoumois,* March 1911.

20. Letter from the Front, dated March 9, 1915, quoted in *Le Feu,* July 1, 1918.

21. Clouard, "Une Jeune Elite sacrifiée," *La Renaissance,* May 12, 1917, p. 12.

22. Henri Lagrange, "Stendhal et la jeunesse," in *Vingt Ans en 1914,* pp. 83–84.

23. Henri Martineau, *Le Coeur de Stendhal* (1953), II, 182; Eugène Marsan, "Politique et psychologie," *Revue critique,* March 1913.

24. Quoted by Jules Pierre in *L'Action Française et ses directions païennes* (1914), p. 15.

25. See Pierre Lasserre in *AF,* Aug. 11, 1908, and *Revue critique,* March 10, 1913; Alfred Capus, quoted in *Revue critique,* April 1913, pp. 87ff.

26. Dimier, *Vingt Ans,* pp. 220–23.

27. Clouard in *La Renaissance,* May 12, 1917, pp. 9–12; *AF,* Feb. 22, 1914.

28. Martineau in *RU,* January 1937; Gilbert Charles in *Revue critique,* March 1924, p. 180.

29. See *AF,* Feb. 17–March 4, 1911.

30. *L'Aurore,* March 17, 1911; *La Petite République,* March 9, 1911; F^7 12862, 7/32 of March 19, 1911; the Bernstein riots found a favorable echo in *La Guerre sociale,* but the latter did not really like anti-Semitism and soon set about organizing an anti-Camelot group, the Jeunes Gardes; *Dépêche de Toulouse,* March 29, April 17, 1911.

31. Maurras in *AF,* Jan. 4, 1911; Marcel Sembat in *L'Humanité,* April 26, 1911.

32. See P.-J. Proudhon, *Théorie de la propriété,* p. 193; Edouard Berth, *Méfaits des intellectuels* (1914), for the Foreword written in 1913; H. Lantz in *Le Libertaire,* Dec. 25, 1910; François Maillard in *L'Action,* Jan. 2, 1911. Léon Vibert in *Le Savoyard de Paris,* January 10, 1914, suggests that the Socialists agree with the Action Française on almost everything but royalism.

33. F^7 12862, 5/38 of May 18, 1910.

34. October 2, 1912.

35. Alfred Capus, *Les Moeurs du temps* (1912); Jacques Bainville in *AF,* Dec. 26, 1912; André Chéradame, *La Crise française* (1912); Berth, *Méfaits des intellectuels,* pp. 14–15.

36. *La Guerre sociale,* July 3, 1912.

37. See *Le Gaulois, La Patrie, La Croix, La Démocratie, La Libre Parole,* May 5–6, 1913; Rocafort, *Résistances,* pp. 140–41.

38. See F^7 12862, 7/39 of March 25, 1911; Gaston Marcellin, *Lettres d'un disparu* (1925), II, 25; *Cahiers des Droits de l'Homme,* XX, No. 22 (Nov. 20, 1920), 3–4.

39. F^7 12862, 5/65 of Sept. 20, 1910.

40. See *AF,* Nov. 13, 1914; April 30, 1917.

41. The letter is quoted in *Eurydice,* No. 24 (Christmas 1936).

42. Alphonse Séché, *Dans la mêlée littéraire,* p. 132; D. W. Brogan, *The French Nation* (New York, 1957), p. 215; Léon Vibert in *Le Savoyard de Paris,* Dec. 13, 1913.

43. Séché, p. 135 (letter of Jan. 14, 1914); *AF,* Jan. 2, 1914.

44. See *AF,* March 20, 29, April 14, May 24, 25, 1914; Paris press of June 20, 1914. For numbers of the Joan of Arc parade, the *AF,* May 25, 1914, claimed 50,000; the *Liberté* agreed, adding that when the head of the column was at the Place de la Concorde the tail was still marching past Saint-Augustin; *L'Intransigeant* and the *Journal des débats* on the evening of May 24 estimated over 30,000.

45. Quoted in *AF,* April 14, 1914.

CHAPTER 4

1. *AF,* July 25, 1914.

2. Faures's words are quoted in *Les Documents politiques,* IV, No. 2 (1923), 49.

3. *Revue des causes célèbres,* 1919, p. 136.

4. *Journal d'un cochon de pessimiste* (1918), pp. 44–47, 115–24.

5. *Revue des causes célèbres,* May 1919; *AF,* July 18, 21, 23, 30, 1914.

6. Villain was ultimately acquitted. For as full an account of the trial as one can get, see *Revue des causes célèbres,* April-May 1919, pp. 131–48, 227–40, 267–308, 389, and the comments of Jean Guiraud in *La Croix,* April 1, 1919.

7. *AF,* Aug. 3, 1914, Jan. 5, 1915; see also Daudet's testimony at Malvy's trial in *Revue des causes célèbres,* 1918, p. 101.

8. *AF,* Oct. 12, 1915; F^7 12863 (1915), 4/52 of May 11, 4/57 of May 20, 4/62 of May 31, 4/67 of June 10.

9. F^7 12863 (1915), 4/38 of March 22, 4/53 of May 14, 4/113 of Sept. 15, 4/116 of Sept. 20.

10. Poincaré, *Au Service de la France,* Vol. IX, Oct. 28, 1917; *Le Procès de Charles Maurras* (1946), pp. 34–35; Emile Constant in *JOC,* Dec. 9, 1915; *AF,* Jan. 13, 1916; *RU,* XXVIII, No. 19 (Jan. 1, 1927), 11–12. F^7 12863, 4/139 of Nov. 12, 1915, reports Maurras's and Daudet's determination to take the warpath on Briand's coming to power, and the intervention of the Duc d'Orléans, on whose formal orders they had to desist. Briand had cannily taken a royalist, Denys Cochin, into his government.

11. See, e.g., *AF,* June 2, 1918.

12. *AF,* April 24, 1915.

13. See, e.g., the issues of March 2, 7, 8, 17, 18, 31, and July 1, 1915.

14. *Frankfurter Zeitung,* April 1, 1915; *L'Echo de Paris,* Dec. 30, 1914; *JOS,* July 22, 23, 1915, p. 361; Juliette Adam to Léon Daudet, Aug. 18, 1916 (F. D. papers); André Gide to Charles Maurras, Nov. 5, 1916, quoted in *Eurydice,* No. 24 (Christmas 1936); see also the letter of the Minister of Supply, Maurice Long, to Daudet in *AF,* Dec. 16, 1914.

15. *JOC,* Nov. 28, 1917, p. 3087; "Procès Malvy," *Revue des causes célèbres,* 1918, p. 96; *Cahiers des Droits de l'Homme,* XX, No. 22 (Nov. 20, 1920), 4.

16. Alphonse Séché, *Dans la melée littéraire,* pp. 188–89, quotes the letter in full.

17. Police report quoted by Malvy in *JOC,* Oct. 4, 1917, p. 2597, the accuracy of which seems to have gone uncontested.

18. *L'Univers,* Dec. 18, 1915; Elie Marty, *Témoignage de Pierre Rousselot* (1940), pp. 323–33; Octave Martin (Maurras), "Adrien Dansette, historien," *Aspects de la France,* Jan. 4, 1952. The paper's steadfast defense of the Pope, when even French prelates held back, ensured it the sympathy of certain ultramontane royalist circles, hitherto suspicious of its wildness. It also put an end—for a decade—to the hostility of the Jesuit order, which had been manifest before the war. F^7 12863, Nos. 1–3 (1912–13) and No. 4 (Feb. 6, 1915).

19. See Bainville in *AF,* Dec. 12, 1914; Daudet, "La Dernière des guerres?" *AF,* Dec. 17, 1914. But Daudet himself had written a good deal of nonsense, as on September 9, 1914.

20. Pierre Nothomb, personal communication; *AF,* May 18, 1915.

21. *AF,* Oct. 31, Nov. 1, 5, 1916.

22. *AF,* April 15, 1917; see also issue of June 17, 1917.

23. Paris press of April 15, 16, 1917; *La Petite République,* April 20, 1917; *Le Journal,* Aug. 4, 1917; *AF,* April 16, Aug. 5, 6, 1917.

24. *AF,* Jan. 11, 31, 1917. For the value of the evidence used by Daudet in his campaigns, see *Cahiers des Droits de l'Homme,* July 10, 1923, which gives R. Réau's account of the accusations brought against Paul Meunier. Gustave Téry, "L'Impunité," *L'Oeuvre,*

Jan. 26, 1918, was right in his bitter complaints against the freedom of calumny that the press enjoyed.

25. See Maurras in *RU*, XXVIII, No. 19 (Jan. 1, 1927), 8–9; Dimier, *Vingt Ans*, pp. 263ff; *AF*, April 20, 27, 1917. But as early as Nov. 5, 1915, Daudet had already singled Vigo out as "a tool of Caillaux and of the Comptoir d'Escompte."

26. See "Procès Malvy," *Revue des causes célèbres*, 1918, pp. 73, 81, 113; *La Vérité*, *L'Humanité*, *La Lanterne*, June 1918; *La Vérité*, Aug. 4, 1918; Jean Longuet in *JOC*, Oct. 4, 1917; Henry Maunoury, *Police de guerre* (1937), pp. 49, 54.

27. See *AF*, June 20 and Nov. 8, 1917, and the testimony of Henry Leroy in the trial of the *Bonnet rouge* staff, confirmed by Marion, in *Revue des causes célèbres*, July 18, 1918, p. 302.

28. *JOC*, Oct. 4, 1917.

29. *Ibid.*, p. 2608.

30. Paul Poncet in *ibid.*, 1917, p. 2600; Téry, in "Le Mouchard du coche," *L'Oeuvre*, Oct. 6, 1917; Maurras in *AF*, Oct. 15, 1917.

31. See *JOC*, Oct. 16, 19, 1917; Sembat in *La Lanterne* and Albert Thomas in *L'Humanité*, quoted in *L'Oeuvre*, Oct. 17, 1917. Note that Painlevé's fall on November 13 came on an issue directly concerned with the Action Française.

32. *AF*, Oct. 28, 29, 1917; Capus in *Le Figaro*, Oct. 28, 1917; Hervé in *La Victoire*, Oct. 29, 1917; *Petit Journal* and *Petit Bleu*, Oct. 30, 1917; Sembat in *L'Humanité*, Oct. 30, 1917; Barrès, *Mes Cahiers*, XII (1949), 253. According to Maunoury, *Police de guerre*, p. 206, Commissaire Faralicq, the police officer in charge of the searches, may himself have been a friend of the Action Française.

33. See *Cahiers des Droits de l'Homme*, Nov. 20, 1920, June 25, 1923; Paul Poncet in *JOC*, Jan. 18, 1918, p. 10. Anne André-Glandy, *Maxime Réal del Sarte* (1955), p. 108, claims that the police who searched Réal's studio found a case of loaded canes but missed one full of guns that was being used as a stand for a statue in progress.

34. Dimier, *Vingt Ans*, pp. 268–69.

35. Pierre Renaudel in *JOC*, Nov. 28, 1917, p. 3086; Bracke in *ibid.*, pp. 3088–89. Maunoury, *Police de guerre*, p. 147, believes in a scarcely disguised alliance between the Church and the royalists.

36. *AF*, Aug. 27, 30, 1914, April 16, 1915, July 21, 1917.

37. *JOC*, Nov. 28, Dec. 11, 1917; *La Victoire*, *AF*, Dec. 12, 1917; Téry in *L'Oeuvre*, Dec. 17, 1917; Raffin-Dugens in *JOC*, Dec. 22, 1917, p. 3494.

38. *JOC*, Jan. 18, 1918, pp. 111, 121, and *passim*.

39. Louis Noguères, *Le Suicide de Philippe Daudet* (1926), pp. 172–73; letter quoted by Maurras in *AF*, Jan. 26, 1919; Jean Cocteau to Léon Daudet (F. D. papers): "Vous ais-je dit que l'AF était la lecture des troupes dans le Nord?"

40. *La Renaissance politique et littéraire*, March 1917; *La Vérité*, July 14, 1918; *AF*, March 6, 1917.

41. Barrès in *L'Echo de Paris*, Sept. 28, 1917: "Droit et liberté, ligue républicaine de défense nationale"; P. Renaudel in *L'Humanité*, Sept. 29, 1917.

42. *Le Canard enchaîné*, Jan. 16, 23, 30, 1918, and *passim*.

CHAPTER 5

1. *AF*, March 12, 1917.

2. *AF*, Jan. 15, 19, 25, 31, 1919. Bainville underestimated the lasting power of Bolshevism; see *AF*, Oct. 16, 26, 1919.

3. *AF*, Jan. 13, 24, 1919, Aug. 27, Sept. 1, 1920.

4. *AF,* May 8, 1919: "Une paix trop douce pour ce qu'elle a de dur." The idea would be repeated and developed in *Les Conséquences politiques de la paix* (1920).

5. See Paul Garcin, *Les Ploutocrates au pouvoir* (Lyon, 1920), and Abel Manouvriez's review of the book in *AF,* April 19, 1920. Maurras in *AF,* Feb. 18, 19, 21, 22, and March 6, 1919.

6. *AF,* March 11, 1919.

7. Quoted in *AF,* March 11, April 2, 1919.

8. See the following in *AF*: Daudet, June 24, 1919; Bainville, Aug. 14, 1919; Valois, Oct. 27, 1919; Maurras, June 13, 1921.

9. *AF,* Jan. 11, Oct. 27, 1920. Etienne Weill-Raynal, *Les Réparations allemandes et la France,* III (1948), 827, 896–97, and *passim.* See also Etienne Mantoux, *The Carthaginian Peace, or the Economic Consequences of Mr. Keynes* (Oxford, 1946).

10. Edouard Bonnefous, *Histoire politique de la 3e République,* III (1959), 192.

11. *AF,* June 5, 10, Oct. 8, 1920. See also Georges Vincène, *Gazette de Lausanne,* quoted in *AF,* Nov. 8, 1920: "derrière la résistance allemande se tient l'Angleterre."

12. *AF,* Feb. 16, March 9, April 10, 1920. For an earlier appreciation of the British alliance, see, e.g., Maurras in *AF,* June 11, 1919; Bainville in *AF,* Jan. 15, 1920.

13. See *Le Temps,* Dec. 13, 1920; *JOC,* Dec. 17, 1920; *AF,* Dec. 17, 1920; *JOC,* Jan. 12, 1921.

14. *Le Temps,* Feb. 7, April 10, 1921. See *AF,* April 12, 1921, delighted to find *Le Temps* echoing its ideas; also *AFD,* April 24, 1921.

15. *AF,* July 18, Aug. 15, Nov. 10, 1921, Jan. 1, 2, 10, April 14, 1922.

16. *JOC,* Jan. 10, 1922. In subsequent vote changing, 72 votes became abstentions, thus giving the results usually quoted, 199–312.

17. See, e.g., *AF,* Aug. 12, 1920, and *Le Temps,* Dec. 13, 1920; *AF,* April 19, 1922.

18. *Il Popolo d'Italia,* April 25, quoted in *AF,* April 29, 1922.

19. Quoted in *AF,* May 1, 1922.

20. *AF,* May 2, 3, 1922.

21. *AF,* May 10, 1922; see the Paris press of May 11–15, e.g., *Le Cri de Paris,* May 14, 1922.

22. *JOC,* May 23–June 2, 1922; *AF,* Oct. 22, 1922.

23. *JOC,* Dec. 15, 1922; Bonnefous, *Histoire politique,* III, 345; Weill-Raynal, *Les Réparations allemandes,* III, 839–41.

24. *AF,* Jan. 14, Feb. 22, Aug. 8, 1923, Jan. 5, 16, 1924.

25. *JOS,* March 2, 1923; *L'Intransigeant,* June 13, 1923.

26. *AF,* June 24, Sept. 7, 1924, Oct. 13, 21, 22, 1925.

CHAPTER 6

1. *Le Canard enchaîné,* July 16, 1919. Friends and critics concur: cf. Eugène Lautier in *L'Homme libre,* July 13, 1922, and André Lugan, *L'Action Française de son origine à nos jours* (1928), pp. 14–17.

2. See the tribute of the *Gazette de Lausanne,* quoted in *AF,* Sept. 2, 1919, and the demands for the death penalty for the traitors in *AFD,* Oct. 19, 1919, and *AF,* April 17, 1920.

3. *Bonsoir,* Oct. 12, 14, 17, 1919; *La Vérité,* Oct. 3, 1919.

4. *AF,* May 12, 25, 1914.

5. *AF,* July 20, 24, Aug. 7, 11, 1919; *Le Temps,* July 28, Aug. 11, 1919.

6. Maurras, *La Contre-révolution spontanée* (Lyon, 1943), pp. 169–71. Maurras would have liked ten or twelve places on the Bloc ticket. Some royalists privately attributed their

failure to join the Bloc to the hostility of Millerand. It is possible that Millerand may have retained a certain prejudice against them from his days as counsel for the Maggi dairies.

7. *AF*, Aug. 7, Sept. 11, 1919; André Lichtenberger in *La Victoire*, Aug. 6, 1919; Yvon Delbos in *Le Pays*, Aug. 12, 1919.

8. Georges Aimel in *La Renaissance*, Sept. 27, 1919; Abbé Godet, publisher, in *La Croix des Deux-Sèvres*, Oct. 11, 1919; Jean Guiraud, editor, in *La Croix*, Oct. 17, 1919.

9. Ludovic-Oscar Frossard, *De Jaurès à Léon Blum* (1943), p. 92; Maurras, *Contre-révolution*, p. 171.

10. See *AFD*, April 11, 1920; *AF*, Aug. 17, Oct. 3, 1922.

11. See Daudet in *AF*, Oct. 24, 1919, and Maurras in *AF*, Oct. 25, 1919.

12. Both Gustave Hervé, who blames the royalists and Jean Guiraud, who blames the conservatives, agree that the splitting of the vote cost the victory of several Bloc candidates. See *La Victoire* and *La Croix* of Dec. 2, 1919; *AF*, Dec. 3, 1919.

13. See *Le Figaro*, Jan. 24, 1920; *AF*, May 25, 1920; *JOC*, May 19, 1920; *Journal de Genève*, May 20–22, 1920.

14. Joseph Lahille, *Lettres d'un autre temps, 1910–1938* (1960), p. 48; *L'Humanité*, May 15, 1920; see also *Le Populaire*, May 21, 1920. The pages of *Bonsoir*, *L'Atelier*, *La Vie ouvrière*, *La Lanterne*, and *Le Journal du peuple* during these days reflect the same fears.

15. *AF*, Feb. 5, March 17, 1920.

16. *AF*, Aug. 21, Oct. 29, 1920; *Le Radical*, April 24, 1920; *Le Rappel*, Sept. 3, 1920.

17. *Bonsoir*, *L'Homme libre*, Jan. 22, 1921; see also *L'Ere nouvelle*, Feb. 18, March 26, 1921, and *AF*, Oct. 24, 1921.

18. *Le Cablogramme*, *La Nation belge*, Jan. 12, 1922; *Le Radical* (Marseille), Jan. 13, 1922; *AF*, Jan. 13, 16, 19, 1922.

19. *La Lanterne*, *Bonsoir*, May 14, 1922; *AF*, *La Croix*, *La Lanterne*, *L'Oeuvre*, *L'Eclair*, *Le Journal du peuple*, May 15, 1922.

20. *L'Ere nouvelle*, July 21, 1922; *L'Internationale*, July 27, 1922; *Le Populaire*, *L'Humanité*, *Le Journal du peuple*, July 28, 1922; cf. *AF*, July 30, 1922.

21, Horace Finaly, director of the Banque de Paris et des Pays-Bas.

22. *AF*, Aug. 4, 14, 1922; see also René Johannet in *RU*, XI, No. 16 (Nov. 15, 1922), 467–73. On March 27, 1921, Bainville had welcomed the first news of Fascist violence as a favorable symptom of Italian recovery.

23. *AF*, Nov. 30, 1922; *AFD*, Nov. 12, 1922.

24. *La Victoire*, Feb. 22, 1923; *Les Nouvelles* (Algiers), May 4, 1923; *Le Quotidien*, Feb. 11, 1924. Royalists, also, sometimes pointed this out, as did M[e]. André Jammes in a talk to the Action Française in Castres (Tarn); see *AF*, April 14, 1923.

25. Gioacchino Volpe, *History of the Fascist Movement* (Rome, 1934?), p. 56 (who quotes Mussolini, speaking in almost Maurrassian terms); Mussolini, "Force and Consent," *Gerarchia*, March 1923 (which also takes issue with Daudet's *Stupide 19e siècle*); Daniel Guérin, *Fascisme et grand capital* (1945), p. 215.

26. Luigi Salvatorelli and Giovanni Mira, *Storia d'Italia nel periodo fascista* (Turin, 1957), p. 17; Pietro Nenni, *Vingt Ans de fascisme* (1960), pp. 30–31.

27. Léon Darcis, *La France va-t-elle au fascisme?* (1923), p. 16; François Berry, *Le Fascisme en France* (1926), p. 19; Clara Zetkin's report to the June 20, 1923, session of the Enlarged Communist Executive and the Executive's final resolutions, in *Bulletin communiste*, 1923, pp. 402–5, 444–46.

28. See *AF*, Oct. 30, Nov. 11, 1922, Feb. 14, 1927, May 17, 1928. Georges Valois, *L'Homme contre l'argent*, p. 83.

CHAPTER 7

1. *AF,* Jan. 11, 1923.

2. *L'Humanité, Le Populaire, L'Ere nouvelle,* Jan. 11, 1923; "Poincaré, Maurras, et la Ruhr," *Le Canard enchaîné,* Feb. 21, 1923; André Berthon in *JOC,* March 23, 1923; *L'Homme libre,* Jan. 15, 1923; *Les Documents politiques,* IV, No. 2 (1923), 50; *Vaterland* (The Hague), Jan. 23, 1923.

3. *AF,* Jan. 15, 1923.

4. See *L'Oeuvre,* Jan. 18, 1923: "Assassiné par les Camelots du Roy"; also *L'Ere nouvelle,* and echoes in, e.g., *Le Petit Parisien,* Jan. 23, 1923.

5. See *Dernières Nouvelles de Strasbourg,* Jan. 25, 1923; *L'Aisne* (Laon), Jan. 25–27, 1923; *Le Radical* (Marseille), Jan. 27, 1923; and *AF,* Jan. 24, 1923, and several days thereafter, especially "Revue de la presse," for copious quotations and some threats.

6. *AF,* Jan. 23, 24, 29, Feb. 14, March 10, April 7, May 17, 1923; *AFD,* Jan. 28, 1923; *Journal de Ruffec,* Feb. 18, 1923.

7. Lautier in *L'Homme libre,* July 13, quoted in *AF,* July 14, 1922.

8. *Paris-Midi,* July 3, 1922; cf. "Revue de la presse," *AF,* June–July 1922.

9. Henry Bordeaux, *Charles Maurras et l'Académie française* (1955), pp. 10, 26, 28, and *passim.* Maurras's supporters were probably Boylesve, Barrès, Bourget, Bazin, Bordeaux, Bonnay, Nolhac, De la Gorce, Poincaré, and Foch. See also *L'Oeuvre, La Liberté, L'Eclair,* April 20, 21, 1923.

10. Ernest Lafont in *JOC,* May 8, 1923; Edouard Herriot and Vincent Auriol in *JOC,* May 11, 1923. On May 24, Lautier in *L'Homme libre* credited Daudet with having saved the Bloc by his defense of Arago. See *JOC,* May 23, 1923

11. *AF,* May 26, 1923.

12. The Paris press of March 24–26, 1921; Marius Moutet in *JOC,* May 11, 1923, p. 1852.

13. Private interview; see also F[7] 12862, 4/82 and *passim,* of June 24, 1909.

14. *AF,* June 1, 2, 1923.

15. *JOC,* June 1, 1923: Herriot, p. 2294; Pierre Deyris, p. 2295; Sangnier, p. 2298; Cachin, p. 2295; Maunoury, p. 2296.

16. *JOC,* June 15, 1923, pp. 2551–53, 2577.

17. *JOC,* pp. 2563, 2566, 2582.

18. Bonnefous, III, 308. But cf. Maurice Privat, *Les Heures d'André Tardieu et la crise des partis* (1930), pp. 44–45.

19. *JOC,* June 2, 1922, Jan. 9, June 1, 15, 1923.

CHAPTER 8

1. *AF,* June 22, July 21, Aug. 3, 1923.

2. *AF,* Aug. 5, 17, 21, 26, 1923.

3. *La Liberté,* July 21, 1923; *L'Eclair,* Nov. 21, 1923; *AF,* Nov. 23, 1923: "Pas d'Elections en 1924! Un avis qui fait du chemin."

4. *Le Quotidien,* Jan. 2, 1924.

5. *JOC,* Feb. 6, 1924; *L'Echo national,* Feb. 7, 1924; *AF,* Feb. 8, 1924.

6. *AF,* Feb. 17, March 13, 1924.

7. *De Maasbode,* quoted in *AF,* April 9, 1924.

8. *Revue hebdomadaire,* April 26, 1924. Unless a specific reference is given, all circulation figures quoted for the years 1921–40 stem from an authoritative private source, the nature of which can be learned upon request.

9. *AF,* April 20, 1924.

10. Bonnefous, III, 435; *AF*, May 11–13, 1924.
11. See Edmond Claris, *Souvenirs de soixante ans de journalisme* (1953), pp. 107–8.
12. *La Liberté*, Nov. 4, 1924.
13. *AF*, Dec. 1, 1925.
14. *L'Humanité*, Dec. 4, 8, 1924.
15. Valois, *L'Homme contre l'argent*, pp. 132–45.
16. See *Le Matin*, *Le Temps*, *L'Echo*, *La Liberté*, *L'Avenir*, *Quotidien*, *AF*, during December 1924; Bonnefous, IV, 51.
17. *AF*, March 12, 13, 1925; Frossard in *Paris-Soir*, March 12, 1925; François de Menthon in *Le Réveil social*, April 11, 1925; *La Croix*, quoted in Bonnefous, IV, 63.
18. See *JOC*, March 31, 1925, and the Paris press of the same day; also *Candide*, April 9, 1925.
19. *JOC*, April 3, 1925. Maurice Bokanowski told Herriot, "C'est l'influence du parti socialiste sur le gouvernement qui préoccupe les épargnants."
20. *AF*, April 12, 1925. Ten months later Calzant was briefly arrested for leading his student cohorts in breaking up a meeting of the Ligue d'Action Universitaire addressed by Scelle. One of those injured in the fray was Pierre Mendès-France, *étudiant*, who was chairman of the meeting. F^7 13198 of Feb. 24, 1926.
21. *AF*, April 19, 21, 1925.
22. *L'Eclair*, April 25, 1925; *Paris-Centre*, April 27, 1925; *Candide*, April 30, 1925; *AF*, April 24, 1925, and the issues following.
23. *La Gazette de l'ouest*, *Le Pays sarthois*, *L'Echo du Roannais*, and *Le Moniteur de Bourgoin* endorsed him. *Le Nouvelliste de Rennes* declared that as a liberal republican publication it owed Daudet its support. See *AF*, May 4, and especially June 6, 7, 23, 28, 1925.
24. *Candide*, Feb. 18, 1926.
25. *AF*, Dec. 8, 1925; *L'Echo de Paris*, Jan. 10, 1926.
26. See *NG*, Aug. 1, 1925; *AF*, March 7, April 25, June 16–19, 1926. In *L'Avenir*, June 19, 1926, Paul Allain echoed their arguments, and frankly admitted that he did so.
27. Georges Suarez, *De Poincaré à Poincaré* (1928), pp. 209–10.
28. *AF*, July 10, 31, 1926.
29. See *AF*, Aug. 9, 11, 12, 1926, for the testimony of men as diverse in opinion as Cardinal Baudrillart, rector of the Catholic Institute; Professor Rémy Perrier, director of the (Pre-Medical) PCN; and Albert Bayet, a professor at the Lycée Louis-le-Grand, as to the tremendous influence of Maurrassian ideas on their students.
30. *AF*, July 22, 28, 1926; *Candide*, July 29, 1926.

CHAPTER 9

1. *AF*, Dec. 2, 1923; compare Maurras's similar reasoning on the day following Ernest Berger's murder, May 27, 1923.
2. *L'Humanité*, Sept. 8, 1925.
3. Maurice Martin du Gard, *Vérités du moment* (1928), p. 133; see also *Le Journal*, Nov. 15, 1925; *Candide*, Nov. 19, 1925.
4. Letter of Gaëtan Sanvoisin to Daudet, dated March 28, 1936 (F. D. papers); Michel Missoffe, personal communication; Gabriel Oberson, *Une Cause célèbre: la mort de Philippe Daudet* (Freibourg, 1926).
5. Letters of June 16, 1926, and May 15, 1927 (F. D. papers). Further details may be found in Paul Dresse, *Léon Daudet vivant* (1947); Maurice Privat, *L'Enigme Philippe Daudet* (1931); Louis Noguères, *Le Suicide de Philippe Daudet* (1926), by Bajot's defender; Seguin and R. Guitton, *Du scandale au meurtre: la mort de Philippe Daudet*

(1925), an early presentation of the Daudet view; René Bréval, *Philippe Daudet a bel et bien été assassiné* (1959), a recent restatement of the same. For skeptical views of Daudet's case from friendly quarters, see F^7 13198 of March 7 and April 15, 1926, and Georges Oltramare, *Les Souvenirs nous vengent* (Geneva, 1956), pp. 122–23.

CHAPTER 10

1. *AF*, July 19, 1922, and Feb. 15, 1923.
2. *RAF*, XXXVII (December 1912), 23; *AF*, Feb. 10, 1914.
3. Dimier, *Vingt Ans*, pp. 233, 265, 336.
4. See Bernanos to Dom Besse, *Bulletin périodique*, No. 11 (July 1952), p. 9.
5. Report to the Eighth Annual Congress, *AF*, June 22, 1921; Report to the Ninth Annual Congress, *AF*, June 8, 1922.
6. See *AF*, Dec. 14, 1920, March 31, April 6, Nov. 21, 1924, Nov. 26, 1925, Nov. 24, 1926, Nov. 24, 1927, Nov. 22, 1928, Nov. 28, 1929.
7. *AF*, Feb. 27, 1923, Feb. 14, 1924, March 25, April 29, 1923, Oct. 27, 1924.
8. *NG*, April 1, May 4, Dec. 15, 1925, April 1, March 15, June 15, Aug. 15, 1926.
9. See *L'Ere nouvelle*, Sept. 21, 1921, for a letter from a Lyon student; *AF*, June 22, 1921; Yves Simon, *La Grande Crise de la République française* (Montreal, 1941), pp. 47ff; Maurice Muret, *Gazette de Lausanne*, June 29, 1921.
10. *AF*, March 20, 1920; *L'Ere nouvelle*, Jan. 12, 13, 23, June 6, 1921.
11. See *Le Temps* and *L'Ere nouvelle*, April 8, 1921.
12. See *AF*, June 27, 1921, quoting *La Documentation catholique*.
13. Reports of Emmanuel Beau and Henri Longnon at the Ninth Annual Congress, *AF*, June 9, 1922; Georges Calzant at the Eleventh Congress, *AF*, Nov. 20, 1924.
14. Calzant in *AF*, Nov. 28, Dec. 4, 1925, Nov. 23, 26, 1926.
15. Gyp, *Le Coup du lapin* (1930), pp. 315–16.
16. *AF*, October 1923, *passim*; *La Croix*, Oct. 10, and *Le Figaro*, Oct. 11, approved their violence.
17. *AF*, April 25, 26, 1926; *Le Canard enchaîné*, April 28, 1926.
18. *NG*, April and September 1925; *AF*, March 15, June 15, 1926; René Benjamin, *Aliborons et démagogues* (1927), pp. 151–218.
19. Gyp, *Le Coup du lapin*, pp. 127–28; Benjamin, pp. 151–218; Marius Plateau to the Eighth Congress, *AF*, June 24, 1921; Paul Courcoural, Louis Jasseron, Elie Jacquet, and Pierre Lecoeur, personal communications.
20. Jean Prévost, *Dix-huitième Année* (1929), p. 138.
21. See *AF*, June 24, Oct. 25, 1921.
22. See *AF*, Aug. 16, 1922, for the report of Emile Devaux (Loire); *AF*, Aug. 30, for that of Jean Jamain (Poitou); *AF*, Sept. 13, for that of Elie Jacquet (Massif Central).
23. *AF*, Dec. 28, 1921; Nov. 5, 1924.
24. *AF*, March 3, Aug. 3, 1924.
25. For subscription and circulation figures, see the following: Archives Nationales, F^7 12863, Nos. 1 and 4/130; F^7 12844, 1917; F^7 13198 of Jan. 13, 27, Feb. 3, Nov. 24, 1926; F^7 13199 of Oct. 7, 1931; reports of the Seventh Annual Congress in *AF*, March 20, 1920, and *Almanach 1921*, pp. 127–28; *AF*, June 22, 1921; Maurras in *AF*, Nov. 2, 1921; Pujo in *AF*, Aug. 3, 1924; Maurras in *AF*, March 3, Dec. 20, 1924, March 7, 10, 1925; reports of the Eleventh Annual Congress in *AF*, Nov. 18–19, 1924; Daudet in *AFD*, April 5, 1925; *AF*, April 16, May 4, June 4, 25, July 15, Aug. 2, Nov. 27, 1925; May 13, Aug. 11, 1926; *Le Canada* (Montreal), Jan. 24, 1923. Cf. Samuel Osgood, *French Royalism Under the Third and Fourth Republics* (The Hague, 1960), p. 115.
26. E.g., *AF*, June 8, 1922, cites the figures of 4,893 propaganda subscriptions for the *Action française* and 1,473 for the *Action française du dimanche* during 1921.

27. See, e.g., *AFD*, April 25, May 30, 1920.
28. *AFD*, June 12, 1921.
29. *AF*, Nov. 18, 19, 1924.
30. In December 1928 it also brought out its own Southern edition, *L'Ordre provençal.*
31. *AF*, Nov. 23, 1927; *Action française agricole*, Nov. 27, 1927, June 3, Nov. 25, 1928, Dec. 1, 1929, Jan. 26, 1930, July 5, 1931. A police report, F⁷ 13199 of October 7, 1931, notes the paper's end, with the remark that it had been printing about 15,000 copies but that since 1927 "bouillonage" had accounted for some three-quarters of that number.
32. Other publications founded to support the Action Française and spread its doctrine were the *Salut national* (Limoges), the *Salut* (Saint-Malo), and Henri de Bruchard's *Midi royaliste*. Bruchard, the only member of the staff of the *Revue critique* who left it after the 1914 break with Maurras, died in the war, and his review died with him.
33. See *AF*, Sept. 27, 1909; "Le mouvement d'Action française," *La Renaissance*, March 3, 1917.
34. See Jacques Kayser, *La Presse de province sous la 3ᵉ République* (1958), pp. 90–95.
35. Lautier in *L'Homme libre*, Jan. 1, 1921; Gyp, *Le Coup du lapin*, pp. 74–75; Abbé Wetterlé in *Le Nouveau Rhin français*, quoted in *AF*, Nov. 26, 1921.
36. One story popular in Maurrassian quarters was of Anatole France's advising a provincial doctor who complained of the poor quality of current writing to read the *Action française*, which is "written in French." See Havard in *RU*, May 1944, p. 447; Vallat, *Charles Maurras*, p. 21.
37. *L'Homme libre*, June 7, 1922; Maurice Muret, quoted in *AF*, April 11, 1921; Gyp, *Le Chambard* (1928), p. 75; Charles Maurras, MS notes of Summer 1950, in the possession of Pierre Boutang.
38. René Bréval, *Philippe Daudet a bel et bien été assassiné*, p. 181, says that the costs of the litigation with Bajot came to about 500,000 francs—equal to some 30 million francs in 1959.
39. Father R. L. Bruckberger in *Les Procès de collaboration* (1948), p. 367.
40. Louis Rambert, *L'Action Française pendant la guerre* (1919), p. 44; *AF*, Dec. 16, 1917; but cf. Téry in *L'Oeuvre*, Dec. 22, 25, 1917.
41. *Cahiers Charles Maurras*, No. 1 (1960), p. 91. The reports of the Sûreté Générale abound in remarks on the League's lamentable financial straits and recurrent financial crises. See, e.g., files F⁷ 13198–99, concerning Action Française activity in the Seine, 1926–32.
42. For Coty's subsidies, see Maurras, *AF*, Sept. 27, 1932; *Contre-révolution*, p. 118; Valois, *L'Homme contre l'argent*, p. 297; Bernanos, *Nous autres français* (1939), pp. 91–93; F⁷ 13199 of Jan. 2, 1932. Coty also gave financial support to Robert Havard's *Rome.*
43. Report of the Ninth Congress, *AF*, June 8, 1922; report of the Twelfth Congress, *AF*, Nov. 26, 1925; report of the Thirteenth Congress, Nov. 24, 1926: this last included the statement that the 5,157 donors contributed a total of 650,000 francs toward the two-million-franc budget of the year.
44. Gyp, *Le Chambard*, pp. 57–58.
45. *AF*, March 21, April 13, 20, 27, May 26, June 10, 1919, April 21, 1921, Jan. 8, Feb. 25, 28, Aug. 28, 1923, May 22, 1924, Sept. 16, 1926. Louis Bringer, a moderate republican and a Freemason, represented the Lozère in the Chamber from 1919 to 1923 and in the Senate from 1932 to 1941.
46. F⁷ 131200 (1926): March 1, Senlis, Oise; March 8, Beauvais, Oise; April 19, Thionville, Moselle.
47. Professor Aulard's son-in-law, Albert Bayet, seems to have kept a weather eye on it: see, e.g., *Le Quotidien*, Aug. 12, 1924.
48. *L'Ere nouvelle*, quoted in *AF*, Jan. 8, 1921; Louis Noguères, *Le Suicide de Philippe Daudet*, pp. 172–73; René Benjamin, "Valentine ou la folie démocratique" in *Minerve et*

le boucher (1926); Jean Anouilh, *Le Hurluberlu* (1959); *AF*, Feb. 28, 1927; *JOC*, April 29, 1923: written question No. 17385 of March 26, 1923. F[7] 13198 (1926) mentions numerous visits paid by officers in mufti to Colonel Georges Larpent and his aides in the Information Service; see, e.g., Jan. 13 and Feb. 25, 1926.

49. See *AF*, November 1922, January 1923, Oct. 15, 1925.

50. *AF*, Jan. 4, 1923.

51. These were often departmental archivists, trained at the Ecole des Chartes, like Louis Biernawski, head archivist of the Loire and a great friend of the Action Française, who, on March 18, 1919, married Margueritte Falcon de Longuevialle, a member of the Lyon group of Jeunes Filles Royalistes. The bride's father, Louis de Longuevialle, was president of the Comité Royaliste du Beaujolais; her sister, Gabrielle, married another integral nationalist, the Vicomte Louis de Saporta.

52. See *AF*, April 1, 1920, Nov. 27, 1927.

53. Report to the Tenth Congress, *AF*, June 21, 1923.

54. Robert Brasillach, *Lettres écrites en prison* (1952), p. 111; *AF*, Oct. 28, 1918; Bernard de Vésins in *Paris patriote à la salle Wagram* (1919), p. 9; Delahaye in *ibid.*, p. 34.

55. Stuart R. Schram, *Protestantism and Politics in France* (Alençon, 1954), pp. 103–7. See Gillouin's *Une Philosophie de l'histoire moderne et française* (1921), *Trois Crises* (1929), and *Le Problème de l'Occident* (Lausanne, 1929).

56. Noël Vesper, *Les Protestants devant la patrie* (1925); Alfred-Henry Chaber, *L'Association Sully—sa doctrine, son but* (1932).

57. "L'Angoisse d'un Juif de France," *AF*, Sept. 6, 1913.

58. *AF*, Oct. 31, 1919.

59. René Groos, *Enquête sur le problème juif* (1924), *passim*; *AF*, Nov. 11, 1926; Gérin-Ricard and Truc, *Histoire de l'Action Française*, pp. 188–89.

60. See, e.g., *AF*, March 4, 1919, Feb. 6, 19, 1923, Oct. 5, 1927, Sept. 27, 1929, May 3, 1931. René Groos, *Réponse à M. Paul Lévy* (1921); Louis Latzarus, *La France veut-elle un Roi?* (1925). Among those attending a monarchist rally at Senlis in January 1932 was a M. Lévy (F[7] 13203 [Oise], Jan. 10, 1932). That summer, a great royalist meeting at Noisy-le-Grand was held on the estate of M. Cahen d'Anvers; see F[7] 13199 (Seine-et-Oise), June 30, 1932.

61. *The Age of Reform* (New York, 1955), pp. 78–79.

62. See Byrnes, *Antisemitism in Modern France*; Georges Bernanos, *La Grande Peur des bien-pensants* (1931).

63. See *La Monarchie française: Lettres et documents politiques (1844–1907)*, (1907), pp. 241–46.

64. Groos, *Enquête sur le problème juif*, pp. 43, 126–29.

65. *Ibid.*, p. 38.

66. Vaugeois in *AF*, Aug. 15, 1900.

67. *Ibid.*; Osgood, *French Royalism*, p. 66; Maurras in *Almanach, 1924*, p. 168.

68. Testimony of Lucien Rebatet; *Almanach 1924*, p. 168; *AF*, Jan. 26, 1925; F[7] 12853, No. 5.

69. See, e.g., *AF*, June 13, July 4, 1920, Oct. 5, 20, 1921. André Blumel, personal communication.

70. *AF*, Jan. 28, 1921; *The Times* (London), Aug. 16–18, 1921; *AF*, Aug. 19, 1921. For a brief history of the *Protocols*, see Paul de Stoecklin in *Cahiers des Droits de l'Homme*, Jan. 1, 1939, pp. 11–21; for an analytical evaluation, see John S. Curtiss, *An Appraisal of the Protocols of Zion* (New York, 1942). As late as 1937 Bernard Grasset published a new edition of the notorious work, translated from the Russian, with an introduction by Lambelin. Much use was also made of it, of course, during the Occupation.

CHAPTER 11

1. See, e.g., *AF*, March 24, June 2, Sept. 1, 1919, March 22, 1930.

2. *AF*, March 22, 1920.

3. Cf., e.g., *La Croix*, May 13, 1920; *Journal de Rouen*, quoted in *AF*, March 24, 1922.

4. See *AF*, November–December 1922 (e.g., Valois, Dec. 4; Maurras, Dec. 7; the great poster reproduced on Dec. 12); Daudet in *JOC*, Dec. 6, 1922; Valois, "Philosophie de la victoire," *RU*, Vol. XIX, No. 16 (Nov. 15, 1924).

5. Valois, *L'Homme contre l'argent*, pp. 74–77; Henry Coston, *Partis, journaux et hommes politiques* (1960), p. 16. See also Maurice Privat, *L'Enigme Philippe Daudet*, pp. 25–26; *Revue hebdomadaire*, April 7, 1923; *Cahiers des Droits de l'Homme*, June 25, 1923, p. 274.

6. Quoted in *L'Homme contre l'argent*, pp. 125–29, where Valois adds: "Cela fit un joli scandale à Paris."

7. *AF*, Oct. 11, 12, 1925; *Le Nouveau Siècle*, Oct. 15, 1925.

8. *AF*, Nov. 10, 26, 1925.

9. *RU*, XI, No. 16 (Nov. 15, 1922), 467–73.

10. *AF*, Jan. 29, 1923.

11. Valois, *Contre le mensonge et la calomnie* (1927), pp. 16–20; *AF*, Oct. 11, Nov. 7, 26, Dec. 8, 1925.

12. See *Il Momento* (Turin), Nov. 7, 1925; *La Tribuna* (Rome), Dec. 8, 1925.

13. *Contre le mensonge*, pp. 21–22.

14. See *L'Ere nouvelle*, Jan. 2, 1926; F^7 13198 (Seine) of January, February, and June, 1926.

15. *AF*, Nov. 22, 1927, Nov. 20, 1928, July 30, 31, 1930.

16. See *AF*, April 5, 12, 1936.

17. Abel Manouvriez, "Néo-Physiocratie," *AF*, Jan. 16, 1920; Maurras, "Agriculture d'abord," *AF*, Aug. 9, 1923.

18. Xavier Vallat, *La Croix, les lys et la peine des hommes* (1960), chap. 11. See also Paul Vignaux, *Corporatisme, traditionalisme et syndicalisme* (New York, 1943), p. 38, concerning Action Française influence in the powerful Union Nationale des Syndicats Agricoles.

19. *AF*, April 7, 1922, Nov. 23, 1927.

20. *AF*, April 1, 1908; *JOC*, April 2, 1924.

21. *AF*, June 30, Aug. 5, 1919, Dec. 20, 1921, April 5, 1922, May 20, 1923, May 11, 1924, Sept. 13, 1925; *JOC*, Feb. 15, 1924.

22. *JOC*, April 4, 1924; *AF*, Aug. 24, 1925; Jean Rateau, *Les Franco-métèques* (1936), pp. 10, 114–15.

23. *Le Dilemme de Marc Sangnier* (1910), p. 14.

24. *AF*, Sept. 19, 1927; UCF, *Tract aux ouvriers*, Aug. 9, 1928; letter of Duc de Guise in *AF*, May 14, 1930.

25. Jean de Kerlecq, "Au-dessus de la haine," *AF*, Nov. 20, 1924.

CHAPTER 12

1. Raissa Maritain, *Les Grandes Amitiés* (New York, 1944), II, 201.

2. See *AF*, March 12, 1925, for a letter from a recruit whose conversion had come about as the result of reading *La Croix* since 1912.

3. J. Brugerette, *Le Prêtre français et la société contemporaine*, III (1938), 684–85.

4. Based on an MS copy of Camille Bellaigue's diary in the possession of Adrien Dansette.

5. See Maurras, *Le Bienheureux Pie X, sauveur de la France* (1953), pp. 68–70; Dimier, *Vingt Ans,* pp. 219–20; F7 12863 No. 3 of Dec. 3, 1913.

6. Monseigneur René Fontenelle, *Sa Sainteté Pie XI* (1937), pp. 189–92.

7. The memoir is quoted in its entirety by Canet-Fontaine, *Saint-Siège, Action Française et Catholiques intégraux,* pp. 121–37.

8. *Ibid.,* p. 35; Maurras, *L'Action Française et le Vatican* (1927), p. 136.

9. See *AF,* Oct. 11, 1919, June 22, 1921, Oct. 11, 29, 1922.

10. *AF,* April 5, 10, Aug. 8, 1919.

11. *AF,* Jan. 17, 1920.

12. *AF,* May 23, 1920. For a view almost as laudatory, see the 1925 edition of the Bloud and Gay *Almanach catholique français,* pp. 439, 453.

13. *AF,* Feb. 11, 1923.

14. *AF,* Dec. 28, 1923, May 3, 1924.

15. See Maurice Vaussard, *Enquête sur le nationalisme* (1924), who quotes a great many Catholics favorable to the Action Française; André Lugan, *L'Action Française de son origine à nos jours* (1928), pp. 11–13; Michel Darbon, *Le Conflit entre la droite et la gauche dans le catholicisme français, 1830–1953* (Toulouse, 1953), pp. 229–30; none of these writers is friendly.

16. Yves Simon, *La Grande Crise de la République française,* pp. 52–53; *Courrier de Genève,* quoted in *AF,* Oct. 23, 1925.

17. Dublaix, *Un apologiste,* pp. 61–62.

18. Letter of Aug. 13, 1922, quoted in Paul Dresse, unpublished MS, III, 6.

19. After the Second World War, Justinien became the editor of *L'Indépendant français,* which in 1952 was combined with *Aspects de la France.* See Maurras, *Lettres,* p. 344.

20. Canet-Fontaine, p. 44.

21. Cardinal Andrieu quoted this in his diocesan bulletin *L'Aquitaine,* Feb. 18, 1922.

22. *AF,* July 9, 1925; *NG,* July 15, 1925.

23. *AF,* July 23, 24, 27, and Aug. 1, 1925.

24. See Lugan, *L'Action Française,* p. 19; Georges Champeaux, *La Croisade des démocraties* (1943), II, 264–67; *Progrès de l'idée royaliste* (1936), p. 101.

25. *L'A.C.J.F. et les mouvements politiques de jeunesse* (Besançon, 1926), pp. 2–3, 5–6, 17–19.

26. Dansette, *Histoire religieuse de la France contemporaine,* II, 582–83.

27. Canon A. Simon, letter to the author, March 4, 1961.

28. *Le Rappel,* July 3, 1925.

29. *XXe Siècle,* July 15, 30, Aug. 4, 1925.

30. Quoted in *La Libre Belgique,* July 24, 1925.

31. *Ibid.,* July 26, Oct. 12, 1925; *Cahiers de la Jeunesse Belge,* Sept. 20, 1925.

32. *La Libre Belgique,* Sept. 19, 23, 1925.

33. See Comte Louis de Lichtervelde in *Revue générale,* Sept. 15, 1925.

34. *L'Indépendance belge,* Oct. 2, 1925; *La Libre Belgique,* Oct. 3, 1925.

35. *La Libre Belgique,* Oct. 16, 1925.

36. *AFD* (Savoy ed.), July 5, 1925.

37. *NG,* April 1, 1926.

38. Charost-Schwerer correspondence, in *Documentation catholique,* March 5, 12, 19, 1927; Canet-Fontaine, p. 76; *Les Documents nationaux,* No. 2, p. 2; Brugerette, *Le Prêtre français,* III, 689–90; Dansette, II, 581–82; Robert Vallery-Radot, *Le Temps de la colère* (1932), p. 173.

39. *NG,* Sept. 15, 1926.

40. *AF,* Sept. 1, 2, 3, 9, 1926.

41. Bernanos to Massis, in a letter written early in September 1926, Société des Amis

de Georges Bernanos, *Bulletin périodique,* No. 17–20 (Christmas 1953), pp. 9–10; *Candide,* Sept. 16, 1925.

42. Undated letter in private collection.
43. Anne André-Glandy, *Le Marquis de Roux* (Poitiers, 1957), p. 149.
44. *AF,* Nov. 22, 23, 1926.
45. Quoted in *AF,* Sept. 27, 1926.
46. *AF,* Oct. 8, 1926.
47. *AF,* Oct. 10, 17, 21, 26, 31, 1926.
48. *AF,* Nov. 1, 9, 1926.
49. See Colonel Georges Larpent, "Que veut-on?" *AF,* Sept. 3, 1926.
50. *AF,* Nov. 10, 17, 1926.
51. Robert Havard, *Chemins de Rome* (1956), p. 207; *AF,* Dec. 4, 1926.
52. Dumont-Wilden in *La Nation belge,* quoted in *AF,* Feb. 19, 1927.
53. *Cyrano,* Jan. 2, 1927; *Candide,* Jan. 13, 1927; Pierre Dominique in *Le Rappel,* Jan. 9, 1927; *AF,* Jan. 6, 1927. See also Dansette, II, 599.
54. *La Croix,* March 8, 1927; *AF,* March 9, 1927.
55. Brugerette, *Le Prêtre français,* III, 697.
56. *La Croix,* March 28, 1927; *AF,* March 29, 1927. Not everyone had, like Maritain, canceled his subscription immediately on seeing the papal decree of January 9; see the copy of Maritain's letter to Maurras, dated Jan. 11, 1927, sent by himself to Gonzague de Reynold, who also submitted (Reynold papers).
57. Vaussard, *Politique religieuse et Action Française* (1927), p. 40.
58. *Courrier de Genève,* Jan. 17, 1927; *AF,* Jan. 22, 1927.
59. Yves Simon, *La Grande Crise,* p. 78; *AF,* Feb. 28, 1927, Jan. 23, 1933.
60. Quoted in Vallery-Radot, *Le Temps de la colère,* pp. 216–19.
61. Quoted from the Aubaret diary in Glandy, *Marquis de Roux,* pp. 155–56.
62. For similar moral dilemmas, see Maurice Clavière, *Léon Daudet ou le contre-courant d'une décadence* (1943), pp. 188ff.
63. Letter of Sept. 9, 1927 (Gay papers). Another point of view was expressed by the vice-president of the 18th section of Paris who told his men "on good authority" that the Pope was half crazy, so contradictory decisions on his part were not surprising (F^7 13199, Jan. 18, 1930).
64. *AF,* Nov. 20, 23, 1927.
65. *AF,* March 5, 1927.
66. See *AF,* June 4, 1927, Feb. 6, March 29, 1928; *Petit Méridional,* Jan. 21, 1928; *Almanach, 1929,* pp. 160–62, 166; Francisque Gay to Monseigneur Maglione, letter of June 3, 1927 (Gay papers); F^7 13204 for many reports of clerical and lay insubmission.
67. *Almanach, 1936,* pp. 103–9.
68. Maurice Bedel, *Molinoff, Indre-et-Loire* (1936), p. 127.

CHAPTER 13

1. See *AF,* Feb. 10, 14, 1927; and, e.g., the circular of royalist and Action Française committees in the Indre, March 30, 1927.
2. Letter quoted in *AF,* Feb. 5, 1927; Lahille, *Lettres,* p. 70 (dated March 28, 1927).
3. Gay to Maglione, June 3, 1927 (Gay papers); General Castelnau, *L'Echo de Paris,* Jan. 7, 1927; Father Doncoeur in *La Croix,* June 2, 1927; also *Le Coup du lapin,* p. 284.
4. Letters to Gay, dated Aug. 8, Sept. 29, 30, Oct. 26, 1927 (Gay papers).
5. Abbé Beaudon to Gay, Oct. 12, 1927 (Gay papers).
6. Toast of Francisque Gay at the banquet of Les Amis de La Vie Catholique, Aug. 6, 1927 (Gay papers).

7. Abbé Beaudon to Gay, Sept. 29, 1927 (Gay Papers); *La Croix,* Sept. 6, 1926.

8. Testimony of Xavier Vallat; Gay to Luigi Maglione, June 9, 1927 (Gay papers); *L'Aube,* Dec. 7, 1927; *La Vie catholique,* Dec. 10, 1927; *La Vie intellectuelle,* Dec. 25, 1932.

9. *AF,* Aug. 25, Oct. 11, 15, 1927; Mermeix, *Le Ralliement et l'Action Française* (1927), p. 455.

10. *La Croix,* Nov. 10, 1927.

11. Private memorandum of the Comte de Nantois, Dec. 14, 1949; communicated by M. René Rancoeur.

12. MM. Louis Jasseron, Roger Joseph, Yves O'Mahony, Pierre Mauriac, personal communications.

13. Nel Ariès, *Episodes et documents—Autour de l'Action Française* (Bordeaux, 1937), p. 9; Gay to Duthoit, Nov. 29, 1930 (Gay papers); F^7 13199 of June 6, 1932.

14. See Charlotte Montard, *Comment j'ai fait évader Léon Daudet* (1932), pp. 58ff. For a detailed report on the Baron's reaction to the condemnation and his compromises between rival alliances, see F^7 13199 of July 22, 1931.

15. *La Vie catholique,* Aug. 26, 1928; Lettre adressée à chaque Evêque français par des professeurs laïques de son diocèse (Strasbourg, June 20, 1928); letter of Henri Carteron, dated Dec. 1, 1928, in Mauriac papers; Georges Lefranc, "L'Action Française et le Vatican," *Politica* (November 1928), p. 353.

16. *AF,* Dec. 12, 1935.

17. Chevrot to Gay, March 2, 3, 1936 (Gay papers).

18. Albert Bayet, *La Lumière,* July 30, 1937.

19. Glandy, *Réal del Sarte,* pp. 144–45; memorandum of the Marquis de Roux, communicated by his son; see also Aristide Cormier, *La Vie intérieure de Charles Maurras* (1954), pp. 123–24.

20. Charles Loiseau in *Europe nouvelle,* quoted in *AF,* Jan. 25, 1936.

21. *Mounier et sa génération* (1956), pp. 176–77; Robert Havard, *Histoire de l'Action Française* (1950), pp. 140–49, and personal communication.

22. Havard, *Histoire,* p. 145, and *Chemin de Rome,* pp. 180–84. See also *Pourquoi le journal "Sept" a été supprimé* (1937).

23. *Extrait des Annales de Sainte Thérèse de Lisieux,* August–September 1939.

24. Letters of Nov. 23, 28, 1938 (private collection).

25. Letters of Robert de Boisfleury (Roux papers).

26. Glandy, *Réal del Sarte,* pp. 146–49. Ministry of Foreign Affairs dispatches, copies in the author's possession: Europe 190, dated May 22; Europe 199, dated June 2; Europe 210, dated June 13, 1939; and Note by Georges Bonnet, summarizing his part in the negotiations.

27. See Rouquette's argument, "Charles Maurras," *Etudes,* p. 405.

28. Quoted in Darbon *Le Conflit entre la droite et la gauche,* p. 240.

29. See his letter to Lucien Corpechot, printed in both *Le Gaulois* and *Le Figaro,* Dec. 4, 1927.

30. Quoted by Jacques Maritain, *Primauté du spirituel* (1927) p. 101.

31. Canet-Fontaine, pp. 43–44; *La Croix,* March 4, 1928.

32. Vallery-Radot, *Le Temps de la colère,* p. 165; Dublaix, *Un Apologiste,* p. 20.

33. Monseigneur Ricard, "Pourquoi l'Eglise a-t-elle condamné l'Action Française?" quoted in Champeaux, *La Croisade des démocraties,* II, 266.

34. See R. Gillouin, "Rome, l'Action Française, et la France," *Le Monde nouveau,* January 1928; also Cardinal Billot's letter quoted in Ariès, *Episodes et documents,* p. 12; Le Floch's letter in *Le Gaulois,* Dec. 4, 1927; and *La Vie catholique,* Dec. 10, 1927. Writing to Maurras on January 20, 1927, Gonzague de Reynold says as much: the conflict was an almost necessary one, and many had seen it coming. "Having built your

apology of the Church on positivistic and pagan foundations, it was impossible that at a given moment this edifice should not sag on its foundations" (G. de R. papers).

35. *La Croix,* Sept. 11, 12, 1927; Paul Vignaux, *Corporatisme, traditionalisme et syndicalisme,* p. 56 and *passim.*

CHAPTER 14

1. Gustav Steinbonner, *Der Ring,* quoted in *AF,* Aug. 13, 1931.

2. *AF,* Aug. 20, 24, Nov. 24, 1927; *NG,* Jan. 1, 1928; *Almanach, 1928,* p. 166. But see F[7] 13198 of Oct. 28, 1926.

3. *La République de l'Oise,* Jan. 25, 1927.

4. *AF,* Nov. 23, 1928.

5. *AF,* Nov. 29, 1929. The report adds: "nos amis ont tort."

6. F[7] 13199 (Seine), July 1, 1929, and (Loire) April 1929; F[7] 13205 (Var), Nov. 29, 1929, and (Vienne) Jan. 20, 1929; F[7] 13202 (Ariège), July 9, 1930; F[7] 13204 (Marne), June 26, 1930, and (Nord) Oct. 13, 1930.

7. But during the same period more meetings were held in Paris itself than had been held in previous years; see *AF,* Nov. 24, 1926, Nov. 28, 1929.

8. *AF,* Dec. 2, 1932.

9. *AF,* Dec. 1, 1930, Dec. 15, 1933.

10. *AF,* Oct. 11, 1931, Nov. 15–17, 1929, Feb. 7, 1930.

11. *Commission d'Enquête chargée de rechercher les causes et les origines des événements du 6 février 1934 et jours suivants, ainsi que toutes les responsabilités encouroues* (1934), *Rapport général,* Annexes, I, 138. In 1931, a lean year, the Dames Royalistes alone collected 340,000 francs for the movement. In particularly tight moments help could be expected from rich supporters like Frédéric Delbecq, the owner of the Château de Changeons near Avranches and a member of the League's board of directors; the Marquis Régis de Vibraye, whose lands and châteaux stood in the Orne, Nièvre, and Loir-et-Cher; and Claude Caruel de Saint-Martin, a *ligueur* of the 17th Arrondissement well known for his liberal support of royalist activities. F[7] 13199 of June 15, 1929.

12. *AF,* April 4, 1930, July 9, 1934, Sept. 13, 1935; Commission d'Enquête, *Rapport géneral,* Annexes, II, 1740.

13. *AF,* July 17, 26, 1928; *Candide,* April 26, 1928.

14. *AF,* March 20, June 11, 1928, June 10, Nov. 29, 1931, June 5, 14, Nov. 28, Dec. 11, 1932, May 16, 1935; Maurras, *Lettres,* p. 274.

15. *AF,* Feb. 10, 25, 1928, July 25, 1929.

16. Bedel, *Molinoff,* pp. 14–15.

17. *Primauté du spirituel,* p. 98; *AF,* March 17, 1927.

18. *Le Figaro, Le Journal, L'Avenir, Le Rappel, L'Homme libre, L'Humanité, L'Ere nouvelle, AF,* May 9, 20, 1927; Charlotte Montard, *Comment j'ai fait évader Léon Daudet,* pp. 65–66.

19. The only papers to take the affair seriously were friendly ones belonging to men like Taittinger, Bailby, and Coty. *Action française agricole,* June 19, 1927, complained that "unlike the Paris papers," the local regional press had, with the exception of *L'Eclair Comtois,* paid no attention to Daudet's siege and arrest, let alone "joined in the protests" raised in Paris against such treatment of a father. For an ironic view of the period and its events, cf. Gyp, *Le Coup du lapin,* which concerns the years 1927–28.

20. See, e.g., *AF,* Nov. 21, 1917, Nov. 3, 23, 1920.

21. Maurice Martin du Gard, *Les Mémorables,* II, 277: "C'est un Bel Ami court sur pattes."

22. *Almanach, 1938,* pp. 101–5. In a talk at Nantes, Delest mentioned that he and Daudet were spared the anthropometric formalities of Bertillon's department and were not even fingerprinted upon arrest. F[7] 13203 (Loire-Inférieure), May 3, 1928.

23. Maurras, *Lettres,* p. 119. For firsthand accounts, see Montard, *Comment j'ai fait évader Léon Daudet,* Joseph Delest, *Pour une grande cause: en prison et en liberté avec Léon Daudet* (1928).

24. *Candide,* June 30, 1927; *Paris-Midi,* Oct. 29, 1928.

25. *AF,* Dec. 20, 21, 1928.

26. *Le Journal, Le Petit Journal, Le Figaro, L'Ami du Peuple, L'Oeuvre, AF,* May 13, 1929.

27. Léon Bérard, addressing the congress of the Alliance Démocratique Républicaine, quoted in *AF,* March 18, 1929.

28. *L'Echo de Paris,* May 18, 20, 1929.

29. *AF,* March 20, 1926, Oct. 6, 1927, March 23, 1928, Sept. 15, 1931.

30. Pierre Benoît in *Aspects de la France,* March 23, 1958.

31. See the Paris press of January 2, 3, 1930.

32. *AF,* Feb. 6, 1930. Vésins was replaced by Admiral Schwerer. A detailed police report of June 5, 1931, on the causes of the troubles of the previous year concluded that the losses which followed upon it, coming after the papal condemnation, had cost the Action Française 35 to 40 per cent of its strength. By September 22, 1931, membership in the section of the 17th Arrondissement in Paris, one of the most flourishing, had fallen from two hundred to forty after the resignation of its president, Roger Sémichon. A report of October 7, 1931, attributes the final collapse of the *Action française agricole* to the departure of Bernard de Vésins, "who had a good deal of influence in the country-side." F[7] 13199.

33. *Comment j'ai fait évader Léon Daudet,* pp. 234–42; F[7] 13199 of March 18, 1930.

34. F[7] 13199 of Dec. 17, 23, 1930, March 16, Sept. 25, 1931.

35. *La Technique du coup d'état* (1931), pp. 262, 290–91, and *passim.*

CHAPTER 15

1. See the devastating analysis of Bainville's works in *Les Idées historiques de M. Jacques Bainville* (1925?), by "Un Professeur agrégé d'Histoire"; also, E. Roussel, *Les Nuées maurrassiennes* (1937).

2. See, e.g., *AF,* Jan. 21, March 21, July 25, Nov. 30, Dec. 7, 28, 1927, July 13, 1929.

3. *AF,* April 6, 1930. The paper never ceased to call for reoccupation of the Rhine-land; see, e.g., June 30, 1930, Dec. 31, 1931, Jan. 1, Nov. 5, 1932, May 20, 1933.

4. *AF,* July 2, 1930.

5. *AF,* Oct. 2, 6, 7, 1930.

6. *AF,* July 5, Nov. 6, 1930.

7. Quoted in *AF,* Dec. 25, 1930.

8. *Le Figaro,* Oct. 22, Nov. 10, 1932.

9. *AF,* April 30, Oct. 10, 1930, March 24, 1931, Aug. 2, 1932.

10. See especially three articles on "Le Parti socialiste-national allemand," *AF,* April 30–May 3, 1930.

11. *AF,* Sept. 15–17, 24–25, Oct. 10, 1930, Oct. 28, Nov. 21, 1931, Feb. 15, April 10, 25, July 24, 1932; *JSP,* Feb. 13, 1932; *RU,* Feb. 15, 1932. On November 26, 1931, Bainville warned that Hitler's accession to power was only a question of time.

12. *Le Populaire* and *L'Humanité,* Aug. 2, 1932; see also *Le Temps,* Aug. 15, 1932, *Le Populaire,* Aug. 18, 1932; *Le Parlement et la Bourse,* Feb. 1, quoted in *AF,* Feb. 2, 1932.

13. *Le Populaire,* Jan. 1, 1933.

14. Daniel Guérin, *Quand le Fascisme nous devançait, 1930–1940* (1955), p. 6; Geneviève Tabouis, *Vingt Ans de suspense diplomatique* (1958), p. 140; Simon, *La Grande Crise,* p. 36.

15. *La Victoire,* Jan. 31, 1933.

16. *AF,* Feb. 1, 8, March 3, 6, 1933.

17. *JSP,* March 18, 1933.

18. *La Liberté,* March 29, 1933; *Candide,* April 13, May 18, 1933; *RU,* Vol. LIV, Nos. 9–12 (1933); *JSP,* April 29, 1933; *AF,* April 15–28, 1933; *Candide,* April 20, 1933.

19. *JSP,* April 29, 1933.

20. *AF,* July 17, 1935.

21. *Le Populaire,* Aug. 30, 1933; *AF,* Sept. 2, 1933.

22. *Europe,* April 15, 1935, quoted in Jean-Marie Carré, *Les Ecrivains français et le mirage allemand* (1947), p. 195.

23. *AF,* Oct. 7, 1933; *L'Etudiant français,* Nov. 25, 1933.

24. *AF,* Sept. 20, 23, 1933.

25. *AF,* Aug. 28, 1931, Dec. 20, 1934, Jan. 24, April 14, 1935; *JSP,* April 20, May 18, 1935. One issue of *Je suis partout* in late 1931 (December 26) was devoted entirely to a warning that the Franco-Soviet pact was a mug's game.

26. See, e.g., *AF,* April 1, 1934.

27. *AF,* Jan. 30, 31, 1935.

28. See *Le Populaire,* Jan. 17, 1935; John T. Marcus, *French Socialism in the Crisis Years, 1933–1936* (New York, 1958), p. 99.

29. *AF,* Jan. 16, 17, 1935.

30. *AF,* Oct. 21, 1935; *Candide,* Jan. 11, 1939; Marcel Proust, *Sodome et Gomorrhe* (1922), Part 2, chap. 1; M. F. Guyard, *L'Image de la Grande Bretagne dans le roman français contemporain, 1914–1939* (1954), p. 251.

31. See *AF,* April 10, July 31, 1920, Aug. 1, 1921, Aug. 7, 1922; *La République française,* July 31, 1921; *La Libre Parole,* Aug. 1, 1921: "La France sous le joug."

32. *AF,* April 17, 1932.

33. Yves Simon, *La Campagne d'Ethiopie et la pensée politique française* (1936), pp. 21–22.

34. *AF,* April 30, July 23, 1934.

35. *AF,* Jan. 8, July 9, Aug. 23, 24, 1935.

36. *AF,* Sept. 1–7, 1935; *Candide,* Sept. 12, 1935.

37. *AF,* Oct. 4, 1935.

38. See *AF,* Oct. 4–6, 1935.

39. *JSP,* Oct. 5, 19, 1935; *AF,* Oct. 10, 18, 1935; *Candide,* Oct. 17, 1935.

40. *AF,* Oct. 23, 1935.

41. *Candide,* Oct. 31, 1935; *JSP,* Nov. 2, 1935.

42. *AF,* Jan. 2, 13, Feb. 12, 1936; *Candide,* Feb. 6, 1936; *L'Eclair,* Feb. 10, 1936.

43. Henry de Montherlant, *L'Equinoxe de septembre* (1938), pp. 28–29; Tabouis, *Vingt Ans de suspense diplomatique,* pp. 262–67; *Le Journal,* April 5, 1936.

44. *AF, March* 7, 9–12, 1936; *Candide,* March 12, 1936.

45. *AF,* March 15, 1936.

46. *Candide,* March 19, 1936.

47. *Le Canard enchaîné,* March 18, 1936.

48. *Marianne,* quoted in *AF,* Jan. 23, 1936; *Le Journal,* March 20, 1936.

49. *Paris-Midi,* Feb. 28, 1936; *AF,* Feb. 29, March 13, 1936.

50. *Savez-vous,* April 5, 1936; *AF,* April 6, 1936.

51. *AF,* Feb. 27, 1936.

52. *AF,* April 26, 1936.

CHAPTER 16

1. *Le Temps,* Sept. 17, 1929.

2. *AF,* Dec. 17, 1930. F7 13199 of December 20, 26, 31, 1930, reports royalist menaces of extreme violence, which, taken literally, would lead one to expect an uprising. But the police were inured to the paper's tone, "toujours très injurieux et plein de menaces."

3. *AF,* Jan. 19, 21, 1931; *L'Echo de Paris,* Jan. 20, 1931; F7 13199 of Jan. 18, 1931.

4. See *AF,* Feb. 14–22, 28, March 1–5, 1931.

5. *Paris-Sport,* Feb. 25, 1931; *La Liberté,* March 2, 1931; the Paris press of March 4, 1931.

6. *AF,* March 5–7, 1931; *La Petite Gironde,* quoted in *AF,* March 11, 1931; *Le Populaire de Nantes,* quoted in *AF,* March 14, 1931; *Le Populaire,* March 6, 1931. On the latter date, see also *Le Quotidien, La République,* and *Le Soir.*

7. *Annales de la Chambre des Députés, Débats Parlementaires,* March 13, 1931, pp. 1931–32; *AF,* March 27–30, 1931.

8. Glandy, *Réal del Sarte,* p. 178; F7 13199: Police reports of April 24, May 7, 8, 9, 12, 1931, showed serious concern about royalist preparations and threats against Briand and his supporters. Notices pasted on the doors of certain deputies and senators warned them against voting for Briand. As early as October 1929 the Action Française had advised its followers to write in violently threatening terms to members of Briand's majority, promising to "have their skins" should they continue to support his un-French policy.

9. Jacques Debu-Bridel, *L'Agonie de la 3e République* (1948), p. 144ff; *AF,* May 14, 15, 1931.

10. *AF,* March 8, 1932.

11. See the Paris press of Nov. 28, 29, 1931; *Frankfurter Zeitung,* Nov. 29, 1931.

12. *La Vie catholique,* Dec. 12, 1931.

13. *NG,* July 15, 1931.

14. See François Goguel, *La Politique des partis sous la 3e République* (1946), p. 256.

15. See *AF, L'Humanité, Le Populaire, Le Quotidien, L'Oeuvre, Le Figaro, L'Ami du Peuple,* on Dec. 12, 1931.

16. *La République,* Feb. 21, 1932; *Frankfurter Zeitung,* Feb. 21, 1932; but see also *AF,* Feb. 22, 29, 1932, denying that Camelots ever shouted for Laval or Tardieu.

17. *La République,* Feb. 28; also *JSP,* Feb. 27, 1932.

18. *JOS,* February 26, 1932.

19. *AF,* May 7, 1932; *NG,* May 1, 15, 1932; *Paris-Midi,* May 2, 1932, claimed that Action Française support caused Louis Marin to lose votes. See also *Le National,* May 17, 1932 and F7 13203, Bordeaux (Gironde) July 15, 1931, and April 13, 1932; Nîmes (Gard) Dec. 5, 1932.

20. André Chéradame in *La France réaliste,* May 24, 1932; *AF,* May 25, 1932.

21. See *L'Intransigeant,* third edition, dated May 7 but published the previous evening.

22. *L'Oeuvre, Le Temps, Pe Populaire, L'Ere nouvelle,* May 9, 1932.

23. *AF,* May 11, 1932.

24. *JOC,* June 7, 1932; see also *La Croix,* June 2: "Glissement à Droite."

25. *AF,* June 12, 1932.

26. Tabouis, *Vingt Ans de suspense diplomatique,* p. 121; see also the informal discussion in Alexander Werth, *France in Ferment* (London, 1934), pp. 29ff.

27. *AF,* Dec. 10–14, 1932; *L'Oeuvre, Le Figaro,* Dec. 11, 1932; *Le Matin, L'Excelsior,* Dec. 13, 1932; *Herald Tribune* (Paris), Dec. 14, 1932; *The Times* (London), Dec. 14, 1932.

28. *Journal des débats,* Dec. 14, 1932; *AF,* Dec. 15, 1932. More important, a police

report of November 4, 1932 (F^7 13199), noted an influx of recruits into the League and the Camelots, practically doubling the numbers of the latter.

29. *La République,* Dec. 16, 1932; *La Patrie,* Dec. 26, 1932; *L'Informateur: Le Journal de Soissons,* quoted in *AF,* Dec. 19, 1932.

30. *L'Homme libre,* July 27, 1932; *AF,* July 28, 1932.

31. *Le Flambeau,* Jan. 1, 1933.

32. *Candide,* Jan. 12, 1933; *La Journée industrielle,* Jan. 20, 1933; *JSP,* Jan. 21, 1933; *AF,* Jan. 25–29, 1933; *Le Réveil des contribuables,* February 1933; *Les Documents politiques,* XIV, No. 2, (1933), 58.

33. *Candide,* Feb. 2, 1933; *Le Quotidien, Le Journal,* Feb. 18, 1933.

34. *AF,* Jan. 30, 31, 1933; *L'Echo de Paris,* Feb. 1, 1933; *Candide,* Feb. 2, 1933.

35. The Paris press of Feb. 3, 1933; *La République* and *L'Action,* quoted in *AF,* Feb. 23, 1933.

36. *Gazette de Lausanne,* Feb. 17, 1933; *Candide,* March 30, 1933; Tabouis, *Vingt Ans,* p. 147.

37. *Revue hebdomadaire,* May 7, June 18, 1933.

38. Georges Roux, "La Jeunesse française," *La Terre Wallonne,* June 1933, p. 83.

39. See reports in *Candide,* May 25, June 1, 1933.

40. Minutes of UNC Congress, May 25–28, 1933, p. 148.

41. *Néo-Socialisme? Ordre—Autorité—Nation* (1933), pp. 30–31, 55, 60. The Action Française was not impressed: see *AF,* July 24, 1923, and *Candide,* July 27, 1933.

42. See Pierre Dominique, *Vente et achat* (1937), pp. 12ff.

43. Pierre Chopine, *Six Ans chez les Croix de Feu* (1935), p. 25 and *passim*; *Le Flambeau,* Dec. 1, 1932; Henri Malherbe, *La Rocque* (1934), pp. 97–98.

44. Commission d'Enquête, *Rapport général, Annexes,* II, 1610–11; *AF,* March 5, 1934.

45. *Paris-Midi,* Oct. 24, 1933; see also *L'Homme libre* of the same date.

46. *Le Pamphlet,* quoted in *AF,* Nov. 7, 1933; *Le Temps,* Nov. 7, 1933; *Candide,* Nov. 9, 1933.

47. *Le Temps,* Nov. 16, 1933; *Le Figaro, AF,* Nov. 17, 1933.

48. Nov. 24, 1933.

49. *Revue hebdomadaire,* Nov. 25, 1933; *Le Capital,* Nov. 28, 1933; *L'Oeuvre, La Volonté, Paris-Midi, Paris-Soir, L'Animateur des temps nouveaux,* Nov. 30, 1933, and the days following; *Bulletin du Redressement français,* December 1933, January 1934; *Candide,* Nov. 30, 1933.

50. *Le National,* Dec. 9, 1933; *JSP,* Dec. 23, 1933; *Journal de Genève,* July 13, 1933; *AF,* July 14, Dec. 2, 13, 1933; *Paris-Midi,* Dec. 5, 1933; Marc Elmer, *Enquête sur la France en danger* (1934).

51. *Le Canard enchaîné,* Dec. 20, 1933, Jan. 3, 1934; *AF,* Dec. 14, 1933; *Candide,* Dec. 14, 1933; Henri Béraud, *Trois Ans de colère* (1937), p. 8.

52. With the Action Française (*AF,* July 4, 5, 1932) claiming 25,000, *Le Figaro,* July 5, estimating 18,000, and *L'Aube* 3,000–4,000, we may be safe in taking an average. For recruitment conditions see an appeal by Nel Ariès, *NG,* May 15, 1932.

53. See *AF,* Jan. 9–11, 1933; *Le Matin,* Jan. 10, 1933.

54. *JSP,* Sept. 9, 1933. In the autumn of 1933 there was a notable revival of activity, both in the provinces and in Paris, where meetings in October and November drew over 10,000 people; see *AF,* Oct. 28, claiming 15,000; Nov. 22, claiming 20,000.

55. *AF,* Dec. 1, 14, 1932.

56. *AF,* Dec. 2, 1932, Dec. 15, 1933.

57. B. M. E. Léger, *Les Opinions politiques des provinces françaises* (1934), pp. 17–18, 33–35.

58. See *L'Ordre provençal,* quoted in *AF,* Jan. 2, 1933.

CHAPTER 17

1. Georges Suarez, *La Grande Peur du 6 février 1934 au Palais Bourbon* (1934), p. 12; *Statistique générale de la France,* January 1935; *JSP,* Jan. 13, 1934; *Les Documents politiques,* XV, No. 1 (1934), 1–2, which cites the list of a future Directory: Weygand, Chiappe, Tardieu, and Flandin; Jean Fabry, *De la Place de la Concorde au Cours de l'Intendance* (1942), p. 31.

2. *AF,* Jan. 3, 1934, and the days following; *JSP* and *Candide,* January 1934, *passim.*

3. Translated in Werth, *France in Ferment,* pp. 90–91. Reprinted by permission of Messrs. Jarrolds Publishers (London) Ltd.

4. See *Journal des débats, Le Matin, Aujourd'hui, Le Journal, Le Petit Parisien, L'Echo de Paris,* and other Paris papers of Jan. 10, 1934.

5. *AF,* Jan. 13, 1934.

6. Werth, *France in Ferment,* pp. 116–17.

7. Chiappe's supporters were well aware of this; see *Candide,* Jan. 25, 1934.

8. *Le Canard enchaîné,* March 15, May 17, June 21, 1933.

9. *JSP,* Jan. 20, 1934; *Le Petit Journal,* Jan. 24, 1934; *La Ville de Paris,* quoted in *AF,* Jan. 25, 1934; *Journal des débats, Le Populaire,* Jan. 27, 1934.

10. *L'Appel,* Feb. 1, 1934; *L'Homme libre,* Jan. 30, 1934; *Le Populaire,* Jan. 28, 1934; *Le Canard enchaîné,* Jan. 31, 1934.

11. *L'Ordre,* Feb. 2, 1934; *Mémorial de la Creuse, Courrier de l'Ain, Vitré-Journal, La Nation belge,* quoted in *AF,* Feb. 2–4, 1934; *Candide,* Feb. 1, 1934; Commission d'Enquête, *Rapport général,* Annexes, I, 189.

12. See *La République, Le Populaire,* Jan. 28; *Le Canard enchaîné,* Jan. 31, 1934; Eugène Frot, personal communication.

13. See Werth, *France in Ferment,* pp. 130–38; Fabry, *De la Place de la Concorde,* p. 46.

14. *Le Matin,* Feb. 4, 17, 1934; *Le Canard enchaîné,* Feb. 7, 1934; *Les Documents politiques,* XV, Nos. 2–3 (1934), 97; also *Le Figaro,* Feb. 4, 1934; *Le Temps, La Liberté,* Feb. 5, 1934.

15. E.g., by Roger Mennevée in his *Documents politiques,* XV, Nos. 2–3, 97.

16. *Ibid.,* p. 101.

17. *AF,* Feb. 3, 5, 1934; *Le Jour,* Feb. 5, 1934; *La Liberté,* Feb. 6, 1934.

18. Augustin Cochin, *Les Sociétés de pensée et la démocratie,* p. 119, quoted in full by Pierre Gaxotte in *JSP,* May 9, 1936.

19. See *AF,* Jan. 11, 1934, for a brief note concerning the Duc de Guise's "reception of royalist leaders and regional delegates, to give them their instructions." The account here given is based on information supplied by the Comte de Paris and M. André Voisin.

20. See Georges Zérapha, *Notre Combat contre l'antisémitisme* (1934), pp. 9–10; and the evidence of Frédéric-Dupont, deputy and municipal councilor of the 7th Arrondissement, before the Fourth Correctional Chamber, March 19, 1940, in a slander action brought by the Action Française against Georges Valois (*AF,* March 20, 1940).

21. See Dorsay in *JSP,* April 7, 1934, who refers to grandiose hopes of attracting a hundred or more deputies to the Hôtel de Ville.

22. Georges Gaudy, personal communication; Pierre Dominique in *La République,* Feb. 7, 1934.

23. Personal communications of the Comte de Paris, Mme Pierre Varillon, and Lucien Rebatet; testimony of Léon Daudet to Commission d'Enquête, *Rapport général,* II, 1778; Gérin-Ricard and Truc, *Histoire de l'Action Française,* pp. 182ff; Benouville, *Le Sacrifice du matin,* pp. 65ff; Lucien Rebatet, *Les Décombres* (1942).

24. "Le Vrai 6 février," *AF,* Feb. 5, 1944.

25. See Daudet's statement in the London *Evening Standard,* Feb. 1, 1934; Pujo in *RU,* LXXIV, No. 8 (July 15, 1938); Xavier Vallat, *Souvenirs d'un homme de droite* (1957), pp. 114ff. Cf. also Jean Goy's statement to UNC Congress, May 1934: *Congrès National de l'UNC* (1934), pp. 482ff.

26. Commission d'Enquête, *Rapport général,* Annexes, II, 2096–97.

27. *Ibid.,* Annexes, I, 52–53; see also more general figures in Louis Ducloux, *Du Chantage à la trahison* (1955), pp. 182–83, who also, pp. 167–90, attributes the main responsibility to the Action Française.

28. See, *Rapport général,* Annexes, II, 1260; *AF,* Feb. 8, 1934.

29. *Rapport général,* Annexes, II, 2097.

30. *RU,* LXXIV, No. 8, July 15, 1938 p. 130.

31. Benouville, *Le Sacrifice du matin,* pp. 65–66; Roger Stéphane, *Chaque Homme est lié au monde,* p. 80.

32. Lahille, *Lettres d'un autre temps,* p. 82.

CHAPTER 18

1. Bertrand de Jouvenel, *Après la défaite* (1941), p. 121; Werth, *France in Ferment,* pp. 171, 213–14.

2. Pierre Lecoeur, personal communication.

3. *Oeuvres de Maurice Thorez,* Vol. II, Bk. 5, p. 256.

4. See *AF, L'Echo de Paris,* Feb. 13, 1934.

5. See, e.g., Thorez in *L'Humanité,* March 10, and the reply of *Le Populaire,* March 12, 1934.

6. *Le Temps,* Feb. 10, 1934.

7. *Le Figaro,* Feb. 8, 1934.

8. *La Liberté,* Feb. 8, 1934; *Revue de Paris,* Feb. 15, 1934.

9. *Candide,* Feb. 22, 1934.

10. *AF,* Feb. 14, 1934.

11. *Candide,* Feb. 15, 1934; see also the text of Philippe Henriot's talk in *Demain,* in the series of the Conférences des Ambassadeurs, March 17, 1934.

12. Roger Nimier, *Le Grand d'Espagne* (1950), pp. 53–55.

13. "La volte-face des gens du monde," *JSP,* April 21, 1934.

14. See *AF,* Feb. 22, 25, 1934; *Journal des débats,* Feb. 22, 1934; *JSP,* Feb. 24, 1934.

15. Debu-Bridel, *L'Agonie de la 3e République,* p. 261.

16. Léon Daudet, *La Police politique* (1934), pp. 64–65, 114, and *passim.*

17. *AF,* March 18, 1934; *NG,* Feb. 15, 1934; *Candide,* March 22, 1934; Bernanos letter dated July 2, 1934, in Société des Amis de Georges Bernanos, *Bulletin periodique,* No. 2–3 (March 1950).

18. Philippe Henriot in *Demain la France* (1934), pp. 29–30; *La Journée industrielle,* quoted in Georges Michon, *Les Puissances d'argent et l'émeute du 6 février* (n.d.), p. 25; Tardieu, "Réformer ou casser," *Revue des Deux Mondes,* March 1, 1934. See also Tardieu's book *L'Heure de la décision* (1934), extolled as essential by influential industrial publications like the *Bulletin quotidien,* March 5, 1934.

19. See, e.g., *Candide,* April 26, May 3, 1934.

20. See reports of its activities in *Candide,* July 5, 1934; *JSP,* July 7, 1934; Commission d'Enquête, *Rapport général,* Annexes, I, 15ff; Henri Pichot, *Les Combattants avaient raison* (Montluçon, 1940), pp. 143, 149, 152.

21. *Dépêche de Brest,* quoted in *AF,* April 25, 1934.

22. Gonzague Truc, *Tableau du 20e siècle* (1934); Daniel Halévy in *1934,* Aug. 27, 1934.

23. E.g., "Revue de la presse," *AF*, Feb. 19, March 1, 2, May 31, 1934.

24. See *Nouvelle Revue de Hongrie*, April 1934.

25. *La Vie intellectuelle*, June 10, 1934, pp. 212–15.

26. Robert Francis, Thierry Maulnier, and J.-P. Maxence in *Demain la France* (1934), a fierce attack upon what they considered the corrupt plutodemocracy of their time and an appeal for national revival through revolution; *AF*, June 30, July 5, 1934; *L'Illustration*, July 21, 1934.

27. *AF*, Oct. 10, 13, 1934; *Candide*, Oct. 11, 18, 1934; *JSP*, Oct. 13, Nov. 3, 1934.

28. See *AF*, Nov. 1, 1934, for an account of a meeting of the Front National in the Salle Wagram.

29. *JSP*, Oct. 20, 1934.

30. See, e.g., *AF*, Nov. 13, 1934; *JSP*, Feb. 2, 1935.

31. *JSP*, Feb. 9, 1935.

32. *JSP*, Jan. 5, 1935; see also *JSP*, June 22, 1935.

33. See *AF*, Jan. 30, Feb. 1, 2, 1935, and the issues following.

34. *Candide*, Jan. 31, Feb. 7, 1935.

35. *Le Temps*, Feb. 3, 1935; April 21, 23, 28, 1935; *L'Humanité*, Nov. 7, 1934; *Le Populaire*, Feb. 13, 18, 1935; *L'Aube*, Feb. 16, 1935; *Le Jour*, March 1, April 26, 1935; *Revue de Paris*, January 1935.

36. *L'Aube*, March 29, 1935.

37. See *Paris-Midi*, May 6, 1935; *Candide*, May 9, 16, 1935. *L'Aube*, May 7, 1935, explained the Catholic vote for Chiappe and against his liberal Catholic opponent Jacques Madaule as showing Action Française influence.

38. *AF*, June 5–7, 1935.

39. See the account of the Radicals' dilemma and their decision in Edouard Herriot, *Jadis* (1952), II, 551.

40. *Candide*, Sept. 6, 1934.

41. *AF*, June 8, 1935.

42. See e.g., *JSP*, June 29, 1935.

43. See my articles, "The Right in France: A Working Hypothesis," *American Historical Review*, LXV, No. 2 (1960); "Un demi-siècle de glissement à droite," *International Review of Social History*, V, No. 2 (1960).

44. *JSP*, June 22, 1935; *Candide*, June 27, 1935.

45. "Inquiétude des partis," *Courrier royal*, Nov. 16, 1935.

46. *Le Jour*, July 28, 1935. See also Paul Marion in *La République*, September 21, 1935, who refers to the Action Française as the oldest and most combative of leagues, and the only one with an original and unified body of doctrine.

47. See Pujo's accusations in his report to the Action Française Congress, *AF*, Dec. 16, 1935.

48. See the interesting way in which the rival parades are described in, e.g., *JSP*, July 20, 1935, and *Candide*, July 18, 1935. Also *AF*, *L'Echo de Paris*, *L'Ordre*, *La République*, *Le Petit Journal*, and the left-wing press of July 15 and 16, 1935, in which the numbers of participants vary by the hundreds of thousands according to the political coloring of the reporter.

49. *Les Etudes*, Aug. 5, 1935; *Courrier royal*, Nov. 23, 1935.

50. See, e.g., *AF*, Nov. 27, 28, Dec. 12, 1935, Jan. 6, 1936; *Candide*, Nov. 28, Dec. 5, 1935.

51. *La Croix*, Dec. 9, 1935; *AF*, Dec. 3–8, 1935; *Candide*, Dec. 12, 1935.

52. See, e.g., *AF*, Feb. 4, 1936.

53. *Candide*, Jan. 23, 1936.

54. Quoted by Roger Salengro in *JOC*, June 30, 1936, p. 1644.

55. *JOC,* Feb. 13, 1936, pp. 379–80.
56. At a meeting held in the Boulevard Montparnasse on February 14, 1936; quoted by Salengro from police reports in *JOC,* June 30, 1936, p. 1644.
57. Tabouis, *Vingt Ans de suspense diplomatique,* p. 283; according to her, Stefan Osusky, the Czech Minister in Paris, heard the remarks in "the most aristocratic of Paris salons" when Jules Sauerwein of *Le Matin* dropped in with the news.
58. See *AF,* Feb. 14, 1936, and the issues following; *JSP,* Feb. 15, 1936; *Candide,* Feb. 20, 1936. *Combat,* March 1936, directed vitriolic attacks against a government, a Parliament, and a regime that had turned against Maurras and against the Action Française, to which "our thinking, thought itself, the French nation and the whole human race owe an inestimable debt."
59. *Le Temps,* Feb. 16, 17, 1936.
60. *Le Canard enchaîné,* Feb. 19, 1936.
61. André Barbot in *Messager de Millau,* quoted in *AF,* March 3, 1936.

CHAPTER 19

1. *Cahiers Charles Maurras,* No. 1, April 1960, p. 91.
2. *AF,* Dec. 12, 1935.
3. The membership of the SFIO also dropped in 1933; see G. Sanvoisin in *Le Figaro,* May 26, 1934.
4. Commission d'Enquête, *Rapport général,* Annexes, I, 134, and II, 2422ff; *AF,* March 7, April 18, 1934, Dec. 13, 1935; Pierre Taittinger and Xavier Vallat, personal communications.
5. Benouville, *Sacrifice du matin,* p. 67; Pierre Lecoeur, Georges Calzant, and Bernard Lecache, personal communications.
6. See *AF,* Jan. 1, 1936.
7. Louis Jasseron, personal communication. There were about two hundred Camelots in Lyon and about four times as many in the surrounding region. See also *AF,* July 11, Sept. 18, 1932, for evidence concerning northern and central France.
8. *La République,* Oct. 25, 1933.
9. Commission d'Enquête, *Rapport général,* Annexes, I, 119ff.
10. *AF,* Dec. 13, 1935.
11. *AF,* April 6, 1930.
12. See, e.g., Philippe Roulland's report to the Eighteenth Congress of the Action Française, Dec. 12, 1931.
13. *AF,* Jan. 1, 1936.
14. *AF,* April 23, 1934.
15. *AF,* March 5, 1936.
16. *AF,* April 25, 1936.
17. See the Paris press of May 11, 1936.
18. See *AF,* April 4, 5, 1936.
19. *AF,* April 5, 1936.
20. *AF,* April 17, 1936. The same arguments appeared in *Le Temps, L'Echo de Paris,* and *Le Petit Parisien*; see Georges Dupeux, *Le Front Populaire et les élections de 1936* (1959), pp. 121–22.
21. *AF,* April 24, 30, May 1, 2, 1936.
22. *L'Humanité,* April 18, 24, 1936; Dupeux, *Le Front Populaire,* p. 110.
23. *L'Humanité,* April 3, 1936; *L'Echo de Paris,* April 2, 14, 1936.
24. See *Le Figaro, L'Ordre, Le Jour,* April 24, 1936.
25. *Le Temps,* April 29, 1936; *AF,* April 30, 1936.

26. *AF,* May 20, 1936.
27. *JOC,* June 6, 1936.
28. *AF,* June 7, 13, 14, 21, 1936.
29. Jean Zay, *Souvenirs et Solitude* (1946), p. 352.
30. *Charivari,* June 20, 1936; *AF,* June 22, 1936; *Le Populaire,* Nov. 13, 1938.
31. Pierre Villette in *Candide,* June 18, 1936.
32. *JSP,* June 27, 1936.
33. *JSP,* July 4, 1936.
34. *AF,* June 27, July 3, 1936; *L'Ere nouvelle,* June 27–July 4, 1936; *Le Matin* and *La République,* June 26, 1936.
35. *Candide,* June 25, 1936.
36. *AF,* June 21, 29, July 5, 1936; *Werth, Destiny of France* (London, 1937), p. 355.
37. See, e.g., *Candide,* June 25, 1936.
38. *La République,* June 24, 1936; *La Croix,* June 25, 1936.
39. Quoted in *JOC,* June 30, 1936, p. 1637.
40. *Ibid.,* p. 1635.
41. *La République,* July 8, 1936.
42. *AF,* July 6, 10, 12, 19, 1936.

CHAPTER 20

1. *AF,* Jan. 4, 1915.
2. *AF,* April 15, 1931, April 8, 1932, April 27, 1934.
3. See José Pemartín, *Ramiro de Maeztu et l'Acción Española* (Madrid, 1931); Stanley G. Payne, *Falange* (Stanford, 1961), p. 68.
4. Pierre Héricourt, "Franco et l'influence de Maurras en Espagne," *Almanach, 1938,* pp. 115–20; Eduardo Aunós, "Les nationalistes espagnols et la France," *Frontières,* Oct. 10, 1936, pp. 501–7; Aldo Garosci, *Gli intellettuali e la guerra di Spagna* (Turin, 1959), p. 234.
5. *AF,* July 19–21, 1936.
6. *AF,* July 22, 1936.
7. *The Second World War* (London, 1948), I, 192–93.
8. Cf. *L'Echo de Paris,* July 23, 1936, and the issues following; *Le Matin, La République, Le Jour, Le Figaro, Le Petit Bleu,* July 24, 1936, and the issues following; *Le Temps,* July 25, 1936, and the issues following. In *Le Figaro,* July 25, 1936, François Mauriac expressed himself passionately against intervention, similarly Victor Margueritte in *La République* of the same day.
9. *AF,* July 25, 26, 1936. See also the information furnished from a different point of view in Hugh Thomas, *The Spanish Civil War* (London, 1961), pp. 223–25.
10. *AF,* July 26, 28, 1936; *L'Humanité,* July 28, 1936.
11. See, e.g., Werth, *Destiny of France,* p. 379; also the important letter of Vincent Auriol in *L'Express,* Sept. 21, 1961.
12. Quoted in Colette Audry, *Léon Blum, ou la politique du juste* (1955), pp. 126–27.
13. See *Journal des débats,* July 26, 1936; *Charivari,* Aug. 1, 1936, quoted in *AF,* Aug. 2, 1936.
14. See, e.g., Pujo in *AF,* July 24, 1936; Gaxotte in *Candide,* July 30, 1936. It should be noted that in December 1936 Blum seems to have endorsed this view when justifying his nonintervention policy to Maurice Thorez.
15. See the aforementioned newspapers on August 2, 3, 1936.
16. See Guy Mollet's admission to J.-R. Tournoux, *Secrets d'état* (1960), p. 155, and Auriol in *L'Express,* Sept. 21, 1961.

17. "La Diplomatie juive," *AF,* Aug. 20, 1936.
18. "En attendant les camions de tueurs," *JSP,* Aug. 8, 1936.
19. *La Croix,* May 8, 1937; *AF,* May 6, 10, 14, 16, 1937.
20. *JSP,* Sept. 10, 1937. See also *AF,* Nov. 13, 1937, for denials of the presence of Italian troops on Majorca.
21. *The Times* (London), Aug. 18, 1937.
22. *AF,* Oct. 2, 1936.
23. *AF,* Jan. 4, 1937; *Almanach, 1938,* p. 120.

CHAPTER 21

1. Philippe Henriot, *La Mort de la trêve* (1934), p. 130; *AF,* July 4, 12, 1936; *AF,* Aug. 30, 1936: "Les Radicaux ne marchent plus."
2. Louise Weiss, *Ce que femme veut: Souvenirs de la 3e République* (1946), p. 232.
3. *AF,* Oct. 19, Nov. 28, 1937.
4. *AF,* Oct. 30, 31, 1936.
5. *Candide,* Nov. 5, 12, 1936.
6. *AF,* Oct. 31, 1936, and personal testimony of friends.
7. *AF,* July 14, Sept. 2, 8, 12, 15, 19, 25, 1936.
8. *AF.* Oct. 22, 29, 31, 1936; *Le Jour, L'Echo de Paris,* Oct. 28, 1936; the Paris press of Oct. 31, 1936.
9. *Le Populaire,* Nov. 19, 1936; *The Times* (London), Nov. 20, 1936.
10. *AF,* Nov. 19, 1936; Yves Simon, *La Grande Crise,* pp. 87–88.
11. *Gringoire,* Nov. 20, 27, 1936; *L'Echo de Paris,* Nov. 24, 1936.
12. *AF, Le Populaire, L'Humanité,* Nov. 22, 1936.
13. See, e.g., *Candide,* April 8, 1937.
14. See *ibid.,* March 16, April 1, Nov. 4, 1937.
15. *Le Jour,* Oct. 27, 1937; see also the Lyon press of Oct. 26, 1937, and the days following, and the Paris press of Nov. 15, 1937, and the days following, and of Jan. 4, 1938.
16. *AF,* Nov. 4, 1937.
17. *Courrier de Genève,* Dec. 8, 1937.
18. *Candide,* Aug. 12, 1937.
19. Two long reviews in *Les Annales de la philosophie chrétienne,* February and April, 1886.
20. See *GK's Weekly,* Feb. 2, 1937; *The Nineteenth Century,* March 1937.
21. French chemist Paul Sabatier of Toulouse, and Swiss physicist Ch.-E. Guillaume of Neuchâtel. See *AF,* May 1, 12, Dec. 29, 1937, Feb. 11, 1938.
22. Jérôme Carcopino, *Souvenirs de sept ans* (1953), p. 31; *AF,* July 1, 1937.
23. See, e.g., *Le Journal,* July 5, 1937; *Candide,* July 8, 1937.
24. *Candide,* July 15, 1937.
25. *AF, L'Echo de Paris, Le Journal, Le Jour, Le Matin, Le Petit Parisien,* of July 9, 1937.
26. *Charivari,* July 10, 1937. This review was consistently sympathetic to the Action Française and often published articles and notes by members and friends of the movement.
27. Quoted in *AF,* July 30, 1937.
28. *La Lumière,* July 23, 30, 1937.
29. See, e.g., *AF,* Aug. 12, Oct. 30, Dec. 15, 1937.
30. Meetings were held on October 29, 1937, at Magic City and on November 20 in the Salle Pleyel. Doriot himself was for the most part friendly, as when he appeared beside Maurras and Daudet in a meeting at the Vel d'Hiv on June 7, 1938; his followers echoed him—see R. Lousteau, "L'Union nécessaire," *L'Emancipation nationale,* June 6, 1938.

31. *AF*, Sept. 12, 1937.

32. *Ce Soir*, Sept. 13, 1937; *AF*, Sept. 13, 1937; *L'Insurgé*, Sept. 15, 1937; *Candide*, Sept. 16, 1937.

33. *Le Matin*, Sept. 14, 1937.

34. *JSP*, Sept. 17, 1937; *AF*, Sept. 17–20, 1937.

35. *Candide*, Sept. 23, 1937; *L'Insurgé*, Sept. 29, 1937.

36. *Candide*, Sept. 30, 1937.

37. *Au Grand Juge de France* (1949), p. 194.

38. *AF*, July 6, 10, 12, 19, 28, 30, Aug. 2, Nov. 20, Dec. 31, 1936.

39. Wartime statement quoted by Coston, *Partis, journaux*, p. 137.

40. Maurras in *AF*, Jan. 14, 1938; see Dr. Martin's declarations to Roger Stéphane, *Chaque Homme*, p. 199; Georges Loustaunau-Lacau, *Mémoires d'un Français rebelle* (1948), pp. 110–28; Ducloux, *Du Chantage*, chap. 7.

41. The Paris press of Nov. 24, 1937; Fontenay, *La Cagoule contre la France* (1938), p. 123; Pujo, "Histoire d'un sursaut national," *RU*, LXXIV, No. 8, 146.

42. Bruckberger in *Les Procès de collaboration*, p. 291.

43. *AF*, Nov. 17, 1937, and the issues following; *Candide*, Nov. 25, Dec. 2, 1937; *JSP*, Nov. 26, 1937.

44. *Candide*, Dec. 9, 1937, Jan. 6, 1938.

45. *Ibid.*, Jan. 13–20, 27, Feb. 3, 1938; *JSP*, Jan. 14, 21, 1938.

46. Feb. 15, 1938. A few months earlier Arbellot had published an interesting study called *Maurras, homme d'action* (1937).

47. André Blumel, personal communication.

CHAPTER 22

1. *AF*, Nov. 23, 1937; *Courrier royal*, Nov. 27, 1937.

2. *AF*, Nov. 26–28, 1937.

3. *AF*, Dec. 3, 1937; *Courrier royal*, Dec. 4, 1937.

4. The Comte de Paris, personal communication.

5. George Téfas, *Les Conceptions économiques des groupements d'Action Française* (1939), p. 489.

6. *Le Petit Journal*, Nov. 28, 1934, July 13, 1935; *Courrier royal*, May 9, 1936; the Comte de Paris, personal communication.

7. See, e.g., *Courrier royal*, June 27, 1936.

8. Quoted in *ibid.*, Nov. 23, 1935.

9. *Ibid.*, March 21, 1936.

10. See *ibid.*, Feb. 22, April 11, May 30, 1936; Duc de Guise's opening message in *Essai sur le gouvernement de demain*.

11. G. Boissière in *Le Canard enchaîné*, Feb. 19, 1936; Yves de la Brière in *Etudes*, Aug. 5, 1936; *Le Voltaire*, Dec. 19, 1936.

12. See *Courrier royal*, March 13, May 1, 1937. Osgood, *French Royalism*, p. 147, speaks of 90,000 subscribers and a peak total circulation of 100,000 reached in 1935. This seems a lot.

13. *Courrier royal*, July 10, Oct. 23, 1937.

14. The Comte de Paris and Pierre Longone, personal communications.

15. Osgood, *French Royalism*, p. 134.

16. *Courrier royal*, Jan. 1, 7, May 7, Nov. 5, 1938, May 6, 1939; *Les Etudes*, Jan. 5, 1938.

17. Personal communication.

18. "L'Etat français," *JSP*, Jan. 7, 1938.

CHAPTER 23

1. *L'Enracinement,* p. 132.

2. Jean Mistler, *JOC,* Feb. 25, 26, 1938; Léon Daudet in *AF,* Feb. 27, 1938; *Le Temps,* Feb. 27, March 11, 1938; C.-J. Gignoux in *La Journée industrielle,* March 10, 1938; Lucien Romier in *Le Figaro,* March 11, 1938.

3. Quoted in *Documents politiques,* XIX, No. 3–4 (1938), 108–9.

4. Tabouis, *Vingt Ans de suspense diplomatique,* pp. 330–32; Debu-Bridel, *L'Agonie de la 3e République,* p. 426; *La République,* March 13, 1938.

5. *Candide,* March 17, 1938. The following day *Je suis partout* asked why Blum should not offer ministries to those eminent Frenchmen, MM. Charles Maurras and Léon Daudet.

6. *Candide,* April 7, 1938, "L'Homme maudit." The same issue denounced "La Dictature de M. Blum," and commiserated with "Duseigneur le martyr."

7. *JSP,* May 13, 1938.

8. *Candide,* May 26, 1938; *Le Populaire,* May 30, 1938; *AF,* May 31, 1938.

9. *Candide,* June 2, 1938.

10. *Politique,* July 1938, pp. 663–65.

11. June 10, quoted in *AF,* June 13, 1938.

12. *Candide,* June 16, 1938.

13. *Ibid.,* July 28, 1938; *Le Temps,* Oct. 19, 1938; *Combat,* October 1938. See Stanley Hoffmann, "The Effects of World War II on French Society and Politics," *French Historical Studies,* II, No. 1 (1961), 36–38.

14. *AF,* Oct. 27, 1938.

15. *Europe nouvelle,* Oct. 1, 1938, p. 1053.

16. On this letter, see the exchange between Maurras and Mauriac in *AF,* Nov. 30, Dec. 1, 1938.

17. *AF, JSP,* Dec. 2, 1938; *Candide,* Dec. 1, 1938. The warmongers of the Right were men like Kerillis and Georges Mandel.

18. *Le Populaire,* Dec. 1, 1938; *Les Documents politiques,* XIX, No. 12 (1938), 1–2; *AF,* Sept. 14, 1935; Jean de La Varende, "Droite et Gauche," *JSP,* Dec. 23, 1938; *Candide,* March 22, 1939.

19. Letter of Aug. 22, 1938 (F. D. papers).

20. *Le Matin,* Aug. 19, 1939; *AF,* Aug. 20, 1939.

21. *Candide,* March 31, 1938.

22. See Osgood, *French Royalism,* p. 153.

23. See *AF,* April 22, Dec. 7, 1936; also Joseph de Pesquidoux in *AF,* May 28, 1937.

24. *AF,* Jan. 1, 1937.

25. These figures are based on a sample of 306 persons approached between January and November 1938; *NG,* Jan. 1, 1939.

26. See Osgood, p. 152–53.

27. Loustaunau-Lacau, *Mémoires,* pp. 130–31; Lahille, *Lettres,* p. 88.

28. *AF,* Jan. 11, 1937.

29. *Le Populaire,* March 25, 1936. See also Blum's statements in *JOC,* March 15, 1935.

30. See, e.g., Geneviève Tabouis in *L'Oeuvre,* Aug. 13, 1936.

31. *JSP,* Dec. 17, 1937.

32. *AF,* March 10, 12, 1936.

33. See Clément Vautel in *Cyrano,* quoted in *AF,* July 13, 1936.

34. *JSP,* April 24, 1937; *AF,* July 4, 1937.

35. See the issues of June 1936 for a debate between *L'Ordre,* the *Lumière,* and the *Action française.*

36. *JSP*, Sept. 19, 1936.
37. *AF*, March 25, 1938; *JSP*, April 15, 1938.
38. *AF*, Aug. 24, Oct. 22, 30, 1936; *JSP*, Nov. 28, 1936.
39. Tabouis, *Vingt Ans de suspense diplomatique*, pp. 327–28; *Candide*, March 3, 1938.
40. *AF*, March 12–15, 1938. Before his death, Bainville issued several warnings against the danger of an alliance with the fragile Czech state; see, e.g., *AF*, May 3, 22, 1935.
41. *AF*, March 17, 1938.
42. *JOS*, March 17, 1938; *AF*, March 19, 21, 1938.
43. See, e.g., "Indépendance tchéque," *Courrier royal*, July 25, 1936; report on alleged Red air bases in Czechoslovakia in *Le Matin*, Nov. 18, 1936; "La Tchécoslovaquie désire-t-elle une guerre européenne?" *JSP*, Nov. 19, 1937.
44. *L'Epoque*, April 17, 1938.
45. *Documents politiques*, XVIII, No. 2 (1937), 53; *AF*, May 1, 1938, and the issues following.
46. *Combat*, July 1938.
47. *Candide*, Aug. 18, Sept. 8, 15, 1938; *JSP*, Sept. 2; *AF*, Sept. 14, 1938.
48. *AF*, Sept. 15–26, 1938; *Le Temps*, Sept. 14, 1938, and the issues following; Daudet in *AF*, Sept. 25, 1938. Berthelot had been Permanent Secretary of the Quai d'Orsay.
49. *JSP*, Sept. 30, 1938.
50. *AF*, Oct. 2, 7, 8, Nov. 1, 1938; *JSP*, Oct. 14, 1938.
51. *Candide*, Oct. 6, 1938; *JSP*, Oct. 7, 14, 1938; *AF*, Nov. 9, 12, 1938.
52. See Albert Petit in *Journal des débats*, Nov. 11, 1938.
53. *Candide*, Nov. 16, 1938.
54. *AF*, Nov. 18, 1938.
55. *Candide*, Jan. 4, 1939; *AF*, March 15, 16, 22, 1939.
56. *JSP*, March 17, 24, 1939.
57. See *Candide*, Jan. 4, 1939; *JSP*, Jan. 6, 1939.
58. *AF*, December 1938–January 1939, *passim*; *JSP*, April 14, 1939.
59. *AF*, April 14, 1939; *Candide*, April 19, 1939; Lucien Rebatet, personal communication.
60. Pierre-Etienne Flandin, *Politique française, 1919–1940* (1947), pp. 307–10; *AF*, Aug. 22, 1939.
61. *Le Procès de Charles Maurras*, p. 87.
62. *AF*, Aug. 29, 1943.
63. Pierre Varillon in *Charles Maurras, 1868–1952* (1953), p. 182; *AF*, Sept. 2, 1939.

CHAPTER 24

1. Alain Laubreaux, *Ecrit pendant la guerre* (1944), pp. 44, 52.
2. *Le Procureur et l'habitant* (1953), p. 61.
3. *AF*, Sept. 3, 8, 9, Oct. 1, 18, 21, 1939.
4. *Le Temps*, Sept. 11, 1939; see also, e.g., *L'Avenir du Plateau central*, Sept. 8, 1939; *Le Journal de la Seine* and *Le Palmier de Hyères*, quoted in *AF*, Sept. 9, 1939; *Le Jour-Echo*, Sept. 20, 1939; *Le Petit Var*, Oct. 5, 1939.
5. See, e.g., *L'Ere nouvelle* and *Dépêche de Toulouse*, Nov. 21, 1939; *AF*, Nov. 22, 1939.
6. See *Le Temps*, Dec. 7, 1939; *AF*, Dec. 8, 9, 1939.
7. See, e.g., Léon Daudet in *AF*, Sept. 9, 1939.
8. Literally: see *Candide*, Feb. 7, 1940.
9. Both in *JSP*, Feb. 9, 1940, a special number devoted to "Heroic Finland."

10. *JSP,* Feb. 23, March 22, 1940. *RU,* March 15, 1940, p. 445, also called for speedy Western intervention in Finland, where a victory could not fail to bring an Allied victory nearer. Suspended from September to December 1939, the *Revue universelle* had not said a word about Poland. But the issue of December 1939 was already concerned with the fate of Finland.

11. *Candide,* Jan. 3, 17, Feb. 7, 28, March 6, 1940.

12. *AF,* Feb. 13, 1940.

13. Fernand Laurent in *JOC,* March 12, 1940; *AF,* March 10–13, 1940. For Daladier's desperate and dishonest attempts to keep Finland fighting, see Max Jakobson, *The Diplomacy of the Winter War* (Cambridge, 1961), pp. 239–40.

14. See, *Le Jour,* March 22, 1940; *AF,* March 23, 1940.

15. *AF,* Jan. 3, 1940.

16. *AF,* April 15, 1940; *Candide,* April 24, 1940.

17. *AF,* May 11, 1940.

18. *AF,* Oct. 31, 1939, April 7, May 13, 1940.

19. *AF,* May 19, 20, 1940.

20. Glandy, *Marie de Roux,* p. 187.

21. After Daladier had lifted political censorship, on February 28, 1940, the paper repeatedly called for a military government. See, e.g., March 14, 15, May 6, 1940.

22. *AF,* July 10–12, 1940.

CHAPTER 25

1. *Le Procès de Charles Maurras,* p. 9.

2. *Le Sémaphore,* Aug. 7, 1940.

3. Pierre Dominique, "Grandeur et décadence du nationalisme de Vichy," *Ecrits de Paris* (June 1953), p. 27; Loustaunau-Lacau, *Mémoires,* p. 214; Bernard de Sérigny, *Trente Ans avec Pétain* (1959), p. 191; Alfred Fabre-Luce and Xavier Vallat, personal communications; Maurice Martin du Gard, *Chronique de Vichy* (1948), p. 386; Robert Aron, *Histoire de Vichy* (1954), pp. 196–203.

4. Maurice Pujo, *L'Action Française contre l'Allemagne* (1946), p. 40; J. Fernet in *Charles Maurras, 1868–1952,* pp. 75–81. Abetz, *Histoire d'une politique franco-allemande* (1953), p. 186, refers to Garde des Sceaux Alibert as "the man to whom it fell to codify Maurrassian ideas," and who particularly enjoyed the Marshal's ear.

5. Pierre Pucheu, *Ma Vie* (1948), p. 44; Xavier Vallat, personal communication. The incidental evidence to be found in the Chambrun Collection of the Hoover Library, esp. Nos. 13, 14, 60, 80, 90, bears this out.

6. Pierre Mendès-France, *Liberté, liberté chérie* (New York), 1943, pp. 180–85.

7. See Gilles Ferry, *Une Expérience de formation de chefs* (1945); Janine Bourdin, "L'Ecole Nationale des Cadres d'Uriage," *Revue française des sciences politiques,* IX, No. 4, (1959), 1029–45; Roger Stéphane, *Chaque Homme,* pp. 165–66; *Mounier et sa génération* (1956), p. 303 and *passim.*

8. *Le Procès de Charles Maurras et de Maurice Pujo* (Lyon, 1945), p. 581.

9. Jean-François Gravier, *Etat, peuple, nation* (1942), p. 13; Jean Guitton, *Journal de capitivité,* quoted by Robert Havard in *RU,* February 1944, pp. 158–60; de La Varende, "L'Immédiat," *Les Cahiers français,* No. 1 (1942), p. 11.

10. The article has since been reprinted with insignificant variations in *De la Colère à la justice* (Geneva, 1942), pp. 85–93; *Aspects de la France,* April 25, 1948; *Cahiers Charles Maurras,* No. 1 (April 1960), pp. 73–74. See also Emile Henriot's contribution to *Ecrit à Lyon,* (Lyon, 1943).

11. Two typed pages, dated Rabat, July 1, 1941 (Rancoeur papers).

12. Robert Poulet, "Adieu au Fascisme," *La Parisienne,* October 1956, pp. 594–602.

13. Champeaux, *La Croisade des démocraties,* II, xiv–xv; *Les Procès de la radio* (1947), pp. 15, 19, 33, 84, 202; Ferdonnet, *La Guerre juive* (1939).

14. Robert Brasillach, *Journal d'un homme occupé* (1955), p. 37.

15. See Georges Claude, *De l'hostilité à la collaboration* (1941), and *La Seule Route* (1942).

16. *Les Procès de collaboration,* p. 288; R. L. Bruckberger, *Nous n'irons plus au bois* (1948); Henry Coston, *Partis, journaux et hommes politiques,* pp. 84–85.

17. *Le Procès de Charles Maurras,* p. 51.

18. From a private letter of Charles Maurras, dated June 1950.

19. *Devenir,* No. 2, March 1944.

20. See, e.g., Jean Agostini, "Maurras le naufrageur," *Jeune Force de France,* July 1, 1944.

21. See *AF,* April 29, 1944; *Au Grand Juge de France,* pp. 172–73; *Le Procès de Charles Maurras,* pp. 51, 72, 232–34.

22. Loustaunau-Lacau, *Mémoires,* pp. 199–200.

23. *AF,* June 8, 1941.

24. Havard, *Histoire de l'Action Française,* pp. 196–97; *AF,* Aug. 15, Sept. 2, 1940.

25. *Le Procès de Charles Maurras et de Maurice Pujo,* p. 517.

26. *AF,* Feb. 15, 1942.

27. Xavier Vallat, *Charles Maurras,* p. 104.

28. *Notre Combat,* March 27, 1943, with articles by Rebatet, Sicard, Ramon Fernandez, etc.

29. *Inter-France,* 7e année, No. 116, May 17, 1944. See also the important article of Sonderführer A. Thiersch, *Spiegel der französischen Presse,* November-December 1943.

30. *AF,* July 20, Aug. 31, 1943.

31. *NG,* Aug. 15, 1942.

32. *La Grande France,* February 1943.

33. *Le Procès de Charles Maurras et de Maurice Pujo,* pp. 292–94; Vallat, *Charles Maurras,* p. 45; Benouville, *Sacrifice du matin,* p. 61, and *passim.* Several royalists even became Compagnons de la Libération, like Michel de Camaret and Armand de Tinguy du Pouët.

34. *Charles Maurras, 1868–1952,* p. 141.

35. Pierre Bloch, *Mes Jours heureux* (1946), p. 179.

36. For Rousseaux, see his *Charles Maurras, ou l'exilé de l'éternel* (1938); *La Littérature au vingtième siècle* (1938), p. 253; *Le Nouveau Siècle,* March 19, 1925; *JSP,* Aug. 12, 1939; *Le Figaro,* Nov. 4, 1944, Jan. 22, 1947. For Claude Roy, who was Brasillach's secretary and at one time also an assistant to Pierre Varillon, and whom *Aspects* insists on calling "le petit rénégat," presumably because he took a long time to change his mind, see *RU,* June 25, 1943; *Les Nouveaux Cahiers de France,* August 1943.

37. *Cinq Années de résistance* (Strasbourg, 1949), *passim,* and especially pp. 8–69. The letter begins on p. 63.

38. *Le Figaro,* Oct. 22, 1932.

39. Letter dated May 21; no year, but probably 1948–50 (Boutang papers).

40. Pierre Gaxotte in *Charles Maurras, 1868–1952,* pp. 14–15.

CHAPTER 26

1. Notes of M. René Rancoeur, transmitted by their author.

2. Personal communication of a royalist organizer, then in charge of the 8th, 9th, and 15th Arrondissements.

3. Letter of Roger Joseph.
4. Quoted in *Aspects,* July 6, 1951. The letter is in the possession of M. Simon Arbellot.
5. *Candide,* July 23, 1941.
6. See Maurras's preface to Jean-Louis Lagor, *La Philosophie politique de Saint-Thomas* (1948), p. 33.
7. *AF,* July 28, 1940; *Candide,* July 24, 1940; Maurras to Colonel Rémy (letter in Boutang papers). The national revolution had been a dream since Valois launched the idea in 1924 in a book of that name and developed it again the following year in the *Almanach, 1925,* pp. 158–64.
8. Henri Boegner, "Le Cercle Fustel de 1939 à 1952," *Cahiers du Cercle Fustel de Coulanges,* December 1955, pp. 165–78; *AF,* Aug. 14, 1940.
9. See, e.g., *AF,* Sept. 27, 1941.
10. See, e.g., *L'Eclair,* Aug. 12, 1940; *AF,* July 21, Aug. 13, 1940.
11. *AF,* Oct. 20, 1941.
12. *AF,* Feb. 27, 1942.
13. *NG,* Feb. 1–15, 1942; *AF,* May 21, 1943.
14. *AF,* Oct. 6, 8, 1941, June 17, Nov. 27, 1942.
15. Havard, "La Question juive," *RU,* September 1942, pp. 350–52.
16. *AF,* Oct, 6, 23, 1942, July 22, 1943.
17. *AF,* Aug. 11, 1940.
18. See *AF,* June 15, 1941, June 20, 1942.
19. *AF,* Aug. 9, 1941.
20. *AF,* Dec. 11. 1941; *AF* and *NG,* Sept. 15–30, 1941; *RU,* Sept. 10, 1941, pp. 358–60.
21. *Paris patriote à la salle Wagram,* p. 44.
22. See *L'Oeuvre,* April 9, 1941, and *Le Procès de Charles Maurras,* pp. 102–7, 110.
23. *AF,* Nov. 1. 1940.
24. Quoted in *Pétain et les Allemands* (1948), pp. 52–53; referred to in *Pour réveiller le grand juge* (1951), p. 19 and *passim.* This same conception of the Action Française as the moving anti-German influence at Vichy reappears in a long, undated memorandum, probably written in 1941, found in German Embassy Archives at the Liberation and quoted in *ibid.,* pp. 23–24. See also in the Chambrun Collection, No. 14, the statement of Roger Perdriat, who was editor of the *Dépêche de Toulouse.*
25. *AF,* Jan. 15, April 26, Dec. 10, 1941.
26. *AF,* Nov. 9, 1942, and the following issues; *Candide,* Nov. 18, 1942.
27. *AF,* Jan. 5, 1943.
28. Quoted by René Benjamin in a private letter to Henri Vallentin, dated Jan. 1, 1943 (Rancoeur papers).
29. *AF,* Nov. 24, Dec. 1, 1942.
30. Letter of René Benjamin cited above.
31. *AF,* June 24, 26, 27, 29, 1942.
32. *AF,* March 18, 1943.
33. See Delebecque, "Illusions funestes," *AF,* Jan. 13, 1944; Havard in *RU,* May 10, 1943, p. 720; Maurras in *AF,* May 8, 1944. In the last citation, my translation may say more than the writer intended: "loucher du côté anglo-américain . . . [c'est] prendre un parti, un mauvais parti."
34. *AF,* Nov. 1, 1940, and *Le Procès de Charles Maurras,* pp. 111–13.
35. Stéphane, *Chaque Homme,* pp. 171–73.
36. François Mauriac, *Oeuvres complètes* (1952), XI, 376–77, 400–402.
37. *AF,* Oct. 8, 1942, March 20, 21, Aug. 30, Sept. 1, 27, Oct. 2, 1943, April 27, 1944.
38. *AF,* Jan. 3, 1944.
39. See *Cinq Années de résistance,* p. 65.
40. *Le Procès de Charles Maurras et de Maurice Pujo,* pp. 470, 506.

41. *Le Procureur et l'habitant,* pp. 41ff and *passim.*

42. As he tells us in *Tragi-comédie de ma surdité* (Aix-en-Provence, 1951).

43. *Franc-Tireur,* Jan. 9, 1945. See also, e.g., *Gavroche,* Jan. 11, 1945; *L'Aube* and *Franc-Tireur,* Jan. 23, 1945; *Résistance,* Jan. 24, 1945; *France-Soir* and *Ce Soir,* Jan. 25, 1945.

44. Letters of Nov. 22 and Dec. 3, 1944 (Gaudy papers).

45. Maurras, *Lettres,* p. 192.

46. Ernst Nolte, "Die Action Française, 1899–1944," *Vierteljahrshefte für Zeitgeschichte,* April 1961, pp. 161–62.

47. See Roger Stéphane, *Fin d'une jeunesse* (1954), p. 56.

CHAPTER 27

1. *Der integrale Nationalismus in Frankreich* (Frankfurt am Main, 1931); *French Royalist Doctrines Since the Revolution* (New York, 1933); *Nationalismus und Demokratie im Frankreich der dritten Republik* (Hamburg, 1933); *Das antiromantische Denken im modernen Frankreich* (Munich, 1935); *The Rise of Integral Nationalism in France* (New York, 1939).

2. Abetz, *Histoire d'une politique franco-allemande,* p. 14.

3. See *Les Procès de la radio,* pp. 52, 93.

4. See, e.g., *AF,* Jan. 5, 1915.

5. See, e.g., Canadian newspapers quoted in *AF,* July 10, 1921, April 22 and July 1, 1923.

6. A correspondent complained about this in *L'Europe nouvelle,* June 16, 1923, p. 749.

7. See *Almanach, 1929,* pp. 267–70.

8. *AF,* March 20, 1938.

9. See the testimony of Maurice Vaussard, *Politique religieuse et Action française,* pp. 8, 33; Joseph Caillaux in *JOC,* Dec. 22, 1917, p. 3480; *Revue des causes célèbres* (1920), p. 168. See also Giuseppe Prezzolini, *La Francia e i Francesi* (Milan, 1913), pp. 329–41; Luigi Tonelli, *Lo Spirito Francese contemporaneo* (Milan, 1917), pp. 303–25.

10. *Opera Omnia di Benito Mussolini* (Florence, 1951——), III, 280; IV, 46.

11. The Duke of Alba was an old friend of Léon Daudet's brother. His letter, dated London, April 11, 1938, is in the F. D. papers.

12. *RAF,* Feb. 15, 1911.

13. Quoted in *AF,* March 3, 1927.

14. *Conceptions économiques,* pp. 759–60.

15. See the Bucharest press during the first half of July 1937.

16. *AF,* July 15, 1926.

17. See Raposo, *Dois Nacionalismos* (Lisbon, 1929).

18. *AF,* March 21, 22, 1914, Aug. 12, 1914.

19. *A Voz,* Aug. 31, 1955.

20. *A Voz,* Oct. 23, 1939; Jacques Ploncard d'Assac, "L'Influence de Charles Maurras au Portugal," *Cahiers Charles Maurras,* No. 1 (April 1960), p. 70.

21. Robert Havard, personal communication.

22. Maurras, *Lettres,* pp. 261–63; *Diario da Manha,* July 20, 1951.

23. In an unpublished MS from which much of the information in the following pages has been drawn.

24. Jacques Serruys, *Sous le signe de l'autorité* (Brussels, 1935), quoted in Dresse MS. On Pierre Nothomb in 1940, see Léon Degrelle, *La Cohue de 1940* (Tangiers, 1949), pp. 211–12.

25. Dresse, personal communication and MS.; Serruys, quoted in Dresse MS.

26. Robert Brasillach, *Léon Degrelle et l'avenir de Rex* (1936), pp. 19, 21; Pierre Daye, *Léon Degrelle et le Rexisme* (1937), pp. 48–51, 59–60, 235.

27. See, e.g., *AF,* June 9, July 11, Oct. 24, 30, 1936; *L'Insurgé,* March 3, April 7, 1937; *JSP,* May 30, Oct. 24, 1936.

28. Brasillach, *Léon Degrelle,* pp. 43–44.

29. Colonel H. Bernard, Paul Dresse, Baron Drion du Chapois, Baron Pierre Nothomb, personal communications.

30. *Journal de Genève,* Nov. 28, 1904.

31. Gonzague de Reynold, MS of an unpublished "Etude sur Maurras" upon which much of this information is based.

32. *La Voix Clémentine,* January 1911, pp. 10, 6.

33. *Ibid.,* pp. 3, 22.

34. Gonzague de Reynold, MS.

35. See quotations in *O Debate,* Nov. 13, 27, 1954; Antonio Sardinha, *Naçao Portuguesa,* May 8, 1914, and *Ao principio era o verbo,* p. xiii.

36. Binet-Valmer died in 1940. See Charlotte Montard, *Quatre Ans à l'Action Française* (1931), pp. 88ff (and private biographical information).

37. *La Suisse libérale,* quoted in *AF,* Feb. 20, 1924.

38. *Nous réactionnaires* (Lausanne, 1929), pp. 21–34.

39. *Ibid.,* pp. 47–56.

40. *Ibid.,* pp. 5–19.

41. *Ibid.,* pp. 35–46.

42. See Eddy Bauer in *Almanach, 1928,* pp. 306–9; *AF,* March 28, 1928, June 15, 1930, July 7, 1933; Maurras, *Dictionnaire politique et critique,* the articles entitled "Suisse" and "Rousseau."

43. See *La Ligue Vaudoise: aux étudiants, aux gymnasiens, aux normaliens* (Lausanne, 1941?).

44. This and other quotations are derived from the two books in which Regamey has outlined his political ideas, *Les Diverses Conceptions de la démocratie* (Lausanne, 1927) and *Essai sur le gouvernement personnel* (Lausanne, 1931), and from conversations with Regamey.

45. Gonzague de Reynold, MS, p. 15.

CHAPTER 28

1. *Nouvelle Revue française,* November 1919.

2. See *Paris-Midi,* July 30, 1919, and *AF,* July 31, 1919.

3. *AF,* June 23, 1921; Massis, *Maurras,* pp. 105–6.

4. See the comments of M. F. Guyard, *L'Image de la Grande Bretagne dans le roman français* (1954)), pp. 94–95, for whom it represented "une fraction peu négligeable de l'opinion."

5. See Montjoye in *RU,* March 1, 1924; E. Gascoyn in *RU,* May 1, 1924.

6. See, e.g., R. Johannet in *RU,* Aug. 1, 1924; Saint-Brice in *RU,* Nov. 15, 1933; Benoist in *RU,* Feb. 1, 1934, Sept. 15, Oct. 1, 1935.

7. See, e.g., Louis Bertrand in *RU,* Feb. 15, 1937.

8. See, e.g., Oct. 15, 1933, April 1, 1934, Oct. 1, 1936; *Le Procès de Charles Maurras,* p. 228.

9. *RU,* Oct. 1, 1937.

10. See R. Garrigou-Lagrange in *RU,* Oct. 25, 1941.

11. Henri Massis, personal communication.

12. Jean Fayard and Pierre Gaxotte, personal communications.

13. See, e.g., Nicias, "Duval et sa Fédération," *Candide,* April 24, 1924. Veber's feature was entitled "Les Quatre Jeudis."

14. See, e.g., "Une belle affaire," *Candide,* Jan. 3, 1929.

15. On May 24, 1928, *Candide* began publication of Mussolini's memoirs.

16. *Candide,* Aug. 12, 1926, Jan. 24, 1929.

17. *Ibid.,* Jan. 25, March 22, 29, Dec. 6, 1934, Jan. 24, 1935. *Candide*'s star reporter, Odette Pannetier, sometimes lectured to Action Française audiences (F^7 13199 of April 19, June 23, 1929). Dr. Guérin introduced her to the section of the 18th Arrondissement as someone "qui est venue parmi nous ces temps derniers et que je considère maintenant non seulement comme une réactionnaire, mais comme une personne de droite."

18. See, e.g., "Gosses bolchevistes," Oct. 14, 1926; "En avez-vous assez des parlementaires?" Sept. 27, 1934. See also Feb. 28, Nov. 7, 1935.

19. *Candide,* May 22, 1940.

20. April 1, 1926.

21. See "L'Anti-Hitler," July 19, 1939.

22. See, e.g., Jan. 2, Feb. 13, 1936.

23. July 31, 1940.

24. *Candide,* Aug. 20, Sept. 3, 1941, Jan. 14, 28, June 10, 1942.

25. Pierre Gaxotte, personal communication; see *Candide,* Nov. 20, 1930, for an announcement of a new periodical to be called *De Partout*; *AF,* Nov. 30, 1930.

26. *JSP,* May 16, 1936; see also *JSP,* May 30, 1936.

27. The account is based on the testimony of MM. Jean Fayard, Fernand Brouty, André Nicolas, J. Lang, and Pierre Longone.

28. Lang also showed interest in Doriot's *Emancipation nationale.*

29. See, e.g., *JSP,* April 29, 1933, Dec. 8, 1934.

30. *AF,* March 19, 1938: "Bravo Gaxotte! Bravo *Je suis partout*!"

31. See Brasillach, *Journal d'un homme occupé,* p. 24.

32. *JSP,* June 9; *AF,* July 1, 1939.

33. *JSP,* Jan. 5, May 17, 1940; *L'Epoque,* Jan. 10, 11, 1940; *AF,* Jan. 7. 1940.

34. Bonnard, "Les Réactionnaires," *JSP,* May 19, 26, 1941.

35. See Jean Servière in *JSP,* Nov. 22, 1941.

36. *JSP,* Oct. 22, Aug. 27, 1943.

37. *JSP,* Oct. 18, 1941. The weekly circulation at that time was 200,000; see Jacques Isorni, *Le Procès de Robert Brasillach* (1946), pp. 67–68.

38. Brasillach, *Journal d'un homme occupé,* pp. 248–49.

39. *JSP,* Oct. 25, 1941; Brasillach, p. 254.

40. For attacks on the reactionary bourgeoisie, see, e.g., *JSP,* April 4, Oct. 18, 1941, Aug. 20, 27, 1943.

41. *JSP,* April 7, 1944; see also "Drumont, notre maître," *JSP,* April 28, 1944.

42. *JSP,* Aug. 27, 1943.

43. The appeal in which the former Maurrassian joined turncoats of both the Socialist and Communist parties appeared in the last number of *JSP,* August 11, 1944.

44. *JSP,* Feb. 10, 1939.

45. Combelle, *Prisons de l'espérance* (1952), pp. 8-9.

46. "Adieu au Fascisme," *La Parisienne,* October 1956, p. 602.

47. *L'Insurgé,* Jan. 13, 1937.

48. *Ibid.,* Feb. 3, 1937.

49. *Ibid.,* Feb. 24, April 14, May 1, 1937.

50. *Ibid.,* Aug. 4, 1947.

51. *Ibid.,* July 21, 1937.

52. *Ibid.,* March 24, 1937.

53. See pp. 203, 207.

54. *Combat,* January 1936.
55. See Brasillach in *Combat,* March 1936; Maulnier in *ibid.,* May 1938.
56. *Combat,* January 1937–June 1938; Maulnier, "Post-scriptum," *La Table ronde,* March 1953, p. 82.
57. Maulnier, *Au-delà du nationalisme* (1938), p. 19.
58. Pol Vandromme, *Robert Brasillach* (1956), pp. 218–20.
59. Paul Peladeau, *On disait en France* (Montreal, 1941), p. 217.
60. *Ibid.,* pp. 213–19.
61. *Les Fins dernières* (1952), p. 24. See also pp. 21–22 of this novel, short on facts but long on psychology, in which, while still a student, Boisdeffre, today one of France's most original right-wing literary critics, sought to defend Brasillach.
62. *La France, la guerre et la paix,* p. 120.
63. "Le Fascisme et son avenir en France," *RU,* LXIV, No. 19 (January 1936), p. 25; see *Demain la France* (1934), pp. 174–75, which expresses similar sentiments.
64. See his two important articles in *RU,* March 15 and April 15, 1933.

CHAPTER 29

1. Georges Bidault in *Un Grand Débat catholique et français: témoignages sur l'Action Française* (1927), pp. 149–50; Yves Simon, *La Grande Crise,* pp. 47–50.
2. C. André in *Un Grand Débat,* p. 80; Jean Grenier, "Réflexions sur Charles Maurras," *NRF,* February 1938, p. 294.
3. Jean Prévost, *Histoire de la France depuis la guerre* (1932), p. 61; Ducloux, *Du Chantage,* p. 76; Pierre Tissier, *I Worked with Laval* (London, 1942), p. 17; Jean Guéhenno, *La Foi difficile* (1957), pp. 50, 148–49.
4. See Pierre Benoît's comments in *Stamboul,* Jan. 20, 1923.
5. *L'Eclair,* Sept. 5, 1925.
6. Introduction to Charles Maurras, *Mademoiselle Monk* (1923). Malraux "m'a spontanément demandé d'écrire votre notice, car il admire profondément *L'Avenir de l'intelligence,*" wrote Florent Fels to Maurras on March 7, 1923 (Maurras papers).
7. *Le Nouveau Mercure,* April 1923, pp. 9, 12.
8. *Ibid.,* and reprinted in the Preface to *L'Exil* (1929). See also his contribution to Varillon and Rambaud's *Enquête* of 1923.
9. *Candide,* Aug. 17, 1933; Dr. Pierre Mauriac, personal communication.
10. In a letter of Oct. 26, 1960.
11. *Le Temps,* March 3, 1926. See also *AF,* Nov. 28, 1928; Maurice Martin du Gard, *Les Mémorables,* II, 304.
12. Pierre Mauriac, personal communication; letters of François Mauriac and his *Mémoires intérieures* (1959); *Revue hebdomadaire,* January 1926, pp. 349–54.
13. *AF,* Oct. 10, 1937; see *ibid.* for statements in the same vein by Louis Marin, J. and J. Tharaud, Pierre Benoît, André Bellessort, Georges Lecomte, and Joseph de Pesquidoux.
14. Letters of May 18, 1926, and Nov. 6, 1937 (F. D. papers); see his public declarations quoted in *AF,* Sept. 19, 1923.
15. "L'Action Française," *Le Document* (1935), p. 15.
16. Régis de Vibraye, *Où mène le nationalisme* (1929), p. 99. Vibraye evidently did not consider royalism an essential issue.
17. *Le Canard enchaîné,* Jan. 6, 1937.
18. See *Candide,* July 23, Aug. 6, 1936.
19. Jean-François Gravier, *Paris et le désert français* (1947); E. Beau de Loménie, *Maurras et son système* (Bourg, 1953), pp. 72–73. See Beau de Loménie's *Nouveaux Essais critiques,* June–December 1926, for the criticism that got him into trouble. The

criticism was well-founded, and it reflects the fundamental ideas later developed in *Les Responsabilités des dynasties bourgeoises* (1947——).

20. Bernanos, "Crépuscule des vieux," *Le Figaro,* Nov. 10, 1932.

21. Maurice Barrès, *Leurs Figures* (1932), p. 311; see also André Gaucher, *L'Honorable Léon Daudet,* p. 8.

22. Bernanos, *Nous autres français* (1939), pp. 66, 93; Société des Amis de Georges Bernanos, *Bulletin périodique,* No. 17–20 (1953), is dedicated to Bernanos and Maurras.

23. André Thérive, *Moralistes de ce temps* (1948), p. 262.

24. *Gazette de France,* March 17, 1900, quoted in Lucien Moreau, *RAF,* May 15, 1900; see also, e.g., *Enquête sur la monarchie,* p. 32.

25. Note on *Aspects de la France,* drawn up in the summer of 1950 (Boutang papers).

26. Maurras, *Le Corps médical français et la restauration nationale* (1933), p. 45.

27. *AF,* Nov. 15, 1934.

28. Quoted in *AF,* Aug. 7, 1920.

29. See pp. 131–33.

30. *AF,* Nov. 13, 1920.

31. *RAF,* Aug. 15, 1900.

CHAPTER 30

1. See Raymond Aron, *L'Opium des intellectuels* (1955), pp. 10, 17, and *passim.*

2. Carl J. Friedrich and Zbigniew K. Brzezinski, *Totalitarian Dictatorship and Autocracy* (Cambridge, 1956), p. 28.

3. Hannah Arendt, *The Origins of Totalitarianism* (New York, 1958), pp. 358–60. For the remarkable coincidence, see the brief, straightforward summary furnished by Curtiss, *Protocols of Zion,* pp. 5–13.

INDEX

INDEX

Paris
Arc de Triomphe
AV. DE LA GRANDE ARMÉE
AV. FOCH
AV. VICTOR HUGO
AV. KLÉBER
AV. D'IÉNA
AV. DE WAGRAM
BOUL. DE COURCELLES
Parc Monceau
St. Augustin
BOUL.
RUE DE ROME
Gare St. Lazare
RUE
AV. DE FRIEDLAND
BOUL.
HAUSSMANN
MALESHERBES
Opéra
Madeleine
FAUBg ST. HONORÉ
Elysée
AV. DES CHAMPS
ÉLYSÉES
ROND-POINT
RUE DU BOCCADOR
AV. MONTAIGNE
Grd. Palais
PLACE DE LA CONCORDE
Jardin des Tuileries
COURS LA REINE
SEINE
QUAI D'ORSAY
Tour Eiffel
Chambre des Députés
Champ de Mars
Hôtel des Invalides
BOUL. DE GRENELLE
École Militaire
AV. DE BRETEUIL
RUE DE SEVRES
BOUL. DE RENNES
RUE DE RENNES
BOUL. DU MONTPARNASSE
RASPAIL
Gare Montparnasse